# Jewish Cu

## Exploring Common and

Zvi Ron

# Jewish Customs

*Exploring Common and Uncommon Minhagim*

Maggid Books

*Jewish Customs*
*Exploring Common and Uncommon Minhagim*

First Edition, 2024

*Maggid Books*
*An imprint of Koren Publishers Jerusalem Ltd.*

POB 8531, New Milford, CT 06776-8531, USA
& POB 4044, Jerusalem 9104001, Israel
www.maggidbooks.com



Cover images courtesy of The National Library of Israel Collections

The publication of this book was made possible
through the generous support of *The Jewish Book Trust.*



ISBN 978-1-59264-631-9, *hardcover*

Printed and bound in the United States

רבי נתן אומר
אין לך אהבה כאהבה של תורה.
ואין לך חכמה כחכמה של דרך ארץ.
ואין לך יופי כיופי של ירושלים.
(אבות דרבי נתן פרק כח)

*Rabbi Natan would say:*
*There is no love like the love of Torah.*
*There is no wisdom like the wisdom of the "way of the world."*
*There is no beauty like the beauty of Jerusalem.*
(Avot D'Rabi Natan, Chapter 28)

*In memory of*

*Avinoam Mordechai Gottlieb z"l*

*To our parents and teachers,*
*for all we have learned from them*

Tilla & Ben Crowne

*Thanks to Rav Ron for the wonderful way*
*he has influenced his talmidim.*

*May the rest of the world now benefit as well.*

A Talmid's Parents

*Donated in honor of*

*Avi Watson and his unit*

*for defending Israel.*

*May we be zokheh for Avi, his unit and the IDF*
*to always be victorious.*
*Am Yisroel Chai!*

Merav and Aharon Watson

*Dedicated in Honor of the Author*

Donny and Tiferet Aaron

Richard Bierig

Steven and Gilli Davis

Shiloh Friedman

Jeremy Gaisin

Eli Guttman

Tzuri and Deena Merzel

Netanel and Ruthie Raden

Avi and Liz Rovinsky

Samuel and Brooke Salamon

Jack and Emma Strulowitz

# *Contents*

# *Preface*

For many generations, the study of Jewish customs consisted primarily of simply recording the various customs, only occasionally giving a reason for the custom. A classic example of this is the very popular *Sefer Taamei HaMinhagim UMekorei HaDinim* by Avraham Sperling, which has been through many editions and expansions since it was first published in 1890. Other similar popular works from previous generations are *Otzar Kol Minhagei Yeshurun* by Avraham Hershovitz (1892), and *Otzar Dinim UMinhagim* by J. D. Eisenstein (1917). A modern version of this type of book is Shmuel Gelbard's *Otzar Taamei HaMinhagim* (1996). It is only in recent years that there has been a growing interest in how customs developed over time, and what influences shaped their development. Rather than taking the custom as a given, researchers now focus on exploring the origin of the custom, the way in which it has been transmitted and popularized, and how it has changed over time, in an attempt to understand how the customs we are familiar with today came to be.

My initial exposure to this approach was the first volume of Daniel Sperber's *Minhagei Yisrael* (Mossad HaRav Kook, 1989). For the first time, customs were presented as being subject to change and development, often from external influences. While this approach may have been found previously in academic literature, for the average practicing Jew, this was a paradigm shift. The fact that this book was disseminated by a respected, traditional publishing house served to popularize this approach among a segment of Jewish society that had not previously encountered this methodology. The book proved popular, becoming an eight-volume series. Other works appeared espousing the same approach, for example, Eric Zimmer's *Olam KeMinhago Noheg* (Zalman Shazar, 1996).

In this book I offer my own research and investigation into a number of popular customs. They were chosen simply because I was curious about or had been asked about these topics, but I could not find a satisfactory treatment of them in the existing literature. I have not sought any particular agenda or hypothesis, although after researching many customs, certain conclusions have emerged. These will be discussed at the end of the book.

There are many new discoveries here, obscure sources and references brought to light, as well as revelations that I found to be remarkable. Sit back and enjoy the fruit of my labor and research, and discover new insights about customs both familiar and arcane.

There are many people to thank for this volume. Foremost among them, my grandfather Rabbi Eliezer Lipa Cohen and my parents, Dr. Shlomo and Ruth Ron, for instilling in me a love and respect for Jewish customs. I grew up in a decidedly non-American home, singing *zemirot* with tunes from the old country that none of my friends were familiar with and which I still proudly use today in my own family, and this is where it all began. With thanks and appreciation to my patient and supportive wife, Sharon, and to my children, Kinamon (and her husband, Nadav), Netanel (and his wife, Karina), Adina, and Shoshana, who are always very encouraging of my research and interests. They all inspire me daily. Our first grandchild, baby Naveh, brings with him a new kind of inspiration. Special thanks also to my students, friends, and neighbors who asked me about various customs; their questions led to the writing of many of the chapters in this book. I'd like to especially thank my students and friends who contributed to support the publication of this book, in particular Dahlia Gottlieb, whose husband Avinoam, of blessed memory, was a source of many insightful discussions about the topics covered in this book. Thank you to Matthew Miller, publisher of Koren Jerusalem, Aryeh Grossman, as well as to the editorial and design team Caryn Meltz, Tomi Mager, Tani Bayer, Debbie Ismailoff, and Esther Shafier, as well as Marc Sherman for the indexes. Lastly, thank you to my dear brother-in-law, Reuven Ziegler, for his constant encouragement and support.

Earlier versions of these chapters appeared in the following publications. My thanks to them all for their permission to reprint revised and updated versions here.

Chapter 1: "The Origin and Development of the Custom for the Bride to Circle the Groom Three or Seven Times," *Zutot* 17 (2019).

Chapter 2: "L'Haim," *Hakirah* 30 (Winter 2021).

Chapter 3: "Covering Mirrors in the Shiva Home," *Hakirah* 13 (Spring 2012).

Chapter 4:"Walking Out for Yizkor," *Zutot* 14 (2017).

Chapter 5: "A Shabbat Candle for Every Family Member," *Hakirah* 30 (Summer 2021).

Chapter 6: "Braided Challa," *Modern Judaism* 42:1 (February 2022).

Chapter 7: "Akhilat Etrog BeRosh HaShana," *Sinai* 142 (Nisan 5768).

Chapter 8: "HaMinhag BeAkhilat Shum BeRosh HaShana," *Sinai* 146 (2014).

Chapter 9: "A Possible Origin of the Eleventh Day of the Eighth Month as the Date of Rachel's Death," *Journal for the Study of the Pseudepigrapha* 24:4 (June 2015).

Chapter 10: "The Story of Judith and the Custom of Eating Dairy Foods on Hanukkah," *Torah U'Maddah Journal* 18 (2020–2021).

Chapter 11: "Ḥanukkah Gelt," *Hakirah* 29 (Winter 2021).

Chapter 12: "The Ashkenazi Custom Not to Slaughter Geese in Tevet and Shevat," *Hakirah* 17 (Summer 2014).

Chapter 13: "Mishloach Manot on Purim and Rosh Hashanah," *Jewish Bible Quarterly* 46, no. 1 (January 2018).

Chapter 14: "The *Bedikat Ḥametz* Kit: Wax Candle, Wooden Spoon and Feather," *Hakirah* 26 (Spring 2019).

Chapter 15: "Our Salty Tears: The History and Significance of an Interpretation of Dipping in Salt Water at the Seder," *Hakirah* 24 (Spring 2018).

Chapter 16: "Our Own Joy Is Lessened and Incomplete – The History of an Interpretation of Sixteen Drops of Wine at the Seder," *Hakirah* 19 (Summer 2015).

Chapter 17: "The Origin of the Custom of Chai Rotl," *Hakirah* 21 (Summer 2016).

Chapter 18: "The Development of the Expanded Tachanun for Monday and Thursday," *European Journal of Jewish Studies* 12 (January 2018).

Chapter 19: "Pointing to the Torah and Other *Hagbaha* Customs," *Hakirah* 15 (Summer 2013).

Chapter 20: "Reciting *Al Tira* After *Aleinu*," *Hakirah* 10 (Summer 2010).

Chapter 21: "Tehillat Hashem and Other Verses Before *Birkat Ha-Mazon*," *Hakirah* 28 (Spring 2020).

Chapter 22: "Minhag Hosafat HaRaḥaman LeShabbat," *HaMaayan* 203 (2012).

Chapter 23: "'Shalom Aleichem' to Three People During *Kiddush Levanah*," *Hakirah* 7 (Winter 2009).

Chapter 25: "Makor Minhag HaKahal Lomar Et Shemot Aseret Bnei Haman BeKol Ram" *HaMaayan* 216 (2015).

Chapter 26: "Reading Shir haShirim, Ruth, Eicha and Kohelet," *Hakirah* 23 (Fall 2017).

Chapter 27: "LaOmer / BaOmer, Shitat Rav Saadia Gaon" *Sinai* 149 (2016).

"Stripes, Hats, and Fashion," *Modern Judaism* 40, no. 3 (October 2020).

# Part 1
# *Life Cycle*

# Chapter 1

# Why the Bride Circles the Groom

In modern times it has become a ubiquitous Ashkenazic custom for a bride to circle the groom under the *ḥuppa*. The custom began as circling three times, with various reasons given for this particular practice and this specific number. With kabbalistic influence, the custom shifted from three circuits to seven, the common custom today. The reasons given also changed over time, reflecting changing attitudes towards the symbolism of the wedding ceremony. We will be building on Dr. Aaron Ahrend's comprehensive study of the custom in his article "Bride Going Around the Bridegroom – Study of a Marriage Custom" (1991).[1]

1 Aaron Ahrend, "Bride Going Around the Bridegroom – Study of a Marriage Custom," *Sidra* 7 (Bar-Ilan University Press, 1991), 5–11 [Hebrew].

## EARLIEST MENTION OF THE CUSTOM

There are many references to this popular Ashkenazic custom[2] for the bride to circle the groom under the *ḥuppa*. The earliest known source to mention this custom is the Torah commentary of Rabbi Dossa the Greek (ר' דוסא היווני), written in 1430. Rabbi Dossa is a little known Romaniote scholar, originally from Vidin, Bulgaria, who spent time in yeshivot in Austria and northern Italy.[3] In his comments to Leviticus 17:11 and 14, where sometimes the word spelled הוא is pronounced as the masculine *hu* and sometimes as the feminine *hi*, he brings the Masoretic mnemonic to remember which is which: "How long will you turn away, wayward daughter? For the Lord will create something new in the world: A woman circles a man (נקבה תסובב גבר)" (Jer. 31:21). This reminds the reader that the feminine surrounds the masculine, meaning that the first and last instances of הוא are feminine, and the two in the middle are masculine.[4] Rabbi Dossa then adds that at a *ḥuppa* in Austria he saw the bride circle the groom three times. When he asked why this was done, he was told that it was based on that same verse, Jeremiah 31:21. Rabbi Dossa writes that this is a nice custom (מנהג יפה).[5]

The meaning of the word *tesovev* in the context of the verse does not actually mean "circling around," but rather refers to courting,[6] and metaphorically refers to the idea that in the future the people will seek

2 Yitzhak Zvi Levovitch, *Shulḥan HaEzer*, vol. 2 (Dej, 1932), 32b, *siman* 7, note 8; Shlomo Zalman Braun's edition of *Kitzur Shulḥan Aruḥ* with his commentary *She'arim Metzuyanim BeHalakha*, vol. 4 (New York: Feldheim, 1951), 59, note 10; Moshe Weinstock, *Siddur HaGeonim VehaMekubalim VehaḤasidim*, vol. 20 (Jerusalem, 1980), 134; *Otzar HaPoskim – Even HaEzer*, vol. 16 (Jerusalem, 1985), 174, *siman* 17; Mordechai Eliyahu stated that Sephardim do not have this custom in his edition of *Kitzur Shulḥan Arukh* (Jerusalem, 2009), 575, note 7.

3 See Shlomo Spitzer, "Yediot al Rabbi Dossa haYevani miChiburo al haTorah," in *Sefer Zikaron LeRav Yitzhak Nissim*, vol. 4 (Jerusalem: Yad HaRav Nissim, 1984), 177–80.

4 This mnemonic is brought by Ḥizkuni in his commentary to Leviticus 17:11.

5 First published by Shlomo Spitzer, "Yediot al Rabbi Dossa HaYevani," 181. It appears in the manuscript of Dossa's commentary on page 138r (Oxford, Bodelian Library MS Mich. 261; Neubauer no. 203; Hebrew University MS 16339). It is included in Shmuel Eliezer Stern, ed., *Meorot HaRishonim*, part 1 (Jerusalem: Machon Yerushalayim, 2001), 322, *siman* 81.

6 See Rashi, David Kimchi, and Malbim here. See also Menachem Buleh, *Daat Mikra: Yirmeyahu* (Jerusalem: Mossad HaRav Kook, 1983), 391.

out God.[7] However, as "encircling" is the common meaning of the word in Hebrew, it was given as a source for the custom. In this earliest source, no explicit reason is given for why it was done three times. It should be noted that the custom was not widespread at the time, even among Ashkenazic communities, as it does not appear in the works of the Maharil and other books of customs from that era.[8] It seems to have begun in eastern Austria and spread from there.[9]

While Rabbi Dossa records no explanation beyond the verse itself, later authorities added additional symbolic meaning. For example, since the verse refers to a future time of messianic redemption, it was considered a particularly auspicious symbol at a wedding,[10] or that it represents the role of the groom as the giver and the bride as the receiver.[11]

In recent times, concerns have arisen that this custom is suggestive of the bride being in some way subordinate to her husband,[12]and as a result contemporary interpretations have emerged that may be more acceptable in light of current attitudes, for example, that wherever the groom looks he will see only his bride, or that in circling her groom the bride reciprocates the affection he showed earlier at the *bedekin*,

7 See Kimchi. There are many explanations for this verse, none of which understand that there is an act of actual circling in the verse. For example, Malbim explains that the Land of Israel will seek out its people and Metzudat David explains that it refers to the Israelites acting with strength to overcome the Chaldeans.

8 *Pardes Eliezer*, vol. 4 (Brooklyn, NY: Machon Damesek Eliezer, 2014), 128.

9 Aaron Ahrend, "Bride Going Around the Bridegroom – Study of a Marriage Custom," *Sidra* 7 (Bar-Ilan University Press, 1991), 9.

10 A. Lewysohn, *Mekorei Minhagim* (Berlin, 1847), 104, *siman* 74; repeated in Y. Lipetz, *Sefer Mataamim* (Warsaw, 1899), 35, *siman* 79; Yitzhak Zeller, *Yalkut Yitzḥak*, vol. 4 (Warsaw, 1900), 97, mitzva 552, *siman* 35, and J. D. Eisenstein, *Otzar Dinim UMinhagim* (New York, 1917), 127.

11 See Dov Ber Schneerson (the Mitteler Rebbe), *Torat Chayyim – Bereshit* (Brooklyn: Otzar Chasidim, 2002), 423, *Vayeshev*, *siman* 16. This idea is quoted in Avraham David Lavut, *Shaar HaKollel* (Brooklyn, NY: Kehot, 2005), 83, 35:5.

12 Anita Diamant, *The Jewish Wedding Now* (New York: Simon and Schuster, 2001), 110; Nancy Wiener, *Beyond Breaking the Glass* (New York: CCAR, 2001), 37 ("Early Reform practice dispensed with this ritual altogether, viewing it as superstitious, non-egalitarian and inessential"); Irit Koren, "The Bride's Voice: Religious Women Challenge the Wedding Ritual," *Nashim* 10 (2005), 31 ("The circling of the groom strikes many as indicating that he is at the center, while the bride is at the margins").

reminiscent also of the verse in Jeremiah.[13] Other opinions propose that "the woman delineates the sacred space of the union,"[14] or that she is demonstrating the creation of a new relationship unit.[15]

## EARLIEST EXPLANATIONS OF THREE CIRCLES

*Tashbetz,* referred to as *Tashbetz Katan* so as to avoid confusion with the compendium of responsa bearing the same name, is a collection of the customs of Rabbi Meir of Rothenberg (c. 1215–93) recorded by one of his students, generally recognized as Samson ben Zadok. Although a version of the book, or parts of it, was apparently already known to the students of Rabbi Meir, it was first published only in 1556.[16] There are many different versions of the book found in earlier manuscripts, and the last group of *simanim* is later material added to the original work.[17]

In this latter part of the book, among wedding-related practices that have numerical significance, the custom to hand the bride over to the groom (למסור כלה לחתן) three times is mentioned. This is explained as corresponding to the three times the Torah uses the expression "When a man marries a woman" (כי יקח איש אשה), in Deuteronomy 22:13, 24:1, and 24:5.[18]

While this *siman* does appear in the first published edition of *Tashbetz* from 1556,[19] it does not appear in earlier manuscripts of *Tashbetz,* and is not even included in some editions published in modern times.[20] This interest in numeric symbolism is in line with that found in other practices of the *Ḥasidei Ashkenaz* in general and Rabbi Meir

13 Yisrael Samet, "The Meaning of *Ḥuppa* Customs – Part 2," *Tzohar* 10 (2001), 166 [Hebrew].

14 This is cited as the explanation given "in some feminist circles," Wiener, *Beyond Breaking the Glass,* 37.

15 Maurice Lamm, *The Jewish Way in Love and Marriage* (New York: Jonathan David, 1980), 214.

16 Shlomo Angel, ed., *Sefer Tashbetz* (Jerusalem: Machon Yerushalayim, 2010), 10–11.

17 Ibid., 12.

18 Ibid., 267, *siman* 467.

19 *Sefer Tashbetz* (Cremona, 1556), 45a.

20 For example, this *siman* is not found in the version of *Tashbetz* published by Mekhon Torah shebi-khetav (Jerusalem 2005), see 353.

in particular,[21] although we do not find this custom mentioned in any of the writings of Rabbi Meir that we have today. An entire section of *remazim* related to the wedding ceremony, however, is found in a fourteenth-century manuscript, comprising a collection of many diverse works. Although it immediately follows a section on the laws of blessings attributed to Rabbi Meir,[22] this particular section is not attributed to any individual. The manuscript is not dated, but it does contain a section dealing with matters pertaining to the calendar and covers the years 1323–1446, so it is reasonable to infer that it is from the early fourteenth century.[23]

The practice of circling the groom three times was included in *Mateh Moshe* (1591) by Rabbi Moshe ben Avraham of Przemyśl, where he uses the same terminology as the *Tashbetz,* and attributes the practice to Rabbi Meir.[24] These earliest sources specify three times rather than seven,[25] and are considered to be the source of the custom quoted in popular classic works which provide explanations for customs, all of which describe circling three times.[26] However, it is important to note that this source does not use the term circling at all, but rather "handing over," and actually refers to a completely different custom, that of having the bride "handed over" to the groom at three distinct times, the first earlier in the day (a practice known as *ḥuppat Main*), the second with the *kiddushin* and blessings, and the third at the *bet yiḥud* where the couple would spend time alone.[27] Later books on customs appropriated the

21 See D. Sperber, *Minhagei Yisrael,* vol. 7 (Jerusalem, 2003), 412.

22 Paris, Bibliothèque nationale de France, Hébreu 391, fol. 108r. See also Shmuel Eliezer Stern, *Seder Erusin VeNisuin LeRabbotenu HaRishonim* (Bnei Brak, 1990), 127.

23 Munk, Derenbourg, Franck, and Zotenberg, *Catalogues des Manuscrits Hébreux et Samaritains de la Bibliothèque Impériale/Manuscrits Orientaux* (Paris, 1866), 52.

24 Moshe ben Avraham of Przemyśl, *Mateh Moshe* (Frankfurt, 1719), 111a, part 3, chapter 1, *siman* 4.

25 Aaron Ahrend, "Bride Going Around the Bridegroom – Study of a Marriage Custom," *Sidra* 7 (Bar-Ilan University Press, 1991), 5, note 1.

26 Avraham Sperling, *Sefer Taamei HaMinhagim UMekorei HaDinim* (Jerusalem: Shai Lamora, 1999), 408; A. Hershovitz, *Sefer Minhagei Yeshurun* (Vilna, 1899), 100, *siman* 176; J. D. Eisenstein, *Otzar Dinim UMinhagim* (New York, 1917), 127.

27 Yaakov Yisrael Setel, ed., *Sefer Gematriot* (Jerusalem, 2005), 308–10, especially note 68; Binyamin Shlomo Hamburger, "Shenei Ḥuppot BeYom HaNisuin," *Or Yisrael* 21

explanation found in *Tashbetz* for this threefold handing over to explain the custom of circling the groom,[28] although this is not what *Tashbetz* was referring to.[29] It is for this reason that despite the manuscript most likely predating Rabbi Dossa, it cannot be considered the earliest mention of the custom of circling the groom.

Over time, many other reasons have been offered to explain why the bride made specifically three circuits. For example, the three circles represent the three words in the original source (נקבה תסובב גבר) in Jeremiah 31:21.[30] Another suggestion is that they represent the three times the word ארשתיך is found in Hosea 2:21–22, "And I will betroth (וארשתיך) you forever, I will betroth (וארשתיך) you with righteousness and justice, and with goodness and mercy. And I will betroth (וארשתיך) you with faithfulness; then you shall be devoted to the Lord."[31] Since this verse is connected to the wearing of *tefillin*, the circles may also represent the three times the *tefillin* are wound around the finger.[32] They are also said to represent the three ways a man can perform *kiddushin*, or the three obligations a husband has to his wife.[33] Other commenta-

---

(Tishrei 5761/2001), 219.

28 Lipetz, *Sefer Mataamim*, 35, *siman* 80; A. Hershovitz, *Sefer Minhagei Yeshurun* (Vilna, 1899) 100, *siman* 176; J. D. Eisenstein, *Otzar Dinim UMinhagim* (New York, 1917) 127; Shmuel Gelbard, *Otzar Taamei Haminhagim* (Petach Tikva: Mifal Rashi, 1996), 443.

29 Aryeh Kaplan, *Made in Heaven* (New York: Moznaim, 1983), 160: "This developed into the bride walking around the groom three times." See also Aaron Ahrend, "Bride Going Around the Bridegroom – Study of a Marriage Custom," *Sidra* 7 (Bar-Ilan University Press, 1991), 7, note 12.

30 Chanoch Zundel ben Yosef, *Mitzhalot Ḥatanim* (Johannesberg, Germany), 11. Although there is no publication date printed, it seems to be around 1854; see the introduction, 5. Chanoch Zundel died in 1859. See also Shlomo Zalman Ehrenreich, ed., *Iggeret HaTiyul* (Jerusalem: HaTechiya, 1957), 217. This is found in a section of additional material not seen in earlier editions of Hayim ben Betzalel's (1530–88) work. See Aaron Ahrend, "Bride Going Around the Bridegroom – Study of a Marriage Custom," *Sidra* 7 (Bar-Ilan University Press, 1991), 9, note 26.

31 A. Lewysohn, *Mekorei Minhagim* (Berlin, 1847), 104, *siman* 74; repeated in J. D. Eisenstein, *Otzar Dinim UMinhagim* (New York, 1917), 127.

32 A. Lewysohn, *Mekorei Minhagim* (Berlin, 1847), 104, *siman* 74, repeated in Shlomo Zvi Schick, *Siddur Rashban* (Vienna, 1894), 15b, *siman* 87.

33 Lewysohn, *Mekorei Minhagim*, 104, *siman* 74, repeated in Schick, *Siddur Rashban*, 15b, *siman* 87 and A. Hershovitz, *Sefer Minhagei Yeshurun* (Vilna, 1899) 100, *siman* 176.

tors say the circles symbolize the three camps that surrounded the Ark of the Covenant in the wilderness, or the layers of darkness, cloud, and fog that surrounded the Divine Presence.[34] It has even been suggested that it gives an opportunity for the groom and two witnesses (three people in total) to catch a glimpse of the bride and make sure she is the right woman.[35] All these reasons are found in books dating from the mid- to late 1800s and early 1900s that give explanations for customs, often without attribution.[36]

## PROTECTION

In Berakhot 54b we find, "R. Yehuda said: Three persons require guarding: a sick person, a groom, and a bride." Rashi explains that in the case of a bride and groom, protection is needed from evil spirits (מזיקין) because they are jealous of them.[37] There are many wedding customs that are based on providing protection for the groom from negative spiritual forces and entities,[38] and the opinion of the folklorists is that the custom of encircling him is one of them. This approach understands that

34 Lipetz, *Sefer Mataamim*, 36, *siman* 92, 93, repeated in Yitzhak Zvi Levovitch, *Shulḥan HaEzer*, vol. 2 (Dej, 1932), 32a, *siman* 7, note 8.

35 Schick, *Siddur Rashban*, 15b, *siman* 87. This approach is ridiculed in S. M. Lehrman, *Jewish Customs and Folklore* (London: Shapiro, Valentine and Co., 1949), 147, where he prefers the explanation found in *Tashbetz* or the one based on וארשתיך.

36 See the notes above where I endeavored to show the earliest source for each explanation.

37 J. Lauterbach, "The Ceremony of Breaking Glass at Weddings," *Hebrew Union College Annual* 2 (1925), 351–80, here 355: "It is the belief that the evil spirits or demons are jealous of human happiness and therefore seek to spoil it or to harm the happy individual."

38 See *Pardes Eliezer*, vol. 4 (Brooklyn, New York: Machon Damesek Eliezer, 2014), 134, note 7, where he brings the idea that the bride's face is covered with a veil in order to protect her from evil forces, and that Psalm 121 is recited under the *ḥuppa* as protection for the bride and groom; Menachem Savitz, *Yismaḥ Lev* (Lakewood, 2004), 191, *siman* 274 and Yitzhak Shechter, *Yashiv Yitzḥak* (Netanya, 2004), *siman* 61, 351–53, regarding not leaving the groom alone due to fear of *mazikin*; Hershovitz, *Sefer Minhagei Yeshurun*, 95, *siman* 171, regarding making sure there are no knots on the clothing of the bride and groom as a protection from witchcraft; Lauterbach, "The Ceremony of Breaking Glass at Weddings," 355–61 regarding a variety of wedding customs. See also Aaron Ahrend, "Bride Going Around the Bridegroom – Study of a Marriage Custom," *Sidra* 7 (Bar-Ilan University Press, 1991), 7, note 17 and Joshua

the custom "was probably originally intended to keep off the demons who were waiting to pounce upon them" by constructing a protective barrier,[39] "a version of the magic circle."[40] Both the numbers three and seven are considered "favored mystical number(s)," and both would be appropriate for the purpose of providing supernatural protection.[41] This is also the conclusion reached by Aaron Ahrend of Bar-Ilan University, in his comprehensive study of this custom.[42] The groom was considered to be in more danger, based on the ancient concern that the demonic forces "would seek to kill the bridegroom or otherwise hurt him and prevent him from joining his bride, in order that they might keep the bride for themselves,"[43] an idea previously found in the Apocryphal work *The Book of Tobit,* understood to have been written by a Jewish author sometime during the third or early second centuries BCE.[44]

At first glance, it would seem that this explanation is not given in any of the early sources, even though other protective practices were explicitly described as such.[45] However, upon closer inspection we see that the element of protection was present from the earliest reference

Trachtenberg, *Jewish Magic and Superstition: A Study in Folk Religion* (New York: Athenium, 1984), 172–74.

39 Joshua Trachtenberg, *Jewish Magic and Superstition: A Study in Folk Religion* (New York: Athenium, 1984), 121.

40 Joshua Trachtenberg, *Jewish Magic and Superstition: A Study in Folk Religion* (New York: Athenium, 1984), 174. "People all around the world from every era of history have believed that circles have magical powers," Wiener, *Beyond Breaking the Glass* 36. See also *Encyclopedia Judaica,* vol. 7, 1154, on *hakafot* in general as an "attempt to dissuade *shedim* from intruding upon the object of attention."

41 See the numerous examples in Trachtenberg, *Jewish Magic and Superstition,* 119–21; see also 174. For rabbinic sources on the power of circles and circling seven times in particular, see Meir Benayahu, *Sefer Zikaron LeRav Yitzhak Nissim,* vol. 6: *Maamadot UMoshavot* (Jerusalem: Yad HaRav Nissim, 1985), 120–25.

42 Aaron Ahrend, "Bride Going Around the Bridegroom – Study of a Marriage Custom," *Sidra* 7 (Bar-Ilan University Press, 1991), 7.

43 Jacob Lauterbach, "The Ceremony of Breaking Glass at Weddings," *Hebrew Union College Annual* 2 (1925), 355.

44 *Tobit,* chapter 6, has the hero concerned that he could not marry Sarah because a demon killed seven men that she had been previously betrothed to. Lawrence M. Wills, ed., *Ancient Jewish Novels: An Anthology* (Oxford: Oxford University Press, 2002), 62, 75–76.

45 See Ahrend, "Bride Going Around the Bridegroom," 8.

to the custom. Yevamot 62b cites Jeremiah 31:21, the verse brought as the earliest source for the bride circling the groom, as a proof text for the idea that an unmarried man "does not have a wall" (בלא חומה). This teaching is well known and appears in the *Tur* in the very beginning of the laws regarding marriage in *Even HaEzer,* and from there was included in a more abbreviated version by Rabbi Moshe Isserles in *Shulḥan Arukh, Even HaEzer* 1:1.

Various explanations were given as to why having a wife is like having a wall,[46] in particular that she protects her husband from sin.[47] This idea can be found in the *Wisdom of Ben Sira* (36:30): "A vineyard with no wall will be overrun; a man with no wife wanders and strays."[48] Many connected the teaching of Yevamot 62b to the bride circling the groom. Rabbi Yosef Shapira (1778–1854) explained that a wife protects her husband from doing stupid things which lead to sin, and to highlight this protection, she circles the groom.[49]

Others viewed this as a supernatural protection for the wedding day.[50] The explanation for the custom reported in the name of Rabbi Shalom Rokeach, the first Belzer Rebbe (1781–1855), is that the bride circles the groom to create a protective barrier, a wall, to protect him from negative spiritual forces (חיצונים), based on Yevamot 62b.[51] Rabbi Shmuel Meir

46 Note that Song of Songs 8:9–10 also compares a woman to a wall.

47 For example, Maharsha understands that a wife protects her husband from the evil inclination and sin. This is in accordance with the statement of Rabbi Ḥiyya in Yevamot 63a–b that a husband should be thankful for his wife since she saves him from sin, which Rashi explains as sexual thoughts. Similarly, in contemporary times, Yisrael Samet, "The Meaning of *Ḥuppa* Customs – Part 2," *Tzohar* 10 (2001), 166 [Hebrew], explains that a wife provides a safe home protected from the dangers of the outside world.

48 Gail Labovitz, *Marriage and Metaphor* (Lanham: Lexington Books, 2009), 139, note 20.

49 *Ḥiddushei Mahari Shapira - Yevamot* (Jerusalem, 1991), 3. Found at the end of the volume of comments on Pesaḥim and Avoda Zara.

50 See note 39 to Yevamot 62b in the ArtScroll Mesorah Schottenstein edition of the Talmud (Brooklyn, NY, 1999).

51 Baruch Mordechai Cooperstein, *Ezer MiKodesh* (Jerusalem, 1993), 139–40, chapter 6, *siman* 46, note 79.

HaKohen Hollander (1888–1964)[52] explains that just as it is customary for members of the *ḥevra kaddisha* to circle around the deceased to chase away negative spiritual forces (לגרש את המקטרגים), so too the bride circles the groom to do the same. He explains that as in the story of Jericho, where seven circuits were needed to break down the wall, so too seven circles are needed to banish the negative forces.[53] He then relates the story of Rabbi Barukh of Medzhybizh, who once dealt with a young man who lost his virility and came to him for help. Rabbi Barukh investigated and discovered that this young man's wife did not circle him at his *ḥuppa*. He ordered the young man to divorce his wife and remarry her, this time with circling. Rabbi Barukh is reported to have said that his grandfather, the Baal Shem Tov, said that the seven circles are needed to chase away a kind of negative wife (זיווג מצד הסיטרא אחרא) associated with the demonic Lilith.[54] A similar story is told of Rabbi Aharon Rokeach, the fourth Belzer Rebbe (1880–1957), where a young couple could not have children, and it was attributed to the fact that because they got married on a snowy day, the *ḥuppa* was rushed and the bride did not circle the groom. In this case they were instructed to do the circling now.[55]

We can now understand that the aspect of protection was indeed implied in the earliest mention of this custom, when Rabbi Dossa was told that Jeremiah 31:21 was the source of the custom.

---

52 For biographical information, see Meir Wunder, *Encyclopedia LeḤakhmei Galitzia*, vol. 2 (Jerusalem, 1982), 96–99.

53 It has also been suggested that seven circles can both destroy a wall, as in Jericho, or build a wall, as in the *ḥuppa*. See *Pardes Eliezer*, vol. 4 (Brooklyn, NY: Machon Damesek Eliezer, 2014), 145. See Meir Benayahu, *Sefer Zikaron LeRav Yitzhak Nissim*, vol. 6: *Maamadot UMoshavot* (Jerusalem: Yad HaRav Nissim, 1985), 121–25 for kabbalistic sources that explain how the same force that destroyed the wall of Jericho can also be used to build and protect. There is also a tradition that Jericho was surrounded by seven walls; see Yaakov Yisrael Stell, "Ḥomot Yeriḥo: Minyanan, Tivan VeInyanan," *Kovetz Ḥitzei Gibborim* 10 (Nisan 5777/2017), 542–85.

54 Shmuel Shavmer, *Siḥot Talmidei Ḥakhamim* (Tel Aviv, 1950), 151, *siman* 86. A much abbreviated version is found in Asher Anshel Katz, *Otzar Minhagei Nisuin* (Williamsburg, 1999), 118–19. Special thanks to Avi Levine who gave me this book as a gift. An expanded version of the story can be found in *Pardes Eliezer*, vol. 4 (Brooklyn, NY: Machon Damesek Eliezer, 2014), 136–37.

55 Baruch Mordechai Cooperstein, *Ezer MiKodesh* (Jerusalem, 1993), 140, chapter 6, *siman* 46, note 79.

## THE SHIFT FROM THREE TO SEVEN CIRCLES

A popular source given for the custom that the bride circles the groom under the *ḥuppa* is Rabbi Shlomo Ganzfried's *Kitzur Shulḥan Arukh,* where he writes that the bride circles the groom three times. This is found in Rabbi Ganzfried's additions to the 1859 edition of *Siddur Derekh HaḤayim,*[56] and was repeated in the first edition of his *Kitzur Shulḥan Arukh,* published in 1864, and appeared in later editions as well.[57] Some versions of the *Kitzur Shulḥan Arukh* have the number of times as seven instead of three.[58] This version began to appear in editions published in Rabbi Ganzfried's lifetime,[59] and in most subsequent editions.[60] Some contemporary editions preserve the original version of three circles.[61]

It would seem that the text was emended in order to conform with the popular custom that the bride circles the groom seven times. Rabbi Ganzfried himself, in the introduction to the Lemberg 1884 edition, writes that he made a few corrections and changes in this edition, and this may be one such change.[62] Whether it mentions three circles

56 Yaakov ben Yaakov Moshe Lorberbaum of Lissa, *Siddur Derekh HaḤayim* (Vienna, 1859), 114b, *siman* 5.

57 In the first edition it appears in 143:5. In subsequent editions, such as the Warsaw 1874 edition, it is found in 147:5.

58 This was noted by Menachem Mendel Pakshar, *Invei HaGefen* (Jerusalem, 1985), 93, note 143, where he attributes it to textual variants. As we will see, the number of circles was intentionally changed over time.

59 For example, the Lemberg 1884 edition, which has an introduction by Rabbi Ganzfried. Rabbi Ganzfried lived from 1804 until 1886.

60 For example, the Lublin 1905 edition; the Vilna 1915 edition; the Hebrew Publishing Company 1927 edition; the Jerusalem 1944 edition; the Basel 1945 edition; Shlomo Zalman Braun's edition with his commentary *She'arim Metzuyanim BeHalakha,* vol. 4 (New York: Feldheim, 1951), 58; Eshkol 1954 edition; the Shabtai Frankel edition (Bnei Brak, 1987), Eliakim Shelneger, *Kitzur Shulḥan Arukh im Divrei Mishna Berura,* vol. 2 (Be'er Yaakov, 1990), 807; and the Shai Lamora edition (Jerusalem, 1999). Seven is also the version in Hyman Goldin's English translation of *Kitzur Shulchan Aruch, Code of Jewish Law,* vol. 4 (New York: Hebrew Publishing Co., 1963), 11.

61 *Kitzur Shulḥan Arukh* (Jerusalem: Mossad HaRav Kook, 1973). This version states on the cover page that it is 'fixed' (מתוקנת). The editions published in Tel Aviv by Sinai Publishing also preserve the three circles. See, for example, the 1967 and 1978 editions.

62 *Kitzur Shulḥan Arukh* (Lemberg, 1884), author's introduction.

or seven, no explanation is given in the *Kitzur Shulḥan Arukh* for the practice.

The custom also appears in Rabbi Yaakov Emden's *Siddur Beit Yaakov,* in the description of the wedding ceremony.[63] In language very similar to that found in the *Kitzur Shulḥan Arukh,* Rabbi Emden writes that it is customary for the bride to circle the groom three times. Although he lived a century before the *Kitzur Shulḥan Arukh* was published, this is not in fact an earlier source for the custom. *Siddur Beit Yaakov* was not actually written by Rabbi Yaakov Emden, and was published in 1881, after the *Kitzur Shulḥan Arukh.* The information found in *Siddur Beit Yaakov* is a combination of commentaries from Rabbi Emden and much later material.[64] This custom was included in it from Rabbi Shlomo Ganzfried's additions to the 1859 edition of *Siddur Derekh HaḤayim* and later incorporated into his *Kitzur Shulḥan Arukh.* This has led to a certain amount of confusion. For example, the Vilna 1902 edition of *Kitzur Shulḥan Arukh* states in the main body of the text that the custom is to circle seven times, but in a note it states that Rabbi Yaakov Emden says it is three times. However, this is not found in the actual writings of Rabbi Yaakov Emden, and the note is actually quoting the version of the custom found in *Siddur Derekh HaḤayim* and earlier editions of *Kitzur Shulḥan Arukh* itself, which was in turn the basis for the passage in *Siddur Beit Yaakov,* and so attributed to Emden.

We have seen that the original custom was for the bride to circle three times, but over the years it changed to seven times, a process that can be seen in the various editions of *Kitzur Shulḥan Arukh.* Although today the prevalent custom is for the bride to circle the groom seven times,[65] the custom of three times persisted until the very recent past. For example, Rabbi Yitzhak Zvi Levovitch reported that in Hungary in the 1930s the custom was to circle three times.[66]

---

63 *Siddur Beit Yaakov* (Lemberg, 1903), 124.

64 See Moshe Zvi Aryeh Bik's introduction to his 1962 facsimile edition of Emden's *Amudei Shamayim,* 1.

65 *Pardes Eliezer,* vol. 4 (Brooklyn, NY: Machon Damesek Eliezer, 2014), 142.

66 Yitzhak Zvi Levovitch, *Shulḥan HaEzer,* vol. 2 (Dej, 1932), 32b, *siman* 7, note 8.

We find a few explanations from the late 1800s and early 1900s for why circling was done seven times. These reasons are not found in earlier sources, and appear to be creations of the various authors to explain the current custom.[67] Rabbi Yaakov Kahane, in his book of responsa, *She'erit Yaakov*, published in 1895, suggests that the word for bride, כלה, appears seven times in the Song of Songs (although it actually appears six times),[68] or that it signifies that the marriage is holy, the seven circles representing God's abode above seven heavens.[69] Other explanations rely on *Gematria*, such as that brought in *Yalkut Yashar*, which states that the last letters of נקבה תסובב add up to seven.[70] Following the idea that circling three times relates to the number of times the word וארשתיך is found in Hosea 2:21–22, it was suggested that seven represents the number of items through which the betrothal is accomplished in those same verses.[71] It has also been proposed that the circles represent the seven days of the week, or the seven times the word *kol* is mentioned in Psalm 29,[72] or that the bride in some fashion represents Shabbat.[73] Kabbalistic explanations were also given, based on the seven lower *sefirot*.[74]

Later, other explanations were offered in line with changing tastes and perspectives. Rabbi Yona Metzger, in his book *BeMaagalei HaḤayim*,

---

67 Aharon Mendel Cohen (1866–1927) in his book *Kelilat Ḥatanim* (Cairo, 1910), 11a, first gives two explanations, with sources, regarding circling three times (*siman* 4), and then provides two explanations for circling seven times with no references (*siman* 5), one of which he explicitly states is his own idea. He explains that it is either symbolic of the seven *ḥuppot* God made for Adam, an explanation later brought in Moshe Weinstock, *Siddur HaGeonim VehaMekubalim VehaḤasidim*, vol. 20 (Jerusalem, 1980), 134, or of seven good things that a wife brings. Note that some sources indicate that God made ten *ḥuppot* for Adam; see *Pardes Eliezer*, vol. 4 (Brooklyn, NY: Machon Damesek Eliezer, 2014), 144, note 13.

68 See the discussion of this discrepancy in *Pardes Eliezer*, 143, note 12.

69 Yaakov Zev Kahane, *She'elot UTeshuvot She'erit Yaakov* (Vilna, 1895), 75a, *Even HaEzer* 18.

70 Yeshaya Rokach, *Yalkut Yashar* (Bilgoraj, Poland, 1937), 111. See there for another explanation, based on the spelling of the word סוכה.

71 Menachem Hacohen, *Sefer Ḥayei Adam – Kelulot* (Jerusalem: Keter, 1986), 63.

72 Menachem Mendel Pakshar, *Invei HaGefen* (Jerusalem, 1985), 93, note 143.

73 Moshe Wolfson, *Emunat Itekha*, vol. 2 (Jerusalem, 2004), 281.

74 See, for example, Avraham Twersky, *Magen Avraham*, vol. 2 (Lublin, 1887), 110 (Koraḥ).

a book on the Jewish life cycle intended for a modern audience, explains that the bride circles the groom seven times in order to break down the barriers between them, as with the walls of Jericho.[75] Rabbi Yaakov Rakovsky, for many years the *rav* of the Hadassah Medical Organization, said in the name of his father, Rabbi Avraham Barukh Abba Rakovsky (1885–1959) that the seven circles represent the idea that every day of the week, at all times and in all directions, the husband will always see only his wife, and not be tempted by others.[76]

Some sources indicate that they were unsure why the custom was indeed seven times if the explanation taken from the *Tashbetz* applies only to three times. For example, Rabbi Yisrael Chaim Friedman of Rakov (1852–1922) gives a complicated kabbalistic explanation for seven times, and concludes by saying that this is all speculation.[77]

### KABBALISTIC REASONS FOR SEVEN CIRCLES

When and why did this custom shift? It seems to have been influenced by various other customs that involved some kind of circling, which for kabbalistic reasons were associated with the number seven rather than three. As these customs became more widespread, circling in general became associated with the number seven.

The first example of this is the *hakafot* on Simḥat Torah. The Mishna (Sukka 4:5) reports that in the Temple, the altar was circled seven times on Hoshana Rabba. This was replicated in the synagogue to remember what was done in Temple times.[78] Rav Saadia Gaon and Rav

---

75 Yona Metzger and Nachum Langental, *BeMaagalei HaḤayim – BeḤaye HaAdam* (Tel Aviv: Yedioth Ahronoth, 1988), 81. It has also been suggested that the seven circles represent in some fashion the creation of the world, showing that a new relationship is being created, Nancy Wiener, *Beyond Breaking the Glass* (New York: CCAR, 2001), 37.

76 Yaakov Rakovsky, *Arukhat Bat Ami*, vol. 4 (Jerusalem, 1993), 384. He brings the same idea in volume 2, 192, but does not state that he heard it from his father there.

77 Yisrael Chaim Friedman, *Likkutei Mahariḥ*, vol. 3 (New York, 1965), 131b, כל זה כתבתי רק בדרך סמך ובדרך אפשר. This is the reason for the seven times referred to in Yitzhak Zvi Levovitch, *Shulḥan HaEzer*, vol. 2 (Dej, 1932), 32a, *siman* 7, note 8. He notes that it is a kabbalistic explanation (על פי סוד) and does not quote it. By contrast, he quotes in full three reasons for three times.

78 *Yalkut Shimoni, Tehillim, remez* 703.

Hai Gaon both report a custom to circle the *bima* three times on each of the intermediate days of the festivals, and seven on Hoshana Rabba.[79] Although this would universally shift to once a day during Ḥol HaMoed,[80] we can see from here that three times was also considered a significant number for circling. This practice of circling the *bima* seven times was carried over into Simḥat Torah by Rabbi Isaac Luria (the Ari) and his students, as reported by Rabbi Hayim Vital.[81] Thus, the practice of the bride circling the groom predated that of *hakafot* on Simḥat Torah. However, at that time the custom was to circle the groom only three times.

Some communities did only three *hakafot* on Simḥat Torah, as reported by Rabbi Eliya Shapira (1660–1712) in his work *Eliya Rabba,* and by Rabbi Joseph ben Meir Teomim (1727–92) in his work *Peri Megadim.*[82] This version of the custom was still reported in various Ashkenazic communities into the late 1800s and early 1900s.[83]

The practice of seven *hakafot* on Simḥat Torah was popularized outside of kabbalistic circles in Israel when it was included in the books *Nagid UMetzaveh,* published in 1712, and *Ḥemdat Yamim,* published in 1731.[84] These books were reprinted multiple times in the 1700s, and *Ḥemdat Yamim* was particularly influential.[85]

Another kabbalistic custom involving seven circles is that of circling the deceased. This parallels the bride circling the groom in that it was done in order "to chase away the forces of impurity."[86] The custom was first mentioned by Rabbi Abraham Saba (1440–1508), who associated it with protection from demonic forces coming from "the side of Lilith," generated from the seed spilled by the deceased throughout his

79 See Avraham Yaari, *Toldot Ḥag Simḥat Torah* (Jerusalem: Mossad HaRav Kook, 1998), 259.

80 Ibid., 291.

81 Ibid., 266.

82 *Eliya Rabba, siman* 669; *Peri Megadim, Eshel Avraham,* siman 669. Yaari, *Toldot Ḥag Simḥat Torah,* 291.

83 Yaari, *Toldot Ḥag Simḥat Torah,* 292.

84 Ibid., 269.

85 Ibid., 268.

86 Moshe Hallamish, *Kabbalah: In Liturgy, Halakha and Customs* (Ramat Gan: Bar-Ilan University Press, 2000), 305.

life.[87] It was understood that there are seven groups of forces of impurity that must be banished.[88] The custom is mentioned by other kabbalists from the time of the Spanish expulsion,[89] and was popularized in extensive discussions by the Italian kabbalist Rabbi Aaron Brechia (d. 1639) in his most famous work, *Maavar Yabok,* which deals with sickness, death, and burial.[90]

The custom of circling the deceased had a very strong impact on the custom of circling the groom, as they both were understood to give protection from forces related to Lilith. In addition, the parallel between the seven days of mourning a death and the seven days of joy for a wedding is well known.[91]

Jeremiah 31:21, the proof text for circling and for the wife as a wall, is cited in the sixth *tikkun* of *Tikkunei Zohar* 23a, in connection with the seven days of Sukkot, when we circle the *bima* seven times while holding the lulav and etrog. Although written earlier, *Tikkunei Zohar* was first published in 1557, the first Zoharic volume to be printed.[92] Many more and newer editions were published in the 1700s.[93]

Due to these multiple associations of circling with the number seven, all circling became associated with seven. Rabbi David ibn Zimra (Radvaz, c. 1479–1573) suggests that the word *hakafa* itself can imply the number seven, writing that another term for a week or a cycle of seven years is *hekef.* He explains that this is why the deceased are circled specifically seven times for protection.[94] It is not surprising that the circles

87 Meir Benayahu, *Sefer Zikaron LeRav Yitzhak Nissim,* vol. 6: *Maamadot UMoshavot* (Jerusalem: Yad HaRav Nissim, 1985), 107.

88 See Benayahu, *Sefer Zikaron,* 114.

89 Ibid., 106.

90 Ibid., 127–28.

91 See ibid., 124. The parallel between mourning and wedding practices is the subject of Shmuel Glick, *Or Noga Aleihem* (Efrat: Keter, 1997). See 188–205 there regarding the parallel between circling the groom and circling the deceased.

92 Boaz Huss, *The Zohar: Reception and Impact* (Oxford: Littman Library of Jewish Civilization, 2016), 99.

93 Ibid., 228.

94 David ibn Zimra, *Magen David* (Amsterdam, 1713), 46a, beginning of letter *kuf.* This book was virtually unknown before being published in 1713, Benayahu, *Sefer Zikaron,* 127. The kabbalistic practice to circle the Shabbat table also shifted to seven

made by the bride would shift from three to seven over time, especially considering that seven was already a significant number for weddings, with the seven blessings and seven days of celebration. It would thus appear that "the prevalent custom of the bride walking around the groom seven times is kabbalistic in origin."[95]

This is why the custom to circle seven times was first reported in hasidic circles in the 1700s.[96] As it became more popular, the custom was changed in the *Kitzur Shulḥan Arukh* in the late 1800s. Although there were fewer reasons for seven circles as opposed to three,[97] and some of those reasons were not very convincing, once the frame of reference for circling was seven, based on Hoshana Rabba, Simḥat Torah,[98] circling the deceased, and *Tikkunei Zohar*, this number was carried over to the wedding custom as well.[99] The custom to circle three times for both Simḥat Torah and under the *ḥuppa* fell into a gradual decline from the 1700s onward, and was replaced with seven in both cases.[100]

While it is not common to see the bride circle the groom three times these days, I saw it happen at a wedding between an Ashkenazic groom and a Sephardic bride. The bride was not interested in circling seven times, as it is not a Sephardic custom. The groom, however, was concerned about ignoring a long-standing custom of his heritage, and

---

times; see the letter in *Alei Zikaron* 31 (Shevat 5777/2017), 81. On this custom and the various numbers associated with it, see Moshe Hallamish, *Hanhagot Kabbaliot BeShabbat* (Jerusalem: Orḥot, 2006), 287–88.

95 Aryeh Kaplan, *Made in Heaven* (New York: Moznaim, 1983), 160, note 69.

96 Shmuel Shavmer, *Siḥot Talmidei Ḥakhamim* (Tel Aviv, 1950), 151, *siman* 86.

97 See Eliyahu Shragai, "Takkanot UMinhagim BeYisrael," in *Shana BeShana* 5748 (1987), 271, who notes that there are many reasons given for circling three times but very few for seven times. He says that they parallel the seven kabbalistic *sefirot*.

98 See Yisrael Samet, "The Meaning of *Ḥuppa* Customs – Part 2," *Tzohar* 10 (2001), 166 [Hebrew]. See also *Pardes Eliezer*, vol. 4 (Brooklyn, NY: Machon Damesek Eliezer, 2014), 148.

99 See Abraham Chill, *The Minhagim* (New York: Sepher-Hermon Press, 1979), 282–83, where he concludes, "While no source can be found, one might surmise that it is in keeping with other encirclements in religious life such as *hakafot*."

100 Note that Yosef Yehuda Charney (*Sefer Masaot* [St. Petersburg, 1884], 300) describes a wedding in Derbent, Dagestan, in the 1860s and notes that the bride went around the groom "a few times" (פעמים אחדות), indicating a possibility that the exact number of times was not always considered particularly important.

he asked Rabbi Avigdor Nebenzahl, then chief rabbi of the Old City of Jerusalem, what to do. Rabbi Nebenzahl advised that, as a compromise, the bride should circle him only three times, as per the original custom, which satisfied both the bride and the groom.[101]

101 For other cases of refusal to circle with different rabbinic responses, see Irit Koren, "The Bride's Voice: Religious Women Challenge the Wedding Ritual," *Nashim* 10 (2005), 41–42; Masud Meshulam, *Mesos Ḥatan* (Tel Aviv, 2008), 16, note 31; Meir Eliyahu Machfutz, *Inyanei Ḥuppa* (Kfar Chabad, 2015), 56. I will note here a practice that I employed when the fathers insisted on standing next to the groom while the bride circled him, that for the last three circles the groom was left alone to be circled by the bride.

## *Chapter 2*

# Saying "*Leḥayim!*"

There is a popular custom to raise a glass of an alcoholic beverage and say, "*Leḥayim!*" at various special occasions. In this chapter we will trace the origin and development of this practice.

### EARLY SOURCES

A version of *leḥayim* as a blessing is found as early as I Samuel 25:6, as part of the greeting David sent to Nabal: "*Leḥai* (לחי)."[1] Although commentators have different explanations as to the exact meaning of this salutation, the common theme is that of a blessed life for Nabal and

1 In the verse it is not completely clear if the greeting phrase is just *leḥai* or the phrase *ko leḥai* (כה לחי), as the section reads: "And David sent ten young men, and David said unto the young men: 'Get you up to Carmel, and go to Nabal, and greet him in my name; and thus ye shall say (כה): "To life! (לחי), Peace be both unto thee, and peace be to thy house, and peace be unto all that thou hast"'" (I Sam. 25:5–6). The term כה may be the introduction to the greeting, as in this JPS English translation, or part of the greeting itself.

his family.[2] However, there is no biblical example of this blessing being connected with drinking wine.

Saying *leḥayim* in the context of drinking wine is found in *Tanḥuma* (*Pekudei* 2). There we are told how the Sanhedrin cross-examined witnesses: "At the time they examined the witnesses concerning a sin an individual had committed, the Sanhedrin and all the Israelites would go out into the public square. They brought there the individual who had been charged with the offense, which required stoning or one of the four death penalties that were imposed by the *beit din*. Two or three of the most distinguished leaders of the community would come forth and question the witness. After they returned from the cross-examination, a member of the Sanhedrin would say to them: '*Savri maranan* (Gentlemen, what do you think?).' They would announce whether he was to live (לחיים) or to die. If he were to be sentenced to stoning, they would bring a pleasant-tasting but potent wine, and give it to him to drink so that he would not suffer pain from the stoning." Further on, this midrash describes a practice to say *leḥayim* at Kiddush and Havdala: "Similarly, when the representative of the community held the Kiddush or Havdala cup in his hand, he would say '*Savri maranan*,' and the congregation would respond: '*Leḥayim*,' that is to say, 'May this cup be for the living.'"

We see that the earliest explanation for the custom, to say *leḥayim* was to distinguish this cup from the cup associated with death. It is the standard explanation brought in the classic works that explain Jewish customs such as *Sefer Taamei HaMinhagim UMekorei HaDinim*,[3] *Otzar Kol Minhagei Yeshurun*,[4] and *Otzar Dinim UMinhagim*.[5]

In *Tanḥuma*, it is the assembled congregation who says *leḥayim* rather than the person drinking. The idea that the person drinking says *leḥayim* is found in Shabbat 67b, in a discussion of what may be considered unlawful due to being categorized as superstitions ("the ways

---

2 See Yehuda Kiel, *Daat Mikra: Shmuel*, vol. 1 (Jerusalem: Mossad HaRav Kook, 1981), 252.

3 Avraham Sperling, *Sefer Taamei HaMinhagim UMekorei HaDinim* (Jerusalem: Shai Lamora, 1999), 137.

4 A. Hershovitz, *Otzar Kol Minhagei Yeshurun* (St. Louis, MO, 1918), *siman* 28:1, 66.

5 J. D. Eisenstein, *Otzar Dinim UMinhagim* (New York, 1917), 192.

of the Amorite"). There we find regarding a person who says while drinking "'Wine and life to the mouth of the Sages,' this does not fall into the category of the ways of the Amorite. There was an incident with R. Akiva, who made a banquet for his son, and over each and every cup he brought he said: 'Wine and life to the mouth of the Sages (חמרא וחיי לפום רבנן), life and wine to the mouth of the Sages and to the mouth of their students.'"[6] The Talmud Yerushalmi (Berakhot 6:8) records another version of this in a discussion on the special blessing *hatov vehameitiv* on wine:[7] "There was an incident with R. Akiva, who made a banquet for Shimon his son, and over each and every barrel that was opened he would bless and say: 'Good wine to the life of the Sages (חמרא טבא לחיי רבנן) and their students.'" Another version is found in Tosefta Shabbat 8:3: "There was an incident with R. Akiva who made a banquet for his son, and over each and every barrel that was opened he would say, 'Wine to the life of the Sages (חמרא לחיי רבננא) and the life of their students.'"

*Tanḥuma* discusses saying "*leḥayim*" as a response to *savri,* which explains the prevalent Sephardic custom of saying *leḥayim* as a response by those hearing the blessing over wine, rather than being said by those drinking themselves. However, the R. Akiva stories do not mention *savri,* and so they indicate that *leḥayim* functions as an independent blessing said by the person pouring or drinking the wine, similar to the prevalent Ashkenazic custom.[8]

No explicit reason is given in the Talmud for R. Akiva's blessing. Rabbi Hayim Yosef David Azulai, the Ḥida (1724–1806), gives two explanations.[9] His primary explanation, which he considers the simple meaning, is based on *Tanḥuma* (*Pekudei* 2), which says that due to the connection between wine and the death penalty noted there, when

6 Regarding the transposing of life and wine in this blessing, see Maharsha and *Iyun Yaakov* here. Many interpretations are found in the literature regarding this switch.

7 On the differences between the two Rabbi Akiva stories, see *Yefeh Einayim* on Shabbat 67b.

8 See Menachem Mendel Landa, *Siddur Tzluta DeAvraham,* vol. 1 (Tel Aviv: Grafika, 1958), 455.

9 Hayim Yosef David Azulai, *Petaḥ Einayim* (Livorno, 1790), 43a.

someone makes Kiddush or Havdala on wine, people say *leḥayim,* and so too at the occasion of R. Akiva's banquet.[10]

These are the earliest examples in Jewish literature of saying a version of *leḥayim* over wine. Rabbi Shmuel Avigdor Tosfaa (1806–66) in his *Minḥat Bikkurim* on the Tosefta, explicitly states that what R. Akiva did was just like the current practice to say, "To your life (לחייכון)" when drinking wine.

### DANGEROUS WINE

Among the *Rishonim* we find other reasons to say *leḥayim,* beyond the idea of distinguishing the wine from the wine drunk by a person sentenced to death. These are all based on the idea that there is danger inherent in drinking wine, thus necessitating saying *leḥayim* to offset potential harm.

*Sefer HaPardes* relates that Rabbi Yitzhak ben Yehuda (eleventh century), one of Rashi's teachers, explained the reason people say *savri* before Kiddush: "Since wine brought a curse to the world in the time of Noah, who became drunk from it and a curse went forth on Canaan," the person about to drink announces, "Understand (*savru*) that I am planning to drink something that brought a curse to the world." When the people respond with *leḥayim,* they are saying, "The drinking should be for you for life and not for any harm."[11] This explanation is also brought by Rabbi Eliezer ben Yoel (Raaviah, c. 1140–1220).[12]

---

10 He also gives a second reason, that it may be that R. Akiva was referring specifically to Nedarim 49a, where we find that rabbis are weak and sickly, and he was saying that they should drink wine for their health.

11 Hayim Yehuda Ehrenreich, ed., *Sefer HaPardes* (Budapest, 1924), 186–87. Also brought in *Shibbolei HaLeket, Seder Berakhot, siman* 140. Note that halakhic reasons are brought in both works for saying *savri* as well, before Rabbi Yitzhak's explanation. See also *Tosafot Berakhot* 43a *hoil.* For an overview of halakhic and other reasons, see Aron Maged, *Beit Aharon,* vol. 13 (New York: Balshon, 1978), *siman* 90, 605–7; Yehuda Ben David, *Shevet MiYehuda,* vol. 1 (Jerusalem, 2018), *siman* 42, note 181, 366–67. The Noah explanation is brought in the *Baḥ, Oraḥ Ḥayim* 174:9 in the name of Menahem of Mirzburg (Mahari Metz, often misquoted as Mahari Mintz, fourteenth century; see *Ḥiddushei UBiurei Maharshal* to *Tur, Oraḥ Ḥayim* 192).

12 David Devilsky, ed., *Sefer Raaviah* vol. 2 (Bnei Brak, 2005), *Pesaḥim, siman* 511. He also mentions in Berakhot, *siman* 120, that *leḥayim* is said because wine "brings a

The commentary of the *Baalei Tosafot* to Leviticus 10:9 states that it is customary that when someone is saying a blessing over wine in public and says, "*Savri maranan*," the congregation responds, "*Leḥayim*," because Adam got drunk on the wine from his marriage blessings (ברכת נישואין) and therefore sinned and was cursed with mortality. *Tosafot* then reference the story above of R. Akiva at his son's banquet, implying that it is for the same reason. Rabbi David Abudraham gives this explanation as well, based on the idea that the forbidden fruit which brought death to the world was grapes (Berakhot 40a; Genesis Rabba 15:17).[13] This same idea appears in *Tikkunei Zohar* (*tikkun* 24), where it is written that one must say, "*Savri maranan*," and the others answer, "*Leḥaye*" (לחיי), "in order to be connected to the tree of life and not the tree of death."[14]

*Tosafot* bring many other negative associations of wine, ending with the teaching in Sanhedrin 70a based on Proverbs 31:6, which states, "Give strong drink to him that is ready to perish, and wine to the bitter in soul," that wine was created to comfort mourners. Ketubot 8b reports the multiple cups of wine that were drunk at the home of the mourner as a component of comforting. Based on that, *leḥayim* expresses the desire to drink not in the context of mourning, but rather in the context of life.[15]

The four major negative associations of wine – the wine drunk by those about to receive capital punishment (*Tanḥuma*), the sin of Adam

---

curse to the world," but he does not specify there what the curse is.

13 Shlomo Wertheimer, ed., *Abudraham HaShalem* (Jerusalem, 1963), 151.

14 Although some sources indicate that the forbidden fruit itself was grapes and that Eve crushed it into wine for Adam (Genesis Rabba 19:5), from the language of *Tosafot* here it appears that they are not following that approach, as they state that Adam got drunk and then sinned, so the drinking itself was not the sin of eating the forbidden fruit. See also Sanhedrin 70b, Numbers Rabba 10:4. However, *Tikkunei Zohar* explicitly states that this explanation is connected to the idea that grapes were the forbidden fruit. Avraham Sperling, *Sefer Taamei HaMinhagim UMekorei HaDinim* (Jerusalem: Shai Lamora, 1999), 137, note *alef*, understands that *Tosafot* here are following that approach as well.

15 See *Baḥ, Oraḥ Ḥayim* 174:9, who brings this idea in the name of the Maharshal. It is found in *Ḥiddushei UBiurei Maharshal* to *Tur, Oraḥ Ḥayim* 182. It is also found in the *Etz Yosef* commentary to *Tanḥuma* by Ḥanoch Zundel ben Joseph (d. 1867).

(*Tosafot*), the curse of Noah (*Sefer HaPardes*),[16] and the connection with mourning – are the standard explanations[17] given in most discussions on the topic of saying *leḥayim*.[18]

There are various customs regarding whether more words are added to the *leḥayim*, such as לחיים טובים ולשלום,[19] and whether a handshake is involved as well.[20] The custom of the Bulgarian rabbi, Rabbi Astruc ben David ibn Sangi (1570–1643),[21] as reported by his student Rabbi Hayim Benvenisti (1603–73) in his book *Shayarei Knesset*

---

16 These three are mentioned by Aaron b. Yaakov HaKohen, *Orḥot Ḥayim* (Jerusalem, 1956), 73, *Hilkhot Birkat HaMazon* 20.

17 For more mystical and *Gematria*-based explanations, see Hayim Palagi, *Kaf HaḤayim, Oraḥ Ḥayim* 167:108.

18 It is because of this that the Munkacs Rebbe, Hayim Elazar Spira (1868–1937) brings in the name of his father, Zvi Hirsch Spira, that it is inappropriate to say *leḥayim* at the Shabbat daytime Kiddush, as it implies that protection from harm is needed, whereas fulfilling a mitzva that needs wine itself provides protection. Since people do not customarily say *leḥayim* at the Friday night kiddush and only in the daytime, it implies that the daytime Kiddush is less of a mitzva. He notes that although R. Akiva said *leḥayim* over wine at a mitzva meal, since there is no particular mitzva to drink wine at such a meal, saying *leḥayim* for protection was warranted, but it should not be said at Kiddush where the mitzva is to use wine. He understands *Tikkunei Zohar* as referring to only wine drunk not in the context of Kiddush, although that entire *tikkun* is in fact talking about Kiddush. He goes on to say that "there is no greater degradation of the daytime Kiddush" than "yelling to each other arf, arf (הב, הב), *leḥayim, leḥayim*, like in a bar." Hayim Elazar Spira, *Nimukei Oraḥ Ḥayim* (Brooklyn, NY: Emes Publishing Institute, 2004), 195–96, *siman* 289, note 2. Still, *Tanḥuma* did explicitly talk about Kiddush and Havdala when discussing saying *savri* and *leḥayim*, and this is the normative practice.

19 See Yissachar Tamar, *Alei Tamar, Yerushalmi: Zera'im*, vol. 1 (Givatayim, Israel: Atir, 1979), Berakhot 6:8, 229–30; Gavriel Zinner, *Nitei Gavriel: Hilkhot Nesuin*, vol. 2 (Jerusalem: Shemesh, 1998), 80:24, 147; Simha Rabinowitz, *Piskei Teshuvot*, vol. 2 (Jerusalem, 2002) 174:15, 518–19.

20 Zinner, *Nitei Gavriel: Hilkhot Nesuin*, 80:23, 147. The handshake is an ancient and well-known "symbol of amity." Raymond Firth, *Symbols: Public and Private* (London: Allen and Unwin, 1973), 137.

21 On this figure, see Matt Goldish, *Jewish Questions: Responsa on Sephardic Life in the Early Modern Period* (Princeton, NJ: Princeton University Press, 2008), lxi; Moshe Amar, *Sefer She'elot UTeshuvot R. Astruc b. David ibn Sangi* (Ramat Gan: Bar-Ilan University Press, 1982).

*HaGedola,* was to say בשמחתכם (in your happiness) instead of *leḥayim.*[22] Thus we find an idea to simply add a positive statement to counter the negative associations of wine, and it does not have to be *leḥayim,* or even a variation of the word *ḥayim* per se.

## *LEḤAYIM* ON LIQUOR

In all of these sources, the reason for *leḥayim* is specific to wine. Because of that, it is not customary for people to say *savri* over other alcoholic drinks, which as we saw was considered the prompt that would generate the response *leḥayim.*[23] Still, nowadays it is common to say *leḥayim* over liquor as well. In hasidic literature, explanations for this can be found in *Gematria* and word play.[24]

Many sources add that beyond the specific incidents with Adam and Noah, the more general reason for saying *leḥayim* is "since wine causes drunkenness and much harm occurs due to drunkenness… he says *savri maranan* that this cup should be for life and not cause matters of death."[25] Rabbi Sinai Sapir, in his *Olat Ḥodesh,* writes that R. Akiva's blessing became the source to say *leḥayim* not only when drinking wine, but any drink that is considered the "wine of the land" (חמר מדינה).[26] Similarly, *Otzar Kol Minhagei Yeshurun* explains that nowadays, liquor often replaces wine, so we say *leḥayim* on liquor as well.[27] This seems to be the simple explanation of the custom; it started with wine and came

22 *Shayarei Knesset HaGedola, Oraḥ Ḥayim* 174:2.

23 See *Baḥ, Oraḥ Ḥayim* 174:9, who brings a quote from Menahem of Mirzburg (Mahari Metz, fourteenth century) that *savri* is not said over beer, and presumably *leḥayim* is not said either, as he connects the two. See also *Ateret Zekenim* on *Oraḥ Ḥayim* 190:1, who says that there are reasons not to say *savri* on anything other than wine, but only gives the reason of Menahem of Mirzburg, which is that wine caused a curse in the time of Noah. See also Elazar Giman, *Sifran shel Tzaddikim* (Lublin, 1928), 1:8, 9, where it is reported that the Baal Shem Tov said not to say *leḥayim* over beer, but no explicit reason is given.

24 Avraham Sperling, *Sefer Taamei HaMinhagim UMekorei HaDinim* (Jerusalem: Shai Lamora, 1999), 496.

25 *Shayarei Knesset HaGedola, Oraḥ Ḥayim, Beit Yosef* 167:4. Similarly in *Shibbolei HaLeket, Seder Berakhot, siman* 140 and *Tanya Rabbati, siman* 24.

26 Sinai Sapir, *Olat Ḥodesh* (Warsaw, 1847), Iyar, *derush* 2, 199.

27 A. Hershovitz, *Otzar Kol Minhagei Yeshurun* (St. Louis, MO, 1918), *siman* 28:1, 65.

to include other alcoholic drinks. We saw that wine was associated with certain negative outcomes, and these concerns apply equally, if not more so, to liquor, so *leḥayim* would be appropriate for liquor as well.

**POISON**

The earliest versions of *Tanḥuma* add a few words when discussing the practice to say *leḥayim* at Kiddush and Havdala:[28] "Similarly, when the representative of the community held the Kiddush or Havdala cup in his hand and he was afraid that there might be poison in the cup (והוא ירא מסם המות שלא יהא בכוס), he would say *savri maranan* And the congregation would respond with *leḥayim*."[29] In some current editions of *Tanḥuma* these words are either left out entirely or included in parentheses.[30]

Why would anyone be afraid that their Kiddush cup was poisoned? There are a number of ways to understand this unusual concern.

It is possible to understand that the reference is not to actual poison, but to the "pleasant-tasting but potent wine" given to those about to be stoned so that their pain is lessened.[31] Although in *Tanḥuma* no substance is added to the wine to make it potent, we do find the idea of adding an ingredient to the wine in Sanhedrin 43a. There we find the statement of R. Ḥisda, "The court gives one who is being led out to be killed a grain of frankincense in a cup of wine in order to confuse his

---

28 Constantinople, 1522, Venice, 1545 (the Bomberg edition), Mantua, 1563, Prague, 1613. This is the version of *Midrash Tanḥuma* also known as *Tanḥuma* C or the "printed *Tanḥuma*," as distinct from the Buber *Tanḥuma*. This *Tanḥuma* is understood to date from the geonic period. See Anat Raizel, *Introduction to the Midrashic Literature* (Alon Shvut, Israel: Tevunot-Michlelet Herzog, 2011), 234–37.

29 This is the version quoted by Ḥida in his discussion of the topic. Hayim Yosef David Azulai, *Petaḥ Einayim* (Livorno, 1790), 43a.

30 These words do not appear in Samuel Berman, *Midrash Tanhuma-Yelammedenu: An English Translation of Genesis and Exodus* (Hoboken, NJ: Ktav, 1996), as he translated based on the Vienna 1863 edition; see x, note 2.

31 Avraham Orenstein, *Encyclopedia Letaarei Kavod BeYisrael*, vol. 3 (Tel Aviv: Netzach, 1963), 1662. This would also be indicated by the fact that the kiddush section in *Tanḥuma* opens with the word וכן (and similarly) indicating a connection to the previous passage about the cup given to the person about to be put to death. See Shmuel Pesah Bagamilsky, "Be'inyan Amirat Savri Maranan," *Kovetz He'arot HaTemimim VeAnshei Shlomenu*, vol. 3 (Morristown, NJ, 1988), 17.

mind, as it is stated: 'Give strong drink to him that is ready to perish, and wine to the bitter in soul' (Prov. 31:6)."[32] It is possible to understand that the term "poison" in *Tanḥuma*, literally "drug of death" (סם המות), is referring to the potent wine or the frankincense given to the person sentenced to death. This basic approach is brought by Rabbi Zedekiah ben Abraham Anav (1210–c. 1280) in his *Shibbolei HaLeket* in the name of his brother Rabbi Binyamin, who heard it from his teacher, Rabbi Yitzhak.[33]

Not only was the cup a cup of death; the frankincense added to it was dangerous on its own, a fact known in the ancient world. The first-century Greek physician Pedanius Dioscorides describes frankincense as "a good medicine, but if drunk by a healthy person brings on madness and, if too much is taken, produces fatal results."[34] Thus it would not be strange for frankincense to be termed a "drug of death." Still, it would be an unusual thing for a person to really worry about, particularly when no trial had taken place, and, in fact, capital punishment was extremely rare (Mishna Makkot 1:10).

Another approach is to view the poisoned cup in a more metaphoric sense as something denoting harm and suffering. The Maharal, in his comments on the R. Akiva episode in Shabbat 67b, gives numerous examples of verses in Tanakh where a cup of wine is used metaphorically to refer to destruction or calamity. Most explicitly, Psalms 60:5 uses the terminology of drinking "bitter/poisoned wine" (יין תרעלה) to describe being subjected to hardships. In this understanding, there is no physical poison in the cup, but more of a general concern that there may be a tragic outcome from the drinking, figuratively termed a cup poisoned with the drug of death.[35] This would bring the statement in *Tanḥuma* in line with the approach we saw of the *Rishonim*, that *leḥayim* is said to offset the dangers associated with wine, here symbolically termed poison.

---

32 Regarding the psychoactive properties of frankincense, see Arieh Moussaieff et al., "Incensole acetate, an incense component, elicits psychoactivity by activating TRPV3 channels in the brain," *FASEB Journal* 22, no.8 (August 2008), 3024–34.

33 *Shibbolei HaLeket, Seder Berakhot, siman* 140.

34 John M. Riddle, *Dioscorides on Pharmacy and Medicine* (Austin, TX: University of Texas Press, 1985), 66.

35 S. Z. Ehrenreich, ed., *Iggeret HaTiyul* (Jerusalem, 1957), 97.

### TOASTS IN THE ANCIENT WORLD

Drinking to good health is a practice found in many cultures around the world. A popular explanation for this is that it was originally done in order to "assure guests that the wine they were about to consume was not poisoned."[36] However, historians have not found evidence to support this assertion.[37]

Drinking, and drinking to health in particular, is attested to as a major component in the ancient Greek symposion, a banquet that took place after the meal.[38] The symposion had an elaborate introductory procedure, which included numerous cups of wine dedicated to pagan gods.[39] The first of these was the *metaniptris,* a cup of undiluted wine "offered to perform a libation to a Good Daemon" (most probably an apotropaic name for the dangerous aspect of Dionysus, god of wine). There was also a cup to honor Hygieia, the goddess of health. Later there was "a triple libation of mixed wine honoring Zeus the Olympian (or another Olympian god), some hero or heroes, and finally Zeus the Savior." This was followed later by "a choral song most often addressed to Apollo in his capacity as a healer or savior of mortals."[40] These basic practices were adopted by the Romans as well,[41] and were found in many cultures in the ancient world.[42]

---

36 Charles Panati, *Extraordinary Origins of Everyday Things* (New York: Harper and Row, 1987), 91.

37 Micah Issitt and Carlyn Main, *Hidden Religion: The Greatest Mysteries and Symbols of the World's Religious Beliefs* (Santa Barbara, CA: ABC-CLIO, 2014), 7.

38 Fiona Hobden, *The Symposion in Ancient Greek Society and Thought* (Cambridge: Cambridge University Press, 2013), 105–7.

39 For examples of these dedication toasts, see S. Douglas Olson, trans., Athenaeus, *The Learned Banqueters* (Cambridge, MA: Harvard University Press, Loeb Classical Library, 2009), Book 11, 367.

40 Marek Wecowski, *The Rise of the Greek Aristocratic Banquet* (Oxford: Oxford University Press, 2014), 38–39.

41 Everett Ferguson, *Backgrounds of Early Christianity* (Grand Rapids, MI: William B. Eerdmans, 2003), 106.

42 For example, the Norse custom where "a toast was first drunk to Odin for victory, then toasts to Njord and Frey for bountiful harvest and peace." Kimberley Christine Patton, *Religion of the Gods: Ritual, Paradox, and Reflexivity* (Oxford: Oxford University Press, 2009), 222.

Note that all of these introductory rites "have something in common, namely an apotropaic character, as if insuring the diners against the dangers inherent in the symposion. This menace is usually understood pragmatically as resulting from the subsequent excessive consumption of wine – the kingdom of Dionysus is a dangerous realm indeed, in which the help of Hygieia becomes truly indispensable."[43] The final cup, to Zeus the Savior, had the particular intention to serve as "a token of gratitude for the safe outcome of the feast and perhaps had the added connotation of averting danger in the future."[44] Beyond this, there was a pagan concern that the gods would be angered by the joy and happiness expressed by the mortals at the banquet, and so must be placated.[45] These ancient toasts were intended as "a dedication to a superior power whose benevolent aid the banqueters desired."[46]

We can now better understand why Shabbat 67b must specifically state that if a person says while drinking, "'Wine and life to the mouth of the Sages,' this does not fall into the category of the ways of the Amorite." There the Talmud previously notes that "one who says: 'My fortune be fortunate [*gad gaddi*] and be not weary by day or by night,' contains an element of the ways of the Amorite. R. Yehuda says: '*Gad* is nothing other than a term of idolatry,' as it is stated: 'And you that forsake the Lord, that forget My holy mountain, that prepare a table for Gad, and that offer mingled wine in full measure unto Meni' (Is. 65:11)." Similarly, saying, "Let my barrels be strengthened [*donu danei*]," contains an element of the ways of the Amorite. "R. Yehuda says: '*Dan* is nothing other than a term of idol worship,' as it is stated: 'They that swear by the sin of Samaria and say: "As your god Dan lives"' (Amos 8:14)." Rashi explains that in both instances R. Yehuda says that these incantations go beyond the "ways of the Amorite" and are actually real idolatry, as the terms *gad* and *dan* here are the names of pagan gods. In the opposing view, these words in the incantation do not refer to the names of pagan gods. In any

43 Wecowski, *The Rise of the Greek Aristocratic Banquet*, 39.

44 Delight Tolles, *The Banquet-libations of the Greeks* (Ann Arbor, MI: Edwards Brothers, 1943), 96.

45 Wecowski, *The Rise of the Greek Aristocratic Banquet*, 40.

46 Delight Tolles, *The Banquet-libations of the Greeks* (Ann Arbor, MI: Edwards Brothers, 1943), 78.

event, we see that there was a fine line between superstitious incantations and actual idolatry.

In the context of this discussion, given that in the ancient world it was customary to drink to the pagan god of wine and to the goddess of health to ensure that no harm would come from the wine, it was important for the Talmud to explicitly state that wishing someone health or life while drinking wine and not referring to any pagan god or superstitious, apotropaic practice is considered appropriate.

We now have an additional insight in the halakhic discussion regarding whether it is appropriate for the one drinking to say *leḥayim* before the blessing is said, or only after drinking a bit directly following the blessing, since it may be considered inappropriate to wish people *leḥayim* before thanking God for the wine.[47] Among pagans the toast was actually an aspect of worship through libation, so its function was similar to the blessing that Jews recite. Placing the *leḥayim* after the blessing and after some wine was drunk would further distance it from the ancient Greek and Roman practice.

## THE JEWISH TOAST

We have seen from numerous early sources that Jews were concerned about potential negative outcomes from drinking wine. Rabbi Shmuel Eliezer Eidels (Maharsha, 1555–1631) explicitly states that the purpose of R. Akiva's blessing was that the Sages "will not come to be in danger" (שלא יבואו לידי סכנה) from drinking wine. A similar idea is found in *Mateh Moshe* (1591), by Rabbi Moshe ben Avraham of Przemyśl. He writes that by saying *savri,* the one saying the blessing is inviting all of the assembled gathering to be part of one group, and when they say *leḥayim,* they are declaring their intention that drinking the wine should not have destructive results. It was important first to establish that they are all part of the group because "the merit of the many is great" and helps protect from any negative outcome from the wine drinking.[48]

47 See *Eliya Rabba, Oraḥ Ḥayim* 174:17; *Peri Megadim, Mishbetzot Zahav, Oraḥ Ḥayim* 174:11. See also J. D. Eisenstein, *Otzar Dinim UMinhagim* (New York, 1917), 192.

48 Moshe ben Avraham of Przemyśl, *Mateh Moshe* (Frankfurt, 1719), *Amud HaAvoda,* part 2, *siman* 349.

This also explains Rashi's comment to the R. Akiva story that his declaration of *leḥayim* is not considered superstitious because it is "just a blessing" (ברכה בעלמא); in other words, it has no particular apotropaic intent. Although the *leḥayim* was said in order for the wine not to have a destructive effect, this was accomplished not in a supernatural or superstitious manner. Rabbi Isaiah Horowitz (1558–1630) in his *Shenei Luḥot HaBrit* similarly explains that R. Akiva said *leḥayim* to remind the Sages that their intention in drinking wine should be for the words of Torah that would thereby come from their mouths, and not for other more mundane purposes.[49]

While both ancient Greeks and Jews recognized the danger inherent in drinking wine, the Greeks reached out to pagan gods for protection, while Jews, exemplified by the practice of R. Akiva, protected themselves by reminding those present that wine should only be used for positive purposes, without need of or recourse to supernatural protection.

---

49 *Shenei Luḥot HaBrit, Shaar HaOtiot, Kedushat HaAḥila, Emek Berakha* 3:10.

*Chapter 3*

# Covering Mirrors in the *Shiva* Home

## CLASSIC RABBINIC EXPLANATIONS

A primary symbol of Jewish mourning is covering the mirrors in a *shiva* house. When my father and teacher, Dr. Shlomo Zalman Ron *z"l*, passed away and we were preparing the house, his caregiver, Melvin Manalo, a native of the Philippines, remarked that they have the same custom in his homeland. When I mentioned this to a neighbor, he wondered if this is a vestige of crypto-Judaism in the Philippines. A short time later I met a native of Sri Lanka, and when I asked him about their customs, he mentioned the same tradition of covering mirrors in a house of mourning. These exchanges spurred me to investigate the origin of this custom.

Ancient mirrors were made of polished metal, like the copper mirrors donated to make the altar in the Tabernacle (Ex. 38:8). Glass mirrors were introduced in fourteenth-century Venice; however, the images were blurred and distorted. The technology to make perfectly reflective full-length mirrors was developed only in the late 1600s.[1] Until this time there is no mention of covering mirrors as a custom of Jewish mourning.

The earliest reference to this custom is found in the writings of Rabbi Moses Sofer (Ḥatam Sofer, 1762–1839), in additional notes placed between a eulogy delivered in March 1832 (II Adar 5592) and another given in December 1834 (Kislev 5595).[2] Here he explains that mirrors are turned around to face the wall based on the mourning practice of *kefiat hamitta*, overturning the beds. In the Talmud Bavli (Moed Katan 15b), Bar Kappara suggests a reason for this practice: Man was created in the image of God; but death may be the result of human sin, causing the divine image to be "overturned." To represent this idea we overturn our beds. In the Talmud Yerushalmi (Moed Katan 3:5), we find another reason. The marital bed is the facilitator for relations between husband and wife to create new life.[3] This facilitator is overturned when a life has ended. The Ḥatam Sofer explains that although we no longer practice overturning the beds,[4] the reasons given in both Talmuds for this custom apply to mirrors as well. Mirrors contain the image of the person looking into them, so mirrors are turned around because the divine image in the deceased has been "overturned." Additionally, Rashi (Ex. 38:8) explains

1 Charles Panati, *Extraordinary Origins of Everyday Things* (New York: Harper and Row, 1987), 229–30.

2 Moses Sofer, *Ḥatam Sofer: Derashot* vol. 2 (New York: Avraham Yitzchak Friedman, 1961), 774. Although it has been reported that the custom of covering mirrors was mentioned already in the 1700s by Yehuda Ayish, a prominent eighteenth-century Algerian rabbi (Yitzhak [Eric] Zimmer, "Kefiat HaMitta BeAvelut VeGilgulei Hilkhata VeHanhagata," *Sinai* 115 [1995], 249), in fact it is the later Algerian rabbi Eliyahu Gig, in his book *Zeh HaShulḥan* (Algeria, 1888), vol. 2, "Laws of Mourning" 78:5, 177, who states that the custom of his community is to cover the mirrors in a house of mourning when the male head of the household dies. The custom is not mentioned by Yehudah Ayish in his own listing of Algerian mourning customs, *Beit Yehudah* (Livorno, 1746), 115b–116. Gig in his introduction to *Zeh HaShulḥan* writes that while he based some of his book on the writings of Ayish, he added many customs, including newer ones, חדשים גם ישנים, not mentioned before. No explanation of the custom is given, or why it applies only if the deceased is male. All subsequent discussions of this custom do not distinguish between males and females. See also note 23 below.

3 Based on the commentary *Korban HaEida* on the Talmud Yerushalmi.

4 For the reasons that *kefiat hamitta* was discontinued, see *Tosafot*, Moed Katan 21a, *eilu*, *Shulḥan Arukh* Y. D. 387:2, and Zimmer's comprehensive article above, note 2.

that in Egypt mirrors facilitated relations between husband and wife just as beds did, so mirrors are turned around in a house of mourning just as beds were overturned in talmudic times.

Note that this explanation applies specifically to turning mirrors around just as beds were overturned, but does not relate to covering mirrors. Although it is not the majority view, based on this explanation some authorities ruled that in fact covering mirrors may not be sufficient; they must be turned around.[5] In addition, if turning mirrors is considered parallel to or a substitute for *kefiat hamitta,* then just as the beds are not overturned on Shabbat, so too the mirrors should not be turned around on Shabbat.[6] This would also mean that every mirror should be covered in the home of a mourner even if it is in a remote part of the house that the mourner does not use, just as all the beds in the home of the mourner were overturned.[7] The association of covering mirrors with *kefiat hamitta* is the explanation favored by Rabbi Joseph B. Soloveitchik (1820–92), albeit expressed in a somewhat different manner. Rabbi Aharon Ziegler explains in the name of Rabbi Soloveitchik the connection between overturned beds and mirrors, pointing out that they are both reminders that intimate relations are suspended during the *shiva;* he adds that mirrors are an expression of vanity and should not be used in a house of mourning.[8]

---

5 Ovadia Yosef in *Yabia Omer,* part 4, *Yoreh De'ah, siman* 35:3, states that it is not necessary to turn the mirrors around; since many mirrors today are attached to walls, covering is enough. However, see Nachum Yevrov, *Kitzur Hilkhot Avelut UBikkur Ḥolim* (Jerusalem, 2001), 439, note 3, and Gavriel Zinner, *Nitei Gavriel: Hilkhot Avelut,* vol. 1 (Jerusalem, 2000), 489, note 16, who explain that turning the mirror around, not just covering, may be needed.

6 This is the opinion of both Rabbis Moshe Feinstein and Joseph B. Soloveitchik; see the article by Hershel Schachter in *Kavod HaRav* (New York: Student Organization of Yeshiva, 1992), 278.

7 Schachter, *Kavod HaRav,* 278. However, see Hayim Goldberg, *Pnei Barukh* (Jerusalem, 1986) 501, who gives the opinion that this is not necessary.

8 Aharon Ziegler, *Halakhic Positions of Rabbi Joseph B. Soloveitchik* (New Jersey: Jason Aronson, 1998), 122. The idea that mirrors as a symbol of vanity should be covered during mourning is given as the primary reason for the custom by Moshe Sternbuch in *Teshuvot VeHanhagot* (Jerusalem, 1994), *Yoreh De'ah, siman* 585, 473. The rationale for covering mirrors is given as the reason for turning around or covering pictures of

Rabbi Moshe Eliezer Dunat (Hungary, 1861–1930) gives another reason for turning mirrors around, suggesting that "mirrors bring joy," which should be avoided by mourners. Again, the custom described is that of turning mirrors around rather than covering them.[9] He does not specify what sort of joy is generated by mirrors.

Rabbi Menachem Pollock (Hungary/United States, 1890–1953) in his book of responsa *Ḥelek Levi*, explains that mirrors are covered in a house of mourning because prayers are usually held there and one should not pray facing a mirror, lest it be thought that he is bowing to the image in the mirror.[10] Here we finally find an explicit reference to covering mirrors rather than turning them around. This is the explanation favored by Rabbi Ovadia Yosef.[11] Note that the prohibition against praying opposite a mirror was already mentioned in the 1500s by the Radbaz (Rabbi David ben Zimra, chief rabbi of Egypt),[12] but the first association between this and covering mirrors in a house of mourning appeared only hundreds of years later.

We have now looked at the three most popular explanations for this custom. Rabbi Leopold Greenwald (Transylvania/Columbus, Ohio, 1888–1955) offers these three explanations in his classic work on Jewish mourning, *Kol Bo al Avelut*, making them the most well-known explanations for covering mirrors,[13] and they are the standard explanations found in halakhic guidebooks intended for popular use, both in Hebrew and in English.[14] It is interesting to note that all of the early

---

people in the *shiva* house as well. See the note by Rabbi Tukachinsky's son in *Gesher HaḤayim*, vol. 1, 50.

9 Moshe Eliezer Dunat (Donath), *Dibburei Emet* (Bardiow: Horovitz, 1931), 42.

10 Menachem Segal Pollack, *Ḥelek Levi* (Szechenyi: Friedman Miskolc, 1934), *Yoreh De'ah, siman* 132, 123a.

11 *Yabia Omer*, part 4, *Yoreh De'ah, siman* 35:3.

12 *Responsa of Radbaz*, part 4, *siman* 107 (1, 178). See the discussion in *Yabia Omer*, part 4, *Yoreh De'ah, siman* 35:3.

13 Yekutiel Yehuda (Leopold) Greenwald, *Kol Bo al Aveilut* (New York: Moria, 1947), 262.

14 See, for example, Hayim Goldberg, *Pnei Barukh* (Jerusalem, 1986) 109, note 8; Maurice Lamm, *The Jewish Way in Death and Mourning* (New York: Jonathan David, 1969) 102–4; Abner Weiss, *Death and Bereavement: A Halakhic Guide* (New York: Union of Orthodox Jewish Congregations of America, 1991) 94.

rabbis who discuss this custom are from the general area of Hungary, Romania, and Transylvania.[15]

## SUPERNATURAL REASONS FOR COVERING MIRRORS

There is, however, another explanation. The Zohar (*Pekudei* 266a–266b) teaches that looking in mirrors too much leads to arrogance and gives power to evil spirits. Rabbi Yonatan Eybeschuetz (1690–1764) develops this idea and states that every picture and graven image has an impure spiritual force (רוח רעה) attached to it. Therefore people should be careful not to have such items in their homes. Furthermore, one must be especially careful not to look into mirrors unnecessarily, since spirits can enter the reflection in the mirror.[16] Based on this idea, Rabbi Joseph Schwartz (Romania, 1875–1944), in his book *Ginzei Yosef*, explains that mirrors are covered in the *shiva* house because evil spirits (מזיקין ורוחות רעות) are commonly found in the home where a death occurred. In order not to see these evil spirits in a mirror, it is turned around.[17] This is also the primary reason for the custom given by Rabbi Gershon Marber (Warsaw/Antwerp, 1872–1941) in his book on the laws of mourning, *Darkhei HaḤayim*. He quotes Rabbi Eybeschuetz and adds that during the *shiva* these spirits can more easily attach themselves to the reflection in a mirror, so they are covered to protect the mourners.[18] This mystical reason is sometimes given in addition to the three nonsupernatural explanations,[19] but appears as the sole reason for the custom in the

15 Zimmer, "Kefiat HaMitta BeAvelut," 250.

16 Yonatan Eybeschuetz, *Ye'arot Devash*, vol. 1 (Jerusalem: Machon Or HaSefer, 1988), *derush* 2, 36. This is also brought as a source for the idea that people should not be photographed; see Ari Wasserman, *Hegyonei haParashah*, vol. 1 (New York: Feldheim, 2008), 97–98; see also *Or Israel*, vol. 21 (Monsey, 2001), 257, for the common practice to be lenient in this matter.

17 Joseph Schwartz, *Ginzei Yosef* (Deva: Markowitz and Friedman, 1930), 320. This explanation was first published by Schwartz in his journal *Vayelaket Yosef* 14, no. 11 (Adar 1912), 83, *siman* 110.

18 Gershon Marber, *Darkhei HaḤayim* (Bilgoraj: Neta Kronenberg, 1937), 128.

19 Rabbis Ovadia Yosef and Moshe Sternbuch bring this explanation but note that it is not the primary reason for the custom. In *Sefer Netivot HaMaarav* by Eliyahu Biton, a book of Moroccan customs (Jerusalem: Makhon Bnei Yissaskhar, 1998), 157, note 34, it is brought as the reason על פי תורת הסוד.

popular books of Jewish customs, *Otzar Kol Minhagei Yeshurun*[20] and *Sefer Taamei HaMinhagim UMekorei HaDinim.*[21]

## SUPERNATURAL REASONS IN DIFFERENT CULTURES

What is the source for the idea that evil spirits may attach themselves to reflections in mirrors? Berakhot 54b (see Rashi) notes that some say mourners need special protection from evil spirits (מזיקין). In the ancient world, spirits were believed to be visible in reflective surfaces. By the sixth century BCE the Greeks had developed a practice of divination called catoptromancy (later adopted by the Romans),[22] where the future was thought to be made visible in a mirror or other reflective surface such as the water in a small bowl. It was considered a very bad omen for the reflective object to fall or break during divination, which is the origin of the superstition that a broken mirror leads to seven years of bad luck.[23] This practice came to include any shiny or reflective surface, such as crystal, fingernails, oil, and even eggshells. There is mention in Sanhedrin 101a of the "princes of oil" and "princes of eggs" that Rashi explains are *shedim* that are asked questions through oil, eggshells, and even thumbnails, but the replies that they give are not to be trusted.[24] Rashi also mentions consulting "princes of cups" through use of glass cups and "princes of thumbs" that were consulted through the use of a knife with a black handle (Rashi on Sanhedrin 67b, s.v. *dekapid*).[25] The idea of consulting spirits through reflective surfaces was well known

20 Avraham Hershovitz, *Otzar Kol Minhagei Yeshurun* (Lemberg, 1929), fourth edition, 303. Note that the custom of covering mirrors is not mentioned in the first three editions of this popular work.

21 Avraham Sperling, *Sefer Taamei HaMinhagim UMekorei HaDinim* (Jerusalem: Shai Lamora, 1999), 434, in the notes on the bottom of the page.

22 The Talmud (Ḥullin 41b) and Midrash note that reflections in water were also significant in pagan worship. See Maharitz Chajes, Ḥullin 41b.

23 Panati, *Extraordinary Origins of Everyday Things*, 11. Note that some associated a broken mirror with death; see, for example, John Brand, *Observations on the Popular Antiquities of Great Britain* (London: George Bell and Sons, 1893), 170: "Breaking a looking-glass betokens a mortality in the family, commonly the master."

24 See also the commentary *Yad Rama* to Sanhedrin 101a.

25 The idea that there is a "prince of thumbnails" may be the origin of the custom to hide the thumbnail when looking at the fingernails by the light of the Havdalah candle;

to both Jews and Gentiles throughout medieval times.[26] Rashi (Gen. 42:14) and Rashbam (44:5) both explain that Joseph claimed to use his special goblet for the purposes of divination,[27] and Radak mentions divining by means of shiny arrowheads, swords, thumbnails, and mirrors (Ezek. 21:26).

Spirits could be seen in all reflective surfaces, but there is no custom for Jewish mourners to cover all reflective surfaces, only mirrors. We do, however, find customs to cover reflective surfaces in other cultures. For example, throughout Scotland in the "death room" it was customary to have "mirrors and windows covered with sheets and curtains."[28] The custom to cover mirrors was reported by the Reverend George Low in his book *History of Orkney*, a study of the Orkney Islands to the north of Scotland. Reverend Low lived in Orkney from 1774 until his death in 1795, decades before the first mention of this custom in Jewish sources. He writes, "Funeral ceremonies [in Orkney] are much the same as in Scotland. The corpse is laid out after being stretched on a board, in a bed and thus continues till it is to be coffined in order to be buried. I know not for what reason they lock up all the cats of the house, and cover all looking glasses as soon as any of the family dies, nor can they give any satisfactory account of it."[29] Similarly, "in some parts of Germany and Belgium after a death not only the mirrors but everything that shines or glitters (windows, clocks, etc.) is covered up."[30] The practice is based

see Joshua Trachtenberg, *Jewish Magic and Superstition: A Study in Folk Religion* (New York: Atheneum, 1984), 308, note 26.

26 Trachtenberg, *Jewish Magic and Superstition*, 219–22.

27 See also Theodor Gaster, *Myth, Legend, and Custom in the Old Testament* (New York: Harper and Row, 1969), 218–22.

28 F. G. Vallee, "Burial and Mourning Customs in a Hebridean Community," *The Journal of the Royal Anthropological Institute of Great Britain and Ireland* 85, no. 1/2 (1955), 123, note 1.

29 George Low, *History of Orkney* (Kirkwall: Orkney Heritage Society, 2001), 55. Thanks to Richard Muirhead for his help with this book. Low is quoted in Richard Gough, *Sepulchral Monuments in Great Britain*, vol. 2 (London: J. Nichols, 1796), ccv, and G. F. Black, *County Folklore*, vol. 3, *Orkney and Shetland Islands* (London: David Nutt, 1903), 216.

30 James Frazer, *The Golden Bough* (New York: MacMillan, 1900), second edition, vol. 1, 294.

on the superstition that the reflection in a mirror, or even in water, can trap a person's soul.[31] This belief was already prevalent in ancient Greece, where "looking at one's reflection could invite death, because the reflection captured the soul."[32]

This idea persisted over many centuries in many cultures. The custom to cover mirrors after a death in the house can be found all over the world, including the countries where the earliest Jewish references to the custom originated, namely Hungary,[33] Romania,[34] and Transylvania.[35] In addition to these countries, the custom has been documented in places as diverse as the Dominican Republic,[36] England,[37] China,[38] India, and Madagascar.[39] It has been reported among Christians, Muslims,[40] and

---

31 Frazer, *The Golden Bough*, 292–95.

32 Sabine Melchior-Bonnet, *The Mirror: A History* (London: Routledge, 2001), 102.

33 Karoly Viski, *Hungarian Peasant Customs* (Budapest: Dr. George Vajna, 1932), 176.

34 A. Murgoci, "Customs Connected with Death and Burial Among the Romanians," *Folklore* 30 (1919), 92.

35 Laurence Rickels, *The Vampire Lectures* (Minneapolis: University of Minnesota Press, 1999), 13.

36 Wayland D. Hand, ed., *The Frank C. Baum Collection of North Carolina Folklore*, vol. 7 (Durham: Duke University Press, 1964), 81.

37 Charlotte Sophia Burne, *The Handbook of Folklore* (London: Sidgwick and Jackson, Ltd., 1914), 66. See also Frazer, *The Golden Bough*, 294. This custom was especially prevalent in rural England; see *The Atlantic Monthly* (Boston: Houghton, Mifflin and Co., 1894), 572.

38 R. F. Johnston, *Lion and Dragon in Northern China* (London: Murray, 1910), 294. The explanation given there is that "every mirror has a mysterious faculty of invisibly retaining and storing up everything that is reflected on its surface, and that if anything so ill-omened as a corpse or ghost were to pass before it, the mirror would thenceforth become a permanent radiator of bad luck." Furthermore, "in some households mirrors are covered up or turned upside down, not only when a corpse is in the house, but after sundown every day, for it is thought that evil spirits and other unlucky influences are free at night to wander whither they will, and that if they pass in front of a mirror that is not covered that mirror will become a source of danger and unhappiness to the family that owns it." In some parts of China, however, mirrors are used for the opposite effect, to frighten spirits away. See, for example, A. R. Wright, "Some Chinese Folklore," *Folklore* 14, no. 3 (Sept. 19, 1903), 297 (see there also the interesting Chinese custom to tie a red string on the wrist of a baby, 298) and Frazer, *The Golden Bough*, 293, note 2.

39 Frazer, *The Golden Bough*, 294.

40 Ibid.

African tribes.[41] The custom was considered "common among Irish Catholics, but not confined to them," and widespread throughout the early United States, among many cultures.[42]

An early visual depiction of this custom is found in a silk embroidery by Prudence Punderson (1758–1784) entitled *The First, Second and Last Scene of Mortality*, long before any mention of it in Jewish sources. The scene represents mortality, showing a coffin with a covered mirror behind it.[43] It was assumed that the viewer understood that a covered mirror represented death and mourning. When President Lincoln's body lay in state at the White House, part of the preparations included covering windows and mirrors. "The East Room, in which the remains were laid, was decorated in mourning... the windows at either end of the room were draped with black barege [a sheer fabric], the frames of the mirrors between the windows, as well as those over the marble mantles, being heavily draped with the same material. The heavy gildings of the frames were entirely enshrouded, while the plates of the mirrors were covered with white crape."[44] The custom also appeared at the funeral of the first United States president to die in office, William Henry Harrison, in 1841.[45]

---

41 Edwin Radford and Mona Radford, *Encyclopedia of Superstitions* (New York: Philosophical Library, 1949), 174, James Macdonald, *Religion and Myth of Africa* (London: D. Nutt, 1883), 24, Jason R. Young, *Rituals of Resistance: African Atlantic Religion in Kongo and the Lowcountry South in the Era of Slavery* (Louisiana State University Press, 2007), 166.

42 Hand, *The Frank C. Baum Collection*, 80–81. Rebecca Shrum, "Mirroring Others/ Fashioning Selves: A History of the Looking Glass in America" (PhD diss., University of South Carolina, 2007), gives numerous reports of mirrors covered after a death among 19th-century (non-Jewish) Americans; see there, 151–52, for reports from freed slaves and 164–66 for instances among whites. She suggests that the custom may have been introduced to America through slaves who brought the custom from Africa.

43 Martha B. Katz-Hyman and Kym S. Rice, eds., *World of a Slave* (Greenwood, 2011), 346: "In a late 18th century Connecticut needlework picture by Prudence Penderson, a covered mirror hangs over a coffin."

44 William T. Coggeshall, *The Journeys of Abraham Lincoln* (Columbus: Ohio State Journal, 1865), 110.

45 Claire A. Faulkner, "Arlington's Ceremonial Horses and Funerals at the White House," *White House History*, 19, 23.

The custom was so widely known that the term "crepe hanger" was used to denote a pessimist, a naysayer.[46]

Another early example comes from the Caribbean, where "the sickroom mirror had to be covered lest the reflection of the corpse attach itself to the glass. The clock, too, was hooded; otherwise the glance of the departing soul would freeze it forever at the instant of death."[47] The reason the sickroom mirror is covered is that "in time of sickness, when the soul might take flight so easily, it is particularly dangerous to project it out of the body by means of the reflection in a mirror."[48] The explanation for "the widespread custom of covering up mirrors or turning them to the wall after a death has taken place in the house" is that "it is feared that the soul, projected out of the person in the shape of his reflection in the mirror, may be carried off by the ghost of the departed."[49] Others have suggested that the custom is "traceable to a fear lest the disembodied spirit, wandering about in search of its former abode, might project itself into the mirror in which it beheld its likeness, and thus be irretrievably injured."[50] These beliefs may also be behind the widespread cross-cultural custom to pour out the water in a house where a person died, since the water provides a reflective surface that can trap a soul.[51]

While the Talmud and medieval Jewish sources discussed *shedim* seen in reflective surfaces, there was no mention of an individual's soul being projected onto or trapped in a reflection. Furthermore, the idea

46 See *World Wide Words*, issue 650, August 2009, where the idiom is explained as being based on the practice of "undertakers' assistants ... literal crêpe hangers, engaged to drape black crêpe across the windows and mirrors of a house in which a person has died."

47 Paul Witcover, *Zora Neale Hurston, Author* (New York: Chelsea House, 1991), 44.

48 This is also the reasoning behind the superstition not to allow a very young baby to look into a mirror, since its soul is not considered to be strongly anchored in its body yet. See Radford, 37, 174.

49 Frazer, *The Golden Bough*, 294–95. This is also the explanation given to me by Melvin Manalo for the practice of covering mirrors in the Philippines.

50 A. P. Bender, "Beliefs, Rites and Customs of the Jews Connected with Death, Burial and Mourning," *The Jewish Quarterly Review* 7 (London: D. Nutt, 1894), 117.

51 Daniel Sperber, *Minhagei Yisrael*, vol. 6 (Jerusalem: Mossad HaRav Kook, 1998), 82, note 2.

that the spirit of the deceased is malevolent and may seek to harm the living through a reflection is alien to Jewish belief. This, however, is a widespread folk belief throughout the Gentile world and led to the custom of covering mirrors in the room of a dying person and the house of mourners. According to this superstition, it is only in the house where the death has taken place that this has to be done, and only until the burial while the ghost of the departed lingers.[52] Since Gentiles would sometimes delay burials for days, the mirrors may have been covered for a while. The idea that souls of the deceased can be seen in reflections is a widespread folk belief even in the present day, and is the foundation of many ghost stories.[53] The superstition has led to the belief that spirits of the deceased can be photographed[54] and that images of the deceased can be permanently imprinted on mirrors.[55]

## HOW COVERING MIRRORS BECAME A JEWISH CUSTOM

The custom to cover mirrors in a house of mourning was not originally mandated by rabbinic authorities. The earliest discussions of this custom relate to a practice that was already widespread but needed some rabbinic approval. It seems that Jews picked up this custom from their neighbors; it resonated with them and eventually became an officially authorized practice.[56] It is not surprising that the Ḥatam Sofer was the first rabbinic authority to provide a halakhic background to the custom. He is well known for both his conservative attitude toward the preservation of Jewish customs[57] and his antagonism to the attempts of the

52 Frazer, *The Golden Bough*, 294.

53 An entire book has been written on the subject, Leslie Rule, *Ghost in the Mirror: Real Cases of Spirit Encounters* (Kansas City: Andrews McMeel Publishing, 2008).

54 See Barbara Allen, "The 'Image on Glass': Technology, Tradition, and the Emergence of Folklore," *Western Folklore* 41, no. 2 (April 1982), 93–102.

55 In folklore studies it is categorized as motif D1323.1.1. Magic mirror reflects the face of whoever dies, Stith Thompson, *The Motif-Index of Folk Literature* (Copenhagen and Bloomington: Indiana University Press, 1955–1958). Variants include the magic mirror, which imprints the face of one who is dying; see Mildred B. Nelson, "An Image: Borrowed and New," *Western Folklore* 29, no. 4 (Oct. 1970), 247, note 2.

56 Zimmer, "Kefiat HaMitta BeAvelut," 250.

57 Sperber, *Minhagei Yisrael*, vol. 2, 17–18, and vol. 3, 5–13.

Reform movement to change them.[58] This led him to provide meaningful Jewish reasons for practices that were observed at the time by religious Jews, even when they originated from local folklore or historical circumstances,[59] in order to show that Jewish customs are always rooted in ancient traditions and not susceptible to change or outside influence.

Although it is in fact non-Jewish in origin, and based on the superstition that souls of the deceased can be drawn into reflections, the real origins of the custom have been forgotten, and covering mirrors is now widely considered one of the signature symbols of Jewish mourning.[60] The idea that this custom was borrowed from other cultures is mentioned in less traditional Jewish writings, but is not generally mentioned in Orthodox literature.[61] However, at least one contemporary Orthodox rabbi, Rabbi Moshe Tzuriel, has written that this is an inappropriate custom and should be discontinued, although he does not explicitly state that it originated outside of Judaism.[62]

Although, as we have seen, the covering of mirrors in the house where a death occurred is a common practice in many cultures

---

58 Ibid., vol. 2, 122–25. See also Assaf Yedidya, "Orthodox Reactions to Wissenschaft Des Judentums," *Modern Judaism* 31, no. 1 (February 2011), 70.

59 See, for example, Ḥatam Sofer's explanation for the custom of not learning Torah on *Nittel Nacht*, Sperber, *Minhagei Yisrael*, vol. 3, 94.

60 See, for example, Sara Carr, *Spirituality, Values and Mental Health* (New Jersey: Jessica Kingsley Publishers, 2007), 85, who writes that it is a Jewish custom that "later passed into Christian tradition."(!)

61 Solomon Freehof, *Recent Reform Responsa* (Cincinnati: Hebrew Union College Press, 1960), 179–82. However, Freehof seems to misinterpret Hershovitz in *Otzar Kol Minhagei Yeshurun* as saying that the reason for covering mirrors is that "the departing spirit might be caught in the mirror," when Hershovitz actually was referring to the idea mentioned by Eybeschuetz that an evil spirit (רוח) would attach itself to the reflection in the mirror, not the departing soul. See also Alfred J. Kolatch, *The Jewish Book of Why* (New York: Jonathan David, 1981), 64, who gives, among other explanations: "The practice of covering mirrors or of turning them to face the wall, which was common among early cultures, has been explained as part of man's primitive belief that a man's soul was his image or shadow. The soul was reflected in a mirror (and in water). Since it was feared that when the soul of a man is projected in a mirror the ghost of the deceased may snatch it away, pains were taken not to allow man's image or shadow to make an appearance, and mirrors were therefore covered."

62 Moshe Tzuriel, *Otzrot HaTorah*, vol. 2 (Bnei Brak, 2005), 1017. See there his long list of mistaken mourning customs, 1006.

throughout the world, the superstitions behind this custom are largely unknown to observant Jews today, who base their practice on the rabbinic interpretations given in the nineteenth and early twentieth centuries. These explanations have given a Jewish context to an otherwise alien observance, helping it to become accepted and continued as a legitimate expression of Jewish mourning.

*Chapter 4*

# Leaving the Synagogue for *Yizkor*

## A BRIEF HISTORY OF *YIZKOR*

A central focus of early Ashkenazic prayer was death and mourning. This is expressed in the role of *Kaddish,* and prayers such as *Av HaRaḥamim* and *Yizkor.*[1] The history of congregational memorial prayers on Shabbat and holidays begins with memorial prayers introduced into Ashkenazic liturgy to follow the Torah reading on the Shabbat before Shavuot, commemorating the martyrs of the Crusades. The time of year was seen as fitting, as this was when many major Rhineland communities were destroyed during the Crusades. The memorial prayers did not take place on Shavuot itself, as this would mar the mandatory holiday joy, so the

1 Israel Ta-Shma, *The Early Ashkenazic Prayer: Literary and Historical Aspects* (Jerusalem, 2003), 13. Regarding the development of Sephardic memorial prayers, see S. Glick, *Or LeAvel* (Efrat, 1991), 134–37. On *Av HaRaḥamim,* see J. I. Lifshitz, "*Av HaRahamim*: On the 'Father of Mercy' Prayer," in S. C. Reif, A. Lehnardt, and A. Bar-Levav, eds., *Death in Jewish Life – Burial and Mourning Customs Among Jews of Europe and Nearby Communities* (Berlin, 2014), 141–54.

preceding Shabbat was chosen.[2] Later, memorial prayers were added on the Shabbat before Tisha BeAv, when there was a massacre of the Mainz community in 1348 during the time of the Black Death.[3] These early communal memorial prayers were said only for martyrs. Additionally, by the twelfth century it had become customary to recite memorial prayers for important members of the community, such as teachers of Torah and donors, inserting them at the same point in the Shabbat service throughout the year.[4] Examples of this are found in the earliest Ashkenazic liturgical works, such as *Maḥzor Vitry*.[5] Individuals could recite prayers for deceased family members on the Shabbat close to the anniversary of their death,[6] but public memorial prayers on Shabbat were recited only for martyrs and important community figures.

Public memorial prayers for deceased relatives only took place on Yom Kippur,[7] when charity was also pledged on behalf of deceased relatives, based on midrashic material that indicates that the deceased can receive atonement for their sins.[8] This midrashic source material is itself of a later date, indicating that the idea of giving charity on behalf

2 See 183–84 in the extensive history of *Yizkor* in S. B. Freehof, "Hazkarath Neshamoth," *Hebrew Union College Annual* 36 (1965), 179–89. It has since been reprinted as "*Hazkarat N'shamot* ('Memorial of Souls'): How It All Began," in L. A. Hoffman, ed., *May God Remember: Memory and Memorializing in Judaism – Yizkor* (Woodstock, VT, 2013), 77–89.

3 Freehof, "Hazkarath Neshamoth," 183; Glick, *Or LeAvel*, 137–38.

4 Glick, *Or LeAvel*, 138.

5 Simon Hurwitz, ed., *Maḥzor Vitry* (Nuremberg: J. Bulka, 1923), 173. The phrase used to describe this custom is וזוכר את המתים, which can mean simply that the names were recited, but it would seem reasonable that at least a brief liturgical element would be part of the recitation of the names of the deceased. On the development and dissemination of the names of Torah scholars added to the list of martyrs, see M. Raffeld, "Components and Combinations in the *Yizkor* Prayers of the North Italian Ashkenaz Community" [Hebrew], *HaMaayan* 53, no. 1 (2012), 63–66.

6 Ismar Elbogen, *Jewish Liturgy: A Comprehensive History* (Philadelphia. 1993), 162.

7 Glick, *Or LeAvel*, 139–40.

8 *Maḥzor Vitry*, 392; S. Buber, ed., *Siddur Rashi* (Berlin, 1911) 99, *siman* 214; B. Shneerson, ed., *Sefer HaRoke'aḥ HaGadol* (Jerusalem, 1967), 112, *siman* 218; *Babylonian Talmud* (Vilna edition), Mordekhai, Yoma, *siman* 727. See also Margaliot, ed., *Sefer Ḥasidim* (Jerusalem. 1991) 578–79, *siman* 1171.

of the deceased may have also arisen at the time of the Crusades.[9] Although an additional reason for holding a memorial service on Yom Kippur was subsequently given, that "recalling death breaks a person's heart" and creates a mood open to repentance,[10] the original reason was to provide atonement for the deceased. This was accomplished through charity. Due to its association with atonement, the component of charity was originally associated exclusively with Yom Kippur and was not part of the Shabbat memorial prayers.[11] The earliest forms of the Yom Kippur memorial service were focused on pledges of charity, and were not accompanied by prayers for the deceased, or any set liturgy.[12]

These special services for the deceased on Shabbat and Yom Kippur were common in Ashkenazic communities, but by no means

9 The idea of charity for the deceased is found in *Midrash Tanḥuma*, but only in the later editions (first added in the Mantua 1563 edition, subsequently the source for the Warsaw edition), Haazinu 1. There *Sifre* is given as the source (erroneously misattributed to *Sifra* or *Torat Kohanim* in most editions), but while *Midrash Tanḥuma* quotes *Sifre* as saying, "From here we learn that the living redeem (פודין) the deceased," implying redemption with money, in our texts of *Sifre* (Shoftim, *piska* 210:8) the teaching is simply: "This teaches that the deceased need atonement (כפרה)." This *Sifre* is given as the source by many medieval sources. See the discussion of this addition in *Midrash Tanḥuma HaShalem*, vol. 4 (Jerusalem, 2008), 189; *Maḥzor Vitry* (ed. Buber) 173, note 1. The source quoted from *Pesikta Rabbati* in *Maḥzor Vitry* regarding giving charity on behalf of the deceased (392) is similarly not found with that formulation in the texts we have. Instead our versions talk about asking for mercy as being effective to help the deceased, but do not mention charity; see *Maḥzor Vitry* (ed. Buber) 173, note 1. There is an earlier reference to giving money on behalf of the deceased in II Maccabees 12:39–45, where Judas collects money on behalf of the fallen soldiers who were found to have been carrying "objects which had been consecrated to the idols of Jamnia, forbidden to Jews by the Torah" (12:40). However, in that event he "sent the money to Jerusalem to be used to bring a sin offering" (12:43). It was the sin offering that was understood to benefit the deceased, not the giving of money itself. See J. A. Goldstein, *II Maccabees – A New Translation with Introduction and Commentary* (New York, 1983), 450.

10 *Kol Bo* (Jerusalem, 1997), 284, *siman* 70. It would seem that this reason would not necessarily contribute to the development of a personal memorial prayer.

11 Freehof, "Hazkarath Neshamoth," 185. See also I. Braun, ed., *Tanya Rabbati* (Jerusalem, 2011), 53, *siman* 17, where he discusses the controversy whether charity on behalf of the deceased should be pledged on Shabbat.

12 *Maḥzor Vitry*, 392; Glick, *Or LeAvel*, 141.

universal.[13] The prayers beginning with the word *yizkor* were composed shortly after the Crusades[14] and were originally found in *Memorbuecher*, the forerunners of the contemporary "*Yizkor* book," which lists the names of the deceased of the community along with prayers to be recited on their behalf.[15] The *Yizkor* paragraph itself is essentially a pledge of charity on behalf of the deceased, the same way a *Mi Sheberakh* is a blessing accompanying a charitable donation, not an independent prayer.[16]

The verb *lizkor* has a double meaning, "to remember" and "to recite." The early *Yizkor* prayer is based on the second meaning, comprising as it did of an elaborate recitation of the name of the deceased along with a donation.[17] Liturgy independent of donations developed only later.[18] Inclusion of family members in the communal *Memorbuch*, the book listing important members of the community who had passed away, was predicated on a charitable offering,[19] as all aspects of *Yizkor* revolved around charity. The connection between the original Yom Kippur custom to pledge charity on behalf of the deceased and the mentioning of their names can be detected in the *Shulḥan Arukh* (*Oraḥ Ḥayim*

13 For example, *Tur* makes no mention of this custom. See Daniel Goldschmidt, *Maḥzor LeYamim HaNora'im – Yom Kippur* (Jerusalem, 1970), 25.

14 Glick, *Or LeAvel*, 145.

15 L. Zunz, *Nachtrag zur Literaturgeschichte der synagogalen Poesie* (Berlin, 1867), 671.

16 See, for example, the classic formulation of *Yizkor* in *Maḥzor Ḥelek Rishon KeMinhag Pihem, Polin, Mehrrin Veshe'arei Kehillot Kedoshot* (Altona, 1744), 212; *Maḥzor Minhag Polin LeYom Kippur* (Roedelheim, 1807), 21a; *Maḥzor Mikol HaShana – LeYom Kippur* (London, 1807), 110, בעבור שאני נודר צדקה בעדו/בעבורו.

17 These prayers still represented "a strong expression of human and personal emotions," but within an "outer shell of language that hides within itself human impulses and emotions." A. Gross, "Liturgy as Personal Memorial for the Victims in 1096," in Reif, ed., *Death in Jewish Life*, 169.

18 Glick, *Or LeAvel*, 138, note 39. Recent studies have not established satisfactorily precisely how, when, and why those two aspects originated and were fused. See S. C. Reif, *Judaism and Hebrew Prayer* (Cambridge, 1993), 219: "The order of development remains unclear but there is no doubt that a number of liturgical customs concerning the deceased are to be traced back to the same period following the Crusades." See also Eric Zimmer, "The Customs of *Matnat Yad* and *Yizkor*," in Joseph Hacker and Yaron Harel, eds., *The Scepter Shall Not Depart from Judah: Leadership, Rabbinate and Community in Jewish History: Studies Presented to Professor Shimon Schwarzfuchs* (Jerusalem: Bialik Institute, 2011), 80–85 [Hebrew].

19 C. Roth, *The Frankfurt Memorbuch* (Jerusalem, 1965), 13.

621:6). Rabbi Joseph Karo, quoting Mordekhai, only writes about the giving of charity on behalf of the deceased on Yom Kippur, while Rabbi Moshe Isserles, based on the *Kol Bo*, adds that it was also customary to recall the deceased (ומזכירין נשמותיהם) at that time.[20]

By the fourteenth century, we find references to memorial donations on the last day of each of the three pilgrimage festivals, not just on Yom Kippur.[21] It is mentioned by Shalom of Neustadt,[22] Rabbi Jacob Moelin (Maharil),[23] and in the *Hagahot HaMinhagim* to Rabbi Isaac Tirnau's *Sefer Minhagim*.[24] Just as pledging charity was the central component of the Yom Kippur memorial service, so it was for the service on the festivals. The names of the deceased were recited as well, as noted by both Maharil and *Hagahot HaMinhagim*,[25] but the central element was still the charitable donation.

We can understand how memorial donations expanded from Yom Kippur to all festivals from a telling statement of the Maharil. He says, "The rule is that on every festival day where we read 'each with his own gift' (Deut. 16:17), we mention the souls of the departed and recite *Av HaRaḥamim*."[26] The thread tying the *Yizkor* services of Yom Kippur and the pilgrimage festivals together is the giving of charity.[27]

---

20 See *Beit Yosef* and *Darkhei Moshe* at the end of *Tur, Oraḥ Ḥayim* 621.

21 Freehof ("Hazkarath Neshamoth," 186) wrote that the earliest source for this expansion is Mordekhai Jaffe in his *Levush* (1530–1612), and thus that it began in Bohemia; however, early Ashkenazic literature shows that it was already known in German sources from a century before. Similarly, in M. Nulman, *The Encyclopedia of Jewish Prayer* (Northvale, NJ, 1996), 187, the expansion of *Yizkor* to all festivals is mistakenly dated in Germany "only since the eighteenth century."

22 S. Spitzer, ed., *Hilkhot UMinhagei Rabbeinu Shalom MeNeustadt* (Jerusalem, 1997), 152, *siman* 510. See note 1 there.

23 S. Spitzer, ed., *Sefer Maharil* (Jerusalem, 1989) 388, *siman* 13.

24 S. Spitzer, ed., *Sefer HaMinhagim LeRabbeinu Isaac Tirnau* (Jerusalem, 2000), 62, note 34. It is not clear exactly who wrote these notes or when, but it seems to be close to the time of Isaac Tirnau, and some may have been written by him; see page 18 in Spitzer's introduction.

25 The term used for the prayers is מזכירין נשמות, similar to the term in *Maḥzor Vitry* for the memorial prayer for the important community members (וזוכר את המתים).

26 Spitzer, *Sefer Maharil*, 388, *siman* 13.

27 Freehof, "Hazkarath Neshamoth," 181.

The idea of pledging charity on the last day of each festival, with no connection to memorial prayers, is an old Ashkenazic custom mentioned by Eleazar (Roke'aḥ) of Worms (c. 1176–1238). It is based on the Torah reading for the additional day of the festival in the Diaspora. He states, "On all festivals we pledge charity when we read the portion *Kol HaBeḥor* because it is written, 'each with his own gift (*matnat yado*), according to the blessing that the Lord your God has bestowed upon you' (Deut. 16:17)."[28] Using the reference to giving gifts to the Temple, these days were seen as a suitable occasion to solicit donations for the synagogue. Sometimes the charity was designated for the needy in the community, or for poor Torah scholars, or for the poor in Israel.[29] Eleazar of Worms himself specifically explains that charity was pledged on behalf of the deceased only as atonement on Yom Kippur, whereas on the other festivals it was a general appeal, not connected with atonement for the deceased.[30]

The expansion of *Yizkor* to the three pilgrimage festivals is rooted in this older custom. The festival gifts were called *matnat yad* after the words in the Torah reading, the same term used for the charity pledged on Yom Kippur in memory of the deceased. The part of the festival service when charitable donations were made was called *Seder Matnat Yad*, when the rabbi or an important member of the congregation would make his way around the synagogue holding the Torah scroll and make an individual *Mi Sheberakh* for each donor.[31] It was a natural progression for the memorial donations on Yom Kippur to expand over time

28 Shneerson, *Sefer HaRoke'aḥ HaGadol*, 164, *siman* 296.

29 Y. Feldman, *Areshet Sefateinu*, vol. 4 (Brooklyn, NY, 1965), 287.

30 Shneerson, *Sefer HaRoke'aḥ HaGadol*, 109, *siman* 217.

31 There were variations of *Seder Matnat Yad* where a *Ḥumash* instead of a Torah scroll was held, or the rabbi stayed by the *bima* and congregants came up to him, but the main idea of an individual *Mi Sheberakh* for every donor is found throughout the varying customs. See Spitzer, *Sefer Maharil*, 150, *siman* 13; Y. S. Feldman, *Sefer Yisrael BeMaamadam* (New Square, NY, 2005), 541; D. Goldschmidt, *Maḥzor Sukkot, Shemini Atzeret VeSimḥat Torah* (Jerusalem, 1981), 398; Y. Tamar, *Alei Tamar, Yerushalmi: Seder Moed*, vol. 1 (Alon Shvut, 1992), 382. Since the rabbi would perform the *Seder Matnat Yad* it was customary in some circles that he be given *gelila* on that day. See B. Hamburger, "Synagogue Customs for Ashkenazim in Israel and the Diaspora," *Yerushatenu* 2 (2008), 427 [Hebrew] and the comprehensive overview of *Seder*

into the appeal for charity on the last day of every festival.[32] In early Ashkenaz it was customary to make even general pledges of charity on behalf of the deceased,[33] so it was normative to associate any giving of charity with the memory of the deceased.

Rabbi Mordekhai Jaffe (1530–1612), in *Levush HaḤur*, explicitly states that the reason memorial prayers are said on the last days of festivals is because of the Torah portion read that day and the associated custom to make appeals, "and since they were pledging charity it was customary to give it in memory of the deceased."[34] Eliezer Waldenberg explains that this is the core reason (עיקר הטעם) the *Yizkor* ceremony expanded to the festivals.[35] This explains how *Yizkor* came to be said on festivals, where mourning is prohibited and memorial prayers seem to go against the joyous mood of the holiday.[36] In fact, Rabbi Yaakov Emden notes that while mourning prayers should not be said on festivals, in this case, since it is the extra day of the festival and a matter of a mitzva, he goes along with the popular custom.[37] In Israel, there was

---

*Matnat Yad*, Yitzhak Zimmer, "The Custom of *Matnat Yad*," *Yerushatenu* 3 (2009), 145–55 [Hebrew].

32 Freehof, "Hazkarath Neshamoth," 188–89. See also H. Schwab, *Jewish Rural Communities in Germany* (London, 1957), 32, where he notes that this practice spread from the north to the south of Germany.

33 Margaliot, *Sefer Ḥasidim*, 176–77, *siman* 170, 578–79, *siman* 1171.

34 M. Jaffe, *Levush HaḤur, Oraḥ Ḥayim*, vol. 2 (Jerusalem, 2004), 148, *siman* 490:9.

35 E. Waldenberg, *Tzitz Eliezer*, vol. 12 (Jerusalem, 1976), 106, *siman* 39:5. For a comprehensive study of the relationship between *Matnat Yad* and *Yizkor*, see Eric Zimmer, "The Customs of *Matnat Yad* and *Yizkor*," in Joseph Hacker and Yaron Harel, eds., *The Scepter Shall Not Depart from Judah: Leadership, Rabbinate and Community in Jewish History: Studies Presented to Professor Shimon Schwarzfuchs* (Jerusalem: Bialik Institute, 2011), 80–85 [Hebrew].

36 More aggadic reasons were given for the custom of reciting *Yizkor* on the festivals. For example, see Z. H. Kaidanover, *Kav HaYashar* (Constantinople, 1732), chapter 86, 109b–110a, where the explanation is based on the idea that in Temple times the souls of the deceased would come to the Temple and replace the Temple in Jerusalem with the heavenly Temple; Bezalel Stern, *BeTzel HaḤokhma*, vol. 4 (Bnei Brak, 1982), 187, *siman* 119. For a conceptual explanation of why *Yizkor* is appropriate on festivals, see A. Ziegler, *Halakhic Positions of Rabbi Joseph B. Soloveitchik*, vol. 2 (Northvale, NJ, 2001), 7–38, where a distinction is made between the *kiyum* and the *maaseh* of mourning.

37 Yaakov Emden, *Siddur Beit Yaakov* (Lemberg, 1904), 268a.

no custom to make charity appeals since there was no additional day of the festival on which *Kol HaBeḥor* was read, but over time it has become customary to recite *Yizkor* on the last day of the festival anyway,[38] despite some opposition.[39]

In some works, an intermediate stage in the expansion of *Yizkor* can be detected. For example, in his thirteenth-century work *Shibbolei HaLeket* (*siman* 239), Rabbi Zedekiah ben Abraham Anav writes that it is customary to pledge charity on the last day of each festival, and in the same *siman* separately discusses the propriety of the custom to pledge charity on behalf of the deceased on these days. It seems the two appeals were on the verge of becoming conflated. Similarly, the sixteenth-century Italian work *Tanya Rabbati* mentions pledging charity on the last day of each festival, connected to the Torah reading, but notes memorial prayers only on the last day of Shavuot.[40]

### LEAVING THE SYNAGOGUE FOR *YIZKOR*

The idea that certain people should leave the synagogue during the *Yizkor* prayer is found in many Ashkenazic sources beginning in the 1800s. For example, it is mentioned in the *Kitzur Shulḥan Arukh* (133:21), in connection with two distinct groups of people: those who have living parents and those in their first year of mourning. At first glance this seems very unusual, since there is no precedent for having a large group leave in the middle of prayer services in any other context, and it seemingly disrupts the solemnity of the service in general.[41] In the earliest rabbinic literature

38 Y. M. Tukachinsky, *Gesher HaḤayim*, vol. 1 (Jerusalem, 1960), 337.

39 See A. Aliner, "Al Minhagei Keriat HaTorah VehaHaftara BaAretz UVagola," in *Shana BeShana* (Jerusalem, 1964), 95–96, esp. note 9.

40 Braun, *Tanya Rabbati* (Jerusalem, 2011), *216*, *siman* 53, 220, *siman* 54, 369, *siman* 88. The reason Shavuot was singled out for memorial prayers seems to be a development of the earlier Ashkenazic custom to recite special memorial prayers for the martyrs of the Crusades on the Shabbat before Shavuot. See Glick, *Or LeAvel*, 137, note 37; Feldman, *Areshet Sefateinu*, 287.

41 There are cases of having priests leave under very particular circumstances (*Shulḥan Arukh, Oraḥ Ḥayim* 129:4, 135:5), and there is a custom for mourners to enter the synagogue only after *Kabbalat Shabbat* during *shiva* (*Be'er HaGola* to *Shulḥan Arukh, Yoreh De'ah* 393:3), but nothing on this level. See N. Vizhonsky, "Should One Leave for *Yizkor*?," *Teḥumin* 17 (1997), 55 [Hebrew].

dealing with this custom, it is always presented as something that has been going on as long as can be remembered; it is not questioned, and it is considered to be deeply rooted and widespread.[42] Various explanations have been given for this custom.

The earliest source to discuss this custom is Barukh Brandeis in his book *Lashon Ḥakhamim*, published in 1815. In the additional notes at the end of volume 1 he includes a question regarding the origin of this custom. The questioner asks why those with living parents should not stay in the synagogue during *Yizkor* and stand silently, instead of leaving the synagogue. The questioner adds, "And if it is because of *niḥush*, 'there is no augury (*naḥash*) in Jacob' (Num. 23:23)." The term *niḥush* is used to describe magical practices; the implication of the questioner is that this custom is based on superstition. Brandeis answers that he did not find "any hint of this custom" in the writings of the *Aḥaronim* , but he feels that "it is possible (דאפשר) that their reason is that maybe perhaps (פן ואולי) if they are there they will come to err and accidentally say it with them, and 'a covenant is made for the lips' (Sanhedrin 102a)," meaning that saying this prayer may result in the death of a parent.[43] The concept of "a covenant made for the lips" is used in the Talmud by Abaye to explain how Jehu was initially righteous but eventually became an idolater. This is because in order to trick the Baal worshippers into gathering in one place, King Jehu declared, "Ahab served Baal little; Jehu shall serve him much" (II Kings 10:18). Abaye explains that the power of the spoken word is such that even utterances made without evil intent are fulfilled, and Jehu ultimately "did not turn away from the sins that Jeroboam had caused Israel to commit" (10:31). Brandeis brings this idea to show that saying an unnecessary *Yizkor* prayer is problematic based on a real concern discussed in the Talmud, and so should not be categorized as a superstition. This explanation would be quoted many times as a justification for the custom.[44]

---

42 For example, B. J. Brandeis, *Leshon Ḥakhamim*, vol. 1 (Prague, 1815), 91b–92a; E. Margaliot, *Shaarei Ephraim* (Dubno, 1820), 10:32; Yitzhak Lipetz, *Sefer Mataamim* (Warsaw, 1890), 21.

43 Brandeis, *Leshon Ḥakhamim*, 91b–92a.

44 It is found in M. Finkelstein, *Tosefet Ḥayim* (on *Ḥayei Adam*) (Warsaw, 1888), *Hilkhot Shabbat* 9, 283; N. Kahane, *Orḥot Ḥayim – Oraḥ Ḥayim*, vol. 2 (Sighet, 1898), 154a,

The custom is also found in Rabbi Ephraim Margaliot's *Shaarei Ephraim* (10:32), first published in 1820. Although no reason is given in the main text, in the author's notes, *Pitḥei She'arim,* he explains that the reason may be that it is not appropriate to stand there silently while others recite *Yizkor*. Although this idea is found in Berakhot 20b regarding the recitation of *Shema,* it may indicate that in general it is not considered appropriate for some of the congregation to be doing nothing while others are praying.[45] In a variation of this approach, staying inside silently may be seen as appearing to transgress the prohibition of *lo titgodedu,* making separate groups within a congregation.[46] However, an individual not reciting a prayer that does not apply to him does not actually constitute *lo titgodedu,*[47] and walking out for a prayer might be seen as even more of a separation.

Rabbi Margaliot adds that there is a small concern (וקצת יש לחוש) that this would invoke the evil eye, as seen in Yevamot 106a, where it is recounted that R. Pappa's parents died when Abaye, an orphan, "set his eyes upon them." This explanation has been quoted in many books on customs and gained widespread popularity.[48]

Yitzhak Lipetz, in his popular *Sefer Mataamim,* published in 1890, brings the above explanations and adds that since it is common for children to be named after deceased forefathers whose names are recited in the *Yizkor* prayers, it is considered "opening one's mouth to the Satan" to mention these names in the presence of the similarly named

---

*siman* 768:7; Lipetz, *Sefer Mataamim,* 21; A. Hershovitz, *Sefer Minhagei Yeshurun* (Vilna, 1899), 20, *siman* 63; Y. Venderofsky, *Minhagei Beit Yaakov* (New York, 1911), 64, *siman* 125; J. D. Eisenstein, *Otzar Dinim UMinhagim* (New York, 1917), 96; A. Sperling, *Taamei HaMinhagim UMekorei HaDinim,* vol. 1 (Lemberg, 1928), 71a. From these sources it went on to be included in virtually every book that discusses this custom.

45 Vizhonsky, "Should One Leave for *Yizkor*?," 55.

46 Tukachinsky, *Gesher HaḤayim,* 337; Hayim Goldberg, *Pnei Barukh* (Jerusalem, 1986), 413.

47 Vizhonsky, "Should One Leave for *Yizkor*?," 55.

48 For example, Lipetz, *Sefer Mataamim,* 21; Eisenstein, *Otzar Dinim UMinhagim,* 96; Sperling, *Taamei HaMinhagim UMekorei HaDinim,* 71a; Y. Greenwald, *Kol Bo al Avelut* (New York, 1947), 404; Tukachinsky, *Gesher HaḤayim,* 337; Goldberg, *Pnei Barukh,* 413.

living descendant.[49] He adds another reason, that if children remain in the synagogue and have nothing to say, instead of being quiet they will "confuse their parents and converse with one another."[50]

Moshe Mordekhai Epstein (1866–1933), in the introduction to his work *Levush Mordekhai* on Bava Kama, explains that for those whose parents are deceased, *Yizkor* is comforting, and appropriate for a festival. However, for those whose parents are still alive, the memorial prayer is one of sorrow and should not be recited on a holiday. If they were to stay in the synagogue, nobody would be able to recite *Yizkor*, the same way nobody recites *Taḥanun* when a groom is attending services, because of his joyous occasion.[51] A popular variation of this general approach is that while *Yizkor* is comforting for those with deceased parents and is thus permitted on a festival,[52] if the non-mourners were to stay inside they would become saddened on the festival, which is prohibited.[53]

In the third edition of *Otzar Kol Minhagei Yeshurun*, published in 1918, an additional reason was given that did not appear in previous editions of this book. Since it is customary for the *gabbai* to announce that it is time to say *Yizkor*, those whose parents are alive walk out, because staying inside would appear as if they are cursing their parents.[54]

Some of these reasons could be obviated by having the children stay in and recite prayers for their deceased forefathers and family members. Meshullam Finkelstein writes that this is what should be done if for some reason people cannot leave the synagogue for *Yizkor*.[55] However,

---

49 This explantation is brought without attribution in later works, Hershovitz, *Sefer Minhagei Yeshurun*, 20, *siman* 63 and Venderofsky, *Minhagei Beit Yaakov*, 64, *siman* 125.

50 Lipetz, *Sefer Mataamim* (Warsaw, 1890), 21.

51 M. M. Epstein, *Levush Mordekhai – Bava Kama* (Jerusalem, 1957), 11.

52 In the same way that crying on Shabbat is permissible if it makes a person feel better (Rema, *Shulḥan Arukh, Oraḥ Ḥayim* 288:2).

53 Venderofsky, *Minhagei Beit Yaakov*, 64–65, *siman* 125; Eisenstein, *Otzar Dinim UMinhagim*, 96; Greenwald, *Kol Bo al Avelut*, 403.

54 A. Hershovitz, *Otzar Kol Minhagei Yeshurun* (St. Louis, MO, 1918), 249, *siman* 27.

55 Finkelstein, *Tosefet Ḥayim, Hilkhot Shabbat* 9, 283–84. The Satmar Rav ruled that one does not have to wake up a child who is sleeping in the synagogue so that they can leave for *Yizkor*; it is sufficient to cover them with a tallit. See G. Zinner, *Nitei Gavriel: Hilkhot Avelut*, vol. 2 (Jerusalem, 2001), 608, *siman* 79:2.

under normal circumstances, it was never the custom to do so.[56] Instead they simply walked out of the synagogue for *Yizkor*.

It should be noted that none of these explanations were presented as the definitive reason for the custom. They are all presented as possible ways to explain a widespread pre-existing practice that had no clear textual or theoretical basis. The majority of early explanations revolve around the idea of fear of death and the evil eye.

### LEAVING *YIZKOR* IN THE FIRST YEAR OF MOURNING

Barukh Brandeis provides the earliest explanation for the custom of those in their first year of mourning to walk out for *Yizkor*. He bases his explanation on the comment of Mordekhai Jaffe that since "the deceased also rest on that day and are not judged, it is appropriate to mention them for rest and blessing and to pray for them."[57] Why is it particularly appropriate to pray for them on a day they are resting? Brandeis explains that it is because then the deceased will pray for the living as well. However, during the first year, when the deceased are being judged (Mishna Eduyot 2:10), this reason does not apply, as the deceased are concerned with their own judgment. Brandeis explains that based on this, once eleven months have passed, and *Kaddish* is no longer recited in order to demonstrate that the deceased is no longer being judged in Gehinnom, the mourner should stay in for *Yizkor*.[58] It seems that although the prevalent custom was to walk out for the entire year, Brandeis felt, based on his explanation, that this should be the case only for the first eleven months.[59]

Solomon Haas in his work *Kerem Shlomo*, first published in 1840, presents the explanation of Brandeis, which he disagrees with, and then brings his own explanation. Based on the idea in Berakhot 58b that the deceased "is only forgotten from the heart after twelve months," he explains that mourners within the first year will "arouse their mourning with cries and yelling and will confuse the others." Additionally, this

56 Waldenberg, *Tzitz Eliezer*, 108, *siman* 39:9.

57 Jaffe, *Levush HaḤur, Oraḥ Ḥayim*, 124, *siman* 284:7.

58 Brandeis, *Leshon Ḥakhamim*, 92a.

59 This explanation is the one brought in Finkelstein, *Tosefet Ḥayim, Hilkhot Shabbat* 9, 283.

will sadden the others, and it is not appropriate to mourn on a festival.[60] This explanation, or a variant of it, is usually the standard explanation given for this custom.[61] Note, however, that this idea would seem to directly contradict the point made above by other authorities that the *Yizkor* prayer is a great comfort to mourners, presumably when not accompanied by extreme wailing, making it appropriate for a festival.

Avraham Hershovitz mentions in the third (1918) edition of *Minhagei Yeshurun* that it is customary for those in their first year of mourning to leave for *Yizkor.* He refers his readers to *Shevut Yaakov* (2:25) by Rabbi Yaakov Reischer (c. 1670–1733) for an explanation. Though this custom is not mentioned there, there is a reference in that responsum to Moed Katan 8a, where we find Shmuel's explanation for the Mishna's ruling that one should not eulogize the deceased thirty days before a festival. Shmuel explains that it is because the deceased will not be forgotten by the time of the festival. Rashi explains that the concern is that the person will then come to eulogize the deceased even on the festival itself. Rabbi Reischer comments that this concern applies only to eulogizing relatives where one's "heart is bitter." Presumably, the connection to a mourner not staying in for *Yizkor* in the first year of mourning is that he too still has a bitter heart, and the *Yizkor* service may cause him to mourn on the festival. This can be seen as a variation of the explanation given by Haas, but rather than focusing on the other people saying *Yizkor* who will be disturbed, it is focused on the problem for the new mourner himself to stay inside the synagogue.

The issue of those in the first year of mourning leaving for *Yizkor* is considered much more problematic than that of those with living parents leaving, and many have expressed opposition to it. For example, Rabbi Eliezer Deitch writes that the custom is erroneous and the deceased need prayers especially during the first year.[62] Similarly, Rabbi Yehiel Mikhel Tukachinsky writes that it is obvious (פשוט הוא) that those in their first year of mourning, even those in their first week of mourning, should recite *Yizkor*. He writes that there is absolutely no basis for the

60 S. Haas, *Kerem Shlomo* (Pressburg, 1848) *Oraḥ Ḥayim* 57a, *siman* 668.

61 Greenwald, *Kol Bo al Avelut*, 404; Nulman, *Encyclopedia of Jewish Prayer*, 381.

62 E. Deitch, *Sefer Duda'ei HaSadeh* (Seini. 1929). 29b–30a, *siman* 85.

custom of leaving, and all the reasons given to support it are weak.[63] Rabbi Yekutiel Greenwald, in his *Kol Bo al Avelut,* brings many authorities who vehemently opposed the custom to leave during the first year of mourning,[64] as does Rabbi Eliezer Waldenberg.[65] Additionally, many books that present the custom of children with living parents leaving for *Yizkor* do not include those in the first year of mourning, indicating that it was not widespread.[66] Based on this, Moses Stern writes that in a place where it is customary for new mourners to leave, the mourner should still say *Yizkor,* but outside the synagogue.[67] Even accepting the idea that it does not make sense to say *Yizkor* during the first year when the memory of the deceased is fresh, some authorities advise saying other memorial prayers instead, ones that do not use the particular term *yizkor,* such as *El Maleh Raḥamim,* rather than skip the entire service.[68]

### FINANCIAL ORIGIN OF THE CUSTOM

Why is there no mention of the custom of children walking out for *Yizkor* in any source earlier than the 1800s? It is possible that the custom as such simply did not exist before then.

Leaving prayer services in the middle is frowned upon in general;[69] however, a break in the services between the Torah reading and Musaf is not unusual. This is the time when the rabbi gives a sermon, when appeals are made, and when a Kiddush may take place on days with particularly long services. All of these are occasions where a child leaving is common and normative, particularly during appeals for money.[70] During

63 Tukachinsky, *Gesher HaḤayim,* 337–38.

64 Greenwald, *Kol Bo al Avelut,* 404.

65 Waldenberg, *Tzitz Eliezer,* 114, *siman* 59:5.

66 For example, it does not appear in Lipetz's *Sefer Mataamim,* Venderofsky's *Minhagei Beit Yaakov,* Eisenstein's *Otzar Dinim UMinhagim,* and it appears only in the later editions of Hershovitz's *Minhagei Yeshurun* and Sperling's *Taamei HaMinhagim UMekorei HaDinim* (those with living parents leaving were mentioned in earlier editions).

67 M. Stern, *Be'er Moshe,* vol. 5 (Jerusalem, 1984), 227, *siman* 152.

68 Sperling, *Taamei HaMinhagim UMekorei HaDinim,* 71a (in note).

69 Vizhonsky, "Should One Leave for *Yizkor*?," 55.

70 I remember as a child in Brooklyn that (good) children were expected to stay in for davening, the Torah reading, and even the Rabbi's sermon, but it was acceptable to leave for "the appeal."

appeals no congregational prayers are being said, and the children are, of course, not expected to pledge any money. The major component of the original *Yizkor* service was pledges of charity rather than prayers,[71] and *Yizkor* expanded to the festivals because of the appeals that would take place on those days. As we have seen, originally there was no independent *Yizkor* service during the festivals; it was the *Seder Matnat Yad*. Over time, *Yizkor* took over and replaced the *Seder Matnat Yad*.[72] In some *maḥzorim*, the Yom Kippur *Yizkor* service was listed as a subsection of the standard appeal, subsumed under the general *Seder Matnat Yad*.[73] It is reasonable that young children, to the extent that they came to services at all, would leave during the appeals, particularly since *Seder Matnat Yad* entailed a lengthy string of *Mi Sheberakhs* for every member of the congregation who pledged charity.[74] They were not walking out of *Yizkor* per se, but rather the appeal. Similarly, adults with living parents could take advantage of this appeal, which did not relate to them, to take a break. It should be noted that, as reported by the Maharil in the fourteenth century[75] and later by Yuspa the Shamash in the 1600s,[76] a *Mi Sheberakh* was only made during *Seder Matnat Yad* for children who were at least thirteen, all the more reason for young children to leave for this part of the service. At the end of the *Seder Matnat Yad* a long *Mi Sheberakh* was said for the women and young children who would not get an individual prayer.[77] It is probable that the children would be called back in for this, as is done with *Kol HaNe'arim* on Simḥat Torah in contemporary times.

In earlier times, when the appeal was still the major component of *Yizkor*, this was clear to all so nobody ever asked why people with living parents were leaving, as the service simply did not apply to them.

---

71 Waldenberg, *Tzitz Eliezer*, 104, *siman* 39:1.

72 See Aliner, "Al Minhagei Keriat HaTorah," 95, note 8; Feldman, *Areshet Sefateinu*, 287.

73 M. M. Konav, *Mincha Ḥadasha – Maḥzor LeYom Kippur* (Krotoschin, 1838), 104a; *Maḥzor LeShemini Atzeret VeleSimḥat Torah* (Roedelheim, 1832), 42.

74 See the description of *Seder Matnat Yad* in Feldman, *Sefer Yisrael BeMaamadam*, 541.

75 Spitzer, *Sefer Maharil*, 150, *siman* 13, note 4.

76 Y. (Shamash) Menatzpach, *Minhagim DeKehillat Kodesh Vermiza*, vol. 1 (Jerusalem, 1988), 59, *siman* 58.

77 Menatzpach, *Minhagim DeKehillat Kodesh Vermiza*, 59, note 1.

Over time, as the prayer component of *Yizkor* became more significant, and the pledge of charity was no longer done in the context of a general appeal in *Seder Matnat Yad* but rather as a line in the *Yizkor* prayer said quietly by each individual ("in the merit that I pledge charity in their name"), the children leaving for the appeal became the children leaving for *Yizkor*.

In the 1700s the formula *bli neder* (without a vow) began to be inserted into the pledge of charity in some texts of *Yizkor*,[78] shifting the focus away from charity and toward *Yizkor* as a prayer. The reason for this is that it was considered inappropriate to make vows in general,[79] and particularly here in case the charity was not given. Rabbi Zvi Hirsch Kaidanover, in his very popular *Kav HaYashar*, first published in 1705, writes that if the pledge is not paid it is a detriment to the soul of the deceased, and so an explicit vow to give charity should not be made.[80] The idea is that just as charity given on behalf of the deceased helps them, because it is as if they gave it themselves, not giving the promised charity would be as if the deceased had not fulfilled a vow. Paying this particular pledge was considered particularly urgent. It was reported that Rabbi Israel Isserlin, author of *Terumot HaDeshen*, would not eat the day after the holiday until he had paid the charity he pledged.[81] Hayim Elazar Spira, the Rebbe of Munkacs, would give the charity pledged at

---

78 I. P. Berlin, *Minei Targuma* (Breslau, 1831), 25a (*Parashat Va'etḥanan*). See also S. Zalman of Liadi, *Siddur Rabbenu HaZaken* (Brooklyn, NY, 2004), 495, note 22; S. Zalman of Liadi, *He'arot HaTemimim Ve'anshei Shelomenu*, vol. 6 (Morristown, NJ, 1989), (589), 13; Zinner, *Nitei Gavriel: Hilkhot Avelut*, 618, *siman* 79:28, note 38.

79 Isaiah Berlin (1725–99) seems to be the first who raised the problem of making a vow to give money in memory of the deceased, noting that he did not find earlier authorities who dealt with this issue specifically regarding the formulation of *Yizkor*. See his *Minei Targuma*, 25a (*Parashat Va'etḥanan*). He notes that although we find that it is customary to make pledges of charity on Shabbat and festivals (Rema, *Shulḥan Arukh, Oraḥ Ḥayim* 306:6), it is best to avoid naming an explicit figure and the term *neder* should not be used.

80 Z. H. Kaidanover, *Kav HaYashar* (Frankfurt/Main, 1706), chapter 86, 178a.

81 I. Weiss, *Kuntres Devek Tov*, *siman* 6, appended to the end of Y. Teichtel's *Mishneh Sakhir* (Baridow, 1924), 108a. This is quoted in the commentary of *Shaarei Ḥayim* by H. Z. Ehrenreich (1875–1937) to *Shaarei Ephraim* (Irsava, 1932), 142, *siman* 10:38.

night, immediately after the holiday ended.[82] It was therefore considered prudent not to make explicit pledges during *Yizkor*. This diminished the appeal aspect, as specific monetary amounts were replaced by a general, nonbinding promise to give charity.[83] Today, *bli neder* is the normative formula in contemporary prayer books,[84] so *Yizkor* is viewed as a prayer, completely independent of a charitable offering.

Based on this, there was never a conscious decision to walk out for memorial prayers, but rather for fundraising. In the 1800s, as the public appeal aspect from *Seder Matnat Yad* was replaced by a private *Yizkor* prayer, the original practice of people with living parents leaving for an appeal was shifted to not being present for memorial prayers.

The Reform prayer book *Seder HaAvoda* (Hamburg, 1819), introduced a longer, more elaborate *Yizkor* liturgy, including selections of verses and psalms, as well as meditations.[85] This had the effect of further marginalizing the charity pledges, and the vow to give charity was entirely omitted from some non-Orthodox *Yizkor* services.[86] Although this began as a Reform innovation, today many of these elements are found in Orthodox *maḥzorim* as well.[87] By the mid-1800s these changes

82 Y. M. Gold, *Darkhei Ḥayim VeShalom* (Brooklyn, NY, 1987), 177, *siman* 506.

83 Berlin, *Minei Targuma*, 23a (*Parashat Va'etḥanan*).

84 S. Ganzfried, *Kitzur Shulḥan Arukh* (Warsaw, 1901), 67:3; B. Z. Alfas, *Mekor Dima – Shas Teḥina Ḥadasha* (Vilna, 1928), 257; Shlomo Tal, *Siddur Rinat Yisrael* (Jerusalem, 1972), 375; N. Scherman, ed., *The Complete ArtScroll Machzor – Yom Kippur* (Brooklyn, NY, 1986), 472. Some prayer books retain the original wording, e.g., *Siddur Tefillat Shai* (Jerusalem, 2001), 296.

85 J. J. Petuchowski, *Prayerbook Reform in Europe* (New York, 1968), 330. This chapter (14) has been reprinted as "*Kaddish* and Memorial Services," in L. A. Hoffman, ed., *May God Remember: Memory and Memorializing in Judaism – Yizkor* (Woodstock, VT, 2013), 90–103.

86 A. M. Boeckler, "'Service for the Souls': The Origin of Modern Memorial Services, 1819 to 1938," in Hoffman, *May God Remember*, 124. See also E. L. Friedland, "*Yizkor*: A Microcosm of Liturgical Interconnectivity," in Hoffman, *May God Remember*, 111, and E. L. Friedland, "The Atonement Memorial Service in the American *Mahzor*," *Hebrew Union College Annual* 55 (1984), 245–82.

87 For example, a collection of verses beginning with Psalms 114:3, introduced in the Reform Hamburg siddur, is found in Scherman, *The Complete ArtScroll Machzor – Yom Kippur*, 470. Above this section is the following note: "Although the following verses are not part of the traditional *Yizkor* service, some congregations have adopted

were being incorporated into Orthodox services, beginning in the German congregations that were in proximity to the Reform innovations.[88] While some have noted that "these flowery but artificial additions have vitiated the simplicity and dignity of the *Yizkor* service,"[89] they are now commonplace. However, as we have seen, even before the Hamburg innovations, the charity element was beginning to be downplayed in Orthodox liturgy. The ready acceptance of the Hamburg innovations among the Orthodox shows that the perception of *Yizkor* as a memorial prayer, rather than as an ancillary component to a charitable pledge, had already taken hold, and as such, people were open to an expansion of the prayer.

Barukh Brandeis describes the custom in some communities in his time (the 1800s) to say memorial prayers on regular Shabbatot, yet he discusses leaving for these prayers only on Yom Kippur and festivals.[90] The simple explanation for this distinction is that because there was no appeal for charity on Shabbat,[91] there was no excuse for children to leave.

Of course, children whose parents passed away would stay inside even during the appeal, in order to pledge charity for the merit of their parents. In this manner, the practice developed that children with living parents left the synagogue for the pledging of charity, while those with deceased parents stayed inside. The practice is thus similar to the custom noted by Rabbi Avraham Gombiner (*Magen Avraham*, 1635–82) of women walking out during the Torah reading, because they do

---

the custom of reciting them before *Yizkor*." These verses are described as a kind of introduction to the "actual prayer of *Yizkor*," recited by "many congregations" in R. J. Abramowitz's "*Yizkor*: The Memorial Prayer Service" on the Orthodox Union website, <www.ou.org/torah/tefillah/yizkor/yizkor-memorial-prayer-service/>. See also S. Raphael, *Yizkor: From Mourning of Mega-Death to Soul-Guiding* (Philadelphia, 2013) 16–17.

88 Boeckler, "Service for the Souls," 118.

89 A. Milgram, *Jewish Worship* (Philadelphia, 1971) 450.

90 Brandeis, *Leshon Ḥakhamim*, 92a.

91 Some communities did have a custom to make appeals on Shabbat along with memorial prayers. See Jaffe, *Levush HaḤur, Oraḥ Ḥayim*, 124, *siman* 284:7. This was subject to controversy; see Braun, *Tanya Rabbati*, 53, *siman* 17, where he discusses the controversy whether charity on behalf of the deceased should be pledged on Shabbat.

not consider themselves obligated to hear it.[92] The synagogue outliers, women and children, who were not active participants in the services to begin with, would leave for parts that they viewed as not necessary for them to be present for.

What of those in their first year of mourning? The same explanation may apply. We find that some communities would not include certain memorial prayers for people who died when they were less than thirteen years old. Since they died before reaching the age of majority it was understood that they had no need for atonement and therefore no need for prayers on their behalf.[93] Although this custom is rejected today,[94] it was found in many communities into the 1800s. This points to an approach that when there is no need for atonement, there is no point in charity or memorial prayers in merit of the deceased.

Since the charity was offered as an atonement for the deceased, this was not considered necessary for someone who recently died, as they are still undergoing their initial penitential period in Gehinnom (Mishna Eduyot 2:10). The controversy over whether or not those in their first year of mourning should stay for *Yizkor* is based on whether the charity offered at this time would have an effect. The majority of authorities ruled that it does, and so mourners should stay in, and many noted that it is particularly in the first year that the deceased need assistance through the charity and prayers of the living.[95]

## CONCLUSION

Many of the traditional reasons given for leaving the synagogue during *Yizkor* in rabbinic literature are related to the evil eye and associated dangers. We have seen that occasions when people would walk out for *Yizkor* were also occasions where appeals were made, and raised the possibility that leaving for *Yizkor* was actually originally leaving for the

---

92 *Magen Avraham, Oraḥ Ḥayim* 282:6.

93 D. Tirani, *Ikkarei HaDat* (Florence, 1806) 114b, *siman* 36:11. See also H. Medini, *Sdeh Ḥemed – Asifat Dinim* (Warsaw, 1896), *Maarekhet Avelut*, 73, *siman* 212, where, based on the same idea, he discusses memorial prayers for someone who died younger than twenty years old.

94 Tukachinsky, *Gesher HaḤayim*, 338.

95 Greenwald, *Kol Bo al Avelut*, 404; Tukachinsky, *Gesher HaḤayim*, 337–38.

appeal. Probably the reason for leaving was due to a combination of factors; for example, if it was common practice for children to leave for the appeal, a child who stayed in would raise concerns related to the evil eye.

Knowing the historical reasons for the development of this custom is unlikely to have an impact on actual practice, since the acceptance of the evil eye explanations is by now deeply rooted and widespread. In recent years, it has been suggested that everyone should stay in during *Yizkor*, and those with living parents can say prayers on behalf of fallen Israeli soldiers or victims of the Holocaust.[96] Recently, prayers to be recited for those with living parents have begun appearing.[97] However, the idea of everyone remaining for *Yizkor* still does not appear to have been widely accepted.[98] Rabbinic authorities have stressed that the custom of people to leave for *Yizkor* should not be changed,[99] and even those who do not find the reasons compelling have admitted that this custom is too deeply rooted to be changed.[100] Additionally, any customs associated with mourning and remembering the deceased are taken very seriously, even when the basis for the custom is tenuous.[101]

---

96 Vizhonsky, "Should One Leave for *Yizkor*?," 57–58.

97 For example, the Tzohar organization in Israel has disseminated a Hebrew version of an English prayer for those with living parents written by Felix Carlebach of Manchester (1911–2008), <upload.kipa.co.il/media-upload/tzohar2/tzohar23372.PDF>.

98 See notes 8 and 9 to Vizhonsky's article, where the editor of *Teḥumin* disagrees with the author of the article.

99 Waldenberg, *Tzitz Eliezer*, 108, *siman* 39:9–10.

100 M. D. Walner, *Ḥemdat Zvi*, vol. 1 (Tel Aviv, 1973), 188, *siman* 34. Walner was the rabbi of Ashkelon at the time. This is the implication at the end of his responsum. It was to this responsum that Eliezer Waldenberg was relating in his *Tzitz Eliezer*, *siman* 39.

101 M. Tzuriel, *Otzrot HaTorah* vol. 2 (Bnei Brak, 2005), 1017. See his long list of mistaken mourning customs on page 1006.

# Part 2

# *Shabbat and the Cycle of the Year*

*Chapter 5*

# A Shabbat Candle for Every Member of the Family

We find in *Shulḥan Arukh, Oraḥ Ḥayim* 263:1, that regarding Shabbat candles, "One should be meticulous to make a beautiful lamp. There are those who use two wicks, one representing 'Remember' and one representing 'Observe.'" Rabbi Moshe Isserles adds, "One may add and light three or four, and this is customary." He then goes on to discuss the custom for a woman who forgot to light Shabbat candles to light an additional candle beyond what she had lit previously.

Today, many, if not most, women light one candle for every member of their family, adding a candle whenever a new child is born. This practice is not mentioned in the *Shulḥan Arukh* or any early sources.[1] It does not even appear in many classic books that describe and explain

1 Simha Rabinovitch, *Piskei Teshuvot*, vol. 3, part 1 (Jerusalem, 2009), 187, 263:2.

Jewish customs, such as *Sefer Taamei HaMinhagim UMekorei HaDinim,*[2] *Otzar Kol Minhagei Yeshurun,*[3] and *Otzar Taamei HaMinhagim.*[4] In this chapter we will trace the origin of this popular custom for Shabbat candle-lighting.

## TWO OR MORE SHABBAT CANDLES

The Talmud always refers to the Shabbat lamp in the singular, and the legal obligation was always understood by authorities to be to light just one lamp.[5] The custom of lighting two candles is recorded in the early Ashkenazic *Rishonim,* and would be adopted by Sephardic communities only later on.[6]

The earliest reference to two candles on Shabbat is Rabbi Eliezer ben Yoel HaLevi of Bonn (Raaviah, 1140–1225). He gives two reasons for this practice. The first explanation is that using one candle to eat by is normal, so another should be added to indicate that they are being lit for a special reason. The second reason is that the two candles represent "Remember" and "Observe," the two terms used in the two versions of the commandment to keep Shabbat in the Ten Commandments.[7] Rabbi Abraham ben Azriel, in his work *Arugat HaBosem,* written c. 1234, also gives two reasons for lighting two Shabbat candles. Firstly, that the numerical value of the word *ner* (candle) is equivalent to 250, twice that is 500, which is the sum total of the traditional number of body parts of a man (248) and woman (252) added together, and so two candles

2 Avraham Sperling, *Sefer Taamei HaMinhagim UMekorei HaDinim* (Jerusalem: Shai Lamora, 1999), 124, only brings the custom to light two Shabbat candles.

3 Avraham Hershovitz, *Otzar Kol Minhagei Yeshurun* (Vilna, 1898), 45, *siman* 77, only states that is it customary to light many Shabbat candles and brings reasons to light seven candles.

4 Shmuel Gelbard, *Otzar Taamei HaMinhagim* (Petach Tikva: Mifal Rashi, 1996), 127–28, discusses only the custom to light two candles.

5 Gedalia Oberlander, *Minhag Avotenu Beyadenu – Shabbat Kodesh* (Monsey: Merkaz Halacha, 2010), 11.

6 Israel Ta-Shma, *Early Franco-German Ritual and Custom* (Jerusalem: Magnes Press, 1999), 126. See there, chapter 2, where he gives the historical reasons why that was the case. A summary can be found in Daniel Sperber, *Minhagei Yisrael,* vol. 3 (Jerusalem: Mossad HaRav Kook, 1994), 77–78.

7 Avigdor Aptowitzer, ed., *Sefer Raaviah,* vol. 1 (Berlin, 1912), 265, *siman* 199.

indicate that the couple should merit to have male and female children. The second reason he gives is that they represent "Remember" and "Observe."[8] This second reason became the most popular explanation for the practice. It is mentioned in the *Tur* (*Oraḥ Ḥayim* 263:1), and from there in the *Shulḥan Arukh* (*Oraḥ Ḥayim* 263:1). It should be noted, though, that this custom took a while to become universal, as Rabbi Yaakov Landau in his *Agur* writes that "the world is not careful about lighting two Shabbat candles."[9]

Another popular explanation for lighting two Shabbat candles is a midrashic idea that on Shabbat many things are doubled.[10] Although the Midrash does not mention two candles, *Kolbo* (*siman* 24) writes that this was understood to be the basis for the custom as recorded in *Sefer Minhagot*, although this particular section of *Sefer Minhagot* is lost today.[11] This explanation was popularized by being quoted in *Beit Yosef* (*Oraḥ Ḥayim* 263:1).

Rabbi Moshe Isserles, when discussing the custom brought by Rabbi Yaakov Moelin (Maharil, 1365–1427) for a woman who forgot to light Shabbat candles one time to always add an extra candle, notes that adding candles actually does not appear to be a good thing, as the special symbolism of two Shabbat candles is no longer apparent.[12] He does note that authorities permitted adding to a fixed number, and based on that in his glosses to the *Shulḥan Arukh* (*Oraḥ Ḥayim* 263:1), Rabbi Moshe Isserles writes that one may add candles beyond the prescribed symbolic number.

Once it was established that more than two candles may be lit, other symbolic numbers were also chosen for the Shabbat candles,

---

8 Ephraim Urbach, ed., *Arugat HaBosem*, vol. 3 (Jerusalem: Ḥevrat Mekitze Nirdamim, 1962), 121.

9 Yaakov Landau, *Agur* (Piotrków, 1883), 37, *siman* 358.

10 He writes that this is from *Midrash Tanḥuma*, but it does not appear in the versions of that midrash that we have today. However, a similar, though not exactly the same, version of this appears in *Midrash Tehillim*, 92:1. See *Sefer Minhagot* in Simha Assaf, ed., *Sifran shel Rishonim* (Jerusalem: Ḥevrat Mekitze Nirdamim, 1934), 178, note 14.

11 See *Sefer Minhagot* in Simha Assaf, ed., *Sifran shel Rishonim* (Jerusalem: Ḥevrat Mekitze Nirdamim, 1934), 125–26, 178.

12 *Darkhei Moshe* (*Oraḥ Ḥayim* 263:1).

especially for kabbalistic reasons. The most popular numbers were seven and ten, as mentioned in *Shenei Luḥot HaBrit*[13] and later in *Magen Avraham* (263:2). Other larger numbers are also found.[14] None of these sources mention the custom that the number of candles should be based on the number of family members.

### YOM KIPPUR CANDLES

Lighting lamps for Yom Kippur depends on local custom, as described in the mishna on Pesaḥim 53b, "In a place where people are accustomed to light a lamp on Yom Kippur evenings, one lights. In a place where people are accustomed not to light a lamp, one does not light. However, one always lights in synagogues and study halls and dark alleyways and next to the sick." While lighting Shabbat and holiday candles in the home is an obligation, lighting Yom Kippur candles is a custom. The Talmud there explains the reason for the custom: "It was taught: Whether they said to light or they said not to light, they both intended to achieve the same objective." This objective, as stated by Rashi, is to distance people from marital relations, which are prohibited on Yom Kippur. Those who lit felt that since people do not engage in relations when there is light, the candles will discourage intimacy. Those who did not light felt that if the couple were not able to see each other, they will not be tempted to engage in marital relations, and so it was better not to have candles lit.

The Maharil writes that it is now customary to light Yom Kippur candles, and they should be lit in the bedroom. If they are lit elsewhere in the home and the bedroom is kept dark it creates the worst situation, defeating the purpose of both those who discouraged relations by lighting and by not lighting, as "he will see her in the house all decorated and will desire her, and when he enters the [bed]room there will be no reminder."[15] This is noted by Rabbi Moshe Isserles (*Oraḥ Ḥayim* 610:1),

---

13 Isaiah Horowitz, *Shenei Luḥot HaBrit* (Jerusalem: Oz Vehadar, 1992), 131, *Shabbat: Torah Or, siman* 29.

14 Moshe Hallamish, *Hanhagot Kabbaliot BeShabbat* (Jerusalem: Orḥot, 2006), 171; Gedalia Oberlander, *Minhag Avotenu BeYadenu – Shabbat Kodesh* (Monsey: Merkaz Halacha, 2010), 16–18.

15 Shlomo Spitzer, *Sefer Maharil* (Jerusalem: Machon Yerushalayim, 1989), 321, *Hilkhot Erev Yom Kippur* 12.

who rules that one who has a candle lit in his house must also have a light in his bedroom.

Because lighting Yom Kippur candles is a custom, there was a debate about whether a blessing should be said over these candles. For example, the Rosh ruled to recite the blessing, and Mordekhai ben Hillel and the Maharil ruled not to.[16] Ultimately *Shulḥan Arukh* (*Oraḥ Ḥayim* 610:2) concurred with the opinion of the Rosh, writing, "Some say that one recites a blessing over lighting Yom Kippur candles."

Other sources refer to lighting candles on Yom Kippur not with reference to the prohibition against marital relations, but rather to ensure survival in the coming year. *Maḥzor Vitry* quotes *Tanḥuma* (*Emor* 17) regarding the *ner tamid* in the Sanctuary: "Do I need your flame? Rather it is to protect your souls, since the soul is compared to a candle, as it says: 'The soul of a man is a candle of God' (Prov. 20:27)." *Maḥzor Vitry* concludes that this is the reason it is customary to light candles on Yom Kippur, for protection.[17] Similarly, Rabbi Abraham ben Azriel, in his *Arugat HaBosem*,[18] writes that one of the reasons to light candles on Yom Kippur eve is "because of the day of judgment; a soul is called a candle, as it is said, 'The soul of a man is a candle of God' (Prov. 20:27)."

"In the early-thirteenth-century work *Sefer HaManhig*, Rabbi Abraham ben Nathan (HaYarḥi) brings a version of the same quote from *Tanḥuma* as a support for the custom "of all Israel" to light a Yom Kippur candle, beyond the halakhic reason to use that fire for Havdala after Yom Kippur. He adds further support for the practice from Keritot 5b and Horayot 12a: "R. Ami said: A person who seeks to know if he will complete his year or if he will not [whether or not he will remain alive

16 See *Tur, Oraḥ Ḥayim* 610:2, and *Beit Yosef* and *Darkhei Moshe* there. Shlomo Spitzer, *Sefer Maharil* (Jerusalem: Machon Yerushalayim, 1989), 320, *Hilkhot Erev Yom Kippur* 11.

17 Simon Hurwitz, ed., *Maḥzor Vitry* (Nuremberg: J. Bulka, 1923), *siman* 340, 373. On the authorship of *Maḥzor Vitry*, see Avraham Grossman, *The Early Sages of France: Their Lives, Leadership and Works* (Jerusalem: Magnes Press, 2001), 395–402 [Hebrew]; Aryeh Goldschmidt, ed., *Maḥzor Vitry*, vol. 1 (Jerusalem: Otzar HaPoskim, 2004), 23–25.

18 Ephraim Urbach, ed., *Arugat HaBosem*, vol. 1 (Jerusalem: Ḥevrat Mekitze Nirdamim, 1939), 11.

in the coming year], let him light a candle during the ten days that are between Rosh HaShana and Yom Kippur, in a room in which wind does not blow. If its light continues to burn, he knows that he will complete his year."[19] Although the practice in the Talmud is connected to the Ten Days of Repentance, Abraham ben Nathan HaYarḥi associates it with Yom Kippur eve specifically.[20] From all these sources we see that there was an association between a lit candle for Yom Kippur and protection and survival during the upcoming year.[21]

This candle representing a person's fate was taken very seriously. Rabbi Yehuda, the son of the Rosh, writes that in the year 1264 his grandfather's Yom Kippur candle blew out early in the night and he died that year on Ḥol HaMoed Sukkot.[22] Due to the perceived gravity of a Yom Kippur candle blowing out, Rabbi Moshe Isserles (*Oraḥ Ḥayim* 610:4) had to specifically warn people not to instruct a non-Jew to rekindle a Yom Kippur candle that was extinguished. Although the *Ḥayei Adam* (144:17), later quoted in the *Mishna Berura* (610:14), writes that one should not be concerned if their Yom Kippur candle blows out, he does note that people take it very seriously, and advises that it is best if the candle is placed somewhere where it cannot be seen so as not to make people worry and perhaps be tempted to ask a non-Jew to relight it.

Lighting Yom Kippur candles is also an expression of honoring the day. Mordekhai ben Hillel (the Mordekhai, 1250–98), in his comments on Yoma (*siman* 725), writes that in addition to the candles lit in rooms in order to discourage marital relations, "We light candles on the table and set the table like on Shabbat," since Yom Kippur is called "Shabbat Shabbaton" (Lev. 23:32). While this is the most well-known

19 Yitzhak Rafael, ed., *Sefer HaManhig LeRabbi Avraham BeRebbi Natan HaYarḥi*, vol. 1 (Jerusalem: Mossad HaRav Kook, 1978), 362–63. Regarding when the book was written, see the introduction there, page 20.

20 See Shlomi Raiskin, "Lighting Lamps on Yom Kippur Eve in the Synagogue," *Magal* 15 (2007), 228.

21 On the powerful symbolism of candles in Judaism in general, see Daniel Sperber, *Minhagei Yisrael*, vol. 3 (Jerusalem: Mossad HaRav Kook, 1994), 140–41.

22 Israel Abrahams, *Hebrew Ethical Wills* (Philadelphia: Jewish Publication Society, 1976), 186. See also the story brought in Daniel Sperber, *Minhagei Yisrael*, vol. 3 (Jerusalem: Mossad HaRav Kook, 1994), 142.

reference to this custom, as it is quoted in *Beit Yosef* (*Oraḥ Ḥayim* 610:2), the same teaching was mentioned earlier by Rabbi Eliezer ben Yoel HaLevi of Bonn[23] and by Samuel ben Barukh of Bamberg (c. 1220).[24] This is in addition to the widespread and early custom of lighting candles in the synagogue for Yom Kippur, as noted in the Mishna.[25]

The idea of lighting candles at home would later be found in the Maharil as well, though he cautioned not to say a blessing over it, following his view not to say a blessing over Yom Kippur candles as it is only a custom, unless it also happens to be Shabbat, in which case it is obligatory.[26] This warning was appropriate, since these candles were being lit in the same place as were the Shabbat candles. Thus, the halakhic distinction between the two candle lightings could be blurred and they could easily be treated the same with a blessing.

## YOM KIPPUR CANDLES FOR EVERY FAMILY MEMBER

Rabbi Eliyahu Spira in his *Eliya Rabba* (*Oraḥ Ḥayim* 610:4) states that lighting candles for every member of the family on Yom Kippur eve is an ancient custom, as the early Ashkenazic work *Amarcal*[27] says that it is mentioned in the *Targum Sheni* of *Megillat Esther*, a work from the geonic period,[28] as part of Haman's description of what he considered negative Jewish customs. Haman's long list of Jewish practices appears

23 David Devlitzky, ed., *Sefer Raaviah*, vol. 2 (Bnei Brak, 2005), Laws of Yom Kippur, *siman* 528:9, 126.

24 Shmuel Eliezer Stern, ed., *Meorot HaRishonim*, vol. 1 (Jerusalem: Machon Yerushalayim, 2001), 115. For biographical information about Samuel ben Barukh, see there, 112.

25 For a full discussion of that practice, see Shlomi Raiskin, "Lighting Lamps on Yom Kippur Eve in the Synagogue," *Magal* 15 (2007), 226–58.

26 Shlomo Spitzer, *Sefer Maharil* (Jerusalem: Machon Yerushalayim, 1989), 320, *Hilkhot Erev Yom Kippur* 11.

27 Regarding the date and authorship of *Amarcal*, see Michael Higger, "Sefer Amarcal al Hilkhot Pesaḥim," in *Sefer HaYovel LeAlexander Marx* (New York: Jewish Theological Seminary, 1950), 144–45.

28 Regarding the dating of *Targum Sheni*, see Bernard Grossfeld, *The Two Targums of Esther* (Collegeville, MN: Liturgical Press, 1991), 20.

in *Targum Sheni* to Esther 3:8,[29] but our current editions of *Targum Sheni* make no reference to candle lighting on Yom Kippur,[30] although there may have been a textual variant that included this.[31] The quote does not appear in any editions of *Amarcal* that we have today.[32] Other works on Esther have been claimed as containing a reference to this custom,[33] but it does not appear in any early work that we have connected to Esther.[34]

Still, the custom to light candles on Yom Kippur for all family members is very old. Mordekhai ben Hillel, in his comments on Yoma (*siman* 723) states that "at this time it is customary to light on Yom Kippur a candle for each and every one because it is the conclusion of judgment." This was popularized by being included in *Beit Yosef* (620:4). On this, Rabbi Moshe Isserles adds in his *Darkhei Moshe* (*Oraḥ Ḥayim* 620:4) the reference from Horayot 12a about determining survival for the year based on a candle lit at this time of year. If the candle burned to the end without going out, it was understood that they would stay alive for the upcoming year. Because of this, it was customary to light a candle for every family member on Yom Kippur as a mechanism to ensure their survival in the upcoming year.

---

29 See Paulus Cassel, *An Explanatory Commentary on Esther: With Four Appendices Consisting of the Second Targum Translated from the Aramaic with notes: Mithra: The Winged Bulls of Persepolis: and Zoroaster* (Edinburgh: T & T Clark, 1888), 310; Mordechai Leib Katzenelbogen, ed., *Torat Ḥayim, Megillat Esther* (Jerusalem: Mossad HaRav Kook, 2006), 247.

30 Yissachar Tamar, *Alei Tamar, Yerushalmi: Seder Moed*, vol. 1 (Alon Shvut: Chorev, 1991), 244, Pesaḥim 4:4.

31 Yaakov Reifman, "Notes on Targum *Megillat Esther* and Kohelet," *Zion: Ephemerides Hebraicae* (1840–1841), 198; Ephraim Zilber, *Sdeh Yerushalayim* (Tchernowitz, 1883), 13.

32 Jacob Freiman, "Sefer Amarcal al Hilkhot Yayin Nesekh" in *LeDavid Zvi* (Berlin, 1914), 423, note 8.

33 For example, Hayim Yosef David Azulai, *Maḥzik Berakha, Oraḥ Ḥayim*, vol. 5 (Jerusalem: Yahadut, 1989), 610:3, 92, states that it is in "Haggada deEsther."

34 Isaac Sternhell, *Kokhavei Yitzḥak*, vol. 1 (Brooklyn: Balshon Printing, 1969), 14, *siman* 1.

Many early authorities, such as Rabbi Meir of Rothenburg,[35] Mahari Weil,[36] and the Maharil[37] mention lighting candles only for male family members,[38]giving various reasons why women are not included in this custom.[39] This is the approach found in Rabbi Moshe Isserles's comments to the *Shulḥan Arukh* (*Oraḥ Ḥayim* 610:4), with *Magen Avraham* (610:3) bringing in the explanations offered by Mahari Weil and the Maharil and adding that "now only married people light a candle,"[40] a view also found in *Arukh HaShulḥan* (*Oraḥ Ḥayim* 610:6).[41] Other sources, for example *Ḥayei Adam* (144:15), mention the custom to light only one candle per household.[42]

Another version of this practice was to light a candle for every family member in the synagogue. This is the custom recorded by Mordekhai Jaffe (c. 1530–1612) in his work *Levush Malkhut* (610:3). This version of the custom is found in various communities. For example, it was the custom of Rabbi Hayim Elazar Spira (1868–1937) the Rebbe of Munkacs,[43] and of the communities of Djerba,[44] Libya,[45] and Yemen.[46]

---

35 Israel Elfenbein, *Sefer Minhagim DeBei Rabbi Meir ben Barukh MiRothenburg* (New York, 1938), 53.

36 Yonatan Shraga Domb, ed., *She'elot UTeshuvot Rabbeinu Yaakov Weil*, vol. 1 (Jerusalem: Machon Yerushalayim, 2000), *siman* 191, 250, *siman* 192, 260.

37 Shlomo Spitzer, *Sefer Maharil* (Jerusalem: Machon Yerushalayim, 1989), 322, *Hilkhot Erev Yom Kippur* 13.

38 This is also the custom described by Yehudah, son of the Rosh; Israel Abrahams, *Hebrew Ethical Wills* (Philadelphia: Jewish Publication Society, 1976), 186.

39 For an overview of these reasons, see Shlomi Raiskin, "Lighting Lamps on Yom Kippur Eve in the Synagogue," *Magal* 15 (2007), 255–56.

40 See ibid., 238, for an innovative alternate reading of *Magen Avraham*.

41 For an overview of the reasons only married men would light, see ibid., 256–58.

42 See also Daniel Sperber, *Minhagei Yisrael*, vol. 4 (Jerusalem: Mossad HaRav Kook, 1995), 52, note 4.

43 Yehiel Mikhel Gold, *Darkhei Ḥayim VeShalom* (Munkacs, 1940), 288, *siman* 743.

44 See Shlomi Raiskin, "Lighting Lamps on Yom Kippur Eve in the Synagogue," *Magal* 15 (2007), 244, note 87.

45 Eliyahu Biton, *Naḥalat Avot* (Biria, 2006), 135, *siman* 11; Refael Zrok, *Zekhor LeRefael* (Bat Yam, 2009), 8.

46 Yitzhak Ratzabi, *Shulḥan Arukh HaMekutzar* (Bnei Brak, 1995), 112:8, 194, especially note 21.

Other variations of this custom include having one wick for every family member, placed in a few candles.[47]

**SHABBAT CANDLES FOR EVERY FAMILY MEMBER**

The earliest references to the custom for a woman to light a Shabbat candle for every member of the family are found in the context of individual family practices. For example, this custom is found in the ethical will of Rabbi Ephraim Segal (1750–1831), head of the rabbinical court in Kolo, Poland. This was first published in 1891 in a limited edition of one hundred copies. It was later republished in 1908 at the end of *Pitḥei She'arim*, written by his son-in-law Rabbi Yissakhar of Chenstochov.[48] Rabbi Segal asks his offspring to "accustom yourselves to light every Shabbat for each child that will be born and that you have."[49] He does not offer a reason for this other than a general idea to add candles in order to honor Shabbat.[50] This was meant as a directive for his family, and does not represent a widespread custom.

Similarly, it was reported that in the home of Rabbi Yehoshua Heschel Rabinowitz, the first Rebbe of Monstrich (1869–1924), thirteen Shabbat candles were lit, corresponding to the members of the family, even in difficult times.[51] This too was a personal custom.

The earliest reference to this as a general custom is found in the second volume of *Likkutei Mahariḥ*, first published in 1899. The author, Rabbi Yisrael Chaim Friedman of Rachov (1852–1922), writes that "the custom of women is that when they give birth to a son or daughter they add a candle," based on Shabbat 23b, where R. Huna states that one who is accustomed to kindle lights on Shabbat will be rewarded by having children who are Torah scholars. Thus, when a child is born, a Shabbat candle is added so that the parents "will merit to have sons and

---

47 This is described in Yair Hayim Bachrach, *Mekor Ḥayim*, vol. 2 (Jerusalem: Machon Yerushalayim, 1983), *Kitzur Halakhot* 605:1, 509; Avraham Zis, *Minhagei Komarna* (Tel Aviv, 1964), 94–95, *simanim* 447, 448.

48 Moshe Rosenfeld, ed., *Birkat Ephraim* (London, 1979), 3.

49 Ibid., 19, *siman* 21.

50 Ibid., 31, *siman* 46.

51 Yehoshua Heschel Rabinowitz, *Erkhei Yehoshua* (Jerusalem, 1995), 241, *Peraḥ Shoshanim*, *siman* 55.

sons-in-law who are Torah scholars."[52] According to this, the candles do not actually represent the children of the woman lighting, but rather her sons and future sons-in-law.

Another early mention of the custom is in the fourth volume of *Torat Ḥayim*, by Rabbi Yaakov Shalom Sofer (1855–1921), first published in 1911. There it is included as one of the various Shabbat candle lighting customs, but with no explicit reason given for the practice.[53]

Rabbi Menashe Klein (1923–2011) connected lighting a candle for every child with the custom that a woman who neglected to light Shabbat candles one week must always add an extra candle as a penalty,[54] since women would generally not light on the Shabbat right after giving birth when they were recuperating. Although a woman who just gave birth and is not feeling well would not be penalized for not lighting candles, there is a variant text of the Maharil which states that a woman who missed candle lighting even due to illness must add an extra candle every week. Rabbi Klein proposes that this is how the custom originated.[55] Similarly, Rabbi Avigdor Nebenzahl suggested that women may have consistently refrained from lighting right after giving birth, as doctors would tell them to rest, and the extra candle is actually to make up for missing candle lighting on that Shabbat.[56]

However, that textual variant of Maharil is considered to be inaccurate, and the correct text refers only to a woman who forgot to light candles, not one who was unable to light.[57] Rabbi Moshe Isserles and other authorities quoted the accurate text of the Maharil, that the penalty applies only to a woman who forgot to light, not who was sick, so that the standard practice is not to penalize a woman who could not

52 Yisrael Chaim Friedman, *Likkutei Mahariḥ*, vol. 2 (Jerusalem, 1965), 26 (13b). This book was first published in 1899.

53 Yaakov Shalom Sofer, *Torat Ḥayim*, vol. 4 (Paks, 1911), *siman* 263:4, 86a.

54 Regarding this practice, see *Darkhei Moshe* (*Oraḥ Ḥayim* 263:1), *Shulḥan Arukh* (*Oraḥ Ḥayim* 263:1), *Mishna Berura* 263:7, and *Shaarei Teshuva* 263:3.

55 Menashe Klein, *Meshane Halakhot*, vol. 7 (Jerusalem, 2008), 69, *siman* 35.

56 Elchanan Printz, *Avnei Derekh*, vol. 8 (Jerusalem, 2014), 173. See also the formulation of this idea in Printz, *Avnei Derekh*, vol. 7 (Jerusalem, 2013), 128.

57 Shlomo Spitzer, *Sefer Maharil* (Jerusalem: Machon Yerushalayim, 1989), 201, *Hilkhot Shabbat* 1, note 15.

light due to a situation that was beyond her control, such as illness or recovering from giving birth.[58] Furthermore, *Mishna Berura* (263:11) states that for the first Shabbat after giving birth, the husband should light instead of the wife,[59] and if her husband lit for her that Shabbat, there is no need to penalize her.[60]

Rabbi Klein and Rabbi Moshe Sternbuch have also suggested that the custom may be related to the Rambam's approach, which is that the head of the household lights Hanukka candles on behalf of the entire family, and so on Shabbat the woman also lights for every member of the family,[61] although if this were the case there would seem to be no need to light on behalf of newborn babies and very young children who are not yet obligated in mitzvot.[62] The simplest explanation for the custom to light a Shabbat candle for every family member is that it spread from the custom to light candles on Yom Kippur for each member of the family.

## SHABBAT AND YOM KIPPUR

Rabbi Avigdor Nebenzahl reported that in his family they lit the same number of candles on Yom Kippur as on Shabbat.[63] This seems to be the prevalent custom today in most households. We have seen that the idea of lighting a candle for every family member on Yom Kippur is already attested to by Ashkenazic *Rishonim*, with symbolism associated with protection on judgment day and survival for the upcoming year. There was no particular symbolism attached to lighting a Shabbat candle for each family member, but since it was customary to light candles at home on Yom Kippur in the same place that the Shabbat candles were lit, and to do so with a blessing, the distinction between Yom Kippur

58 *Darkhei Moshe* (*Oraḥ Ḥayim* 263:1); *Shulḥan Arukh* (*Oraḥ Ḥayim* 263:1); *Mishna Berura* 263:7; *Shaarei Teshuva* 263:3.

59 See also *Arukh HaShulḥan, Oraḥ Ḥayim* 263:7; Binyamin Zilber, *Az Nidabru*, vol. 11 (Bnei Brak, 1980), 9–10, *siman* 2; Yitzhak Zilberstein and Moshe Rothschild, *Torat HaYoledet* (Bnei Brak: Machon Halakha VeRefua, 2011), 180–81, 38:6, and especially note 7.

60 Yehoshua Neuwirth, *Shemirat Shabbat KeHilkhatah*, vol. 2 (Jerusalem: Moriah, 1988), 38, 43:9, end of note 51.

61 Menashe Klein, *Meshane Halakhot*, vol. 7 (Jerusalem, 2008), 69, *siman* 35.

62 See Moshe Sternbuch, *Teshuvot VeHanhagot* (Jerusalem, 1993), 123, *siman* 157:10.

63 Moshe Harari, *Mikra'ei Kodesh: Yom Kippur* (Jerusalem, 2003), 60, note 90.

and Shabbat candles became blurred. Most people now view lighting Yom Kippur candles as just another occasion of candle lighting, like on any other holiday or Shabbat. This may have contributed to the decline nowadays in the practice of the ancient custom to light Yom Kippur candles in the synagogue. The fact that lighting Yom Kippur candles is only a custom, and that there is a difference of opinion regarding whether or not a blessing should be recited over them, is something most people are not aware of today.

This situation has led people to view the lighting of Yom Kippur candles and lighting Shabbat candles in much the same way, so that the Yom Kippur custom of lighting a candle for every family member became a Shabbat and holiday practice as well. This was noted by Rabbi Yehuda Blum, in a responsum from 1911, where he writes that "in my humble opinion the custom of women to add candles has nothing to do with honoring Shabbat; it is a new teaching (תורה חדשה) that they developed that when a new baby is born or when a baby is sick they add candles, and I did not see in any place that there is even a hint of a mitzva here." He goes on to say that lighting a candle for every family member is connected to Yom Kippur only, and not to Shabbat. Although some modern sources[64] give *Targum Sheni* as quoted by the halakhic work *Eliya Rabba* as a source for lighting a candle for every family member on Shabbat,[65] the fact is that that source discusses only lighting candles on Yom Kippur, and the actual reason for lighting a candle for every member of the family on Shabbat is a conflation of these two candle-lighting occasions.

Though nowadays lighting a candle for every family member is widespread and appears to be the dominant Ashkenazic custom, as recently as in pre-World War II Europe there were many different local customs in various communities. For example, just within the Siebengemeinden, the seven Jewish communities in Eisenstadt and the surrounding area, the communities of Eisenstadt, Frauenkirchen, and Deutschkreutz (Tzeilem) are reported to have lit a candle for every

64 Yehuda Zvi Blum, *She'erit Yehuda* (Jerusalem, 1972), 14, *siman* 23.

65 See Eliyakim Devoraks, *BeShvilei HaMinhag*, vol. 2 (Jerusalem: Imrei David, 1997), 45; Elchanan Printz, *Avnei Derekh*, vol. 7 (Jerusalem, 2013), 128, and vol. 8 (Jerusalem, 2014), 173.

family member; Lackenbach and Kittsee lit three and Mattersdorf lit ten.[66]

Why is this custom reported only from the late 1800s? It would seem to be related to the fact that advances in candle-making technology made candles more affordable at the time, so people could allow themselves the luxury of burning multiple candles. In 1834, Joseph Morgan, considered one of the "innovators of the Industrial Revolution," invented a candle-molding machine that allowed for the continuous production of candles, up to fifteen hundred an hour, lowering costs considerably.[67]

Added to this was the discovery of paraffin in the mid-1800s which revolutionized candles and their manufacture.[68] Paraffin, a waxy substance produced as residue from the petroleum refinement process, "burned brightly, consistently and relatively cleanly. It left no odor and was less costly to produce than any other candle fuel of the time."[69]

It appears that the custom of lighting a Shabbat candle for every member of the family began as the practice of a few families, was viewed as something nice and meaningful, and was originally borrowed from Yom Kippur. The custom caught on and spread because it resonated with people and became less expensive. Within a few generations it has become the most dominant candle-lighting custom, despite the fact that, unlike Yom Kippur, there is no traditional symbolism for lighting a Shabbat candle for every member of the family.

## BORROWING FROM THE HIGH HOLY DAYS

A candle for every family member is not the only practice that transitioned from Yom Kippur to more general usage. The powerful declaration *Aleinu* is now used as the concluding prayer of the three daily

66 Yehiel Goldhaber, *Sefer Minhagei HaKehillot*, vol. 2 (Jerusalem, 2007), 173, note 12b.

67 Kristin Hutchins, "Candle Making," in Wendy Martin, ed., *All Things Dickinson: An Encyclopedia of Emily Dickinsons's World*, vol. 1 (Santa Barbara: Greenwood, 2014), 147; Paul Wonning, *Brief History of Candle Making* (Mossy Feet Books, 2012), 5.

68 Robert Routledge, *Discoveries and Inventions of the Nineteenth Century* (London: George Routledge and Sons, 1876), 547–49; Mark Anthony Benvenuto, *Industrial Organic Chemistry* (Berlin: Walter de Gruyter, 2017), 67.

69 Hutchins, "Candle Making," 146.

services as well as on other occasions, such as the circumcision ceremony and *Kiddush Levana*. Originally, it served only as part of the Rosh HaShana *Amida* in Musaf and in its repetition, as well as in the repetition of the Yom Kippur Musaf *Amida*. In France and Germany it was part of the *maamadot* prayers recited by individuals after the regular morning service concluded, and over time became one of the portions of the *maamadot* prayers that were added to the service itself.[70] It was included in the eleventh-century work *Maḥzor Vitry*,[71] and by Rabbi Yehuda HeḤasid (1150–1217)[72] and his student Rabbi Eleazar of Worms (c. 1176–1238)[73] as the conclusion of the daily morning service.[74] The practice to say it at the end of the daily services took some time to catch on fully, and later spread to Spain.[75] Rabbi Yoel Sirkes (*Bayit Ḥadash, Oraḥ Ḥayim* 133:1) explains that *Aleinu* was added to the daily service "in order to fix in our hearts before we return home the Oneness of God's kingship, and to strengthen our faith that He will one day remove detestable idolatry from the earth and false gods will be utterly cut off," and also that despite Jewish people's daily business dealings with Gentiles they should not have doubts about their faith. This prayer had "high religious significance" and so became part of the daily service.[76]

Lighting a candle for every family member, as well as the daily *Aleinu*, both began as High Holiday practices, later expanded by Ashkenazic Jews. Both were adopted for more common use because they

70 Israel Ta-Shma, *The Early Ashkenazic Prayer: Literary and Historical Aspects* (Jerusalem: Magnes Press, 2003), 143–44.

71 Simon Hurwitz, ed., *Maḥzor Vitry* (Nuremberg: J. Bulka, 1923), 75, *siman* 99. On this reference, see Israel Ta-Shma, *The Early Ashkenazic Prayer: Literary and Historical Aspects* (Jerusalem: Magnes Press, 2003), 140, note 4.

72 Ephraim Urbach, ed., *Arugat HaBosem*, vol. 4 (Jerusalem: Ḥevrat Mekitze Nirdamim, 1963), 98, note 65.

73 Elazar of Worms, *Sefer HaRoke'aḥ HaGadol* (Jerusalem, 1966), 221, *siman* 324.

74 See also Barry Freundel, *Why We Pray What We Pray* (Jerusalem: Urim, 2010), 227, note 94.

75 Israel Ta-Shma, *The Early Ashkenazic Prayer: Literary and Historical Aspects* (Jerusalem: Magnes Press, 2003), 140–41.

76 Ismar Elbogen, *Jewish Liturgy, A Comprehensive History* (Philadelphia: Jewish Publication Society, 1993), 71.

were considered particularly meaningful, so much so that by now they are associated more with Shabbat and the daily prayers than their holiday of origin.

*Chapter 6*

# Braided Challa

A loaf of yeast-leavened bread, braided or twisted, and traditionally used by Ashekanzic Jews on Shabbat is commonly known as challa. While challa is formed in various shapes, the braided appearance remains an essential and distinctive component of this bread. This defining characteristic of challa was adopted from the baking styles of the neighboring societies of Ashkenazic Jews.

In this chapter we will explore the origins of this particular custom.

## CHALLA

The original use of the word *challa* referred to the portion of bread given to a priest during Temple times. (For an example, see Num. 15:20.)

The earliest use of the word *challa* as we know it today, denoting the bread used at the Shabbat meal, is found in the work *Leket Yosher* by Rabbi Yosef bar Moshe. *Leket Yosher* contains the practices of Rabbi Israel Isserlin (1390–1460), author of *Terumat HaDeshen*. There we find that on his Shabbat table were "three fine challot kneaded with eggs, oil, and a little water."[1] These challot aren't described as braided, reflecting the fact that braided challa was not yet widespread at that time.

The original Ashkenazic challot were plain round loaves,[2] as they would remain in Sephardic lands,[3] similar to the bread that was baked during the week.[4] Some of the many reasons offered for why the Shabbat bread is called challa[5] are based on the original round shape of the bread. Rabbi Raḥamim Palagi (1813–1907) suggests that the term "challa" may specifically indicate something that is round shaped, as found in the commentary of Ibn Ezra to Leviticus 2:4, who explains the (plural) word "challot," "Some say they are round, from the word *ḥalila* (rotation) in the words of our ancestors."[6] Additionally, round loaves for Shabbat may have been understood to symbolize the manna, which is described by Rabbi Asi in Yoma 75a as "round like coriander seed."[7]

---

1 Yosef bar Moshe, *Leket Yosher* (Berlin, 1873), 49.

2 Note that although he does not mention braided challot, Avraham Sperling, in his *Sefer Taamei HaMinhagim UMekorei HaDinim* (Jerusalem: Shai Lamora, 1999), 550, notes the use of round challot on Shabbat from Rosh HaShana until Hoshana Rabba.

3 John Cooper, *Eat and Be Satisfied* (Northvale, NJ: Jason Aronson, 1993), 174. On a family trip to Croatia, we purchased Shabbat food from the local Jewish community in Zagreb. The challot supplied were large, round and basically flat, in accordance with Sephardic tradition.

4 Gil Marks, *The World of Jewish Cooking* (New York: Simon and Schuster, 1996), 276. See the Yemenite work by Yitzhak Ratzabi, *Shulḥan Arukh HaMekutzar* (Bnei Brak, 1995), *Oraḥ Ḥayim*, vol. 2, 6, note 21, which explicitly states, "But our simple custom is that they are round loaves, as they are also on weekdays."

5 See Yosef Lewy, *Minhag Yisrael Torah*, vol. 2 (Jerusalem: Frank, 1994), *siman* 274:1, 85. Yitzhak Lipetz, in his work on Jewish customs, *Sefer Mataamim* (Warsaw, 1894), 112, *siman* 32, 33, gives homiletic reasons why the bread is called challa, either as a reference to the Shabbat bride (*kalla*) or as a reference to the mishna read Friday night (Shabbat 2:6) which mentions the mitzva of separating *challa*. The challa/*kalla* connection was also used to explain the old Ashkenazic custom for women to dance holding challot at weddings, see Avraham Levinson, "LeRikkudei Am BeYisrael," *Reshumot*, vol. 3 (Tel Aviv: Dvir, 1947), 157, note 17. On conducting the wedding dance with a braided challa, see Daniel Sperber, *Minhagei Yisrael*, vol. 7 (Jerusalem: Mossad HaRav Kook, 2003), 346.

6 For example, Sukka 55b, חוזרין חלילה. Rahamim Palagi, *Yafeh LaLev*, vol. 2 (Izmir, 1876), 242:2, 11a.

7 Yaakov Weil, *Torat Shabbat*, vol. 2 (Karlsruhe, Germany, 1839), 274:1:2, 53a.

It was only in the fifteenth century that Ashkenazic Jews in Austria and southern Germany started braiding their bread for Shabbat.[8] Even so, the braiding would not be accorded significance in rabbinic literature for many years, and even now is not noted in many classic works on Jewish customs.[9]

The earliest explanation for braided challa is given by Rabbi Yair Hayim Bacharach (1639–1702). He explains that it is the custom "in all the lands of Poland, Bohemia and Moravia" to braid the challa because it is often in contact with the meat dishes being prepared for Shabbat. In other words, the special braided form is based on the idea in Pesaḥim 36a that such bread must have an unusual shape to remind people not to eat it with dairy.[10] This is the only explanation for braided challa mentioned by Rabbi Simha Rabinowitz in his *Piskei Teshuvot*.[11] Over time, as this shape became more commonplace, it would no longer be able to serve as an unusual shape to remind people that it may have been in contact with meat.

The kabbalistic tradition to have twelve loaves at the Shabbat table, parallel to the twelve showbreads on the table in the Temple,[12] forms the basis for the most popular explanation for braided challa. Of course, producing twelve loaves of bread for every Shabbat meal is not necessarily an easy feat, and so creative solutions were devised.

---

8 Freda Reider, *The Hallah Book: Recipes, History, and Traditions* (New York: Ktav, 1987), 13.

9 For example, Avraham Sperling, *Sefer Taamei HaMinhagim UMekorei HaDinim* (Jerusalem: Shai Lamora, 1999); Yitzhak Lipetz, *Sefer Mataamim* (Warsaw, 1894); A. Hershovitz, *Sefer Minhagei Yeshurun* (Vilna, 1899); J. D. Eisenstein, *Otzar Dinim UMinhagim* (New York, 1917); Shmuel Gelbard, *Otzar Taamei HaMinhagim* (Petach Tikva: Mifal Rashi, 1996).

10 *Mekor Ḥayim*, commentary to *Tur, Oraḥ Ḥayim* 274, introduction. *Peri Megadim, Oraḥ Ḥayim* 242:1 notes a practice to add fat to the bread used for Shabbat, and explains that it is permitted since the bread is unusual, although he doesn't say exactly in what manner it looks different.

11 Simha Rabinowitz, *Piskei Teshuvot*, vol. 3a (Jerusalem, 2011), 242:11, 10, note 105. While this work mentions braided challa in a note, the earlier edition from 1991 doesn't mention the custom at all.

12 On the history and symbolism of this practice, see Moshe Hallamish, *Hanhagot Kabbaliot BeShabbat* (Jerusalem: Orḥot, 2006), 329–30.

Rabbi Elhanan Broda, in his eighteenth-century kabbalistic work *Leket HaPardes*, writes that it is customary to make the Shabbat loaves "nice and long, not round like the weekday bread," in order to appear like the letter *vav*, with the numerical value of six. The two loaves together would thus constitute the numerical value of twelve, representing the twelve loaves mandated by kabbalistic practice. Alternatively, the symbolism of a *vav* shaped loaf is that along with the five fingers of each hand holding the bread at the time of the blessing representing the letter *heh* two times, and the piece torn off representing the letter *yod*, the four-letter name of God is spelled out.[13] Another approach to a simplified way of making twelve loaves was the Ukrainian hasidic custom to make a large loaf called a *yud-betnik* that consisted of twelve smaller, pull-apart pieces.[14] A somewhat similar idea was noted by Rabbi Shmariah Brendris (1780–1857), who explained that the challot could be braided with six strands each, and so the two together, with twelve strands, would represent the twelve loaves of the showbread.[15] This explanation was popularized when it was quoted by Rabbi Yisrael Chaim Friedman of Rachov (1852–1922) in the second volume of his *Likkutei Maharih̤*.[16] It applies only to the six-strand braided challa, not the less elaborate versions that have a smaller number of strands. Since the twelve loaves of the showbread were associated with Shabbat and not holidays, there is a custom not to use braided challa on holidays.[17]

Other explanations may be found in more contemporary works, for example, that the braided challa in a mystical manner represents

---

13 Hallamish, *Hanhagot Kabbaliot BeShabbat*, 332.

14 Aharon Wertheim, *Halakhot VeHalikhot BeH̤asidut* (Jerusalem: Mossad HaRav Kook, 2003), 150.

15 Shmariah Brendris, *Iyun Tefilla* (Lvov, 1849), 20. This is a hasidic work. Brendris was *Av Beit Din* of Trembovla and Rimlov (Ukraine).

16 Yisrael Chaim Friedman, *Likkutei Maharih̤*, vol. 2 (Jerusalem, 1965), 54 (27b). This book was first published in 1899. He also brings the idea that two long loaves that each look like a *vav* also symbolize the number twelve. These same two explanations are brought by Hayim Zvi Ehrenreich (1875–1937) in his *Ketzei HaMateh*, a commentary on the *Mateh Ephraim* (New York: Kol Aryeh, 1959), 625:83.

17 Yosef Lewy, *Minhag Yisrael Torah*, vol. 2 (Jerusalem: Frank, 1994), *siman* 274:1, 83; Gavriel Zinner, *Nitei Gavriel: Yom Tov*, vol. 2 (Jerusalem: Shemesh, 1998), 7:6, note 10, 71.

"connecting the right and the left,"[18] but the explanations that the braiding serves as a reminder that the bread is in contact with meat and that it represents the twelve loaves of the showbread remain the standard reasons.

Over time, many different customs arose regarding the particular size and arrangement of the challot,[19] including using a nonbraided loaf for the Friday night meal, and a fancier braided challa for Shabbat day, in order to show more honor to the Shabbat day meal, as found in Pesaḥim 105a.[20]

Some Ashkenazic communities preserved the original practice of using nonbraided bread on Shabbat. This was the custom in Frankfurt am Main, where braided bread was eaten only after Shabbat.[21] This was understood to represent the difference between Shabbat and the regular weekday, as explained by Rabbi Yair Hayim Bacharach, since it has the appearance of the braided Havdala candle.[22] Note that Rabbi Joseph Juspa Hahn (d. 1637), in his book *Sefer Yosef Ometz,* an important collection of the customs of the Frankfurt am Main community, describes special bread made for Shabbat, but it is not braided. He mentions that loaves made for Shabbat had holes punched into them with a knife, which he explains was to make them look different in case they came into contact with meat, and that rich people made "long and wide" loaves seasoned with many kinds of spices.[23]

### BRAIDED BREAD IN EUROPE

The use of breads fashioned into braids dates back to ancient times.[24] They were served on special occasions, such as those mentioned by the

18 Avner Tunic, *Mayim Ḥayim* (Bnei Brak, 2003), 51, note 5.

19 There is an entire book on the subject: Avigdor Berger, *Minhagei Betziat Leḥem Mishneh* (Jerusalem: Dfus Alon, 2002).

20 See Yosef Lewy, *Minhag Yisrael Torah,* vol. 2 (Jerusalem: Frank, 1994), *siman* 274:1, 84–85, where he also adds kabbalistic reasons for this.

21 *Yerushatenu,* vol. 3 (Bnei Brak: Machon Moreshet Ashkenaz, 2009), 403.

22 *Mekor Ḥayim, Kitzur Halakhot,* commentary to *Tur, Oraḥ Ḥayim* 274.

23 Amichai Kinarti, ed., Joseph Juspa Hahn, *Sefer Yosef Ometz* (Shaalvim: Machon Shlomo Aumann, 2016), *siman* 573, 163. The book was first published in 1723.

24 See the comment regarding ancient Assyrian braided bread in Nicholas Postgate, "The Bread of Assur," *Iraq* 77 (2015), 165.

Greek Athenaeus of Naucratis (ca. 2–3 CE) in his *Deipnosophistae*: "Nice twisted loaves, solemnizing the Lenæan festival, and the Potfeast at the Anthesteria ...," two festivals associated with the worship of Dionysus.[25]

The Romans also baked braided breads for festive occasions.[26] The *bracellus* (meaning bracelet, ultimately from the Latin word for arm, *brachium*), was an early Roman twisted bread.[27] It represented a baker's artistry and was used as an emblem for his bakery, a practice that persists to this day in some parts of Europe. This bread is often presented as the origin of the more familiar twisted pretzel,[28] itself a food associated with the special season of Lent in Austria, Germany, and Poland.[29]

Seasonal decorative breads are well known in Germany, Austria, and Switzerland.[30] The *Allerheiligenstriezel* (All Saint's braid), often referred to as *streizel*, is a type of braided yeast bread used to commemorate All Saint's Day[31] and Lent.[32] Different shapes of braided bread were made for the different Christian holidays. Some shapes derived from ancient symbols, such as a wheel or wreath to symbolize the sun and eternity.[33]

25 C. D. Yonge, trans., *The Deipnosophists, or Banquet of the Learned* (London: R. Clay, 1854), book 4, 5:214. Lenaia was an important festival that took place in January, where Dionysus was worshipped and new theatrical pieces premiered. The Anthesteria was another festival in honor of Dionysus held around the time of the January or February full moon. See Susan Guettel Cole, "Finding Dionysus," in Daniel Ogden, ed., *A Companion to Greek Religion* (Oxford: Blackwell, 2010), 336.

26 Josephine Bacon, "Kalach, Kolatch, Kulitch – Challah?," in Harlan Walker, ed., *Oxford Symposium on Food and Cookery, 1990: Feasting and Fasting: Proceedings* (London: Prospect Books, 1990), 53.

27 Bacon, "Kalach, Kolatch, Kulitch – Challah?," 53.

28 Phyllis Raybin Emert, *The Pretzel Book* (New Hope, PA: Woodsong Graphics, 1984), 14.

29 Emert, *The Pretzel Book*, 109.

30 Sarah Kelly "Specialty Baking in Germany, Austria and Switzerland," in Alan Davidson, ed. *National and Regional Styles of Cookery: Proceedings: Oxford Symposium 1981* (London: Prospect Books, 1981), 162.

31 Victoria R. Williams, *Celebrating Life Customs around the World: From Baby Showers to Funerals*, vol. 1 (Santa Barbara, CA: ABC-CLIO, 2017), 265.

32 James Dow, *German Folklore: A Handbook* (Westport, CT: Greenwood, 2006), 169.

33 Kelly "Specialty Baking in Germany, Austria and Switzerland," 162.

The Swiss *zopf* is a braided bread, considered Switzerland's "Sunday bread." It is also served on special occasions, and sometimes has seasonal variants of particular shapes, such as a bunny shape for Easter.[34] Until the 1600s it was prohibited for bakers to make this special bread on days other than religious feast days.[35] The German Sunday bread is the braided *hepezopf*.[36]

*Vánočka* is a braided bread baked in the Czech Republic and Slovakia (in Slovak it is called *vianočka*) traditionally at Christmas time. It was first mentioned by a Benedictine monk, Jan of Holešov (d. 1436), in his work *Treatise on Christmas Eve*.[37] The bread is named after *Vánoce*, meaning Christmas in Czech (*Vianoce* in Slovak).[38]

In Ukrainian culture there are many traditional braided breads, to the extent that braided bread is often presented as a classic symbol of traditional Ukrainian cuisine.[39] For example, the *paska* is a special bread, made in various shapes but usually braided, served at Easter and at memorial services. The *kolach*, or *kalach*, was used in various ceremonies, particularly Christmas. The name itself is derived from the Ukrainian *kolo*, meaning a circle, and the braided loaf is often made in a circular shape, understood to symbolize eternity and general well-being.[40] It is also served on special occasions, such as at weddings, funerals, and to welcome important guests. The *korovai* is a special, decorated braided

---

34 Heddi Nieuwsma, Dorian Rollin, *Swiss Bread* (Basel: Helvetiq, 2020), 59.

35 Andie Pilot, *Helvetic Kitchen: Swiss Cooking* (Basel: Bergli, 2017), 10.

36 Ursula Heinzelmann, *Food Culture in Germany* (Westport, CT: Greenwood, 2008), 133.

37 Josef Hrabák, *Výbor z české literatury od počátků po dobu Husovu* (Committee on Czech Literature: From the Beginning to the Time of Hus), (Prague: Czechoslovak Academy of Sciences, 1957), 745.

38 Miriam Elizabeth Lowenberg, *Food and People* (Hoboken, NJ: Wiley, 1979), 135.

39 See the cover of the classic work on the subject by Savella Stechishin, *Traditional Ukrainian Cookery* (London: Trident Press, 1991), which is illustrated by a braided loaf.

40 Josephine Bacon, "Kalach, Kolatch, Kulitch – Challah?" in Harlan Walker, ed., *Oxford Symposium on Food and Cookery, 1990: Feasting and Fasting: Proceedings* (London: Prospect Books, 1990), 53.

bread used at weddings.[41] These breads are placed on the table with candles either inside them or next to them.[42]

## EXPLANATIONS FOR BRAIDED BREAD

The simple reason that braided bread was used for special occasions throughout Europe was that it looked fancy and allowed for the making of even more elaborate shapes and designs. "Braiding is a favorite technique used in many of the decorative breads," as "the braid binds the unruly dough in a specific shape, helping the baker to control his art work."[43] Additionally, braided breads stay fresh somewhat longer, so they could be baked in advance of holidays and Sundays, when bakers usually didn't work.[44]

Various folkloric explanations were given as well. For example, Romans viewed braided bread as "shaped to represent the crossed arms of the Roman at prayer," where arms were crossed in front of the heart,[45] making it particularly appropriate for religious festivals. This basic concept has also been appropriated to explain how braided challa symbolizes Shabbat, since "when your arms are folded, you are at rest, you can't work."[46]

The most popular folkloric explanations make a connection between braided bread and the braided hair of women. The German braided bread called *perchisbrod* or *berchisbrod*[47] was associated with the

41 Jo Maries Powers, "Ukrainian-Canadian Breads: Shape, Symbolism and Spirituality," in Harlan Walker, ed., *Look and Feel: Studies in Texture, Appearance and Incidental Characteristics of Food* (Devon: Prospect Books, 1994), 149–51.

42 Bacon, "Kalach, Kolatch, Kulitch – Challah?," 54.

43 Sarah Kelly, "Specialty Baking in Germany, Austria and Switzerland," in Alan Davidson, ed., *National and Regional Styles of Cookery: Proceedings: Oxford Symposium 1981* (London: Prospect Books, 1981), 162.

44 Ursula Heinzelmann, *Food Culture in Germany* (Westport, CT: Greenwood, 2008), 133.

45 Bacon, "Kalach, Kolatch, Kulitch – Challah?," 53.

46 Martha Zimmerman, *Celebrating Biblical Feasts: In Your Home or Church* (Minneapolis: Bethany House, 2004), 28.

47 Samuel Krauss, "Aus Der Jüdischen Volksküche" (From the Jewish National Cuisine), *Mitteilungen Zur Jüdischen Volkskunde* 18, no. 1/2 (53) (1915), 3–5, proposes that *berchisbrod* was abbreviated to form the German term for challa, *berches*. For

figure of Perchta or Berchta, a female bogeyman as it were, who punished naughty children at Christmas by cutting open their stomachs and filling them with trash.[48] An additional equivalent was Holle, also known as Holda or Hulda, another frightening figure with many associations,[49] but generally conceived as a kind of demonic witch who ate children and was considered responsible for tangling loose hair at night while people slept.[50] The braided bread was thought to be connected to the braided hair of Holle.[51] In another connection to braided hair, the Swiss *zopf* was understood to be derived from an ancient practice that the wife of a warrior who died would be killed and buried with him, after a braid of her hair was cut off as a symbol of mourning. The braided bread was seen as a symbolic substitute for the actual hair and wife.[52] A connection

the traditional interpretation of *berches*, see Yosef Lewy, *Minhag Yisrael Torah*, vol. 2 (Jerusalem: Frank, 1994), *siman* 274:1, 85.

48 On this figure, see John B. Smith, "Perchta the Belly-Slitter and Her Kin: A View of Some Traditional Threatening Figures, Threats and Punishments," *Folklore* 115, no. 2 (2004), 167–86, and Thomas D. Hill, "Perchta the Belly Slitter and Án Hrísmagi: 'Laxdœla Saga' Cap. 48–49," *The Journal of English and Germanic Philology* 106, no. 4 (2007), 518–19.

49 See the comprehensive study by Jill Hammer, "Holle's Cry: Unearthing a Birth Goddess in a German Jewish Naming Ceremony," *Nashim: A Journal of Jewish Women's Studies and Gender Issues*, no. 9 (2005), 62–87.

50 This figure was well known to German Jews, who adopted the custom of the Hollekreisch, where the child received his secular name. This custom involved lifting the baby, sometimes with the cradle, while shouting out a magical formula mentioning Holle. The ceremony was originally intended to protect the child from this demonic figure. See Joshua Trachtenberg, *Jewish Magic and Superstition* (New York: Athenium, 1984), 41–42. Paul Wexler, *Two-Tiered Relexification in Yiddish* (Berlin: Walter de Gruyter, 2002), 289, proposes that the term "challa" "was Hebraized in an attempt to eliminate the pagan pre-Christian symbolism of the plaited bread term" named after Holle. On this controversial suggestion, see Ghilad Zuckermann, "'Ety*myth*ological Othering' and the Power of 'Lexical Engineering' in Judaism, Islam and Christianity: A Socio-Philo(sopho)logical Perspective," in Tope Omoniyi, Joshua A. Fishman, eds., *Explorations in the Sociology of Language and Religion* (Amsterdam: John Benjamins, 2006), 252.

51 Gil Marks, *Encyclopedia of Jewish Food* (Boston: Houghton Mifflin Harcourt, 2010), 97–98.

52 Sarah Kelly "Specialty Baking in Germany, Austria and Switzerland," in Alan Davidson, ed., *National and Regional Styles of Cookery: Proceedings: Oxford Symposium 1981* (London: Prospect Books, 1981), 162.

between braided hair and challa even appears in contemporary Jewish sources, where the braided challa is explained as a reference to Eve, since the Talmud in Berakhot 61b mentions that God braided her hair before presenting her to Adam.[53]

## JEWISH BRAIDED BREAD

Braided challa dates to the fifteenth century, when Ashkenazic Jews in Austria and Southern Germany began modeling their challa on the local decorative breads baked throughout the central European and Slavic countries.[54] Ashkenazic Jews lived in countries where braided bread was made to commemorate special occasions, both religious festivals and life-cycle events, influencing them to adopt the practice of making braided challa for Shabbat, holidays, and special occasions. Sephardic Jews did not adopt the custom of making braided challa for special occasions[55] until they themselves were exposed to this practice through interaction with Ashkenazic Jews.[56] The instructions for braiding and final appearance of these traditional European breads remain remarkably similar to the familiar Ashkenazic braided challa.[57]

Although the most widespread term for this bread among Jews today is "challa," other terms used for the Shabbat bread hearken back to the particular local breads they were modeled after. For example, the *kulitsch* is a braided Christmas bread, often stuffed with raisins and glazed with sugar, known in Bohemia, Moravia, Poland, and the Ukraine. This

---

53 See Avraham Zvi Kluger, *Rav Ḥesed* (Beit Shemesh, 2018), 23. There he explains that this is a reason to eat braided challa on Rosh HaShana, the day Eve was created.

54 Freda Reider, *The Hallah Book: Recipes, History, and Traditions* (New York: Ktav, 1987), 13.

55 Sephardic Jews didn't even have a special term for the bread used on Shabbat. Samuel Krauss, "Aus Der Jüdischen Volksküche" (From the Jewish National Cuisine), *Mitteilungen Zur Jüdischen Volkskunde* 18, no. 1/2 (53) (1915), 2.

56 See the contemporary Yemenite halakhic work by Yitzhak Ratzabi, *Shulḥan Arukh HaMekutzar* (Bnei Brak, 2006), *Even HaEzer*, vol. 2, 350, note 19, who points out a few times that braided challa is not customary in the Yemenite community, noting that "I wrote this only for the next generation, that this doesn't have the status of a custom for us."

57 For example, see the instructions for the Swiss *zopf* here: https://tinyurl.com/432c7tbo.

term is preserved as the Yiddish *koylatsh* and used in Poland, Ukraine, and Russia to denote challot, particularly the very large ones used in weddings and celebrations.[58] Jewish bakers would even make these special braided loaves for their Christian neighbors at Christmas.[59] Note that the suggestion that two six-braided loaves of challa represent twelve loaves at the Shabbat meal originated with Rabbi Shmariah Brendris, who was head of the *beit din* of Trembovla and Rimlov in the Ukraine, where braided bread was most elaborate and used widely.

## CONCLUSION

While Jews are generally thought to be conservative in their religious practices and wary of outside influences, adopting culinary practices such as braided bread from their neighbors wasn't seen as problematic. There was no association with idolatry per se, and Jewish people didn't necessarily believe in the local folklore that Gentiles associated with their braided bread.[60] It was simply that they were exposed to the cultural norm of braided bread as a signifier of a festive meal and incorporated it into their holidays as well. Just as these days we wouldn't be surprised to find hot dogs, sushi, or eggrolls at a smorgasbord at a Jewish wedding or even an elaborate Kiddush, alongside more traditional Jewish fare such as kugel and herring, it is not surprising that braided

---

58 Bacon, "Kalach, Kolatch, Kulitch – Challah?," 54. Eliezer Meir Lifshitz, *Ktavim*, vol. 1 (Jerusalem: Mossad HaRav Kook, 1947), 330, note 18. See, for example, David Cohen, *Shpola* (Haifa: Sokolofsky, 1965), 155, where he describes the special "Purim *koylatsh*" baked in Shpola, Ukraine; Shneur Zalman Berger, *Noda BeShe'arim* (2010), 305, regarding a *koylatsh* for the celebration of 19 Kislev; Shlomo Eliram, *Harei At Mekudeshet* (Jerusalem, 1993), 128, *siman* 43, who refers to the wedding *koylatsh* broken at the entrance to the *yiḥud* room.

59 See the description of Reb Meir the baker from Hlynjány, Ukraine, in Asher Korech, *Kehillat Galina* (Jerusalem: Weiss, 1950), 67.

60 Samuel Krauss, "Aus Der Jüdischen Volksküche" (From the Jewish National Cuisine), *Mitteilungen Zur Jüdischen Volkskunde* 18, no. 1/2 (53) (1915), 4–5; Joshua Trachtenberg, *Jewish Magic and Superstition* (New York: Athenium, 1984), 40–41; John Cooper, *Eat and Be Satisfied* (Northvale, NJ: Jason Aronson, 1993), 174. It is interesting to note that Yehuda Asad (1794–1866, Hungary) notes that round-shaped matza, and by extension round-shaped bread, symbolizes the unity and eternity of God and serves to counter old pagan ideas, *She'elot UTeshuvot Yehuda Yaaleh, Oraḥ Ḥayim* (Lemberg, 1873), *siman* 157, 48b.

bread was adopted by Jews in countries where such bread was used to commemorate special occasions.

Although it is considered "a curious fact that the Jewish religion, always so quick to distance itself from other faiths in custom and practice, should have adopted a symbolic food from another culture" as part of festive meals,[61] the reality is that just as with clothing fashions,[62] Jews adopted the culinary styles of their neighbors, within the limitations of dietary laws.

In this way challa joins a long list of foods considered traditional by Jews today, but are in fact historical remnants of contact with the surrounding communities in generations past. For example, the familiar *rugelach* are based on the medieval Polish crescent-shaped rolls (*rogal* means "horn" in Polish).[63] Today these are often filled with chocolate and are a common Shabbat treat. Although they are a staple of traditional Jewish bakeries and generally associated with Shabbat and festive occasions, these pastries and their shape were never accorded any particular Jewish symbolism or meaning. Because of this, it wouldn't surprise anyone to learn that it is based on a Polish treat that Jews adopted. Such is the case with challa as well, notwithstanding the explanations about the braiding of challa over the years.

61 Bacon, "Kalach, Kolatch, Kulitch – Challah?," 54.

62 See chapter 28.

63 Maria Dembińska, *Food and Drink in Medieval Poland* (Philadelphia: University of Pennsylvania Press, 1999), 116. See David Cohen, *Shpola* (Haifa: Sokolofsky, 1965), 155, where he describes *rugelach* as "cakes in the shape of a half moon." Special thanks to my student Talia Davis who asked the question that inspired this chapter.

*Chapter 7*

# Eating an Etrog on Rosh HaShana

## ETROG AS A GOOD SIGN ON ROSH HASHANA

The *Tur* (*Oraḥ Ḥayim* 583) quotes a statement by Abaye in Keritot 6a that certain foods traditionally eaten on Rosh HaShana are seen as "good omens," but adds a particular fruit to the list that is not mentioned by Abaye: the etrog. The *Tur* writes, "Abaye said, 'Now that you have said that an omen is a [significant] matter, a person should accustom himself to eating etrog, squash, beans, leeks, beets, and dates on Rosh HaShana.'" Rabbi Yosef Karo, in his commentary *Beit Yosef*, notes that our texts of the Talmud do not mention the etrog. In fact, the etrog is not included in the list of auspicious foods eaten on Rosh HaShana in any edition of the Talmud.[1]

Some commentaries on the *Tur* suggest that the word "etrog" was a scribal error. For example, Rabbi Mordekhai Karmi (1749–1825),

1 Although the work *Dikdukei Soferim* by R. N. Rabbinovicz did not include a volume of textual variants in Keritot, the parallel section of Abaye's statement in Horayot 12a has no variants which include the etrog, R. N. Rabbinovicz, *Dikdukei Soferim*, vol. 10 (Munich, 1879), Horayot 12a, 40.

in his commentary *Maamar Mordekhai*, points out that while all the other omens are explained, no explanation is given for the etrog, and no special symbolism is associated with it in the text of the *Tur*.[2] However, all manuscripts and printed editions of the *Tur* do include etrog in the list, so it seems to have been a deliberate addition.[3]

Attempts have been made to explain how an etrog can be seen as a good omen. Rabbi Yehoshua Falk Cohen (1555–1614), in his commentary *Perisha*, explains that since an etrog is called "the product of goodly trees" (Lev. 23:40), and since Mordekhai ben Hillel (known as the Mordekhai) wrote that it is customary to eat "all manner of sweet foods so that our upcoming year will be sweet,"[4] the etrog can be considered a nice omen for a good year. Rabbi Yosef Escapa (1570–1662) explains that we eat an etrog so that we will merit doing the mitzva of the four species on the upcoming holiday of Sukkot, or that we should merit that our own "fruits," our children, are goodly, just as the etrog is described as "goodly fruit."[5]

Rabbi Hayim Palagi, in his book *Ruaḥ Ḥayim*, brings a few explanations for why it may be auspicious to eat an etrog on Rosh HaShana: "Since on Rosh HaShana the first man was created and he sinned with the Tree of Knowledge, and there is an opinion that it was an etrog (Genesis Rabba 15:7), therefore, to repair this sin we eat it with a blessing. Alternatively, it is as our Sages taught (Leviticus Rabba 30:12), there are four types of Jews, and the etrog represents those who have both taste and smell, the Jews who have Torah and mitzvot, and consequently we eat it so that we will be worthy of being like an etrog, filled with Torah and good deeds."[6] Some sources indicate that the etrog was used as the new fruit for *Sheheḥeyanu* on the second night of Rosh HaShana.[7]

---

2 Mordekhai Karmi, *Maamar Mordekhai*, vol. 4 (Jerusalem: Oz Vehadar, 1995), 247.

3 See note 4 in the Machon Yerushalayim edition of the *Tur*.

4 Mordekhai, Yoma, *remez* 723.

5 Yosef Escapa, *Rosh Yosef* (Izmir, 1658), 101a. This explanation is explicitly rejected in *Maamar Mordekhai*.

6 Hayim Palagi, *Ruach Ḥayim* (Izmir, 1876), 91a. Based on this, the *Yehi Ratzon* prayer said when eating the etrog is "that we should be written in the book of the righteous," since the etrog symbolizes the righteous among Israel. See *Kovetz Beit Aharon*, vol. 49, Tishrei 5754, 133.

7 See Hayim Yosef David Azulai, *Otzrot Ḥayim: Tikkun Seuda* (Jerusalem: Ahavat Shalom, 1999), 111. Regarding the *Sheheḥeyanu* blessing on an etrog, see Yoel Malka,

## A NEW UNDERSTANDING OF THIS CUSTOM

It is possible to explain the "good sign" of the etrog in another way, and to view it as the source of one of the most popular Rosh HaShana customs, dipping an apple in honey. After recording the foods listed by Abaye and the various hints found in their names, the *Tur* (*Oraḥ Ḥayim* 583) writes, "And from this there are many customs, each place according to its custom, like in Ashkenaz where it is customary to eat an apple dipped in honey at the beginning of the meal and to say, 'A sweet year should be renewed for us.'" The Maharil (Rabbi Yaakov ben Moshe Levi Moelin, 1365–1427) explains the custom to specifically use an apple as a reference to the "field of apples" known to the kabbalists: "The smell of my son is like the smell of the fields" (Gen. 27:27).[8] The "field of apples" is a kabbalistic term denoting the place of the Divine Presence, the *Shekhina*. During the High Holidays "the King is in the field" and we feel the Divine Presence. In order to demonstrate that this feeling is sweet and pleasant to us, we dip the apple, representing the Divine Presence, in the sweet honey.[9]

The source for the idea that the "smell of the fields" (Gen. 27:27) is an apple orchard is found in Taanit 29b, where R. Yehuda in the name of Rav interprets the verse that way. On the words *shel tapuḥim*, *Tosafot* state, "Some explain *tapuḥim* as the smell of etrogim." This is the approach of Rabbeinu Tam, who explained that whereas the term *tapuaḥ* is generally translated as "apple," it actually refers to an etrog, as found in *Tosafot*, Shabbat 85a (*pirio kodem*). There, Rabbi Ḥama interprets the verse "Like an apple (*tapuaḥ*) among the trees of the forest, so is my beloved among the maidens" (Song 2:3) as a reference to the Jewish people, suggesting that "just as with a *tapuaḥ* the fruit precedes the leaves, so too Israel said "we will do" (*naaseh*) before "we will hear" (*nishma*) when receiving the Torah. *Tosafot* bring the explanation of Rabbeinu Tam, that *tapuaḥ* in this context cannot mean an apple, as "we see

---

*Netivei Halakha* (Emmanuel, 1994), 235, note 18.

8 Shlomo Spitzer, *Sefer Maharil* (Jerusalem: Machon Yerushalayim, 1989), 276, *siman* 7.

9 See also the homiletic explanation offered in Yaakov Greenwald, *VaYaged Yaakov* (Brooklyn, 2008), 147–48.

that it grows like all other trees with the fruit appearing after the leaves," and must mean an etrog, since "the etrog remains on the tree from year to year," and stays there as old leaves fall and new ones grow; thus the fruit precedes the new leaves.[10] This opinion of Rabbeinu Tam is also found in his *Sefer HaYashar, siman* 263. Similarly, the *Targum* to Song of Songs 2:3 translates *tapuaḥ* as an etrog.[11]

Although many interpret the *tapuaḥ* in Song of Songs as the fruit we call an apple,[12] this is not the approach of Rabbeinu Tam, who translates *tapuaḥ* as etrog. In his responsa, Rabbi Hanoch Teitelbaum (1884–1943)[13] explained that this is the source for adding etrog as an ingredient in *ḥaroset,* as the Rema stated in *Oraḥ Ḥayim* 473:5 that "we make the *ḥaroset* out of fruits that Israel is compared to, like *tapuḥim,*" and according to Rabbeinu Tam, the *tapuaḥ* that the children of Israel are likened to is an etrog.[14]

Support for the approach of Rabbeinu Tam may be found in Genesis Rabba 15:7. There, in a discussion about the identity of the fruit of the Tree of Knowledge, Rabbi Abba of Akko says: "It was an etrog, as it states: 'The woman saw that the tree was good for eating' (Gen. 3:6). Go and see, which tree is eaten like its fruit? You can find nothing other than the etrog." Regarding the "smell of the fields" (Gen. 27:27) that Isaac smelled, in Genesis Rabba 65:22 Rabbi Yoḥanan asks how Isaac could

---

10 Yisrael Hopstein (1737–1814), the Maggid of Kozhnitz, in his commentary to this passage in the Talmud resolves the problem of Rabbeinu Tam by explaining that the correct version of this homiletical teaching is the parallel version found in Song of Songs Rabba: "The *tapuaḥ* buds before its leaves," not that the entire apple is ready before the leaves. See Hanoch Teitelbaum, *She'elot UTeshuvot Yad Ḥanokh* 8:2.

11 Although *Tosafot* there refer to the *Targum* of Song of Songs 7:9, there the *Targum* does not translate *tapuaḥ* as etrog. In *She'elot UTeshuvot Yad Ḥanokh* 8:3 this reference in *Tosafot* is understood to be a scribal error, and the intent was Song of Songs 2:3. Perhaps *Tosafot* had a different version of the *Targum* to Song of Songs. See also *Yad Ḥanokh* 8:8.

12 Yehuda Feliks, *Nature and Land in the Bible* (Jerusalem: Reuven Mass, 1992), 364, note 3 [Hebrew].

13 *She'elot UTeshuvot Yad Ḥanokh* 8:1.

14 See *She'elot UTeshuvot Yad Ḥanokh* 8:6 regarding whether the *tapuaḥ* mentioned in Pesaḥim 116a as the tree under which the Israelite women gave birth when hiding from Egyptians is considered to be an apple or an etrog.

have enjoyed the smell of Jacob, since he was disguised using goat skins, which smell awful. Rabbi Yoḥanan explains that "when our father Jacob entered to his father, the smell of the Garden of Eden entered with him," and this is what is meant by the "smell of the fields." We saw that this smell is described in Taanit 29b as the smell of *tapuḥim*, which is now reasonable to understand as the smell of etrog, the smell of the fruit of the Tree of Knowledge in the Garden of Eden.[15]

Based on this, it may well be that the custom recorded in the *Tur* of eating an etrog on Rosh HaShana has been replaced today with eating an apple dipped in honey, according to Rabbeinu Tam's approach that the *tapuaḥ* is an etrog rather than an apple. If so, the *Tur* himself provides an explanation for eating an etrog on Rosh HaShana when he writes, "And from this there are many customs, each place according to its custom, like in Ashkenaz where it is customary to eat an apple dipped in honey at the beginning of the meal and to say, 'A sweet year should be renewed for us.'" In other words, in Ashkenaz an apple is eaten instead of an etrog.[16]

15 This conflation of etrog and *tapuaḥ* may have contributed to the Christian association of the apple with the forbidden fruit.

16 See also Shemtob Gaguine, *Keter Shem Tov*, vol. 6 (London, 1955), 97, who reached the same conclusion and understood that the early authorities relied on the *Tur* to use apples as a substitute for an etrog when none were available.

*Chapter 8*

# Different Approaches to Eating Garlic on Rosh HaShana

## AVOIDING GARLIC ON ROSH HASHANA

The *Kol Bo* (*siman* 64) discusses the custom to eat certain foods on Rosh HaShana as a good omen, based on Keritot 6a and Horayot 12a. In addition to the foods mentioned in the Talmud, he notes that there is a custom to eat the head and lungs of a ram, and adds, "And this was what Rabbi Meir (of Rothenburg, 1215–93) customarily did, and he was not careful about eating garlic, nuts, or anything."[1] The *Tashbetz HaKatan*, written by Rabbi Meir's student, generally identified as Rabbi Shimshon ben Tzaddok, similarly writes (*siman* 118), "Rabbi Meir of blessed memory would customarily eat the head of a ram on the first night of Rosh

1 This is also found in *Orḥot Ḥayim, Hilkhot Rosh HaShana, siman* 5. It is also brought in Yitzhak Zev Kahane, ed., *Teshuvot, Pesakim UMinhagim shel Rav Meir ben Rav Barukh MiRothenburg* (Jerusalem: Mossad HaRav Kook, 1957), 296, *siman* 522. Regarding eating nuts, see Daniel Sperber, *Minhagei Yisrael*, vol. 3 (Jerusalem: Mossad HaRav Kook, 1994), 41–49.

HaShana, recalling the ram of Isaac. He was not careful to avoid eating garlic, onions, or nuts or anything else." The custom not to eat nuts on Rosh HaShana is well known from the Maharil (*Minhagim, Hilkhot Shofar* 2) and the Rema in the *Shulḥan Arukh* (*Oraḥ Ḥayim*, 583:2), where it is explained that nuts increase spit and phlegm, and spitting interrupts and distracts one from prayer, or causes difficulty hearing the shofar blasts. Avoiding garlic is not mentioned by the Maharil or the Rema.

It is not clear from the *Kol Bo* and *Tashbetz HaKatan* why some people were careful not to eat garlic on Rosh HaShana. An explanation is found in a book of Rabbi Meir of Rothenburg's practices, *Minhagim DeBei Maharam*. There we find: "Some have the custom not to eat garlic or onions and similar things that have a bitter taste."[2] Note that there it is presented as something that some people do, although Rabbi Meir himself did not follow this custom. At first glance, it would seem that this practice is reminiscent of the custom mentioned in an earlier source in the responsa of Rabbi Natronai Gaon: "We do not cook any dish that contains vinegar" on Rosh HaShana, as a sign "that we should have a year that is completely sweet and pleasant and that there should be nothing bad or troublesome in it."[3] This custom persisted over time. For example, in the nineteenth century *Mateh Ephraim* writes, "It is customary not to eat sour or bitter things" (583:3); so too in the *Arukh HaShulḥan* (583:3).

In reality, garlic is not sour or bitter. It is more correctly categorized as sharp, and so it would not fall under the category of foods mentioned by Rabbi Natronai Gaon. However, avoiding sharp foods on Rosh HaShana is mentioned in *Leket Yosher* by Rabbi Yosef ben Moshe as the custom of his teacher, Rabbi Israel Isserlin (1390–1460) author of *Terumat HaDeshen*. He states, "This is the general principle: anything sharp

2 Israel Elfenbein, ed., *Minhagim DeBei Rabbi Meir ben Barukh MiRothenburg* (New York: Jewish Theological Seminary of America, 1938), 45.

3 Robert Brody, ed., *Responsa of Rabbi Natronai Gaon*, vol. 1 (Jerusalem: Ofeq Institute, 1994), *siman* 179. This also appears in *Sefer Abudraham* (*Tefillat Rosh HaShana*), "We do not cook in vinegar." Ḥida in *Tov Ayin*, *siman* 18, writes that the custom not to eat sour things "is ancient, from geonic times." Regarding foods not eaten on Rosh HaShana because they are sour or bitter, see the comprehensive article by Gedalia Oberlander, "Avoiding Eating Nuts and Sour Foods on the High Holidays," *Kovetz Or Yisrael* 1, no. 17 (Tishrei 5760/1999, year 5), 135–45 [Hebrew].

was not eaten during the Ten Days of Repentance, only sweet things and new fruits; he did not even want to eat cooked onions."[4]

The earliest record of the custom not to eat sharp foods in particular, including garlic, comes from the time of Rabbi Meir of Rothenburg, as we saw in the *Kol Bo* and *Tashbetz HaKatan*, and those sources come specifically to negate that practice. This indicates that avoiding garlic began as a folk custom with no rabbinic source, as a natural expansion of the good omens found in the Talmud and the avoidance of sour foods found in the geonic period. This practice was rejected by Rabbi Meir in the thirteenth century, but later on, by the time of Rabbi Israel Isserlin, it had come to receive rabbinic approval, albeit as an individual practice worthy of note. *Leket Yosher* notes that even for Rabbi Israel Isserlin the practice was undergoing development over time: "But the fish called 'salted fish' (זולץ וויש) and peppers he ate even on Rosh HaShana, because they are significant foods, but the following year he did not want to eat those fish because of the vinegar in them."

An explanation for the fact that Rabbi Meir of Rothenburg did not avoid garlic,[5] nuts, or sleeping on Rosh HaShana but did care about other omens may be found in *Sefer Ḥasidim*. It is known that Rabbi Meir of Rothenburg was heavily influenced by the German Pietists (*Ḥasidei Ashkenaz*) and followed their approach in his halakhic decisions and worldview.[6] In *Sefer Ḥasidim* we find strong objections to superstitious practices, which are categorized as the biblically forbidden *niḥush*: "You shall not practice divination (לא תנחשו) or soothsaying" (Lev. 19:26). He notes that one should pay heed only to omens that appear in rabbinic works: "We may not use *niḥush* as an omen, except for what the Sages said, like eating the head of a ram on Rosh HaShana, that we should be

4 *Leket Yosher* (Berlin, 1903), 124.

5 See *Baḥ, Oraḥ Ḥayim* 597, where he gives a few explanations for the custom not to sleep during Rosh HaShana, and then reports that Rabbi Meir would sleep on Rosh HaShana just as he would on other holidays, and that *Tashbetz* reported this as well. Regarding the custom not to sleep on Rosh HaShana, see Eliakim Devoraks, *BeShvilei HaMinhag*, vol. 2 (Jerusalem, 1997), 94–97 and vol. 3, 77–79.

6 See Ephraim Kanarfogel, *Peering through the Lattices: Mystical, Magical, and Pietistic Dimensions in the Tosafist Period* (Detroit: Wayne University Press, 2000), 115–24, 234–39.

like a head, etc., and sweet foods for a sweet year."[7] Note that the *Kol Bo* mentioned the ram's head specifically as something Rabbi Meir would eat on Rosh HaShana, which although not mentioned in the Talmud was an accepted practice of the German Pietists.[8]

This approach appears to care about the "good omens" but to disregard the "bad omens." Indeed, *Sefer Ḥasidim* does not mention any foods or practices to be avoided on Rosh HaShana as a bad omen. This approach would be explicitly delineated years later by Rabbi Shmuel Eliezer Eidels (Maharsha, 1555–1631) in his *Ḥiddushei HaMaharsha* to Horayot, where he explains the difference between eating particular foods as a good omen on Rosh HaShana, which is permitted, and the prohibited practice of *niḥush*. The difference is that doing something for yourself as a positive sign is not *niḥush*, but "bad signs" do not indicate anything (אין בהם שום הוראה) and are prohibited as *niḥush*.

The approach of Rabbi Meir appears to be reflected in the commentary of the Meiri (1249–1306) to Horayot 12a, where he writes: "Many things that appear to be *niḥush* are sometimes permitted, and they are not divination, God forbid; rather, they are a sign used to awaken our hearts to a good behavior. And this is what they instructed to put on our table on Rosh HaShana night: squash, beans, leeks, beets, and dates. Some of these grow quickly, and some grow a lot, and in order that they do not become a stumbling block to use in the manner of *niḥush* it was established to say over them words that awaken us to repentance… and it is known that all of this is only to show that it is all dependent on what is stated alone, only repentance and good deeds. But things done in the matter of *niḥush*, God forbid, are undoubtedly prohibited." Based on this, the *Yehi Ratzon* statements customarily made over the special Rosh HaShana foods function to remove the entire practice from the realm of *niḥush*, turning the tradition into a way to inspire the participants to change their ways in the upcoming new year. Accordingly, since the "bad signs" have no prayer component, there is a strong reason not to

---

7 Reuven Margaliot, *Sefer Ḥasidim* (Jerusalem: Mossad HaRav Kook, 1990), *siman* 59, 119–20.

8 Regarding the custom to eat a ram's head, see Yehiel Avraham Zilber, *Birur Halakha Talitaa* (Bnei Brak, 1995), *Oraḥ Ḥayim* 583, 248.

pay any attention to them, as they could be considered a form of *niḥush*. As the Meiri writes, "It is not appropriate to rely on these vain things, and performing them is forbidden."

Besides the idea that garlic is sharp, another reason was suggested to avoid eating it on Rosh HaShana. Rabbi Eliyahu Spira (1660–1712), in his work *Eliya Rabba* (583:5), explains: "But in *Kol Bo* it says that Rabbi Meir would not be careful about eating garlic, nuts or anything that increases sperm."[9] This additional reason to avoid garlic is not found in the *Kol Bo* or *Orḥot Ḥayim*, which do not give any explanation for not eating garlic. The idea that garlic increases sperm is found in Bava Kama 82a as the explanation for why Ezra instituted that garlic should be eaten on Friday night. There among the qualities listed for garlic are that it increases sperm and acts as an aphrodisiac.

The issue of avoiding foods that were understood to increase the sperm count is raised in the *Shulḥan Arukh* by the Rema (*Oraḥ Ḥayim* 608:4), citing the Maharil, but only in connection with the meal eaten before Yom Kippur, where he states that on the morning of Erev Yom Kippur it is still fine to eat garlic.[10] The *Taz* (608:3) comments that garlic should not be eaten even on the morning of Erev Yom Kippur. He explains that since it is reported that *talmidei ḥakhamim* would eat garlic on Friday morning in order to increase their sperm count for that evening, it should not be eaten even on the morning before Yom Kippur when relations are prohibited. He adds that the same rule applies to eggs, which the Talmud in Yoma 18b indicates increase sperm as well. Although we find the idea to avoid garlic before Yom Kippur, prior to its mention in *Eliya Rabba* there is no record that this prohibition extends to Rosh HaShana as well, when relations are not expressly forbidden.[11] It is true that the Maharil is said to have eaten squash (קישואין) at his Rosh HaShana meals, both at night and in the day, since they have a

9 Note that there is no source in rabbinic literature that indicates that nuts increase sperm, and that explanation may be referring to garlic only and not nuts.

10 The idea of avoiding foods that can possibly result in seminal emissions before Yom Kippur is found in Yoma 18a regarding foods that the high priest avoided before Yom Kippur. Note that one of the foods listed there is an etrog, which was customarily eaten on Rosh HaShana. See previous chapter.

11 See *Magen Avraham, Oraḥ Ḥayim* 581:15.

"cooling effect" and act as an anti-aphrodisiac of sorts,[12] but avoiding garlic was not reported.

### EATING GARLIC ON ROSH HASHANA

On the other hand, there are sources which indicate that garlic should be eaten on Rosh HaShana. Menahem ben Zerach, a student of Rabbi Yehuda, son of the Rosh, in his book *Tzeida LaDerekh*, brings the special Rosh HaShana foods mentioned in the Talmud,[13] but in place of dates (תמרים) he has garlic (תומי in Aramaic). He associates the *Yehi Ratzon* customarily said on dates (that our enemies come to an end, יתמו אויבינו) with garlic. It appears that he had a different text of the Talmud which replaced dates with garlic, although we have no record of such a textual variant. The same substitution is found in the Constantinople 1519 printing of *Sefer HaManhig*. *Keter Shem Tov* explains that the *Yehi Ratzon* actually makes more sense to say over garlic, as the word for garlic (תומי) is just like the word for "come to an end" (יתמו) in the *Yehi Ratzon*, while with dates there is a letter *resh* not represented in the term יתמו.[14]

While we might be justified in writing off both of these sources as printing errors, the fact is that the eating of both dates and garlic is mentioned by some Spanish *Rishonim*. Rabbi Yitzhak Karkosha, a student of the Ramban, in his commentary to the Rif, states, "Garlic and dates: our transgressions should end (תומי ותמרי יתמו עונינו)."[15] Rabbi Hayim ben Shmuel from Tudela, a student of Rashba, in his book *Tzror HaḤayim*, mentions them both as well.[16] Since multiple sources referred

---

12 Shlomo Spitzer, ed., *Sefer Maharil* (Jerusalem: Machon Yerushalayim, 1989), 277 (*siman* 8), 279 (*siman* 12).

13 *Sefer Tzeida LaDerekh* (Livorno, 1859), *maamar* 4, *klal* 5, end of the first chapter, 108b. Menahem ben Zerah was born in France and moved to Spain, where he studied with Rabbi Yehuda.

14 Shemtob Gaguine, *Keter Shem Tov*, vol. 6 (London, 1955), 100. The notes to the Mossad HaRav Kook edition of *Sefer HaManhig*, 304, note 60, state that the version with garlic can be discounted. In light of the fact that this substitution is also found in *Tzeida LaDerekh* about a hundred years after *Sefer HaManhig*, there may be room for the approach of *Keter Shem Tov*.

15 Machon Ofeq, "Peirush Rabbeinu Yitzḥak Karkosha LeHilkhot HaRif LeMasekhet Rosh HaShana," *Yeshurun* 6 (Av 5759/1999), 42.

16 Shmuel Yerushalmi, ed., *Tzror HaḤayim* (Jerusalem, 1966), *derekh* 4, *siman* 3, 82.

to eating garlic, some contemporary rabbinic authorities recommended that "it is appropriate to take dates and also tasty cooked garlic" on Rosh HaShana.[17] Eating garlic on Rosh HaShana is known among Tunisian Jews, who would dip it in honey and recite the *Yehi Ratzon* that our enemies should come to an end (יתמו אויבינו ושונאינו).[18]

## DIVIDED SIGNS

We now see that alongside the Ashkenazic custom not to eat garlic, disregarded by Rabbi Meir, there was a Sephardic custom to purposely eat garlic on Rosh HaShana. At first glance, it might seem unusual that the same food can be considered a positive omen in one community and a negative omen in another, but this dichotomy applies to many foods associated with Rosh HaShana. As in the case of garlic, the division is between Ashkenazic and Sephardic customs. For example, among the Jews of Morocco we find that some would avoid carrots (גזר) on Rosh HaShana because it recalls evil decrees (גזרות),[19] while among Ashkenazim this is a positive traditional Rosh HaShana food.[20] Similarly, *Birkei Yosef* (583:5) brings in the name of Rabbi Shimon ben Tzemach Duran that one should not eat fish on Rosh HaShana, since in Nehemiah 13:16 it is spelled with an *alef* (דאג), which indicates worry (דאגה), while the Ashkenazic *Mateh Ephraim* (583:3) states that "in our countries people look for fish, and there is a hint to being fruitful and multiplying like fish." These differences touched even the most classic of Rosh HaShana food, the apple, as the Turkish Rabbi Rahamim Palagi (1813–1907) recommends limiting apple consumption on Rosh HaShana, as it may lead to nocturnal emissions![21]

---

17 Yosef Ezra Zlicha, "Regarding the Signs Eaten on Rosh HaShana Night," *Or Torah* 13, no. 296 (Elul 5752/1992), 914 [Hebrew].

18 Refael Ben-Simchon, *Yahadut Magreb* (Jerusalem: Machon Bnei Yissachar, 1998), 350. In modern-day Arabic garlic is called תום.

19 Eliyahu Biton, *Netivot HaMaarav HaShalem* (Jerusalem, 2007), *siman* 29, 117.

20 Avraham Danzig, *Ḥayei Adam* 139:6. The Yiddish term for carrots (מערן) recalls growth/more (ריבוי) and so the *Yehi Ratzon* brought is: "that our merits should increase" (שירבו זכויותינו).

21 *Yafeh Lalev*, vol. 2 (Izmir, 1876), 583:10. He also says not to eat an etrog on Rosh HaShana, although the *Tur* writes that one should eat it. See the previous chapter in this book.

*Chapter 9*

# The Eleventh of Ḥeshvan as the *Yahrzeit* of Rachel

**THE RABBINIC VIEW**

The Torah does not record the date of Rachel's death. Instead, the narrative focuses on the location of her burial place; she was buried "on the road to Efrat, which is Bethlehem" (Gen. 35:19). Interestingly, a few verses earlier the Torah uses an unusual word to describe how far from Efrat Rachel's death took place: "There was still a stretch of land (*kivrat haaretz*) to go to Efrat" (Gen. 35:16). Generally, *kivrat aretz* is understood to mean a long distance, related to the word *kabir*, "great."[1] However, the midrashic literature connects the word *kivrat* to the word *kavra*, "sieve." Genesis Rabba 82:7 explains that *kivrat aretz* refers to "the time of year when the land is hollowed out like a sieve," when the land is cut through with furrows. This time of year is described as after the rains but before the dry heat of the summer. *Pesikta Rabbati* 3:67 explains that this is the time of year between Passover and Shavuot. Thus, according to the rabbinic midrash, Rachel died in the springtime or early summer.

1 This is the interpretation of Menahem ben Saruk quoted in Rashi on Gen. 35:16.

### THE VIEW OF JUBILEES

In Israel today, an alternative date is popularly commemorated as the day of Rachel's death, the eleventh day of the eighth month, Ḥeshvan. This date is recorded in some versions of the commentary of the fourteenth-century sage Rabbeinu Bahya to Exodus 1:6.[2] There we find birthdays given for all twelve tribes, and the birthday of Benjamin is given as the eleventh of Ḥeshvan, which is also the day Rachel died. This same basic list is found in the midrashic collection *Yalkut Shimoni* (Ex. 1). Rabbeinu Bahya writes that he found this list in *Midrash Tadshe*.[3] *Midrash Tadshe* contains many midrashic ideas not found in the standard rabbinic literature and makes use of material found in the Book of Jubilees;[4] in fact the birthdates listed in *Midrash Tadshe* closely parallel those in Jubilees, with the few differences attributable to scribal errors.[5]

The Book of Jubilees is a retelling of Genesis and the beginning of Exodus in the form of an angel speaking to Moses. It was written in Hebrew by a Jewish person sometime around the early second century BCE, perhaps even earlier. The original Hebrew is lost to us today; our translations are based primarily on Ethiopic texts. The main focus of the work is to demonstrate that the narratives in the early part of the Bible contain legal instruction, though the legal elements are hidden in the biblical narrative.[6] Jubilees often supplements the biblical narratives with additional information, much like the Midrash does, for example, providing names of women and exact dates of events not explicated in

---

2 Hayim Chavel, ed., *Rabbeinu Baḥye, Biur al HaTorah*, vol. 2 (Jerusalem: Mossad HaRav Kook, 1990), 9, note 57.

3 J. D. Eisenstein, *Otzar Midrashim*, vol. 2 (New York, 1915), 481, *Pinḥas ben Yair*, 15.

4 See Anat Reizel, *Introduction to the Midrashic Literature* (Alon Shvut: Tevunot, 2010), 411–13 [Hebrew]; Abraham Epstein, *MiKadmonot HaYehudim*, vol. 1 (Vienna, 1887), xxiii. See also Samuel Belkin, "*Midrash Tadshe* or *Midrash deRav Pinḥas ben Yair*, an Ancient Hellenistic Midrash," *Horeb* 11 (Nisan 1951), 2–3 [Hebrew].

5 Epstein, *MiKadmonot HaYehudim*, vol. 1, xxiii, notes 1–9. For example, the birthday of Asher in the Book of Jubilees is "the second day of the eleventh month" (28:21), whereas in *Midrash Tadshe* it is the twentieth day of the eleventh month. The letter *bet* representing the number two is very similar to the letter *kaf*, which represents the number twenty.

6 James Kugel, *The Bible as It Was* (Cambridge, MA: Harvard University Press, 1997), 38–39.

the Torah. Jubilees also provides resolutions to some difficulties in the biblical text, another concern of Midrash. As such, the Book of Jubilees may be categorized as an early form of midrashic literature.[7] Some of the interpretations in Jubilees are in fact preserved in later midrashic literature. The title, Book of Jubilees, reflects the author's particular way of viewing the chronology of the world as a series of forty-nine year cycles, but it was also sometimes referred to as "the Little Genesis" (*Bereshit Zuta* in Aramaic),[8] since it is an abbreviated retelling of Genesis.[9] Jubilees was not incorporated into rabbinic literature because it differs in some very fundamental legal points, most famously, regarding the insistence on a purely solar calendar as opposed to the rabbinic lunar/solar model[10] and stringencies regarding Shabbat observance.[11]

Jubilees in chapter 28 records the birthdays of most of Jacob's children, and Jubilees 32:33 records the death of Rachel while giving birth to Benjamin, "on the eleventh of the eighth month." However, the calendar system of the Book of Jubilees included months of thirty-one days, something that never occurs in the current Jewish calendar. By this reckoning, the eleventh day of the eighth month did not fall on the same day as the eleventh of Ḥeshvan, but later Jewish sources simply transferred the date in Jubilees to the eighth month of the Jewish calendar. This is the earliest source for setting the date of the eleventh of Ḥeshvan as the day of Rachel's death.[12]

7 O. S. Wintermute, "Jubilees: A New Translation and Introduction," in James H. Charlesworth, ed., *The Old Testament Pseudepigrapha*, vol. 2 (New York: Doubleday, 1985), 39–40.

8 S. Herr and S. Shrira, *Toldot HaSifrut HaTalmudit* (Tel Aviv: Haskala LaAm, 1937), 247.

9 Wintermute, "Jubilees," 41.

10 See A. Z. Aescoly, *Sefer HaFalashim* (Jerusalem: Reuven Mass, 1943), 29, 60, and Michael Stone, "Astronomy in the Apocrypha," *Maḥanayim* 125 (Tishrei 1971), 108 [Hebrew].

11 Avraham Goldberg, "Rabbinic and Biblical Shabbat Prohibitions," *Sinai* 46 (Tishrei 1959), 183 [Hebrew].

12 Some versions of *Midrash Tadshe* do not include the birthday for Benjamin, apparently because the author made use only of the information found in the Book of Jubilees, chapter 28, Epstein, *Mikadmonot HaYehudim*, vol.1, xxiii, note 9.

Thus there are two traditions regarding the time of Rachel's death: the early summer, as found in the rabbinic midrash, and the eleventh of Ḥeshvan using the approach based on the Book of Jubilees. Apparently not realizing that the eleventh of Ḥeshvan is not a date originating in rabbinic literature, some contemporary rabbinic writers who noted this difference of opinion attempted to harmonize the two dates.[13]

## THE ORIGIN OF THE JUBILEES APPROACH

Is there any significance in the date of the eleventh day of the eighth month, or was it chosen arbitrarily by the author of Jubilees? When we look at the birthdays of Jacob's children in Jubilees, we see that while most appear to have been assigned seemingly arbitrary birthdates, some were born on significant dates. Levi was born "on the first day of the first month" (28:14), Judah "on the fifteenth of the third month" (28:15), and Joseph "on the first of the fourth month" (28:24). Thus, Levi and Joseph were born on dates which mark the beginning of a season, considered festival days according to Jubilees 6:23, and Judah was born on the day that according to Jubilees marks the holiday of Shavuot, the day of the covenant.[14] None of the other children were born on either the first or middle day of the month, and their birthdates seem to be incidental.[15] It appears that only the "special" tribes were assigned significant birthdays.

If Benjamin was considered one of the "special tribes," we would expect his birth date, the day of Rachel's death, to be a significant date. We know that Jubilees has much in common with the texts found in the Qumran Caves, and many copies of it were indeed found there. While it is not clear if the author of Jubilees was an Essene, the book represents

---

13 See Yehuda Sheinfeld, *Oseri LeGefen*, vol. 12 (Jerusalem, 2006), 67, who suggests that Rachel began her pregnancy difficulties in the summer, but actually died giving birth on the eleventh of Ḥeshvan. The contradiction is also mentioned in Eliyahu Shlezinger, *Eleh Hem Moadai* (Jerusalem, 2001), 260, and Yitzhak Kuperstock, *Meorot Natan* (Jerusalem, 1998), 12–13.

14 Michael Segal, *The Book of Jubilees: Rewritten Bible, Redaction, Ideology and Theology* (Leiden: Brill, 2007), 90, note 17.

15 Jonathan Ben-Dov, "Tradition and Innovation in the Calendar of Jubilees," in Gabrielle Boccaccini and Giovanni Ibba, eds., *Enoch and the Mosaic Torah: The Evidence of Jubilees* (Leiden: Brill, 2007), 286.

a similar tradition and similar beliefs.[16] In particular, the Temple Scroll of the Qumran community and the Book of Jubilees have much in common. Both claim heavenly ascription and rewrite sections of the Torah as if God or an angel were speaking in the first person.[17] Jubilees is, effectively, the narrative parallel of the Temple Scroll.[18] For our purposes, there are a few points of commonality that are particularly significant, including the 364-day solar calendar,[19] the celebration of a spring new year on the first day of the first month (Nisan),[20] the date of the fifteenth of the third month for the holiday of Shavuot,[21] and the exaltation of Levi[22] and Judah in Jubilees (they receive special blessings in Jub. 31.11–20), paralleled with the idea of two messiahs, one from each of these tribes, as found in the Qumran literature.[23] We know that the tribe of Benjamin was considered significant to the Qumran community: during the six-day Wood Festival described in the Temple Scroll, Levi and Judah bring sacrifices on the first day, followed by Benjamin and the sons of Joseph on the second day.[24] Three of these four special tribes clearly have significant birthdays in Jubilees, but it is left to determine the significance of Benjamin's birthday.

Benjamin's birthday is also the day of Rachel's death, and so we must also examine the dates recorded in the Book of Jubilees for the deaths of other biblical characters. Jubilees rarely mentions an exact day

16 James C. VanderKam, *The Book of Jubilees* (Sheffield: Sheffield Academic Press, 2001), 143.

17 Hindy Najman, *Seconding Sinai: The Development of Mosaic Discourse in Second Temple Judaism* (Leiden: Brill, 2003), 66, note 61.

18 Ida Frohlich, "Enoch and Jubilees," in Gabriele Boccaccini, ed., *Enoch and Qumran Origins: New Light on a Forgotten Connection* (Grand Rapids, MI: William B. Eerdmans, 2005), 146.

19 Yigael Yadin, *The Temple Scroll*, vol. 1 (Jerusalem: Israel Exploration Society, 1977), 81; E. P. Sanders, *Judaism: Practice and Belief 63 BCE–66 CE* (London: SCM Press, 1994), 360.

20 Sidnie White Crawford, *The Temple Scroll and Related Texts* (Sheffield: Sheffield Academic Press, 2000), 78.

21 VanderKam, *Jubilees*, 146.

22 Crawford, *The Temple Scroll*, 78.

23 VanderKam, *Jubilees*, 146.

24 Johann Maier, *The Temple Scroll* (Sheffield: JSOT, 1985), 83.

when a person dies; usually it is only the year of death that is noted, as in the Tanakh. The three exceptions to this are all women: Deborah, Rachel, and Bilha. In Jub. 32:30, just a few verses before the death of Rachel is described, the death of Rebecca's nurse, Deborah, is recorded as taking place on the "twenty-third of that month," the day after the Festival of Booths and the additional feast day described just previously in Jubilees 32:27–29. The death of Bilha occurs on the day Joseph's death was reported to Jacob (Jub. 34:15), which according to Jubilees 34:18–19 is the tenth day of the seventh month, the Day of Atonement. Note also that Abraham is described in Jubilees as dying right after celebrating Shavuot, although it is not explicitly stated that he died the day after the festival (Jub. 22:1, 23:1). Thus we see that in Jubilees, whenever a specific date is associated with the death of a biblical figure, that date is always significant as either a holiday or the day after a holiday. The holidays themselves also represent the end of the previous season and the beginning of a new era. Sukkot marks the beginning of the rainy season, the Day of Atonement begins a new judicial cycle, and a new covenantal and agricultural cycle begins with Shavuot. What of the day of Rachel's death?

We know from the Temple Scroll that the Qumran community celebrated additional first fruit festivals not found in the Bible at fifty-day intervals. The Feast of the Waving of the Sheaf (celebrating the first fruits of barley) took place on the twenty-sixth of the first month, Nisan, and the First Fruits of Wheat (Shavuot) was on the fifteenth of the third month, Sivan. Additionally, the First Fruits of Wine was commemorated on the third day of the fifth month, Av, and fifty days later the First Fruits of Oil was celebrated on the twenty-second day of the sixth month, Elul.[25] These additional festivals are attested to in other texts found in Qumran as well.[26] The method of calculation was to count fifty days from the previous first fruit festival, with the day of the holiday itself counting as both the last day of the previous cycle of fifty days and the first day of the next cycle of fifty days.[27]

25 Yadin, *The Temple Scroll*, vol. 1, 95.

26 Crawford, *The Temple Scroll*, 51.

27 Yadin, *The Temple Scroll*, vol. 1, 85. See also Marvin A. Sweeney, "*Sefirah* at Qumran: Aspects of the Counting Formulas for the First-Fruits Festivals in the Temple Scroll."

Although there are no overt signs of a pentecontad (fifty-day cycle) calendar in the Book of Jubilees, the units of fifty are counted the same way as in the Temple Scroll. The Temple Scroll counts the fiftieth day as both the last day of one unity of fifty and the first day of the next one, the same method that Jubilees applies to count the fiftieth year of one Jubilee period as the first year of the next one.[28] In this calendar system, the 364-day year is divided into quarters of ninety-one days each, with each three-month quarter beginning with two months of thirty days and ending with one month of thirty-one days.[29] While the whole calendar is not based on repeating units of fifty days and is thus not a strictly pentecontad calendar, the Temple Scroll lists four feasts which punctuate three consecutive fifty-day periods.

If we calculate an additional fifty-day unit from the apparently final fruit festival mentioned, the First Fruits of Oil, we arrive at the tenth of the eighth month, Ḥeshvan. It is telling that the day of Rachel's death follows the day that would have been the next first fruit festival. Thus, in the same chapter, just a few verses apart, Jubilees describes two women dying on the day after a festival, Deborah and Rachel. All three characters whose exact date of death is mentioned die on a significant day: Deborah dies on the day after the additional feast day which follows Sukkot, Rachel on the day after the fifty-day count from the Feast of Oil, and Bilha on the Day of Atonement. While it is certainly possible that the date of Rachel's death is coincidental, the fact that it is specifically mentioned, which is a rare occurrence in Jubilees, and it is noted just a few verses after the significant date of Deborah's death indicates that it represents something of importance.

The pentecontad calendar, which divided the year into seven periods of fifty days, is well attested in the late Hellenistic period in certain Jewish sectarian groups.[30] We do not have records of specific

---

*Bulletin of the American Schools of Oriental Research*, no. 251 (1983), 61–66.

28 Joseph Baumgarten, "The Calendars of the *Book of Jubilees* and the Temple Scroll," *VT* 37 (1987), 71–78 (73).

29 Yadin, *The Temple Scroll*, vol. 1, 95.

30 Jonathan Ben-Dov, "The History of Pentecontad Time Units (I)," in Eric F. Mason, ed., *A Teacher for All Generations: Essays in Honor of James C. VanderKam*, vol. 1 (Leiden: Brill, 2007), 94–95.

additional holidays commemorating fifty-day periods beyond the four in the Temple Scroll;[31] however, the Jewish sect known as the Therapeutae are reported as holding a feast to commemorate every pentecontad.[32] The seven-pentecontad calendar is preserved in the Nestorian Christian calendar[33] as well as in the Palestinian folk calendar[34] and the liturgical calendar of the Ethiopian Jews.[35] There are hints to other possible fiftieth day festivals. The Ethiopian Jews, who were greatly influenced by the Book of Jubilees,[36] celebrate the holiday of Sigd fifty days after Yom Kippur.[37] There is even a possible rabbinic hint to the idea of additional pentecontad festivals, as it states in Song of Songs Rabba 7.2.2 that ideally there should have been a holiday fifty days after Sukkot.

Even though we do not have parallels to the additional harvest festivals from the Temple Scroll in the Book of Jubilees,[38] Jubilees, like the Temple Scroll, does use the harvest seasons of grain, wine, and oil as the cutoff times for tithes (Jub. 32:11–13).[39] While it has been suggested that this may indicate that Jubilees assumes the same system of festivals

---

31 However, there seems to be evidence of such festivals in the ancient Near East. See Hildegard Lewy and Julius Lewy, "The Origin of the Week and the Oldest West Asiatic Calendar," *Hebrew Union College Annual* 17 (1943), 1–152 (123), remarking on the Old Assyrian calendar, "each pentecontad ended with a festival on which a percentage of the products gathered during the respective period was brought to the sanctuary as a thanks offering."

32 Philo, *On the Contemplative Life* 8.65; see C. D. Younge (trans.), *The Works of Philo* (Peabody, MA: Hendrikson, 1993), 704; Lewy and Lewy, "Origin of the Week," 102–3.

33 Lewy and Lewy, "Origin of the Week," 100.

34 Lewy and Lewy, "Origin of the week," 99.

35 Ibid., 117.

36 See Michael Corinaldi, "The Relationship between the *Beta Yisrael* Tradition and the *Book of Jubilees*," in Oliver Leaman, ed., *Jews of Ethiopia* (New York: Routledge, 2005), 193–204; Steven Kaplan, *The Beta Israel (Falasha) in Ethiopia: From Earliest Times to the Twentieth Century* (New York: New York University Press, 1992), 29, 74; Sharon Shalom, *From Sinai to Ethiopia* (Tel Aviv: Miskal-Yedioth Ahronoth Books, 2012), 57, 161, 268, 334.

37 Shalom, *From Sinai to Ethiopia*, 209.

38 Lawrence Schiffman, *The Courtyards of the House of the Lord: Studies on the Temple Scroll* (Leiden: Brill, 2008), 12.

39 Schiffman, *Courtyards*, 114.

as exists in the Temple Scroll,[40] even if it does not, Jubilees considered these harvest periods significant regarding tithes, and also regarding the timing of the offerings of the first fruits of wine and oil in the fourth year (Jub. 7:36).[41] The harvest periods themselves were significant in the Book of Jubilees; punctuating them with festivals seems to be an innovation found in the Temple Scroll.[42] It has been suggested that both works are based on an earlier source, which Jubilees interpreted as referring to harvest seasons and the Temple Scroll understood as referring to harvest festivals.[43] Even if it is not commemorated by a festival, the fiftieth day after the final harvest can be seen as numerically significant, signifying the complete termination of the harvest season.

This conforms with one of the themes of the Book of Jubilees, that the holidays and commandments observed by the Israelites were also significant in the pre-Sinai era. For example, according to Jubilees, Noah, Abraham, Isaac, and Jacob celebrated Shavuot (Jub. 6:17–19; 15:1; 22:1–2), Abraham celebrated Sukkot (16:20–21), as did Jacob (32:4–7), and the sale of Joseph is associated with the Day of Atonement (34:18–19). The offerings of the first fruits in the fourth year after planting, including wine and oil, and the law of the Sabbatical year were commanded to Noah (7:36–28). We now have the additional idea of deaths occurring on significant dates which would later be associated with festivals, or harvest seasons. It seems that in Jubilees, in the same way that the death of Deborah was connected to the day after a significant festival day, so too was Rachel's, with the next significant date after her death being the eleventh day of the eighth month, the day after the date representing the complete conclusion of the harvest period.

## CONCLUSION

It is clear that the eleventh of Ḥeshvan as the date of Rachel's death originated in the Book of Jubilees, and it reflects certain attitudes and

40 Yadin, *The Temple Scroll*, vol. 1, 114; Schiffman, *Courtyards of the House of the Lord* 15; Baumgarten, "Calendars," 73; Maier, *The Temple Scroll*, 80.

41 Schiffman, *Courtyards of the House of the Lord*, 113–14.

42 Ibid., 114.

43 Michael Owen Wise, *A Critical Study of the Temple Scroll from Qumran Cave 11* (Chicago, IL: The Oriental Institute of the University of Chicago, 1990), 97–98.

approaches held by the author of that work. Jubilees represents an approach at odds with rabbinic Judaism, and it would at first blush seem very unusual that traditional Jews today have adopted the Jubilees's date for Rachel's *yahrzeit* rather than the season found in the rabbinic midrash.

The reasons for this are twofold. First of all, many Jews today are completely unfamiliar with the Book of Jubilees and do not understand that this book opposes rabbinic attitudes. Furthermore, the birthdays recorded in Jubilees made their way into later rabbinic literature, and in this way were given a de facto seal of approval.

Additionally, Jubilees provides a precise, specific date on which to commemorate the death of Rachel, while the midrash provides only a season. Among certain Orthodox Jews, the search for a definite answer is very important, and in any situation, an exact mode of behavior is desired. This type of approach, where exact directions are sought for many aspects of life, can extend into interpretations of texts as well. In this case, the rabbinic interpretation was considered too ambiguous, with Rachel dying sometime in the spring, and so instead, many Orthodox Jews today commemorate the *yahrzeit* of Rachel on the eleventh of Ḥeshvan, based on the Book of Jubilees.

*Chapter 10*

# The Story of Judith and Eating Dairy Foods on Hanukka

Rabbi Moshe Isserles (the Rema) writes in his glosses to the *Shulḥan Arukh*: "Some say it is customary to eat cheese on Hanukka because the miracle was done with the milk that Judith fed the enemy."[1]

The sources given for this ruling of the Rema in the parentheses following his gloss are the commentaries of Rabbi Nissim (the Ran) on the Rif and the *Kol Bo*. These sources were not provided by Rabbi Isserles himself, but rather by the printers of the *Shulḥan Arukh* beginning in the early 1600s.[2] Although these sources are sometimes imprecise, in this case they appear to be accurate.

1 Rema, *Oraḥ Ḥayim* 670:2.

2 See Yitzhak Nissim, "*HaHagahot al Shulḥan Arukh*," in Yitzhak Refael, ed., *Rabbi Yosef Karo* (Jerusalem: Mossad HaRav Kook, 1969), 70–71.

Rabbi Nissim discusses the following story in the context of explaining that women are also obligated to light Hanukka candles because they were involved in the miracle of Hanukka:

> "The Greeks decreed that all virgins getting married must sleep with the governor (hegmon) first, and through a woman a miracle occurred, as it is said in the Midrash that the daughter of Yoḥanan fed the chief of the enemies cheese in order to get him [to drink wine, and so make him] drunk, and she cut off his head and they all fled, and because of this it is customary to eat cheese on Hanukka."[3]

The *Kol Bo* has a slightly expanded version of the story in his explanation of the obligation of women to light Hanukka candles and the custom to eat cheese on Hanukka:

> Yoḥanan the high priest had a very, very beautiful daughter, and the king of Greece wanted to sleep with her. She fed him a dish of cheese in order to make him thirsty, so that he would drink a lot and get drunk and lie down and fall asleep. That is what happened; he lay down and fell asleep. She took his sword and cut off his head and brought it to Jerusalem. When the army saw that their hero was deceased, they fled.[4]

What is the source of this story found in the Rema, the Ran, and the *Kol Bo*? The story of Judith is mentioned by numerous early authorities as

3 Ran (1320–76), Shabbat 10a in the Rif's pages, s.v. *she'af hen*, commenting on Shabbat 23b. Ran also mentions this in his commentary to Megilla 4a, but without mentioning many of the details found in his comments on Tractate Shabbat. See the overview in Deborah Levine Gera, "The Jewish Textual Traditions," in *The Sword of Judith: Jewish Studies Across the Disciplines*, ed. Kevin Brine, Elena Ciletti, and Hernike Lähnemann (Cambridge: Open Book Publishers, 2010), 35–36.

4 David Abraham, ed., *Kol Bo*, vol. 1 (Jerusalem, 2007), 162, *siman* 44. The date and authorship of *Kol Bo* is uncertain, but it seems to be from the thirteenth century. See the introduction by Shlomo Zalman Havlin in *Sefer Kol Bo* (Jerusalem: Even Yisroel, 1997), 7–10. The same story, with very similar wording, is found in *Orḥot Ḥayim, Hilkhot Ḥanukka, siman* 12 (Jerusalem: Sela, 1956), 262.

the reason that women are obligated to light Hanukka candles: "because they were involved in the miracle." Without elaborating on the details of the story, Judith is mentioned in *Tosafot* in the name of the Rashbam,[5] *Sefer Mitzvot Gadol*,[6] Mordekhai,[7] the Ritva, and the Meiri,[8] as well as in many other early sources.[9] However, none of these sources mention that she was the daughter of the high priest or that she gave the Greek leader milk or cheese; their only concern is using Judith as a proof that women participated in the Hanukka miracle.

## THE BOOK OF JUDITH

The Book of Judith is a book of the Apocrypha that recounts the story of how Nebuchadnezzar sent his general Holofernes to attack Israel, and Judith, a pious and beautiful widow, saved her town of Betulia. Judith is identified as the daughter of Merari and the widow of Menashe (Judith 8:1–2), from the tribe of Shimon (9:2).[10] Using her beauty and cunning, she ingratiated herself with Holofernes and then managed to behead him with his own sword after he fell into a drunken slumber at a party. Taking the severed head with her, Judith used it to inspire the Jews and demoralize the enemy troops, leading to a Jewish victory.

5 *Tosafot*, Megilla 4a, s.v. *she'af hen*. See also *Tosafot*, Pesaḥim 108b, s.v. *hayu*.

6 *Sefer Mitzvot Gadol*, positive commandments, rabbinic commandment 5.

7 Mordekhai, in the additions to Pesaḥim 108b.

8 Ritva and Meiri, Megilla 4a.

9 Judith is also mentioned in *Sefer Abudraham* (Jerusalem, 1995), 32, in the context of the obligation of women to light Hanukka candles with a blessing. There it is stated that she cut off the head of Antiokhus. Judith is mentioned as a member of the Hasmonean family in *Sefer HaManhig*, ed. Yitzhak Rafael (Jerusalem: Mossad HaRav Kook, 1978), *Hilkhot Megilla*, 249. The story is also cited in Moshe and Yehudah Hershler, eds., *Peirushei Siddur HaTefillah LaRoke'aḥ*, vol. 2 (Jerusalem: Makhon HaRav Hershler, 1992), *siman* 141, 717–18. There the story is abbreviated and stops before the dairy element of the story. However, Judith is definitively not presented as the daughter of the high priest, and in some manuscripts her name is given as Hannah, not Judith.

10 In some versions, she is from the tribe of Reuven; see A. M. Dubarle, *Judith: Formes et Sens des Diverses Traditions – Tome II: Textes* (Rome: Institut Biblique Pontifical, 1966), 47, version E. She is also described as being from the tribe of Reuven in some midrashic and liturgical versions of the story (Dubarle, *Judith*, 126, midrash 7a; 132, midrash 7b; 168).

The story itself has no obvious connection to Hanukka or the Greeks; the enemies are identified as Assyrians, although the book was probably written around the second century BCE[11] and seems to reflect the Maccabean times.[12] The Book of Judith follows the style of numerous Apocryphal works based on plot elements already found in the Bible, with many components that are essentially rewritten biblical narratives.[13] These elements are also found in abundance in later retellings of the story.[14] The work is generally considered a historical drama, or at best a fictionalized account of a historical event,[15] filled with literary artistry.[16]

The Book of Judith cannot be the source for the Rema, the Ran, or the *Kol Bo* since it is missing some key elements that they mention – the most obvious being that the enemies in the Book of Judith are not Greeks. While some versions of the Book of Judith have her bringing cheese along as part of her personal food supply when going to the camp of Holofernes, in no version is she reported to have fed him milk or cheese.[17] Furthermore, while the Book of Judith does include the character of a high priest, he is named Joakim,[18] or in some versions Eliakim,[19] and is a minor character with no family relationship to Judith.

---

11 Lawrence M. Wills, *Ancient Jewish Novels* (Oxford: Oxford University Press, 2002), 89.

12 See Benedikt Otzen, *Tobit and Judith* (London: Sheffield Academic Press, 2002), 57, 78, 86, 96, 132–34.

13 See, for example, Erich Gruen, *Heritage and Hellenism* (Berkley: University of California Press, 1998), 124–25.

14 Susan Weingarten, "Food, Sex, and Redemption in *Megillat Yehudit* (the Scroll of Judith)," in Kevin Brine et al., eds., *The Sword of Judith* (Cambridge: Open Book Publishers, 2010), 97–109.

15 Carey A. Moore, *Judith – Anchor Bible Series* (Garden City, NY: Doubleday, 1985), 46–49; see Otzen, *Tobit and Judith*, 81–87, particularly 82, note d; Deborah Levine Gera, *Judith* (Berlin: Walter de Gruyter, 2014), 26–30.

16 For a detailed discussion of the literary elements, see Toni Craven, *Artistry and Faith in the Book of Judith* (Chico, CA: Scholars Press, 1983), 47–112.

17 Gera, *Judith*, 333–34.

18 Ibid., 174–75.

19 Solomon Zeitlin, ed., *The Book of Judith* (Leiden: Brill, 1972), 45.

## THE STORY OF JUDITH IN MEDIEVAL TIMES

Although there is no mention of Judith in the Talmud or standard collections of the Midrash,[20] there are more than a dozen variants of the Judith story that have been published in more recent collections of midrashic material, although some are only fragments.[21] These have been categorized into a few basic versions.[22] These retellings and reworkings of the material in the Apocrypha generally place the story of Judith in Maccabean times, switching the enemies from Assyrians to Greeks,[23] and were known to the *Rishonim*.[24]

The central element of the beautiful Jewish woman beheading the enemy leader appears in all of the versions, but just about every other plot element is subject to change. For example, in the version recorded by Rabbi David HaNaggid, grandson of the Rambam, the woman is not named, and is identified only as being from the priestly Hasmonean family. Here, the villain is the Greek general Nicanor, and the Jewish woman put sleep-inducing drugs into his wine to knock him out.[25]

Most of the Judith narratives can be immediately ruled out as the source for the Rema, the Ran, and the *Kol Bo* because they do not suggest that Judith gave the enemy leader milk or cheese.[26] Rather, in these accounts, as in the Apocryphal Book of Judith, the Greek leader

---

20 Moshe Leiter, *Mamlekhet Kohanim* (Modiin Illit, 2002), 361.

21 See the introduction and bibliography in Michael Higger, *Halakhot VeAggadot* (New York, 1933), 91–94; Dubarle, *Judith*, 98–100; and the overview in Moore, *Judith – Anchor Bible Series*, 103–7.

22 Yehoshua Grintz, *Sefer Yehudit* (Jerusalem: Bialik Institute, 1957), 197–208; Gera, "The Jewish Textual Traditions," 32–34.

23 David Samuel Lowinger, *Yehudit – Shoshana* (Budapest, 1940), 5–6; Otzen, *Tobit and Judith*, 139.

24 Moshe Hershler, "Maaseh Yehudit," in *Genuzot I* (Jerusalem, Moznaim, 1984), 165.

25 *Midrash Rabbi David HaNaggid – Bereshit*, ed. Avraham Yitzhak Katz (Jerusalem: Mossad HaRav Kook, 1964), 199.

26 Samuel Mirsky, *She'iltot – Genesis 2* (Jerusalem: Sura, 1961), 189; J. D. Eisenstein, *Otzar Midrashim*, vol. 1 (New York, 1915), 192–93; Higger, *Halakhot VeAggadot*, 99–100, 110–11; A. Habermann, *Ḥadashim Gam Yeshanim* (Jerusalem: Reuven Mass, 1971), 52, 56, 60; Hershler, *Maaseh Yehudit*, 167. In the version found in the writings of Rambam's grandson, David HaNaggid, the Jewish heroine (unnamed in that version) puts a sleep-inducing drug in the wine of the Greek general (Nicanor in that version); see Leiter, *Mamlekhet Kohanim*, 419.

falls into a drunken stupor without the help of a dairy product.[27] While the Syriac version of Judith includes cheese (*gavta*) as one of the foods that Judith brings, it is not connected to making the villain thirsty and then drunk.[28]

Furthermore, in these versions Judith is generally identified as the daughter of Merari, as she appears in the Vulgate Book of Judith,[29] and sometimes as the daughter of Be'eri (such that she has the same name as Judith the daughter of Be'eri, the wife of Esau, Gen. 26:34),[30] or the daughter of Mordekhai,[31] or even the daughter of Matityahu[32] – but never as the daughter of the high priest Yoḥanan.[33] For example, in *Midrash LeḤanukka*, which is included in the collection *Batei Midrash*, although the story takes place during the time of Greek oppression, Judith is identified only as a widow, and the enemy gets drunk at his party without eating cheese or drinking milk first.[34]

What, then, is the source of the oft-quoted story that serves as the reason for eating dairy on Hanukka? There is one extant version of the Judith story in which she gives the Greek leader milk prior to his getting drunk. This version, *Maaseh Yehudit*, states that Judith gave Holofernes[35]

27 Moshe Hayim Leiter, "She'iltot BeInyanei Ḥanukka," *Yeshurun* 19 (2007), 42.

28 Weingarten, "Food, Sex, and Redemption," 98, note 8. Cheese appears also in the Latin version, but as in the Syriac, it is not connected with getting Holofernes drunk. See Zeitlin, *The Book of Judith*, 35.

29 Habermann, *Ḥadashim Gam Yeshanim*, 52; Dubarle, *Judith*, 46–47, Vulgate and version B.

30 Adolph Jellinek, *Beit HaMidrash* (Jerusalem: Wahrman Books, 1967), 2:15; Dubarle, *Judith*, 46, version C. On this identification of Judith, see Grintz, *Sefer Yehudit*, 204.

31 Dubarle, *Judith*, 47, version E, and 126, midrash 7a; *Likkutei Aggadot* (Oxford, Bodelian Library, Heb. D.47), 36–39.

32 Dubarle, *Judith*, 170, midrash 12.

33 It has also been suggested that when Judith is described as the daughter of the High Priest Yoḥanan, what is meant is that she is his descendant; he was actually her grandfather or some other ancestor. See Leiter, *Mamlekhet Kohanim*, 375.

34 Jellinek, *Beit HaMidrash* 1:133–34.

35 In the Hebrew text, his name is Eliporni, a Hebrew version of Holofernes, the general in the Apocryphal Book of Judith; see Dubarle, *Judith*, 24–25, 140. He is sometimes referred to as Olopirno or Oliporno (see Grintz, *Sefer Yehudit*, 6, 201), Olopirnes (Dubarle, 120), Elipirni (Dubarle, 152), or Elporna (see David Ganz, *Tzemaḥ David* [Warsaw, 1878], vol. 1, 29).

a skin of milk (*nod*) to drink from.[36] This is a reference to Yael's actions in Judges 4:19, where Yael makes Sisera sleepy by feeding him milk from a skin, and then kills him by striking him in the head with a tent peg.[37] This version seems to have been used by Menahem ben Makhir of Ratisbon (eleventh century) when composing the poem "*Ein Moshia VeGo'el*."[38]

Note that while the Rema writes that it is customary to eat cheese on Hanukka, he states that it is "because the miracle was done with milk that Judith fed the enemy," unlike the Ran and the *Kol Bo*, who write that Judith fed the enemy cheese.[39] Thus the story that correlates with the statement of the Rema is this version of *Maaseh Yehudit*. This may also have been the source for the authorities who note a custom to eat dairy on Hanukka but do not specify that it be cheese.[40]

We now see that it is imprecise to say that the Rema's statement is based on the Ran and the *Kol Bo*, as recorded in the parentheses in the published editions of *Shulḥan Arukh*. In the Rema's version, Judith fed the enemy milk, as recorded in *Maaseh Yehudit*, not cheese, as stated by the Ran and the *Kol Bo*. Having found the narrative source for the custom noted by the Rema, we must still locate the source for the Ran and the *Kol Bo*.[41]

---

36 Jellinek, *Beit HaMidrash* 2:19; Eisenstein, *Otzar Midrashim*, 1:207. In this version of the story, Judith is identified as the daughter of Be'eri.

37 Another variant of the Yael and Judith plot is found in the pseudepigraphal *Words of Gad the Seer*, chap. 13, where Tamar kills Pirshaz, king of Geshur, after lulling him to sleep with her harp playing. See Meir Bar-Ilan, *Divrei Gad HaḤozeh* (Rehovot: Meir Bar-Ilan, 2015), 301–3.

38 Grintz, *Sefer Yehudit*, 198. However, the poem does not contain a reference to milk. This poem has also been attributed to Ephraim ben Isaac of Regensburg (twelfth century); see Macy Nulman, *The Encyclopedia of Jewish Prayer* (Northvale, NJ: Jason Aronson, 1996), 74.

39 Moshe Rosenwasser, "Hidden *Midrashim* as Sources for the *Piyut Odekha*," *HaMaayan* 43:2 (2002), 30.

40 See the list in Chaim Simons, "Eating Cheese and *Levivot* on Hanukka," *Sinai* 115 (1995), 62–63.

41 Note that the specific motif of cheese rather than milk is so strong that Menahem Azarya da Fano – who in his *Sefer Gilgulei Neshamot* (Lublin, 1907), 25–26, writes that Judith was a reincarnation of Yael – still points out that Yael gave Sisera milk, while Judith gave the enemy cheese.

In the medieval *Megillat Yehudit*, Holofernes is served cheese. There we are told that Judith's maidservant prepared two fritters (*levivot*)[42] that were overly salted, together with cheese (*ḥaritzei ḥalav*) before the feast. Judith gives this to Holofernes, who then drinks wine, gets drunk, and falls asleep.[43] The manuscript this was taken from ends with a colophon giving the scribe's name as Moshe Dascola, and stating that the year it was written, or copied from an earlier document, was 1402.[44] This seems to be the only currently known version of the story to record that Judith fed the enemy cheese specifically.[45]

The term for cheese here, *ḥaritzei ḥalav*, appears as one of the foods that David brought to the captain at the beginning of the Goliath episode (I Sam. 17:18). Its use in the Book of Judith is just one of the many allusions to the episode of Goliath, who was also beheaded by his own sword (ibid. 17:50).[46]

However, even this version cannot be the source for the Ran and the *Kol Bo*, since here Judith is not identified as the daughter of the high priest Yoḥanan, but only as "one of the wives of the *benei hanevi'im*," the disciples of the prophets.[47]

### A POSSIBLE SOURCE?

In the beginning of his account of the story of Judith, the Ran mentions a decree that virgin brides had to sleep with the Greek governor before going to their husbands. This plot element is not found in the Apocryphal Book of Judith, and appears in only a few of the later versions. It also does not appear in the version of the story in the *Kol Bo*, which simply states that the Greek leader desired her, a plot element found

42 A reference to the two *levivot* that Tamar prepared for Amnon (II Sam. 13:6, 8, 10). See Weingarten, "Food, Sex, and Redemption," 104.

43 Dubarle, *Judith*, 148, midrash 8; Habermann, *Ḥadashim Gam Yeshanim*, 45.

44 Susan Weingarten, "Appendix to Chapter 6: *Megillat Yehudit* (the Scroll of Judith)," in Kevin Brine et al., *The Sword of Judith*, 110; Habermann, *Ḥadashim Gam Yeshanim*, 46.

45 Dubarle, *Judith*, 93; Simons, "Eating Cheese and *Levivot* on Hanukka," 60; Weingarten, "Food, Sex, and Redemption," 100. See also Catherine Donnely, ed., *The Oxford Companion to Cheese* (Oxford: Oxford University Press, 2016), 68.

46 Weingarten, "Food, Sex, and Redemption," 100.

47 Habermann, *Ḥadashim Gam Yeshanim*, 43.

in all versions from the Apocrypha on.[48] However, the decree on virgin brides is found in other midrashic works related to Hanukka.[49] For example, *Midrash LeḤanukka* (version 3) relates that the daughter of the high priest Matityahu, named as Hannah later in the story, inspired her brothers, led by Judah, to kill the Greek leader so that she wouldn't be forced to sleep with him on her wedding night.[50] Another version of *Midrash LeḤanukka* does not give the bride's name at all, but identifies her father as the high priest Yoḥanan and her brother as Judah. The story then segues into a second story, a version of the Judith narrative,[51] something found in other versions as well with certain variations.[52] This is the closest connection we have between Yoḥanan and Judith in a single narrative,[53] and even here it is in a place where two distinct narratives were strung together.

It is possible that a version of *Midrash LeḤanukka* that we are not currently aware of further conflates the two episodes, inserting the name Judith as the name of the bride, the daughter of the high priest Yoḥanan, in the first part of the story.[54] Conflation of narrative elements

---

48 Simons, "Eating Cheese and *Levivot* on Hanukka," 61.

49 See the overview in *HaMaayan*, 28.

50 Adolph Jellinek, *Beit HaMidrash* (Vienna, 1878), 6:2; Eisenstein, *Otzar Midrashim*, vol. 1, 190 (as *Midrash Maaseh Ḥanukka*). The story also appears in *Megillat Taanit* (regarding Elul 17), but there the bride is not named; she is identified only as the daughter of the high priest Matityahu. Note that in a version of the Judith story brought by Roke'aḥ, the heroine is called Hannah. See Moshe and Yehudah Hershler, eds., *Pirushei Siddur HaTefillah LaRoke'aḥ*, vol. 2, *siman* 141, 717–18; Leiter, *Mamlekhet Kohanim*, 418.

51 Jellinek, *Beit HaMidrash* 6: 133–34. In this version, there is no mention of Judith giving cheese or milk to the Greek general.

52 Deborah Levine Gera, "Shorter Medieval Hebrew Tales of Judith," in *The Sword of Judith*, ed. Kevin Brine et al., 87–88; Leiter, *Mamlekhet Kohanim*, 371. See, for example, Hershler, "*Maaseh Yehudit*," 165, where the bride is not named and is identified as "a daughter of the Hasmoneans," and Judah comes to her aid, although he is not her brother.

53 Tuvia Friend, *Moadim LeSimḥa* (Jerusalem: Otzar HaPoskim, 2000), 2:286–87.

54 Simons, "Eating Cheese and *Levivot* on Hanukka," 61. Azarya de Rossi, *Meor Einayim*, vol. 2 (Vilna, 1865), 159, suggests that once the special days in *Megillat Taanit* were canceled, all of the miraculous salvations from the Greek period were commemorated on Hanukka, leading to a possible conflation of what were completely different events – the Judith story and the story about the bride who was the daughter of the high

from similar stories is not unusual in ancient literature.[55] Even so, the element of serving cheese appears only in *Megillat Yehudit* and not in *Midrash LeHanukka*.

In order for all elements noted by the Ran to be included – the decree on brides, serving cheese, and Judith being the daughter of Yoḥanan – the most probable assumption is that he had a version of the story that is lost to us today. This holds true for the *Kol Bo* as well, since there is currently no known version that mentions both cheese and the daughter of Yoḥanan.[56]

The conflated narrative emerged in additional works after the advent of printing. For example, it can be found in the book *Ḥanukkat HaBayit* by Rabbi Shaul ben David (c. 1570–c. 1641), first published in 1616.[57] Here Judith is mentioned in a few places, and putting the references together, we see that the rabbi took Judith to be the sister of Judah the Maccabee. In his telling of the story, as a bride she refused to sleep with the Greek leader, instead cutting off his head, thus inspiring her brother to wage war against the Greeks.[58] He also has her serving the Greek leader cheese.[59]

This is the version of the story familiar to many today through its inclusion in the *Mishna Berura*. All the elements from the Ran are included there, even those not mentioned by the Rema:

---

priest. Yaakov Emden takes this idea further and proposes that there was a conflation of the Judith episode from Assyrian times with events from the Greek period; see *Mor UKetzia*, ed. Avraham Bombach (Jerusalem: Machon Yerushalayim, 1996), *Oraḥ Ḥayim* 670, 520.

55 See, for example, Frank Docken, *Herod as a Composite Character in Luke-Acts* (Tubingen, Germany: Mohr Siebeck, 2014), 70.

56 Leiter, *Mamlekhet Kohanim*, 374.

57 Very little biographical data is known about him. See the introduction to the new edition of his work *Tal Orot HaKadmon*, ed. Menachem Adler (Jerusalem, 1996), 8–9. See also Menachem Adler, ed., *Tal Orot HaKadmon* (Jerusalem: HaKetav VehaMikhtav, 1996), 7–19. See also Eliezer Brodt, "A Forgotten Work on Hanukka: חנוכת הבית," Seforim Blog, December 18, 2006, https://seforimblog.com/2006/12/forgotten-work-on-chanuka/.

58 Hershler, Shimon, ed., *Ḥanukkat HaBayit* (Bnei Brak: Makhon Nachlat Zvi, 1991), 79, 85.

59 Ibid., 94.

> "Judith was the daughter of Yoḥanan the High Priest, and there was a decree that every engaged woman must first sleep with the governor, and she gave cheese to the leader of the enemy to get him [to drink wine, and so make him] drunk and cut off his head, and they all fled."[60]

In this way, the Ran's version of the story of Judith became the most familiar to contemporary Jews, even though it does not match any early versions of the Judith story that we have in our possession today.

60 *Mishna Berura* 670:10.

## *Chapter 11*

# *Ḥanukka Gelt*

Although not mentioned in many classic works on Jewish customs,[1] there is a popular custom to give children money at Hanukka time. Giving this money, called *Ḥanukka gelt* (*gelt* in Yiddish means "money"), is considered a more authentic Jewish practice than giving gifts, which is understood to be influenced by Christmas. *Ḥanukka gelt* has become a symbol found in various Hanukka decorations, stickers and magnets, as well as appearing as chocolate coins wrapped in foil. In this chapter we will explore the origin and development of this widespread custom.[2]

### CHARITY ON HANUKKA

The Rambam in *Hilkhot Ḥanukka* 4:12 rules that even a person who receives charity for food must borrow money or sell his clothing to

1 For example, it is not mentioned in *Sefer Taamei HaMinhagim UMekorei HaDinim*, *Otzar Kol Minhagei Yeshurun* and *Otzar Taamei HaMinhagim*.

2 An excellent overview of this issue can be found in David Golinkin, *Responsa in a Moment*, vol. 4 (Jerusalem: Schechter Institute of Jewish Studies, 2017), 157–70. I am indebted to that article for pointing me in the direction of many valuable sources.

purchase oil and candles to light on Hanukka. This is because lighting Hanukka candles publicizes the miracle (*pirsumei nisa*), and is similar to the obligation to have four cups of wine at the Seder, even if this comes from charity.[3] This would later be codified in the *Shulḥan Arukh* (*Oraḥ Ḥayim* 671:1). It is thus not unusual to find early sources that describe Hanukka as a time of year when charity is distributed to the poor.

The earliest mentions of giving money on Hanukka concern the distribution of charity to the needy at this time. For example, Rabbi Shlomo ibn Aderet (the Rashba, 1235–1310) discusses a case in a responsum involving a benefactor who would distribute money on Hanukka to poor people, widows, and orphans.[4] The simple explanation is that this was done to enable the impoverished to celebrate Hanukka festively.[5]

It was particularly significant to give charity to poor Torah scholars for Hanukka. Many sources, dating from the 1500s, detail the practice in Italian and Sephardic communities to collect money for clothing for teachers and poor students at Hanukka time.[6]

Ashkenazic sources also note the practice of rabbis, synagogue wardens, cantors, ritual slaughterers, and teachers to collect money and sometimes food by going door to door on Hanukka.[7] Rabbi Yitzhak Lipetz writes that the practice of communal workers going door to door to

---

3 *Maggid Mishneh, Hilkhot Hanukka* 4:12.

4 Aharon Zeleznik, ed., *She'elot UTeshuvot Rashba,* vol. 3 (Jerusalem: Machon Yerushalayim, 1996), 164, *siman* 297. In the Worms community, the new *gabba'ei tzedaka* were appointed on Hanukka. See Avraham Meir Haberman, "Minhagei HaKehilla BeVermiza Mitokh Sefer HaMinhagim shel Rav Yuspa Shamash," *Sinai* 79, nos. 5–6 (1976), 258.

5 See Ephraim Greenblatt, *Rivevos Ephraim,* vol. 1 (Memphis, TN, 1975), *siman* 440:3, 350; David Cohen, *Gvul Yaavetz,* vol. 1 (Brooklyn, NY, 1987), 158. See also Sidney Hoenig, *Hanukkah: The Feast of Lights* (Philadelphia: Jewish Publication Society of America, 1937), 116: "Hanukkah shares with Purim in being a time in which gifts of money are distributed among those in need."

6 Shmuel di Medina (Maharashdam, 1505–89) discusses a case where the amount of wool collected for a teacher was not enough for Hanukka clothing, *She'elot UTeshuvot Maharshadam, Ḥoshen Mishpat* 372. See also Simha Assaf, *Mekorot LeToldot HaḤinukh BeYisrael,* vol. 2 (Tel Aviv: Dvir, 1925), 135, item 2, 168, item 19.

7 See Isaac Rifkind, *Yidishe Gelt* (New York: Academy for Jewish Research, 1959), 103–4. Regarding Rifkind and this book, see Shimeon Brisman, *A History and Guide to Judaic Dictionaries and Concordances,* part 1 (Hoboken, NJ: Ktav, 2000), 153.

collect money specifically on Purim and Hanukka was instituted as one of the ways to ensure they had a livelihood.[8] The custom of educators and students collecting money on Hanukka has persisted into modern times.[9]

The particular connection between educators in general and Hanukka is explained in various ways. Some point to the connection between the word "Hanukka" and the word *ḥinukh* (education).[10] Another explanation is noted by Rabbi Ephraim Greenblatt, who writes that Rabbi Menashe Klein suggests that since the miracle of Hanukka occurred because of Jews persisting to learn Torah (עוסקי תורתך), it is significant to support poor Torah scholars in particular on Hanukka.[11]

However, a major factor influencing this custom seems to be the practice of having a school break during Hanukka. This is noted in the eighteenth-century work *Ḥemdat Yamim*, where the author specifically explains that the Hanukka break from school was used as an opportunity to collect funds on behalf of impoverished students and poor Torah scholars. He says that over time this transformed into students going door to door asking for money to give to their teachers and poor people, not just scholars,.[12]

Rabbi Yaakov Yosef of Polonne (1710–84), a student of the Baal Shem Tov, in his classic work *Toldot Yaakov Yosef*, describes how rabbis would visit smaller communities on Hanukka to teach them Torah, and the members of the community would give them donations. Over time

8 Yitzhak Lipetz, *Sefer Mataamim* (Warsaw, 1910), 26, item 7. Homiletical explanations for this practice are given there on 26, *siman* 8 and 27, *siman* 13.

9 Nachum Wahrmann, *Ḥagei Yisrael UMoadeihem* (Tel Aviv: Achiasaf, 1970), 97, reports that this still took place in Jerusalem "a generation ago."

10 See Zvi Elimelech Spira of Dinov in his *Bnei Yissaskhar*, Kislev-Tevet, *maamar* 2, *Or Torah, siman* 16; Avraham Yitzhak Kook, *Ein Ayah – Shabbat*, vol. 1 (Jerusalem: Machon HaRav Zvi Yehuda Kook, 1993), 63, *siman* 8. See also Paul Steinberg, *Celebrating the Jewish Year: The Winter Holidays: Hanukkah, Tu B'shevat, Purim* (Philadelphia: Jewish Publication Society, 2007), 33.

11 Ephraim Greenblatt, *Rivevos Ephraim*, vol. 1 (Memphis, TN, 1975), *siman* 440:3, 350.

12 *Ḥemdat Yamim*, vol. 2 (Bnei Brak: Machon Ḥemdat Yamim, 2010), 205, *simanim* 29–31. Regarding the controversy surrounding this book, see Moshe Fogel, "The Sabbatean Character of Ḥemdat Yamim: A Reexamination," *Jerusalem Studies in Jewish Thought* 16, no. 2 (2001), 365–422 [Hebrew].

they would just send donations to rabbis and educators on Hanukka, irrespective of a communal visit.[13]

In his book *Yesod VeShoresh HaAvoda,* the eighteenth-century kabbalist Rabbi Alexander Susskind of Grodno notes that giving charity on Hanukka, particularly to poor Torah scholars, repairs the "blemishes of the soul."[14] He explains this based on mystical concepts. This is also found in the *Kitzur Shulḥan Arukh* (139:1).

## YOUNG MEN GOING DOOR TO DOOR

Rabbi Avraham Gombiner (c. 1635–82), in *Magen Avraham* (*siman* 670), his commentary to the *Shulḥan Arukh,* mentions that it is the custom of poor young men (נערים) to go door to door collecting money on Hanukka.[15] Based on this, *Be'er Heitev* (670:3) and *Mishna Berura* (670:1) also mention that poor people go door to door on Hanukka, but do not single out young men in particular. Many historical sources attest that it was normal for the needy to go door to door asking for money on Hanukka just as on Purim.[16]

Rabbi Abraham David Wahrman (1770–1840) in his *Eshel Avraham,* explains that the Greeks wanted to destroy the three pillars of the world, Torah (i.e., Torah study), *avoda* (prayer), and *gemilut ḥasadim* (which includes giving charity) (*Avot* 1:2). For this reason, these three activities must be increased on Hanukka.[17] This is the reason brought in the contemporary work on Jewish customs, *Otzar Taamei HaMinhagim,*

13 Yaakov Yosef of Polonne, *Toldot Yaakov Yosef,* vol. 1 (Jerusalem: Machon Daat UTevuna, 2009), *Parashat Tzav,* 401.

14 Alexander Susskind of Grodno, *Yesod VeShoresh HaAvoda* (Jerusalem, 1940), 12:1, 261.

15 As restated in Abraham Bloch, *The Biblical and Historical Background of Jewish Customs and Ceremonies* (NY: Ktav, 1980), 277, "According to *Magen Avraham* (18th century), it was the custom for poor yeshiva students to visit homes of Jewish benefactors who dispensed Hanukkah money."

16 See Isaac Rifkind, *Yidishe Gelt* (New York: Academy for Jewish Research, 1959), 105. See there also regarding Yiddish folksongs that mention begging for money on Hanukka.

17 Yehuda Zinger, in his *Ziv HaMinhagim* (Jerusalem: Dror, 1970), gives a more expanded version of this idea. He writes that to represent Torah, *avoda,* and *gemilut ḥasadim,* Jews established the lighting of Hanukka candles (based on Prov. 6:23, which

for giving charity particularly on Hanukka.[18] Note that these sources do not specify that those collecting were Torah scholars or educators.

However, *Magen Avraham* and *Be'er Heitev* themselves refer the reader to the book *Ḥanukkat HaBayit* by Rabbi Shaul ben David (c. 1570–1641), first printed in 1616, for an explanation of the custom.[19] There the author writes that in the *at-bash Gematria* (where the letters of the first half of the Hebrew alphabet are substituted with the numerical value of the letters in the second half of the alphabet and vice versa), the word Hanukka has the same value (269) as סוד צדקה (the secret of charity) which hints at the connection between charity and Hanukka. He writes that it is particularly important to give charity to young men who learn Torah, and therefore "young men go door to door on Hanukka and sing." These young men represent the small jug filled with pure oil through which the miracle was performed. They go door to door to publicize the miracle.[20]

### GIVING *ḤANUKKA GELT* TO CHILDREN

Later sources discuss giving money to children on Hanukka, regardless of their financial need. It is sometimes noted as a hasidic custom,[21] and was recorded as early as the 1800s.[22] The custom was particularly associated

---

says that a light symbolizes Torah), the recital of Hallel and *Al HaNissim* (*avoda* is understood to refer to prayer), and giving charity (as an act of *gemilut ḥasadim*).

18 Shmuel Gelbard, *Otzar Taamei HaMinhagim* (Petach Tikva: Mifal Rashi, 1996), 338.

19 For biographical information on this relatively unknown figure, see the end of the previous chapter.

20 Shimon Hershler, ed., *Ḥanukkat HaBayit* (Bnei Brak: Makhon Nachlat Zvi, 1991), 72.

21 See Asher Waserteil, ed., *Yalkut Minhagim* (Jerusalem: Ministry of Education and Culture, 1977), in the sections on hasidic customs by Tuvia Bloi, 145, 8:5, 169, 9:6; Gavriel Zinner, *Nitei Gavriel: Hanukka* (Jerusalem, 1999), 308, 51:5, note 7.

22 Pauline Wengeroff (1833–1916) describes receiving *Ḥanukka gelt* as a child on the fifth night of Hanukka. See her memoir, translated by Shulamit Magnus, *Memoirs of a Grandmother: Scenes from the Cultural History of the Jews of Russia in the Nineteenth Century*, vol. 1 (Stanford: Stanford University Press, 2010), 108. On the significance of this memoir, see Shulamit Magnus, "Pauline Wengeroff and the Voice of Jewish Modernity," in Tamar Rudavsky, ed., *Gender and Judaism* (New York: NYU Press, 1995), 181–90; Shulamit Magnus, "*Kol Ishah*: Women and Pauline Wengeroff's Writing of an Age," *Nashim* 7 (2004), 28–64.

with the fifth night of Hanukka,[23] which was considered to be a night of special spiritual significance.[24] It had additional significance for the custom of giving *gelt* since the fifth night of Hanukka cannot fall on Shabbat.[25] The Lubavitcher Rebbe, Rabbi Menachem Mendel Schneerson, notes that originally money was given to children only once, on either the fourth or fifth night, in order to keep the practice exciting.[26] Based on this, the significance of those particular nights seems to be that they are in the middle of the holiday, an appropriate time to inject some extra festivity. The simple explanation for the custom is that money is given to children to increase the joy of Hanukka and in this way add to the popularization of the Hanukka miracle.[27] Rabbi David Cohen adds a layer of significance by suggesting that giving money to children in general was done so that the needy would not be embarrassed to receive charity.[28]

This developed as an outgrowth of the earlier forms of the custom, giving money to the needy, Torah scholars, teachers, and students. At first, parents would "give money to their small children for distribution to their teachers. In time, as children demanded their due, money was also given to children to keep for themselves."[29] Still, originally the *gelt* was given to children "with the expectation that they would give some of it to their teachers."[30]

A more spiritual explanation of the evolution of the custom is brought by Rabbi Menachem Mendel Schneerson. He teaches that money is given to children in order to encourage them to learn Torah.

---

23 Hayyim Schauss, *Guide to Jewish Holy Days* (New York: Schocken Books, 1938), 233.

24 See Yom Tov Lewinsky, *Sefer HaMoadim: Rosh Ḥodesh, Ḥanukka, Ḥamisha Asar BiShvat* (Tel Aviv: Dvir, 1961), 257, 260, 261.

25 It is reported that Yaakov Kanievsky (the Steipler Gaon), gave *Ḥanukka gelt* specifically on the fifth day of Hanukka since it never falls on Shabbat. Gavriel Zinner, *Nitei Gavriel: Hanukka* (Jerusalem, 1999), 308, 51:5, note 7.

26 Menachem Mendel Schneerson, *Shaarei Halakha UMinhag – Oraḥ Ḥayim*, vol. 2 (Jerusalem: Heichal Menachem, 1993), 280–81, *siman* 283.

27 Zinner, *Nitei Gavriel: Hanukka*, 308, 51:5, note 7. והטעם הפשוט כדי לפרסם הנס ביותר

28 David Cohen, *Gvul Yaavetz*, vol. 1 (Brooklyn, NY, 1987), 158.

29 Abraham Bloch, *The Biblical and Historical Background of Jewish Customs and Ceremonies* (New York: Ktav, 1980), 277.

30 Dianne Ashton, *Hanukkah in America: A History* (New York: New York University Press, 2013), 10.

It is important to do so at this time because Hanukka is "a time of renewal of the Torah after the decree of the Greeks who wanted Torah to be forgotten."[31] He notes that although originally it was given on only one night, because of the "increased darkness of exile, including and particularly regarding the deterioration of the state of education," the custom should be increased to each day of Hanukka, except of course Shabbat.[32] This is the explanation given in the contemporary work on Jewish customs *Otzar Taamei HaMinhagim*.[33] A similar idea was stated by Rabbi Yosef Shlomo Kahaneman, the Ponevezher Rebbe, where he noted that when the Maccabees defeated the Greeks, they gave Jewish children a little money to encourage them to return to learning Torah, which he states is the function of *Ḥanukka gelt* today.[34]

In this manner the custom expanded from giving money to Torah scholars to giving money to children to encourage them to become Torah scholars, retaining the original theme of emphasizing the importance of Torah study.[35]

## FROM *GELT* TO GIFTS

Although "we have no idea when the first families began to exchange gifts, it seemed to grow more common in the 1880s."[36] "By the 1920s, though, it came into its own ... as an exercise in consumption."[37] Today,

31 Menachem Mendel Schneerson, *Shaarei Halakha UMinhag – Oraḥ Ḥayim*, vol. 2 (Jerusalem: Heichal Menachem, 1993), 279, *siman* 283.

32 Ibid., 280–81, *siman* 283.

33 Shmuel Gelbard, *Otzar Taamei HaMinhagim* (Petach Tikva: Mifal Rashi, 1996), 338.

34 Hayim Friedlander, *Siftei Ḥayim: Moadim*, vol. 2 (Bnei Brak, 1993), 134.

35 Ron Wolfson, *Hanukkah: The Family Guide to Spiritual Celebration* (Woodstock, VT: Jewish Lights, 2001), 125.

36 Dianne Ashton, *Hanukkah in America: A History* (New York: New York University Press, 2013), 97. Note that the practice of giving Christmas presents themselves developed only in the early 1800s; see Stephen Nissenbaum, *The Battle for Christmas* (New York: Vintage Books, 1997), 136.

37 Jenna Weissman Joselit, *The Wonders of America: Reinventing Jewish Culture, 1880–1950* (New York, 1994), 233. This timeline parallels the prominence of chocolate *gelt* as well; see Deborah R. Prinz, *On the Chocolate Trail: A Delicious Adventure Connecting Jews, Religions, History, Travel, Rituals and Recipes to the Magic of Cacao* (Woodstock, VT: Jewish Lights, 2012), 63–64. Note that this also seems to have originated as a

giving gifts on Hanukka is considered "a new American Jewish trend, supplanting the European custom of bestowing *gelt* on children during Hanukka,"[38] although it was also reported to have been practiced in Western Europe, particularly Germany, where more assimilated Jews were concerned that their children would be envious of the Christmas gifts their neighbors received.[39] This created a major shift in the evolution of giving *Ḥanukka gelt*, which although given to children was still expected to be given to teachers. Now, "objects specially selected to please children or fulfill their needs became popular."[40]

This led to the widespread concern that Hanukka was slowly being turned into "Christmas times eight."[41] Presents have insinuated themselves into the American celebration of Hanukka even among Orthodox families, along with other Christmas staples such as special sweaters and decorations for the home, elements not associated with other Jewish holidays.[42]

In contemporary times, the excessive gift giving in some circles has created a backlash, and in many modern holiday guides, it is recommended that children engage in a *tzedaka* (charity) project as a way of commemorating Hanukka.[43] In this fashion the custom has come full circle, from charity to *gelt* to gifts and back to charity again.

---

Jewish version of the giving of chocolate coins associated with Christmas and Saint Nicholas Day; see there, pages 60, 65.

38 Ashton, *Hanukkah in America*, 112.

39 Nachum Wahrmann, *Ḥagei Yisrael UMoadeihem* (Tel Aviv: Achiasaf, 1970), 97. See Joselit, *The Wonders of America*, 235, where it says that in the 1940s, Jewish parents were instructed that "Jewish children should be showered with gifts, Hanukkah gifts, as a perhaps primitive but most effective means of making them immune against envy of the Christian children and their Christmas presents."

40 Ashton, *Hanukka in America*, 112.

41 Irving Greenberg, *The Jewish Way: Living the Holidays* (New York: Simon and Schuster, 1988), 276.

42 This includes the Christmas "Secret Santa" gift-giving practice, turned into "Mystery Maccabee." Daniel Cohen, *What Will They Say About You When You're Gone?: Creating a Life of Legacy* (Deerfield Beach, FL: Health Communications, 2016), 120.

43 See for example, Sharon Duke Estroff, *Can I Have a Cell Phone for Hanukka?: The Essential Scoop on Raising Modern Jewish Kids* (New York: Broadway Books, 2007), 232; Paul Kipnes and Michelle November, *Jewish Spiritual Parenting: Wisdom, Activities, Rituals and Prayers for Raising Children with Spiritual Balance and Emotional Wholeness*

**HISTORICAL EXPLANATIONS**

Some works attribute the significance of gold coins as a Hanukka symbol to the coins minted by the Maccabees demonstrating their independence from and victory over the Greeks.[44] The right to mint their own coins is specifically mentioned in I Maccabees 15:6 as a liberty granted by Antiochus VII to Simon the Maccabee.[45] While it is true that this right was part of the Maccabean struggle,[46] historically Jews did not consider these coins particularly significant and they are not the inspiration for *Ḥanukka gelt.*

It has also been suggested that *Ḥanukka gelt* is just the Jewish version of the ancient Roman practice of giving gifts at the time of their winter solstice holidays.[47] These gifts, called *strenae,* included honey and fruit as well as gold coins.[48] Although the practice of *strenae* was known to, and possibly even practiced by, some Jews in Roman times,[49] there is no evidence that this persisted for centuries until the time when *Ḥanukka gelt* became customary.

The most significant clue to the origin of the practice to give money at Hanukka time is found in the early Ashkenazic sources of the custom referenced above, *Magen Avraham* and his source *Ḥanukkat HaBayit.* Note that *Magen Avraham* stated that poor young men (נערים) went door to door collecting money on Hanukka, whereas in *Ḥanukkat HaBayit* it was observed that "young men go door to door on Hanukka and sing." This unusual phrasing led to homiletical interpretations of the term "young men" used here.[50] These sources do not specify that

(Woodstock, VT: Jewish Lights, 2015), 181; Lawrence Bush and Jeffrey Dekro, "From *Gelt* to *Tzedakah,*" *Tikkun* 15, no. 6 (2000), 49.

44 Ronald Isaacs, *Bubbe Meises: Jewish Myths, Jewish Realities* (Jersey City, NJ: Ktav, 2008), 81.

45 Ron Wolfson, *Hanukka: The Family Guide to Spiritual Celebration* (Woodstock, VT: Jewish Lights, 2001), 125.

46 See Solomon Grayzel, "Hasmonean Coins," in Emily Solis-Cohen, *Hanukka: The Feast of Lights* (Philadelphia: Jewish Publication Society of America, 1965), 91–92.

47 Yom Tov Lewinsky, *Eileh Moadei Yisrael* (Tel Aviv: Achiasaf, 1987), 113.

48 Tad Tuleja, *Curious Customs* (New York: Harmony, 1987), 180.

49 Leonard Victor Rutgers, *The Jews in Late Ancient Rome: Evidence of Cultural Interaction in the Roman Diaspora* (Leiden: Brill, 1995), 85.

50 See Yissachar Shlomo Teichtel, *Mishneh Sakhir,* vol. 2 (Jerusalem: Machon Keren Re'em, 2013), *simanim* 298, 366.

the young men were teachers, students, scholars or connected to Torah study. Both of these practices recall the custom, known by a variety of names including *wassailing*, wherein gifts and money would be given to "roving bands of youthful males" who would go singing from door to door in the winter,[51] a custom that would evolve into the Christmas caroling performed outside people's homes.[52]

Wassailing itself was one of the various aspects of social inversion associated with the Roman wintertime celebration of Saturnalia, which was the predecessor of Christmas. This was a celebration where regular social norms and roles were reversed, including those of men and women and master and servant.[53] One of the aspects of this merrymaking was that "prosperous and powerful people were expected to offer the fruits of their harvest bounty to their poorer neighbors and dependents,"[54] reversing the normal hierarchy of the poor bringing tributes to the rich. The way in which this occurred was that "the poor – most often bands of boys and young men – claimed the right to march to the houses of the well-to-do" in order to receive gifts. In exchange, the young men would offer "their goodwill" in the form of "the performance of songs."[55]

Door-to-door begging was not considered socially acceptable in many communities, so allowing it at this time of year was an exception and part of the theme of the inversion of standard social norms. This is found in Jewish sources as well; for example, the communal *takkanot* of Eisenstadt from 1732 and 1736 noted that Hanukka and Purim (another time of social inversion) are the exceptions to the general rule prohibiting door-to-door begging.[56]

51 Stephen Nissenbaum, *The Battle for Christmas* (New York: Vintage Books, 1997), 9.

52 Torstein O. Kvamme, *The Christmas Carolers' Book in Song and Story* (Miami, FL: Hall and McCreary, 1935), 6.

53 See Carole E. Newlands, *Statius' Silvae and the Poetics of Empire* (Cambridge: Cambridge University Press, 2004), 227–29; Bruce David Forbes, *Christmas: A Candid History* (Los Angeles: University of California Press, 2007), 9.

54 Stephen Nissenbaum, *The Battle for Christmas* (New York: Vintage Books, 1997), 8–9.

55 Ibid., 9.

56 See Isaac Rifkind, *Yidishe Gelt* (New York: Academy for Jewish Research, 1959), 105.

The aspect of giving money to poor students at this time of year, in conjunction with door-to-door singing, is attested to in early European sources. "In Munich, authorized street singing for money to support students' upkeep is documented at least as early as 1526."[57]

Giving charity to the poor specifically at this time of year originated with the Roman celebration of Saturnalia, when "the wealthy were obliged to share with the poor."[58] Of course it is not surprising that the needy would require special assistance during the cold winter season, and donations at this time of year were not unusual. However, the early Ashkenazic sources of this practice, which specifically note the elements of young men going door to door and singing, connect it to the custom of wassailing. These elements do not appear in the Sephardic references to the practice to give charity on Hanukka, which emphasize collecting for poor students and teachers but do not mention young men doing the collecting or singing door to door.

The door to door collecting and singing, although noted in seventeenth-century Ashkenazic sources, dissipated over time, obscuring the connection between *Ḥanukka gelt* and wassailing. Since this shared origin has been forgotten, the giving of *Ḥanukka gelt* is considered appropriate for traditional Jewish families. On the other hand, these same families retain a resistance to and disapproval of gift giving on Hanukka, since its connection to Christmas is still remembered.

57 Alexander J. Fisher, *Music, Piety, and Propaganda: The Soundscape of Counter-Reformation Bavaria* (Oxford: Oxford University Press, 2014), 213.

58 Tad Tuleja, *Curious Customs* (New York: Harmony, 1987), 180.

*Chapter 12*

# The Custom Not to Slaughter Geese in Tevet and Shevat

## AN EARLY ASHKENAZIC CUSTOM

The notes of Rabbi Moshe Isserles supplement the *Shulḥan Arukh* by bringing the rulings and customs of Ashkenazi authorities. Scattered throughout his comments are references to various folkloric practices. These include ideas such as the beliefs that placing the keys of the synagogue under a sick person's head will cause them to pass away (*Yoreh De'ah* 339:1),[1] that blessing two grooms at once can bring on the evil eye (*Even HaEzer* 62:3),[2] and that a person can tell if they will survive the upcoming year by checking their shadow in the moonlight on Hoshana

---

1 See the discussion in Yaakov Yisrael Stell, "Tefillat Neshamot HaNiftarim BeVeit HaKnesset," *Yerushatenu* 3 (Elul 5769/2009), 217–18.

2 See the discussion in Gavriel Zinner, "BeDin Birkat Erusin VeNisuin LeKama Ḥatanim BeVat Eḥad," *Kovetz Beit Aharon VeYisrael* 81, no. 3 (Shevat-Adar 5759/1999), 75–78.

Rabba (*Oraḥ Ḥayim* 664:1).[3] In this chapter we will trace the origin of one such custom which is virtually forgotten today.

Rabbi Yehuda HeḤasid of Regensberg (1140–1217), a leading figure among the German Pietists (*Ḥasidei Ashkenaz*), is named as the source of an unusual Ashkenazic custom regarding the slaughter of geese. Rabbi Moshe Isserles, in his commentary to the *Tur* (*Darkhei Moshe, Yoreh De'ah* 11:2) notes that he found in the name of Rabbi Yehuda HeḤasid that some slaughterers are careful not to slaughter geese during the month of Shevat. This is based on a tradition that whoever slaughters a goose during a particular hour in this month would die within the year. Since the precise hour is not known, slaughtering geese is avoided during the entire month. This is the reason people are careful not to eat geese during Shevat, lest they come to slaughter a goose during the dangerous hour. Some are careful not to eat geese during the month of Tevet as well.

The way to counteract this death sentence is by having the slaughterer eat the heart of the goose he slaughters. Rabbi Isserles mentions this custom not to slaughter geese during Tevet and Shevat in his glosses to the *Shulḥan Arukh* (*Yoreh De'ah* 11:4) as well, noting that this led to the custom of slaughterers eating the hearts of the geese they slaughter during Tevet and Shevat.

The only source we have for this custom in the writings of Rabbi Yehuda HeḤasid is *Tzavaat Rabbi Yehuda HeḤasid,* an ethical will attributed to him, but of contested authorship.[4] Item 41 in the document[5] warns not to slaughter geese in the month of Shevat, and that one family is careful not to slaughter geese in Tevet. The will concludes by following the custom to avoid slaughtering geese in Shevat.

3 See the discussion in Yisrael Weinstock, *Maagalei HaNigleh VehaNistar* (Jerusalem: Mossad HaRav Kook, 1970), 249–70.

4 On the authorship of *Tzavaat Rabbi Yehuda HeḤasid* , see Reuven Margaliot, *Sefer Ḥasidim* (Jerusalem: Mossad HaRav Kook, 1990), 3–6, and Abrahams, Israel, "Jewish Ethical Wills," *The Jewish Quarterly Review* 3, no. 3 (Apr., 1891), 472: "There can be little doubt that the testament is spurious, but whoever be the author it contains a mass of superstitions." It was first printed in Venice in the sixteenth century.

5 In some editions it is found as items 48 and 49.

This custom is also mentioned in the glosses to Rabbi Isaac Tyrnau's *Sefer HaMinhagim*.[6] There we find that geese are not slaughtered in Shevat, and if they are, then the liver should be given to the slaughterer. While *Sefer HaMinhagim* is a late-fourteenth-century work, it is not clear when the glosses were written, or by whom. Opinions range from the time that *Sefer HaMinhagim* was compiled to the mid-seventeenth century.[7]

The gloss mentions that the *Tashbetz* states in the name of Rabbi Yehuda HeḤasid that there is one hour in Shevat when whoever slaughters a goose dies. *Tashbetz* is a collection of the customs of Rabbi Meir of Rothenburg (c. 1215–93) recorded by a student whose identity is not entirely clear. Some editions of the *Tashbetz* include a statement that Rabbi Yehuda HeḤasid taught that it is dangerous to eat geese on the eighth of Shevat, and that there is one hour in Shevat when it is dangerous to slaughter geese; therefore, some people are careful not to eat geese all of Shevat, lest they come to slaughter a goose.[8] The *Tashbetz* has undergone many editions, and the statements about slaughtering geese do not appear in the editions currently available.[9] In the glosses of Rabbi Moshe Isserles, the *Tashbetz* quoting Rabbi Yehuda HeḤasid is given as the source for the custom not to eat geese in Tevet and Shevat.

All the early sources that mention this custom are of unknown or contested authorship, and it is not clear when they were written. The time of the prohibition, Shevat or Tevet or both, is a matter of debate,

---

6 Shlomo Spitzer, ed., *Sefer HaMinhagim LeRabbeinu Isaac Tirnau* (Jerusalem: Mossad HaRav Kook, 2000), 143, Shevat, note 41.

7 See Spitzer, , introduction, 17–18.

8 *Tashbetz, siman* 555 as *Sefer HaMinhagim* quoted in *Shivi'im Temarim* by Hayim Shimon Dov Zivon, a commentary on *Tzavaat Rabbi Yehuda HeḤasid* (Warsaw, 1900), 106. This is also quoted by Ḥida in the name of Yehuda HeḤasid in *Birkei Yosef, Yoreh De'ah* 11:5 (Livorno, 1776), although other editions give the date of 5 Shevat (Jerusalem: Siach Yisrael, 2005). An interesting explanation for refraining from eating a goose on the eighth of Shevat based on the idea that rabbis are sometimes referred to metaphorically as "white geese" is found in Natan Neta Olevski, *Neta Revai* (Jerusalem: Machon Yerushalayim, 1995), *siman* 23, 414.

9 See Spitzer, *Sefer HaMinhagim*, 143, note 41. See also Menashe Lehmann, "Maḥzor Ketav Yad Lehmann VehaTashbetz Shebetokho," 188–89, in *Kovetz al Yad*, vol. 11 (Jerusalem: Ḥevrat Mekitze Nirdamim, 1985) (21).

as is the way to prevent death, i.e., eating the goose's liver or its heart. What is clear is that by the sixteenth century this Ashkenazic custom was understood to have originated with Rabbi Yehuda HeḤasid and had been incorporated into the *Shulḥan Arukh*.[10]

There are variants of this practice regarding which part of the goose to eat in order to avoid danger. The *Shakh* (Rabbi Shabtai HaKohen, 1621–63) stated that he saw that the legs of the geese were eaten by the slaughterers;[11] Rabbi Yonatan Eybeschuetz declared that in Prague the custom was for the slaughterers to take some fat from the goose.[12] Further leniencies are mentioned, for example that it suffices if one of the slaughterer's family members partakes of the goose, or even that the slaughterer may be given money instead of part of the goose.[13] There are also various traditions regarding when it is dangerous to slaughter geese. The *Taz* writes that he found in an old book in the name of Rabbi Yehuda HeḤasid that it is dangerous to engage in bloodletting and slaughtering or eating a goose on the first day of the months of Iyar, Elul, and Tevet when it falls on either a Monday or a Wednesday, and in a different book that the dangerous time is the fifteenth of Tevet when it falls on a Sunday.[14]

## WINTERTIME GEESE

We have seen that this custom has many variants, but the primary component is that there is a time when it is dangerous to slaughter geese

---

10 Over time, the custom spread to the community of Sephardic Jews as well. See, for example, Refael Aharon Ben Shimon (1848–1928), *Nahar Mitzrayim*, vol. 1 (Alexandria, 1908), *Hilkhot Sheḥita, siman* 18, 57; Hayim Palagi, *Sefer Nefesh HaḤayim* (Jerusalem: Chen Ḥayim, 2004), 193.

11 *Shakh, Yoreh De'ah* 11:7.

12 *Kreiti UPleiti, Kreiti* 11:14.

13 See the responsa of Ḥatam Sofer, *Kovetz Teshuvot,* 27, and the responsa of Ketav Sofer, *Yoreh De'ah* 12, which state that the slaughterer should eat from the goose to avoid danger, but whoever is unconcerned about this may take money instead. See also *Darkhei Teshuva, Yoreh De'ah* 11:49.

14 *Taz, Yoreh De'ah* 116:6. Different editions of *Shulḥan Arukh* contain textual variants regarding the exact dates mentioned by the *Taz,* based on the similarity between the letters *alef* (denoting the first day of the month) and *ḥet* (denoting the eighth day) in Rashi script, thus making the eighth, not the first, of Iyar, Elul and Tevet dangerous days. See, for example, *Shivi'im Temarim,* 107.

unless a part of it is given to the slaughterer. To clarify matters, we must first understand the connection between geese and the months of Tevet and Shevat. Geese were a significant source of food for Jews in early medieval Rhineland. Owning them was considered more advantageous than owning chickens since they live longer, can be sustained on lower-quality feed, can be herded rather than carried, are less prone to disease, and provide more fat for schmaltz. Goose schmaltz was the predominant cooking fat at the time. Only centuries later, with the movement of Jews to Eastern Europe, did chickens replace geese as the fowl of choice.[15]

Geese gorge themselves in the months preceding the winter migration, eating as much as possible in anticipation of the long journey ahead. The liver and skin are the principal repositories of the fat geese use to store energy. In addition to this, geese were manually fattened by their owners through the autumn months. Typically, the geese were free-range for several months, during which time the keratin of their esophagus firmed. Then, in late autumn, in order to secure as much fat as possible from each goose, excess grains and bread were massaged down the throats of the animals on a regular basis. By the very end of autumn, through a combination of the instinctive premigration gorging together with the force-feeding by their owners, geese were at the peak of their fatness. Historically, most geese were slaughtered shortly before the onset of winter, in order to take maximum advantage of the fattened goose. Any domesticated geese not slaughtered by then would not be slaughtered during the ensuing winter months when their fat levels fell. Those remaining geese were intended for future procreation.[16]

This led to the popularity of roast goose on Hanukka among German Jews.[17] Gentiles also feasted on geese on their autumn and winter holidays: on Michaelmas, the feast commemorating the autumnal equinox at the end of September, on Samhain (Halloween) at the

---

15 Gil Marks, *Encyclopedia of Jewish Food* (Hoboken, NJ: John Wiley and Sons, 2010), 233.

16 Gil Marks, personal correspondence, Oct. 3, 2010. See also Nigel Pennick, *The Pagan Book of Days* (Rochester, VT: Destiny Books, 1992), 123: "The Anglo-Saxon name for November was Blotmonath, the month of sacrifice, the time for killing the livestock that could not be kept through the winter months."

17 Marks, 74.

end of October, on Martinmas in November,[18] and on the Germanic Yule, originally the first day of the new year.[19] The German Martinmas goose was later incorporated into Christmas celebrations.[20] Special "roast goose fairs" were held in the fall.[21] Tevet and Shevat coincided with the time of year when slaughtering the geese had, for the most part, been completed.

### SUGGESTED EXPLANATIONS FOR THE CUSTOM

Why would slaughtering a goose at that particular time be dangerous? Trachtenberg, in his classic work *Jewish Magic and Superstition*, suggests that while "the origin of this notion is obscure," it has something to do with the fact that the months of Tevet and Shevat cover the time of the winter solstice, a transitional period given great significance in the ancient world.[22] Indeed, we find many goose-related customs in the Gentile festivals noted above that take place in the period of time from the autumnal equinox to the winter solstice. The geese served at these European holiday meals had a supernatural component as well. Geese had sacred associations among the ancient Greeks, Romans, and Britons, ideas that survived into medieval Europe.[23] "A sacrifice of geese at the transition from one season to another was a universal custom in Europe."[24] Rituals included sprinkling the blood of the goose across the

---

18 Maguelonne Toussaint-Samat, *A History of Food* (Chichester, West Sussex: John Wiley and Sons, 2009), 320. See also Leland Duncan, "Fairy Beliefs and Other Folklore: Notes from County Leitrim," *Folklore* 7 (1896), 179, and Thomas J. Westropp, "A Folklore Survey of County Clare," *Folklore* 22 (1911), 207.

19 Tamara Andrews, *Nectar and Ambrosia: An Encyclopedia of Food in World Mythology* (Santa Barbara, CA: ABC-CLIO, 2000), 105–6.

20 William Sansom, *A Book of Christmas* (New York: McGraw-Hill, 1968), 144–45.

21 M. A. Courtney, "Cornish Feasts and Feasten Customs," *Folklore* 4 (1886), 111.

22 Joshua Trachtenberg, *Jewish Magic and Superstition* (New York: Athenium, 1984), 258.

23 James Hastings, ed., *Encyclopedia of Religion and Ethics*, vol. 8 (New York: Charles Scribner's Sons, 1916), 623. See also N. W. Thomas, "Animal Superstitions and Totemism," *Folklore* 11 (1900), 242, 243, 253, 259.

24 Toussaint-Samat, *A History of Food*, 320. An annual sacrifice of geese in connection to crops is found beyond Europe as well, for example, in India; see Col. J. Shakespear, "The Religion of Manipur," *Folklore* 7 (1896), 433.

threshold and in the four corners of the house.[25] The goose was considered an offering to ensure the regeneration of vegetation after the winter months. A harvest festival would be considered incomplete without the traditional goose.[26]

The idea that food and drink may be adversely affected by the changing of the *tekufot,* the solstices and equinoxes, and be rendered dangerous for consumption is found in many medieval sources, both Jewish and Gentile.[27] However, if the slaughter of a goose was considered dangerous due to the winter solstice and this was indeed the "particular hour" warned about by Rabbi Moshe Isserles, why would the custom extend to the entire month of Tevet? All other sources that mention the dangers of the *tekufot* limit the hazard to the exact hour of the *tekufa,* or at most from sunset to midnight,[28] and do not extend the danger to the entire month, and certainly not a month after the solstice to Shevat. Furthermore, the time of the *tekufa* was well known, but the "particular hour" when it was considered dangerous to slaughter geese was in fact, according to Rabbi Isserles, unknown. An additional problem with this theory is that we have seen that rather than avoiding slaughtering geese at the autumnal equinox and winter solstice, people considered slaughtering geese an integral component of the festivities held at those times of year.

Rabbi Reuven Margaliot, in his notes to *Tzavaat Rabbi Yehuda HeḤasid* , explains that the custom is related to an idea found multiple times in the Zohar, that Tevet is one of the months where negative spiritual forces and stern judgment are found in the world.[29] According to Rabbi Margaliot, this causes the slaughter of geese to be dangerous at this time. However, the Zohar includes the months of Tamuz and Av along with Tevet as dangerous times, but the custom did not extend to these

---

25 C. C. Bell, "Fifth of November Customs," *Folklore* 14 (1903), 186, describing St. Martin's Eve in November.

26 Toussaint-Samat, *A History of Food,* 133.

27 See Trachtenberg, *Jewish Magic and Superstition,* 257–58. See also, for example, *Kitzur Shulḥan Arukh* 33:8.

28 See, for example, Rabbeinu Bahya on Genesis 4:22, s.v. *ve'achot.*

29 Reuven Margaliot, *Sefer Ḥasidim* (Jerusalem: Mossad HaRav Kook, 1990), 23, note 57.

two months. Furthermore, why would the danger affect the slaughter of geese more than of any other animal?[30]

The mystical work *Sefer HaKaneh* explains[31] that during the month of Shevat the "angel of geese" has dominion, and whoever slaughters a goose will be slaughtered in turn.[32] This is stated directly after declaring that it is prohibited to kill a black cat. It is not clear who wrote *Sefer HaKaneh* and where or when it was written. It is generally understood to be a Spanish or Greek work from the late fourteenth or early fifteenth century.[33] The idea of a vengeful "angel of geese" is not found in other sources;[34] however, this idea was popularized by being quoted in *Be'er Heitev* (*Yoreh De'ah* 11:7).

Rabbi Yonatan Eybeschuetz explains that this is a superstitious practice, not based on any logic or natural law, and it falls under the category of "the ways of the Amorite," which Jewish people should not follow. He states that in the time of Rabbi Yehuda HeḤasid, witchcraft involving geese was common, and perhaps this custom came to negate their power, but this is no longer a concern.[35] This approach is quoted by the Ḥida,[36] Rabbi Yechiel Michel Epstein in his *Arukh HaShulḥan*,[37] and others[38] as the reason this practice is no longer observed.[39]

---

30 See *Ḥodesh BeḤodsho* (Brooklyn, NY: Ichud Chassidei Munkacs, 2000), Shevat 5760, vol. 6, no. 71, 7, for these and other criticisms of the idea that the custom is based on the Zohar.

31 *Sefer HaKaneh* (Cracow: Yosef Fischer, 1894), *Sod Hilkhot Tereifot*, 278.

32 וכן ארז"ל שלא לשחוט אווזים בזמן שיש לשר שלהם הממשלה והכח והוא חודש שבט כי הממית ימות.

33 See Israel Ta-Shma, "Where were *Sefer HaKaneh* and the *Pelia* composed?" [Hebrew], in *The Jacob Katz Jubilee Volume* (Jerusalem: Magnes Press, 1980), 56–60.

34 There is some controversy surrounding the authenticity and reliability of *Sefer HaKaneh*. See, for example, David Avitan, ed., *Birkei Yosef* (Jerusalem: Siach Yisrael, 2005), *Yoreh De'ah* 11:5, 11, note 7.

35 *Kreiti UPleiti*, *Kreiti* 11:14 and *Pleiti* 11:5.

36 *Birkei Yosef*, *Yoreh De'ah* 11:5.

37 *Arukh HaShulḥan*, *Yoreh De'ah* 11:15.

38 Pinhas Simha Kornfeld, *Maarekhet HaShulḥan*, vol. 1 (Bnei Brak, 1995), 126, note 19. See also Gavriel Zinner, *Nitei Gavriel: Hilkhot Purim* (Jerusalem: Cong. Nitei Gavriel, 2000), 51, note 7. See also *Shivi'im Temarim*, 108–9, who disagrees with Yonatan Eybeschuetz, explaining that there is a טעם נורא for this custom.

39 This is also the explanation offered by contemporary *kashrut* organizations as to why the custom is no longer observed (personal communication from Rabbi Mordechai

The idea of permitting sorcery to combat sorcery is well represented in Jewish legal writings. For example, the Maharshal writes in a responsum: "The Torah did not prohibit sorcery in this manner, which comes only to expel and nullify (other) sorcery."[40] Similarly, the *Kitzur Shulḥan Arukh* (166:5) rules that "it is forbidden to consult sorcerers except... if a sickness was the result of witchcraft."[41] Seemingly illogical and theurgic practices can be justified only when warding off malevolent supernatural forces, such as witchcraft. In the absence of these malevolent forces, the techniques once used to combat them are downgraded from legitimate means of protection to simple superstition, and should thus be abandoned.[42]

## EGYPTIAN DAYS

The idea that certain days are dangerous for eating geese is found in European folklore. Many records of so-called "Egyptian days," in other words unlucky days, include three days on which it was inauspicious to engage in certain activities, such as bloodletting, beginning a new business venture, and eating geese. These lists are dated as early as 354 CE and were very popular through medieval times.[43] They were known as *dies mali,* which is the origin of the English adjective "dismal."[44]

The idea of evil days dates back to ancient times. Counting from the new moon, the Babylonian calendar identified the 7th, 14th, 21st, and 28th day of each month as *umu limnu,* an "evil day," making it unsuitable for certain activities. A religious calendar from the library of Ashurbanipal (650 BCE) in Nineveh details the activities prohibited on these

Frankel, Institute of Halacha at the Star-K, January 8, 2014).

40 Shlomo Luria, *She'elot UTeshuvot Maharshal,* 3.

41 See J. H. Chajes, *Between Worlds: Dybbuks, Exorcists, and Early Modern Judaism* (Philadelphia: University of Pennsylvania Press, 2003), 93, 94.

42 Hayim Palagi writes that this custom is based on scientists (המחקר חכמי) stating that these are difficult days, *Sefer Nefesh HaḤayim* (Jerusalem: Chen Chayyim, 2004), 193. Based on this, if it is now demonstrated that the science behind the custom is in error, the custom need not be observed.

43 Laszlo Sandor Chardonnens, *Anglo-Saxon Prognostics, 900–1100* (Leiden: Brill, 2007), 331. See also Nigel Pennick, *The Pagan Book of Days* (Rochester, VT: Destiny Books, 1992), 7.

44 Chardonnens, *Anglo-Saxon Prognostics,* 330.

days, mostly applied to people of superior position. Regarding officials it says, "He shall not eat salted meat cooked over embers, he shall not change his body clothing, he shall not be clothed in white, he shall not offer a sacrifice." "The king shall not ride in a chariot, he shall not talk victoriously. The seer shall not make declaration with regard to a sacred place. A physician shall not touch a sick man." The only prohibition that applied to ordinary people was that "it is not suitable to make a wish." On each of these days, offerings were made to a different god and goddess, apparently at nightfall to avoid the prohibitions. Even more fearsome was the 19th day of the month, which was "a week of weeks" (forty-nine days) from the start of the previous month, an *umu uggati*, "a day of anger."[45] Lists of unlucky days are common in medieval works; they were understood to be based on the ancient Egyptian calendar and were determined on astrological grounds, hence the term "Egyptian days."[46]

We find that the last day of April, the first day of August, and the last day of December were considered especially dangerous, "and if they eat any goose in these three days, within forty days they shall die."[47] Another list mentions the last Monday of April, the first of August and the first Monday in the second half of the month of December as days when "he that tastes of goose-flesh, within forty days space his life he will end."[48] This is reminiscent of the list of dangerous days that the *Taz* found in an old book in the name of Rabbi Yehuda HeḤasid, with its dangerous Mondays.[49]

We can now understand that what the *Taz* found was simply a list of Egyptian days translated into the Jewish calendar, with the

45 T. G. Pinches, "Sabbath (Babylonian)," in James Hastings, ed., *Encyclopedia of Religion and Ethics*, vol. 10 (New York: Charles Scribner's Sons, 1919), 889–90.

46 Trachtenberg, 254. See also Pennick, 7.

47 Robert Chambers, *Book of Days: A Miscellany of Popular Antiquities in Connection with the Calendar* (Whitefish, MT: Kessinger, 2004, reprint of the original 1869 edition), part 1, 42, quoting a Saxon MS (Cott. MS. Vitell, C. viii. fo. 20).

48 Chambers, 41, quoting *The Book of Knowledge*. See also Laurence Gomme, "Rules Concerning Perilous Days," *Folklore* 24 (1913), 122.

49 Later I found that this same conclusion has been reached by Justine Isserles, "Some Hygiene and Dietary Calendars in Hebrew Manuscripts from Medieval Ashkenaz," in Sacha Stern and Charles Burnett, eds., *Time, Astronomy, and Calendars in the Jewish Tradition* (Leiden: Brill, 2014), 273–85.

months of Iyar, Elul, and Tevet substituting for April, August and December. The same goes for the eighth of Shevat as reported in the name of the *Tashbetz*. The multiple versions of perilous days recorded by the *Tashbetz* and the *Taz* are reflective of the different traditions regarding Egyptian days. The main difference is that the Jewish versions of this custom focus on the danger involved in slaughtering geese, whereas the Gentile versions talk only about the danger of consuming geese.[50] The *Tashbetz* and the *Taz* mention the danger in eating geese as well as slaughtering them; other Jewish sources discuss only the slaughter. This follows the approach of Rabbi Isserles, who notes that we refrain from eating geese in order to avoid the danger involved in slaughtering them.[51]

We now have the source for the custom reported in the *Taz* of particular days when a goose should not be slaughtered, but what of the more popular custom mentioned by Rabbi Isserles that the entire months of Tevet and Shevat are considered dangerous? The source of this custom is the conflicting lists of Egyptian days regarding the dangerous day to slaughter geese,[52] along with the additional difficulty of translating this day into a particular Hebrew calendar date, especially since the first Monday of the second half of December was not tied to a particular calendar date at all. Since the day of peril was disputed in various lists, with some mentioning, for example, the first Monday of the second half of December and some the last day of December, the whole month was considered off-limits. Even authors of non-Jewish accounts of Egyptian days had difficulty navigating when they fell, based

50 The exception to this is Hayim Palagi, who states that the danger is in eating goose flesh because the meat is difficult to digest and therefore should be avoided on days of ill omen, *Sefer Nefesh HaḤayim* (Jerusalem: Chen Chayyim, 2004), 193. He lists a number of particular activities that should be avoided on these days, such as making *shidduchim* and beginning any endeavor in general.

51 *Darkhei Moshe, Yoreh De'ah* 11:2.

52 This is the reason given in *Shivi'im Temarim*, 107, that because of the different versions of the dangerous day found in *Tashbetz* and *Taz* we are cautious during the entire months of Tevet and Shevat. Modern scholarship has failed to find a formula underlying the Egyptian days or a resolution to the conflicting lists. See Chardonnens, *Anglo-Saxon Prognostics*, 356–58.

on varying traditions and the complication of making the switch from the Julian to the Gregorian calendar.[53]

If this is the case, why don't we have any warnings related to slaughtering geese in the months of April and August, as found in the lists of Egyptian days? We do find such days recorded by the *Taz,* but not by Rabbi Isserles. The reason could be a practical one. The season for slaughtering geese was the end of the fall and beginning of winter, and it was important to know which days to avoid during this season. In practice, the dangerous days for slaughtering geese in the spring and summer were largely irrelevant, as very little slaughtering took place then. This prohibition may also have had the added benefit of encouraging people to slaughter their geese at the peak of their fatness, at the end of the autumn right before winter begins.

The Egyptian days regarding eating goose included days in late December, often coinciding with Tevet, making it understandable that this month was considered dangerous for slaughtering geese. How did the month of Shevat come to be included in the prohibition? In fact, there are multiple lists of Egyptian days, some listing just three unlucky days, some twelve, and some as many as twenty-four.[54] These expanded lists include even more days when it is perilous to eat goose, such as the 1st and 25th days of January,[55] and the 8th day of February.[56] Based on these expanded lists of Egyptian days, the month of Shevat also contains days when it is considered dangerous to eat goose. We can now understand why *Tzavaat Rabbi Yehuda HeḤasid* mentions that some people were cautious regarding Tevet and others Shevat: it all depended on which list of Egyptian days was being consulted.[57] What of the "particular hour" of danger mentioned by Rabbi Isserles? This too is mentioned in certain lists of Egyptian days, where the 11th hour of the 1st of January and the

53 John Aubrey, *Remains of Gentilism and Judaism, 1686–87* (London: Satchell, Peyton and Co., 1881), 94.

54 Chardonnens, *Anglo-Saxon Prognostics,* 330, 349.

55 Ibid., 356.

56 Ibid., 365.

57 This is the simple reason that there are so many divergent and conflicting customs regarding the perilous days in Jewish sources. See also Aron Maged, *Beit Aharon,* vol. 3 (Brooklyn: E. Grossman's, 1965), 152–53.

6th hour of the 25th of January are mentioned as the dangerous times to eat geese on those particular days.[58] Texts including the exact hour of danger are rare,[59] and as noted before, the dangerous dates themselves were a matter of dispute, leading Rabbi Isserles to write that the particular hour of peril is not known.

We now see that the Ashkenazi custom not to slaughter geese during Tevet and Shevat is based on the popular tradition of Egyptian days of bad luck and danger. We even find certain Latin texts of Egyptian days that mention the months of Tevet and Shevat by name as corresponding to the months of January and February.[60] As Rabbi Yonatan Eybeschuetz explained, it is a superstitious practice, "the ways of the Amorite."

Why was the goose singled out for special consideration on the Egyptian days? Although their true origin is unknown, the Egyptian days were believed to be based on Egyptian beliefs and astrology, or on the seasonal changes in Egypt.[61] Some scholars have attempted to trace the prohibition of goose to Egyptian traditions.[62] The goose figures prominently in Egyptian creation myths as laying the primeval egg from which the Earth was hatched.[63] Additionally, "the goose was commonly killed as a victim to the gods, for no animal is more frequently seen in the sculptured representations of sacrifices."[64] These beliefs may have figured in an Egyptian taboo of geese. Others relate the prohibition against geese to a taboo among some Celtic tribes against eating geese in general, or to an Irish belief that eating geese after bloodletting is dangerous,[65] or that goose flesh is difficult to digest and therefore should be avoided

58 Noted on page 135 of Chardonnens's doctoral dissertation at Leiden University, "Anglo-Saxon Prognostics: A Study of the Genre with a Text Edition" (2006), upon which his book *Anglo-Saxon Prognostics* is based.

59 Chardonnens, *Anglo-Saxon Prognostics*, 246.

60 Ibid., 231.

61 See Chardonnens, *Anglo-Saxon Prognostics*, 333, 348, 349.

62 Chardonnens, *Anglo-Saxon Prognostics*, 333, 339.

63 Pat Remler, *Egyptian Mythology A-Z* (New York: Chelsea House, 2000), 72.

64 J. C. Prichard, *An Analysis of the Egyptian Mythology* (London: John and Arthur Arch, 1819), 319.

65 J. H. G. Grattan, and C. W. Singer, *Anglo-Saxon Magic and Medicine, Illustrated Specially from the Semi-Pagan* (London: Oxford University Press, 1952), 43.

during inauspicious times.[66] All of these explanations are considered inconclusive, modern scholarship having failed to provide a convincing rationale for the custom to avoid eating geese on certain days.[67]

One part of the Ashkenazic custom not mentioned in the lists of Egyptian days is that eating the heart, liver, or some other part of the goose serves to cancel the danger involved in slaughtering the goose. What is the origin of this protective measure? There are precedents in the world of ancient and medieval medicine for the idea that "only by harnessing the powers that inflicted the wound can the wound itself be mollified."[68] This concept is found in Jewish sources as well. For example, consuming part of a dog's liver to cure a person who was bitten by a rabid dog is discussed in the Mishna (Yoma 8:6).[69] The therapeutic use of parts of a rabid animal, particularly the liver, to cure a person bitten by such an animal is found in the writings of Galen and many other ancient physicians.[70] The underlying belief is that part of the animal that caused harm has the power to undo that harm, a belief echoed today in homeopathics.[71] Rabbi Mordekhai Jaffe (the Levush) explains that eating the heart of a goose saves the slaughterer from death since "the essence of life is in it."[72] The heart and liver were considered the ideal protective measures given to slaughterers, since they are the main blood organs and were understood to have the power to negate any harm originating from geese.[73] Other parts of the goose suggested to have medicinal powers also hearken back to ancient beliefs. Goose fat was believed to have special curative powers,[74] and

---

66 Hayim Palagi, *Sefer Nefesh HaḤayim* (Jerusalem: Chen Chayyim, 2004), 193.

67 Chardonnens, *Anglo-Saxon Prognostics*, 339.

68 J. H. Chajes, *Between Worlds: Dybbuks, Exorcists, and Early Modern Judaism* (Philadelphia: University of Pennsylvania Press, 2003), 78.

69 See also Y. Yoma 8:5, where such a cure was administered unsuccessfully.

70 See Fred Rosner, *Medicine in the Bible and Talmud* (Hoboken, NJ: Ktav, 1977), 50.

71 Rosner, *Medicine in the Bible*, 50.

72 *Levush, Yoreh De'ah* 11:4, עיקר החיות תלוי בו.

73 However, many Jewish sources indicate that it is customary not to eat the heart, or liver, of any animal since it causes forgetfulness. See the discussions in *Yabia Omer*, vol. 2, *Yoreh De'ah* 8, and *Meshaneh Halakhot* 3:61, *Shivi'im Temarim*, 107–8.

74 See *Yoma* 84a and Fred Rosner, ed., Julius Preuss, *Biblical and Talmudic Medicine* (Northvale, NJ: Aronson, 1993), 172, note 289.

goose feet figured in homeopathic magic, having the power to ward off supernatural danger.[75]

The Ashkenazic custom to refrain from slaughtering geese during Tevet and Shevat is based on when it was considered dangerous to eat geese according to the superstition of unlucky Egyptian days. The protective measures suggested to ward off the alleged danger are rooted in ancient belief in effecting a cure using a part of the object that caused the harm. In the words of Rabbi Yonatan Eybeschuetz, "Heaven forfend that we should be strict about this; you should be perfectly faithful to the Lord your God" (Deut. 18:13).[76]

75 A. Ela, "Working Evil by a Duck's Foot," *Folklore* 28 (1917), 322.
76 *Kreiti UPleiti, Pleiti* 11:5, חס ושלום להקפיד על זה, תמים תהיה וכו'.

## *Chapter 13*

# Purim Festivities

### *MISHLOAḤ MANOT* ON PURIM AND ROSH HASHANA

The practice of sending food gifts to one another on a holiday is generally associated with Purim, as it is mentioned in Esther 9:22, "They were to observe them as days of feasting and merrymaking, and as an occasion for sending gifts (*mishloaḥ manot*) to one another and presents to the poor." The practice was codified in Megilla 7a, described by Rabbi Yosef as an obligation to send two portions of food to one other person.

However, this term, *mishloaḥ manot*, also appears in Nehemiah, chapter 8, in connection to the observance of what we now call Rosh HaShana. There we are told that when Ezra read the Torah to the people "on the first day of the seventh month" (Neh. 8:2), the people began weeping and had to be instructed that "this day is holy to the Lord your God; you must not mourn or weep" (Neh. 8:9). Instead, they were to "eat choice foods and drink sweet drinks and send portions (*veshilḥu manot*) to whoever has nothing prepared, for the day is holy to our Lord" (Neh. 8:10). And so the people "went to eat and drink and send portions (*uleshalaḥ manot*) and make great merriment" (Neh. 8:12).

A further connection between the *mishloaḥ manot* of Esther and Nehemiah is the twinning of this practice with providing food for the needy. In Esther 9:22 we find that Purim is "an occasion for sending gifts (*mishloaḥ manot*) to one another and presents to the poor," and in Nehemiah 8:2 the people are told to "send portions (*veshilḥu manot*) to whoever has nothing prepared."

Based on this, it would seem that sending *mishloaḥ manot* was a standard component of any holiday celebration.[1] It ensured that everyone had food to eat as part of their festivities. This practice of sending portions on all holidays has been preserved in rabbinic literature, since it is referred to in the Mishna (Beitza 1:9), where the terminology *meshalḥin manot* is used in a general holiday context.[2]

Of course, distribution of food among celebrants is a fairly obvious way of expressing a festive mood, as seen for example in the book of Samuel: "He then distributed a ring of bread, a share of meat, and a cake of raisins to all the people – to all the multitudes of Israel, every single man and woman" (II Sam. 6:19). However, the specific terminology of *mishloaḥ manot* is used in the Bible only in Esther and Nehemiah. The fact that both of these works take place in the Persian era may well indicate that this practice was a standard method of celebration in the Persian milieu.

Thus, it is not surprising that many have identified this practice, and even the holiday of Purim in general, with Persian celebrations. A number of different holidays have been suggested,[3] most prominently Nowruz, the Persian New Year festival, which takes place at the vernal equinox,[4] a time when it was customary to send portions of sweet foods

1 Alter Hilevitz, *Ḥikkrei Zemanim*, vol. 1 (Jerusalem: Mossad HaRav Kook, 1976), 14–15. See also Refael Kook, *Kehunat Refael* (Jerusalem, 2008), 147.

2 See David Henshke, *Festival Joy in Tannaitic Discourse* (Jerusalem: Magnes Press, 2007), 39, note 68.

3 A.W. Streane, *Cambridge Bible for Schools and Colleges – Esther* (Cambridge: Cambridge University Press, 1907), 67–68; Adele Berlin, *The JPS Bible Commentary – Esther* (Philadelphia: Jewish Publication Society, 2001), xlvi; Dan Shapira, "Judaeo-Persian Translations of Old Persian Lexica: A Case of Linguistic Discontinuity," in Ludwig Paul, ed., *Persian Origins – Early Judaeo-Persian and the Emergence of New Persian* (Wiesbaden: Harrassowitz Verlag, 2003), 231.

4 Carey Moore, *The Anchor Bible – Esther* (Garden City, NY: Doubleday and Company, 1971), xlvii; Lewis Patton, ed., *The International Critical Commentary – The Book of Esther* (Edinburgh: T & T Clark, 1976), 85.

to others.[5] This Persian holiday can be connected to both biblical mentions of *mishloaḥ manot.* Since it is a Persian New Year celebration, it can be connected to the celebration of the new year in Nehemiah; and in terms of when it is celebrated, it falls around the time of Purim. This connection is, in fact, found in a note in the traditional *Daat Mikra* commentary.[6]

However, although they may have certain practices in common, one should not mistake Purim for a Jewish version of a Persian holiday. From Nehemiah we see that *mishloaḥ manot* were considered a standard component of holiday celebrations in Persian times, and not exclusively associated with the celebration of Purim. Thus, when explaining to the Jewish people that the first day of the seventh month is to be treated as a festive day, it is reasonable that a description of these festivities would include elements of Persian culture associated with expressions of joy. So too with Purim: Since it was established as a festival during the Persian era, the festivities are described in a manner acceptable and reasonable for that time and place. It was not a celebration based on a Persian holiday; it is a Jewish holiday that used local contemporary expressions of joy and festivity.[7]

Over time, as Jews settled among other cultures in different times, concepts of holiday celebrations adapted and changed. However, the ruling to celebrate Purim by sending *mishloaḥ manot,* as required in Esther 9:22 and codified by the Sages, continued to be observed. Taken out of its original Persian context where this was a standard holiday practice, it became more ritualized and associated specifically with the holiday of Purim, so that the *mishloaḥ manot* mentioned in Nehemiah, chapter 8, could seem strange, as they are connected to an entirely different holiday there.[8] Yet both these instances of *mishloaḥ manot* originated

5 Abraham Yahuda, *Ever VaArev* (New York: Shulsinger Bros., 1946), 91.

6 Mordechai Zer-Kavod, *Daat Mikra: Ezra Neḥemya* (Jerusalem: Mossad HaRav Kook, 1994), 106, note 13*. The reference given there is to Abraham Yahuda, *Ever VaArev*; see above note.

7 Yahuda, *Ever VaArev*, 91.

8 See David Henshke, *Festival Joy in Tannaitic Discourse* (Jerusalem: Magnes Press, 2007), 37–40. Note that Hizkiya da Silva, the *Pri Ḥadash* (1659–98) states that he would in fact send *mishloaḥ manot* to poor people before Rosh HaShana based on

the same way, as an expression of festivity that Jews living in a Persian world were very familiar with.

## JUMPING OVER FIRE

Another example of this phenomenon can be found in Purim itself. The Talmud in Sanhedrin 64b records an unusual Purim custom while describing the idolatrous Molekh worship, which involved children passing through fire. There are two opinions as to how Molekh worship was performed: "Abaye said: There was a loose pile of bricks in the middle, and fire on either side of it. Rava said: It was like the leaping about on Purim." Rashi explains that according to Rava, a pit was dug and a bonfire was lit inside, and children leaped over it. Apparently this was something that Jews did on Purim, with no connection to Molekh worship. The practice is described in greater detail in the eleventh-century dictionary of Aramaic, *Arukh*. "It is a custom in Babylonia and Elam that young lads make a dummy of Haman and hang it from their roofs for four or five days. On Purim they make a bonfire and throw the dummy into it and they stand around and sing. And they have a ring hanging in the fire and they hang on it and jump from one side of the fire to the other."[9]

This unusual custom recalls the Chahar Shanbeh Suri, which was on the Wednesday before Nowruz, when children jumped over bonfires to ensure a lucky new year.[10] The practice took place a little before the

---

the verses in Nehemiah, *Oraḥ Ḥayim* 581:4. For a discussion of the possible halakhic obligation to give *mishloaḥ manot* on Rosh HaShana, see Shemtob Gaguine, *Keter Shem Tov*, vol. 6 (London: Shraga, 1955), 60; Yosef Cohen, *Sefer Vayeshev Yosef* printed in *BeKaneh Eḥad*, vol. 3 (Ashdod, 2016), 248, *siman* 38.

9 Natan ben Yeḥiel, *Sefer HaArukh* (Tel Aviv), 551. Note that according to the *Arukh* the lads jumped over the bonfire using the ring; they did not just wave the ring back and forth over the fire as found in Israel Abrahams, *The Book of Delight and Other Papers* (Philadelphia, 1912), 266, and J. G. Frazer, *The Golden Bough*, vol. 9 (Cambridge: Cambridge University Press, 1913), 393. The Aramaic term for this is *mashvarta d'Puriah*; *shavar* means "to jump."

10 William Crump, *Encyclopedia of New Year's Holidays Worldwide* (Jefferson, NC: McFarland, 2008), 120. Celebrations involving bonfires, including passing children through fire for good luck, have also been associated with European summer pagan rituals from the Middle Ages into the eighteenth century; see Jeffrey Kacirk, *Forgotten English* (New York: Quill, 1997), 39. See also the discussion of bonfires on Lag

vernal equinox and was something Jews living in Persia would have seen happening among their neighbors close to Purim. Although children jumping over bonfires seems to the modern mind to be an unusual and possibly inappropriate way to mark a festive occasion, for Jews living in Persia, this was a culturally appropriate way to express holiday joy. They were not celebrating Purim as a Judaized Chabar Shanbeh Suri; rather, they incorporated a local way of expressing holiday happiness into their celebration of Purim.[11]

## COSTUMES

One of the most renowned Purim customs is dressing up in costume; it is even mentioned by the Rema (*Shulḥan Arukh, Oraḥ Ḥayim* 696:8). He writes that there is no prohibition for men and women to wear clothing of the opposite gender on Purim, despite the prohibition that "a woman must not put on man's apparel, nor shall a man wear women's clothing" (Deut. 22:5). On Purim it is permitted because "the intention is only for joy." While to the casual reader it may seem that the Rema is addressing a very particular detail relating to the custom of masquerading on Purim, in fact the earliest sources that describe Jews dressing up on Purim speak of cross-dressing, and it would appear that the costumes were indeed based on this.

The earliest source to mention dressing up on Purim is found in a book of *musar, Even Boḥen*, by Klonymus ben Klonymus, who lived from 1286 to sometime in the early 1300s. He was born in France, but traveled in Europe, writing *Even Boḥen* while in Spain, and then moving to Italy.[12] There he criticizes various forms of Purim excess, including men dressing up in women's dresses and jewelry.[13]

---

BaOmer in Shlomo Zevin, *HaMoadim BeHalakha* (Jerusalem: Machon HaTalmud HaYisraeli HaShalem, 1980), 363.

11 See Daniel Sperber, *Minhagei Yisrael*, vol. 1 (Jerusalem: Mossad HaRav Kook, 1989), 16–18 for other possible origins of the custom to jump over a bonfire on festival occasions, all based on external cultural influences.

12 See the extensive biography in A. Haberman, ed., *Even Boḥen* (Tel Aviv: Machbaroth Lesifrut Publishing House, 1956), 170–87.

13 Haberman, *Even Boḥen*, 30.

The earliest positive view of this practice is found in the responsa of Rabbi Yehuda Minz (Mahari Minz, c. 1405–1508). He was born in Germany, but moved to Italy where he was the rabbi of Paua for forty-seven years. He discusses the practice of people wearing masks and cross-dressing on Purim and writes that he saw this growing up among the children of saintly people, and it is permitted, as the biblical prohibition does not apply if the intent is for joy and not licentiousness.[14] He compares it to the stealing of food that youngsters would engage in on Purim, which is not prosecuted as it is considered part of the Purim fun.[15] This is the standard defense of the practice, and it is the authority the Rema quotes in the *Shulḥan Arukh*, although dissenting stricter views are presented in the *Taz* (*Yoreh De'ah* 182:3) and the *Mishna Berura* (696:30).

Many sources indicate that what really should be worn on Purim are festive clothes. The Maharil would wear Shabbat clothing on Purim,[16] a practice the Rema included in his *Darkhei Moshe* (*Oraḥ Ḥayim* 695:1) and in his glosses to the *Shulḥan Arukh* (*Oraḥ Ḥayim* 695:2): "There are those who are accustomed to wear Shabbat and Yom Tov clothes on Purim, and this is correct."[17] Rabbi Eliya Shapira (1660–1712), in his *Eliya Rabba,* explains that the reason we change into "important clothing" on Purim may be to remind us that Mordekhai wore royal clothing (Est. 8:15). This practice is also represented in Sephardic authorities, for example in the *Ben Ish Ḥai.*[18] All this indicates that cross-dressing, and costumes in general, on Purim was a folk custom that some rabbinic authorities tried to justify, but the actual rabbinically prescribed attire was Shabbat clothing.

---

14 Note that in anthropological studies a similar distinction is made between transvestism, "the practice of wearing the clothing of the opposite sex for emotional or sexual expression," and cross-dressing, which is done "to make a comment on society or to entertain." See Attila Kiss, ed., *The Iconography of the Fantastic: Eastern and Western Traditions of European Iconography* 2 (Szeged: University of Szeged, 2002), 301.

15 *She'elot UTeshuvot Mahari Minz* (Munkacs, 1898), *siman* 17, 80b–82b.

16 S. Spitzer, ed., *Sefer Maharil* (Jerusalem: Machon Yerushalayim, 1989), 426, *siman* 9.

17 Regarding the distinction between Shabbat clothes and Yom Tov clothes on Purim, see Eliakim Devoraks, *BeShvilei HaMinhag – Shabbat UMoadim*, vol. 3 (Jerusalem, 1998), 123–25.

18 Yosef Hayim of Baghdad, *Sefer Ben Ish Ḥai* (Baghdad, 1902), year 1, *Tetzaveh* 22, 48a.

Why did the earliest sources to mention costumes on Purim talk specifically about the problematic practice of cross-dressing? Note that in these early sources no reason is given for wearing costumes on Purim, other than that it was an expression of joy. Only much later would explanations be offered for wearing costumes on Purim,[19] and even these do not address cross-dressing specifically. Why was cross-dressing seen by some as an acceptable expression of joy and festivity? The reason is that this is the way Gentiles celebrated some of their own festive occasions. The Roman festivities of Kalends, the beginning of a new month, included "men imitating women in dress and behavior," reported by Asterius of Amasea in the fourth century CE.[20] Kalends was "most unusually, celebrated Empire wide, in town and countryside alike."[21] Similar practices were associated with the Roman festivals of Saturnalia and Consualia.[22] The practice persisted into the Middle Ages, becoming associated with carnival settings.[23]

This origin of Purim costumes has been noted by some rabbinic authorities. For example, Rabbi Shemtob Gaguine writes that "it is an inheritance from the Italian Jews ... who inherited it from the Romans."[24] Based on this, some authorities characterized Purim costumes as *ḥukkot hagoyim*, a prohibited Gentile practice.[25] On the other hand, despite evidence to the contrary, some rabbinic authorities claimed that

---

19 See Shmuel Gelbard, *Otzar Taamei HaMinhagim* (Petach Tikva: Mifal Rashi, 1996), 341–42 and Eliakim Devoraks, *BeShvilei HaMinhag – Shabbat UMoadim*, vol. 2 (Jerusalem, 1997), 176, where many reasons are given, all dating long after the *Shulḥan Arukh*.

20 Lucy Grig, *Popular Culture in the Ancient World* (Cambridge: Cambridge University Press, 2017), 242.

21 Ibid., 237.

22 Christian Roy, *Traditional Festivals: A Multicultural Encyclopedia*, vol. 1 (Santa Barbara: ABC-CLIO, 2005), 425.

23 Daniel Pigg, "Imagining Urban Life and Its Discontents," in Albrecht Classen, ed., *Urban Space in the Middle Ages and the Early Modern Age* (Berlin: Walter de Gruyter, 2009), 398. See also Rudolf Dekker and Lotte van de Pol, *The Tradition of Female Cross-Dressing in Early Modern Europe* (London: Macmillan, 1989), 7.

24 Shemtob Gaguine, *Keter Shem Tov*, vol. 2 (London, 1934), 545, note 622. See there, where he writes that "in London and Amsterdam this matter [wearing costumes] has been completely forgotten" (!).

25 See Reuven Kamil, *Shaar Reuven*, vol. 1 (Jerusalem, 2006), 206, *siman* 18, note 22.

costumes began as a Jewish custom which was then taken on by Gentiles.[26]

Cross-dressing was part of a larger festive theme of "topsy-turvydom," or role reversal. Part of the Roman Saturnalia was the election of a "mock king" who set the rules for that day, a practice recorded even before the destruction of the Second Temple. This would later lead to the medieval festival figures of the Lord of the Revels, the Lord of Misrule, the Abbot of Fools, and others.[27] Other aspects of "social inversion" associated with these celebrations were slaves "given temporary liberty to do as they liked."[28] In keeping with the theme of "the world turned upside down" was "cross-dressing, men dressed as women, or, more crudely, as clothes worn back to front, often indecently revealing parts of the body."[29]

Additionally, these festivals were a time for satire, poking fun at authority figures and making skits. Slaves were allowed to speak insolently to their masters, and were even invited to do so.[30] We have records of early Christian authorities writing against these activities in the fourth century CE.[31] Through "a controlled and provisional reversal of social norms," these celebrations "actually reinforced the existing roles and boundaries."[32]

26 Avraham Horvitz, *Orḥot Rabbeinu HaKehillot Yaakov*, vol. 3 (Bnei Brak, 1998), 60, *siman* 104. See also the online Ask the Rabbi column: ḥttp://www.yesḥiva.co/ask/?id=4869, where costumes are considered "an ancient Jewish custom" that "you cannot disapprove of" (July 2017).

27 John Aubrey, *Remains of Gentilism and Judaism, 1686–87* (London: Satchell, Peyton and Co., 1881), 122; Samuel L. Macey, *Patriarchs of Time* (Athens, GA: University of Georgia Press, 2010), 122–23.

28 Timothy Insoll, *Case Studies in Archaeology and World Religion* (Cambridge, 1999), 178.

29 Francoise Piponnier and Perrine Mane, *Dress in the Middle Ages* (New Haven: Yale University Press, 1997), 142–43.

30 John Clarke, *Looking at Laughter: Humor, Power and Transgression in Roman Visual Culture* (Berkley: University of California Press, 2007), 20.

31 Lucy Grig, *Popular Culture in the Ancient World* (Cambridge: Cambridge University Press, 2017), 242.

32 Filippo Carla-Uhink, "Between the Human and the Divine: Cross-dressing and Transgender Dynamics in the Graeco-Roman World," in *TransAntiquity: Cross-Dressing and Transgender Dynamics in the Ancient World* (London: Routledge, 2017), 15.

It is easy to see how these practices from the local culture became integrated into the Purim festivities, when "the opposite happened (ונהפוך הוא) and the Jews got their enemies in their power" (Est. 9:1). Besides costumes, other traditions such as the "Purim Rav" who heads the yeshiva for a day,[33] children taking over the leadership positions in the synagogue,[34] Purim plays poking fun at authority figures,[35] and even the contemporary practice of schoolchildren making rules that teachers must follow are all Purim versions of the mock king and general social inversion of Roman and medieval celebrations.

Since these kinds of celebrations were widespread in Christian countries, and there are no Muslim traditions of wearing costumes on festivals, they had much less impact on Sephardic Jews, particularly those who lived outside Europe, in North Africa.[36] Rabbi Ovadia Yosef wrote against cross-dressing on Purim, as well as the "custom that has spread recently" to appoint a "Purim Rav" and make satirical plays.[37] These kinds of activities were not associated with joy and festivity for Sephardic Jews, because they were not exposed to the same cultural practices.

## CONCLUSION

Purim is a festive holiday. The question of how to express a festive spirit depends on the cultural context that Jews are familiar with. When it came to Purim joy, Jews naturally chose to express their happiness in ways that festivity was expressed in the broader society of their time and place. This was so from the very beginning with the custom of *mishloaḥ manot,* and continued with costumes. Note that the Purim custom of jumping over fire was mentioned in the Talmud as a way to describe Molekh worship, yet it was deemed appropriate for Purim when it was taken out of the context of idolatry and performed "just for fun." This is the same reasoning that was applied to cross-dressing

33 J. D. Eisenstein, *Otzar Dinim UMinhagim* (New York, 1917), 337.

34 See Yospe Shammash, *Minhagim of the Worms Community* (Jerusalem: Machon Yerushalayim, 1988), *siman* 224, 265–67, where the children took over the synagogue on the Shabbat after Purim.

35 Simha Rabinowitz, *Piskei Teshuvot,* vol. 6 (Jerusalem, 1997), 696:14, 601.

36 *Torat Imekha: Ḥodesh Adar VePurim,* number 8, 2.

37 *Yeḥaveh Daat* 5:50.

on Purim: it is biblically prohibited, but leniencies can be found when it is classified as an expression of joy. Cultural context continues to impact Purim, for example, in the choice of costumes depicting figures from literature and pop culture, which are remarkably similar to the kinds of outfits Gentiles wear in their celebrations today that call for costumes of their own.

*Chapter 14*

# The *Bedikat Ḥametz* Kit: Wax Candle, Wooden Spoon, and Feather

In this chapter we will trace the development and significance of each element of the *bedikat ḥametz* kit commonly used today: the wax candle, wooden spoon, and feather.

## WAX CANDLE

The Mishna (Pesaḥim 1:1) speaks about checking for *ḥametz* "by the light of the candle." The Talmud in Pesaḥim 7b–8a provides verses to demonstrate that searching should be done by candlelight, and that candlelight is superior to sunlight, moonlight, and torchlight. Although it was suggested among the *Rishonim* that an oil lamp may cast better light for searching, the Raavad,[1] the Rosh,[2] and Rabbeinu Yeruḥam[3] all rule that it is best to use a wax candle for searching. This is because it is assumed that people would not search so thoroughly with an oil or tallow candle as they are difficult to use for checking in narrow crevices, as well as not wanting the oil or fat to drip on their household utensils. The use of a wax candle was codified in the *Tur* and the *Shulḥan Arukh* (*Oraḥ Ḥayim* 433:2), and is therefore the most basic, and well-attested, element of a *bedikat ḥametz* kit.[4]

## WOODEN SPOON

Rabbi Yaakov Moelin (the Maharil, 1365–1427) writes that if one did not find any *ḥametz* during one's search, one should at least burn the utensil that was used during the search in order to have a "remembrance of burning."[5] This is based on the proposition raised in Pesaḥim 7a that it would be plausible to wait to nullify the *ḥametz* at the sixth hour, which Rashi writes is theoretically a foolproof time, since nobody would be negligent and forget to nullify then. Rashi explains that since people are burning their *ḥametz* at that time, they will be reminded to nullify it as well. The Maharil asks, How can we be so sure that burning is taking place at that time? Perhaps all the *ḥametz* was consumed or destroyed earlier? He concludes that either a little *ḥametz* was always left over to burn at the later time,[6] or that even if there was no *ḥametz*, a vessel would be burned at that time.[7] This vessel is described by the Maharil as a bowl (קערה).[8]

1 *Kol Bo, siman* 48.
2 *Tur, Oraḥ Ḥayim* 433:2.
3 *Bayit Ḥadash, Oraḥ Ḥayim* 433:4, *vekatav*.
4 Mystical and homiletical reasons were also given for using wax candles specifically; see Simha Rabinovitch, *Piskei Teshuvot*, vol. 5 (Jerusalem, 1995), 12, note 4.
5 Shlomo Spitzer, *Sefer Maharil* (Jerusalem: Machon Yerushalayim, 1989), 40, *siman* 8.
6 This is his explanation for the custom to specifically put out *ḥametz* to be found during *bedikat ḥametz*, in order to have something to burn the next day.
7 Yitzhak Seff, ed., *She'elot UTeshuvot Maharil HaḤadashot* (Jerusalem: Machon Yerushalayim, 1991), 58, *siman* 48.
8 *She'elot UTeshuvot Maharil HaḤadashot*, 58, *siman* 48.

Use of a bowl for collecting the *ḥametz* during the *bedika* is found in illustrated Haggadot even before the time of the Maharil, dating back to the early 1300s.[9] However, only once the Maharil recommended burning the bowl do we find an illustration of people using specifically a broken bowl for *bedikat ḥametz,* as it would be destroyed anyway.[10] This avoids the prohibition of *bal tashḥit,* destroying a perfectly good utensil, as noted by Rabbi Yaakov Hayim Sofer.[11]

The idea of burning the bowl in which the *ḥametz* was collected was included in the notes to Rabbi Issac Tirnau's *Sefer HaMinhagim.*[12] Rabbi Moshe Isserles mentions this idea of the Maharil in *Darkhei Moshe* (*Oraḥ Ḥayim* 432:2) and in the *Shulḥan Arukh* (*Oraḥ Ḥayim* 445:3). Not everyone accepted this approach. *Peri Ḥadash* comments that "there is no reason or support for this," and *Arukh HaShulḥan* (*Oraḥ Ḥayim* 445:11) similarly writes that since we customarily put out *ḥametz* to find and later burn, there is no need to burn a utensil. Despite these detractors, it was customary to burn the utensil in which the *ḥametz* was collected along with the *ḥametz* itself.[13]

Although some modern works, particularly Sephardic ones, still refer to using a bowl for *bedikat ḥametz,*[14] nowadays wooden bowls

---

9 Daniel Sperber, *Minhagei Yisrael,* vol. 7 (Jerusalem: Mossad HaRav Kook, 2003), 175.

10 Ibid., 170, 174. See there for the idea that once it became customary to use ten pieces of *ḥametz* for the *bedika* there would always be something to burn whatever the case, and the burning of the bowls was less prominent.

11 *Kaf HaḤayim* 432:32.

12 Shlomo Spitzer, ed., *Sefer HaMinhagim LeRabbeinu Isaac Tirnau* (Jerusalem: Mossad HaRav Kook, 2000), 36–37. On the authorship of these notes, see 17–18 of the introduction.

13 See Hayim Yehuda Deitch, *Seder Haggada shel Pesaḥ: Kol Yehuda* (Satmar, 1937), 5–6, where the Belzer Rebbe explained that since the spoon and feather came into contact with *ḥametz* it makes sense that they should be burned. He gives a homiletic explanation as to why the candle is burned as well.

14 For example, see the instructions in Yitzhak Ben-Shushan, *BeFi Yesharim – Haggada shel Pesaḥ* (Rishon LeZion: Agudat Maḥzikei Torah Etz HaḤayim, 1986), 105; *Ishei Yisrael – Nisan* (Bnei Brak: Kollel Rabbeinu HaAri, 1997), 189; Ephraim Oved, *Haggada shel Pesaḥ* (Bnei Brak, 2004), 20; Yosef Hayim Mizrahi, *Od Yosef Ḥai* (Jerusalem, 2005), 36; *Haggada shel Pesaḥ – Shaar Binyamin* (Machon Shaar Binyamin, 2013), 34. Regarding the Sephardic custom to have salt in the bowl, see Avner Afjin, *Divrei Shalom,* vol. 4 (Rosh HaAyin, 2003), 493; Bentzion Mutzfi, *Shivat Tziyon – Shabbat,*

are not a very common household item, certainly not as common and inexpensive as a wooden spoon. Because of this, the spoon has taken over the role of the utensil burned along with the *ḥametz*. Since there is no way to make a wooden spoon used for cooking *ḥametz* kosher for Passover, it would have to be destroyed anyway before the festival, so there was no financial loss involved in using it for *bedikat ḥametz* as well.[15] However, since a shallow spoon is not as effective as a bowl for collecting and storing *ḥametz*, another item, usually a bag of some sort, was added to actually hold the *ḥametz*,[16] relegating the spoon to having almost no functionality and having only ceremonial value at this point.

The current ceremonial role of the wooden spoon can be seen in the book of Chabad customs, *Sefer HaMinhagim*. There, the instructions for *bedikat ḥametz* say that one is to "check by the light of a wax candle, and with a bird's feather. The checker places the *ḥametz* that he finds in a small paper bag. When he finishes checking for *ḥametz*, this bag, the feather, and the remnant of the candle, if there is any, are placed in the hollow of a wooden spoon, and then it is all wrapped in paper (except the handle of the spoon, which remains unwrapped)," which is then tied shut.[17] The spoon is not used for actually checking the *ḥametz*. Similarly, contemporary guides to Jewish observance written for laypeople struggle to find a role for the wooden spoon. For example, "a feather [is used] to brush the *ḥametz* into a wooden spoon, with which they scoop the discovered *ḥametz* into a napkin for disposal."[18] Note that there is nothing that the spoon actually does in these descriptions that could not be accomplished by the napkin or paper bag already in use.

---

vol. 1 (Jerusalem, 2005), *Yoshev Tziyon*, 17; Yitzchak Chazzan, *She'elot UTeshuvot Yeḥaveh Daat*, vol. 3 (Jerusalem: Otiot, 2008), "Customs of Morocco," 36.

15 Yitzhak Lieberman, *Sefer Ḥag HaMatzot – Halakhot UMinhagim* (Bnei Brak, 2003), 138, note 31*.

16 Nissan David Dubnow, *Eḥad Mi Yode'a* (Tzfat: Chish, 2008), 117.

17 *Sefer HaMinhagim* (Brooklyn: Kehot Publication Society, 1993), 37, first published in 1966.

18 Wayne Dosick, *Living Judaism: The Complete Guide to Jewish Belief, Tradition and Practice* (New York: HarperOne, 1995), 165. So too in Mordechai Becher, *Gateway to Judaism* (New York: Shaar Press, 2005), 204: "He brushes it into a wooden spoon using a feather, then transfers the pieces into a paper bag."

In modern times, as the wooden spoon became more ceremonial and less functional, homiletical explanations were offered for its presence. Rabbi Shaul Brach, the Kashoer Rav (1865–1940) brings two such explanations.[19] He states that the spoon (כף) hints to "the fruit of your labors (יגיע כפיך)" (Ps. 128:2), referring to work done throughout the year. Wood (עץ) has the same numerical value as money (כסף). Burning the wooden spoon is a symbolic representation of the idea that all our prosperity comes from God rather than from our own efforts. He also states that there is a connection between destroying *ḥametz* and destroying Amalek, and the wooden spoon hints to the destruction of Amalek through the raised hands (כף) of Moses, and through being hanged on the tree (עץ) that Haman had prepared.[20] Rabbi Yehoshua Zev Zaffrin (d. 1996), a member of the inner circle of the Bobover Rebbe, Rabbi Shlomo Halberstam, explained that the word for spoon, *kaf*, recalls the idea of *kefia* (כפיה), to be forced. Here it teaches that we must force ourselves to check thoroughly for *ḥametz* even though it can be very burdensome to do so.[21]

The use of a wooden spoon is particularly prominent in hasidic writings, where it is reported, for example, that in 1955 the Belzer Rebbe would not begin *bedikat ḥametz* until he had a wooden spoon.[22]

---

19 Shaul Brach, *Tov Devarkha* (Munkacs, 1940), 2b, *siman* 3.

20 Although he brings both explanations in his book *Tov Devarkha*, only the second one is mentioned in *Yalkut Moadei Kodshekha – Pesaḥ* (Kahal Ittav Lev, 2006), 89, and Chaim Ben-Zion Folger, *Shevaḥ Pesaḥ* (Monsey, NY: Eastern Book Press, 2013), 173.

21 Folger, *Shevaḥ Pesaḥ*, 173; Aharon Pelov, *Otzroteihem shel Tzaddikim*, vol. 2 (Jerusalem, 2012), 625. See *Tosafot*, Pesaḥim 4b *himnuhu*, for the idea that checking for *ḥametz* is particularly burdensome. It is also reported that in 1973 the Bobover Rebbe, Shlomo Halberstam, explained that everything must have a vessel prepared to receive it, and the hidden *ḥametz* can be found only if there is a vessel prepared for it, in this case the spoon. *Haggada shel Pesaḥ – Beit Tzaddikim* (Monsey: Eastern Book Press, 2003), 162, note 24. See also Moshe Deutsch, *Or Ganuz*, vol. 2 (London, 1996), 74, *siman* 3, where a hint to using a spoon for the ten pieces of *ḥametz* is found in Numbers 7:14: "one *kaf* of ten."

22 Aharon Pollack, *Beito Naaveh Kodesh*, vol.1 (Bnei Brak: Machon Zichron Aharon, 1999), 272–73.

Another popular reason given for the custom to use a wooden spoon is based on the opinion of Rabbi Yehuda in Pesaḥim 27b, which is that the destruction of *ḥametz* must be accomplished specifically by burning it, as he compares it to *notar*, leftover sacrifices, that must be burned. Rabbi Shmuel Strashun (the Rashash, 1794–1872) explains that since *notar* must be burned with wood, it follows that according to Rabbi Yehuda, *ḥametz* must also be burned with wood, rather than, for example, pouring fuel on the *ḥametz* and setting it alight.[23] The wooden spoon is thus employed during *bedikat ḥametz* to ensure that there is wood burned along with the *ḥametz*. The first to make this connection seems to have been Rabbi Eliezer Zvi Zigelman in his book *Naḥalei Emuna*, published in 1935,[24] and it has since been repeated in many places.[25]

This does not, however, appear to have been the original reason for the custom, as the concept found in the Maharil preceded the innovative notion of the Rashash by a few centuries, and the idea of connecting the opinion of the Rashash to the wooden spoon is of very recent vintage.[26] It may be that this explanation originated only after bowls were no longer used, in order to explain the use of the wooden spoon, which we have noted has very limited functional value in the *bedika*.

### FEATHER

Rabbi Avraham Gombiner (*Magen Avraham*, 1635–82) is the first authority to mention feathers as a component of *bedikat ḥametz*. Commenting

23 Rashah, Shabbat 66a, *kaveret*.

24 Eliezer Zvi Zigelman, *Naḥalei Emuna* (Lublin, 1935), 37. Zigelman is best known for his books collecting hasidic teachings and stories, *Ohel Emuna* (1909) and *Beit Tzaddik* (1910). The book *Ḥok LeYisrael* by Yisrael Waltz is often given as a source for this explanation, but although this book was published in Budapest in 1927, and later in 1930 and 1950, the explanation was included only in much later editions; see Yisrael Waltz, *Ḥok LeYisrael* (Jerusalem, 1974), 38, note 33.

25 Shmuel Gelbard, *Otzar Taamei HaMinhagim* (Petach Tikvah: Mifal Rashi, 1996), 271; Gavriel Zinner, *Nitei Gavriel: Hilkhot Pesaḥ*, vol. 1 (Jerusalem: Shemesh, 2002), 74, note 19. See also Yisrael Dandroivitch, "Are We Really Not Fulfilling the Commandment to Burn *Ḥametz*?" [Hebrew], *Moriah* vols. 10–12 (2016), 304.

26 See also Yitzhak Weiss, *Minḥat Yitzḥak*, vol. 2 (Jerusalem, 1993), 106, *siman* 53, where he writes that the innovative idea of Rashash, that wood is needed for burning *ḥametz*, is a "very big stringency" (חומרא גדולה).

on the ruling of the Rema (*Oraḥ Ḥayim* 433:11) that all areas that may have had *ḥametz* in them must be cleaned prior to *bedikat ḥametz*, he writes, "Therefore it is customary to take feathers and clean."[27] Although the cleaning referred to by the Rema takes place prior to *bedikat ḥametz*, the feathers are still a valuable tool during *bedikat ḥametz* for cleaning up any remaining *ḥametz*.[28] *Magen Avraham* is quoted in *Mishna Berura* (*Oraḥ Ḥayim* 433:46), although feathers were used for *bedikat ḥametz* hundreds of years before *Magen Avraham* mentioned the practice, as can be seen in illustrations of *bedikat ḥametz* going back to the 1400s.[29]

Some sources, particularly hasidic sources, are very specific about the use of the feather. We find reports that three feathers should be taken and be held in the right hand,[30] or that feathers from the chickens of *kapparot* should be used.[31] On the other hand, the Vizhnitzer Rav (Rabbi Mordekhai Hager, Monsey) explained that taking feathers for *bedikat ḥametz* is a new innovation, and actually it is simply the ויש פעדערין, a small broom made with feathers used for cleaning year round.[32] In an illustrated fifteenth-century Haggada, the person doing *bedikat ḥametz* is shown holding a bundle of feathers, like a feather duster without a handle.[33] For this reason, while using a feather is very popular among many Jewish communities, it is not customary among Yemenites[34] or

27 *Magen Avraham, Oraḥ Ḥayim* 433:21.

28 *Ḥok Yaakov* (433:25) (Berlin, 1767), points out that while a feather may be fine to remove crumbs from cracks and crevices during *bedikat ḥametz*, to actually clean the house for *ḥametz*, a large, broomlike cleaning implement made of large feathers bound together should be used.

29 Daniel Sperber, *Minhagei Yisrael*, vol. 7 (Jerusalem: Mossad HaRav Kook, 2003), 167–68, 174; Avraham Maimon, *Brit Avraham* (2005), 273.

30 Yosef Weinberger, *Edut BeYehosef* (Bnei Brak, 2006), 91; Chaim Ben-Zion Folger, *Shevaḥ Pesaḥ* (Monsey, NY: Eastern Book Press, 2013), 173.

31 See *Orḥot HaToldot Rav Mordekhai Eliyahu Sluschitz* (2011), 19, *siman* 4. Sluschitz (1912–66) was a rabbinic and communal figure in Jerusalem. See David Tidhar, *Encyclopedia of the Founders and Builders of Israel*, vol. 16 (Tel Aviv, 1997), 4960 [Hebrew].

32 Weinberger, *Edut BeYehosef*, 91, note 17. He is reported to have said this in 2002. See also Yehuda Taub, *Otzar HaHalakhot – Pesaḥ*, part 1 (Jerusalem, 1983), 154, note 145, where the feathers are described as a kind of broom.

33 Daniel Sperber, *Minhagei Yisrael*, vol. 7 (Jerusalem: Mossad HaRav Kook, 2003), 174.

34 Yitzhak Ratzabi, *Shulḥan Arukh HaMekutzar – Oraḥ Ḥayim*, vol. 3 (Bnei Brak, 2001), 8, *siman* 81:8.

Moroccans,[35] where small feather brooms were not popular cleaning implements.

Clearly, although the feather is not considered integral to the *bedika*, it does serve a strictly functional purpose.[36] Although E. E. Hoag is considered the first person to bind turkey feathers to a short broom handle, creating the feather duster in 1870,[37] and Susan Hibbard's design for mass-produced feather dusters was granted a patent in 1876,[38] feathers were used for cleaning long before the commercial feather duster was invented, particularly for items which "any harsh substance would injure."[39] For example, feathers as cleaning tools were documented in the fourteenth-century work *The Good Wife's Guide*,[40] and goose feathers are included by the Rema in a list of examples of soft cleaning tools (*Oraḥ Ḥayim* 337:2), without any connection to Passover.

Since the feather was originally used simply as a mechanism to sweep up the *ḥametz*, it is not unusual to find sources which refer to additional items employed during the *bedika* for cleaning, such as a rag,[41] a brush, or even a knife or screwdriver to remove *ḥametz* from cracks.[42]

In recent times, because using feathers for general cleaning is uncommon, more homiletic explanations have appeared for the use of a feather during *bedikat ḥametz*. For example, since the feather is

---

35 Yitzhak Chazzan, *Ko LeḤai – Haggada shel Pesaḥ* (Jerusalem: Alfa, 1986), 40, *Bedikat Ḥametz, siman* 4, note 2, "In Morocco there are no set customs regarding this."

36 Arye Forta, *Examining Religions: Judaism* (Oxford: Heinemann Educational, 1995), 49; Gamliel Rabinowitz, *Gam Ani Odekha – Responsa of Rabbi Yisrael Pesah Feinhandler* (Bnei Brak, 2016), 233, *siman* 129:4; Yosef David Weingarten, *Darkhei Horaa*, vol. 7 (Jerusalem, 2006), 42, *siman* 5:3.

37 Robert McClain Corbit, *History of Jones County, Iowa*, vol. 1 (Chicago: S. J. Clarke, 1910), 477.

38 Mary Ellen Snodgrass, *Encyclopedia of Kitchen History* (New York: Fitzroy Dearborn, 2004), 124.

39 Thomas Webster, *An Encyclopedia of Domestic Economy* (New York: Harper and Brothers, 1845), 372–73.

40 Gina L. Greco and Christine M. Rose, trans., *The Good Wife's Guide: A Medieval Household Book* (London: Cornell University Press, 2009), 220.

41 Shalom Gross, *Afiat Matza HaShalem* (Jerusalem, 1983), 10, chapter 6, *siman* 14, in the section "Customs of the *Tzaddikkim*," where this is brought as a custom of the Belzer Rebbe.

42 Yehuda Teshenzer, *Shaarei Yemei HaPesaḥ* (Ofakim, 2008), 38, *siman* 18.

an object of negligible value and smells bad when burned, as noted in Rashi on Leviticus 1:17, quoting Leviticus Rabba 3:5, the use of a feather teaches that even lowly items can be elevated when used properly to fulfill God's will.[43] It has also been suggested that the feather reminds us that we can soar to great heights, or conversely, that we burn a chicken feather to indicate that we should not act like "chickens pecking in trash" (Avoda Zara 4b), spending their time bringing impurity to different places.[44]

### THE CURRENT SITUATION

We have seen that explanations regarding these items and instructions for their use are found especially in hasidic works, and many sources refer to these three elements as a hasidic custom,[45] probably because Hasidim are particularly careful not to change earlier practices. Even so, in the wider Jewish community as well, the wax candle, wooden spoon, and feather are regarded as the normative components of *bedikat ḥametz* and can be found in stores as a kit[46] and are the subject of projects for young schoolchildren.[47]

It is interesting to note that other elements never caught on as part of the *bedikat ḥametz* kit. For example, we pointed out that some sources refer to a rag[48] that was used to tie up the *ḥametz* at the end of the *bedika* and would be burned along with the *hametz.*[49] Today, a small paper bag is used instead, which is sometimes included in the *bedikat*

43 Shimon Hershler, *Seh LaBayit* (London, 2010), 282.

44 Michael Aryeh Rand, *KeHilkhot Pesaḥ* (Ashdod, 2011), 61–62, note 25.

45 See Gross, *Afiat Matza HaShalem*, 10, chapter 6, *siman* 14, in the section "Customs of the Tzaddikkim," where this is brought as a custom of the Belzer Rebbe; Asher Waserteil, ed., *Yalkut Minhagim* (Jerusalem: Ministry of Education and Culture, 1977), in the section on hasidic customs by Tuvia Bloi, 146, 11:5.

46 Sol Scharfstein, *Understanding Jewish Holidays and Customs* (Hoboken, NJ: Ktav, 1999), 77.

47 Maxine Segal Handelman, *Jewish Every Day: The Complete Handbook for Early Childhood Teachers* (Denver: ARE Publishing, 2000), 229.

48 Israel Klopholtz and Natan Ortner, eds., *Haggada shel Pesaḥ – Midrash BeḤiddush* (Bnei Brak, 1965), 13.

49 Waserteil, *Yalkut Minhagim*, in the section on hasidic customs by Tuvia Bloi, 146, 11:5.

*ḥametz* kit. It is not considered necessarily more traditional to prefer a rag over a paper bag. Since the rag is still clearly recognized as a cleaning element with no possible symbolic or ceremonial value, it is easily excluded from *bedikat ḥametz*. This is not the case with the feather and the wooden spoon however, which by now are simply part of the ritual, irrespective of functionality. In fact, the less obviously functional an item is, the better the chances that it will remain intact as part of *bedikat ḥametz*, as it will be viewed as ceremonially important.

We also saw that some sources talk about taking along a knife for *bedikat ḥametz* in order to scrape any *ḥametz* out of cracks and crevices,[50] but this also did not catch on as a *bedikat ḥametz* kit staple, probably since walking around with a knife in the dark with children is perceived as inappropriate according to modern sensibilities.

The feather and wooden spoon began as the cleaning and collecting tools used in *bedikat ḥametz*. Today they remain part of *bedikat ḥametz* as an expression of nostalgia more than anything else.[51] This does not necessarily mean that we should take these items lightly, as the continued use of a wax candle in the dark for *bedikat ḥametz* could also be viewed as nostalgic. It is reported in the name of Rabbi Shlomo Zalman Auerbach that one may, and perhaps even should, leave the electric lights on during *bedikat ḥametz* to make it more effective.[52] Furthermore, Rabbi Auerbach ruled that while one should use a candle, because that is what the Mishna says to do, one can use a flashlight if no candles are available.[53] Despite these sensible rulings, since *bedikat ḥametz* today

50 Yitzhak Chazzan, *Ko LeḤai – Haggada shel Pesaḥ* (Jerusalem: Alfa, 1986), 40, *Bedikat Ḥametz, siman* 4, note 2.

51 Wayne Dosick, *Living Judaism: The Complete Guide to Jewish Belief, Tradition and Practice* (New York: HarperOne, 1995), 165.

52 Tuvia Prener, *Shalmei Moed* (Jerusalem, 2004), 312. See note 12 there, where it is reported that once when Rabbi Auerbach was doing *bedikat ḥametz* and a lightbulb went out, he waited to continue until it was replaced. See also Avigdor Nebenzal, *Yerushlayim BeMoadeha – Pesaḥ* (Jerusalem: Machon Keren Re'em, 2006), 32, where differing accounts are reported.

53 Tuvia Prener, *Shalmei Moed* (Jerusalem, 2004), 312; Aharon Auerbach and Yitzhak Triger, eds., *Halikhot Shlomo: Nisan-Av* (Jerusalem: Yeshivat Halikhot Shlomo, 2007), 110; see note 19.

generally comes long after the house has been thoroughly cleaned for Passover, it mainly serves a ritual and ceremonial function rather than a practical one. This being the case, a wax candle, wooden spoon, and feather are actually ideal tools for *bedikat ḥametz.*

*Chapter 15*

# "Our Salty Tears": Dipping in Salt Water at the Seder

K*arpas* is the term used in the Haggada for the vegetable which is customarily dipped in salt water at the beginning of the Seder. The *ArtScroll Youth Haggadah* states that "salt water is used instead of fancy dressing to remind us of our salty tears and sweat when we were slaves in Egypt."[1] This explanation is found in many Haggadot, both in Hebrew[2] and English,[3] and is usually the only explanation given for why

1 Nosson and Yitzchok Zev Scherman, *ArtScroll Youth Haggadah* (Brooklyn, NY: Mesorah, 1995), 14.

2 For example, Matityahu Solomon, "This Night Two Times," *Kol HaTorah* vol. 13 (Nisan, 1983), 62; Dov Goldberger, *Osim Seder – Haggada shel Pesaḥ* (Tel Aviv: Yedioth Ahronoth, 2004), 17; Shneur Zalman Havelin, *Haggada shel Pesaḥ – Shoel KeInyan* (Jerusalem: Wagshal, 2006), 29; Meir Yehuda Mandel, *Pninei Yeḥezkel* (Ashdod, 2008), 473; Nachman Wilhelm, *Haggada shel Pesaḥ – Ata Beḥartanu* (Bnei Brak, 2010), 32.

3 For example, Morris Silverman, *Passover Haggadah with Explanatory Notes and Original Readings* (Hartford, CT: Prayer Book Press, 1959), 5; Shlomo Riskin, *The Passover Haggadah* (New York: Ktav, 1983), 35; Reuven Bulka, *The Haggadah for Pesah* (Jerusalem: Machon Pri Haaretz, 1985), 22: "We also dip the vegetable in salt

we dip in salt water. However, it is generally offered without any attribution. In this chapter we will trace the development and significance of this interpretation of this Seder night custom.

## WHAT IS THE DIP?

The Mishna (Pesaḥim 10:3) speaks briefly about the first dip: "He dips the lettuce (*ḥazeret*) before he reaches the course of food." Rashi explains that the Mishna is discussing a case where a person has only a bitter vegetable to use for both the first dip and the *maror* dipped in *ḥaroset* later on.[4] The Talmud speaks of using "other vegetables" for the first dip, but does not specify which vegetables are preferable.[5] A list of appropriate vegetables was first presented by Rav Amram Gaon and developed from there.[6]

---

water, giving us a taste of the tears shed by our ancestral parents during their agonizing enslavement"; Steven Cohen and Kenneth Brander, eds., *The Yeshiva University Haggada* (New York: Student Organization of Yeshiva, 1985), 2. Shoshana Silberman, *A Family Haggadah* (Minneapolis, MN: Kar-Ben, 1987), 17: "The salt water reminds us of the tears our ancestors shed in Egypt"; Chanan Simon and Yosef Fridman, *The Why Haggadah* (New York: Beit Shammai, 1989), 17; John Levi, *A Family Haggadah* (Melbourne, Australia: Melbourne Books, 2002), 14; Berel Wein, *The Pesach Haggadah: Through the Prism of Experience and History* (New York: Shaar Press, 2004), 42: "The salt water represents the tears shed by the Jewish people"; Matthew Berkowitz, *The Lovell Haggadah* (Jerusalem: The Schechter Institute of Jewish Studies, 2008), 39; Sarah Rochel Hewitt, ed., *Beginners Passover Haggadah* (New York: National Jewish Outreach Program, 2010), 57: "The salt water is meant to remind us of the tears of the Jewish slaves." It is the only explanation brought in the Haggadot published by the Central Conference of American Rabbis, representing the Reform movement; see Alan Yoffie, *Sharing the Journey: The Haggadah for the Contemporary Family* (New York, NY: CCAR, 2012), 24; Howard Berman, *The New Union Haggadah – Revised Edition* (New York, NY: CCAR, 2014), 24. The explanation does not appear in the earlier editions of CCAR Haggadot, from 1923 and 1974.

4 Pesaḥim 114a, *metabel.*

5 Y. Pesaḥim 10:3 reports that Rav would use *tered* (beet leaves) as the first vegetable, but there is no mention that this specific vegetable is preferable for any reason. See Joseph Tabory, *The Passover Ritual Throughout the Generations* (Tel Aviv: HaKibbutz HaMeuḥad, 2002), 256–57.

6 See Heinrich Guggenheimer, *The Scholar's Haggadah* (Northvale, NJ: Jason Aronson, 1998), 228–29.

The Talmud does not explicitly mention what the vegetable is dipped into. Rav Amram Gaon suggests that the vegetable at the beginning of the Seder is dipped into *ḥaroset,* just as the *maror* is later on.[7] This opinion is followed by Rabbeinu Hananel,[8] Rashi,[9] the Rambam,[10] the Ritva,[11] Rabbeinu Nissim and many early *Rishonim.*[12] Their reasoning is that since the Talmud did not specify what dip should be used, it must be the same dip as used for *maror,* which is *ḥaroset.*[13] This seems to be have been the original custom.[14]

However, the Rashbam determined that the vegetable was not dipped in *ḥaroset,* as the *ḥaroset* was brought out only later for the *maror.*[15] This is also the opinion of Roke'aḥ, the Rosh, Rabbeinu Yona, and other *Rishonim.*[16] What, then, should the vegetable be dipped into? *Tosafot* write that Rabbeinu Tam would dip "either into vinegar or salt water."[17] In practice, it seems that the French sages used vinegar.[18] While *Tosafot* explain why *ḥaroset* should not be used, since it functions specifically to offset the bitterness of the *maror,* no explanation is given as to why vinegar or salt water in particular should be used instead. Rabbi Yosef Karo explains in *Beit Yosef* (Tur, *Oraḥ Ḥayim* 472:6), that since there is a difference of opinion whether *ḥaroset* should be used for the first dip,

7 Daniel Goldschmidt, ed., *Seder Rav Amram Gaon* (Jerusalem: Mossad HaRav Kook, 2004), 112.

8 Pesaḥim 114a, *heviyu.*

9 Pesaḥim 114a, *metabel.*

10 *Hilkhot Ḥametz UMatza* 8:2.

11 Yehuda Leibovitz, ed., *Ritva – Hilkhot Seder HaHaggada* (Jerusalem: Mossad HaRav Kook, 1983), 9.

12 Leibovitz, *Ritva – Hilkhot Seder HaHaggada,* 9, note 41. See also *Hagahot Meimoniot, Hilkhot Ḥametz UMatza* 8:3.

13 See also *Baḥ* to *Tur Oraḥ Ḥayim* 473, *uma shekatav.*

14 See Joseph Tabory, *The Passover Ritual Throughout the Generations* (Tel Aviv: HaKibbutz HaMeuḥad, 2002), 259.

15 Pesaḥim 114a, *metabel.*

16 Leibovitz., *Ritva – Hilkhot Seder HaHaggada,* 9, note 41. See also *Hagahot Meimoniot, Hilkhot Ḥametz UMatza* 8:3, where it discusses whether Rabbeinu Tam meant that one does not *have to* dip in *ḥaroset,* or that one *should not* dip in *ḥaroset.*

17 Pesaḥim 114a, *metabel.*

18 Joseph Tabory, *The JPS Commentary on the Haggadah* (Philadelphia: Jewish Publication Society, 2008), 24.

it is best to follow the approach of Rabbeinu Tam, since all agree that vinegar and salt water are acceptable. This is the opinion presented in the *Shulḥan Arukh* (*Oraḥ Ḥayim* 472:6).[19]

## SYMBOLIC EXPLANATIONS

Why use specifically salt water or vinegar? No explanation is brought in *Tosafot*, other *Rishonim* or early *Aḥaronim*. Even in the modern era, many Haggadot explain only the symbolism of the *karpas* vegetable itself and not the dip.[20]

The earliest explanation commonly quoted was offered by Rabbi Aharon Teomim (1630–90), based on a kabbalistic concept that water represents *raḥamim* (mercy) and salt represents *din* (justice).[21] This is the only explanation given in the main text of the classic work on Jewish customs, *Otzar Taamei HaMinhagim*.[22] However, it should be noted that this should not necessarily be considered the reason for the custom; rather it adds a meaningful insight about the ritual. Kabbalistic meanings were given to many mitzvot, rituals, and customs, even those with seemingly simple explanations, enriching them with an additional layer of mystical significance.[23]

Rabbi Yosef Hayim, the Ben Ish Ḥai (1835–1909), explained that both vinegar and salt water are "strong" substances, and represent the

19 There only vinegar is mentioned explicitly, but the same would apply to salt water. Both the term "salt water" and the term "vinegar" are added in parenthesis in *Shulḥan Arukh, Oraḥ Ḥayim* 472:4. Regarding parenthetical additions to the *Shulḥan Arukh*, see Daniel Sperber, *Minhagei Yisrael*, vol. 1 (Jerusalem: Mossad HaRav Kook, 1989), 179, note 6.

20 See, for example, Yosef Kenapo, *Haggada shel Pesaḥ – Zevaḥ Pesaḥ* (Livorno, 1875), 98a.

21 Aharon Teomim, *Mateh Aharon* (Frankfurt am Main, 1710), 10.

22 Avraham Sperling, *Otzar Taamei HaMinhagim UMekorei HaDinim* (Lemberg, 1928), 229, *siman* 522.

23 Similarly, Yosef Karo explained dipping the vegetable into vinegar as a kabbalistic action against the *sitra aḥra*, Yehiel Bar-Lev, ed., *Maggid Meisharim* (Petach Tikvah, 1990), 218, *Parashat Tzav*. On kabbalistic meanings given to mitzvot and rituals, see chapter 6 of Lawrence Fine, *Physician of the Soul, Healer of the Cosmos: Isaac Luria and His Kabbalistic Fellowship* (Stanford, CA: Stanford University Press, 2003).

difficult servitude that the Israelites endured.[24] A similar explanation is found in Rabbi Tavala Bandi's Haggada, published in 1898, where it is explained that the Egyptians "embittered our lives with slavery like vinegar and salt water."[25]

Other explanations centered on the idea that the salt water symbolizes a body of water. The first Belzer Rebbe, Rabbi Sholom Rokeach (1781–1855), explains that the salt water recalls the water the Israelites used to immerse themselves in after being circumcised, prior to offering the Passover sacrifice. He writes that the Jews all immersed themselves in the Nile River, giving it the turbid appearance of briny water.[26] This explanation is found in notes of *Otzar Taamei HaMinhagim*.[27] According to Rabbi Yosef Hayim Sonnenfeld (1848–1932), the salt water reminds us of the miracle of crossing the Sea of Reeds.[28]

Rabbi Isaac Baer Levinsohn (1788–1860), a leader in the Russian Enlightenment, explains in his book *Yalkut Ribal* that we use salt water specifically because salt was forbidden to Egyptian priests, and by consuming it we show that we are free of Egypt and reject its ways.[29] This

24 Yosef Hayim, *Otzrot Ḥayim – Yamim UZemanim – Moadim 1* (Jerusalem: Ahavat Shalom, 1996), 247; Yosef Hayim, *Sefer Ben Ish Ḥai HaMeshulav* (Bnei Brak: Machon HaRav Matzliach, 2005), 40, *siman* 9.

25 Tavala Bandi, *Haggada shel Pesaḥ* (Slavatsky: Frankfurt am Main, 1898), 7. A similar idea is found in the contemporary work by Yitzhak Tawil, *Mekadesh Yisrael VehaZemanim* (Jerusalem, 2005), 199. See also the symbolism offered in Shlomo Gross, ed., *Divrei Torah al Haggada shel Pesaḥ* (Ramat Beit Shemesh: Or Yechezkel, 2008), 13, based on the idea that these substances "have an aspect of bitterness."

26 Israel Klopholtz, ed., *Maharash (Imrei Kodesh)* (Tel Aviv, 1965), 91.

27 Sperling, *Otzar Taamei HaMinhagim*, 229, *siman* 522, note 32. It is also the explanation quoted in Hayim Yehuda Segal Deitch, *Haggada shel Pesaḥ – Kol Yehuda* (Satmar, 1937), 29.

28 Yosef Hayim Sonnenfeld, *Ḥokhmat Ḥayim* (Jerusalem, 2002), 177. This is the explanation brought in *Haggada shel Pesaḥ – Shoel KeInyan* (Jerusalem: Machon Derech Eliezer, 2006), 29. A version of this explanation which also involves *Gematria* can be found in Yehiel Rothschild, *Yemei HaḤag*, vol. 2 (2009), 91.

29 Isaac Baer Levinsohn, *Yalkut Ribal* (Warsaw, 1878), 79. See there on page 78 his remarkable explanation for having a piece of meat and a bowl of salt water on the table, that it is a remnant of an ancient custom during festive meals where riddles were asked, where meat would be given as a reward to whoever answered questions correctly, and salt water drunk as a penalty for those who answered incorrectly. On Levinsohn, see Israel Zinberg, *A History of Jewish Literature: The Haskalah Movement*

explanation has gained a certain amount of popularity, as it is cited in *Minhagei Yeshurun*, another classic work explaining customs.[30]

Other more homiletical explanations have been offered, for example, that the salt water symbolizes Torah,[31] that it represents the idea that Torah must be studied with humility,[32] that dipping a vegetable in salt water hints at the concept that we must financially support Torah scholars,[33] that it represents the small amount of the evil inclination necessary for the world to function properly,[34] or that we should be satisfied with minimal physical pleasures.[35]

None of these works offer the allusion to salty tears that is so popular today.

## SALTY TEARS

The explanation that salt water represents salty tears is found in the teachings of Rabbi Shmuel Zvi Dancyger (1860–1923), the third Rebbe in the Aleksander dynasty. He explains that the salt water symbolizes the tears that a true penitent sheds, and recalls the repentance process of the Israelites, who were raising themselves up from the forty-ninth level of

---

*in Russia* (Cincinnati, OH: Hebrew Union College Press, 1978), chapter 2. Plutarch listed salt as a food considered impure by Egyptian priests (as well as pork, onions, and beans); see Peter Garnsey, *Food and Society in Classical Antiquity* (Cambridge: Cambridge University Press, 1999), 90; for differing opinions as to whether this is historically accurate, see Emily Teeter, *Religion and Ritual in Ancient Egypt* (Cambridge: Cambridge University Press, 2011), 33–34.

30 Avraham Hershovitz, *Sefer Minhagei Yeshurun* (Warsaw, 1899), 67, *siman* 119. Later works no longer attribute this idea to Levinsohn. See, for example, David Efraim Greenboim, *Haggada VeAggadta* (Modiin Illit, 2004), 82.

31 Aryeh Leib Shapira, ed., *Haggada shel Pesaḥ – Olellot Ephraim* (Zhitomir, 1863), 14. This commentary was written by Shlomo Ephraim Luntschitz (1550–1619), author of *Kli Yakar*. Note that here the salt water is actually considered sweet, in contrast to the other explanations, where it was termed strong or sharp. See also Yissachar Avraham, *Haggada shel Pesaḥ – Mateh Yissakhar* (Pietrikov, 1913), 15, where the water represents the "covenant of Torah."

32 David Rabinowitz, *Haggada shel Pesaḥ – Livnat Sapir* (Brooklyn, NY, 1949), 32.

33 David Tevele Schiff, *Lashon Zahav* (London: Mechon Rav Chesed Trust, 1997), 362–63, first published in 1822.

34 Yonatan Binyamin Cohen, *Haggada shel Pesaḥ – Nefesh Yonatan* (Sighet, 1925), 3b.

35 Elazar Hacohen, *Haggada Zikhron Niflaot* (Warsaw, 1880), 18.

impurity.[36] The suggestion that the salt water reminds us of the tears of sorrow shed during slavery does not appear in his symbolic explanation.

The idea that the salt water represents the tears shed by the Israelites during their oppressive slavery is first found in the *Ishei Yisrael* Haggada, first published in Warsaw in 1938. This Haggada contains two running commentaries by Modzitz Rebbe'im: *Divrei Yisrael* by Rabbi Yisrael Taub, and *Yisa Berakha* by his son Rabbi Shaul Yedidya Elazar Taub (1886–1947).

Rabbi Shaul Yedidya Elazar Taub became leader of the Modzitz Hasidim in 1920.[37] He escaped from Vilna using a Japanese visa issued by Consul Sugihara in Kovno.[38] His introduction to the republished version of this Haggada in New York is dated 23 Shevat 5707 (February 23, 1947), which is when he was living in Brooklyn.[39] He passed away a few months later, on 16 Kislev 5708 (November 29, 1947), the day the UN passed its partition plan for Israel, soon after fulfilling his dream of settling in Israel. He is reported to have been the last person to be buried on the Mount of Olives until after the Six-Day War, when a monument was finally put on his grave.[40]

In the *Ishei Yisrael* Haggada, Rabbi Shaul Taub offers two explanations as to why salt water is used. The first is based on the idea expressed in Berakhot 40a, that at the conclusion of every meal salt should be consumed and water drunk to ensure that no harm will come to the participants. Rabbi Taub suggests that since the Seder night is a time of protection from all harm, and since nothing must be eaten after the *Afikoman*, salt and water are placed on the table at the very beginning to remind us that the meal on this night differs from the way meals are usually eaten. He then offers a second explanation, that the same way

36 Azriel Hayim Zamlong, *Eser Niflaot* (Piotrkow, 1932), 57, *siman* 131; Reuven Landau, *HaOtzar MiSippurei Tzadikkim* (Warsaw, 1937), 94, *siman* 20.

37 Mordechai Staiman, *"His Name is Aaron" and Other Amazing Chassidic Stories and Songs* (Brooklyn: Otzar Sifrei Lubavitch, 2002), 209.

38 Esther Farbstein, *Hidden in Thunder: Perspectives on Faith, Halachah and Leadership During the Holocaust* (Jerusalem: Mossad HaRav Kook, 2007), 101, note 116.

39 Shaul Yedidya Elazar Taub, *Haggada Shel Pesaḥ – Ishei Yisrael* (Brooklyn, New York: Vaad Agudat Chasidei Modzitz, 1947), alef (before the numbering begins).

40 See David Mendelbaum, *Gibborei HaḤayil* (Bnei Brak, 2009), 163.

the *ḥaroset* that we dip *maror* into reminds us of the building materials that the Israelite slaves used, so too the salt water used for the *karpas* reminds us of the tears shed by the Israelites during their slavery.[41]

This explanation would be repeated with slight variations, and without attribution, in many discussions of the symbolism of the Passover Seder.[42] Before the publication of the *Ishei Yisrael* Haggada, this explanation did not appear in Haggadot. English-language Haggadot published for general audiences that today bring this explanation as a matter of course did not offer any symbolic explanation for the salt water prior to the appearance of the republished *Ishei Yisrael* Haggada in New York in 1947.[43] It seems that the explanation gained widespread popularity only after being included, without attribution, in the 1959 *Passover Haggada* by Morris Silverman: "The salt water into which the *karpas* is dipped to make it palatable has been interpreted as salty tears, to remind us of the tears shed by the oppressed Israelites."[44] Silverman was a prominent Conservative rabbi responsible for the movement's *Sabbath and Festival Prayerbook*, whose "name had become synonymous with Conservative Judaism's liturgy."[45] It may be significant that Silverman augmented the traditional text "with an extensive section on the Holocaust, the birth of the State of Israel, and numerous comments about America,"[46] so this explanation may have been chosen

---

41 Shaul Yedidya Elazar Taub, *Haggada shel Pesaḥ – Ishei Yisrael* (Warsaw, 1938), 6–7. כן י"ל הטבילה במי מלח לזכר איך היו טבולים בדמעות, אשר שפכו מצרת השעבוד.

42 See notes 2 and 3 above.

43 For example, Mordechai Kaplan's *New Haggadah* (New York: Behrman's, 1941), whose goal was to present "compelling content of present day idealism and aspiration" (vii), explains that the *karpas* itself comes to symbolize "the coming of Spring, and suggest the perpetual renewal of life" (xi), but gives no explanation for the salt water. Compare with Lawrence Hoffman and David Arnow, eds., *My People's Passover Haggadah* (Woodstock, VT: Jewish Lights, 2008), which has a similar goal, and presents both the spring symbolism of *karpas* and the tears symbolism of the salt water, 143.

44 Morris Silverman, *Passover Haggadah with Explanatory Notes and Original Readings* (Hartford, CT: Prayer Book Press, 1959), 5.

45 Lawrence Hoffman and David Arnow, eds., *My People's Passover Haggadah: Traditional Texts, Modern Commentaries*, vol. 1 (Woodstock, VT: Jewish Lights, 2008), 83.

46 Joel Gereboff, "One Nation, with Liberty and Haggadahs for All," in Jack Kugelmass, ed., *Key Texts in American Jewish Culture* (New Jersey: Rutgers University Press, 2003), 284.

as one that would be particularly meaningful for American Jews in a modern setting.

Today the salt water in which we dip the vegetable is typically associated with the tears of the enslaved Israelites before their liberation."[47] It is such a well-known interpretation that it is sometimes retrofitted into earlier commentaries. For example, the contemporary *Mystical Haggada*, in a section "adapted from" the Haggada of Rabbi Isaiah Horowitz, the Shelah (c. 1565–1630), states that the dipping in salt water is a reminder of "the tears of our suffering in bondage,"[48] whereas in the original *Haggadat HaShelah* there is no mention of salt water or tears. There only vinegar is mentioned, explained as representing the hardship of slavery in general,[49] a symbolism that would later be applied to salt water as well, as we saw above.

The reason that today "the prevalent custom is to use salt water"[50] rather than vinegar is at least partially due to the fact that salt water now carries a powerful and simply stated symbolism, whereas no such equivalent interpretation was given for vinegar.

## WHY USE SALT WATER AND VINEGAR?

These symbolic explanations are relatively modern, most dating from the nineteenth and twentieth centuries.[51] Even in modern times, many

---

47 Hoffman and Arnow, *My People's Passover Haggadah*, 143. It even appears in explicitly nonreligious Haggadot, for example, Edwin Mishkin, *A Haggadah for the Non-Observant* (2012), 17: "The salt water is often connected to the tears the Jewish people cried in Egypt."

48 Eliyahu Klein, *A Mystical Haggadah* (Berkley, CA: North Atlantic Books, 2008), 44.

49 Isaiah Horowitz, *Haggadat HaShelah HaShalem* (Jerusalem: Ahavat Shalom, 2001), 54. Joseph Elias, *ArtScroll Mesorah Series Haggadah* (Brooklyn, NY: Mesorah, 1977), 63, more correctly states that according to the Shelah it is "to remind us of the bitterness of the bondage," although he brings this symbolism to explain salt water, not vinegar, as in the actual Shelah.

50 Yosef Zvi Rimon, *Haggada MiMekorah* (Jerusalem: Mossad HaRav Kook, 2002), 115.

51 The explanation often quoted in the name of Maharal, that the salt water symbolizes the kabbalistic concept *Yesod*, is found in the Maharal Haggada (*Divrei Neggidim*), which is actually a forgery by Yehuda Rosenberg (1859–1935), first published in 1905. See Yitzhak Lieberman, *Sefer Ḥag HaMatzot* (Bnei Brak, 2003), 393, note 34; Shlomo Fisher, "Do Not Let Wickedness Dwell in Our Tents" (On Forgeries in Books and Books Containing Deceptive Ideas), *Tzfunot* 3 (Nisan 5749), 69. This is the same

works on Jewish customs do not provide any explanation for choosing salt water for dipping.[52] Why are no explanations found in the *Rishonim* and early *Aḥaronim*?

An important insight is gained from the *Leket Yosher.* This book was compiled by Rabbi Yosef ben Moshe (1423–c. 1490) and records the customs and rulings of his teacher, Rabbi Israel Isserlein (1390–1460). He states, "There is no mitzva to use salt water rather than vinegar, and the opposite seems to be true, for we in our time and in our land are not accustomed all year long to dip into salt water, and most of our dipping is in vinegar; it is better to dip in vinegar.... And if you should say that we should make a big change in order to arouse the children's astonishment, we should only make the changes that the sages mentioned, and the sages only mentioned dipping, and the simple understanding is that they meant the regular dip."[53] Using vinegar for dipping is found as far back as the book of Ruth (2:14), further demonstrating that the reason vinegar was chosen for dipping is that it was commonly used, not because it was particularly sharp or possessed some other quality.[54]

The *karpas* is dipped into something that was considered normative to dip vegetables into. In the original formulation of the well-known Four Questions, found in the Mishna and traditionally sung by the youngest child present at the beginning of the Seder, the question is asked, why is food dipped *twice*, not why is it dipped into an unusual liquid, suggesting that the idea of dipping was not remarkable.[55] No explanation was needed because the reason was obvious; those were the

forger responsible for many fanciful tales about the Maharal; see Leiman, S. Z., "The Adventure of the Maharal of Prague in London: R. Yudl Rosenberg and the Golem of Prague," *Tradition* 36:1, 2002.

52 For example, J. D. Eisenstein, *Otzar Dinim UMinhagim* (New York, 1917); Shmuel Gelbart, *Otzar Taamei HaMinhagim* (Petach Tikvah: Mifal Rashi, 1996); Gavriel Zinner, *Nitei Gavriel: Hilkhot Pesaḥ*, vol. 2 (Jerusalem: Shemesh, 1997).

53 Yaakov Friedman, ed., *Leket Yosher – Oraḥ Ḥayim* (Berlin, 1903), 89.

54 Meir Nathanson, "The Law Regarding Preparing Salt Water for Seder Night, Particularly When It Falls on Shabbat," *Tzohar* 2 (1998), 80 [Hebrew]. Dipping into salt water or vinegar is called "a wholesome Orientalism" in Aaron Green, *The Revised Haggadah* (London: George Routledge and Sons, 1929), 19.

55 Mishna Pesaḥim 10:4: "On all other nights we dip once; on this night twice." This was emended in the Mishna printed in the Talmud with parenthetical additions.

normative salad dressings at the time. As Rabbi David Feinstein states, "In those days it was quite normal to eat a vegetable dipped in salt water before the main course."[56]

In the time of the Greeks, when mixed greens were eaten they were seasoned with vinegar, salt, oil, and herbs. The Romans called this dish *herba salata* (salted greens), which is the origin of the modern English word "salad."[57] The salt was sometimes added to the salad in the form of brine, salty water, so that it would stick.[58] These dressings remained standard throughout medieval times; more complex salads and salad dressings were developed only later. Most of the dressings popular today, such as Thousand Island, ranch, and Caesar, date from the 1900s.[59] While the *ArtScroll Youth Haggada* writes that "salt water is used instead of fancy dressing to remind us of our salty tears and sweat when we were slaves in Egypt,"[60] the fact is that the opposite is true, and salt water and vinegar were chosen precisely because they were very normative dressings in earlier times.

In the time of the *Rishonim* and early *Aḥaronim*, when salt water was still recognized as a standard dip for vegetables, there was no need to provide a symbolic meaning for the dips. As time passed and salt water was no longer obviously recognized as a simple and standard salad dressing, symbolic explanations began to be offered for this popular choice of dip.

---

56 David Feinstein, *The Kol Dodi Haggadah* (Brooklyn, NY: Mesorah, 1990), 39. This simple explanation is recorded in the early English-language Haggada, William Rosenau, *Home Service for Passover Eve* (New York: Bloch, 1905), 8: "The salt water or vinegar, into which the parsley is dipped, is provided to lend palatability to the parsley."

57 Amy Brown, *Understanding Food: Principles and Preparation* (Stamford, CT: Cengage Learning, 2015), 338; James L. Morgan, *Culinary Creation* (New York: Buttersworth-Heinemann, 2006), 185.

58 Kate Burridge, *Weeds in the Garden of Words* (Cambridge: Cambridge University Press, 2005), 61.

59 Andrew Smith, ed., *The Oxford Companion to American Food and Drink* (New York: Oxford University Press, 2007), 514.

60 Nosson and Yitzchok Zev Scherman, *ArtScroll Youth Haggadah* (Brooklyn, NY: Mesorah, 1995), 14.

## CREATING JEWISH CUSTOMS

Based on this, it would seem that today people should be dipping the *karpas* into a commonly used, contemporary salad dressing[61] rather than the now unusual salt water. The fact that this is not done is a testament to the conservative nature and endurance of the practices of the Jewish people. The changing trends of the contemporary world have had little impact on the people who are steadfast in perpetuating the traditions of their parents and grandparents. Due to this phenomenon, over time the Jewish people have become the contemporary bearers of what was once a widespread culinary custom, to season vegetables with salt water.

61 As long as it is composed of substances that would require washing when used as a dip. See Moshe Katz, *VaYaged Moshe* (Jerusalem, 1973), 35.

*Chapter 16*

# Sixteen Drops of Wine at the Seder

## INTRODUCTION

There is a well-known custom to remove sixteen drops of wine from the cup as we recite the names of the ten plagues and words associated with them. The *ArtScroll Youth Haggadah* states that "we don't want our cups to be full when we tell about other people's pain."[1] The idea that we remove some wine to show that we cannot fully rejoice when our enemies are destroyed is also found in the *ArtScroll Mesorah Series Haggadah*: "Abrabanel, however, explains that we should remove the wine because 'You should not rejoice when your enemy falls' (Prov. 24:17)."[2] However, this idea does not actually appear in Abrabanel's commentary to the Haggada, or in any of his writings. In fact, this explanation for the custom of removing sixteen drops from the cup of wine is a recent innovation. By now it is so entrenched in Haggadot that it is often the only explanation offered. The idea is most commonly presented

1 Nosson and Yitzchok Zev Scherman, *ArtScroll Youth Haggadah* (Brooklyn, NY: Mesorah, 1995), 25.

2 Joseph Elias, *ArtScroll Mesorah Series Haggadah* (Brooklyn, NY: Mesorah, 1977), 127.

as follows: "By spilling a drop of wine from the Passover cup for each plague, we acknowledge that our own joy is lessened and incomplete, for our redemption had to come by means of the punishment of other human beings. Even though these are just punishments for evil acts, it says, 'Do not rejoice at the fall of your enemy' (Prov. 24:17)."[3] In this chapter we will trace the development of this interpretation of this cherished Seder-night custom.

## ORIGIN OF THE CUSTOM

The earliest reference to this custom and to an explanation for it is found in a Passover sermon of Rabbi Eleazer of Worms (Roke'aḥ, c. 1176–1238): "For each word a finger [goes] into the cup of wine and they spill out a drop, matching the sword of the Holy One, blessed be He, which has sixteen sides. And the sixteen mentions of plague in Jeremiah. [This custom] teaches us that we will not be injured. Based upon [this] our ancestors created this custom. And sixteen times the word *ḥayim* [appears in Psalm 119], and sixteen people read from the Torah each week,[4] matching the sixteen lambs that are sacrificed in a week. Also, 'She is [in Hebrew, הי״א, which has a *Gematria* of 16] a tree of life to those who grasp her' (Prov. 3:18). And one should not ridicule the custom of our holy ancestors."[5] This explanation is quoted in *Sefer Amarcal* in the name of the Roke'aḥ, along with a list of rabbis who observed this custom.[6] That the Roke'aḥ emphasized not to belittle this custom, and that *Sefer Amarcal* brought

3 Noam Zion and David Dishon, *The Family Participation Haggadah: A Different Night* (Jerusalem: Shalom Hartman Institute, 1997), 101.

4 Seven people read it on Shabbat morning, three on Shabbat afternoon, and three each read it on Monday and Thursday.

5 Simha Emanuel, ed., *Rabbi Eleazar of Worms: Derasha LePesaḥ* (Jerusalem: Ḥevrat Mekitze Nirdamim, 2006), 101. Translation based on the English version in Joshua Kulp and David Golinkin, *The Schechter Haggadah: Art, History and Commentary* (Jerusalem: Schechter Institute of Jewish Studies, 2009), 233.

6 Michael Higger, ed., "Sefer Amarcal al Hilkhot Pesaḥim," *siman* 30, 164, in *Alexander Marx Jubilee Volume* – Hebrew Section (New York: Jewish Theological Seminary, 1950). The author of *Sefer Amarcal* is unknown.

"an impressive array of names of the German Hasidim"[7] who observed it indicates that it was one of the customs of *Ḥasidei Ashkenaz* (the German Pietists) that were indeed subject to ridicule.[8] The custom is mentioned in *Sefer Maharil,* quoting the Roke'aḥ and others, where the idea is explained that God should "save us from all these and they should fall upon our enemies."[9] Thus, the sixteen drops are intended to ward off the danger from the sixteen-faced sword of God.[10] The custom is mentioned by Rabbi Moshe Isserles in his comments on the *Tur* (*Darkhei Moshe, Oraḥ Ḥayim* 473:18) and in his glosses to the *Shulḥan Arukh* (*Oraḥ Ḥayim* 473:7). In *Darkhei Moshe* he quotes the Maharil, and adds that this custom alludes to the "the angel in charge of vengeance."

The original explanation can be somewhat difficult to present to participants in the context of a family Seder, as it is based on the idea of the sixteen-sided sword of God and the general symbolism behind the number sixteen, something not widely known or easily related. In the late nineteenth and early twentieth centuries a simpler reason was offered in popular books of explanations for customs, that the removal of drops of wine from the cup parallels the Egyptians, who were diminished with every plague. This explanation is found in widely read books

---

7 Heinrich Guggenheimer, *The Scholar's Haggadah* (Northvale, NJ: Jason Aronson, Inc., 1998), 302.

8 Avraham Grossman, *The Early Sages of Ashkenaz* (Jerusalem: Magnes Press, 2001), 230, note 105.

9 Shlomo Spitzer, ed., *Sefer Maharil* (Jerusalem: Machon Yerushalayim, 1989), 106–7.

10 Joshua Trachtenberg, *Jewish Magic and Superstition* (New York: Athenium, 1984), 167; Kulp and Golinkin, *The Schechter Haggadah,* 233. In light of this, there may be an additional reason for the custom to use the pinky finger to remove the drops. *Magen Avraham* (*Oraḥ Ḥayim* 473:28) brings opinions that either the index, ring, or little finger is used. It is known that the little finger was understood to have apotropaic powers in European folk culture; see A. B. Strachov, "Miscellanea Meterologica Slavica: "Breaking" the Rainbow in Poles'e," *Die Welt der Slaven* 33 (1988), 338–39, where the little finger is used to ward off demonic forces and spells from water and wedding feasts. See also the chapter "Pointing to the Torah with the Little Finger and Other *Hagbaha* Customs."

explaining customs, including *Sefer Mataamim*,[11] *Minhagei Yeshurun*,[12] *Sefer Taamei HaMinhagim*[13] and *Otzar Dinim UMinhagim*.[14]

The *Mishna Berura* explains that the sixteen drops represent the first two letters of God's name (*Oraḥ Ḥayim* 473:75). Rabbi Reuven Margaliot, in his Haggada commentary *Be'er Miriam* (1937), explains that the removal of drops represents the idea that the plagues were only a small drop from the cups of retribution and punishment that nations that persecute Israel will drink from in the future.[15] These explanations generally relate the custom to some aspect of vengeance against enemies.[16] They contain no trace of the idea of "incomplete joy" due to the suffering of the Egyptians, and, in fact, seem diametrically opposed to it.

### ABBREVIATED HALLEL

Disseminators of the explanation centered on "incomplete joy" generally relate it to a reason given in the Midrash for the recitation of the full Hallel on every day of Sukkot but only on the first day of Passover, with the abbreviated Hallel recited on the rest of the festival. The halakhic reason given for this in the Talmud (Arakhin 10a–b), is that on Sukkot different *musaf* sacrifices are offered each day, so each day of Sukkot is considered a distinct holiday, whereas on Passover the same *musaf* sacrifice is offered every day. Another answer, however, is found in the midrashic literature. The thirteenth-century work *Shibbolei HaLeket* (*siman* 174),

---

11 Yitzhak Lipetz, *Sefer Mataamim* (Warsaw, 1890), 56, item 55. Although he seems to reference the *Hagahot HaMinhagim* to Issac Tirnau's *Sefer Minhagim* as his source, the custom is found there (note 98) but without an explanation. In Haggadot that are more careful about quoting sources, this explanation is cited as being "in the name of *Sefer Minhagim*" rather than actually appearing there. See Abraham Natan Barnett, *Haggada shel Pesaḥ im Likkutim Neḥemadim* (Jerusalem, 1959), 3.

12 Avraham Hershovitz, *Otzar Kol Minhagei Yeshurun* (Vilna, 1899), 34, *siman* 120.

13 Avraham Sperling, *Sefer Taamei HaMinhagim UMekorei HaDinim* (Lemberg, 1928), 66, *siman* 538.

14 J. D. Eisenstein, *Otzar Dinim UMinhagim* (New York, 1917), 282.

15 Reuven Margaliot, *Haggada shel Pesaḥ – Be'er Miriam, Kehillat Moshe* (Tel Aviv: Margaliot, 1937), 40. This explanation is sometimes attributed to the Vilna Gaon, since it may be hinted to in *Biur HaGra, Oraḥ Ḥayim* 473:45.

16 Israel Yuval, "Vengeance and Damnation, Blood and Defamation: From Jewish Martyrdom to Blood Libel Accusations," *Zion* 58, no. 1 (1993), 38 [Hebrew].

quoted by Rabbi Yosef Karo (*Beit Yosef, Oraḥ Ḥayim* 490:4), brings in the name of *Midrash Harninu* (a midrash collection lost to us today),[17] that Shmuel b. Abba taught that the reason only an abbreviated Hallel is recited after the first day of Passover is that the Egyptians drowned and "if your enemy falls do not exult" (Prov. 24:17). This seems to be based on the episode mentioned in Megilla 10b and Sanhedrin 39b, that when the Egyptians were drowning in the Sea of Reeds, God silenced the angels who wanted to sing, saying that it is not appropriate to do so when His "handiwork is drowning in the sea." It should be noted, however, that the Israelites themselves sang *Shirat HaYam* at this point, and this was not viewed as problematic. Whatever the merits of this particular midrashic explanation for not reciting the full Hallel throughout Passover,[18] it does not seem to apply to the custom of removing drops of wine from the cup, since that is done on Seder night, when we do in fact recite the full Hallel and do not seem to limit our joy.

This explanation for the abbreviated Hallel is also found in some versions of *Pesikta DeRav Kahane*[19] and in *Yalkut Shimoni* (*Emor, remez* 654), but there the midrash begins by asking why the Torah uses the term *simḥa*, joy, three times relating to Sukkot but not even once relating to Passover. Two answers are given. The first is that since judgment is passed on the crops on Passover and people do not know if their fields will produce crops in the coming year, they cannot have complete joy

17 See J. D. Eisenstein, *Otzar Midrashim* (New York: Noble Offset Printers, 1915), 137.

18 See the excellent overview of this midrashic explanation by Avi Zivotofsky in "What's the Truth About... Hallel on Pesach?," *Jewish Action* 60, no. 3 (Spring 5760/2000). See also the comments of Avigdor Nebenzahl, *Yerushalayim BeMoadehah – Pesaḥ* (Jerusalem: Machon Keren Re'em, 2006), 160. It is worth noting that the idea of displaying mercy toward Egyptian adversaries is also found in the pseudepigrapha, in *Joseph and Asenath*, a first-century Jewish romance written in Egypt. In the story, when Benjamin is ready to kill Pharaoh's firstborn son, the villain of the story, he is stopped by Levi, who explains, "By no means, brother, will you do this deed, because we are men who worship God, and it does not befit a man who worships God to repay evil for evil nor to trample underfoot a fallen (man) nor to oppress his enemy till death" (29:3). See E. P. Sanders, *Judaism: Practice and Belief 63 BCE–66 CE* (London: SCM Press, 1994), 234.

19 Bernard Mandelbaum, ed., *Pesikta de Rav Kahane* (New York: Jewish Theological Seminary of America, 1987), 458.

on Passover. The second answer given is "because the Egyptians died." The midrash then states that this is also why only the abbreviated Hallel is recited after the first day of Passover, while on Sukkot, full Hallel is said every day. This expanded version of the midrash is more relevant to the explanation of "incomplete joy." The version in *Shibbolei HaLeket* relates only to the abbreviated Hallel, making it irrelevant to the first day of Passover. In the expanded version, the Torah's omission of the term *simḥa* when dealing with the holiday of Passover indicates that even on the first day of Passover there is a lack of joy because of the death of the Egyptians.

## ENGLISH-LANGUAGE HAGGADOT

The explanation of "incomplete joy" was popularized by being the only one presented in many early English-language Haggadot intended for laypeople. A 1929 English-translation Haggada published by the Austrian/Hungarian Schlesinger publishing house explains the custom as indicating that "we cannot celebrate the feast of our deliverance full of joy when so many thousands of human beings have perished," and states that "from this cause also, in the last days of Passover, Hallel, the prayer of thanksgiving, is recited only to the half."[20] The Schlesinger prayer books "were especially popular" throughout the early 1900s.[21] Variations of this Haggada were continually reprinted and expanded over the years in English-language Haggadot published in Israel after the Schlesinger publishing company moved to Tel Aviv in the late 1930s and changed its name to the Sinai Publishing Company.[22]

20 Joseph Loewy and Joseph Guens, *Service for the First Nights of Passover* (Vienna: Joseph Schlesinger, 1929), 20.

21 Kinga Frojimovics, ed., *Jewish Budapest: Monuments, Rites and History* (Budapest: Central European University Press, 1999), 179.

22 In some later editions the authors of the notes are not even named. *The Bezalel Haggada*, illustrated by Zeev Raban (Tel Aviv: Sinai, 1965), 31, for example, gives this explanation word for word, but no author is listed anywhere in the book. On the history of the Schlesinger publishing company, see Frojimovics, 179; Istvan Ormos, "David Kaufmann and His Collection" in Eva Apor, ed., *David Kaufmann Memorial Volume* (Budapest: Library of the Hungarian Academy of Sciences, 2002), 140, note 44.

In the 1940s, 50s, and 60s this explanation became ubiquitous in American Haggadot.[23] The explanation is presented in the introductory note by Louis Finkelstein to a 1942 English-translation Haggada: "The spilling of wine at the mention of the plagues is interpreted as a symbol of regret that the victory had to be purchased by the death of the Egyptians."[24] Finkelstein was "the dominant figure of Conservative Judaism in the twentieth century," and was chancellor of the Jewish Theological Seminary at the time he wrote that introduction.[25] The Haggada edited by David and Tamar De Sola Pool, first published in 1943 by the National Jewish Welfare Board "for members of the armed forces of the United States," similarly explains that "a drop of wine of rejoicing is diminished from the cup in sign of pity for the suffering Egyptians."[26] This Haggada, composed by a committee of Orthodox, Conservative, and Reform rabbis for Jewish soldiers who were fighting in World War II, addresses the "compatibility of Jewish and American values."[27] The American value here is "the liberal ethic, believing that all people are

23 Earlier English-translation Haggadot generally either do not explain the reason for the custom, or still give explanations closer to the original one. For example, J .D. Eisenstein's *Haggada: Seder Ritual for Passover Eve* (New York: Hebrew Publishing Company, 1928), 18, explains that "we spill out a drop of wine at the mention of each plague to indicate we are immune from the plagues."

24 Maurice Samuel, *Haggadah for Passover* (New York: Hebrew Publishing Company, 1942), xvii.

25 Lawrence Hoffman and David Arnow, eds., *My People's Passover Haggadah: Traditional Texts, Modern Commentaries, volume 1* (Woodstock, VT: Jewish Lights, 2008), 83.

26 David and Tamar De Sola Pool, *The Haggadah of Passover* (New York: Jewish Welfare Board, 1943), 38. This Haggada contains essentially no commentary and this explanation was written as part of the instructions before reciting the ten plagues. The Haggada was reprinted throughout the 1940s and 1950s.

27 Joel Gereboff, "One Nation, with Liberty and Haggadahs for All," in Jack Kugelmass, ed., *Key Texts in American Jewish Culture* (New Jersey: Rutgers University Press, 2003), 285. Translated Haggadot often dealt with the changing sensibilities of their intended readership. See, for example, Aaron Green, *The Revised Hagada* (London: George Routledge and Sons, 1897), 3, where the author explains that he did not translate "nine months of pregnancy" in the song *Eḥad Mi Yode'a* and instead "substituted the nine Jewish festivals as more in consonance with our modern ideas of what is adapted for the perusal of children."

essentially good," so that punishing the Egyptians "seems so vindictive and vengeful."[28]

The Haggada edited by Philip Birnbaum for the Hebrew Publishing Company in 1953 also states that the custom "is intended to stress the idea that we must not rejoice over the misfortunes that befell our foes."[29] The Birnbaum Haggada was considered the standard traditional Haggada for English speakers until the first ArtScroll Haggada was published in 1977[30] and, as noted above, also included this explanation. This explanation is also presented in the 1959 *Passover Haggada* by Morris Silverman,[31] a Conservative rabbi responsible for the movement's *Sabbath and Festival Prayerbook*, whose "name had become synonymous with Conservative Judaism's liturgy."[32] Rabbi Shlomo Kahn's 1960 Haggada, *From Twilight to Dawn*, billed "the traditional Passover Haggada," also explains this custom as a sign of limiting our joy, reminding us that the Egyptians, "although our enemies and tormentors, were fellow human beings nevertheless."[33] This Haggada, reprinted in 1969, is the only English-language Haggada published prior to the late 1970s that "includes much longer translations of traditional commentaries,"[34] so that this explanation reached an even more scholarly audience.

We can say that since World War II, every American Haggada aimed at a primarily English-speaking audience and offering an explanation for this custom mentioned the idea of "incomplete joy," and in most such Haggadot it was the only explanation offered.[35] By now

---

28 Nathan Laufer, *Leading the Passover Journey: The Seder's Meaning Revealed, The Haggadah's Story Retold* (Woodstock, VT: Jewish Lights, 2005), 92. See there his critique of this entire approach to the plagues.

29 Philip Birnbaum, *Haggadah* (New York: Hebrew Publishing Company, 1953), 38.

30 Hoffman and Arnow, *My People's Passover Haggadah*, 84.

31 Morris Silverman, *Passover Haggadah* (Hartford, CT: Prayer Book Press, 1959), 20.

32 Hoffman and Arnow, *My People's Passover Haggadah*, 83.

33 Shlomo Kahn, *From Twilight to Dawn* (New York: Scribe, 1960), 60.

34 Gereboff, "One Nation," 283.

35 There are almost as many examples as there are English-language Haggadot. See, for example, Sidney Hoenig, *The Haggadah of Passover with Introductory Notes and Supplement* (New York: Shulsinger Brothers, 1950), 11, which states: "It may also show that we symbolically cast a tear at the mention of each plague." Arthur Gilbert, *The Passover Seder: Pathways Through the Haggadah* (New York: Ktav, 1965), 31, says that

the explanation is widespread and more well-known than the original one. Today Wikipedia even gives this explanation in its entry "Passover Seder"![36]

This approach is found in more scholarly Orthodox literature as well.[37] It is particularly prevalent in works written by people connected to English-speaking countries, where this idea was most widely popularized. It is included, for example, in Rabbi David Feinstein's *The Kol Dodi Haggada*[38] and Rabbi Yaakov Wehl's *The Haggada with Answers,*

it is a "symbol of regret that the victory had to be purchased through misfortune visited upon God's creatures, the Egyptians." This seems to be based on Finkelstein's phrasing. Alfred J. Kolatch, *The Family Seder – A Traditional Passover Haggadah for the Modern Home* (New York: Jonathan David, 1967), 38, states, "This practice has been explained as an expression of our unhappiness over the misfortune suffered by the Egyptians.... The thought of rejoicing over the suffering of others is alien to Judaism, even where punishment may be justified." Zev Schostak, *Why Is This Night Different?* (New York: ArtScroll Studios, 1977), 57, says, "As we recall the downfall of our enemies, we recall that they were creatures of God and our joy is incomplete." The famed *Maxwell House Haggadah* does not mention this explanation, nor did it even note the custom in its earlier editions. Later editions instruct that wine be removed from the cup but offer no explanation. The "incomplete joy" explanation is also brought in Yiddish in the Yiddish-and-English-translated *Passover Haggadah* by Nathan Mandel (New York, 1954), 65; the source given is "I have heard." This explanation is featured in other translated Haggadot from this time period as well, and is the only one offered in the French *La Haggadah de Paque* by Joseph Bloch (Paris, 1950), 36. It is also the only explanation found in the National Jewish Outreach Program's *Beginners Passover Haggadah* (New York: NJOP Publications, 2010), 18.

36 "With the recital of the Ten Plagues, each participant removes a drop of wine from his or her cup using a fingertip. Although this night is one of salvation, the sages explain that one cannot be completely joyous when some of God's creatures had to suffer." http://en.wikipedia.org/wiki/Passover_Seder (April, 2014).

37 To name a few, it is brought in the name of Abrabanel in Yaakov Weingarten, *HaSeder HaArukh*, vol. 2 (Jerusalem: Machon Otzar HaMoadim, 1992), 178, 179; it is brought without attribution in Ephraim Greenblatt, *Rivevos Ephraim, Oraḥ Ḥayim* , vol. 2 (Brooklyn, NY: Deutsch Printing and Publishing Co., 1978), *siman* 137, 361; Moshe Zvi Holzberg, "Biur Makkot Mitzrayim," in *Kovetz Beit Aharon* 33, Shevat-Adar 5751/1991, 50; and in the name of Abrabanel in Yoel Chaim Friedman, "Yayin shel Shvi'it Beleil HaSeder," in *Emunat Itecha* 3, Shevat-Adar 5755/1995, reprinted in Yoel Friedman, ed., *HaTorah VehaAretz* (Jerusalem: Hemed, 2001), 227.

38 David Feinstein, *The Kol Dodi Haggadah* (Brooklyn, NY: Mesorah in conjunction with Mesivta Tifereth Jerusalem, 1990), 106. There it states that the wine is removed "in consideration for the losses caused by the plagues." This appears in the Hebrew

in both the Hebrew and English versions.[39] Rabbi Yehezkel Abramsky discusses it and explains, "The four cups were instituted by the Sages as a demonstration of our joy over having been redeemed from Egyptian servitude and our becoming God's chosen people in the process. In order to ensure that there is no trace of other emotions involved in our celebration of the exodus, so that there will be no gloating over the misfortune of the Egyptians rather than joy at our own good fortune, some wine is spilled as we recount the frightful plagues that were visited upon our former tormentors. The spilled wine represents a symbolic reduction in the tone of our joy, to remind us to keep our celebrations within the limits of propriety and sensitivity."[40] The Bostoner Rebbe, Rabbi Levi Yitzhak Horowitz, gave a similar explanation: "Our cup is also lacking when God strikes them."[41] The idea of "incomplete joy" is the only explanation offered in some Modern Orthodox Haggadot. *The Yeshivah University Haggada* brings it in the name of Abrabanel.[42] Rabbi Jonathan Sacks calls it "the most beautiful" explanation for the custom, and does not offer alternative explanations.[43] Rabbi Shlomo Riskin includes it in his Haggada, stating that "it symbolizes our sadness at the loss of human life – even that of our enemies." [44] It is also found on Orthodox "Ask the Rabbi" forums on the Internet.[45] By now it

---

original (New York: Tiferet, 1970), 21, as the somewhat more ambiguous נוהגים ששופכים לאיבוד המכות.

39 Yaakov Wehl, *The Haggadah with Answers* (Brooklyn, NY: Mesorah, 1997), 143. Not attributed to any authority, it is introduced by the words "It is also possible to suggest another reason..." The Hebrew original, *Haggadat Ki Yishalḥa Binkha* (Brooklyn, NY: Tova Press, 1993), 202, introduces the explanation with לכאורה אולי יש לומר.

40 Yaakov Blinder, *The Haggadah of the Roshei Yeshivah – Book Two* (Brooklyn, NY: Mesorah, 1999), 136, 137, translated from Asher Bergman, *Haggada shel Pesaḥ – Arzei HaLevanon*, vol. 2 (Bnei Brak: Mishor, 1999), 154; Yehezkel Abramsky, *Ḥazon Yeḥezkel* (Bnei Brak, 2009), 398.

41 *Seder Haggada Shel Pesaḥ – Ezrat Avoteinu* (Jerusalem: New England Chassidic Center, 1997), 146.

42 Steven Cohen and Kenneth Brander, eds., *The Yeshiva University Haggada* (New York: Student Organization of Yeshiva, 1985), 19.

43 Jonathan Sacks, *Rabbi Jonathan Sacks's Haggadah* (New York: Continuum, 2010), 36.

44 Shlomo Riskin, *The Passover Haggadah* (New York: Ktav, 1983), 90.

45 This is the answer given in the Ohr Somayach "Ask the Rabbi" question on "Drops of Wine": "While we rejoice at our salvation, we nonetheless retain our sensitivities to

appears in many mainstream scholarly Hebrew Haggadot, with a version brought in the recently published Haggada based on the teachings of Rabbi Yosef Shalom Elyashiv.[46]

## ABRABANEL AND ABUDRAHAM

Some Haggadot attribute this explanation to Abrabanel. The earliest such attribution seems to be in the *Fun Unzer Alten Otzar* column of the Warsaw newspaper *Haynt* from March 26, 1937. This was a column, considered innovative at the time, that Moshe Bunem Justman (1889–1942) began writing in 1930, collecting short ideas related to the weekly Torah portion or an upcoming holiday.[47] These were later collated in the *Fun Unzer Alten Otzar* series of books. In the Haggada of this series, published in Warsaw in 1938, the explanation of "incomplete joy" is presented in the name of Don Isaac Abrabanel, as it appeared in the newspaper column a year before.[48]

This explanation is included in a Hebrew translation of material on the holidays and *Pirkei Avot* compiled from Justman's books, *MeOtzareinu HaYashan*,[49] first published in 1965, and from there has made it to various collections of material on Passover.[50] The same expla-

---

the suffering of the Egyptians by diminishing our joy, if only in the mildest extent." https://ohr.edu/ask_db/ask_main.php/273/Q3/ (April 2014). It is worth noting that the Chabad "Ask the Rabbi" site does not give the "incomplete joy" explanation, but one more closely resembling the original explanation: "The Ten Plagues, describing the affliction of the Egyptians, represent negative energy that we would rather not bring into our system. So after reading each plague we spill wine from the cup, banishing the forces of punishment and its curses, and leaving the cup with only blessings. The spilled wine should then be discarded, for drinking it would be drinking in the plagues." http://www.chabad.org/holidays/passover/pesach_cdo/aid/1814212/jewish/Why-Do-We-Spill-Wine-on-Passover-Night.htm (April 2014).

46 Moshe Israelzon, *Haggada shel Pesaḥ* (Jerusalem: Machon Keren Re'em, 2006), 106. There it is introduced with ואפשר לומר and suggests that God is unhappy because of the death of the Egyptians.

47 H. Justus (Justman), *MeOtzareinu HaYashan – Bereshit* (Tel Aviv: Mofet, 1976), 8.

48 B. Yoashson (Moshe Bunem Justman), *Haggada shel Pesaḥ mit a Modern Yiddish Iberzetzing – Fun Unzer Alten Otzar* (Warsaw: Yehudiah, 1938), 57. It was republished in New York by Saphrograph in 1947.

49 Shimshon Meltzer, trans., *MeOtzareinu HaYashan* (Tel Aviv: Modiin, 1976), 109.

50 To name two, the exact formulation is copied in Hayim Zuckerman, *Birkat Ḥayim al Moadim*, vol. 2 (Tel Aviv, 1971), 133, and Chanan Levi, *BeShvilei HaḤodashim*

nation, worded slightly differently, also appears in the name of Abrabanel in the "overwhelmingly popular"[51] Hebrew *Yalkut Tov* Haggada by Rabbi Eliyahu Kitov, first published in 1961 and reprinted many times since.[52] From there it was copied word for word in *Yalkut LeMoadim: Haggada shel Pesaḥ*, compiled by Rabbi Hayim Becker and published in 1968,[53] part of a series of books he wrote collecting short ideas relating to each holiday. From there it was copied for later collections.[54] Rabbi Kitov is also the source for the commentary in the 1977 ArtScroll Haggada.[55] These two slightly different Hebrew texts of this "quote" from Abrabanel seem to be based on different ways to rephrase Justman's original Yiddish misattributed text.

In the *Haggadah Treasury* (ArtScroll, 1978), this explanation is given in the name of Abudraham,[56] an approach followed by Rabbi Jona-

---

(Rechasim: Tiferet Ram, 2001), 923.

51 Introduction to the Feldheim English translation of the Kitov Haggada (Jerusalem: Feldheim, 1999), vi.

52 Eliyahu Kitov, *Haggada shel Pesaḥ: Yalkut Tov* (Jerusalem: Alef, 1961), 79.

53 Hayim S. Becker, *Yalkut LeMoadim: Haggada shel Pesaḥ* (Jerusalem: HaTeḥiya, 1968), 103. He also copies the *Meshekh Ḥokhma* brought right after from the Kitov Haggada, as well as the same exact formulation of the Maharil's explanation. The book *Yalkut LeMoadim: Haggada shel Pesaḥ* was not very meticulous about citing references. On the same page he gives the Vilna Gaon as the source for the explanation found in *Sefer Mataamim* that the custom symbolizes the diminishing of the Egyptians, an idea not found in the writings of the Vilna Gaon. See Yosef Eliyahu Halevi Movshovitz, ed., *Haggada shel Pesaḥ im Peirush HaGra* (Jerusalem: Mossad HaRav Kook, 2009), 63. The source of the confusion, it seems, is Yosef Leser's *Haggada shel Pesaḥ – Maatayim Sheloshim VeShemoneh Peirushim* (Cracow, Poland, 1905), 39, where two paragraphs in small print are found under the large print heading "From Rabbeinu the Gra," but the second paragraph actually begins with the words "In the name of *Sefer HaMinhagim*" and gives the explanation found in *Sefer Mataamim* in the name of *Sefer HaMinhagim*.

54 Two examples: Bezalel Landau, *Haggada shel Pesaḥ – LeAvot ULebanim* (Jerusalem: Mifal Torah MiTziyon, 1972), 49; Meir Cohen, *Sefer Pesaḥ KeHalakha* (Ashdod, 1997), 130.

55 Kitov is listed in the bibliography of the *ArtScroll Haggadah*, and in a footnote to the explanation of Abrabanel, the *ArtScroll Haggadah* brings an idea from the *Meshekh Ḥokhma*, which in *Yalkut Tov* is also brought immediately after the Abrabanel.

56 Nosson Scherman, ed., *The Haggadah Treasury* (New York: Mesorah in conjunction with Zeirei Agudath Israel of America, 1978), 92.

than Sacks in his Haggada.[57] Since this idea does not actually appear in the writings of either Abudraham or Abrabanel,[58] or even in the later additions to the commentary of Abrabanel on the Haggada,[59] scholarly works that bring this explanation are generally careful not to attribute it to a particular early rabbinic authority. Instead they attribute it to ambiguous "later sources"[60] or "the opinion of some,"[61] or state that "it is commonly said."[62] Modern English-language Haggadot that give Abudraham or Abrabanel as the source for the explanation of "incomplete joy" seem to be using the ArtScroll Haggadot from the 1970s as their source.

## THE EARLIEST SOURCES

Where does this explanation for the custom originate? Since it seems to be particularly politically correct, some claim that this interpretation was started by Reform rabbis, an idea propagated by the Reform movement itself. It was claimed that this "beautiful and moving interpretation" of the removal of drops of wine as symbolizing "the diminishing of our joy at our own redemption as we recall the sufferings of our oppressors" was "originated by Rabbi Herbert Bronstein in the 1974 CCAR Haggada."[63] We have seen, however, that this interpretation was already popular decades before that.

In the introduction to his 1947 commentary on the Haggada, Daniel Goldschmidt writes that "in recent times an attempt has been made to explain this custom in a more ethical manner, and give it a meaning that is appropriate for modern sensibilities, as if we are symbolically

57 Jonathan Sacks, *Rabbi Jonathan Sacks's Haggadah* (New York: Continuum, 2010), 36.

58 David Arnow, in *Creating Lively Passover Seders* (Woodstock, VT: Jewish Lights, 2004), 192, correctly notes that it is "widely (but questionably) attributed to Isaac Abrabanel."

59 Israel Meir Perser, *Haggada shel Pesaḥ Abrabanel – Zevaḥ Pesaḥ* (Jerusalem: Mossad HaRav Kook, 2007), 13.

60 Joseph Tabory, *The JPS Commentary on the Haggadah: Historical Introduction, Translation and Commentary* (Philadelphia: Jewish Publication Society, 2008), 27.

61 Menachem Kasher, *The Passover Haggadah* (New York, 1957), 159.

62 Lawrence Hoffman and David Arnow, eds., *My People's Passover Haggadah: Traditional Texts, Modern Commentaries*, vol. 2 (Woodstock, VT: Jewish Lights, 2008), 45.

63 "Selections from the *New Union Haggadah*," *The Reform Advocate* 6, no. 1 (Spring 2014), 3.

lessening the joy of the holiday due to consideration of the downfall of the Egyptians, based on the verse 'If your enemy falls do not exult' (Proverbs 24:17)." In a note he attributes this explanation to Rabbi Hirsch and Rabbi Dr. Eduard Baneth.[64] We do not find this reason for the custom of taking out drops of wine in the writings of the former,[65] but we do find it in the writings of the latter.

Eduard Ezekiel Baneth (1855–1930) studied at the Rabbinical Seminary in Berlin and was ordained by Rabbi Israel Hildesheimer.[66] He served as the rabbi of Krotoszyn, Poland, and later became a professor of Talmud at the Lehranstalt für die Wissenschaft des Judentums in Berlin, where he was succeeded by Hanoch Albeck.[67] Eduard Baneth was known in Germany as a *talmid ḥakham* and an academic. While he was completely observant and a member of Mizrachi (he was one of the

64 Daniel Goldschmidt, *Haggada shel Pesaḥ* (Tel Aviv: Schocken, 1947), 20–21. This is also noted in the English-language Passover Haggada edited by Nahum Glatzer, published in 1953, which incorporated Goldschmidt's comments: "In recent times an attempt has been made by S. R. Hirsch and Eduard Baneth to interpret this custom as a symbolic tempering of the joy of the evening in order to show sympathy for the misfortune of the Egyptians." Nahum Glatzer, ed., *The Passover Haggadah* (New York: Schocken Books, 1953), 41.

65 In the original German edition of his Schocken Haggada, *Die Pessach-Haggada* (Berlin: Schoken, 1937), 23, 24, Goldschmidt attributed this explanation to Hirsch but did not provide a source for that attribution. Hirsch did not write a commentary on the Haggada, as noted in the introduction to the Feldheim *Hirsch Haggadah*. He does discuss the idea expressed in the verse "If your enemy falls do not exult" (Prov. 24:17) in his commentary on *Pirkei Avot* 4:23, but he does not connect it to this Passover custom. In the material on this verse brought in the collection of Hirsch's writings on Proverbs, *From the Wisdom of Mishlei* (New York: Feldheim, 2000), there is also nothing related to Passover. The explanation is also brought in the name of Hirsch, but likewise with no actual reference, in Yehuda David Zinger, *Ziv HaMinhagim* (Jerusalem: Kollel Ziv haMinhagim, 2000), 125.

66 *Jewish Encyclopedia*, vol.2 (New York: Funk and Wagnalls, 1906), 489. A photo of Baneth can be found in *The Universal Jewish Encyclopedia*, vol. 2 (New York: Universal Jewish Encyclopedia, 1948), 63. An early Hebrew-language Haggada with this explanation, but without any attribution, is Zev Klein, *Haggada shel Pesaḥ – Ḥokhma im Naḥala* (Buenos Aires: Julio Kaufman, 1948), 38. It is significant that Klein was a member of Kahal Adass Yisroel in Berlin, led by Hildesheimer, and often quotes Hirsch in his Haggada.

67 Dan Cohn-Sherbok, *Dictionary of Jewish Biography* (New York: Continuum, 2005), 22.

founders of the weekly national-religious Hebrew newspaper *HaIvri*),[68] he was not considered part of the official Orthodox establishment due to his position at the Lehranstalt für die Wissenschaft des Judentums, a liberal institution.[69] Today he is mostly remembered for giving a score of "Good" to Regina Jones's paper "Can a Woman Hold Rabbinical Office?" shortly before his death. Regina Jones went on to become the first woman ordained as a rabbi in 1935.[70]

Eduard Baneth mentions the explanation "incomplete joy" for removing some wine from the cup at the Seder in his lecture on the Passover Seder, "*Der Sederabend: Ein Vortrag*," published in Berlin in 1904, a work considered significant in its time.[71] There he writes that when he was "still a boy, the strange custom was explained" to mean that wine is a symbol of joy, and because each plague caused our tormentors to suffer on our account, we diminish our joy over our own liberation. He notes that "whether this explanation may make claim to historical truth" is an open question, but "one must recognize the poetic truth" and that it "breathes the spirit of Judaism" as reflected in the midrash quoted in *Beit Yosef, Oraḥ Ḥayim* 490.[72]

One of Baneth's contemporaries, Rabbi Eliyahu Klatzkin (1852–1932), the famed "*ilui* (genius) from Shklov" who served as chief rabbi

68 Baneth's connection to Mizrachi may have contributed to the inclusion of this explanation in the German guidebook on the Seder for Mizrachi youth. Bernhard S. Jacobson, *Pesach: Arbeitsplan und Stoffsammlung* (Hamburg, 1936), 25. Bernhard Jacobson would go on to write the *Netiv Bina* series on the prayers as Yissachar Yaakovson.

69 Meir Bar-Ilan, *From Volozhin to Jerusalem*, vol. 2 (Tel Aviv: Pilei, 1939), 394 [Hebrew].

70 See Michael Meyer, "Women in the Thought and Practice of the European Jewish Reform Movement," in Marion Kaplan and Deborah Dash Moore, eds., *Gender and Jewish History* (Bloomington, IN: Indiana University Press, 2011), 152; Tiffany Wayne, ed., *Feminist Writings from Ancient Times to the Modern World: A Global Sourcebook and History* (Santa Barbara, CA: ABC-CLIO, LLC, 2011), 504; George Kohler, *Reading Maimonides' Philosophy in 19th Century Germany: The Guide to Religious Reform* (New York: Springer, 2012), 8, note 22.

71 Glatzer considered it worthy of "special attention." Nahum Glatzer, ed., *The Passover Haggadah* (New York: Schocken Books, 1953), 14. It is noted as "a penetrating analysis" in Goldschmidt, "Studies on Jewish Liturgy by German Jewish Scholars," *Leo Baeck Institute Yearbook* (1957), 2 (1), 129.

72 Eduard Baneth, *Der Sederabend: Ein Vortrag* (Berlin: Poppelauer, 1904), 28–29.

of Lublin from 1910–28,[73] also mentions this explanation. Rabbi Klatzkin authored many books, and was considered a major halakhic authority, particularly in the area of releasing *agunot*.[74] He was also known for his knowledge of medicine, pharmacology, mathematics, history, and geography, and was conversant in Greek, Latin, German, French, English, Russian, and Polish.[75] *Kuntres LeDugma* is a twenty-four-page booklet of miscellaneous material from works that Rabbi Klatzkin began writing but never completed. The beginning section contains homiletic material related to the weekly Torah reading, and in the section on *Parashat Va'era* he writes that "we do not act like the Gentiles who are joyous at the downfall of their enemies when they... kill them, rather we follow the ways of the Holy One Blessed be He (Sota 14a), and it is written, 'The Holy One Blessed be He is not happy at the destruction of the wicked... He said to them "My handiwork is drowning in the sea and you sing before me"' (Sanhedrin 39b), and when we mention and tell of the plagues... we pour out and diminish the cup through dripping out drop by drop." He continues that in addition to the original reason for the custom given by the Roke'aḥ, "it makes sense to say that it is also to show that... when we recall this we are pained... and to remember the pain mixed with joy, we take away from the cup."[76]

73 See Jacob Klatzkin, "Eliyahu Klatzkin," in Leo Jung, ed., *Jewish Leaders, 1750–1940* (New York: Bloch, 1954), 340; Aviad Hacohen, *The Tears of the Oppressed* (Jersey City, NJ: Ktav, 2004), 62, note 125.

74 See, for example, Shimon Yosef Meller, *The Brisker Rav: The Life and Times of Maran HaGaon HaRav Yitzḥak Ze'ev HaLevi Soloveichik zt"l*, vol. 1 (Jerusalem: Feldheim, 2007), 233, note 2.

75 Shnayer Z. Leiman, "Rabbinic Openness to General Culture in the Early Modern Period in Western and Central Europe," in Jacob J. Schacter, ed., *Judaism's Encounter with Other Cultures* (Northvale, NJ: Jason Aronson, 1997), 213, note 178.

76 Eliyahu Klatzkin, *Kuntres LeDugma* (Lublin, 1921), 4, 5. Rabbi Klatzkin moved to Jerusalem in 1928, and this explanation is included in his name in Haggadot that focus on the rabbis of Jerusalem. See Shabbtai Rosenthal, *Haggada shel Pesaḥ – Geonei VeḤakhmei Yerushalayim* (Jerusalem: Mifal Moreshet Yerushalayim, 1996), 95, 96; Shlomo Verner, *MiShulḥanam shel Gedolei Yerushalayim* (Jerusalem: Machon Keren Re'em, 2008), 121. Both books change the order of the sentences in Rabbi Klatzkin's original formulation, but are otherwise true to the source material. Klatzkin is also quoted in Pinhas Issac, *Peninei Pardes – Haggada shel Pesaḥ* (Rishon LeZion, 1995), 87, 88.

Both Rabbis Klatzkin and Baneth indicate that this explanation is not the historical reason for the custom, an assessment echoed in *The Schechter Haggadah*, which, after attributing this explanation to Abrabanel, states that "although it does not seem that this is the origin of the custom, it is a notion connected to Passover in classical rabbinic sources" and proceeds to quote the midrashim mentioned earlier.[77] It should be noted, however, that although this idea might be connected to Passover in general, until the innovation of the "incomplete joy" explanation, the message of the plagues was understood to emphasize that "only the exercise of overwhelming force... ultimately succeeded in freeing the Jewish people from slavery."[78]

While it is clear that the latter formulations of this idea were derived from Rabbi Baneth, as they make reference to the recitation of the partial Hallel, an idea noted in the discussion of the custom by Rabbi Baneth but not mentioned by Rabbi Klatzkin, we now see that the idea of diminished joy was being discussed by learned Orthodox rabbis in the early 1900s. As Eduard Baneth was only three years younger than Eliyahu Klatzkin, Rabbi Klatzkin could not have been the source of the explanation that Rabbi Baneth reported hearing as a young boy at the Seder.

### THE TRUE ORIGIN

Is there any way of determining who originated the idea that was told to a young Eduard Baneth? The book *Divrei Yirmeyahu – Derashot* is a collection of the homilies of Rabbi Yirmeyahu Löw (1812–74), compiled by his grandson, Rabbi Binyamin Zev Lev (Löw). In the last pages of the book, some extra material is added "in order not to leave blank pages." There Rabbi Binyamin Zev Lev brings the "incomplete joy" explanation in the name of his grandfather, indicating that it was a nice idea that his grandfather originated.[79] He writes that his grandfather explained that "since the Jewish people are merciful, and since through the rescue from Egypt many of God's creations were destroyed and drowned, although

77 Joshua Kulp and David Golinkin, *The Schechter Haggadah: Art, History and Commentary* (Jerusalem: Schechter Institute of Jewish Studies, 2009), 233.

78 Laufer, 98.

79 He writes that his grandfather "gave a nice explanation" (נתן טעם לשבח).

it is a great joy for us that God took us out of Egypt and redeemed us, it is still painful for us that through this others were destroyed... and if God would have rescued us without the destruction and death of others it would be a greater joy for us. Therefore our joy is a little diminished, and to show that Israel are merciful and the children of [the] merciful, we pour out a little [wine] at every plague."[80]

Although this book was published in 1934, making Rabbi Baneth's record of this explanation published in 1904 the earliest, this represents the first legitimate named attribution for this interpretation, placing its origin in the 1800s. It does not connect the drops of wine to the midrashic explanation for the abbreviated Hallel; that connection was made by Baneth. In the formulation of Rabbi Yirmeyahu Löw, there is nothing inherently unethical or inappropriate about celebrating the destruction of their enemies, but "since the Jewish people are merciful" and "to show that Israel are merciful and the children of [the] merciful," we go beyond normal moral standards and express diminished joy because of the deaths of the Egyptians. This aspect was also stressed by Rabbi Klatzkin, who emphasizes that not expressing joy at the death of enemies is a particularly Jewish trait. It would seem that the ultimate origin of the "incomplete joy" explanation is Rabbi Yirmeyahu Löw. Although the "incomplete joy" explanation seems to express modern sensibilities and possibly political correctness, Rabbi Löw was not known for these characteristics, and in fact was considered a "recognized leader of Hungarian Orthodoxy," and a vigorous opponent of Hasidism, the Reform movement,[81] and the Enlightenment.[82]

---

80 Binyamin Zev Lev (Löw), *Sefer Divrei Yirmeyahu – Derashot* (Satmar: Meir Lev Hirsch, 1934), 42b. In Shaul Yechezkel Weiss, *Haggada Shel Pesaḥ – Otzar Divrei HaMefarshim* (London, 2010), 321, he mistakenly attributes this explanation to Elazar Löw of Santov in the name of his own grandfather, but the writer of this particular section is the compiler of the book, Binyamin Wolf. It is clear that he is referring to his own grandfather, whom he calls זקני הקדוש ז"ל, as distinct from his great-grandfather, Binyamin Wolf, whom he refers to as זקני הקדוש בעל שערי תורה ז"ל in the very next paragraph.

81 *The Universal Jewish Encyclopedia*, vol. 7 (New York: Universal Jewish Encyclopedia, 1948), 213.

82 See Yehiel Mikhel Stern, *Sefer Gedolei HaDorot* (Jerusalem: Minchat Yisrael, 1996), 690, and David Halachmi, *Ḥakhmei Yisrael* (Bnei Brak: Tiferet Hasefer, 1980), 303.

Eduard Baneth was nineteen years old when Rabbi Yirmeyahu Löw passed away, and it is reasonable that a member of the Baneth family related an explanation heard from Rabbi Löw. The rabbinical figures in the Löw and Baneth families were connected for generations. Rabbi Yirmeyahu Löw's grandfather, Rabbi Elazar Löw (1758–1837, author of *Shemen Roke'aḥ*), became the rabbi of the Moravian community of Triesch at the recommendation of his friend, the famed Rabbi Mordekhai Benet of Nikolsburg (1753–1829),[83] and his aunt Gittel married Rabbi Mordekhai Benet's son Yeshayahu.[84] Rabbi Benet gave one of the *haskamot* to the first volume of *Shaarei Torah* by Rabbi Yirmeyahu Löw's father, Rabbi Binyamin Wolf.[85] Most significantly, both Rabbi Löw and his brother studied under Rabbi Mordekhai Benet.[86] Rabbi Mordekhai Benet's cousin Joachim Markus (Yaakov) Banet (1750–1812) was the great-grandfather of Eduard Baneth.[87] Thus it is certainly possible that young Eduard Baneth heard the explanation of Rabbi Yirmeyahu Löw through a relative at a family Seder.

Many of the elements found in the "incomplete joy" explanation as stated by Rabbis Löw, Klatzkin, and Baneth are found in the book *Meshekh Ḥokhma*, written by their contemporary, Rabbi Meir Simha of Dvinsk (1843–1926). In his commentary to Exodus 12:16,[88] Rabbi Meir Simha explains that the Israelites were told about the festival on the

83 Zahava Stessel, *Wine and Thorns in Tokay Valley: Jewish Life in Hungary* (Cranbury, NJ: Associated University Presses, 1995), 120. Mordekhai Benet also recommended to Elazar Löw not to rewrite his commentary on *Ḥoshen Mishpat* after the manuscript was lost once, then rewritten and burned in a fire. Benet said this should be taken as a divine sign not to rewrite this work so that scholars would have to study the original source material, 121.

84 Moshe Samet, *HaḤadash Assur min HaTorah* (Jerusalem: Carmel, 2005), 272; Stessel, *Wine and Thorns in Tokay Valley*, 126.

85 Yitzchak Yosef Cohen, *Ḥakhmei Hungaria VehaSafrut HaToranit Bah* (Jerusalem: Machon Yerushalayim, 1997), 254.

86 Stessel, *Wine and Thorns in Tokay Valley*, 124; Yirmiyahu Feldman, *Divrei Yirmeyahu – Kiddushin* (Jerusalem: Machon Yerushalayim, 1984), 12.

87 Benet, Banet, and Baneth are all variant spellings of the same name and were variously used by the different members of the extended family. Benzion Kaganoff, *A Dictionary of Jewish Names and Their History* (Northvale, NJ: Jason Aronson, 1996), 131.

88 In some editions it is attached to the comments on Exodus 12:15.

seventh day of Passover while still in Egypt, "to teach that the holiday is not due to the downfall of the Egyptians at the sea, for God commanded them before the Egyptians drowned ... and so it is explained in *Yalkut Shimoni* (*remez* 654), that this is the reason that *simḥa* is not written regarding Passover and we do not recite the complete Hallel on all seven days because 'if your enemy falls do not exult' (Prov. 24:17)." He specifically declares that other nations establish holidays to celebrate the downfall of their enemies, but Jews do not do this, a sentiment shared by Rabbis Löw and Klatzkin. Although he does not refer to the custom of spilling some drops of wine, there is a clear affinity between the commentary from the *Meshekh Ḥokhma* and the "incomplete joy" explanation, showing that the essence of this explanation was known during this time period. This connection was noted by Rabbi Kitov, who included the idea from the *Meshekh Ḥokhma* in his Haggada following the explanation from Abrabanel.[89] Given that the first part of *Meshekh Ḥokhma* was published decades after the death of Rabbi Löw,[90] Löw remains the earliest representative of this interpretive approach.

It remains unclear how the explanation offered to the young Eduard Baneth came to be associated with Abrabanel and Abudraham. What these authorities have in common is that their names begin with the letters אב, the same letters as the Hebrew initials of Eduard Baneth. Thus it is possible that a writer saw this explanation written in Hebrew in the name of ר' אב and misunderstood these letters as referring to the first two letters of either Abrabanel or Abudraham.

We have seen that the modern popularity of the "incomplete joy" explanation can be traced back to an approach originating with Rabbi Yirmeyahu Löw and related to the young Eduard Baneth, then reported by him years later in a lecture. Eduard Baneth is the earliest written source for this explanation. Although sometimes claimed to originate with Reform rabbis, it actually originated with an Orthodox rabbi in the 1800s. It resonated with the sensibilities of English-speaking American

89 Kitov, *Haggada shel Pesaḥ: Yalkut Tov*, 79. It also appears there in the 1977 *ArtScroll Haggadah*, which used Kitov as a source.

90 The earliest date that any part of the *Meshekh Ḥokhma* was printed was 1902. See the introduction to the *Meshekh Ḥokhma* by Avraham in the Feldheim edition.

Jews in particular, and was popularized through being presented as the only explanation for the custom in American Haggadot from the 1940s onward. This interpretation came to be seen as more humane and understandable than the original explanation, which states that this represents the sixteen-faceted sword of God, and by now has eclipsed the original meaning of the custom, certainly in the English-speaking Jewish world.[91]

91 Thanks to Beinish Ginsburg for asking me about the source of this explanation, an inquiry that led to my researching this topic; to Claudia Bollag for helping translate German material; and to my students Ephraim Hollander, Eli Genauer, and Avi Hoffman who helped me go through all the Haggadot at the Hebrew Union College library in Jerusalem. Special thanks to my friend Avi Levine for all-around help and for the many stimulating conversations we had about this issue, which opened up new areas of research.

## Chapter 17

# *Ḥai Rotel* on Lag BaOmer

### INTRODUCTION

There is a custom, which seems to gain more and more publicity each year, to distribute "*ḥai* (eighteen) *rotel*" of drinks in Meron on Lag BaOmer as a *segula* (a supernatural aid) to have children. The custom was not widespread until recent years,[1] affording a rare opportunity to trace the origin and development of a custom as it grows before our eyes.

The *rotel* is a unit of weight that was widely used in the Mediterranean region, but it was measured differently in different countries, and even in different parts of the same country,[2] varying between one and six-plus pounds.[3] Regarding this custom, a *rotel* is understood to be

1 When asked about the custom, Hayim Kanievsky said that "we never knew about it at all." Zvi Yevrov, *Derekh Siḥa* (Bnei Brak: Or HaḤayim, 2004), 429; Yishai Mezlomian, *Segulot Rabboteinu* (Holon, 2014), 321.

2 Housni Alkhateeb Shehada, *Mamluks and Animals: Veterinary Medicine in Medieval Islam* (Leiden: Brill, 2013), 291, note 15; Naval Intelligence Division, *Palestine and Transjordan* (London: Kegan Paul, 2006), 554; Kalman Kahana, *Ḥeker VeIyun* (Tel Aviv: Melen, 1960), 227.

3 Moshe Behar and Zvi Ben-Dor Benite, eds., *Modern Middle Eastern Jewish Thought* (Waltham, MA: Brandeis University Press, 2013), 43, note 18; Mordekhai Diskin, *Divrei Mordekhai* (Jerusalem, 1889), 11a; A. M. Luncz, "History of the Jews in Palestine, Part I," *Jerusalem Year Book* 2 (1887), 18, note 52.

equivalent to three liters, a value at the higher end of the *rotel* scale, so that eighteen *rotel* of drinks is equivalent to fifty-four liters.[4]

These days, the *ḥai rotel segula* is featured in a considerable amount of publicity material disseminated by charitable organizations connected with Lag BaOmer and Meron. For example, on its website, Kupat Tzidkat Rashbi tells us: "The distribution of *ḥai rotel mashkeh* (drinks) to individuals who come to Rabbi Shimon's burial place on Lag BaOmer ensures wonderful merit for the provider. People who distribute *ḥai rotel mashkeh,* fifty-four liters of drink, to the celebrants, earn Rabbi Shimon Bar Yoḥai's berakha and blessing."[5] Similarly, the Yeshuos Rashbi organization states that "the *Taamei HaMinhagim* says that numerous people who have had difficulty having children, finding a *shiddukh,* recovering from an illness or attaining a livelihood were successful only after they donated *ḥai rotel* for the Lag BaOmer celebration in Meron."[6] This practice is distinct from the meritorious act of giving charity, as the drinks are distributed not to the poor and needy, but rather to whoever happens to be celebrating in Meron.[7]

The source commonly quoted for this custom is a letter written by Rabbi Benzion Halberstam, the second Bobover Rebbe (1874–1941), on Sunday, April 21, 1912. He wrote that someone heard that the "Jews in Israel have a tradition that a *segula* for barren couples is to vow to bring eighteen *rotel* of drink (*mashkeh*) on the day of the *hilula* at the grave of the divine *Tanna* Rashbi." The Bobover Rebbe had been asked to perform the *segula.* The Rebbe asks the recipient of the letter, Rabbi Yaakov Yisrael Shmerler,[8] to be his "*shaliaḥ mitzva* to mention the couple Meir ben Ḥaya Leah with his wife Sara bat Sheindel, that God should give them viable offspring speedily with no obstacle or harm, and vow on their behalf eighteen *rotel* of drinks as is customary. And when God assists them and they are redeemed speedily, they are prepared to happily

4 Yaakov Kokhavi, *Darakh Kokhav MiYaakov* (Bnei Brak, 2006), 104.

5 http://www.rashbi.org/page_e.php?id=13 (March 2016).

6 http://www.yeshuosrashbi.com/segula.html (March 2016).

7 *Ohel Avraham* (Bnei Brak, 2011), 227.

8 Regarding this righteous figure, see Natan Anshin, *Sippurim Yerushalmi'im,* vol. 4 (Jerusalem: Daat-HaMeimei, 1997), 132.

repay their vow."[9] Apparently, the vow had to be made at the grave of Rashbi, which is why the Bobover Rebbe appointed a messenger to do this on behalf of the couple. It is understood that the beverages purchased would refresh the visitors to Meron on Rabbi Shimon bar Yoḥai's *hilula*, and is therefore an appropriate way to give thanks for the prayer being answered.[10]

Since the Bobover Rebbe's letter mentions *mashkeh*, a term commonly used for alcoholic beverages, the drink was generally understood to be wine.[11] Old Bobover Hasidim reported that beer was referred to as *mashkeh*, which at the time was sold in cases of a *rotel*.[12] More recent sources mention bringing grape juice,[13] and even soda or chocolate milk[14] – anything that may be considered a significant and refreshing beverage.

This letter is reproduced in the well-known book of customs, *Sefer Taamei HaMinhagim*.[15] The original book was compiled by Rabbi Avraham Sperling (1851–1921), but the chapter about Lag BaOmer customs was added in the 1957 edition, as the commemoration of Lag BaOmer became more popular and elaborate during the years since the book was first written. The new chapter was compiled by Rabbi Shlomo Eliezer Margaliot, based mostly on the works of his father, Rabbi Yeshaya Asher

9 ב"ה, א׳ אח"ק י"ט במב"י תרע"ב באבוב יע"א, שלום רב לידידי האברך המופלג הירא היוחסין כ"ש מו"ה יעקב ישראל נ"י שמערלר, נדרשתי מאחד מאנ"ש יחיה בענין נשגב, היות ששמע מפי אנשי אה"ק ת"ו שקבלה בידם סגולה לחשוכי בנים רח"ל, לנדב ח"י ראטל משקה ביומא דהילולא על ציון התנא האלקי רשב"י זי"ע ועכ"י. לכן בחרתי בו לעשותו שליח מצוה להזכיר לטובה את הזוג מאיר בן חיה לאה עם זוגתו שרה בת שינדל שיפקוד השי"ת אותם בזש"ק במהרה בלי שום מכשול ונזק. וינדב עבורם ח"י ראטל משקה כנהוג. וכאשר יעזור השי"ת ויפקדם בישועה במהרה, מוכנים המה לשלם נדבת לבבם בשמחה. ובזה הנני מברכו בישועה בכ"ע ויזכה לישב על אדמת הקודש במנוחה והשקט ובטח וברוב נחת והרחבה. ידידו"ש באהבה בן ציון הלברשטאם

10 Moshe Bublil, *Simḥat Banim* (2006), 25.

11 Yehuda Sheinfeld, *Oseri LeGefen*, vol. 8 (Jerusalem, 2002), 377, *siman* 403.

12 *Davar BeItto*, 5768 (Bnei Brak, 2008), 847.

13 Yaakov Kokhavi, *Darakh Kokhav MiYaakov* (Bnei Brak, 2006), 104.

14 Bublil, *Simḥat Banim*, 25.

15 Avraham Sperling, *Sefer Taamei HaMinhagim UMekorei HaDinim* (Jerusalem: Eshkol, 1957), 263, in the footnote.

Zelig Margaliot (Riaz, 1894–1969), a major promoter of commemorating Lag BaOmer in Meron.[16]

### EXPLANATIONS FOR THIS CUSTOM

In his letter, the Bobover Rebbe refers to a custom that was already in place, although the letter indicates that he himself knew of this *segula* only because someone had just told him about it. When did it originate, and who started it?

Rabbi Yosef Messas (1892–1974) recounted a legend about the birth of Rabbi Shimon bar Yoḥai based on what he recalled from various books. According to the story, Rabbi Shimon Bar Yoḥai's mother, Sarah, was barren, and her husband, Yoḥai, was considering divorcing her and marrying someone else. Sarah cried and prayed for a child. The story continues:

On the night of Rosh HaShana Yoḥai had a dream, and in the dream he was standing in a large forest. The forest had many thousands of trees; some of them were fresh with fruit and some were dry. Yoḥai was leaning on a dry tree and he lifted his eyes and saw a man of stature, of awesome appearance, carrying a jug filled with water on his shoulder. He watered some of the dry trees and some he skipped over and left as they were. When the man came to water the tree Yoḥai was leaning on, he took out a little plate filled with pure water and watered the tree and blessed it. Yoḥai felt the blessing in the little bit of water. The water kept the tree and its surroundings covered and the tree immediately produced large apples.... When Yoḥai woke up he told his wife about the dream. He told her that he understood that the forest represented the world and the trees represented women, some fertile and some barren like the dry trees... and his wife was the tree he leaned on and she

16 Ibid., 255. Regarding Yeshaya Asher Zelig Margaliot, an ideological leader of the Eda Ḥaredit, see chapter 3 in Raphael Patai and Emanuel Goldsmith, *Thinkers and Teachers of Modern Judaism* (New York: Paragon House, 1994); Aviezer Ravitzky, "Covenant of Faith or Covenant of Fate? Competing Orthodox Conceptions of Secular Jews," in Rachel Elior and Peter Schafer, eds., *Creation and Re-Creation in Jewish Thought* (Tubingen, Germany: Mohr Siebeck, 2005), 283–84; Motti Inbari, *Messianic Religious Zionism Confronts Israeli Territorial Compromises* (Cambridge: Cambridge University Press, 2012), 146–47.

was now watered with the spring of blessing.... But what was the reason that the man watered all the other trees with a jug and the tree he leaned on was watered with a little plate? His wife suggested going to Rabbi Akiva and asking for an explanation of the dream. Rabbi Akiva explained that the little bit of water the man used were the tears Sarah cried when she prayed, that's why it was used only for this tree. He told them she would get pregnant that very year. And so it happened. Yoḥai and Sarah had a baby boy born on Shavuot. They called him Shimon, since God heard her prayers.[17]

Although this story is sometimes brought as a source for the *segula,*[18] it actually contains nothing about donating drinks or making a vow of any kind connected to having children. Furthermore, the story itself is of questionable provenance, as it does not appear in any classical sources nor in any written source prior to Rabbi Messas.

Another source given for the custom is a letter written by Rabbi Ovadia of Bartenura in 1489, where he responds to his brother's query regarding miracles associated with the Temple Mount and graves of saintly people. The general tenor is to deny the miracles his brother asked about. In his discussion of alleged miracles, he notes that on the 28th of Iyar people gather at the grave of Samuel the prophet, and he never heard of any miracles associated with that site "other than people saying that many barren women have conceived and sick people were healed after a vow or promise was made there, or their prayers there were answered." He concludes that the authenticity of these reports cannot be verified.[19] In earlier, corrupted versions of this letter, the date was switched to the 18th of Iyar, and Rabbi Shimon bar Yoḥai was substituted for Samuel the prophet,[20] leading to an association of Lag BaOmer with Meron.[21] In actuality, Rabbi Ovadia specifically writes that he did not visit the northern part of Israel, and the only comment he makes about Tzfat

17 Yosef Messas, *Naḥalat Avot*, vol. 3 (Jerusalem: Otzrot Yosef, 1977), 31–32.

18 Ilan Smila, *Ilana DeḤaye* (Lod, 2012), 247–48.

19 Avraham Yaari, ed., *Iggerot Eretz Yisrael* (Ramat Gan: Massada, 1971), 139, letter 22.

20 Ovadia MiBartenura, *Darkhei Tziyon* (Kolomya, 1886), 17b; errors repeated in the Petrikov, 1928 edition, 26.

21 See the discussion by Hanokh Tobias in *Alim LeTrufa*, no. 381, 3 Av 5763 (2003), 3; *Davar BeItto*, 5768 (Bnei Brak, 2008), 846.

and the north in this letter is that he heard that the Jews and Muslims live there peacefully.[22]

## THE ORIGIN AND DEVELOPMENT OF THE CUSTOM

The earliest recorded mention of this practice is in the book *Tal Yerushalayim,* published in 1873. It was written by Rabbi Yehuda Ornstein (1814–89), formerly the *Av Beit Din* of Faltishen (Falticeni), Romania, who moved to Jerusalem and headed the court of the hasidic community there.[23] The book describes the customs of the people living in Jerusalem, and Israel in general, at that time. In the book, the author records a visit to Meron on Lag BaOmer, noting the celebrations and practices he saw there. The author reports that he saw with his own eyes, "two men who had a lot of *mashkeh,* and they would ask every person to drink their *mashkeh.* I asked what this was about, and I was told that one of the men had brought his young son for a festive haircut. He did not have children for fourteen years. One time the men were [in Meron for] Lag BaOmer and in a festive mood. One said in a loud voice that he vowed to bring eighteen *rotel* of *mashkeh* to the celebration of Rabbi Shimon bar Yoḥai so he should help the man have a son this year, and the crowd answered 'Amen!' That year his wife became pregnant and gave birth to a son. Now that it was time for his son's haircut he repaid his vow. The other man did not have children for ten years, he made the same vow as the first man, and God helped him too. I heard this from the men themselves."[24]

---

22 Yaari, *Iggerot Eretz Yisrael,* 139–40, letter 22.

23 Yehuda Orenstein, *Tal Yerushalayim* (Jerusalem, 1988), 2–3. See the biographical information in Barukh Traktin and Zev Hershkovitz, *Encyclopedia LeYahadut Romania,* vol. 1 (Jerusalem: Mossad HaRav Kook, 2012), 424; Meir Wunder, *Encyclopedia LeḤachmei Galicia,* vol. 6 (Jerusalem: Machon LeHantzaḥat Yahadut Galicia, 2005), 43–44; *Od Yosef Ḥai – Memorial Volume* (Jerusalem, 1989), 71–72.

24 Orenstein, *Tal Yerushalayim* (Jerusalem, 1873), 10a–b. More recently reprinted in Jerusalem, 1988, 39–40.
והנה בשמחה זו ראיתי בעיני שהיו שני אנשים שהיו להם משקה הרבה, והיו מבקשים לכל איש שישתה משקה שלהם, ושאלתי מה זה וסיפרו לי שאחד הביא קטן שלו על שמחת התג־לחת, והוא לא היו לו ילדים ארבעה עשר שנים, ופעם אחת היו בל״ג בעומר ובתוך השמחה ענה בקול אני מנדר שמונה עשר ראטיל משקה על שמחת רשב״י שיעזור לי ה׳ בזו השנה בן

Since there is no earlier mention of this custom, and the author seemed surprised and intrigued by what he saw and the explanation he received, it is clear that this was not a pre-existing, well-known custom, but rather seems to have been a spontaneous vow made by one man, perhaps when he was a bit tipsy, which was seconded by another man. In the well-known series on Jewish customs, *Nitei Gavriel,* this vow was understood to be a pledge to make a *seuda* with eighteen *rotel* of drinks at the time of the child's first haircut.[25] Thus, the vow of eighteen *rotel* of *mashkeh* is comparable to someone today vowing to make a Kiddush with eighteen bottles of scotch, or pledging $180 at an appeal.

The payment of the vow was a big event that year on Lag BaOmer, and thanks to the author, the story became known to a wider audience. In the years between the publication of *Tal Yerushalayim* and the Bobover Rebbe's writing his letter, word of this particular vow had spread to the extent that others followed suit, and it was transformed from a personal vow into a *segula.* It cannot be considered an ancient custom.[26]

Adding to the popularity of the practice, the original story from *Tal Yerushalayim* was quoted in the book *Masa Meron,* published in 1966. This book is based on the 1889 book *Masa Meron* by Rabbi Menachem Mendel Rubin, in which he describes his trip to Meron.[27] The 1966 version was published by the local council in Israel in which Meron is located, Merom HaGalil, and contained much additional material beyond the original travelogue, such as songs and prayers associated with Rashbi, as well as tales of salvation, including the story of the two childless men.[28] The book was aimed at encouraging and

---

זכר, וענו כל העם בקול אמן. בשנה זו נתעברה זוגתו וילדה לו בן, וכעת הגיע זמן ההתגלחת ושילם נדרו כאשר נדר, ואיש השני לא היו לו ילדים עשר שנים. ענה אחריו כנ"ל ועזר לו ד' גם כן. שמעתי מפיהם בעצמם.

25 Gavriel Zinner, *Nitei Gavriel: Children's Haircuts, Bringing Them to Cheder and Chumash Parties* (Jerusalem, 2001), 73, note 13.

26 David Russof, *VeAmartem Ko LeḤai* (Jerusalem: Otzar HaTorah, 2006), 329.

27 Menachem Mendel Rubin, *Masa Meron* (Jerusalem, 1889).

28 Bezalel Landoy, *Masa Meron* (Jerusalem: Usha, 1966), 112.

supporting people visiting Meron on Lag BaOmer.[29] Multiple editions of this book have appeared since then.[30]

In the original story we see all the elements that made it into the 1912 letter: the vow was made in Meron on Lag BaOmer, there was a plea to have a child, and the vow was repaid only after the prayer was answered, in the original episode only when the child got his first haircut years later. We can now trace the development of this custom. It began as a spontaneous individual vow by two childless men in the mid- to late 1800s. The episode was recorded in the book *Tal Yerushalayim*. Others heard or read about this and word of the vow spread, so that the Bobover Rebbe had heard of it by the early 1900s. The custom was then included in the 1957 edition, and all subsequent editions, of the very popular *Sefer Taamei HaMinhagim*. The original story was recounted in the various editions of *Masa Meron* from the 1960s onward.

Note that the original sources of this *segula* only refer to having children, nothing else, and more significantly, the drinks were purchased and distributed only after the prayers were answered.[31] Today, the *segula* is used as a pretext for organizations to ask for donations on Lag BaOmer by subtly shifting the donation of eighteen *rotel* from after the prayer is answered to before the prayer is answered, which brings us to the contemporary version of this *segula*.[32] Modern books that repeat the contents of the Bobover Rebbe's letter even misquote the request in order to match the current practice. While in the original letter the Bobover Rebbe asked Rabbi Shmerler only to make the vow at Meron for the couple to have a child, this has been changed to a request "to distribute eighteen *rotel* of drinks... in Meron."[33] Although the original sources talk about this only as a *segula* to have children, now it is

---

29 Ibid., dedication on inside cover.

30 For example, *Masa Meron* (Jerusalem: Torah MiTziyon, 1983) and *Masa Meron* (Jerusalem: Wagshal, 1989).

31 That is, when the woman becomes pregnant. See Asher Chananiah, *She'elot UTeshuvot Shaarei Yosher*, vol. 3 (Jerusalem, 2005), 349, *Yoreh De'ah, siman* 16.

32 See, for example, Aharon Tzoref, *Mevasser Tov* (2010), 52–53; *Davar BeItto*, 5768 (Bnei Brak, 2008), 847.

33 Baruch Lev, *There Is No Such Thing as Coincidence* (Jerusalem: Feldheim, 2003), 45. There the date of the letter is mistakenly given as 1932.

advertised as helping with *shiddukhim* and livelihood as well,[34] which were never mentioned in the original sources or the literature that faithfully recounted those original sources. These alterations to the original version of the vow may have been made in good faith or can be viewed in a more cynical manner.

What began as a spontaneous vow by a childless man in the 1800s has now become a cure-all *segula* and fundraising tool directed at a population that is fundamentally unaware that this *segula* never really existed.

34 Ibid., 45. The author states that he was told by a representative of Agudas Ohel HaRashbi that this *segula* also works to find a spouse or cure illnesses, after they "had given eighteen *rotel* of drinks." Special thanks to my neighbor Mordechai Holtz who asked the question that inspired this chapter.

# Part 3
## *Liturgy*

*Chapter 18*

# The Expanded *Taḥanun* for Monday and Thursday

The Talmud in Berakhot (16b–17a) gives many examples of personal additional prayers that the Sages added to follow the *Amida*. This point in the service was designated for individual expression. At first it took the form of an epilogue to the *Amida* but eventually took on a distinct structure as *Taḥanun*, also known as *Nefilat Apayim*.[1] These penitential prayers (*Taḥanunim*) began as private supplications but became more standardized over time. The earliest post-talmudic versions of the daily *Taḥanun* were based on two sources; the personal prayers of the Sages recorded in the Talmud, and the benedictions of the *Amida*. Either or both of these provided the basis for the weekday *Taḥanun* found in the writings of ben Baboi, *Seder Rav Amram Gaon*,

1 Solomon Freehof, "The Origin of the Tahanun," *Hebrew Union College Annual*, vol. 2 (1925), 341–42. Regarding one's posture during *Nefilat Apayim*, which literally means to "fall on one's nostrils," see Ruth Langer, "We Do Not Even Know What to Do: A Foray into the Early History of Tahanun," 48–49, in *Seeking the Favor of God: Volume 3: The Impact on Penitential Prayer Beyond Second Temple Judaism*, ed. Mark J. Boda et al. (Atlanta: Society of Biblical Literature, 2008), 39–69.

*Siddur Rav Saadia Gaon*, and *geniza* fragments from the geonic period.[2] This reflects the original connection of *Taḥanun* to the part of the liturgy that preceded it, the *Amida.*

On Mondays and Thursdays, long prayers of supplication are added to the regular *Taḥanun* of the morning service. These are the days when, according to tradition, both the earthly and heavenly courts sit in judgment.[3] While Mondays and Thursdays are already mentioned in the Tosefta[4] as designated for public fasts, and individuals typically chose them as fast days in talmudic times,[5] special prayers for Mondays and Thursdays on which fasts did not take place are not noted in the Talmud.

The additional *Taḥanunim* for Mondays and Thursdays are divided in contemporary Ashkenazic prayer books into eight liturgical units.[6] The first is a collection of verses beginning with *Vehu Raḥum.* This is followed by a passage from the book of Daniel (9:15–19). Next is a supplication beginning with the words *Avinu Av HaRaḥaman,* followed by a short prayer, *Habet Na Raḥem Na.* The next supplication begins with

---

2 Freehof, "The Origin of the Tahanun," 345–48.

3 Shabbat 129b.

4 Tosefta Taanit 2:5. The Mishna (Taanit 1:4) mentions three fast days when there is a drought but does not explicitly state that they take place on Mondays and Thursdays. An early version of Taanit Esther took place on the Monday, Thursday, and Monday following Purim (Soferim 21:1).

5 See Taanit 12a and *Megillat Taanit,* end of chapter 12, where a case is discussed dealing with a person who accepted upon himself to fast every Monday and Thursday of the year. Soferim 21:3 states that "scholars fast on Mondays and Thursdays [throughout the year] on account of the desecration of the name of God and for the honor of the Temple which was burnt." See also the *Tur, Oraḥ Ḥayim* 429:2, which connects this with the custom to fast on these days following the holidays of Passover and Sukkot. Regarding the origin of Mondays and Thursdays as days appropriate for fasting and supplication, see *Sefer HaManhig, siman* 69 (p. 102); *Tur, Oraḥ Ḥayim* 134:1; Rema, *Shulḥan Arukh, Oraḥ Ḥayim* 134:1; and *Be'er Heitev* 134:1. See also Ismar Elbogen, *Jewish Liturgy, A Comprehensive History* (Philadelphia: Jewish Publication Society, 1993), 69; Clemens Leonhard, *The Jewish Pesach and the Origins of the Christian Easter* (Berlin: Walter de Gruyter, 2006), 131–32, note 29; Yonah Frenkel, *Midrash VeAggada,* vol. 3 (Tel Aviv: The Open University of Israel, 1996), 616–19. See also Alter Hilevitz, "Taanit Esther," *Sinai* 64 (1968): 238–39, where the idea of Monday/Thursday fasts is understood as a custom of Eretz Yisrael not accepted in Babylonia.

6 Nosson Scherman, *The ArtScroll Siddur* (New York: Mesorah, 1990), 124–32; Shlomo Tal, *Siddur Rinat Yisrael* (Jerusalem: Moreshet, 1981), 82–87.

*Ana Melekh Raḥum Veḥanun,* followed by the three prayers *El Raḥum, Ein Kamokha,* and *HaPote'aḥ Yad,* each its own liturgical unit. Unlike the basic *Taḥanun* of the rest of the weekdays, the blessings of the *Amida* and the prayers of the Sages do not form the basis for the Monday and Thursday additions. In this chapter, we will trace the origin of the special *Taḥanun* prayers recited on these days in addition to the standard weekday *Nefilat Apayim.*

### THE THREE AUTHORS

There are three primary versions of the legendary origin of these prayers, and it is difficult to determine the historical truth behind them.[7] One version appears in the twelfth-century works *Sefer HaManhig,*[8] *Orḥot Ḥayim*[9] and *Kol Bo.*[10] *Sefer HaManhig* has a very terse version of the story; *Orḥot Ḥayim* and *Kol Bo* have a greatly expanded and more detailed narrative. The version in *Orḥot Ḥayim,* which is nearly identical word for word to the version in *Kol Bo,* reads:

> An episode happened with a Jewish ship that came from the exile of Jerusalem to a place with a tyrant. He asked them, "What nation are you from?" They replied, "From the Jewish nation." He told them, "If you are from the Jewish nation, I want to test you as Ḥananya, Mishael, and Azarya were tested in a fiery furnace" (Dan. 3). They said to him, "Give us thirty days." He gave them time. They fasted and every day whoever had a dream would relate it before the community. At the end of the thirty days, there was

7 Eliezer Landshut, *Siddur Hegayon Lev* (Königsberg: Adolph Samter, 1845), 89.

8 Yitzhak Rafael, ed., *Sefer HaManhig LeRabbi Avraham BeRebbi Natan HaYarḥi,* vol. 1 (Jerusalem: Mossad HaRav Kook, 1978), 102. Abudraham quotes the story from *Sefer HaManhig, Sefer Abudraham HaShalem,* vol. 1 (Jerusalem: Even Israel, 1995), 140–41. It is very briefly mentioned in the thirteenth-century work *Sefer HaMaḥkim* by Natan ben Yehuda; Jacob Freiman, ed., *The Sefer HaMaḥkim of R. Nathan ben Yehuda* (Kharkov, 1909), 14.

9 Aharon HaKohen, *Orḥot Ḥayim* (Jerusalem: Sela, 1956), 47.

10 David Abraham, ed., *Kol Bo,* vol. 1 (Jerusalem, 2007), 335–36, *siman* 18. The date and authorship of *Kol Bo* is uncertain but seems to be from the thirteenth century. See the introduction by Shlomo Zalman Havlin in *Sefer Kol Bo* (Jerusalem: Even Yisroel, 1997), 7–10.

> an old man who feared sin but was not very wise, who said, "I saw in a dream that a verse was read to me with the word *ki* (כי) written twice and the word *lo* (לא) written three times, and I do not know what it is." One wise old man said, "This is certainly the verse that you were shown from heaven: 'When (כי) thou passest through the waters, I will be with thee, and through the rivers, they shall not (לא) overflow thee; when (כי) thou walkest through the fire, thou shalt not (לא) be burned, neither (לא) shall the flame kindle upon thee' (Isa. 43:2). You will certainly be able to go into the fire and be rescued, since you are safe."[11] They built at the king's command a great fire at the crossroads, and the old man who dreamt that dream went in the fire and it split into three paths, and the three righteous ones entered them to meet the old man. These three elders praised and said *Vehu Raḥum*. The first said until *Ana Melekh Raḥum Veḥanun*, the second until *Ein Kamokha*, the third from there on. The Sages established to say this on Mondays and Thursdays, which are days of judgment.[12]

The eight liturgical units of the Monday/Thursday *Taḥanun* were understood to represent subdivisions of these three primary divisions. *Vehu Raḥum* contains sections one to four, *Ana Melekh Raḥum Veḥanun* covers sections five and six, and *Ein Kamokha* contains sections seven and eight.[13]

A second version of this story is first mentioned by Rabbi Eliezer ben Natan of Mainz (1090–1170), an early Tosafist, in a commentary he wrote on some of the prayers. He seems to be quoting the story from

---

11 In *Kol Bo* it says, "Since this is from heaven."

12 Berliner notes that the text of these prayers does not indicate any rescue from fire, and the story should be regarded as without historical basis. Abraham Berliner, *Ketavim Nivḥarim*, vol. 1 (Jerusalem: Mossad HaRav Kook, 1989), 66.

13 *Kol Bo* adds that each of the three liturgical units begins and ends with a passage containing the word *raḥum*. This is true of the first two units and the beginning of the third unit. The versions of the Monday and Thursday *Taḥanun* that we have today do not conclude with a passage containing the word *raḥum*, but it is possible that what is meant is that the third section segues into the regular weekday *Nefilat Apayim* that does have a *raḥum* reference toward the beginning.

another source.[14] The most well-known source of this story is *Siddur Avodat Yisrael,* which quotes the story from a prayer book manuscript dated 1407 by Rabbi Yehudah ben Eliezer Zvi, a student of Rabbi Menahem, the prayer leader (*shaliaḥ tzibbur*) of Troyes:[15]

> "*Vehu Raḥum,* etc., which we recite on Monday and Thursday while standing, was established by men of stature who were exiled from Jerusalem during the destruction of the Second Temple. They were exiled by Vespasian, may his bones be ground to dust, who ordered three boats built and filled them with Jews with no captain and set them adrift in the ocean. A wind sent each one to a land in a different area; one landed in Lepanto, one in Arles, and one in Bordeaux.[16] Those who landed in Bordeaux were welcomed by the ruler and he gave them fields and vineyards,

---

14 Ephraim Urbach, *Sefer Arugat HaBosem,* vol. 4 (Jerusalem: Ḥevrat Mekitzei Nirdamim, 1963), 25, note 29. This version is also found in Moshe Hershler and Yehudah Hershler, eds., *Pirushei Siddur HaTefilla LaRoke'aḥ* (Jerusalem: Machon HaRav Hershler, 1992), 369–70.

15 Seligman Baer, *Siddur Avodat Yisrael* (Roedelheim, 1868), 112–13. Berliner (*Ketavim Nivḥarim,* vol. 1, 66) states that he found the source of this story referred to as "the responsa of the *Geonim.*" This is the preface found in *Peirushei Siddur HaTefilla LaRoke'aḥ.* Many books that took their information from Berliner copy this attribution. However, the Ashkenazic sages that use this term here are not referring to the *Geonim* of the Babylonian yeshivot but to the early sages of Mainz, a usage found elsewhere in the writings of the Roke'aḥ; see Urbach, *Sefer Arugat HaBosem,* vol. 4, 25, note 29.

16 The names of these three French cities are as found in Baer's *Siddur Avodat Yisrael.* Baer is not sure of the identification of the third place, written in Hebrew as מדינת בורדייי"ל. He writes that it may be Portugal or Bordeaux. In the version written by Eliezer ben Natan of Mainz it is spelled בודייאיש. Zunz, Neubauer, and Urbach identify it as Bordeaux, and the other two cities as Lyons and Arles (Leopold Zunz, *Literaturgeschichte der Synagogalen Poesie* [Frankfurt am Main: Gerschel, 1865], 17). This is in accordance with Zunz's view that the historical basis for the story is the oppression of the Jews at the hands of the Franks and Goths in the seventh century. See note 12 infra. Johann Bodenschatz identifies it as Portugal; see Landshut, *Siddur Hegayon Lev,* 89. This is utterly rejected in Abraham Neubauer, "The Settlement of the Jews in Southern Italy," *The Jewish Quarterly Review* 4 (1892), 620. See also Gerson David Cohen, "The Story of the Four Captives," *Proceedings of the American Academy for Jewish Research* 29 (1960–1961), 27–30.

> and they were there for many days in peace, until that ruler died and a new king arose. What the first ruler established for them the second one destroyed and he made new decrees. There were there two brothers, Yosef and Binyamin, along with Shmuel their cousin, and they were from the people of Jerusalem. They cried out to God in their distress, and they fasted and wore sackcloth on their bodies and they established *Vehu Raḥum* among the three of them. Yosef composed *Vehu Raḥum* up to *Melekh Raḥum Veḥanun Atta* (1–4), Binyamin composed from *Ana* to *Ein Kamokha* (5–6), and Shmuel composed all the rest, up to *Hashem Eḥad* (7–8). Afterward, God saved them and redeemed them and killed the evil oppressor through an unnatural and difficult death. They informed everyone of the whole episode in all places where Jews lived, and they also wrote the prayer and told it to them, and they took it upon themselves to recite it on Monday and Thursday, and so is the custom of all Israel."[17]

Zunz understands that while clearly legendary, this story has a historical basis: the oppression of the Jews at the hands of the Franks and Goths in the seventh century.[18] However, this approach is difficult, as there is no historical record affirming that these supplications were said at such an early date, and as we will see, the ninth century *Seder Rav Amram Gaon* includes only one section of these prayers. Furthermore, the motif of connections between poetic liturgy and historic persecutions is today understood to be "a legendary device, habitually used to explain contemporary practices"[19] in geonic times.[20] Since "medieval Jews explained

17 Translated from Seligman Baer, *Siddur Avodat Yisrael*, 112–13.

18 Leopold Zunz, *Die Ritus Synagogalen Gottesdientes* (Berlin: J. Springer, 1859), 10. This is discussed in Berliner, *Ketavim Nivḥarim*, vol. 1, 66; and Elbogen, *Jewish Liturgy, A Comprehensive History*, 69.

19 Lawrence Hoffman, *The Canonization of the Synagogue Service* (Notre Dame: University of Notre Dame Press, 1979), 84. See also page 212, no. 38 there.

20 Ruth Langer, *To Worship God Properly: Tensions Between Liturgical Custom and Halakhah in Judaism* (Cincinnati: Hebrew Union College Press, 1998), 122–23. See also Louis Ginzberg, *Genizah Studies in Memory of Doctor Solomon Schechter*, vol. 2 (New York: Jewish Theological Seminary, 1929), 526–27.

pretty much everything for which they had no historical record as a response to persecution,"[21] these stories about the origin of *Taḥanun* can thus be relegated to a folkloric motif.

The basic narrative of three individuals cast into fire who recited three distinct parts of a prayer is found in the Talmud, where Ḥananya, Mishael, and Azarya are described as each reciting different parts of Psalms 115 and 117 when they went into and then emerged unscathed from the fiery furnace.[22] The idea of a Gentile ruler challenging Jews by saying a version of "If you are from the Jewish nation, I want to test you as Ḥananya, Mishael, and Azarya" is found in Taanit 18b. The accounts are also reminiscent of the well-known story "The Four Captives," about scholars traveling by ship who were captured by Arabs and later redeemed by different Jewish communities, thus spreading Torah knowledge across the Mediterranean region.[23] In all the stories, helpless Jewish captives are taken by ship to three foreign ports.[24]

In his study of these accounts, G. D. Cohen concluded that the *Taḥanun* stories are at least a century older than the Four Captives story and the themes date back to talmudic times.[25] For example, *Avot DeRabbi Natan* records that Titus sent three ships filled with men, women, and

---

21 Lawrence Hoffman, ed., *My People's Prayer Book: Tachanun and Concluding Prayers* (Woodstock, VT: Jewish Lights, 2002), 55.

22 Pesaḥim 118a. Although the tradition about the prayers recited by Ḥananya, Mishael, and Azarya already appears in the Apocryphal additions to the book of Daniel, much before the Talmud, there they all recite the same prayer together, "Then in unison the three praised and glorified and blessed God" (3:28 [51]). Carey A. Moore, *Daniel, Esther and Jeremiah: The Additions – The Anchor Bible* (New York: Doubleday, 1977), 63. See also Johanna Manley, *Grace After Grace: The Psalter and the Holy Fathers* (Crestwood, NY: Monastery Books, 2003), 663. In the talmudic account, they each recite a different prayer, which were later combined to form Psalms 115:1, 2 and 117:1, 2, similar to the legendary account of the composition of the long *Taḥanun*.

23 The story of the Four Captives is found in chapter 7 of *Sefer HaKabbala* by Abraham ibn Daud (c. 1110–80).

24 Note that in relating the story of the Four Captives, Ibn Daud does not know the name or the port of the fourth scholar, so only three are recounted. See the discussion of this in Gerson David Cohen, "The Story of the Four Captives," *Proceedings of the American Academy for Jewish Research* 29 (1960–1961), 32–40.

25 Cohen, "The Story of the Four Captives," 23–30.

children to Rome in order to boast of his triumph in Jerusalem.[26] Lamentations Rabba (1:45) tells how Vespasian filled three ships with men from Jerusalem, sending them to Rome to be used for promiscuity. The men of each ship decided to commit suicide by jumping into the sea. Besides the motif of three ships of exiles, the Midrash records that the first group recited a verse from Psalms (44:21) as they jumped into the sea, the second group recited Psalms 44:23, and the third Psalms 44:22. Here we see each group reciting a different section of a larger prayer, similar to the idea found in the *Taḥanun* stories as well. The motif of the rudderless ship containing exiles from Jerusalem and set adrift is also found as early as the 1100s.[27]

The legends of the origin of the *Taḥanun* prayers thus match preexisting themes in midrashic literature. Variants of these two basic stories are found in other medieval works.[28] Both of these legendary stories of the creation of *Taḥanun* share certain elements: the ships of Jews exiled to foreign lands, the three authors, miraculous salvation from an oppressive ruler, and the same three divisions of *Taḥanun*. A third version relates:

> Some say that the prayer *Vehu Raḥum* was composed by three great men, Rabbi Amitai, Rabbi Shefatiah and Rabbi Yosphia,[29]

26 *Avot DeRabbi Natan*, version B, chapter 7.

27 See Cohen, "The Story of the Four Captives," 25–26.

28 In *Siddur Rabbeinu Shlomo*, attributed to the eleventh-century sage Shlomo ben Shimshon of Worms, both stories are recounted with differences in certain details. In the first story, three ships were sent out which arrived in three different countries, and the three sages who wound up in Africa were to be tested in a fiery furnace. The sages requested three days, rather than thirty, to prepare. They spent these days in prison. One of the sages had the dream, and he knew the verse. Only he was thrown into the furnace and was miraculously saved, after which the king released all three. In the second story, it is Titus, rather than Vespasian, who sets the Jews adrift. Moshe Hershler, ed., *Siddur Rabbeinu Shlomo* (Jerusalem, 1972), 127–28. See the introduction there for a discussion regarding the dating of this work. These versions are discussed in Abraham Neubauer, "The Settlement of the Jews in Southern Italy," *The Jewish Quarterly Review* 4 (1891), 617–20. Johann Bodenschatz also brings Titus as the one who sets the Jews adrift; see Landshut, *Siddur Hegayon Lev*, 88.

29 Elbogen understands that the names Amitai, Shefatiah, and Yosphia "would point to southern Italy, but they do not appear to be correct." Elbogen, *Jewish Liturgy, A Comprehensive History*, 69.

> who were amongst the exiles of Jerusalem in the time of the wicked Titus. They lived a long time after the destruction of the Temple. When Titus died of grievous sickness there was no king in Rome for many years, as is found in the book *Yossipon*. In the twenty-eighth year of the destruction of the Temple, the world stood without a king. When thus the fear of the king ceased, enemies arose, and diverse calamities came upon Israel. At that time, these three pillars of the world rose and composed the prayer mentioned above, one as far as the words *Ana Melekh* (1–4); the second the continuation to *Ein Kamokha* (5–6); and the third continued to the end of the prayer (7–8). They wrote letters, and sent them into captivity, asking that this prayer should be recited with deep feeling of heart on the days when the Torah is read in the assembly of the nation (Monday and Thursday).[30]

As in the other stories, this version has a connection to the destruction of the Temple and the idea of three authors, but does not have the ships taking them to foreign lands.

The idea of multiple authors is reasonable in light of the fact that some elements in these prayers are repeated, such as Psalms 20:10, which appears in the first section (1), and slightly altered in the third section (7), and a variation of part of Nehemiah 9:31 is used at the conclusion of both the first (4) and second sections (6). There are also different styles in the three sections; the first section (1–4) is much more heavily based on biblical quotes and variations of them than the other two sections. Themes repeat themselves throughout the different sections in different words and styles, with no evidence of any editorial attempts to condense the repetitious prayer.[31] Even if we do not accept these stories as historically accurate, the idea that these were originally independent prayers composed by different individuals and later adopted as part of the public prayer service is evident.[32]

30 Neubauer, "The Settlement of the Jews in Southern Italy," 616–18.

31 Eliyahu Munk, *Olam HaTefillot*, vol. 1 (Jerusalem: Mossad HaRav Kook, 1992), 173.

32 Baer, *Siddur Avodat Yisrael*, 113; Elbogen, *Jewish Liturgy, A Comprehensive History*, 69. See also Zvi Karl, *Meḥkarim BeToldot HaTefilla* (Tel Aviv: Twersky, 1950), 101.

### SEDER RAV AMRAM GAON

While the Talmud presupposes that the *Taḥanunim* after the *Amida* are meant to be personal and individualized, the *Geonim* began to provide standardized texts for people to recite.[33] The earliest version of a *Taḥanun* prayer for Mondays and Thursdays is found in the ninth-century work *Seder Rav Amram Gaon.*[34] Rav Amram Gaon wrote the first known complete prayer book[35] as a responsum to a Jewish community in Spain. This work was part of the pursuit of conformity in the liturgy in the ninth and tenth centuries CE, which would be followed by Rav Saadia Gaon's order of prayers.[36] Although it is unclear whether Rav Amram ever achieved unanimous recognition as Gaon of Sura, his was the first attempt to produce a comprehensive prayer book by any kind of recognized authority.[37] This work achieved great popularity in Europe, but as a result of its position of authority, copyists permitted themselves to modify the text in accordance with local custom, leading to multiple manuscripts and difficulty in ascertaining the original text.[38]

In three of the four manuscripts of *Seder Rav Amram Gaon*, before the recitation of the Thirteen Attributes of Mercy, two paragraphs are given as options for the opening supplication on Mondays and Thursdays. The first option is a collection of verses beginning with Jeremiah 14:7 and Psalms 130:3–4. The paragraph serves a function similar to the current first paragraph of *Taḥanun, Vehu Raḥum* (section 1), although that classic opening verse taken from Psalms 78:38 does not appear in these manuscripts. Still, both paragraphs are a collection of verses focusing on God's mercy. The manuscripts then bring Daniel's prayer from Daniel 9:15–19 as another option for the opening paragraph, noting that

33 Richard Sarason, "The Persistence and Trajectories of Penitential Prayer in Rabbinic Judaism," in *Seeking the Favor of God: Volume 3: The Impact on Penitential Prayer Beyond Second Temple Judaism*, eds. Mark Boda et al. (Atlanta, GA: Society of Biblical Literature, 2008), 15.

34 Daniel Goldschmidt, ed., *Seder Rav Amram Gaon* (Jerusalem: Mossad HaRav Kook, 2004), 55–58.

35 Elbogen, *Jewish Liturgy, A Comprehensive History*, 8.

36 Hoffman, *The Canonization of the Synagogue Service*, 5.

37 Robert Brody, *The Geonim of Babylonia and the Shaping of Medieval Jewish Culture* (New Haven: Yale University Press, 1998), 41, 191, 192.

38 Brody, *Geonim*, 192; Goldschmidt, *Seder Rav Amram Gaon*, 16–18.

it is recited by some. This paragraph also appears in current prayer books (section 2), but as an additional supplication rather than as an alternative. This selection from Daniel is the only opening supplication found in the liturgy of the Jews of Rome.[39] Daniel's prayer was considered particularly appropriate for *Taḥanun*, as Daniel himself prefaces his prayer by explicitly stating that it is a supplication (*Taḥanunim*) (Dan. 9:3). It is clear that the basic concept was that some additional supplications should be said on Mondays and Thursdays, and at the time there were different options for which *Taḥanun* prayer could be recited, either a collection of verses from the Bible or the section from Daniel. This "significant reliance on biblical models of penitential prayer, in vocabulary, in theme and by allusion or direct quotation" represents the earliest form of the Monday/Thursday *Taḥanun*.[40]

These manuscripts of *Seder Rav Amram Gaon* do not include all the prayers that are attributed to the legendary three elders; rather, there are elements from what was attributed to the first author presented as two different communal customs. While the idea of three authors is not represented in *Seder Rav Amram Gaon*, we do see that there was more than one source for these prayers.

The one manuscript of *Seder Rav Amram Gaon* that includes the full *Taḥanun* recited today is the British Museum manuscript. There, after the first two options brought in the other manuscripts, a third option is presented: the full *Taḥanun* beginning with the familiar *Vehu Raḥum*.[41] This is the manuscript which formed the basis of the first printed edition of *Seder Rav Amram Gaon*.[42] While it is the most ancient manuscript, it contains many later additions,[43] this being one of them.[44]

Other *Geonim* did relate to *Taḥanun*, but none as thoroughly as Rav Amram Gaon. His predecessor Rabbi Natronai Gaon simply states that *Nefilat Apayim* is completely optional, and he does not relate to the

---

39 Aryeh Loeb Frumkin, *Seder Tefilla KeMinhag Ashkenaz im Seder Rav Amram HaShalem*, vol. 1 (Jerusalem, 1912), 301.

40 Langer, "We Do Not Even Know What to Do," 51–52.

41 Nachman Nathan Coronel, ed., *Seder Rav Amram Gaon* (Warsaw, 1865), 20.

42 Goldschmidt, *Seder Rav Amram Gaon*, 19–20.

43 Ibid., 11–12.

44 Frumkin, *Seder Tefilla KeMinhag Ashkenaz*, vol. 1, 395.

liturgical content of this prayer.[45] About half a century after Rav Amram Gaon's time, Rav Saadia Gaon wrote of *Nefilat Apayim* as obligatory and included a liturgy for *Taḥanun* in his prayer book, but he did not describe any additional penitential prayers for the Monday and Thursday *Taḥanun*.[46] Only Rav Amram Gaon noted these additional penitential prayers, and he gave options for what was appropriate to include. It would seem that while the general trend in geonic literature was toward a more uniform and obligatory communal liturgy,[47] certain parts, such as these additional penitential prayers, retained their original fluidity and remained in the realm of the individual's discretion.

### MAḤZOR VITRY

Describing the *Taḥanun* prayers after the *Amida*, the Rambam writes: "He sits on the ground, falls with his face toward the earth, and utters all the supplications that he desires" (*Hilkhot Tefilla* 5:13). This continues the geonic idea that the particular prayers recited for the daily *Taḥanun* was a personal choice, with multiple options.[48] Similarly, the *Tur* quotes Rabbi Natronai Gaon's view that the very recitation of *Nefilat Apayim* was optional.[49] Reflecting this approach, there are

---

45 Robert Brody, *Teshuvot Rav Natronai Bar Hilai Gaon* (Jerusalem: Ofeq Institute, 1994), 145.

46 Israel Davidson, Simha Assaf, and Yissachar Yoel, eds., *Siddur Rav Saadia Gaon* (Jerusalem: Reuven Mass, 2000), 24; Karl, *Meḥkarim BeToldot HaTefilla*, 100; Sarason, "The Persistence and Trajectories of Penitential Prayer in Rabbinic Judaism," 15.

47 See Hoffman, *Canonization*, 5; Ruth Langer, "Biblical Texts in Jewish Prayers: Their History and Function," in *Jewish and Christian Liturgy and Worship: New Insights into Its History and Interaction*, ed. Albert Gerhards and Clemens Leonhard (Leiden: Brill, 2007), 63–90 (72).

48 Elbogen, *Jewish Liturgy, A Comprehensive History*, 67; see also Gabriel Cohn and Harold Fisch, eds., *Prayer in Judaism: Continuity and Change* (Northvale, NJ: Jason Aronson, 1996), 47–48.

49 *Tur, Oraḥ Ḥayim* 131:3. This is a factor in the ruling in *Birkei Yosef* (131:13) that in cases of doubt, *Taḥanun* should be omitted, and also in the hasidic custom to omit *Taḥanun* when traveling or when an important visitor arrives to pray with the congregation; see Ephraim Stein, *Sefer Avodat Ephraim*, vol. 1 (Bnei Brak: Machon Zecher Shaul, 1996), 328–30; Avraham Tsevi Friedman, *Sefer Otzar Halakhot*, vol. 2 (Brooklyn: Hamatik Printing, 2007), 66, note 127.

Sephardic customs which include some prayers for Mondays and others for Thursdays.[50]

However, the idea of having options and taking into account personal preferences with respect to reciting *Taḥanun* prayers quickly disappeared among Ashkenazic authorities. The next work to deal with a special Monday and Thursday *Taḥanun* was *Maḥzor Vitry*, dated to the eleventh century and compiled by Rashi's student Rabbi Simha of Vitry.[51] Based on earlier material from the students of Rashi, *Maḥzor Vitry* provided extended *Taḥanunim* built upon the earlier versions from the geonic period.[52] As part of this approach, it followed the precedent of Rav Amram Gaon and listed additional penitential prayers for Monday and Thursday, considerably expanding them.[53] The *Taḥanun* found there is more or less as it appears in current prayer books, with no indication that one may pick and choose from among the prayers.[54] The fluidity of the *Taḥanunim* that existed from the earliest mentions of these penitential prayers in rabbinic literature and that was retained in the form of the options presented by Rav Amram Gaon disappeared in *Maḥzor Vitry*.[55]

The notes to Rabbi Issac Tirnau's *Sefer HaMinhagim* states that each of the three sections of *Taḥanun* mentions God's name eighteen times, paralleling the benedictions of the *Amida*. This is given as a reason to say the *Taḥanun* prayers silently while standing, in the same way that

50 Frumkin, *Seder Tefilla KeMinhag Ashkenaz*, vol. 1, 30; see also Langer, "We Do Not Even Know What to Do," 42.

51 On the authorship of *Maḥzor Vitry*, see Avraham Grossman, *The Early Sages of France: Their Lives, Leadership, and Works* (Jerusalem: Magnes Press, 2001), 395–402 [Hebrew]; Aryeh Goldschmidt, ed., *Maḥzor Vitry*, vol. 1 (Jerusalem: Otzar HaPoskim, 2004), 23–25.

52 Freehof, "The Origin of the Tahanun," 349; Simon Hurwitz, ed., *Maḥzor Vitry* (Nuremberg: J. Bulka, 1923), liv.

53 Sarason, "The Persistence and Trajectories of Penitential Prayer in Rabbinic Judaism," 15.

54 Hurwitz, *Maḥzor Vitry*, *siman* 93, 68–70; Goldschmidt, *Maḥzor Vitry*, vol. 1, 116–19, has very slight changes based on other manuscripts.

55 Other works on the liturgy from the students of Rashi do not elaborate on the *Taḥanun* for Monday and Thursday. See Salomon Buber, ed., *Siddur Rashi* (Berlin: Ḥevrat Mekitze Nirdamim, 1911), 209, *siman* 418, where it says that extra prayers are recited but does not detail what they are beyond the fact that they begin with *Vehu Raḥum*.

the *Amida* is recited.[56] This would seem to indicate that there are indeed three sources for these prayers. However, each section contains a different number of God's names, and only one, the first section in *Maḥzor Vitry* (1–4), has eighteen. This seems intentional, as the wording of Psalms 106:47 in (1) was changed in the *Maḥzor Vitry Taḥanun* in order not to have the name of God in it, apparently so as to keep the number down to eighteen. In contemporary prayer books, this quote was "corrected," and God's name was also inserted after the words יכירו וידעו כל הגוים כי אתה in (3),[57] so the first section of *Taḥanun* now has twenty mentions of God's name, thus eliminating the parallelism to the *Amida*.

As noted above, the concept that *Taḥanun* should in some way parallel the *Amida* is already found in the Talmud, where the private supplications that individual Sages recited after the *Amida*, recorded in Berakhot 16b–17a, correspond to various blessings of the *Amida* in their theme or language. The earliest post-talmudic *Taḥanun* recorded, that of ben Baboi,[58] also parallels the *Amida*.[59] This first section of the Monday/Thursday *Taḥanun* follows this approach, not in theme or wording, but in the symbolism of the number of divine names.

---

56 Shlomo Spitzer, ed., *Sefer HaMinhagim LeRabbeinu Isaac Tirnau* (Jerusalem: Mossad HaRav Kook, 2000), 13. On the authorship of these notes, see pages 17–18 of the introduction. The idea that these prayers parallel the *Amida* is brought in *Magen Avraham* 131:1. Note that the *Shulḥan Arukh* rules that *Vehu Raḥum* is said aloud, while Rema states that it is said quietly (*Oraḥ Ḥayim* 131:1). This is based on the idea that the Ashkenazic liturgy has *Vehu Raḥum* recited immediately after the *Amida*, so it can be seen as an extension of it, while the Sephardic custom is to have the *Vidui* and Thirteen Attributes recited first, so that *Vehu Raḥum* is seen as separate from the *Amida*. See Simha Rabinowitz, *Piskei Teshuvot*, vol. 2 (Jerusalem, 2002), 103.

57 Scherman, *The ArtScroll Siddur*, 126; Tal, *Siddur Rinat Yisrael*, 84. This addition of God's name is already found in some manuscripts of *Maḥzor Vitry*, see Aryeh Goldschmidt, *Maḥzor Vitry*, vol. 1, 117. However, even nineteen mentions of God's name can be viewed as a parallel to the *Amida*, since the latter contains nineteen blessings once the additional *Birkat HaMinim* is taken into account (see Berakhot 28b).

58 Pirqoi ben Baboi (c. 800 CE) was a Babylonian scholar known mainly for his polemical tract against the customs practiced in Israel which were at variance with Babylonian customs. See Adele Berlin, ed., *The Oxford Dictionary of the Jewish Religion*, 2nd ed. (Oxford: Oxford University Press, 2011), 568.

59 Freehof, "The Origin of the Tahanun," 341–46.

This first section is the one that most closely resembles the earlier version in *Seder Rav Amram Gaon,* as it includes almost all the verses given there as the first option for *Taḥanun* on Mondays and Thursdays as well as the section from Daniel. Thus, the core of the section attributed to the first author in the legendary accounts is a combination of the two options given in *Seder Rav Amram Gaon.* In *Maḥzor Vitry* they were joined, and additional verses were added to create a unit with eighteen names of God, apparently in order to parallel the *Amida.* The fact that only this section (1–4) uses the symbolism of numbers, coupled with the tradition that it was composed by someone separately from the other parts of *Taḥanun,* indicates that indeed this part of *Taḥanun* was once considered a stand-alone unit.

There is one other parallel between *Maḥzor Vitry* and *Seder Rav Amram Gaon.* After the opening sentence of the third and final part of *Taḥanun* (7), *Maḥzor Vitry* continues with variations of the last three sentences of Rav Amram Gaon's first version. This would seem to further indicate that the supplications recorded in *Maḥzor Vitry* used the *Taḥanun* in *Seder Rav Amram Gaon* as a basic template, the first part (1) beginning with a variation of the *Taḥanun* brought by Rav Amram Gaon, then continuing with the verses from Daniel (2), also found in *Seder Rav Amram Gaon,* and ending with variations of the ending from Rav Amram Gaon (7). It is only the second section (5–6) that is not related at all to the supplications found in *Seder Rav Amram Gaon.*

## SOURCES OF THE LITURGY

Where did the parts of *Taḥanun* not found in *Seder Rav Amram Gaon* come from? These other sections of *Taḥanun* are often explained to have been based on and taken from supplications originally recited on fast days.[60] Tosefta Berakhot 3:6 mentions that after the *Amida* one may add more material "even like the Yom Kippur *Vidui* (confession)." While this

60 Elbogen, *Jewish Liturgy, A Comprehensive History,* 69. The post-geonic elements of *Taḥanun* were probably "originally supplications for fast days." See also Daniel Keith Falk, *Daily, Sabbath and Festival Prayers in the Dead Sea Scrolls* (Leiden: Brill, 1998), 74–75.

seems to simply state that one may add a long prayer, it may indicate that fast day prayers were a source for texts for personal supplications.

Regarding the opening paragraph (1), *Vehu Raḥum* is indeed also found in the context of fast day prayers in *Sefer HaPardes*, a work edited by Rabbi Shemaya, a student of Rashi, around the time of the compilation of the *Maḥzor Vitry*.[61] It is mentioned there as part of a responsa of Rabbi Yitzhak ben Yehuda regarding the prayers omitted from the standard fast day liturgy when a *brit mila* falls on a fast day.[62] However, it is also reasonable to assume that *Vehu Raḥum* was originally composed for Mondays and Thursdays. As we have noted, *Vehu Raḥum* is closely related to the first option brought by Rav Amram Gaon, and it may be that it was copied from the prayers recited on Mondays and Thursdays to be added to the fast day liturgy. Mondays and Thursdays were commonly chosen as personal fast days,[63] and a strong connection existed between the two. For example, Rabbi Abraham ben Isaac of Narbonne (c. 1110–79), in *Sefer HaEshkol*, groups the laws of regular Mondays and Thursdays in one section together with the laws of fast days.[64] Thus an interchange between the two liturgies is very possible.

In *Siddur Rav Saadia Gaon Vehu Raḥum* is part of the regular weekday *Taḥanun*,[65] which may have been the initial reason for using this verse on all the other occasions – Mondays, Thursdays and fast days. Furthermore, it was standard practice in early medieval liturgy to begin personal prayers with *Vehu Raḥum* (Psalms 78:38).[66] Thus, it is probable that certain liturgical elements originally associated with the supplications for a particular occasion were later added to the supplications on other occasions. Prayers passed between versions of the weekday *Taḥanun*, Monday/Thursday *Taḥanun*, and fast day prayers, each influencing the other. Remnants of this can still be detected. It has even been suggested that *Nefilat Apayim* itself began as a prayer recited only

61 Berliner, *Ketavim Nivḥarim*, vol. 1, 66.

62 Hayim Yehuda Ehrenreich, ed., *Sefer HaPardes* (Budapest, 1924), 76.

63 Landshut, *Siddur Hegayon Lev*, 84.

64 Shalom Albeck, ed., *Sefer HaEshkol*, vol. 1 (Jerusalem: Wagschall, 1984), 123.

65 Israel Davidson, Simha Assaf and Yissachar Yoel, eds., *Siddur Rav Saadia Gaon*, 25.

66 Israel Ta-Shma, *Early Franco-German Ritual and Custom* (Jerusalem: Magnes Press, 1999), 303 [Hebrew].

on Mondays and Thursdays by people who were fasting, then began to be said by everyone on all regular Mondays and Thursdays, and finally became incorporated into the prayers for every day of the week.[67]

Repeating themes can be detected in the post–*Seder Rav Amram Gaon* additions, which may shed light on their possible point of origin. The second section, which is not related to the supplications found in *Seder Rav Amram Gaon*, is composed of two paragraphs (5–6). The first, *Ana Melekh Raḥum Veḥanun Atta* (5) emphasizes the covenant made with Abraham and the *Akeida*.[68] It seems to be a special supplication initially recited at times of persecution and plague[69] that from there was brought into the standard Monday and Thursday liturgy.

The next paragraph (6) asks God to save His people from enemies, distress, and woe, and not to abandon the Jewish people. These general ideas are also found in the third section of *Taḥanun* (7–8). Its first paragraph, *Ein Kamokha* (7), mentions the Patriarchs and begs for salvation from punishment and troubles. The final paragraph (8) incorporates prayers to save the Jewish people from their enemies and from distress. It is the most emotional of the prayers, describing the Jewish people suffering in exile and hoping for redemption.[70] It is very possible that this last paragraph was composed independently of the paragraph before it, and so there may even be four original liturgical sources for the extended *Taḥanun*.[71] These basic themes are found in the *Vehu Raḥum* section of *Taḥanun* as well (1–4), though without the emphasis on the Patriarchs. We can conclude that all the sections of *Taḥanun* contain the basic elements of asking God for forgiveness and salvation from troubles. It would seem that in terms of reciting a heartfelt supplication, any of the three traditional sections, and even just one of the paragraphs within each section, would be adequate. The first section (1–4) relies more on biblical quotations than the others, but as a whole they all seem to serve the same function.

67 Karl, *Meḥkarim BeToldot HaTefilla*, 99.

68 Scherman, *The ArtScroll Siddur*, 128.

69 Yissachar Jacobson, *Netiv Bina*, vol. 1 (Tel Aviv: Sinai, 1991), 350.

70 Ibid.

71 Karl, *Meḥkarim BeToldot HaTefilla*, 102.

The fact that they all have very similar themes and can function independently of each other is indicative of their origin as distinct penitential prayers which were later fused together. There are multiple variations in the regular weekday *Taḥanun* liturgy attested to in a number of different sources, ranging from ancient fragments found in the Cairo Geniza, to a variety of communal rites today.[72] Even though there is no clear evidence in the *geniza* for variations of the Monday/Thursday *Taḥanun,* it should not be surprising that like the regular weekday *Taḥanun,* it too is composed of disparate elements from various authors.[73] Thus, while part of the *Taḥanun* in *Maḥzor Vitry* is based on the two options brought in *Seder Rav Amram Gaon,* the additional sections seem to have been based on other versions of *Taḥanun* found elsewhere.

In summary, the elements added to the *Seder Rav Amram Gaon Taḥanun* in *Maḥzor Vitry* seem to have come from two sources; special supplications for fast days and times of distress, and standard *Taḥanun* prayers that were in use locally by other communities.

## THE SHIFT

What took place between ninth-century Babylonia and eleventh-century France that caused these supplications to shift from relatively short collections of verses that the individual could choose from to a much longer series of prayers that allowed no room for individual choice? Although "the tendency to conflate competing versions" of the same prayer "is one of the most commonplace phenomena in liturgical literature,"[74] why did *Taḥanun* undergo this process at this particular juncture?

We do not know much about the period between the *Geonim* and early *Rishonim* in the West, the era between Rav Amram Gaon and *Maḥzor Vitry*. Rabbi Lawrence A. Hoffman hypothesizes that the expansion of *Taḥanun* is a result of the pietistic revival and Christian persecutions that took place in the High Middle Ages throughout Europe,

---

72 See Langer, "We Do Not Even Know What to Do," 39–69.

73 See ibid., 51, on the regular weekday *Taḥanun*: "Private recitation of much of this rite generated the enormous variety in some parts."

74 See Daniel Sperber, *On Changes in Jewish Liturgy* (Jerusalem: Urim, 2010), 125, note 5, where he discusses this phenomenon regarding *Modim DeRabbanan.*

and particularly in France. One effect of the high level of popular piety among Christians and increased actions against Jews was the increase in Jewish penitential prayers.[75] In general, early Ashkenazic prayer is typified by many additional requests and supplications, particularly before and after the obligatory parts of the prayer service.[76] Furthermore, the prayers of earlier sages were seen as being more holy and effective than any that an individual would be able to compose on his own.[77] The idea that the long composite *Taḥanun* developed as a result of the European pietistic revival and Christian persecutions would explain why in Italian and Yemenite liturgies these prayers are much shorter. They remain closer to the original version, before all the supplications were added,[78] despite the influence that different liturgical customs had on each other.[79]

An additional element that helps to explain the long composite *Taḥanun* in *Maḥzor Vitry* is that it is one of the very first Ashkenazic prayer books ever written. Rashi's students were very involved in the genre of *maḥzorim*, collections of the texts of prayers, commentaries to the prayers, as well as laws and customs relating to prayer and the yearly cycle of holidays. These works were written at the time to instruct the growing Jewish population, particularly in France, as to what the proper customs and formulas for prayers were.[80] Before *Maḥzor Vitry* and contemporaneous early Ashkenazic prayer books, prayer seems to have occurred mostly without a written text. Once a written text was created, various penitential prayers, originally designed to be performed on a single occasion, spontaneously or by an individual, now became

75 Hoffman, *My People's Prayer Book: Tachanun and Concluding Prayers*, 55.

76 Israel Ta-Shma, *The Early Ashkenazic Prayer: Literary and Historical Aspects* (Jerusalem: Magnes Press, 2003), 13.

77 Arnold Rosenberg, *Jewish Liturgy as a Spiritual System* (Lanham, MD: Rowman and Littlefield, 2004), 111. See also Hoffman, *The Canonization of the Synagogue Service*, 170, regarding the veneration later generations had for the *Geonim* and their rulings.

78 See Langer, "We Do Not Even Know What To Do," 41–44.

79 See Hirsch Jacob Zimmels, *Ashkenazim and Sephardim: Their Relations, Differences, and Problems as Reflected in the Rabbinical Responsa* (Hoboken, NJ: Ktav, 1996), 122, especially notes 13 and 14.

80 Avraham Grossman, *The Early Sages of France: Their Lives, Leadership and Works* (Jerusalem: Magnes Press, 1995) 402 [Hebrew].

standardized.[81] This process resulted in a collection of differing traditions of supplications written by various authors becoming transformed into one expanded *Taḥanun*. This "trend toward maximalism" is also found in the development of other penitential prayers and poems, such as *piyutim*. They too began as ad hoc individual prayers with fluid texts, over time transforming into a common, fixed liturgical canon.[82]

It seems that the long *Taḥanun* emerged in eleventh-century Ashkenazic liturgy as a result of an increase in penitential prayers coupled with the emergence of a standardized written liturgy. Once an authoritative text coalesced, it would be difficult to go back to the original shorter, individualized *Taḥanun* prayers. However, though it is no longer the norm, even after the time of *Maḥzor Vitry* there are echoes of the earlier idea that options existed within *Taḥanun*. For example, toward the end of the weekday *Taḥanun* the *Kol Bo* (*siman* 19) instructs the *ḥazan* (cantor or prayer leader) to say one of the poetic supplications (ואחת מהתחנות המפוייטות), apparently leaving the exact choice up to the discretion of the *ḥazan*. Today, this poetic supplication has been standardized, and the poem *Habet Mishamayim* is recited. It is interesting to note that Rabbi Zechariah Agmati (c. 1189), in his commentary to Berakhot 29b, writes that *Taḥanun* should sometimes be longer or shorter depending on the individual's circumstances, and that a standardized *Taḥanun* makes it a rote recitation rather than a true supplication.[83] This statement was made

81 Talya Fishman, "Rhineland Pietist Approaches to Prayer and the Textualization of Rabbinic Culture in Medieval Northern Europe," *Jewish Studies Quarterly* 11, no. 4 (2004): 325–26. See also Freehof, "The Origin of the Tahanun," 339: "Frequently such prayers outlast the need which called them forth and are preserved by tradition to serve as spiritual guides for men less articulate."

82 Laura Lieber, "Confessing from A to Z: Penitential Forms in Early Synagogue Poetry," 104, in *Seeking the Favor of God: Volume 3: The Impact on Penitential Prayer Beyond Second Temple Judaism*, ed. Mark J. Boda et al. (Atlanta: Society of Biblical Literature, 2008), 99–125.

83 Meir David Ben-Shem, ed., *Sefer HaNer LeRav Zechariah ben Rav Yehuda Agmati* (Jerusalem: Machon Torah Shleimah, 1958), 55; Issachar Tamar (*Alei Tamar, Yerushalmi: Zera'im*, vol. 1 [Givatayim, Israel: Atir, 1979], 162), notes that the ideal of individualized supplication found in the Talmud and Genizah fragments gave way to conformity so that "people would not make mistakes."

at a turning point, when the recitation of an individualized *Taḥanun* was replaced by a standardized version.

Today, the idea of returning to the original individualized and shorter *Taḥanun* is not represented in halakhic literature. However, echoes of the early form of *Taḥanun* can still be found. Abraham Berliner (1833–1915), a professor at the Hildesheimer Rabbinical Seminary, recommended that the long *Taḥanun* prayer be divided into two smaller units, one for Monday (1–5) and one for Thursday (6–8). This would increase the *kavana* (intention) people have when saying these prayers, which are often very rushed.[84] Variations on this approach are commonplace among people who find themselves unable to keep up with the pace of the congregation during *Taḥanun* and consulted with their synagogue rabbis or teachers for advice.

This is also the reason why there is no concept of "compensating for" these prayers if the congregation went at a pace too fast for the individual. While the *Shulḥan Arukh* (*Oraḥ Ḥayim* 134:1) writes that it is a communal *takana* to recite these prayers, the *Mishna Berura* (134:3) states that only omitting the prayer altogether is considered going against the *takana*. Saying some of the supplications seems to be sufficient.[85]

While there is no clear understanding of exactly how, when, and why the expanded *Taḥanun* for Mondays and Thursdays developed, the general trajectory was from a relatively short, individualized prayer to the much longer, standardized composite version in use today.

---

84 Berliner, *Ketavim Nivḥarim*, vol. 1, 67. See also Lawrence A. Hoffman, "The Liturgy of Confession: What It Is and Why We Say It," in *We Have Sinned: Sin and Confession in Judaism*, ed. Lawrence A. Hoffman (Woodstock, VT: Jewish Lights, 2012), 5, where he notes that Jews whose prayer books do include *Taḥanun* "are likely to rush through it."

85 See Simha Rabinowitz, *Piskei Teshuvot*, vol. 2 (Jerusalem, 2002), 103, note 9, where he seems to indicate that *Vehu Raḥum* must be made up for, but that might be only if it was skipped entirely.

*Chapter 19*

# Pointing to the Torah with the Little Finger and other *Hagbaha* Customs

## WHEN TO DO *HAGBAHA*

The tradition of lifting the Torah scroll and displaying it to the listening congregation (*hagbaha*) started as early as the days of the Tanakh. Before Ezra read to the assembled Jews from the Torah scroll, we are told that "Ezra opened the scroll before the eyes of the people… and when he opened it, all the people stood silent. Ezra blessed the Lord God, and all the people answered, 'Amen! Amen!' with their hands upraised; then they bowed and prostrated themselves before the Lord, faces to the ground" (Neh. 8:5–6). It is not clear if this event was intended as a onetime occurrence or a routine that would accompany every public Torah reading. Nevertheless, this source forms the basis of the custom of displaying the Torah scroll as codified in *Masekhet Soferim* 14:13.[1] Just

1 *Masekhet Soferim* is one of the minor tractates, and it presents rulings and customs from the middle of the geonic period, around the eighth or ninth century. See M. B. Lerner, "Massekhet Soferim," in *The Literature of the Sages. First Part: Mishna, Tosefta,*

as reported in Nehemiah, *Masekhet Soferim* instructs that the Torah is to be shown before the reading, at which time the congregation should bow: "It is a mitzva for all the men and women to see the writing, bow, and say, 'This is the Torah that Moses placed before the children of Israel' (Deut. 4:44); 'The Torah of the Lord is perfect, restoring the soul' (Psalms 19:8)." This source is quoted by the Ramban in his discussion of *hagbaha*,[2] as well as by other *Rishonim*.[3] *Masekhet Soferim* forms the basis for the law as formulated in the *Shulḥan Arukh* (*Oraḥ Ḥayim* 134:2). In all of these sources the only actions incumbent upon the congregation during *hagbaha* are bowing and reciting two verses.

There are a few differences between the way *Masekhet Soferim* describes *hagbaha* and current practice. In accordance with *Masekhet Soferim*, Rabbi Yosef Karo in the *Shulḥan Arukh* has *hagbaha* taking place before the Torah reading, the universal custom in talmudic times.[4] Rabbi Moshe Isserles adds that the Ashkenazic custom is to do *hagbaha* after the Torah reading, even though the early Ashkenazic work *Kol Bo*, quoting *Masekhet Soferim*, indicates that *hagbaha* is done before the reading.[5] It seems that some textual variants of *Masekhet Soferim* state that *hagbaha* is done after the Torah reading, reflective of the different customs.[6] Rabbi Hayim Benvenisti (1603–73), an important Turkish halakhist, explains in his book *Shayarei Knesset HaGedola* that the Ashkenazic custom to do *hagbaha* after the Torah reading originated because uneducated people

---

*Talmud, External Tractates*, S. Safrai and P. J. Tomson, eds. (Assen/Maastricht and Philadelphia: van Gorcum, 1987), 397–400. On the custom to display the Torah scroll, see Mordechai Zer-Kavod, *Daat Mikra: Ezra Neḥemia* (Jerusalem: Mossad HaRav Kook, 1994), 105, note 6. See there also an alternate interpretation that the word *vayiftaḥ* in this verse means "began reading" rather than "opened." According to that interpretation there was not necessarily a public display of the Torah at this event, and the people reacted to hearing the words of the Torah rather than to seeing the scroll. See also Daniel Sperber, *Minhagei Yisrael*, vol. 1 (Jerusalem: Mossad HaRav Kook, 1989), 78–81.

2 Ramban, commentary to Deut. 27:26.

3 See *Beit Yosef, Oraḥ Ḥayim* 134:2.

4 *Arukh HaShulḥan, Oraḥ Ḥayim* 147:9.

5 *Kol Bo, siman* 20. *Darkhei Moshe, Oraḥ Ḥayim* 147:4.

6 See *Bayit Chadash, Oraḥ Ḥayim* 147:3. See also *Talmudic Encyclopedia*, vol. 8 (Jerusalem: Talmudic Encyclopedia Publishing Ltd., 1957), 167, note 12.

thought that seeing the Torah at *hagbaha* was more important than hearing the Torah reading, so they would walk out of the synagogue right after *hagbaha*. By postponing *hagbaha*, people would leave only after the Torah reading.[7] Some Sephardic authorities approved of the Ashkenazic custom,[8] and in some Ashkenazic communities *hagbaha* is still done before the Torah reading.[9]

### VERSES RECITED DURING *HAGBAHA*

*Masekhet Soferim* offers two verses (Deut. 4:44 and Psalms 19:8) for the congregation to recite during *hagbaha*. These are still found today in Ashkenazic and Sephardic prayer books, along with various additional verses.[10] Some editions of *Masekhet Soferim* have the word "or" between the two verses, indicating that either verse can be said, and it is not necessary to recite both, so it is not surprising that many prayer books omit Psalms 19:8.[11]

Contemporary Ashkenazic prayer books generally add the words "According to the word of the Lord through Moses" to the verse

---

7 *Shayarei Knesset HaGedolah, Beit Yosef, Oraḥ Ḥayim* 134:2. This is similar to the contemporary practice in some synagogues to place *Anim Zemirot* in the middle of the service rather than at the end so that people do not walk out of the synagogue while the Ark is open. For more on Benvenisti, see Bezalel Naor, *Post-Sabbatian Sabbatianism* (Spring Valley, NY: Orot, 1999), 167.

8 Hayim Yosef David Azulai, *LeDavid Emet* (Jerusalem, 1847), 4:2. He notes also that in some communities it was customary not to do *hagbaha* at all for fear that the Torah may be dropped or touched with bare hands, 4:1. See also *Talmudic Encyclopedia*, vol. 8, 167, notes 5–7.

9 See *Kaf HaḤayim, Oraḥ Ḥayim* 134:17, Simha Rabinowitz, *Piskei Teshuvot*, vol. 2 (Jerusalem, 2002), 134:9, 107, note 42. The differences in the placement of *hagbaha* in the prayer service may also be related to the different customs found in Israel and Babylonia regarding standing when the Torah is taken out and returned to the ark; see Daniel Sperber, *Minhagei Yisrael*, vol. 8 (Jerusalem: Mossad Harav Kook, 2007), 142–45.

10 Daniel Sperber, *Minhagei Yisrael*, vol. 3 (Jerusalem: Mossad Harav Kook, 1994), 99, note 75.

11 The word "or" appears in parentheses in the standard Vilna edition of *Masekhet Soferim*; however, the Vilna Gaon in his notes to *Masekhet Soferim* deletes that word. The version of *Masekhet Soferim* found in *Maḥzor Vitry* indicates that both verses are said (p. 707). See also *Piskei Teshuvot*, vol. 2, 134:8, 107, note 38.

from Deut. 4:44, and leave out the verse from Psalms.[12] This addition is found in the very influential prayer book composed by Rabbi Isaiah Horowitz, author of *Shenei Luḥot HaBrit* (Shelah, 1565–1630),[13] but is considered unusual since it is only a fragment of a verse with seemingly no connection to Deut. 4:44 or to *hagbaha*.[14] It does not appear to be a kabbalistic addition since it is not found in kabbalistic prayer books before the Shelah.[15] Although this phrase appears multiple times in the Torah,[16] some prayer books note that these words are taken specifically from Num. 9:23: "According to the word of the Lord would they encamp, and according to the word of the Lord would they journey; the charge of the Lord would they safeguard, according to the word of the Lord through Moses."[17] Rabbi Hayim of Volozhin was of the opinion that originally this entire verse was said, but it was mistakenly abbreviated.[18] This verse was considered appropriate for when the Torah is in motion, that is, during *hagbaha* and on the way to the ark.[19] It would then be seen as part of the collection of verses recited about the Ark with the tablets being in motion, said when the Torah is being removed (Num. 10:35) and returned (10:36). There is no evidence from any early prayer book that the whole verse was ever recited. It has been suggested that the additional words proclaiming that this is the complete, divine

---

12 Psalms 19:8 is included in some prayer books at the end of the formula for calling up a congregant for the first *aliya*, which begins with the words *vetigaleh*. This is already found in works of the *Rishonim*; see, for example, *Sefer Abudraham* (Jerusalem: Frank, 1995), 142, and *Peirushei Siddur HaTefillah LaRoke'aḥ* (Jerusalem: Machon Harav Hershler, 1992), 422.

13 *Siddur HaShelah, Shaar HaShamayim* (Amsterdam, 1717), 117b. The Shelah does not comment on the addition.

14 See, for example, *Arukh HaShulḥan, Oraḥ Ḥayim* 134:3, and Eliyahu Munk, *Olam HaTefillot*, vol. 1 (Jerusalem: Mossad HaRav Kook, 1992), 185.

15 Daniel Mordechai Reimer, *Sefer Tefillat Ḥayim* (Beitar: Tzror HaḤayim, 2004), 107.

16 Num. 4:37, 4:45, 9:23, 10:13, and once in Josh. 22:9.

17 See *ArtScroll Siddur*, 146. *Rinat Yisrael*, which usually provides chapter references, does not do so for this passage.

18 Menachem Mendel Landa, *Siddur Tzluta DeAvraham* (Tel-Aviv: Grafika, 1958), 373.

19 Yitzhak Landa, *Mikra Soferim* (Suwalki, Poland, 1862), 13:4; see also his commentary *Dover Shalom* in *Otzar HaTefillot*, 422. Based on this, in *Ishei Yisrael*, a prayer book based on the teachings of the Vilna Gaon, the entire verse is brought, Isaac Moltzin, *Ishei Yisrael* (Tel Aviv: Yakov Landa, 1968), 164.

Torah were added in Ashkenazic lands to negate the theology of their Christian neighbors.[20]

## POINTING TO THE TORAH

While *Masekhet Soferim* instructs the congregation to bow during *hagbaha*, it is more common today to see people pointing at the Torah during *hagbaha*, despite the explicit statement by the *Shulḥan Arukh* (*Oraḥ Ḥayim* 134:2) that one should bow. Rabbi Moshe Isserles writes that bowing was the custom of the Maharil as well.[21] One bows the same way one bows during *Modim* in the *Amida*.[22] Some authorities have decried the fact that many people today do not bow during *hagbaha*.[23]

Various reasons have been offered to justify this. Rabbi Isaiah di Trani (Riaz, c. 1235–1300), is quoted in *Shiltei HaGibborim* (Kiddushin 14b) as saying that one should stand for the Torah but not bow to the Torah. He explains that there is no source anywhere that indicates that people should bow to the Torah or the ark.[24] Some authorities understood this to mean that it is in fact prohibited to bow to the Torah and only standing for the Torah is allowed.[25] This ruling is considered the main justification for those who do not bow during *hagbaha*.[26] This statement of the Riaz seems to be in direct conflict with *Masekhet Soferim*, a source that clearly mandates bowing. The Ḥida reconciles this blatant conflict by explaining that the Riaz was not referring to an open Torah scroll, but to a closed one, and thus one should in fact bow to the open Torah during *hagbaha*.[27] Others have justified not bowing during *hagbaha* because of the possibility the Torah scroll may not be

20 Daniel Sperber, *Minhagei Yisrael*, vol. 3 (Jerusalem: Mossad HaRav Kook, 1994), 95–102.

21 *Darkhei Moshe, Oraḥ Ḥayim* 147:4.

22 *Talmudic Encyclopedia*, vol. 8, 170, note 44.

23 See Yehuda Levi Ben-David, *Sefer Kara Ravatz* (Jerusalem: Birkei Yosef, 1996), 267.

24 ולא נמצא בכל התורה שמשתחוין אפילו לארון הקודש.

25 See Hayim Yosef David Azulai, *Birkei Yosef*, 134:3, where he discusses this at length.

26 Simha Rabinowitz, *Piskei Teshuvot*, vol. 2, 134:7, 105, note 28. See also Saul Liebermann, *Shki'in* (Jerusalem: Shalem Books. 1992), 9, regarding Karaite opposition to what they considered the Rabbinate practice of bowing to the Torah.

27 Hayim Yosef David Azulai, *Birkei Yosef*, 134:3.

kosher,[28] or because the person lifting the Torah is standing between the congregation and the Torah scroll,[29] or that *Masekhet Soferim* only meant that it is good to bow during *hagbaha* but not obligatory.[30] Whatever the justification, today in many congregations pointing is much more prevalent than bowing.

Pointing during *hagbaha* is not mentioned in any early sources and is not found in the *Shulḥan Arukh*, nor indeed in any of the traditional commentaries on the *Shulḥan Arukh*. Some works claim that there is no real source for this custom and it should be avoided.[31] Certain rabbinic leaders in modern times, such as Rabbi Shlomo Zalman Auerbach and Rabbi Eliyashiv, would not point to the Torah during *hagbaha*.[32]

An early commentary sometimes brought as the source for pointing during *hagbaha* is *Divrei Mordekhai*, a book of responsa by Rabbi Mordekhai Krispin, a rabbi in Rhodes in the 1800s. In this responsum he explains why it is appropriate to point to the Torah during what he refers to as הקס"ת. This abbreviation can be understood as referring to *hagbaha* (הקמת ספר תורה) or the reading of the Torah (הקראת ספר תורה), so it is not entirely clear if he is discussing *hagbaha* at all. Furthermore, in justifying why it is not inappropriate to point to the Torah while reading it, he indicates that it was, in fact, generally considered improper. Rabbi Krispin explains that in this case it is appropriate, based on Numbers Rabba (2:3), where R. Ḥanina explains that while it is usually considered insolent and punishable by death to point to the image of a king using a finger, because of His great love for the Jewish people, God allows young children to point to His name in the house of study. Rabbi Krispin writes that this is the opinion people rely on when they point to the Torah.[33]

---

28 Yekutiel Yehudah Halberstam, *Divrei Yatziv* (Jerusalem: Shefa Ḥayim, 1997), *Oraḥ Ḥayim*, vol. 1, 76:6.

29 *Piskei Teshuvot*, vol. 2, 134:7, 106, note 29. This would explain why bowing during *hagbaha* is more prevalent in Sephardic congregations where the person doing *hagbaha* is not blocking any of the writing.

30 *Sefer Kara Ravatz*, 267.

31 Yehuda Chesner, *Siaḥ Tefilla* (Ofakim, 2003), 248.

32 Avraham Schigel, *Doleh UMashkeh* (Kiryat Sefer, 2007), 95, note 272.

33 Mordekhai Krispin, *Divrei Mordekhai* (Salonika, 1836), *siman* 9.

This justification is quoted by Rabbi Hayim Palagi (1788–1869), who served as the *ḥakham bashi,* the chief rabbi, of the Ottoman Empire, in his book *Sefer Ḥayim.*[34] This work is the most common source referenced for the custom.[35] He interprets the abbreviation הקס"ת in *Divrei Mordekhai* as referring to *hagbaha,* even though he himself uses that same abbreviation on occasion to mean the reading of the Torah.[36]

Rabbi Palagi discusses this custom in other works as well. In his book *Ruaḥ Ḥayim,* he explains that pointing with a finger is not considered inappropriate in connection with God, bringing proof from the Talmud and Midrash, for example, the famous comment at the end of Taanit 31a, based on Isaiah 25:9, that in the Garden of Eden the righteous will form a circle around God and point to Him with their finger.[37] He also references *Divrei Mordekhai.*[38] In his book *Lev Ḥayim,* Rabbi Palagi once again discusses the custom of pointing to the Torah, referencing *Divrei Mordekhai.* This time he explains that the most appropriate finger to point with is the index finger, since it is the second finger if we begin counting with the thumb, corresponding to the second word in the series of five-word statements describing the Torah in Psalms 19:8–10. In Hebrew, for each of the six statements, the second word is the name of God. For example, "The Torah of the Lord is perfect, restoring the soul; The testimony of the Lord is trustworthy, making the simple wise" (תורת ה' תמימה משיבת נפש, עדות ה' נאמנה מחכימת פתי) (Psalms 19:8). Pointing with the second finger is therefore ideal since the entire Torah is understood to be the name of God.[39]

34 Hayim Palagi, *Sefer Ḥayim* (Salonika, 1863), 3:6. This book is often mistakenly referred to as *Sefer HaḤayim.*

35 See, for example, Schigel, *Doleh UMashkeh* (Kiryat Sefer, 2007), 95, and *Aliba DeHilkhata* 31, Shevat-Adar 5769, 34, where Hayim Kanievsky references Palagi as the source of the custom.

36 See Hayim Palagi, *Lev Ḥayim,* vol. 2 (Izmir, 1876), 117a, *Oraḥ Ḥayim* 167:16.

37 A similar exposition of Psalms 48:15 found in the Talmud (Y. Moed Katan 3:7) is suggested by Jacob Neusner to be the source for pointing as showing respect and thus pointing to the Torah. See Noam Neusner, "The Pinkie Paradox," *Jerusalem Post Magazine,* June 13, 2003.

38 Hayim Palagi, *Ruaḥ Ḥayim* (Izmir, 1876), *Yoreh De'ah* 285: 4.

39 Palagi, *Lev Ḥayim,* vol. 2, 116b, *Oraḥ Ḥayim* 167:3:6.

A popular explanation for the custom to point is based on the idea found in Menaḥot 29a that the word *zeh* in the Torah implies pointing with a finger. "A *Tanna* of the school of R. Ishmael stated, 'Three things presented difficulties to Moses, until the Holy One, blessed be He, showed Moses with His finger, and these are they: the Menora, the new moon, and the creeping things. The Menora, as it is written, "And this was (*vezeh*) the work of the candlestick" (Num. 8:4). The new moon, as it is written, "This (*hazeh*) month shall be unto you the beginning of months" (Ex. 12:2). The creeping things, as it is written, "And these are (*vezeh*) they which are unclean" (Lev. 11:29). Others add, also the rules for slaughtering beasts, as it is written, "Now this is (*vezeh*) that which thou shall offer upon the altar" (Ex. 29:38)."[40] Thus, when reciting the verse "This is (*zot*) the Torah that Moses placed before the children of Israel" (Deut. 4:44) during *hagbaha,* people point with their finger.'"[41]

Other *derashot* connecting the word *zeh* to pointing with a finger are found in rabbinic literature,[42] but always only in connection with the word *zeh,* never *zot.* This would make pointing irrelevant to *hagbaha,* where the verse recited uses the word *zot* and not *zeh.* Still, in a comment on the verse in Leviticus (11:2), "These are (*zot*) the creatures that you may eat from among the animals that are upon the earth," Rabbi Eliyahu Mizrahi (1435–1526) indicates that the idea of pointing can be learned from both *zeh* and *zot,* so this is considered by some a support for the custom.[43] However, in a discussion of this same verse in Ḥullin

40 Exodus Rabba 15:28 adds a fourth, the anointing oil, based on the verse "This (*zeh*) shall remain for Me oil of sacred anointment for your generations" (Ex. 30:31).

41 Yosef Lewy, *Minhag Yisrael Torah,* vol. 1 (Brooklyn, NY: Fink Graphics, 1990), 181. He introduces his discussion of the custom by stating that he searched through many books and could not find anywhere a reference to pointing during *hagbaha.*

42 See *Torah Temima,* Gen. 25, note 30 and Ex. 13, note 29, for examples from the Talmud Yerushalmi and midrashic literature. There the custom to point to the matza and *maror* at the Seder is explained based on the verse "And you shall tell your son on that day, 'It is because of this (*zeh*) that the Lord acted on my behalf when I left Egypt'" (Ex. 13:8). Similarly, *Tiferet Yisrael* on the Mishna (Sanhedrin 8:4) explains that when the parents of a rebellious son (*ben sorer umoreh*) declare "This (*zeh*) son of ours" (Deut. 21:20), they point to their child with their finger.

43 *Minhag Yisrael Torah* also references the commentary *Iyun Yaakov* to *Ein Yaakov,* Ḥullin 42a, where the word *zot* in Lev. 11:2 is understood as indicating pointing with

42a, it says only that God showed Moses the kinds of *tereifot* without specifically mentioning pointing to them with a finger. Nonetheless, this explanation is very popular, and seems to resonate with many people. This reasoning, along with the opinion of *Divrei Mordekhai* as quoted by Rabbi Palagi, are the explanations given in the popular *Otzar Taamei HaMinhagim.*[44]

The sources we have seen are concerned with justifying and bringing support for a preexisting, commonly performed practice, but raise the question why people started pointing to the Torah in the first place.[45] It has been suggested that it arose from the practice of kissing the Torah as it is taken from the ark to the *bima,* the place where the Torah is read. People who were far away and could not reach the Torah would hold their hands out in the direction of the Torah, sometimes holding their tzitzit, and then kiss the tzitzit or their finger. In Sephardic congregations, where *hagbaha* takes place right after the Torah arrives at the *bima,* some people would still be holding their hands out during *hagbaha,* possibly leading to the impression that people should point to the Torah during *hagbaha.* This would explain why all the early references to the custom of pointing appear in Sephardic sources.[46] Rabbi Palagi specifically notes that most people hold their tzitzit in their hand when pointing to the Torah (although he explains that it is not necessary to do so),[47] and the custom in many Sephardic congregations today is to lift the tzitzit toward the Torah during *hagbaha* with or without a finger extended,[48] further indicating that the custom may have arisen as a way of kissing the Torah from afar on its way to the *bima.*

Another factor that may have contributed to the prevalence of pointing is the practice of looking at letters in the Torah during *hagbaha.* The kabbalistic work *Shaar HaKavanot,* compiled by Rabbi Shmuel Vital, son of Rabbi Hayim Vital, relates that Rabbi Isaac Luria, the Ari,

---

a finger. See also Efraim Greenblatt, *Rivevos Ephraim* (Brooklyn, NY: Mazel, 1993) *Oraḥ Ḥayim,* vol. 6, no. 4.

44 Shmuel Gelbard, *Otzar Taamei HaMinhagim* (Petach Tikva: Mifal Rashi, 1996), 224.

45 Yehuda Chesner, *Siaḥ Tefilla* (Ofakim, 2003) 248, note 65.

46 Ibid., 249, note 65.

47 *Sefer Ḥayim* 3:6.

48 *Sefer Kara Ravatz,* 275.

would get close to the Torah during *hagbaha* so that he could see the actual letters, and that this practice draws down a great light.[49] This was quoted by Rabbi Abraham Gombiner (c. 1633–1683) in his commentary *Magen Avraham* (*Oraḥ Ḥayim* 134:3), and was later included in *Shaarei Ephraim* (10:13) and the *Mishna Berura* (134:11). Previous to kabbalistic influence, an indistinct view of the text of the Torah during *hagbaha* was considered sufficient, and making out individual letters was not stressed.[50] By being included in the *Magen Avraham* and *Mishna Berura*, this kabbalistic custom became well known and widely practiced.

Rabbi Yosef Hayim of Baghdad (Ben Ish Ḥai, 1832–1909) adds that he saw in a book that during *hagbaha* a person should look for a word in the Torah that begins with the first letter of his name.[51] This idea is included in Rabbi Yaakov Hayim Sofer's *Kaf HaḤayim* (*Oraḥ Ḥayim* 134:13). While none of these sources instruct people to point to the Torah, pointing is a natural way for people to make sure they can make out an actual letter, and certainly to find a particular letter. Justifications for pointing to the Torah are found only after the time of *Magen Avraham*, when the kabbalistic practice of looking at the letters during *hagbaha* became more widely known.

## POINTING WITH THE LITTLE FINGER

In contemporary synagogues, when the Torah is opened and lifted up during *hagbaha*, many congregants can be seen pointing to the Torah with their little finger. The earliest reference to this custom is found in the encyclopedic work *Yalkut MeAm Loez*, a Ladino commentary on the Tanakh. This work was begun by Rabbi Yaakov Culi in the 1700s to facilitate Torah study among Turkish Jews who were not fluent in Hebrew. Rabbi Culi died in 1732, having completed the commentary on Genesis and most of Exodus. The rest of *Yalkut MeAm Loez* on the Torah was written by different authors. The custom of pointing to the Torah using

49 Hayim Vital, *Shaar HaKavanot* (Jerusalem: Yerid HaSefarim, 2005), *Inyan Keriat HaTorah, derush alef*, 48b.

50 Moshe Hallamish, *Kabbala: In Liturgy, Halakha, and Customs* (Ramat Gan: Bar-Ilan University, 2000), 311 [Hebrew].

51 Yosef Hayim of Baghdad, *Sefer Ben Ish Ḥai* (Jerusalem, 1932), year 2, *Toledot* 16, 19a.

the little finger is mentioned as part of the commentary on *Parashat Ki Tavo* (Deut. 27:26) in a discussion of customs related to *hagbaha*.[52] There it simply states, "It is customary to point to the writing with the little finger and to kiss it." No explanation is given for the custom.

Rabbi Isaac Behar Arguiti of Constantinople began work on *Yalkut MeAm Loez* on Deuteronomy and he completed his commentary in 1772. However, beyond the commentary on the first three portions of Deuteronomy, *Devarim, Va'etḥanan,* and *Ekev,* only a few pages of his work were found. The rest of the *Yalkut MeAm Loez* commentary on Deuteronomy, including the discussion of *hagbaha,* was written by Rabbi Shmuel Kroizer (1921–97),[53] a fifth-generation Jerusalemite who lived most of his life in the Beit HaKerem neighborhood of Jerusalem.[54] Rabbi Kroizer was a well-known Jerusalem rabbi and *talmid ḥakham* who was on the staff of the *Talmudic Encyclopedia* at a very young age. He authored many books and was responsible for translating *Yalkut MeAm Loez* from Ladino to Hebrew. He wrote the *Yalkut MeAm Loez* commentary for the remainder of Deuteronomy, and, in fact, for much of the Tanakh. Due to his great modesty he often used pseudonyms; on the title page of *Yalkut MeAm Loez* he goes by Shmuel Yerushalmi.

Thus, the earliest reference in writing to the custom of pointing to the Torah with the little finger is in fact in the book *Yalkut MeAm Loez,* although that particular section of the work dates to 1969, making this a very recent source. Pointing with the little finger was popular enough by Kroizer's time that he called it "customary" (נהגו); however, it was never considered significant enough to be mentioned as a legitimate custom in any halakhic work or book of Jewish customs before he wrote about it. The author of the contemporary halakhic work *Piskei Teshuvot* claims that the custom of pointing to the Torah with the little finger has an ancient source ( מקורו קדמון), apparently not realizing that Rabbi Kroizer is the

52 *Yalkut MeAm Loez, Devarim: Volume 3* (Jerusalem: Wagshal, 1969), 1037.

53 *Yalkut MeAm Loez, Devarim: Volume 1* (Jerusalem: Wagshal, 1969), introduction, 5–6.

54 Kroizer's wife was the daughter of Yisrael Ber Odesser, famous for his discovery of the "Letter from Heaven," containing the now ubiquitous *na nach* phrase based on the name of Rebbe Nachman of Breslov. For an overview of the life and works of Shmuel Kroizer, see the article in *Haaretz,* May 5, 2010.

author of this part of *Yalkut MeAm Loez*.[55] On the other hand, Yehuda Chesner, in his book *Siaḥ Tefilla*, correctly points out that this part of *Yalkut MeAm Loez* was written recently, and the custom has no ancient sources at all (ואין בזה שום מקור קדמון).[56] Since *Yalkut MeAm Loez* is a Sephardic work, many people assume that using the little finger to point is a Sephardic custom; however, Rabbi Kroizer is Ashkenazic, and the sections that he wrote draw upon both Sephardic and Ashkenazic customs. In the same section he notes the differences between Sephardic and Ashkenazic congregations regarding when to do *hagbaha* and the custom of the Ari to move close enough to see the actual letters.

Pointing with the little finger can be seen in many congregations today, but there is no clear reason for it.[57] Generally people explain that they do it because they have seen others doing so, even though they were never specifically taught to point to the Torah with their little finger.[58] In recent years, a few explanations have been offered for this custom. One popular explanation is that pointing to the Torah with the littlest finger demonstrates the classic teaching that only a humble person can acquire Torah greatness.[59] Other approaches are somewhat more obscure. The ten fingers can be seen as representing the Ten Commandments, and if we begin counting the fingers with our hands palms down, the little finger on the right hand corresponds to the First Commandment, making it an appropriate finger to point to the Torah.[60] However, this way of counting on our fingers isn't common, and it also differs from the method Rabbi Palagi noted earlier, where counting begins with the thumb.[61]

55 *Piskei Teshuvot*, vol. 2 (Jerusalem, 2002), 134:3, 104.

56 *Siaḥ Tefilla*, 248, note 65.

57 Correspondence with the son of Kroizer, friends, and neighbors did not shed any light on the custom. It may be that Kroizer himself did not know of a reason for the custom, since unlike other customs, he did not provide a reason for this one in *Yalkut MeAm Loez*.

58 See Noam Neusner, "The Pinkie Paradox," *Jerusalem Post Magazine*, June 13, 2003.

59 Nissim Dayan, *Naeh Zivam* (Bnei Brak, 2002), 43. The exact same text also appears in Dayan's book *Shavatenu Kabel* (Bnei Brak, 2009), 184.

60 *Sefer Kara Ravatz*, 275.

61 On the various places to begin counting via fingers, see Oliver Lindemann, Ahmad Alipour, and Martin H. Fischer, "Finger Counting Habits in Middle Eastern and Western Individuals," *Journal of Cross-Cultural Psychology* 42, no. 4 (May 2011), 566–78.

Rabbeinu Bahya, in his commentary on the Torah (Lev. 8:23) mentions an idea current among scientists of his time that each finger assists one of the five senses. For example, the index finger is commonly used to clean out nostrils, so it serves the sense of smell; the ring finger is used to clean out the eyes, so it serves the sense of sight. The little finger is used for cleaning out the ear, thus serving the sense of hearing. Based on this, it has been suggested in some contemporary sources that pointing with the little finger recalls the Israelites saying "*naaseh venishma*"(we will do and we will listen) at the giving of the Torah at Mount Sinai.[62] However, the connection between cleaning out one's ears and pointing to the Torah seems tenuous. In general these explanations do not seem particularly satisfying, but the prevalence of the custom demands some sort of explanation.[63]

### A CULTURAL EXPLANATION

There may be another reason for the choice of using the little finger to point to the Torah. Finger pointing sometimes has negative connotations in Tanakh. For example, the verse "If you remove from your midst perversion, finger pointing, and evil speech" (Is. 58:9) is explained by the Radak as referring to the way belligerent people point a finger at each

62 *Sefer Kara Ravatz*, 275. The connection between the little finger and ear cleaning is found in many cultures. The Anglo-Saxons called the little finger the ear finger; it is also known as the auricular finger (*Brewer's Dictionary of Phrase and Fable* [New York: Harper Collins, 2005], 509). It is interesting to note that in medieval times, a raised little finger indicated that an actor in a play was eavesdropping on another character; see Charles Reginald Dodwell, *Anglo-Saxon Gestures and the Roman Stage* (Cambridge: Cambridge University Press, 2000), 23.

63 Rabbi Yehuda Schwartz explains that actually people are making the *kemitza* sign with their hand, folding down the middle three fingers, as the priests did when preparing the meal offering: "And so, we can say that the pinky is not pointing at all. Rather it is the result of forming that *kometz* with our fingers as the Torah is being returned, in effect, as we seek to 'take with us' that little portion of the Torah that we are able to, a *kometz* so to speak, to carry us through until the next reading" (personal correspondence). See his letter in the *Jerusalem Post Magazine*, June 20, 2003. Other quaint explanations are given for the custom, such as the idea that since all the other body parts have mitzvot to do but not the little finger, it was decided to leave this for the little finger to perform.

other. In Proverbs 6:13, finger pointing is listed as one of the actions of a lawless man.

Islamic and European cultures of both the modern and the ancient world, have generally considered pointing at someone with the index finger offensive.[64] There are some positive references to finger pointing in rabbinic literature, such as Taanit 31a noted above,[65] but negative connotations are found as well, such as the midrash mentioned by *Divrei Mordekhai,* which says that it was considered an unpardonable offense to point to the likeness of a king. The reason for this is that "pointing with the finger is often held to be of magical efficacy, the power streaming, as it were, from operator to victim ... hence it is indecorous to point with a finger toward, for example, the heavenly bodies or other worshipful objects or at friends or superiors."[66] Even in modern times, in many cultures pointing with the finger to what were considered supernaturally powerful objects, such as the sun,[67] moon, stars,[68] rainbows,[69]

---

64 When I was serving in the IDF and was responsible for training a group of new *olim* from Ethiopia, we were specifically instructed not to point to them, as it was considered a very offensive gesture in Ethiopia. Regarding the negative associations of pointing among ancient cultures in biblical times, see Aron Maged, *Beit Aharon: Klalei HaShas,* vol. 10 (Brooklyn, NY: Deutsch, 1975), 712. Regarding the pointing taboo in the modern era, see Larry A. Samovar, *Communication Between Cultures* (Boston, MA: Wadsworth, 2007), 257; Mai Moua, *Culturally Intelligent Leadership: Leading Through Intercultural Interactions* (New York: Business Expert Press, 2010), 123; Lillian Glass, *Say It Right* (New York: Putnam's Sons, 1991), 164; J.K. Yates, *Global Engineering and Construction* (Hoboken, NJ: John Wiley and Sons, 2007) 32; Craig Steven Cravens, *Culture and Customs of the Czech Republic and Slovakia* (Westport, CT: Greenwood, 2006), 63.

65 See also Hanoch Zundel Grossberg, *Zer HaTorah* (Jerusalem, 1979), 12, note 8.

66 James Hastings, ed., *Encyclopaedia of Religion and Ethics,* vol. 6 (Edinburgh: T & T Clark, 1913), 496. The taboo to point "with the forefinger at the god-protector" is found in ancient Babylonia, see A. B. Strachov, "Miscellenea Meteorologica Slavica: Breaking the Rainbow in Poles'e," *Die Welt der Slaven,* vol. 33 (1988), 341.

67 Frank A. Kmietowicz, *Slavic Mythical Beliefs* (1982) 174; Strachov, "Miscellenea Meteorologica Slavica," 340.

68 James Frazer, "Some Popular Superstitions of the Ancients," *Folklore* 1 (1890), 151–52; Strachov, "Miscellenea Meteorologica Slavica," 340.

69 Francisco Demetrio, *Encyclopedia of Philippine Folk Beliefs and Customs,* vol. 2 (Cagayan de Oro City, Philippines: Xavier University, 1991), 19; Strachov, "Miscellenea Meteorologica Slavica," 339.

and tombstones,[70] is considered inappropriate and a source of misfortune. This is extended to pointing to anything considered of value, such as ships in fishing cultures[71] and livestock among herders and farmers.[72] The index finger was considered a particularly offensive finger to use for pointing.[73] Because of this some people bend their index finger down a bit so that they are not directly pointing at the Torah with it.

It may be that once the custom of pointing to the Torah became prevalent, it was considered inappropriate to use the index finger for pointing because of widespread negative cultural connotations. The use of other fingers have their own negative and vulgar cultural connotations, and it is difficult to use the ring finger for pointing, leaving the little finger as an alternative with no offensive connotations.[74] Additionally, with some European folk customs, the little finger is considered to have a very positive effect in countering demonic forces and magic, in contrast to the index finger, which has a number of negative associations.[75] The fact that the little finger, affectionately known as the pinky,[76] is considered cute is probably a factor in the popularity of this custom.

---

70 Wayland Debs, *Popular Beliefs and Superstitions: A Compendium of American Folklore*, vol. 1 (G. K. Hall, 1981), 1241.

71 See Morag Cameron, "Highland Fisher-Folk and Their Superstitions," *Folklore* 14 (1903), 303, regarding not pointing to boats going out to sea. See John Rhys, "Manx Folklore and Superstitions," *Folklore* 3 (1892), 84, regarding the superstition of fishermen not to point to anything with a finger.

72 Strachov, "Miscellenea Meteorologica Slavica," 340–41.

73 Charlotte S. Burne, "Presidential Address," *Folklore* 22 (1911), 27, notes that the index finger is considered poisonous.

74 See *Sefer Kara Ravatz*, 275, where the author explains that it is not standard to point with the thumb. Dr. Roman Katsman of Bar-Ilan University confirmed that the gesture of pointing with the little finger is "positively a non-offensive one." There have been some reports of a German custom of using the little finger to point in general; see Geraldine Michael and Frank N. Wills, Jr., "The Development of Gestures in Three Subcultural Groups," *Journal of Social Psychology* 79, no. 1 (1969), 39. This is repeated in many books about gestures but in fact appears to be very uncommon and unrelated to the development of the custom to point to the Torah with the little finger.

75 Strachov, "Miscellenea Meteorologica Slavica," 338–39.

76 The term "pinky" for little finger derives from the Scottish use of the word "pink" to mean "small"; this is also the derivation of "pink eye," meaning a small or contracted eye. See John Jamieson, *An Etymological Dictionary of the Scottish Language* (Edinburgh: Abernathy and Walker, 1818), under "pinkie."

As we have seen, the original custom to bow to the Torah during *hagbaha*, codified in the *Shulḥan Arukh*, has in many congregations been substituted with finger pointing. Finger pointing with the index finger during *hagbaha* first appeared in sources from the 1800s. Today many people point with the little finger, a custom attested to in writing for the first time in 1969. The reasons for using specifically the little finger seem to be cultural and sociological.

*Chapter 20*

# Reciting *Al Tira* After *Aleinu*

## THE STANDARD SOURCE OF THE POPULAR PRACTICE

Many Ashkenazic prayer books indicate that it is customary to recite three verses after *Aleinu*: Proverbs 3:25, Isaiah 8:10, and Isaiah 46:4.[1] How did this custom originate, and what purpose do these three verses serve at the conclusion of the prayer service?

The three verses are first found linked together in Esther Rabba 7:17. There it is related that after the decrees against the Jews were sealed and handed over to Haman, he and his cohorts were filled with joy. They happened upon Mordekhai, who was walking in front of them. Just then, Mordekhai saw three young children on their way home from school. Mordekhai ran over to them, and Haman and his friends followed to see what Mordekhai wanted from the children. Mordekhai asked the children, "*Pesok li pesuk'kha,* Tell me what verse you are studying in school." The first child quoted Proverbs 3:25, "You will not fear sudden terror, or the holocaust of the wicked when it comes." The second child quoted

1 See, for example, *Siddur Avodat Yisrael,* 132, *Siddur Rinat Yisrael,* 102, *Siddur Tefillat Shai,* 70, *ArtScroll Siddur,* 160.

Isaiah 8:10, "Plan a conspiracy and it shall be annulled; speak your piece and it shall not stand, for God is with us." The third child quoted Isaiah 46:4, "Until your old age I am unchanged, and until your hoary years I will carry you; I made you and I will bear you, I will carry you and I will rescue you." When Mordekhai heard this he laughed and was filled with great joy. Haman asked him what he found so joyful in the words of the children, and Mordekhai replied that he was just informed that he should not fear Haman's plots against the Jews. This infuriated Haman, who then decided to kill the Jewish children first.

The custom to recite these three verses after *Aleinu* is recorded in many books, all referencing one of a few major sources. The earliest source generally given for this custom is the sixteenth-century work *Manot HaLevi*, a commentary on the book of Esther written by Rabbi Shlomo Alkabetz. Alkabetz was one of the kabbalists of Tzfat, a contemporary of Rabbi Yosef Karo and brother-in-law of Rabbi Moshe Cordovero. He is best known as the author of *Lekha Dodi*. In his commentary to Esther 3:15, he quotes and explains the story above from Esther Rabba 7:17. During the course of his explanation he mentions that Rabbi Yehuda ibn Shushan wrote in his own commentary that based on this midrash, the people of Provence would add these three verses to the "end of their prayers" every day, a custom that he too adopted.[2]

Ibn Shushan's commentary to the five *megillot* is lost to us today.[3] Excerpts from this work are incorporated throughout Alkabetz's commentaries.[4] Not much is known about Rabbi Yehuda ibn Shushan. His work on the laws of blessings, *Birkat HaNehenin*, dated 1495, states that his full name was Rabbi Yehuda ben Yitzhak ben Avraham ben Shushan HaSefaradi. According to most biographers, he was among the exiles from Spain.[5] Ibn Shushan mentions in *Birkat HaNehenin* that he left

---

2 Shlomo Alkabetz, *Manot HaLevi* (Jerusalem, 2002), 231.

3 Avraham Chavatzelet, "Birkat HaNehenin LeR. Yehuda ibn Shushan," *Moriah* 72 (1983), 41.

4 Alkabetz thus saved elements of many works that would otherwise be totally lost today. See Gedaliah Nigal, "Peirusho shel R. Yosef Yaavatz LeRut," *Sinai* 76 (1975), 155.

5 Naftali Yaakov Hacohen, *Otzar HaGedolim* (Bnei Brak, 1966), 103, part 4, section 250. While it is very probable that Ibn Shushan was among the Spanish exiles, there

his homeland, and that at the time of writing this work he was living in Provence.[6] According to some sources he later settled in Turkey[7] and was possibly among the Jewish exiles from Provence in 1501. Ibn Shushan was a great scholar and is cited by Rabbi Yosef Karo in his *Kesef Mishneh*[8] and *Beit Yosef*.[9] He was considered a saintly figure and is sometimes referred to as HaḤasid Rabbi Yehuda ibn Shushan. An oft-quoted story about Ibn Shushan is related in the sixteenth-century kabbalistic *musar* book *Reshit Ḥokhma* by Rabbi Eliyahu de Vidas. He writes that Rabbi Shabtai Lapidot, one of the great kabbalists of Tzfat and a colleague of Rabbi Yosef Karo, reported to Rabbi Moshe Cordovero that he was visited by Ibn Shushan in a dream sometime after the latter's death. Ibn Shushan's face was "glowing like the sun, and each and every hair of his beard was glowing as if it were a torch." When Rabbi Lapidot asked him how he merited such an honor, Ibn Shushan replied that it was because his trait of silence meant that he had never engaged in frivolous conversation.[10] While we do not know much about Ibn Shushan, it is clear that he was well known and highly regarded by the Tzfat kabbalists.

## THE SOURCE OF THE PROVENCE COMMUNITY

But where did the Jews of Provence that Ibn Shushan observed learn this custom? One of the earliest forms of Jewish public worship was the institution of the *maamadot* during the time of the Temple. Representatives of the people would come to Jerusalem to attend the daily sacrifices. These sacrifices took place in the presence of and with the participation of representatives from all over the Land of Israel, which meant they were viewed as a communal undertaking. The people were divided into twenty-four districts, whose members would take turns

is no conclusive evidence of this. See Chavatzelet, "Birkat HaNehenin," 39, 40. Ibn Shushan is mentioned in passing in David Conforte's *Korei Ha-Dorot* (Jerusalem: Ahavat Shalom, Yad Samuel Franco, 2008), 109, 123.

6 Chavatzelet, "Birkat HaNehenin," 40.

7 *Otzar HaGedolim*, 103.

8 *Kesef Mishneh*, *Hilkhot Sheḥita* 3:13, *Hilkhot Berakhot* 3:8.

9 *Beit Yosef*, *Oraḥ Ḥayim* 168:10.

10 Eliyahu de Vidas, *Reshit Ḥokhma* (Mukachevo, 1943) *Shaar HaAhava*, chapter 6, 71b, 72a.

every week sending representatives to "stand over" (עמדו על גביו) the sacrifices in the Temple, and so they were called *maamadot* (literally "standings"). These representatives recited special prayers. Although it is not clear exactly what prayers the *maamad* liturgy consisted of, some of the service is described in Mishna Taanit 4:1, where we find that the special services included readings from Genesis and the *Birkat Kohanim*.[11]

Even after the Temple was destroyed, the practice of reciting a *maamad* service continued. Prayer books from the Middle Ages indicate that it was customary for individuals in France and Germany to recite a *maamadot* prayer after morning services.[12] This prayer was based on an approximation of what the *maamad* service was in Temple times. It consisted of readings from Genesis, various selections from the Prophets and Psalms, readings relating to sacrifices, *Ein Kelokeinu, Pitum HaKetoret,* the psalm of the day, the Torah portion describing the manna, the Ten Commandments, and various verses said for protection. These verses of protection took many forms; some services included eleven verses that begin and end with the letter *nun*, verses that can be read both forward and backward, and other verses that were considered for some reason significant. The *maamad* service concluded with *Aleinu*. At the time, the public morning service concluded with the *Kaddish* after *Kedusha DeSidra*, and then individuals who wanted to would say the *maamadot* service.

Toward the end of the twelfth century, a process began whereby some of this *maamad* service became incorporated into the main body of the public prayer (*Ein Kelokeinu, Pitum HaKetoret,* the psalm of the day, *Aleinu*). Some parts remained as additions after the service to be recited by individuals (the Torah portion describing the manna, the Ten Commandments) and some parts were left out altogether (readings from Genesis, various selections from the Prophets).

What happened to the verses recited for protection? This is where our three verses come in. A British prayer book following the French custom, dated from around 1190 (Ms. Corpus Christi College, 133), provides an example of an early *maamad* service that was incorporated into

11 Ismar Elbogen, *Jewish Liturgy* (Philadelphia: Jewish Publication Society, 1993), 190–91.

12 Ephraim Urbach, "*Mishmarot* and *Maamadot*," *Tarbiz* 42, nos. 3–4 (1973), 313–27.

the regular public service. The last elements of this section are a string of verses, Isaiah 8:10, Proverbs 3:25, Isaiah 46:4, I Kings 8:54– 60, and Micah 4:5, followed by *Aleinu.*[13] Three of these are the familiar verses listed in our prayer books, but in a different order. We can now understand what Ibn Shushan saw in Provence: it was a remnant of a *maamad* service that had been incorporated into the public service.

Rabbi David ben Shmuel HaLevi (*Taz,* c. 1586–1667) writes in *Turei Zahav,* his commentary to the *Shulḥan Arukh,* that he would recite these three verses while the *ḥazan* said *Sim Shalom* in his repetition of the *Amida.* He refers to the story found in Esther Rabba and says that in Provence they would say these verses every day.[14] It is interesting to note that certain customs placed elements of the *maamad* service (including *Ein Kelokeinu* and *Pitum HaKetoret*) after the *ḥazan*'s recital of *Sim Shalom,*[15] as this was considered the end of the official *tefilla.* We see here an echo of the idea that the recitation of these verses have their origin in the *maamadot* prayers, and so they were said at this point in the service.

## THE CUSTOM BECOMES MORE POPULAR

Any connection between these verses and the *maamadot* was quickly forgotten. The custom to say these verses is mentioned in *Or Tzaddikim* by Rabbi Meir Popperos, first published in 1690. Popperos was a popularizer of the kabbalistic teachings of the Ari. He states that "the sages of Israel" established the custom to say these three verses before leaving the synagogue. He explains that the purpose of the verses is to awaken divine mercy and hasten redemption.[16] The sages to whom Popperos refers are most probably the Jerusalem kabbalists with whom he studied.[17] It is this work that is quoted as the source of the custom in the popular book of

13 Israel Ta-Shma, *The Early Ashkenazic Prayer: Literary and Historical Aspects* (Jerusalem: Magnes Press, 2003), 139–53.

14 *Shulḥan Arukh, Turei Zahav, Oraḥ Ḥayim* 132:2.

15 See the Warsaw 1865 edition of *Seder Rav Amram Gaon,* 14, and the note on the bottom of the page.

16 Meir Popperos, *Or Tzaddikim* (Warsaw, 1889), *Tikkun HaTefillah, siman* 84, 33.

17 Noach Aminach and Yosef Nitzan, *Gedolei HaAchronim* (Jerusalem: Jewish Agency, 2000), 19.

customs *Sefer Taamei HaMinhagim UMekorei HaDinim.*[18] By the 1700s the verses were simply understood as a mystical formula for protection.

Another major source for this custom is the book *Avodat HaKodesh* by the eighteenth-century sage Rabbi Hayim Yosef David Azulai (Ḥida). In the second section of this work, entitled *Tziporen Shamir,* he writes: "The people of Provence have a custom to say these three verses every day at the end of their prayers."[19] He references Rabbi Yehuda ibn Shushan and *Manot HaLevi* as the source for this custom. He then adds that the seventeenth-century kabbalist, Rabbi Moshe Zacuto (the Ramaz), would follow this custom and add a short personal prayer of his own.[20] In all sources seen so far there is no mention of adding these prayers specifically after *Aleinu.*

## PLACEMENT OF THE VERSES AFTER *ALEINU*

Modern siddurim instruct us to say these three verses specifically after *Aleinu.* The association of these verses with *Aleinu* comes from the book that is most often quoted as a source for this custom, *Zikhron Tziyon,* published around 1680 by Yehiel Mikhel ben Avraham Berekh.[21] *Zikhron Tziyon* is a twenty-two page booklet of prayers and *segulot* based on the teachings of Lurianic Kabbala, in particular the classic kabbalistic work by Rabbi Isaiah Horowitz, author of *Shenei Luḥot HaBrit.* It contains prayers for the amelioration of a bad dream and supplications to be said on various occasions. It is here that we find for the first time an explicit instruction to recite the three verses after *Aleinu.* On page 17, under the heading "After *Aleinu* recite," the three verses are listed, with

18 Avraham Sperling, *Sefer Taamei HaMinhagim UMekorei HaDinim* (Jerusalem: Shai Lamora, 1999), section 148, 63.

19 Hayim Yosef David Azulai, *Avodat HaKodesh* (Warsaw, 1874), *Tziporen Shamir* 2:35, 19.

20 רבון העולמים זכנו לעסוק בתורה לשמה ובמצוות וגמילות חסדים ולהשכים בהם ולהעריב בהם וזכנו לראות בבנין מקדשנו החרב או"א הראנו בבנינו וכו' עד תמידין כהלכתן.

21 Bodleian Library, Opp. 8vo (2). There is no publication date listed anywhere in the booklet, only a note that it was published in Prague during the reign of Leopold I (1658–1705). Isaac Yudlov, director of the Institute for Hebrew Bibliography at Hebrew University, understands that it was published around 1680. My thanks to Rahel Kasemaa, assistant to the Hebraica and Judaica Librarian at the Bodleian Library, Oxford, for her assistance.

no explanation or additional instructions. At this point these verses, which were originally recited as part of the *maamad* service specifically before *Aleinu*, have been shifted to after *Aleinu*.

In 1683, the first edition of *Kitzur Shenei Luḥot HaBrit* by Rabbi Yechiel Michel Epstein was published. This work was written in order to make the practices contained in *Shenei Luḥot HaBrit* more accessible and widely known, and included various customs and practices from other works as well. It became very popular and was republished many times.[22] After discussing *Aleinu*, he quotes the custom of the *Taz* to recite these verses while the *ḥazan* says *Sim Shalom*. He adds that through the recitation of these verses a person will be saved from all evil decrees. In a gloss, *Zikhron Tziyon* is quoted as stating that the verses are to be said after *Aleinu*. He adds that they are a "wonderful *segula*" and contain many great secrets. If, for some reason, the verses could not be said directly after *Aleinu*, they should be said before leaving the synagogue.[23] Rabbi Yaakov Emden included the book *Kitzur Shenei Luḥot HaBrit* in a list of Sabbatean works.[24] However, there was never a concern that this particular custom of reciting these three verses after *Aleinu* was in any way connected to Sabbateanism.

This custom was also included in *Sefer Zekhira VeInyanei Segulot*, a collection of *segulot* first published in 1709 and written for a general audience. Although the book claims to be quoting *Zikhron Tziyon*, it is actually quoting *Kitzur Shenei Luḥot HaBrit*, using the same terminology to say that the verses are a "wonderful *segula*" and contain many great secrets.[25] The same quote, this time including the idea that these verses save the supplicant from evil decrees, attributed to *Zikhron Tziyon* but again actually from *Kitzur Shenei Luḥot HaBrit*, was included in *Otzar HaTefillot*, a very popular nineteenth-century prayer book printed by the Widow and Brothers Romm, publishers of the Vilna edition of the Babylonian Talmud.[26] These sources were then quoted in later books,

22 Yechiel Michel Epstein, *Kitzur Shenei Luḥot HaBrit* (Jerusalem, 1944), 3, author's introduction.

23 *Kitzur Shenei Luḥot HaBrit, Inyanei Tefilla*, 133.

24 Shnayer Z. Leiman, "Sefarim HaḤashudim BeShabtaut," in *Sefer HaZikaron LeRav Moshe Lipshitz* (New York, 1996), 889, note 12.

25 Zecharia Simner, *Sefer Zekhira VeInyanei Segulot* (Hamburg, 1709), 29.

26 *Otzar HaTefillot* (Vilna, 1928), 437.

and so the custom to say the verses after *Aleinu* became better known. All of these works stress that it is important to say these verses before leaving the synagogue. Since *Zikhron Tziyon* was a short booklet and was not readily available after its initial publication, *Kitzur Shenei Luḥot HaBrit* became the main source for information about this custom and contributed to its widespread popularity.

Various homiletic connections have been made between *Aleinu* and the three supplementary verses, for example, that as long as Amalek exists in the world, God's name cannot be complete, and therefore the three verses indicating the downfall of Amalek (Haman) come straight after *Aleinu*, where we speak of a time when the name of God is complete.[27] However, there was never an essential connection between the three verses and *Aleinu*. It was simply that by the late 1600s the custom was to say these verses directly before leaving the synagogue, and *Aleinu* happened to be the last part of the service. In contemporary prayer books, the Mourners' Kaddish after *Aleinu* is placed either before or after the *Al Tira* verses. Since these verses have no intrinsic connection to *Aleinu* and must simply be said before leaving the synagogue, it would seem that they should ideally be said after the *Kaddish*.

## THE ORIGIN OF THE CURRENT POPULAR PRACTICE

From these sources it is clear that this custom began as part of the *maamad* service. It was observed and noted by Ibn Shushan and adopted by kabbalists who held him in high regard, such as Rabbi Alkabetz, Rabbi Popperos, the Ramaz and the Ḥida. The general population was made aware of the custom through works such as *Kitzur Shenei Luḥot HaBrit* and *Sefer Zekhira*, books that were written with the aim of spreading kabbalistic practices among the masses.[28] Kabbalistic prayer books that appeared before the publication of these popular works do not include these verses.[29] Originally, the verses were recited at the end of the prayer service before *Aleinu*, but over time, as *Aleinu* came to be seen more and

27 David Cohen, "He'arot BeInyanei Tefilla," *HaDarom* 50 (1980), 232, 233.

28 *Kitzur Shenei Luḥot HaBrit*, 4, 5, publisher's introduction.

29 For example, the verses are not included in *Siddur HaMekubal HaRav Herz Shliaḥ Tzibbur ztz"l* (Bnei Brak: Morgenstern, 1971), first published in 1560.

more as integral to the morning service, the verses were placed exclusively after *Aleinu*. This assured that the verses would be said before leaving the synagogue. The connection to *Aleinu* was first established in *Zikhron Tziyon* and popularized in *Kitzur Shenei Luḥot HaBrit*. All the subsequent books that quote *Zikhron Tziyon* connect the verses to *Aleinu*, and the books that do not reference *Zikhron Tziyon* associate the verses with the end of the service, but not specifically with *Aleinu*.

What was seen as the role of these verses and why was it considered so important not to leave the synagogue without saying them? *Kitzur Shenei Luḥot HaBrit* mentions the secrets contained within the verses, adding that they are a "wonderful *segula* to rescue one from many evil decrees." This explanation is quoted in *Otzar HaTefillot*.[30] Similarly, Rabbi Popperos in *Or Tzaddikim* notes that these verses awaken divine mercy. According to this reasoning, as long as a person is still in the synagogue he remains "safe" to a certain level, but once he goes out into the world he may be at the mercy of any number of "evil decrees." Therefore, these verses of protection must be said before going into the dangerous outside world. Since these verses indicated to Mordekhai that he should not fear the decree of Haman, they now function as a mystical formula to annul all evil decrees. This was the role of these verses going back to the time of the medieval *maamad* service, when they were part of a series of verses of protection. In fact, a French siddur from the late 1200s adds a prayer specifically against evil decrees after the *maamad* service.[31]

Once this reasoning is understood, it is easy to see why this custom captured the imagination of Ibn Shushan, who first saw this custom after being expelled from Spain. The evil decree of expulsion decimated the great Jewish community of Spain, sending tens of thousands into forced exile from their adopted homeland. The verses that comforted Mordekhai at the time of Haman's evil decree were now observed being recited by the Jews of Provence. Ibn Shushan adopted this custom at

30 *Kitzur Shenei Luḥot HaBrit, Inyanei Tefillah*, 133, *Otzar HaTefillot*, 437.

31 Ephraim Urbach, "*Mishmarot* and *Maamadot*," *Tarbiz* 42, nos. 3–4 (1973), 317. The prayer concludes: ופדנו מכל גזירות רעות הבאות ומתרגשות בעולם ותושיע ברחמיך ברבים משיח צדקך ועמך.

the time of an evil decree in his own land. Over time, these verses were popularized as a general kabbalistic *segula* to reverse evil decrees.[32]

Although the custom was originally mentioned by Sephardic mystics, it was popularized through Ashkenazic books, and the verses did not become entrenched in Sephardic prayer books, which contain different verses that are to be recited after *Aleinu*, and for other purposes.[33]

Having seen the origin of the recitation of the three verses, we know that originally they were said only as part of the morning service, when individuals would say the *maamadot*. The current custom to recite these three verses after *Aleinu* developed over many centuries, from the *maamadot* service of Provence when they were said before *Aleinu*, through Ibn Shushan to the Tzfat kabbalists; then through the popularity of a Sabbatean book of mystical customs they became forever associated with *Aleinu*. Once these verses became seen as a complement to *Aleinu*, it became customary to recite them at the end of Minḥa and Maariv as well, and any other occasion when *Aleinu* is recited, such as after *Kiddush Levana*.

---

32 Rabbi Chaim Malinowitz informed me that he inaugurated the public recitation of these verses after *Aleinu* in his synagogue Beit Tefillah, Ramat Beit Shemesh, during the time of the Gaza disengagement in Israel. Even though he did not know the full history of this custom at the time, it is particularly fitting when we consider that it was originally popularized by a Jew who was expelled from his own home in Spain. Thanks to Rabbi Beinish Ginsburg for calling my attention to this practice from his shul.

33 Macy Nulman, *The Encyclopedia of Jewish Prayer* (Northvale, NJ: Jason Aronson, 1996), 23.

*Chapter 21*

# *Tehillat Hashem* and Other Verses Before *Birkat HaMazon*

In this chapter we investigate the origin and development of saying various psalms and selected verses from Psalms before *Birkat HaMazon*. In particular, we will attempt to explain the practice of some Ashkenazic Jews to add Psalms 145:21, 115:18, 118:1 and 106:2 after the customary Psalm 126 (*Shir HaMaalot*) preceding *Birkat HaMazon*.

## PSALMS 137 AND 126 BEFORE *BIRKAT HAMAZON*

The earliest source for reciting Psalm 137 (*Al Naharot Bavel*) before *Birkat HaMazon* is found in the list of practices of the Tzfat kabbalist Rabbi Moshe Cordovero (1522–70). There are different versions of this list, but all versions include the practice of saying *Al Naharot Bavel*.[1]

1 Moshe Hallamish, *Kabbalah in Liturgy, Halakhah, and Customs* (Ramat Gan: Bar-Ilan University Press, 2000), 349, 353 [Hebrew].

Some versions specifically note that this is to recall the destruction of the Temple,[2] some versions state that the psalm is supposed to be said at the meal, though not necessarily right before *Birkat HaMazon*,[3] and some versions state that the psalm is said only on weekdays, though no alternative psalm is offered for Shabbat and holidays.[4] Although the exact provenance of this list is not clear, the parts of it referring to the recitation of Psalm 137 were already popularized by 1577.[5]

The mystical work *Seder HaYom*, by the sixteenth-century Tzfat kabbalist Rabbi Moshe ben Makhir, was first published in 1599. He mentions saying *Al Naharot Bavel* at a meal in order to recall the destruction of the Temple, and adds that "on Shabbat and holidays, when sorrow and sighing should not be mentioned, mention verses of the comfort of Zion and Jerusalem and the psalm 'When the Lord brought back those that returned to Zion' (*Shir HaMaalot*, Psalm 126)."[6]

The recitation of *Al Naharot Bavel* before *Birkat HaMazon* was next included in the work *Seder HaShulḥan* by Rabbi Naftali ben David Zekharya, published in 1603, as the introductory part of a small *bencher*, making it the earliest *bencher* to include this custom.[7] There he writes that the custom is based on the Zohar, *Teruma* 157b, which states, "One who has pleasure at his table, and has pleasure from the food, should remember and worry about the holiness of the Holy Land and the palace of the King which is destroyed; and on account of the sorrow which he experiences at his table along with the same joy and feasting which

2 Ibid., 349, MS 1691, item 13.

3 Ibid., 349, MS 1961, item 13.

4 Ibid., 353, MS 1955, item 22.

5 Ibid., 347.

6 Moshe ben Makhir, *Seder HaYom* (Venice, 1599), 29b. Some kabbalists already refrained from reciting Psalm 137 from Friday afternoon; see Moshe Hallamish, *Hanhagot Kabbaliot BeShabbat* (Jerusalem: Orḥot, 2006), 49, note 21 [Hebrew]; *Mishna Berura* 267:1.

7 Abraham Berliner, *Ketavim Nivḥarim*, vol. 1 (Jerusalem: Mossad HaRav Kook, 1969), 31; Yissachar Jacobson, *Netiv Bina*, vol. 2 (Tel Aviv: Sinai, 1987), 134. Note that Naftali ben David Zekharya only brings the custom to recite *Al Naharot Bavel*, not *Shir HaMaalot*. On Naftali, see Reuven David Gershon and Moshe David Shvicha, "Seder HaShulḥan LeRabbi Naftali" in *Birkat Menaḥem* (Cleveland: Machon Nahor Safra, 2007), 77–79.

is there, the Holy One, blessed be He, will consider it as if he built His House and built all of the ruins of the Temple; fortunate is his lot."[8]

This practice was then included in *Shenei Luḥot HaBrit* by Rabbi Isaiah Horowitz (the Shelah, c. 1555–1630), first published in 1648 by his son. He puts together all the elements previously seen, bringing the quote from the Zohar as the source of the idea, and explains, "We recite the psalm 'By the rivers of Babylon' (*Al Naharot Bavel*, Psalm 137) before *Birkat HaMazon*... and on Shabbat and holidays we recite the psalm 'When the Lord brought back those that returned to Zion' (*Shir HaMaalot*, Psalm 126)."[9]

This idea was quoted in the name of the Shelah by halakhic authorities in the 1600s, with *Magen Avraham* (*Oraḥ Ḥayim* 1:5)[10] and *Eliya Rabba* (181:9) popularizing it outside of mystical circles. *Magen Avraham* was in turn quoted in the *Mishna Berura* (*Oraḥ Ḥayim* 1:11), and for this reason, popular works often attribute the origin of this practice to the Shelah.[11]

Other psalms were suggested to fulfill the purpose of recalling the Temple. For example, for Shabbat and holidays, the Maharshal suggests reciting Psalm 87,[12] while Rabbi Yaakov Emden suggests Psalm 122.[13] Different psalms were suggested in other kabbalistic sources,[14] but Psalms 126 and 137 proved to be the most popular. Even so, many early prayer

---

8 Naftali ben David Zekharya, *Birkat HaMazon* (Venice, 1603), 13a. *Al Naharot Bavel* is brought there on 16a–16b.

9 Isaiah Horowitz, *Shenei Luḥot HaBrit* (Jerusalem: Machon Shaarei Ziv, 1993), *Shaar HaOtiot, Kuf – Kedushat HaAkhila, siman* 88, 369.

10 Avraham Gombiner in his *Magen Avraham* often includes kabbalistic works as halakhic sources; see Hayim Tchernowitz, *Toldot HaPoskim*, vol. 3 (New York, 1947), 172.

11 See, for example, Eliyahu Munk, *Olam HaTefillot*, vol. 1 (Jerusalem: Mossad HaRav Kook, 1992), 227; Macy Nulman, *The Encyclopedia of Jewish Prayer* (Northvale: Jason Aronson, 1996), 304, note 2; Nosson Scherman, *Zemiros and Bircas Hamazon* (Brooklyn: Mesorah, 1998), 260.

12 Menachem Mendel Landa, *Siddur Tzluta DeAvraham*, vol. 2 (Tel Aviv: Grafika, 1961) 389.

13 Yaakov Emden, *Amudei Shamayim* (1962 facsimile edition), 23b.

14 Avraham Landa, *Siddur Tzluta DeAvraham*, vol. 2 (Tel Aviv, 1961), 495. Psalm 87 was chosen for this purpose among Karlin-Stolin Hasidim (Yaakov Yisraeli, *Beit Karlin-Stolin* [Tel Aviv: Keren Yaakov VeRachel, 1982], 90).

books and *benchers* did not include any Psalms before *Birkat HaMazon*, demonstrating that it was not a universal custom.[15] For various reasons, some persisted in omitting *Al Naharot Bavel*[16] and even *Shir HaMaalot*.[17]

We can now understand the development of this custom. At first it was noted that one should recall the destruction of the Temple during the meal, and reciting Psalm 137 was used to fulfill this. Since this psalm was considered sad and thus inappropriate for Shabbat and holidays, a

15 Although the earliest *bencher* was published before the time of Shelah (Prague, 1515), even much after, these psalms were not included. For example, they are not found in *Birkat HaMazon* (Amsterdam, 1723); *Birkat HaMazon KeMinhag Ashkenaz UPolin* (Frankfurt am Main, 1727); Yitzhak Stanov, *Siddur VaYe'ater Yitzḥak* (Berlin, 1785), 151a; *Birkat HaMazon* (Dyhernfurth, 1811); Naftali Hertz HaLevi, *Siddur HaGra* (Jerusalem, 1895), 157b.

16 In certain circles it is rare to find people who say *Al Naharot Bavel* before *Birkat HaMazon*; see Pinhas Ben-Harush, *Mei Pinḥas* (Ashdod, 2011), 134, note 13. Some said it only on the eve of Tisha BeAv; see Aharon Pinchuk, *Mateh Aharon* (Jerusalem, 1980), 17. Shlomo Zalman Auerbach is also reported to not have said *Al Naharot Bavel*. See Shlomo Aviner, *Piskei Shlomo*, vol. 1 (Beit El: Sifriat Chava, 2013), 89. Zvi Yehuda Kook replaced *Al Naharot Bavel* with *Shir HaMaalot*, which according to Yaakov Ariel, *rav* of Ramat Gan, is something that many in Israel do. See Mordechai Zion, *Kum Hithalekh BaAretz* (Maale Adumim, 2015), 394. Regarding Hasidim who do not say Psalm 137, see the oft-repeated anecdote regarding Reb Hillel Paritcher (1795–1864) in *R. Hillel MiParitch–Sippurim* (Heichal HaNegina, 2015), 56–57; *Kovetz Sippurim*, vol. 2 (Brooklyn: Beit Midrash Lubavitch, 1988), *siman* 63, 45. On the hasidic custom, reported in the name of the Baal Shem Tov, to always say *Shir HaMaalot* instead of *Al Naharot Bavel*, see the comprehensive discussion in Yosef Lowy, *Minhag Yisrael Torah*, vol. 1 (Brooklyn, 1994), 1:4, 43–44; see also Natan Perlman, "Minhag Rabboteinu SheEin Omrim HaPiyut Dvai Haser," *Kovetz Beit Aharon VeYisrael* 180 (Elul 5771/2011), 155, note 28; Meir Yisrael, *Birkat HaMazon HaMevoar* (Bnei Brak: Keter Chaim, 2011), 144; Levi Yitzhak Raskin, *Seder Birkat HaMazon* (London, 2013), 4, note 3. See also Zev Goldberger, *Darkhi HaYashar VehaTov* (1910), 23b, who reports that Zvi Hirsch Friedman of Lesko (d. 1874) always said *Shir HaMaalot* before *Birkat HaMazon*, even on weekdays.

17 It is reported that Hayim of Volozhin would not say *Shir HaMaalot*, as it is still referring to exile and so not appropriate for Shabbat; Avraham Halevi Horowitz, *Orḥot Rabbeinu*, vol. 1 (Bnei Brak, 1991), 115. The Ḥatam Sofer said neither psalm; Yehuda Nachshoni, *Rabbeinu Moshe Sofer* (Jerusalem: Mashabim, 1981), 441, *siman* 75. Regarding Hasidim who do not say Ps. 126, see Eliezer Brandwein, *Degel Maḥane Yehuda* (Brooklyn, 2011), 360, note 26; Eran Moshe Margalit, *Haggadat Likkutei Sfat Emet* (Or Etzion, 2009), 201, note 129. See also *Rebbe Velvel* (Bnei Brak, 2003) 335.

different psalm was chosen to fill this role on those festive days.[18] The psalms then were moved to immediately before *Birkat HaMazon*. These psalms do not have any particular connection to *Birkat HaMazon*,[19] and they were slotted in at this point just to ensure that they would be said during the meal and not forgotten. However, there is a natural connection between these psalms and some parts of *Birkat HaMazon*, as the second blessing of *Birkat HaMazon* (*Birkat HaZan*) is focused on thanking God for the Land of Israel, and the third blessing (*Birkat Neḥama*) focuses on Jerusalem and the Temple, ideas central to Psalms 137 and 126, so it was reasonable to view them all as one extended unit.

## ADDITIONAL VERSES BEFORE *BIRKAT HAMAZON*

Some people say additional verses after Psalm 126 before *Birkat HaMazon*, the most prevalent being Psalms 145:21 תהלת ה' ידבר פי ויברך כל בשר שם קדשו לעולם ועד, "My mouth shall speak the praise of the Lord; and let all flesh bless His holy name for ever and ever," and Psalms 115:18 ואנחנו נברך י־ה מעתה ועד עולם הללוי־ה, "But we will bless the Lord from this time forth and forever, Hallelujah." This is often reported as the Ashkenazic custom.[20] What is the source for this addition?

The earliest reference to reciting these particular verses before *Birkat HaMazon* is found in the work *Shaar HaMitzvot* by the Tzfat kabbalist Rabbi Hayim Vital (1542–1620).[21] There he reported that Rabbi Isaac Luria (the Ari) told him that certain verses should be said after washing *mayim aḥaronim* and before *Birkat HaMazon*.[22] First Psalm 67 should be recited in its entirety. This is followed by Psalms 34:2, which

---

18 See Moshe Hallamish, *Hanhagot Kabbaliot BeShabbat* (Jerusalem, Orḥot, 2006) 354.

19 See Moshe Barzam, *Imrot Moshe* (Bnei Brak, 2004) 134, *siman* 3; Natan Einfeld, *Minḥat Natan – Aggada* (Bnei Brak, 2007), 48; Moshe Shlezinger, *Zimrat HaLevi* (Zikhron Meir, 2010), 27, *siman* 3. Attempts have been made to show a conceptual connection between these two chapters of Psalms and *Birkat HaMazon*. See, for example, Yitzhak Etshalom, "Al HaDima Ve'al HaRina – Iyun BeMizmor 126," *Megadim* 42 (2005), 58–59.

20 Avigdor Unna, "Customs of the Jews of Germany," in Asher Waserteil, ed., *Yalkut Minhagim* (Jerusalem: Ministry of Education, 1996), 71.

21 This book is the fifth of the *Shemoneh She'arim*, which as a whole are sometimes referred to as *Etz Ḥayim*.

22 Hayim Vital, *Shaar HaMitzvot* (Jerusalem, 1905), *Ekev*, 45a.

functions to banish the forces of evil (*sitra aḥra*) present at the table, then Ecclesiastes 12:13, Psalms 145:21 and 115:18, and the end of Ezekiel 41:22. Thus, these two verses popularly recited are actually the middle part of the Ari's kabbalistic pre-*Birkat HaMazon* prayer.

This Lurianic practice was also reported by Rabbi Meir Poppers (c. 1624–62),[23] who wrote many works based on the teachings of Rabbi Isaac Luria. It was later noted by the prominent Sephardic authorities Rabbi Yosef of Baghdad (the Ben Ish Ḥai, 1832–1909)[24] and Rabbi Yaakov Hayim Sofer (the Kaf HaḤayim, 1870–1939).[25] This entire pre-*Birkat HaMazon* recitation is found in many prayer books and *benchers,* particularly those reflecting Sephardic practice.[26] Some sources are particular not to add any other psalms or verses to the ones listed by the Ari.[27]

Note that all of the customs to say psalms and verses before *Birkat HaMazon* originated with Tzfat kabbalists in the 1500s: the Ari, Rabbi Moshe Cordovero, Rabbi Hayim Vital, and Rabbi Moshe ben Makhir. While the recitation of psalms mentioned by Moshe Cordovero, Moshe ben Makhir, and the Shelah is focused on remembering the destruction of the Temple, those chosen by the Ari – Psalm 67 and the five verses – are focused on the theme of blessing, praising God, and an awareness of His Presence.[28] The current custom of reciting two of these verses before *Birkat HaMazon* can be understood to be a remnant of the custom of the Ari, appended to the end of the psalm that Rabbi Moshe ben Makhir suggested.[29] Thus it is an amalgam of both kabbalistic practices. This development of different versions of additional mealtime prayers would then parallel the development of the *Kabbalat Shabbat*

---

23 Meir Poppers, *Or Tzaddikim* (Warsaw, 1889), 59, *siman* 23, item 35. This book was first published in Hamburg in 1690.

24 *Ben Ish Ḥai, Shelaḥ,* first year, *siman* 15.

25 *Kaf HaḤayim* 157:22.

26 *Zemirot Shabbat VeSeder Birkat HaMazon* (New York: Otzar Hasefarim, 1968), 30; Mikhael Peretz, *Siddur Ohalei Shem* (Jerusalem, 2007), 255; Zvi Yevrov, *Birkat HaMazon im Biur MiMaran HaGraḥ Kanievsky* (Bnei Brak, 2009), 4; *Siddur Kavanat HaLev* (Elad: Machon Shira Ḥadasha, 2014), 423.

27 See Barukh Cohen, *Barukh HaShulḥan,* vol. 4 (Bnei Brak, 1986), 50, note 25 there.

28 Shem Tov Gaguine, *Keter Shem Tov,* vol. 1 (Jerusalem, 1960), 141, note 188.

29 See Daniel Goldschmidt, *Yeshuat Daniel* (Modiin Illit, 2013) 264, *siman* 185, note 1.

service, with Rabbi Cordovero and the Ari each choosing additional psalms to be recited as *Kabbalat Shabbat,* with our current practice being a combination of both customs.[30]

Some sources suggest that these verses function to fulfill the obligation to say words of Torah at a meal,[31] but that was not the original intent expressed in the first sources to mention these practices. In fact, works which provide lists of verses to say in order to fulfill the requirement to speak words of Torah at a meal give entirely different verses from the ones brought in the name of the Ari.[32] The Shelah also discusses the idea of speaking words of Torah at the meal, independent of the psalms recited to remember the Temple. He specifically mentions that ideally, psalms should not be recited for this purpose, and if Psalms are said, as in the case of unlearned people, they should choose something related to the meal.[33]Additional pre-*Birkat HaMazon* verses are found in other works,[34] for example, a list of ten verses to be said before those of the Ari, which are "a *segula* that one will not lack sustenance all the days of his life,"[35] or the two verses (Lev. 26:5 and Ex. 23:26) which Rabbi

30 Moshe Hallamish, *Kabbalah in Liturgy, Halakha, and Customs* (Ramat Gan: Bar-Ilan University Press, 2000), 319 [Hebrew].

31 See *Avot* 3:3. Seligman Baer, *Seder Avodat Yisrael* (Roedelheim, 1901), 553; Shem Tov Gaguine, *Keter Shem Tov,* vol. 1 (Jerusalem, 1960), 141, note 188; Eliyahu Munk, *Olam HaTefillot,* vol. 1 (Jerusalem: Mossad HaRav Kook, 1992), 227. See also *Arukh HaShulḥan, Oraḥ Ḥayim* 170:1, which states that even *Al Naharot Bavel* and *Shir HaMaalot* can function as the words of Torah at a meal, although actual Torah study is preferable.

32 See Yechiel Michel Epstein, *Kitzur Shenei Luḥot HaBrit* (Amsterdam, 1721), 23b. This became popularized by being included in Avraham Sperling, *Sefer Taamei HaMinhagim UMekorei HaDinim* (Lemberg, 1928), 23a. For the development of the practice to be careful about saying words of Torah at a meal, see Ze'ev Gries, *Safrut HaHanhagot* (Jerusalem: Bialik Institute, 1989), 18–22 (the outcome of which is quoted in Daniel Sperber, *Minhagei Yisrael,* vol. 2 [Jerusalem: Mossad HaRav Kook, 1991], 46–47) and Daniel Sperber, *Minhagei Yisrael,* vol. 3 (Jerusalem: Mossad HaRav Kook, 1994), 162–65.

33 Isaiah Horowitz, *Shenei Luḥot HaBrit* (Jerusalem: Machon Shaarei Ziv, 1993), *Shaar HaOtiot, Kuf – Kedushat HaAkhila,* 385.

34 Moshe Hallamish, *Hanhagot Kabbaliot BeShabbat* (Jerusalem: Orḥot, 2006), 354, 355; Adin Steinsaltz, *HaSiddur VehaTefilla* (Tel Aviv: Yedioth Ahronoth, 1994), 266.

35 Eliyahu Hacohen, *Shevet Musar* (Jerusalem, 1989), 31:37, 442–43; *Siddur KeMinhag Polin* (Ostroh, 1876), 95a; *Siddur Otzar HaTefillot,* vol. 1 (Vilna, 1911), 474.

David of Lida reported the great men of Jerusalem would say before the five verses of the Ari,[36] and the verses brought in *Kitzur Shenei Luḥot HaBrit* that were traditionally recited both after completing a *masekhet* and also on finishing a meal.[37] However, those of the Ari proved to be the most popular.

**THE TWO VERSES**

The question is, why were only these two verses retained from the five that the Ari declared should be recited? There is no clear explanation for this found in the literature,[38] but when certain factors are taken into account, a few possible explanations emerge.

First of all, these two verses are much more familiar to people than the other three in the group of verses, as they form the ending of *Ashrei*, recited three times a day during prayers. The addition of Psalms 115:18 to the end of *Ashrei* is already noted in the first siddur, *Seder Rav Amram Gaon*, where it is explained that this was done so that *Ashrei* will end with "Hallelujah," like the parts of *Pesukei DeZimra* which follow.[39] If any verses were to endure, it would be this very familiar duet.

Another factor is introduced in the *Shulḥan Arukh* of the Ari. Here it states that one should recite the four verses, and then it discusses holding the cup of wine and explains that one should recite the end of Ezekiel 41:22 just before placing the cup in one's right hand.[40] This version of the custom was popularized when it was quoted in *Eliya Rabba* (183:7). The custom is described in the same way in the well-known *Likkutei*

36 David ben Aryeh Leib of Lida, *Divrei David* (Brooklyn: Tiferet Bachurim d-Bobov, 2006), 16, *siman* 77.

37 Yechiel Michel Epstein, *Kitzur Shenei Luḥot HaBrit, Zikhron Tzaddikim* edition, 43–44.

38 Yitzhak Satz, David Yitzhaki, David Salmon, eds., *Birkat HaMazon LeMoreinu HaRav Shabbtai Sofer* (Toronto: Otzreinu, 2002), 2, note 1.

39 Daniel Goldschmidt, ed., *Seder Rav Amram Gaon* (Jerusalem: Mossad HaRav Kook, 2004), 9.

40 *Shulḥan Arukh shel Rabbeinu Yitzhak Luria* (Frankfort, 1691), 34b. These instructions are also found in Daniel Mordechai Reimer, ed., *Siddur Tefillat Ḥayim* (Beitar: Tzror HaḤayim, 2004), 108, a siddur based on the teachings Hayim Vital received from Isaac Luria.

*Maharikh.*[41] We can see from these sources that the Ezekiel section was considered a somewhat distinct element.

Many sources separate the Ezekiel verse, describing it as being recited after *mayim aḥaronim* while the four others are said before it,[42] even though Rabbi Hayim Vital reported that the Ari said they should all be recited after *mayim aḥaronim.*[43] It is likely that only this particular verse was kept by some after *mayim aḥaronim* while the other four were recited before in order to minimize any perceived interruption between *mayim aḥaronim* and *Birkat HaMazon.*[44]

Once the Ezekiel verse was considered a separate unit, we find that it was completely omitted in some prayer books and *benchers,* with no explanation offered.[45] Another reason to leave out the Ezekiel section is that it is not a full verse, and recitation of incomplete verses is avoided.[46]

Thus, the group of verses to be said before *Birkat HaMazon* can be viewed as a unit ending with Psalms 145:21 and 115:18, with Ezekiel 41:22

---

41 Yisrael Chaim Friedman, *Likkutei Maharih,* vol. 1 (Jerusalem, 2013), 506, first published in 1900.

42 Yaakov Emden, *Siddur Yaavetz, Amudei Shamayim* (Altona, 1745), 296b; *Siddur Tefilla im Likkutei Torah* (Vilna: Romm, 1912); Moshe Yair Weinstock, *Siddur HaGeonim VehaMekubalim VehaḤasidim,* vol. 18 (Jerusalem, 1981), 90–91; Levi Bistritzky, *Siddur Shaar Menaḥem* (Tzfat: Ḥasdei Lev, 2008), 127, 283; *Birkat HaMazon VeSheva Berakhot* (Brooklyn: Empire Press), 2; *Megillat Esther UBirkat HaMazon* (Brooklyn: Empire Press), 54. The Chabad custom is to recite this verse after *mayim aḥaronim;* see Yehoshua Mondshein, *Otzar Minhagei Ḥabad, Nisan Iyar Sivan* (Jerusalem: Heikhal Menachem, 1996), 189.

43 Hayim Vital, *Shaar HaMitzvot* (Jerusalem, 1905), *Ekev,* 45a. See also Lior Rosenruas, *Birkat HaShulḥan* (Bnei Brak, 2011) 113, 4:7. The ruling of Ari was not universally accepted, and some sources indicate that all the verses should be said before *mayim aḥaronim.* See Avraham Hayim Naeh, *Ketzot HaShulḥan* (Jerusalem, 1928) 29b, vol. 2, *siman* 43:1.

44 Levi Yitzhak Raskin, ed., *Siddur Rabbeinu HaZaken* (Brooklyn: Kehot, 2004), 365, note 2 and 366, note 9; Levi Yitzhak Raskin, *Seder Birkat HaMazon* (London, 2013), 3, note 2.

45 Israel Ricardo, *Tefillat Kol Peh* (Amsterdam, 1993), 184; Yitzhak Satz, David Yitzhaki, David Salmon, eds., *Birkat HaMazon LeMoreinu HaRav Shabbtai Sofer,* 4; Hanoch Vidislefsky and Aryeh Leib Pepper, eds., *Birkat HaMazon–Peninei Maharal* (Ashdod: Mechon Maharal Tzintz, 2010), 8.

46 This is the reason Shmuel Aharon Yudelvitz (1907–79) omitted the part from Ezekiel. See Shalom Meir Wallach, *Me'ilo shel Shmuel* (Bnei Brak, 1998), 275.

coming after on its own, if at all. Additionally, since the *Shulḥan Arukh* of the Ari associates this verse with lifting the cup for *Birkat HaMazon*, and other sources recite it after *mayim aḥaronim*, those who were not accustomed to doing either of these prior to *Birkat HaMazon* may simply have omitted the verse associated with these practices. Some siddurim preface the recitation of Ezekiel 41:22 with instructions to say this verse only if *Birkat HaMazon* is being said over a glass of wine.[47]

Another verse that could be considered a distinct element is Psalms 34:2, which Rabbi Hayim Vital explains functions to remove the *sitra aḥra* (impure or evil force) that is present at the table, "and in order to banish it you must say '*hav lan venavarikh*'... that is why we say אברכה את ה׳ בכל עת."[48] Based on this, when people say, "*Rabbotai nevarekh*," as is customary today, Psalms 34:2 may not be necessary,[49] and so this verse would also be omitted. Furthermore, there are sources that indicate that some people recited only a few of the Ari verses rather than all of them.[50] Additionally, it is not difficult to imagine a scenario where the first verses in the group were said quietly and only the last two aloud, in the style of Ashkenazic *Pesukei DeZimra*, thus focusing attention on these two verses to the exclusion of others that came before. Based on this understanding, the current Ashkenazic recitation of Psalms 145:21 and 115:18 is considered a remnant of the five verses chosen by the Ari.

---

47 See, for example, Menachem Mendel Landa, *Siddur Tzluta DeAvraham*, vol. 2 (Tel Aviv, 1961), 495–96, אם מברכים על הכוס, מוזגים קודם ואח״כ נוטלין הידים ואומרים: וידבר אלי זה השלחן אשר לפני ה׳; Yechezkel Bing, *Siddur HaRashash* (Bnei Brak: Divrei Shalom, 2009), 79, כשיש לו כוס, יקח הכוס בידו ויאמר: וידבר אלי זה השלחן אשר לפני ה׳. See also Yitzhak Satz, David Yitzhaki, David Salmon, eds., *Birkat HaMazon LeMoreinu HaRav Shabbtai Sofer*, 2, end of note 2.

48 Hayim Vital, *Shaar HaMitzvot* (Jerusalem, 1905), *Ekev*, 45a.

49 Yitzhak Satz, David Yitzhaki, David Salmon, eds., *Birkat HaMazon LeMoreinu HaRav Shabbtai Sofer*, 2, note 2. In Hizkiya Dachbash, *Tiklal* (Shami) (Rosh HaAyin, 2005), 706, the instructions are to say the verse when there is no *zimmun*. See the discussion of omitting the *zimmun* when reciting this verse in *Or Torah*, Elul 5762 (2002), vol. 12 (418), *siman* 138, 788–92.

50 See Shushan Hacohen, *Peraḥ Shushan* (Jerusalem, 1977), 17 in the biographical section, where only Ps. 34:2, Eccl. 12:13 and the end of Ezek. 41:22 are said.

## ANOTHER TWO VERSES

Some *benchers* add two additional verses to Psalms 145:21 and 115:18: Psalm 118:1, הודו לה׳ כי־טוב: כי לעולם חסדו, "Give thanks unto the Lord, for He is good, for His mercy endures forever," and Psalm 106:2, מי ימלל גבורות ה׳ ישמיע כל תהלתו, "Who can express the mighty acts of the Lord, or make all His praise to be heard?" No source is ever provided for the recitation of these particular verses.[51] For example, the verses appear in *Siddur Aliyot Eliyahu*, a modern-day siddur which is intended to represent the rulings of the Vilna Gaon and *Mishna Berura*; however, no references are brought there for the source, or reason for their inclusion.[52]

The addition of these two verses is generally referred to as a German custom.[53] It should be noted that Joseph Juspa Hahn included the recital of *Al Naharot Bavel* and *Shir HaMaalot* before *Birkat HaMazon* in his book *Sefer Yosef Ometz*, an important collection of the customs of the Frankfurt am Main community.[54] This work was completed around 1630, before *Shenei Luḥot HaBrit* was published, although it was published only later in 1723.[55] This attests to the early acceptance of the practice of saying *Al Naharot Bavel* and *Shir HaMaalot* among German Jews. However, there are no early references to these additional verses.

In *Seder Zemirot Yeshurun*, a work representing the German Ashkenazic tradition, three different versions of this custom are brought.

---

51 Shlomo Riskin, *Around the Family Table* (Jerusalem: Urim, 2005), 12; *The Koren Birkon* (Jerusalem: Koren Jerusalem, 2010), 153; Natan Zvi Yarom, *Birkat HaMazon BeMeḥitzat HaḤafetz Ḥayim* (Modiin Illit: Mechon Mishnat HaḤafetz Ḥayim, 2014), 5; Aaron Perlov, *Birkat HaMazon–Karnei Hod* (Jerusalem, 2014), 9; *Birkon Koren–Shir Zion Edition* (Jerusalem: Koren Jerusalem, 2016), 178. Regarding the Tunisian custom to say Ps. 118:1 before *Birkat HaMazon* on holidays, see David Setbon, *Alei Hadas* (Kiryat Sefer, 2010), 586, *siman* 13.

52 *Siddur Aliyot Eliyahu* (Jerusalem: Machon Aliyot Eliyahu, 2013), 141. When contacted, the various *bencher* and siddur editors replied that although they do not know the source of these verses, they included them because they are commonly said. This response is illustrative: לא מצאתי כעת מקור פסוקים האחרים, אבל היות שדשו בו רבים לא נמנענו מלהביאם.

53 Yitzhak Satz, David Yitzhaki, David Salmon, eds., *Birkat HaMazon LeMoreinu HaRav Shabbtai Sofer*, 2, note 1.

54 Joseph Juspa Hahn, *Sefer Yosef Ometz* (Frankfurt am Main, 1723), 21b, *siman* 154.

55 Dean Phillip Bell, *Jewish Identity in Early Modern Germany: Memory, Power and Community* (New York: Routledge, 2016), 48–49.

In all the versions, two additional verses are added after *Shir HaMaalot* and Psalms 145:21 and 115:18. The difference lies in which two verses are said and in what order. In one version, Psalms 118:1 and 106:2 are recited. The other has Psalms 106:2 followed by Psalms 150:6 כל הנשמה תהלל י־ה הללוי־ה, "Let everything that hath breath praise the Lord, Hallelujah." The Amsterdam custom reported has the order switched: Psalms 150:6 is said first, followed by Psalms 106:2.[56] In this work as well, no sources are given for the recitation of these verses.[57]

This custom is also presented without any source in the contemporary work *Otzar Taamei HaMinhagim*, with the explanation that these particular verses may have been chosen because each parallels one of the four blessings of *Birkat HaMazon*. Psalms 145:21 and the first blessing both contain the phrase "all flesh" (כל בשר); Psalms 115:18 and the second blessing both have the term "we" (אנחנו), referring to blessing or thanking God; Psalms 118:1 and the third blessing both contain the phrase "forever" (לעולם); and Psalms 106:2, which refers to "all the praises" (כל תהלתו), parallels the multiple descriptions of praise accorded to God in the fourth blessing (מלכנו, אדירנו, בוראנו, גואלנו).[58] Some of these connections are clearly forced, as the terms "we" (אנחנו) and "forever" (לעולם) are fairly common in liturgical contexts.

The kabbalistic work *Ḥemdat Yamim* gives extensive and detailed lists of psalms and verses that are to be recited before *Birkat HaMazon*, with different selections based on the day and time. For example, on Shabbat night a selection of verses are recited followed by Psalm 87;[59] on Shabbat day Psalms 121, 45, and 24 are said along with the verses from the night meal,[60] and a different selection of psalms are recited for

56 Shlomo Hofmeister, *Seder Zemirot Yeshurun* (Vienna: Yeshurun, 2016), 57.

57 Personal queries to the editor of *Seder Zemirot Yeshurun* went unanswered. The additional verses are also found in the new edition of the German prayer book, Joseph Scheuer, ed., *Siddur Schma Kolenu* (Basel: Morascha Verlag, 2000), 106, but not in early editions.

58 Shmuel Gelbard, *Otzar Taamei HaMinhagim* (Petach Tikva: Mifal Rashi, 1996), 105–6.

59 *Ḥemdat Yamim*, vol. 1 (Bnei Brak: Machon Ḥemdat Yamim, 2011), 192.

60 Ibid., 291.

*Seuda Shelishit*.[61] Holidays have their own psalms as well; for example, on Purim, Psalm 98 is recited before *Birkat HaMazon*.[62]

For Rosh Ḥodesh, the verses chosen begin with the letters that spell out the Hebrew word *Adonai* in its *milui* (filled) form. For example, the first letter of the word, *alef*, is divided into the three letters that spell the word *alef*: *alef, lamed, peh*. Then each of these letters is itself spelled out, *alef* becomes *alef, lamed, peh*; *lamed* becomes *lamed, mem, dalet*; *peh* becomes *peh, heh*. A verse is chosen beginning with each letter of this expanded spelling. In this list of verses, Psalm 106:2 (מי ימלל) is the verse for the *mem* in the middle of the *lamed*, and Psalm 118:1 (הודו) appears as the verse for the *heh* at the end of the *peh* of *alef*. Furthermore, Psalm 145:21 (תהלת) also appears here as the verse for the *tav* from the spelled-out *dalet*.

*Ḥemdat Yamim* is a kabbalistic work of unclear authorship first published in Turkey in the early 1730s under the auspices of Rabbi Israel Yaakov Algazi. For years, the book was the subject of much controversy stemming from allegations that it represents Sabbatean ideas. The controversy continues to this day. However, the current view is that the work is quite possibly a collection of customs and practices based on the students of the Ari, often brought without attribution, and is not necessarily a Sabbatean work.[63] We therefore have a kabbalistic source for reciting these verses before *Birkat HaMazon*. However, this cannot be the source of the addition of the two verses, as *Ḥemdat Yamim* specifies that they are for Rosh Ḥodesh, not for other occasions, and furthermore they appear in a very long list of verses, the rest of which are not recited.

## POSSIBLE EXPLANATIONS: MELODIES AND ZIONISM

A possible explanation for the addition of two verses may be indicated by the fact that, although there are variations in the verses and their order in communities of Germany and Amsterdam, in all cases there is a total of four verses added to Psalm 126. This has led to speculation that the extra

61 Ibid., 332.

62 *Ḥemdat Yamim*, vol. 2 (Bnei Brak: Machon Ḥemdat Yamim, 2011), 347.

63 See Moshe Fogel, "The Sabbatean Character of Hemdat Yamim: A Reexamination," *Jerusalem Studies in Jewish Thought* 16:2 (2001), 365–422.

verses are actually added because of the tunes used for *Shir HaMaalot* among German Jews. Many of the popular Ashkenazic *Shir HaMaalot* tunes work well with a song divided into four-line stanzas. If two of the Ari verses are added, the tune no longer fits well, so adding yet another two verses makes the tune fit nicely.[64] This would be the reason that, although the verses themselves may differ between Ashkenazic communities, there are always two more added to the standard extra two verses.

Why these particular ones? It is documented that the German Jewish community had distinct tunes for *Shir HaMaalot* for different holidays, special Shabbatot, and certain times of year.[65] These tunes were used not only for *Shir HaMaalot,* but also for other liturgical elements on Shabbat, for example, *Lekha Dodi.*[66] The *Shir HaMaalot* tunes for Sukkot, Passover, and Shavuot were often the same tunes used for the responsive sections of Hallel said on those days, which includes the refrain הודו לה׳ כי־טוב: כי לעולם חסדו (Ps. 136:1).[67] Thus, among German Jews, there was a natural connection between *Shir HaMaalot* and *Hodu*: they shared the same tune on festivals. Therefore, if a verse needed to be added to make the *Shir HaMaalot* tune fit melodically, it would seem very appropriate to add this one. These tunes even outlasted their original liturgical context: "By the second half of the twentieth century, when many German-Jewish liturgical traditions fell into oblivion, the original melodies of the festive *piyutim* were no longer performed in synagogue services. Therefore, the survival of these melodies as a marker of liturgical

---

64 See Steve Epstein, "The Source of the Addition of *Tehillat Hashem* After *Shir HaMaalot,*" in *Ḥiddushei Torah © NDS* 12 (2011), 163, note 16 [Hebrew].

65 Yaakov Rothschild, "Shabbat *Zemirot* of the Jews of Southern Germany and the Customs Connected to Them," *Duchan* 7 (1964), 100 [Hebrew]. For a list with sound samples, see Naomi Cohn-Zentner, "*Shir HaMaalot* – the Umbilical Cord Between Liturgical and Domestic Soundspheres in Ashkenazi Culture," July 2014, Jewish Music Research Center, Hebrew University, http://www.jewish-music.huji.ac.il/content/shir-hama%E2%80%99alot-umbilical-cord-between-liturgical-and-domestic-soundspheres-ashkenazi-culture.

66 Uri Aharon, "Melodies for *Shir HaMaalot* in Frankfurt am Main," *Duchan* 16, (2005), 296–97 [Hebrew]; Yair Goldreich, "Sidrei Tefilla BaKehilla," *Shnot Ḥayim* (2007), 71, detailing the practices of the Mekor Ḥayim community in Petach Tikvah, following the Frankfurt am Main customs.

67 Aharon, "Melodies for *Shir HaMaalot,*" 302–4.

time remained alive through their continuous practice in the domestic sphere among families of German origin."[68]

Psalms 106:2, מי ימלל גבורות ה׳ ישמיע כל תהלתו, "Who can articulate the Lord's mighty acts; who can express all His praise?" is also a reasonable, appropriate verse to add to make up a four-verse stanza, as it declares that in our recitation of these verses we still have not sung all the praises due to God. This verse is also appended to *Anim Zemirot*, where it serves a similar function.[69]

Another fairly popular explanation for the addition of these verses is that they were chosen to stress that God should be praised irrespective of any connection to our return to the Land of Israel. Thus, the verses were added as an "anti-Zionist" expression, to lessen the focus on Israel found in *Shir HaMaalot*.

We saw that the kabbalistic addition of Psalms 137 and 126 to the meal was to emphasize "the holiness of the Holy Land and the palace of the King" (Zohar, *Teruma* 157b), themes already found in the second and third blessings of *Birkat HaMazon*.[70] *Shir HaMaalot* in particular, with its description of actually returning to the Land of Israel, especially resonated with the early Zionists. Rabbi Kook noted that the secret behind reciting this psalm before *Birkat HaMazon* is to demonstrate a yearning to come to Israel, thus tapping into the *shefa* (bounty) of the Land of Israel even when eating food from outside of Israel.[71] Connections were also made between *Shir HaMaalot* and the national anthem of Israel, "HaTikva." It has been reported many times that early Zionists would sing *Shir HaMaalot* before *Birkat HaMazon* to the tune of "HaTikva,"[72]

---

68 Cohn-Zentner, "*Shir HaMaalot*."

69 See Elchanan Adler, *Zvi Tifara* (Passaic, 2017), 145.

70 See Avi Erlich, *Ancient Zionism: The Biblical Origins of the National Idea* (New York: Free Press, 1995), 14.

71 Abraham Isaac Kook, *Orot HaKodesh*, vol. 3 (Jerusalem: Mossad HaRav Kook, 1950), 295. See on this Moshe Tzuriel, *Otzrot HaRaya*, vol. 3 (Rishon LeZion: Yeshivat Hesder Rishon LeZion, 2002), 362; Hayim Drukman, *Netiot Haaretz* (Kfar Darom: Makhon HaTorah VehaAretz, 2004), 185.

72 See, for example, Yaakov Efrati, *Vavim LeAmudim*, vol. 3 (Jerusalem, 2002), 153, note 1; Michael Englishman, *163256: A Memoir of Resistance* (Ontario: Wilfrid Laurier University Press, 2007) 4; Joseph Reider, "Secular Currents in Synagogal Chant in America (1918)," in Jonathan L. Friedman, ed., *The Value of Sacred Music* (Jefferson:

and there were authorities who opposed this.[73] The exchange of melodies worked both ways; it is reported that Bialik wanted to use Yossele Rosenblatt's tune for *Shir HaMaalot* for "HaTikva" after hearing him sing it on a trip to Israel.[74] *Shir HaMaalot* was even suggested as the national anthem instead of "HaTikva."[75]

It is reported that Rabbi Dr. Mordechai HaLevi (Markus) Horovitz (1844–1910), the Hungarian-born Orthodox rabbi of Frankfurt from 1878–1910, although regarded as one the most prominent *Protest Rabbiner* against organized Zionism,[76] would sing the first stanza of "HaTikva" after *Shir HaMaalot*.[77] It was also reported among some Jews in Amsterdam that "HaTikva" was sung at the end of the Shabbat meal.[78] Even with these connections, there is no documentation that verses were ever added after *Shir HaMaalot* specifically to mitigate any Zionist message, and historically this explanation cannot be accurate as two of the verses were added much earlier, in the 1600s.[79]

---

McFarland, 2009), 146; Raymond Apple, *Let's Ask the Rabbi* (AuthorHouse, 2011), 140. Ps. 126 sung to the tune of "HaTikva" became part of the Yom HaAtzma'ut evening service, right from the very first Yom HaAtzma'ut; see Maimon, "Pirkei Zikhronot al HaTzionut," *Sinai* 34 (1953), 277. See also *Seder HaTefillot VehaHodayot* (Jerusalem: Ministry of Religion, 1952), 9 and Shmuel Katz, ed., *HaRabbanut HaReshit LeYisrael: Shivim Shana LeYisoda*, vol. 2 (Jerusalem, 2002), 839.

73 Avraham Weinfeld, *Lev Avraham*, vol. 1 (Brooklyn: Balshon, 1977), *siman* 133, 229–30. This was vehemently opposed in the Neturei Karta literature, as expected; see *Mishmeret Ḥomoteinu*, vol. 8 (1956), 37 (5). See the description of a dispute that broke out over singing *Shir HaMaalot* after a meal to this tune on the first Yom HaAtzma'ut in Miriam Sperber, *MiSippurei HaSavta* (Jerusalem, 1986), 143.

74 Shmuel Rosenblatt, *Yossele Rosenblatt* (2007), 248.

75 Goel Rappel, *Moreshet Am VeAretz* (Tel Aviv: Yedioth Ahronoth, 2002), 134.

76 Matthias Morgenstern, *From Frankfurt to Jerusalem* (Leiden: Brill, 2002), 18.

77 Mordechai HaLevi (Markus) Horovitz, *Rabbanei Frankfurt* (Jerusalem: Mossad HaRav Kook, 1972), 340, in the additional material added by Joseph Unna after the passing of Horovitz. On this work and this description of Horovitz, see the review by Ernest Simon in the Joseph Unna memorial volume, *Zikhron Yosef* (Kfar Haroeh, 1983), 498.

78 Suzanne Mehler Whiteley, *Appel Is Forever: A Child's Memoir* (Detroit: Wayne State University Press, 1999), 25.

79 See the discussion in Steve Epstein, "The Source of the Addition of *Tehillat Hashem* after *Shir HaMaalot*" [Hebrew], in *Ḥiddushei Torah © NDS* 12 (2011), 161–63, particularly note 16.

## THE PURPOSE OF ADDITIONAL VERSES

There may be another explanation for the added verses. They all share a common theme; praising God. This might not seem unusual, but note that *Al Naharot Bavel* and *Shir HaMaalot* were instituted to recall the destruction of the Temple. They refer either to the destruction of Israel at the hands of the Babylonians or the future redemption, but not specifically to praising God.

We have records of other verses and psalms being recited just before *Birkat HaMazon* by different communities. For example, Psalms 34:2: "I will bless the Lord at all times; His praise shall continually be in my mouth," and Nehemiah 9:5: "Let them bless Thy glorious Name, which is exalted above all blessing and praise," in the Yemenite tradition,[80] or Psalm 33 among the Skolye Hasidim,[81] and Psalm 111 and Psalm 121 among some Jews of Amsterdam.[82] All of these have the common element of blessing or calling out to God.

The idea that it is particularly important to recall that one is thanking and praising God while reciting *Birkat HaMazon* is specifically noted in a number of sources, most popularly with the statement of Rabbi Yitzhak Meir Alter (1799–1866), the first Ger Rebbe. He declared that "if a person eats before God and then recites *Birkat HaMazon* and knows before whom he is blessing, and thanks the One who gave him the food, there are no greater words of Torah than this."[83] We have seen that some sources relied on the verses said before *Birkat HaMazon* to fulfill the custom of saying words of Torah at the meal. Those verses are

---

80 Yitzhak Mualem, *Aggadata DePisḥa* (Beitar Illit: Machon Ohalei Avraham Yaakov, 2003), 120. Regarding the various psalms and verses added into the Yemenite liturgy before *Birkat HaMazon*, see Moshe Gavra, *Meḥkarim BeSiddurei Teiman* (Bnei Brak: HaMakhon LeḤeker Ḥakhmei Teiman, 2010), 365; Moshe Gavra, *HaTiklal HaMadai HaMehudar* (Bnei Brak: HaMakhon LeḤeker Ḥakhmei Teiman, 2012), 365.

81 Yissachar Ringel, *Adir BaMarom* (Brooklyn: Makhon Tal Orot, 2003), 231, *siman* 509.

82 Yehuda Brillman, *Minhagei Amsterdam* (Jerusalem: Machon Yerushalayim, 2001), 235, 2:3.

83 Yoetz Kim Kadish Rakocz, *Siaḥ Sarfei Kodesh*, vol. 3 (Bnei Brak, 1989), item 16, 16; Yehuda Leib Levin, *Ḥiddushei HaRim* (Jerusalem: Nachliel, 1965), 300. This idea is brought in many sources, see for example, Yehuda Arye Leib Heina, *Likkutei Yehuda, Devarim* I (Jerusalem, 1972), 68; Elchanan Printz, *She'elot UTeshuvot Avnei Derekh*, vol. 7 (Jerusalem, 2014), 85.

even more significant when they also remind us that God is the source of our food, and it behooves us to praise and thank Him for that. In fact, many of the verses prescribed by the Ari fulfill this purpose as well. The recitation of these four verses after *Shir HaMaalot* would therefore not necessarily be a conscious selection of two verses from the Ari with two extra verses added on, but rather a collection of verses suitable for the purpose of praising God, two of which happen to be the verses favored by the Ari.[84]

This is the explanation offered by Rabbi Yosef Tzvi Halevi Dunner (1913–2007), regarding the various additional verses recited by Jews in Germany and Amsterdam after *Shir HaMaalot*. He was a graduate of the Hildesheimer Rabbinical Seminary in Berlin and chief rabbi of East Prussia before moving to England and ultimately serving as head of the Union of Orthodox Hebrew Congregations. A family member reports that at a meal once, Rabbi Dunner explained that in his father's family, "they were accustomed to say Psalms 150:6 (כל הנשמה תהלל י־ה הללוי־ה) and other verses, and today it is customary to say Psalms 145:21 (תהלת ה׳ ידבר פי ויברך כל בשר שם קדשו לעולם ועד) and others, but the point of all these verses is the same, to awaken us to understand and feel that we are coming to bless and thank the Holy One, blessed be He."[85]

We can now understand that there were different verses and psalms used by various communities to fulfill the dual function of speaking words of Torah at a meal and as a reminder that we are now blessing God. The verses that were added varied, and may have been chosen either with or without regard to the verses of the Ari. The particular number of four verses popular among the Jews of Germany and Amsterdam is probably related to the tunes used for singing *Shir HaMaalot*.

84 It is interesting to note, *lehavdil*, that among Lutherans, the blessing before the meal includes selections from Ps. 145, and the thanksgiving after includes selections from Ps. 106, indicating that these psalms are particularly meaningful in the context of praising God at a meal. See Frank Senn, "Lutheran Spirituality," in his *Protestant Spiritual Traditions* (Eugene, OR: Wipf and Stock, 2000), 37.

85 *Kol HaTorah* 65 (Nisan 5768/2008), 173.

*Chapter 22*

# Adding *HaRaḥaman* to *Birkat HaMazon* on Shabbat and Holidays

## INTRODUCTION

It is commonly thought that the Ashkenazic custom of adding *HaRaḥaman* at the end of *Birkat HaMazon* for special occasions is a late development that began about three hundred years ago.[1] In fact, a special *HaRaḥaman* for holidays is found in *benchers* from the time that printing began. The earliest known printed *bencher*, produced five hundred years ago, contains the same *HaRaḥaman* for Shabbat, Yom Tov, Rosh HaShana, and Sukkot that we have in our contemporary *benchers*.[2] A few decades later, *Birkat HaMazon* with the commentary of Rabbi Nathan Natan Spira (1585–1633) was printed; this also included the *HaRaḥaman*

1 This is the approach of Abraham Berliner, *Ketavim Nivḥarim*, vol. 1 (Jerusalem: Mossad HaRav Kook, 1969), 64. He writes that *HaRaḥaman* is found in print only from the beginning of the eighteenth century. Regarding the *HaRaḥaman* blessing before *BaMarom*, see Menachem Mendel Landa, *Siddur Tzluta DeAvraham*, vol. 2 (Tel Aviv: Grafika, 1958), 542.

2 *Birkat HaMazon UZemirot* (Prague, 1514), 7.

prayers,[3] as did *benchers* printed later.[4] *HaRaḥaman* also appears in the first printed kabbalistic siddur, *Siddur HaPardes* (1765), but as we have seen, these prayers precede the Tzfat kabbalists.[5]

The *HaRaḥaman* additions to *Birkat HaMazon*, including those for Shabbat and holidays, did not originally have a standard formula. It appears that during the time of the *Rishonim* it was not even considered necessary to standardize them. For example, Rabbi Yosef ben Moshe, in his *Leket Yosher*, described the formula for *Birkat HaMazon* of his teacher, Rabbi Israel Isserlin (1390–1460), up to the section *HaRaḥaman*. Rabbi Isserlin stated that beyond that point "there is no difference" regarding what is said, and there is no need to set down an exact text."[6]

## SHABBAT

The end of the last mishna of Tractate Tamid includes an exegesis of Psalm 92: "On Shabbat they would say [Psalm 92], 'A Psalm, a Song for the Sabbath day,' a psalm for the future, for the day that is completely Shabbat and rest for all eternity." This entire mishna was included in *Seder Rav Amram Gaon* as part of the conclusion of the weekday morning service, after *Pitum HaKetoret*.[7] The Ashkenazic *Rishonim* included

3 *Seder Birkat HaMazon im Peirush Moreinu Rav Natan Spira MiHorodna* (Lublin, 1574), 30. So too in *Birkat HaMazon im Peirush Rav Natan Ashkenazi* (Lublin, 1575); *Birkat HaMazon UZemirot UPeirusheihem* (Cracow, 1580); *Seder Birkat HaMazon* (Lublin, 1599).

4 For example, *Seder Birkat HaMazon* (Italy, 1649), JTS#4644; *Seder Birkat HaMazon* (Amsterdam, 1723); Yaakov Emden, *Siddur Amudei Shamayim* (Altona, 1748).

5 So too *Siddur HaAri shel Ḥakhmei HaKloiz DeKehillat Kodesh Brod* (Zhovka, 1781); *Siddur HaAri shel R. Asher ben R. Shlomo Margaliot* (Lemberg, 1788). In *Siddur Tzluta DeAvraham*, vol. 2 (Tel Aviv: Grafika, 1958), 554, regarding the *HaRaḥaman* for Sukkot, he writes that although he gave only kabbalistic sources for this, "we can assume that there is an earlier source," which he writes that he leaves for others to find.

6 *Leket Yosher* (Berlin, 1903), 37. This approach of Isserlin is also found in his *Terumat HaDeshen* (*siman* 39), that *Birkat HaMazon* concludes with the end of the fourth blessing and whatever is said after that does not have the status of being "officially" part of *Birkat HaMazon*. There are in fact many variations in the *HaRaḥaman* section; see the comprehensive discussion in Pinhas Musabi, *Pinḥas Yepallel* (Jerusalem, 2006), 62–67.

7 *Seder Rav Amram Gaon*, ed. Daniel Goldschmidt (Jerusalem: Mossad HaRav Kook, 2004), 40.

this only in the Shabbat service, as seen in *Siddur Rashi* (*siman* 512) and *Maḥzor Vitry* (*siman* 134). None of these sources mention saying a special *HaRaḥaman* in *Birkat HaMazon* on Shabbat, and it appears that it made its way into *Birkat HaMazon* from this part of the Shabbat liturgy.

In the *Birkat HaMazon* printed at the beginning of the edition of the book of Psalms published in Bologna, Italy, in 1480, we find the formula, "May the Merciful One let us inherit forever a world which will be all Shabbat" (הרחמן הוא ינחילנו לעולם שכולו שבת). However, this prayer is part of the *HaRaḥaman* petitions connected to the coming of the Messiah, with no particular connection to Shabbat. In fact, this text of *Birkat HaMazon* has no special *HaRaḥaman* for any special day or occasion. It was only later that this *HaRaḥaman* would become a special prayer recited only on Shabbat.

There are a number of variations of *HaRaḥaman* for Shabbat. Rabbi Natan Ashkenazi, who published a *bencher* with commentary in 1575, writes: "Know that in this matter there are divided opinions; some customarily say, 'He will let us inherit a day that is completely Shabbat' (הוא ינחילנו יום שכולו שבת) and no more, and some add, 'He will let us inherit a day that is completely Shabbat and rest for eternal life' (הוא ינחילנו יום שכולו שבת ומנוחה לחיי עולמים)." He notes that there are also two versions of the phrase לחיי עולמים, with either one *yod* or two. He concludes by saying, "And whatever you pick is holy." There is no decision made in favor of one particular formula.[8] It was only later, in the mid-1600s and afterward, that halakhic authorities addressed the *HaRaḥaman* blessings.[9]

### ROSH ḤODESH AND ROSH HASHANA

As with *HaRaḥaman* for Shabbat, *HaRaḥaman* for Rosh Ḥodesh and Rosh HaShana first appeared in rabbinic literature as a prayer or saying and was later transferred to *Birkat HaMazon*. The Rosh Ḥodesh

8 *Birkat HaMazon im Peirush R. Ashkenazi* (Lublin, 1575). In the introduction he laments the errors that made their way into the texts of *Birkat HaMazon*, something he seeks to correct in his work. But even so, when it comes to the *HaRaḥaman* blessings he does not make an effort to choose a particular version.

9 See *Ḥok Yaakov* 490:4; *Eshel Avraham* 490:1.

*HaRaḥaman* is based on the formula for the blessing of the new month as presented in *Seder Rav Amram Gaon* (p. 88b): "Renew this month for us for goodness and blessing (חדש עלינו את החודש הזה לטובה ולברכה)." This phrase is also the basis for the Rosh HaShana *HaRaḥaman,* which simply replaces "month" with "year."

Among the customs of Rabbi Israel Isserlin brought by Rabbi Yosef ben Moshe in his *Leket Yosher* we find the statement "I remember that when it was Rosh Ḥodesh he would bless 'May the Merciful One renew this month for us for goodness and blessing.'"[10] This indicates that in Rabbi Isserlin's time in the fifteenth century, saying a particular *HaRaḥaman* for Rosh Ḥodesh was not yet a widespread custom, and was considered a custom of note of Rabbi Isserlin. It appears that the recital of these special *HaRaḥaman* blessings began as something certain individuals would add, based on well-known parts of the liturgy, and became popular primarily through inclusion in printed *benchers,* which reached a wide audience.

## YOM TOV

The *HaRaḥaman* for Yom Tov comes from a teaching found in Kiddushin 39b and Ḥullin 142a based on Deut. 5:16: "'That it may be well with you' means in the world where all is well (לעולם שכולו טוב), and 'that your days may be long' is referring to the world that is entirely long (לעולם שכולו ארוך)." Rabbi Yechiel Michel Epstein quotes this in his *Kitzur Shenei Luḥot HaBrit,* explaining that it is a special *HaRaḥaman* for the Seder night.[11] He writes that he "found in the name of Maharil that on Seder night, before the *HaRaḥaman* about the Messiah, we add, 'May the Merciful One let us inherit a day that is all well (ליום שכולו טוב), a day that is entirely long (ליום שכולו ארוך), a day when the righteous sit with their crowns upon their heads, enjoying the splendor of the Divine Presence, and our portion should be with them." The additional

10 *Leket Yosher* (Berlin, 1903), 39. Menachem Mendel Landa (*Siddur Tzluta DeAvraham* [Tel Aviv: Grafika, 1958], vol. 2, 552) notes that based on the phrasing in *Leket Yosher,* the author understood that Rabbi Isserlin originated this *HaRaḥaman.* See also the *Birkat HaMazon* of Shabbtai Sofer (28) from the sixteenth century, which includes a *HaRaḥaman* for Shabbat, but still has nothing for Rosh Ḥodesh or holidays.

11 Yechiel Michel Epstein, *Kitzur Shenei Luḥot HaBrit* (Jerusalem, 1944), 142.

elements are based on Berakhot 17a: "Rav was wont to say: The World-to-Come is not like this world. In the World-to-Come there is no eating, no drinking, no procreation, no business negotiation, no jealousy, no hatred, and no competition. Rather, the righteous sit with their crowns upon their heads, enjoying the splendor of the Divine Presence, as it is stated: 'And they beheld God, and they ate and drank' (Ex. 24:11)." This blessing is not found in the writings of the Maharil that we have today, but it is plausible that he did follow this custom, since we find that Rabbi Isserlin included special *HaRaḥaman* prayers, and he had contact with the teachings of the Maharil through Rabbi Yaakov Weil.

Although this *HaRaḥaman* is mentioned only in *Kitzur Shenei Luḥot HaBrit* for Seder night, there is no reason why it cannot be said on the other days of Passover or on other holidays. In fact, many authorities expanded its recitation beyond the Seder night.[12] Still, the more prevalent custom is to say an abbreviated version on Yom Tov: "May the Merciful One let us inherit a day that is all well (ליום שכולו טוב)," and use the longer form only at the Seder.[13]

Although the Yom Tov *HaRaḥaman* may be viewed as an abbreviated form of the original Seder night *HaRaḥaman,* the opposite is true. In Haggadot published prior to 1683, when the *Kitzur Shenei Luḥot HaBrit* was first published in Amsterdam, we find only the short form[14] or no *HaRaḥaman* at all.[15] It would seem that even if the Maharil recited this prayer, it was not widespread prior to the publication of the *Kitzur Shenei*

12 For example, the custom of Hayim Elazar Spira of Munkacs was to say it throughout Pesaḥ and also on Yom Tov. See Yehiel Mikhel Gald, *Sefer Darkhei Ḥayim VeShalom* (Munkacs, 1940), customs of Pesaḥ night, *siman* 608, 194.

13 Landa, *Siddur Tzluta DeAvraham,* 553.

14 See, for example, in the earliest printed Haggada, in Guadalajara, Spain (c. 1480); *Haggada shel Pesaḥ* (Prague, 1526); Yoel ben Shimon Veibesh Ashkenazi, *Haggada shel Pesaḥ – 15th century manuscript.* The long form is found in *Seder Haggada shel Pesaḥ* (Metz, 1764) in smaller letters, after the short version.

15 For example, *Haggada shel Pesaḥ* (Venice, 1609). Even after the publication of *Kitzur Shenei Luḥot HaBrit* there were many Haggadot which included only the shorter form, for example, *Haggada Avodat HaGefen* (Offenbach am Main, 1722); *Haggada shel Pesaḥ* (Itingen, 1729). And some included no *HaRaḥaman* at all, for example, *Haggada shel Pesaḥ* (Amsterdam, 1695); *Haggada shel Pesaḥ* (Copenhagen, 1739); *Haggada shel Pesaḥ* (Furth, 1741); *Haggada shel Pesaḥ* (Sulzbach, 1755). Even into

*Luḥot HaBrit*, and it is clear that the shorter Yom Tov version predated the longer Seder night version.

As with other *HaRaḥaman* blessings, the text was not set. In the *Sefer Minhagim* of the Worms community, written by Rabbi Yospe Shammash in the seventeenth century, he writes, "After saying, 'May the Merciful One let us inherit a day that is all well' (יום שכולו טוב), on Passover we add: 'May the Merciful One take us from slavery to freedom' (הרחמן הוא יוציאנו מעבדות לחירות)."[16] Others added a similar formula on Passover: "May the Merciful One take us from exile to freedom" (הרחמן הוא יוציאנו מגלות לחירות),[17] and on Yom Tov: "May the Merciful One bring us to the upcoming holidays in peace" (הרחמן הוא יגיענו למועדים הבאים לקראתנו לשלום).[18] These formulas are grounded on the prayers found in the Haggada before and after the first part of Hallel, and are based on Pesaḥim 116b: "Therefore it is our duty to thank, praise, laud, glorify, exalt, honor, bless, extol, and adore He who wrought all these miracles for our fathers and ourselves; He brought us forth from slavery to freedom, from sorrow to joy, from mourning to festivity, from darkness to great light, and from servitude to redemption, therefore let us say before Him, Hallelujah!" and the version of R. Akiva: "So may the Lord our God and God of our fathers bring us to the upcoming holidays and festivals in peace."

As with the other *HaRaḥaman* prayers, this one appears in halakhic literature as an accepted custom only much later on. For example, *Magen Avraham* (*Oraḥ Ḥayim* 490:1) rules that "the intermediate days are not considered Yom Tov and therefore we do not say in *Birkat HaMazon* 'May the Merciful One let us inherit a day that is all well' (יום שכולו טוב)."[19]

---

the nineteenth century there are some Haggadot with no *HaRaḥaman* at all, even for Shabbat, such as the Bordeaux Haggada from 1813.

16 Yospe Shammash, *Minhagim of the Worms Community* (Jerusalem: Machon Yerushalayim, 1988), *siman* 77, 87.

17 Yair Hayim Bachrach, *Mekor Ḥayim* (Jerusalem: Machon Yerushalayim, 1983), part 2, *kitzur halakhot, siman* 188, 331.

18 Yitzhak Meir Lieberman, *Sefer Ḥag HaMatzot – Halakhot UMinhagim* (Bnei Brak, 2003), *siman* 45:21, 727.

19 See also *Eliya Rabba* 490:4.

**SUKKOT**

The *Shenei Luḥot HaBrit* states, "We pray, 'Raise for us the sukka of David that is fallen' (יקים לנו סוכת דוד הנופלת), meaning the kingdom of the House of David."[20] In later printings, a parenthetical addition appears which states that this is added to *Birkat HaMazon*. However, the original intent may well have been that this is something we add to our general prayers, not necessarily in *Birkat HaMazon*.

The phrase "the sukka of David that is fallen" (סוכת דוד הנופלת) is not mentioned by the *Rishonim* in connection with *Birkat HaMazon*. However, it is mentioned in *Maḥzor Vitry* (siman 265) in a discussion about mourning as an expression of comfort. This shows that praying for redemption using the term "the sukka of David that is fallen" existed before it had any connection to the holiday of Sukkot or to *Birkat HaMazon*.

The first time the expression is found as the *HaRaḥaman* for Sukkot is in the *Sefer Minhagim* of the Worms community: "All the days of the holiday one says *Yaaleh VeYavo* in *Birkat HaMazon*. And regarding *HaRaḥaman* he says, 'May the Merciful One raise for us the sukka of David that is fallen.' On Yom Tov he adds, 'May the Merciful One let us inherit a day that is all well' before saying, 'Raise for us the sukka,' as is customary on every holiday. On the intermediate days he says immediately, 'May the Merciful One raise for us'... and he does not say 'Let us inherit' on the intermediate days."[21] Later on this would appear in halakhic literature by Rabbi Avraham Wahrmann (1771–1840) in *Eshel Avraham* (*Oraḥ Ḥayim* 490:1), where he states that in terms of the order of the *HaRaḥaman* prayers, they should be said in order of frequency, so that if it is Sukkot and Shabbat, first the Shabbat *HaRaḥaman* is said, then that of Yom Tov, then Sukkot.

Although the *HaRaḥaman* for Sukkot is based on Amos 9:11, "In that day will I raise up the sukka of David that is fallen, and close up the breaches thereof, and I will raise up his ruins, and I will build it as in the days of old," there is no connection between this verse and the holiday

---

20 *Shenei Luḥot HaBrit, Masekhet Pesaḥim, Matza Ashira, derush* 7.

21 Yospe Shammash, *Minhagim of the Worms Community* (Jerusalem: Machon Yerushalayim, 1988), *siman* 170, 202.

of Sukkot. Most commentators explain that the verse is either referring to the Davidic monarchy (*Targum Yonatan*, Rashi, Radak, Malbim), the Divine Presence (Alsheikh), or the Temple (Mahari Kara), none of which are directly connected to Sukkot. Although many have tried homiletically to make a connection between "the sukka of David that is fallen" and the holiday of Sukkot, the only obvious connection is the word "sukka" itself.[22]

It appears that this *HaRaḥaman* also began as a custom of certain individuals and later became more widespread. Rabbi Hayim Kanievsky, when asked about the connection between "the sukka of David," the Temple, and the holiday of Sukkot, replied that the connection is only in the same term, "sukka."[23]

We saw that according to *Eshel Avraham* this *HaRaḥaman* is said on all the days of Sukkot, but the Ḥatam Sofer[24] and other authorities determined that it should be said only on the intermediate days,[25] basing their opinion on the understanding that "the sukka of David" refers to the Temple, which is not built on Shabbat or Yom Tov. Rabbi Yedidya Weil (son of the author of the *Korban Netanel*) emphasizes that although "many people" have this practice, there is no basis for it, since according to Rashi (Rosh HaShana 30a, *meḥatzot hayom*), that restriction applies only to human construction of the Temple, not the future Temple "that is in the hands of Heaven."[26]

As with the *HaRaḥaman* for Shabbat, Passover, and Yom Tov, there are also different versions of the *HaRaḥaman* for Sukkot.[27] They include such variations as "May the Merciful One allow us to merit to sit in the sukka of Leviathan" (הרחמן הוא יזכנו לישב בסוכה של לויתן),

---

22 See, for example, Meir Zvi Bergman, *Sefer Shaarei Ora* (Jerusalem, 2001), 318–19; David Quait, *Sefer Sukkat David* (Jerusalem, 2005), 322–23; Shimon Korsia, *Sefer Orot HaḤag* (Jerusalem, 2006), 35. Note that many of these *derashot* are from contemporary times; earlier it was understood that the only connection is lexical.

23 David Falk, *Sefer Inyano shel Yom* (Jerusalem, 2004), *Moadim*, 27 (כי זה לשון סוכה).

24 Yosha Leib Shillel, *Minhagei Baal HaḤatam Sofer* (Pressburg, 1930), chapter 8, note 11.

25 Ephraim Greenblatt, *Rivevos Ephraim* (Brooklyn, NY: Mazel, 1995) *Oraḥ Ḥayim*, vol. 7, *siman* 177. He writes that this was the custom in Holland.

26 Yedidya Weil, *Haggada shel Pesaḥ im Biur Marbeh LeSapper* (Karlsruhe, 1791), 42.

27 Yitzhak Lieberman, *Sefer Ḥag HaAssif – Halakhot UMinhagim* (Bnei Brak, 1991), 341.

based on the prayer said at the conclusion of Sukkot (*Kol Bo, siman* 71); "May the Merciful One spread over us the sukka of peace" (הרחמן הוא יפרוס עלינו סוכת שלום), familiar from the *Hashkivenu* blessing in the Friday night prayers; and "May the Merciful One send us holy and pure emanations from the seven holy *Ushpizin,* may their merit shield us" (הרחמן הוא ישפיע עלינו שפע קדושה וטהרה משבעה אושפיזין עלאין קדישין זכותם תהא מגן וצינה עלינו), based on the *Ushpizin* prayer.[28] These are all founded on earlier prayers that were well known to the masses, just like all other *HaRaḥaman* prayers, and have either a lexical or more essential connection to Sukkot.

## HANUKKA AND PURIM

*Kol Bo, siman* 25, mentions a special *HaRaḥaman* for Hanukka and Purim: "May the Merciful One make miracles and wonders for us as He made for our forefathers, in those days, at this time" (הרחמן יעשה לנו נסים ונפלאות כמו שעשית לאבותינו בימים ההם בזמן הזה). However, it is not clear if this was meant as an independent *HaRaḥaman* to be recited regularly on Hanukka and Purim, since it is mentioned here only in a discussion of a person who forgot to add *Al HaNissim* in *Birkat HaMazon.* The *Kol Bo* writes that if forgotten earlier, *Al HaNissim* can be added at the end of this *HaRaḥaman,* which segues into the opening phrase of *Al HaNissim.*[29] This ruling is brought in *Beit Yosef* (*Oraḥ Ḥayim* 187),[30] and the Rema (*Oraḥ Ḥayim* 187:4 and 682:1),[31] again not as a *HaRaḥaman* to be said routinely, but as a way to make up for a forgotten *Al HaNissim.*

Whatever the case, we see again that the *HaRaḥaman* is based on a previously existing prayer, this time the blessing of "who performed

28 *Siddur Kol Eliyahu HaShalem* (based on the rulings of Mordechai Eliyahu) (Jerusalem: Darkei Horaa LeRabbanim, 2002), 462.

29 His phrasing is:
שכח ולא אמרו כאן אין מחזירין אותו, ויש אומרים כשסיים, אבל אם לא סיים כשיגיע להרחמן יאמר הרחמן יעשה לנו נסים ונפלאות כמו שעשית לאבותינו בימים ההם בזמן הזה, בימי מתיתיהו וכו' ואחר כך משלים.

30 At the end of *uma shekatav ve'im shakhaḥ.*

31 Rema also notes an option of making up a forgotten *Yaaleh VeYavo* in *Birkat HaMazon* on the intermediate days of a holiday, but rules that we do not do that (*Oraḥ Ḥayim* 188:7).

miracles for our forefathers in those days, at this time" (שעשה ניסים לאבותינו בימים ההם בזמן הזה).

Rabbi Yair Hayim Bachrach (1639–1702), at the end of his book *Mekor Ḥayim,* notes that on Hanukka and Purim we recite "will make for us miracles" (יעשה עמנו ניסים).[32] This is an unequivocal source for a special *HaRaḥaman* on those days, to be recited irrespective of a forgotten *Al HaNissim.* However, recital of this *HaRaḥaman* is not very common, and is generally known only as a way to add another *Al HaNissim.* This is mainly because it has not been published in many *benchers,* and as we have noted, inclusion in printed *benchers* was the primary way the *HaRaḥaman* prayers became customary.[33]

## CONCLUSION

The *HaRaḥaman* prayers for special days were already known in Ashkenazic countries from the end of the period of the *Rishonim.* All of them are based on well-known prayers or phrases and began as additions recited by individuals, which over time caught on among the general population. Only later did they begin to appear in halakhic literature. The publication of *benchers* made this practice more common, and was instrumental in determining the exact text of these prayers.

32 Yair Hayim Bachrach, *Mekor Ḥayim* (Jerusalem: Machon Yerushalayim, 1984), part 2, *kitzur halakhot, siman* 188, 331. See also *Kovetz Beit Aharon VeYisrael,* vol. 99:3, Shevat-Adar 5762, 115, where it is mentioned that it is the custom of Karlin-Stolin Hasidim to say this *HaRaḥaman* in *Birkat HaMazon,* implying that it is not a widespread general custom. Regarding saying this *HaRaḥaman* on the 16th of Adar on Purim Meshulash, see Gavriel Zinner, *Nitei Gavriel: Hilkhot Purim* (Jerusalem: Cong. Nitei Gavriel, 2000), 450; Moshe Mordechai Karp, *Hilkhot Ḥag BeḤag – Purim* (Jerusalem, 2002), 107–8, note 14.

33 Some saw in this *HaRaḥaman* a request for a miracle, which would be inappropriate. See *Shaarei Teshuva* (end of *siman* 187), which explains why this formula of *HaRaḥaman* is in fact appropriate. On this topic, see also Refael Rubenstein, *Sefer Birkat Refael BeInyanei Ḥanukka* (Jerusalem, 1984), 221; David Cohen, *Sefer Yemei Ḥanukka* (Jerusalem, 2005), 8–9.

*Chapter 23*

# Saying "*Shalom Aleikhem*" to Three People During *Kiddush Levana*

### THE ORIGINAL FORM OF *KIDDUSH LEVANA*

The blessing recited over seeing the new moon is found in the Talmud, Sanhedrin 42a:

> R. Aha said to R. Ashi: In "the West" they pronounce the following benediction: "Blessed is He who renews the moons." Whereupon he retorted: Such a blessing even our women folk pronounce! But [one should rather say the following], in accordance with R. Yehuda, who gives it thus: "Praised, etc. who created the heavens with His word, and all their hosts with the breath of His mouth. He appointed unto them fixed laws and times, that they should not change their ordinance. They rejoice and are glad to do the will of their Creator. They work truthfully, for their action is truth. The moon He ordered that it should renew itself as a crown of beauty for those whom He sustains from the womb, and who will, like it, be renewed in the future, and magnify their Maker in the name of

> the glory of His kingdom. Blessed are You, O Lord, who renews the moons."

In addition to the basic blessing, additional prayers were added, including a series of statements that are each repeated three times. The earliest source for these repeated statements is *Masekhet Soferim* 20:2:

> Then one says three times, "A good sign, a good sign, shall it be for all Israel. Blessed is He who formed you, blessed is He who made you, blessed is He who owns you, blessed is He who created you." Turning in the direction of the moon, he leaps three times and exclaims three times, "Just as I leap toward you but cannot touch you, so may none of my enemies be able to touch me to do me harm. May fear and dread fall upon them, and may this be retrospective, Amen, Amen, Selah. Hallelujah." He then says "shalom" (peace) three times to his fellow and goes home with a cheerful heart.

These additions do not appear in *Seder Rav Amram Gaon,*[1] and are absent from some early Ashkenazic siddurim[2] but are found in others.[3]

*Maḥzor Vitry,*[4] Roke'aḥ,[5] *Or Zarua,*[6] *Shibbolei HaLeket,*[7] and the *Tur*[8] all copy these prayers from *Masekhet Soferim,* based on the version of the text that has the greeting "*Shalom alekha*" (Peace be with you), rather than just "Shalom." Rabbi Yoel Sirkes, in his commentary to the *Tur,* specifically notes that "*Shalom alekha*" is the correct form of the greeting.[9] Rabbi Moshe Isserles concurs in the *Shulḥan Arukh.*[10]

---

1 Daniel Goldschmidt, ed., *Seder Rav Amram Gaon* (Jerusalem: Mossad HaRav Kook, 2004), 90.

2 Moshe Hershler, ed., *Siddur of R. Solomon ben Samson of Garmaise* (Jerusalem: Hemed, 1971), 196.

3 Moshe Hershler, Yehuda A. Hershler, eds., *Peirushei Siddur HaTefilla LaRoke'aḥ* (Jerusalem: Machon HaRav Hershler, 1992), 605.

4 *Maḥzor Vitry,* vol. 1, 183.

5 Roke'aḥ, Laws of Rosh Ḥodesh, *siman* 229.

6 *Or Zarua,* vol. 2, Laws of Rosh Ḥodesh, *siman* 456.

7 *Shibbolei HaLeket,* Rosh Ḥodesh, *siman* 167.

8 *Tur, Oraḥ Ḥayim* 426:2.

9 *Oraḥ Ḥayim* 426:2.

10 Rema, *Shulḥan Arukh, Oraḥ Ḥayim* 426:2.

## THE CURRENT POPULAR PRACTICE

The greeting as found in these sources differs from current practice in two significant ways. First, printed prayer books today use the plural form of the greeting "*Shalom aleikhem*."[11] This is also the form of the greeting referred to in the relatively more recent halakhic works of *Eliya Rabba*,[12] *Shulḥan Arukh HaRav*,[13] and *Arukh HaShulḥan*.[14] However, although the greeting "*Shalom alekha*" is found in various contexts in the Talmud,[15] we never find the plural form to address an individual in the Talmud. This has led to some discussion over the reason why the plural form "*Shalom aleikhem*" is commonly used in *Kiddush Levana*.[16]

The second major difference is that it is common practice nowadays to greet three different people during *Kiddush Levana*, whereas the early sources above indicated that you should greet one friend three times, just as the other statements in the prayer are repeated three times.

The practice to greet three different people is found in some contemporary prayer books.[17] This custom has also been the subject of a certain amount of discussion,[18] with some authorities deciding that it is of recent vintage and not necessary.[19]

How did the current practice develop? The earliest source for the custom of greeting three different people during *Kiddush Levana* is from the thirteenth century, in the writings of Rabbi Hayim Eliezer, the son of the *Or Zarua*. While the *Or Zarua* does not mention that different people should be greeted, his son Rabbi Hayim Eliezer writes: "He greets three people, and if there is only one person, he greets him three times."[20]

---

11 See, for example, *Siddur Beit Yaakov*, 220, *Siddur Avodat Yisrael*, 338, *Siddur Rinat Yisrael*, 373, *ArtScroll Siddur*, 614.

12 *Eliya Rabba* 426:4.

13 *Shulḥan Arukh HaRav, Piskei HaSiddur, Kiddush Levana.*

14 *Arukh HaShulḥan, Oraḥ Ḥayim* 426:4.

15 For example, Middot 1:2, Berakhot 3a, Bava Kama 73b.

16 Bezalel Stern, *Ohalekha BeAmitekha* (Jerusalem, 2005), 218, chapter 22, note 9.

17 *ArtScroll Siddur*, 614.

18 Seriah Devlitzky, *Zeh HaShulḥan* (Bnei Brak, 1958), *Oraḥ Ḥayim* 38, no. 426, and Efraim Greenblatt, *Rivevos Ephraim* (Brooklyn, NY: Mazel, 1995), *Oraḥ Ḥayim* , vol. 7, no. 134.

19 Yisrael Feinhandler, *Avnei Yashpeh* (Jerusalem, 1999), vol. 3, no. 50:2, 88.

20 Isaak S. Lange, ed., *Derashot Maharaḥ Or Zarua* (Jerusalem, 1972), Ekev, 67.

This practice is next mentioned in the fourteenth century, among the customs of Rabbi Shalom of Neustadt, teacher of the Maharil. He states: "Three people must be greeted, and if they are only two people (the person saying the blessing and one other) he says to his friend three times '*Shalom aleikhem*,' and if they are three he says to one friend twice '*Shalom aleikhem*' and to the other once."[21] This is also the earliest source for using the plural form of the greeting, "*Shalom aleikhem*," in this prayer. This then is the earliest record of the popular custom to greet three different people by saying "*Shalom aleikhem*."

This custom is mentioned in the sixteenth-century work *Mateh Moshe* by Rabbi Moshe of Przemyśl: "He says three times '*Shalom aleikhem*' and if there are not three people with him he greets one person three times."[22] Since the earlier works of Rabbi Hayim Eliezer and Rabbi Shalom of Neustadt were not readily available for many years, *Mateh Moshe* is commonly referenced as the source for the custom.[23]

Why did the custom shift from saying "*Shalom alekha*" three times to one person to saying "*Shalom aleikhem*" one time each to three different people? And more fundamentally, why have a greeting at all during this blessing? The Maharil explains: "Since this is such a great mitzva and is considered like greeting the *Shekhina*, it is appropriate to greet one another out of joy and good feeling."[24] *Mateh Moshe* cites the explanation of the Maharil, and adds an explanation in the name of the kabbalist Rabbi Herz that "after cursing [our enemies] by saying, 'Let terror and dread fall upon them,' it is appropriate to say to his friend, 'Not on you; only peace and peace.'"[25] This explanation is found in the commentary of Rabbi Herz to his siddur, first printed in 1560. There he states that after praying for the coming of the Messiah by saying, "'David, king of Israel, lives and endures,' since the birth pangs of the Messiah are

---

21 Shlomo Spitzer, ed., *Hilkhot UMinhagei Rabbeinu Shalom MeNeustadt* (Jerusalem: Machon Yerushalayim, 1997), no. 364.

22 *Mateh Moshe*, no. 540.

23 See, for example, Yissachar Dov Eichorn, *Pi Kohen*, Berakhot, vol. 3 (Jerusalem, 2010), 12:1.

24 Yitzhak Satz, ed., *New Responsa of Rabbi Yaacov Molin – Maharil* (Jerusalem: Machon Yerushalayim, 1977) no. 47, 57.

25 *Mateh Moshe*, no. 540.

many, it is incumbent upon us to pray and say each person to his friend, '*Shalom aleikhem, aleikhem Shalom.*'"[26] These reasons, popularized by their inclusion in *Mateh Moshe,* are associated with those who advocate saying "*Shalom aleikhem*" to three different people.

The Maharil was the student of Rabbi Shalom, and *Mateh Moshe* also follows the approach of Rabbi Shalom. Even though Rabbi Herz does not say explicitly that the greeting should be said to three different people, since it was included in the *Mateh Moshe* that reason became connected to the practice of greeting multiple people as well.[27] It may be that since the greeting was understood to be an expression of joy or reassurance, it makes more sense to greet many people rather than only one, in order to spread happiness and comfort among more people. The popularity of *Mateh Moshe* contributed to the expansion of the custom to greet three different people.

While the early sources who advocate saying the singular form of the greeting, "*Shalom alekha,*" three times to one person did not give a reason for this practice, a threefold repetition is typical of acts with supernatural significance, as seen, for example, in the prayers added to the bedtime *Shema* for protection from evil as well as in the text at the end of *Tefillat HaDerekh.*[28] If the greeting is understood to be a mystical statement like the prayers that precede it there is no need to greet many people, just to repeat the special phrase three times. Rabbi Herz's approach as stated in *Mateh Moshe* gained popularity by being quoted in the *Perisha*[29] and *Magen Avraham.*[30] Since no specific reason was given for greeting only one person three times, and since the popular reasons for the custom of greeting at all were associated with greeting three different people, this approach gradually became more acceptable.

---

26 *Siddur HaMekubal HaRav Herz Shliaḥ Tzibbur ztz"l* (Bnei Brak: Morgenstern, 1971), 277.

27 Note that in the siddur of Herz, while the commentary speaks of the greeting as "*Shalom aleikhem,*" the text of the prayer itself uses the form "*Shalom aleikha.*" There are no instructions in this siddur regarding how many people to greet.

28 See Rashi, Shabbat 66b, *kol minyanei.* Also Joshua Trachtenberg, *Jewish Magic and Superstition* (New York: Athenium, 1984), 119, 156, 256.

29 *Perisha, Tur, Oraḥ Ḥayim* 426:4.

30 *Magen Avraham, Oraḥ Ḥayim* 426:11.

The question is, why did the form of the greeting itself change from the singular to the plural? This is related to the emergence of the use of the plural form in Hebrew as a sign of respect. As noted above, the Talmud does not record the use of the plural form to greet an individual, even an individual who is entitled to great respect, such as a teacher.[31] Use of the plural form when speaking to an individual as a sign of respect, *pluralis majestatis,* is common in languages which have a what is known as a "T-V distinction," a different way of addressing peers and those to whom one wishes to show respect. This usage is not originally found in Hebrew or Aramaic[32] but rather was borrowed from other languages, in this case German.[33] The Jewish communities in German-speaking areas adopted this form of greeting. Both Rabbi Hayim Eliezer and Rabbi Shalom of Neustadt lived in German-speaking Austria.

There was a certain amount of opposition to greeting people in the plural. Rabbi Yair Hayim Bachrach (d. 1702) in his *Mekor Ḥayim* writes, "'*Shalom aleikhem,*' which is commonly said, is not correct for an individual in Hebrew, and the error comes from foreign languages."[34] He notes that the Rema preserved the original Hebrew expression "*Shalom alekha*" when writing about *Kiddush Levana,* and that Rabbi Yosef Karo used the singular Hebrew form when writing about greeting a rabbi.[35] Despite this, over time the plural form of greeting became accepted as appropriate. Various reasons were given to explain the special spiritual significance of greeting in the plural form, for example, as a greeting to both body and soul.[36] Eventually, the foreign influence was forgotten and the plural form became normative. By the nineteenth century, Rabbi Yechiel Michel Epstein simply states that "in ancient times people would always speak to each other in the second person, saying '*Shalom alekha,*

31 Sanhedrin 98a.

32 Except for referring to God, as in *Elohim.*

33 "Peace in the Plural," *Forward,* January 26, 2007.

34 Eliyahu Dov Pinchas, ed., *Mekor Ḥayim,* vol. 2 (Jerusalem: Machon Yerushalayim, 1984), no. 110, at the end.

35 Rema, *Shulḥan Arukh, Oraḥ Ḥayim* 426:2, *Shulḥan Arukh, Yoreh De'ah* 242:16.

36 J. D. Eisenstein, *Otzar Dinim UMinhagim* (New York, 1917), 417.

*Rebbi*,' but today we address an honored individual in the plural form and say '*Shalom aleikhem*.'"[37]

The original custom to say "*Shalom alekha*" three times to one person has been transformed over time. The influence of foreign languages and shifting perceptions of the reason for the greeting have led to the current popularity of the custom of Rabbi Shalom of Neustadt to greet three different people by saying "*Shalom aleikhem*." Although the Rema does not codify the plural form or the idea to say it to three people, and in fact uses the form "*Shalom alekha*" and states that it is said to one person,[38] this approach is almost universally ignored today, to the extent that when the Brisker Rav, Rabbi Yitzchok Zev Halevi Soloveitchik and later Rabbi Joseph B. Soloveitchik were observed saying the greeting three times to one person it was reported as a remarkable practice.[39]

37 *Arukh HaShulḥan, Yoreh De'ah* 242:38.

38 Rema, *Shulḥan Arukh, Oraḥ Ḥayim* 426:2.

39 Hershel Schachter, *MiPeninei HaRav* (New York, 2001), 81.

*Chapter 24*

# *Barkhi Nafshi* on Rosh Ḥodesh

The Talmud in Sukka 54b notes that a special psalm was said in the Temple on Rosh Ḥodesh, but does not indicate which particular psalm was recited. The practice today of reciting *Barkhi Nafshi*, Psalm 104, on Rosh Ḥodesh is found in neither the Talmud Bavli nor the Talmud Yerushalmi, nor in any early rabbinic literature. *Masekhet Soferim* (17:10)[1] does describe the practice of adding special psalms for Rosh Ḥodesh and holidays, but the additions for Rosh Ḥodesh listed there are Psalm 98 and I Chronicles 16, inserted into *Pesukei DeZimra*, reflecting an old custom of the Land of Israel.[2] In some versions of *Masekhet Soferim* Psalm 104 is given as the special psalm for Yom Kippur, along

1 In some versions it is in 18:1.

2 Michael Higger, ed., *Masekhet Soferim* (New York: Dbei Rabanan, 1937), p, 29. The Yemenite custom is to recite Psalms 98–99 on the day of Rosh Ḥodesh and *Barkhi Nafshi* in the evening; see Amos Chacham, *Daat Mikra: Sefer Tehillim*, vol. 2 (Jerusalem: Mossad HaRav Kook, 1990), 265, note 40a.

with Psalm 130.[3] In *Seder Rav Amram Gaon* we indeed find Psalm 104 included in the Yom Kippur liturgy,[4] but not for Rosh Ḥodesh.[5]

The earliest mention of the familiar custom of reciting Psalm 104 on Rosh Ḥodesh is found in the early thirteenth-century work, *Sefer HaManhig*.[6] Rabbi Abraham ben Nathan (HaYarḥi) writes that he "saw a nice custom in Toledo and its surroundings to say after the prayer psalms according to the day. On weekdays: 'A prayer for David. Incline Your ear, O Lord, answer me' (תפלה לדוד הטה ה׳ אזנך ענני) (Ps. 86).... On Rosh Ḥodesh: 'Bless the Lord my soul' (ברכי נפשי את ה׳) (Ps. 104), since it says there, 'He made a moon for the seasons' (עשה ירח למועדים) (verse 19) and talks about Creation. On Ḥol Hamoed: 'Like a hind crying' (כאייל תערוג) (Ps. 42), because it is written there: 'With joyous shouts of praise the throng celebrates' (בקול רנה ותודה המון חוגג) (verse 5).... On Hanukka: 'A psalm of David. A song for the dedication of the House' (מזמור שיר חנוכת הבית לדוד) (Ps. 30).... On Purim: 'The doe of the morning' (על איילת השחר) (Ps. 22), which is talking about Esther[7] ... and it makes sense to do this, and it is correct in my opinion."

In *Orḥot Ḥayim,* Rabbi Aharon HaKohen discusses the halakhot of Shabbat, Rosh Ḥodesh, and the festivals, and mentions these psalms, each in reference to the designated occasion described above, explaining that in some places there is a custom to recite them.[8]

---

3 See Higger, *Masekhet Soferim*, p. 323, 18:11. This version was rejected by the Vilna Gaon. See the variants noted in Shmuel Wasserstein, ed., *Masekhet Soferim* (Jerusalem, 2001), 167–68, 19:2. Menahem Azarya da Fano understood the reference to be to Ps. 103, *She'elot UTeshuvot HaRema MiPano* (Jerusalem, 1963), *siman* 25, 40. *Arukh HaShulḥan* (*Oraḥ Ḥayim* 424:3) suggests that the text in *Soferim* should be emended, and that Ps. 104 should be attributed to Rosh Ḥodesh rather than Yom Kippur.

4 Daniel Goldschmidt, ed., *Seder Rav Amram Gaon* (Jerusalem: Mossad HaRav Kook, 2004), 165.

5 See Meir Weiss, "*Barkhi Nafshi*: Ps. 104," in *Mikraot KeKavanatam* (Jerusalem: Mossad Bialik, 1988), 222, where he discusses this and other non–Rosh Ḥodesh recitations of Ps. 104.

6 Yitzhak Rafael, ed., *SeferHaManhig LeRabbi Avraham BeRebbi Natan HaYarḥi*, vol. 1 (Jerusalem: Mossad HaRav Kook, 1978), 107, *siman* 77. Regarding when the book was written, see the introduction there, page 20.

7 See Yoma 29a.

8 *Orḥot Ḥayim*, part 1, *Din HaTeḥinot VehaMizmorim She'omrim Aḥar Shemoneh Esreh, siman* 5 (Ps. 86); *Hilkhot Rosh Ḥodesh, siman* 2 (Ps. 104); *Hilkhot Ḥolo shel Moed, siman*

This entire list as found in *Sefer HaManhig* is brought in the *Tur* (*Oraḥ Ḥayim* 123) and is referred to there as the Spanish custom.

The Abudraham also mentions the recital of these psalms, each mentioned separately in the relevant sections of his book.[9] He gives the same reasons for saying *Barkhi Nafshi* on Rosh Ḥodesh as in *Sefer HaManhig*.[10] He also provides additional psalms appropriate for fast days for *Shiva Asar BeTamuz* (Psalm 79), Tisha BeAv (Psalm 127),[11] the Fast of Gedalia and *Asara BeTevet* (Psalm 83), and *Taanit Esther* (Psalm 22).[12] All of these special psalms were compiled in one list by Rabbi Isaac Aboab (fourteenth century) in his *Menorat HaMe'or*.[13]

To this day, these psalms are found in Sephardic prayer books at the end of Shaḥarit, with Psalm 86 placed after *UVa LeTziyon* and before the Psalm of the Day.[14] This is also mentioned in *Arukh HaShulḥan* (*Oraḥ Ḥayim* 133:4), as the Sephardic custom. In addition to *Barkhi Nafshi* on Rosh Ḥodesh,[15] which is still familiar to Ashkenazim, Sephardic prayer books also have the noted psalms for Purim, Hanukka, and the fast days

36 (Ps. 42); *Hilkhot Ḥanukka, siman* 23 (Ps. 30); *Hilkhot Megilla VePurim, siman* 33 (Ps. 22). Ismar Elbogen (*Jewish Liturgy: A Comprehensive History* [Philadelphia: Jewish Publication Society, 1993], 106) mistakenly writes that *Orḥot Ḥayim* is the oldest source naming Ps. 104 as the psalm recited on Rosh Ḥodesh. As expected, *Kol Bo* also brings these customs, *siman* 15 (Ps. 86), *siman* 43 (Ps. 104), *siman* 44 (Ps. 30), and *siman* 45 (Ps. 22).

9 *Sefer Abudraham*, vol.1 (Jerusalem: Even Israel, 1995), 137 (Ps. 86), 217 (*Barkhi Nafshi*), 224 (Ḥanukka), 229 (Purim), 270 (Ḥol HaMoed).

10 *Sefer Abudraham*, vol.1 (Jerusalem: Even Israel, 1995), 217.

11 Ibid., 286.

12 Ibid., 284.

13 *Menorat HaMeor*, chapter 2, *Nefilat Apayim*, 160. He does make one change, giving the standard fast day psalm (83) as the one for the Fast of Esther as well, as opposed to Abudraham, who gives the Purim psalm (22) for the Fast of Esther.

14 *Siddur Rinat Yisrael – Sefaradi* (Jerusalem: Moreshet, 1984), 89; *Tefillat Bnei Tziyon* (Tel Aviv: Sinai, 1980), 94; *Siddur Koren KeMinhag Sefaradim* (Jerusalem: Koren Jerusalem, 2013), 101; *Siddur Kavanat HaLev* (Petach Tikvah: Machon Shira Chadasha, 2014), 208.

15 *Siddur Rinat Yisrael – Sefaradi*, 388; *Siddur Koren KeMinhag Sefaradim*, 109; *Siddur Kavanat HaLev*, 646.

as listed by the Abudraham.[16] The practice is discussed extensively in *Ben Ish Ḥai*.[17]

Of the psalms listed in *Sefer HaManhig*, Psalm 86 received special attention from Rabbi Isaac Luria (the Ari). Rabbi Hayim Vital, in his *Pri Etz Ḥayim*, notes that the Ari warned him that the weekday psalm, Psalm 86, "must be said with great intent" due to its kabbalistic significance.[18] Later, in his mystical-halakhic work *Seder HaYom*, the sixteenth-century Tzfat kabbalist Moshe ibn Yehuda HaMakhiri stressed the importance of saying Psalm 86 every day.[19] Psalm 86 appears in all prayer books today that are based on the teachings of the Ari.[20]

Rabbi Hayim Vital does not note any particular instruction from the Ari regarding saying Psalm 104 (*Barkhi Nafshi*) on Rosh Ḥodesh. However, it was understood that it should be included in the prayers, as it appears in the Sephardic siddur published in Venice in 1524 that Rabbi Hayim Vital used as the basic template for any changes and additions of the Ari.[21]

There is a Sephardic custom to say Psalm 104 on the night of Rosh Ḥodesh as well. The Yemenite scholar Rabbi Yihye Salah (Maharitz, 1804–59) notes that adding it here indicates that it is not connected to the Psalm of the Day. He explains that there is a mystical idea that people are susceptible to negative spiritual forces at the renewal of the moon, and the evening recital of Psalm 104 is for the purposes of protection.[22]

---

16 *Siddur Rinat Yisrael – Sefaradi*, 96–99; *Siddur Koren KeMinhag Sefaradim*, 106–8; *Siddur Kavanat HaLev*, 219–23.

17 Yosef Hayim, *Ben Ish Ḥai – Halakhot* (Jerusalem: Siach Yisrael, 1985), first year, *Ki Tissa, siman* 17, 173.

18 Hayim Vital, *Pri Etz Ḥayim* (Dubrovno, 1804), 73a, *Shaar Keriat HaTorah*, chapter 5.

19 *Sefer Seder HaYom, Seder Ashrei UVa LeTziyon*.

20 Menachem Mendel Landa, *Siddur Tzluta DeAvraham*, vol. 1 (Tel Aviv: Grafika, 1958), 389.

21 Hayim Vital, *Shaar HaKavanot* (Jerusalem, 1961), 328; Daniel Mordechai Reimer, *Sefer Tefillat Ḥayim* (Beitar: Tzror HaḤayim, 2004), 210.

22 Sagiv Mahfud, ed., *Tiklal – Etz Ḥayim* (Bnei Brak: Nusaḥ Teiman, 2012), 358.

Of the large group of special psalms, the only one[23] that made it into the Ashkenazic liturgy is *Barkhi Nafshi* for Rosh Ḥodesh. The *Shulḥan Arukh* (*Oraḥ Ḥayim* 423:3) mentions reciting Psalm 104 on Rosh Ḥodesh and Rabbi Moshe Isserles made no comment there.[24] However, Rabbi Avraham Gombiner (1635–82) in *Magen Avraham* (423:5) states that in a few places it is not customary to say it. Rabbi Abraham David Buchach (1770–1840) in *Eshel Avraham* (422:2) describes it as a practice of "recent generations." It does not appear in early Ashkenazic prayer books, for example, in the prayer book of Rabbi Shabtai Sofer, first published in the early 1600s, nor in *Siddur Derekh Siaḥ HaSadeh* (1704). Over time, however, the practice did become more accepted among Ashkenazim. By the 1800s we find that reciting Psalm 104 on Rosh Ḥodesh is mentioned with no caveats in *Ḥayei Adam* (118:12). However, note that while the *Arukh HaShulḥan* says that "some recite *Barkhi Nafshi*" on Rosh Ḥodesh (423:5), not connecting it with Sephardic practice in particular, he does call it a Sephardic practice in 133:3. All this shows that it took a significant amount of time for the addition of *Barkhi Nafshi*, which originated with Sephardim, to become accepted by Ashkenazim.

Why is *Barkhi Nafshi* the only special psalm to be incorporated by Ashkenazim? Even Psalm 30, the Psalm for Hanukka in *Masekhet Soferim* (18:3),[25] the only psalm for a special day that is the same in *Masekhet Soferim* and *Sefer HaManhig*,[26] did not make it into the standard Ashkenazic liturgy. There have been other customs regarding the special psalm for Rosh Ḥodesh. For example, Meiri writes that the special psalm for Rosh Ḥodesh is Psalm 81.[27] The Italian custom is to say Psalm 8 on Rosh

23 With the exception of the *nusaḥ* based on the teachings of the Vilna Gaon, who includes psalms for special days.

24 Presumably indicating that this was the Ashkenazic custom as well. See Amos Chacham, *Daat Mikra: Sefer Tehillim*, vol. 2 (Jerusalem: Mossad HaRav Kook, 1990), 265, note 40a.

25 In some versions 18:2.

26 *Masekhet Soferim* 18:3 lists Psalm 7 or 83 for Purim and Psalm 148 for Ḥol Hamoed of Passover, whereas different Psalms are listed in *Sefer HaManhig*.

27 On Rosh HaShana 31a. This may be a typographical error and should read Rosh HaShana (the abbreviation ה"ר mistaken for ח"ר), as that is the Psalm for Rosh Hashana in the Talmud (Rosh HaShana 30b) and Meiri on Sukka 54b explicitly refers to *Masekhet Soferim* for the psalm for Rosh Ḥodesh.

Ḥodesh, whose contents are similar to Psalm 104, and it mentions the moon in verse 4, but it is much shorter.[28] Nevertheless, despite its length, Psalm 104 proved to be the universally accepted psalm for Rosh Ḥodesh.

There seem to be two factors which helped to popularize *Barkhi Nafshi* and led to its inclusion by Ashkenazim. In addition to mentioning *Barkhi Nafshi* in the list of the special Psalms, the *Tur* also mentions it in the end of the section on Rosh Ḥodesh (*Oraḥ Ḥayim* 423) as the Spanish custom. This explains why, of all the additional psalms mentioned in *Sefer HaManhig* and *Tur*, only *Barkhi Nafshi* is mentioned in the *Shulḥan Arukh* (*Oraḥ Ḥayim* 423:3). Rabbi Yosef Karo did not incorporate the list of psalms provided in the *Tur* (*Oraḥ Ḥayim* 123), but when Psalm 104 was mentioned again in the *Tur* (423), Rabbi Yosef Karo included it in his work. This brought the psalm to the attention of the many readers of the *Shulḥan Arukh*, while the other special psalms remained obscure.[29]

Additionally, although not mentioned in all the early references of this custom, a kabbalistic reason for reciting *Barkhi Nafshi* served to increase its popularity. The Zohar (*Midrash HaNe'elam*,[30] *Vayera* 97b) presents a teaching of R. Eliezer: "Every Rosh Ḥodesh, the Blessed Holy One ventures forth... and when the soul beholds... her Master's *Shekhina*, she offers blessings and bows down before Him, as is written, 'Bless the Lord O my soul' (*Barkhi Nafshi*) (Psalms 104:1)." To this R. Akiva adds, "The soul utters this entire passage of praise before the Blessed Holy One... the entire chapter until the end."[31] In other words, the soul sings Psalm 104 to God every Rosh Ḥodesh.

The kabbalist Rabbi Menahem Azarya da Fano (Rema MiPano) (1548–1620) cites *Midrash HaNe'elam* as the reason he prefers Psalm

---

28 Chacham, *Daat Mikra: Sefer Tehillim*, vol. 2, 265, note 40a.

29 See Ephraim Greenblatt, *Rivevos Ephraim*, vol. 1 (Memphis, TN, 1975), *siman* 288, 225.

30 On *Midrash HaNe'elam* and its relationship to the main body of the Zohar, see Gershom Scholem, *Major Trends in Jewish Mysticism* (Jerusalem: Schocken Books, 1954), 181–86; Boaz Huss, *The Zohar: Reception and Impact* (Oxford: Littman Library of Jewish Civilization, 2016), 104, 108.

31 Nathan Wolski, trans., *The Zohar: Pritzker Edition*, vol. 10 (Stanford, CA: Stanford University Press, 2016), 318.

104 for Rosh Ḥodesh over the psalm suggested in *Masekhet Soferim*.[32] Later, the Vilna Gaon (1720–97) in *Yahel Or*,[33] Rabbi Zvi Elimelekh Spira (1783–1841) in *Bnei Yissaskhar*[34] and Rabbi Abraham David Lavut (1815–90) in his work *Shaar HaKollel*[35] all gave this description from the Zohar as the primary reason to say Psalm 104 on Rosh Ḥodesh, and each became a popular reference as the source of the custom. It would appear that the increase in popularity of reciting Psalm 104 on Rosh Ḥodesh among Ashkenazim can also be attributed, at least in part, to the influence of these kabbalistic sources.[36]

There are some variations regarding saying *Barkhi Nafshi* on Rosh Ḥodesh. The Vilna Gaon ruled that only one special psalm should be recited in association with the day, and Psalm 104 on Rosh Ḥodesh trumps the Psalm of the Day, even on Shabbat, whereas others simply add *Barkhi Nafshi* after the regular psalm.[37]

Either way, saying Psalm 104 during the morning prayers on Rosh Ḥodesh is an almost universal custom among Ashkenazim today,[38] despite its origin as a purely Sephardic practice.

---

32 *She'elot UTeshuvot HaRema MiPano* (Jerusalem, 1963), *siman* 25, 40. Note that he does not give the exact place in *Midrash HaNe'elam* that he is referring to.

33 Eliyahu of Vilna, *Yahel Or* (Vilna: Romm, 1882), 26b, *Vayera*.

34 Zvi Elimelech Spira, *Bnei Yissaskhar* (Oz VeHadar, 2014), *maamarei Rosh Ḥodesh, maamar* 3, 58.

35 This reference is often mistakenly given as 93b due to a typo and misquote in Abraham David Lavut's *Shaar HaKollel* (Vilna, 1912), 37 (19a), 11:27. Because of this, it is sometimes understood that there are two sources in the Zohar for saying *Barkhi Nafshi* on Rosh Ḥodesh. See, for example, Menachem Mendel Landa, *Siddur Tzluta DeAvraham* (Tel Aviv: Grafika, 1958), 399. The reference in *Shaar HaKollel* is corrected in Levi Yitzhak Raskin, *Siddur Rabbeinu HaZaken im Tziyunim Mekoros VeHe'aros* (Brooklyn: Kehot Publication Society, 2004), 482, note 37.

36 Moshe Hallamish, *Kabbalah: In Liturgy, Halakhah and Customs* (Ramat Gan: Bar-Ilan University Press, 2000), 290 [Hebrew].

37 Yosef Eliyahu Halevi Movshovitz, *Maaseh Rav* (Jerusalem: Mossad HaRav Kook, 2016), *siman* 157, 158, 175–77. See the discussion in See Ephraim Greenblatt, *Rivevos Ephraim*, vol. 1 (Memphis, TN, 1975), *siman* 288, 224–25.

38 It is reported that *Barkhi Nafshi* was not said on Rosh Ḥodesh in the Telshe Yeshiva, see Manuel Poliakoff, *Minhagei Lita: Customs of Lithuanian Jewry* (Baltimore, 2008), 39. However, see Moshe Mordechai Karp, *Hilkhot Ḥag BeḤag – Rosh Ḥodesh VeKiddush Levana* (Jerusalem, 2015), 151, and Mordechai Gross, *Iggreta DeḤedvata*, vol. 18 (Bnei Brak, 2105), 29 who report that the Lithuanian custom is to say it, based on the approach of the Vilna Gaon.

## *Chapter 25*

# Saying the Names of Haman's Sons Aloud

### OPPOSITION TO THE PRACTICE

The Talmud in Megilla (16b) states: "R. Adda from Jaffa said: The ten sons of Haman and the word 'ten' [which follows] should be said in one breath. What is the reason? Because their souls all departed together." This was codified in the *Shulḥan Arukh* (*Oraḥ Ḥayim* 690:15), with the instruction directed at the *shaliaḥ tzibbur* reading *Megillat Esther* on behalf of the congregation.

In many synagogues today it is customary for the entire congregation to say the names of Haman's ten sons out loud right before the *shaliaḥ tzibbur* reads them in one breath.[1] This practice is not found in the writings of the *Rishonim*, or in the *Shulḥan Arukh* and its commentaries. It appears that the practice did not yet exist at that time; however,

---

1 Moshe Sternbuch (*Teshuvot VeHanhagot*, vol. 2 [Jerusalem, 1994], *Oraḥ Ḥayim, siman* 358, 301), states that this is the custom today. So too states Yehoshua Yoel Weinberg ("Hilkhot UMinhagei Keriat HaMegilla," in *Paamei Yaakov BeSdeh HaHalakha* [Kislev 5766 (2005)], 241): "In many places it is customary to say this out loud, and that is our custom."

the Rema writes that there are four other verses that it is customary to say aloud: Esther 2:5, 8:15, 8:16, and 10:3.[2]

The earliest well-known mention of the practice to say the names of Haman's sons aloud seems to be Rabbi Avraham Danzig in the first printing of his book *Ḥayei Adam* in 1810. There (151:21) it is mentioned as a practice that should be abolished: "The custom in a few places that the entire congregation says the names of the ten sons of Haman is a stupid custom (מנהג שטות); rather, the reader alone says them and the congregation listens, like all of the Megilla."[3] In later editions of *Ḥayei Adam* the language was softened, and the phrase "stupid custom" was replaced with "is not a custom" (אינו מנהג).[4] It is described in the *Kitzur Shulḥan Arukh* (141:14) as an improper custom (אינו מנהג נכון), and also in *Mishna Berura* (690:52), quoting *Ḥayei Adam* that it "is not a custom."[5]

Still, it is a practice that is seen in many communities nowadays. What is the origin and rationale for this custom that persevered despite opposition from major Ashkenazic halakhic authorities?

## THE POPULAR EXPLANATION FOR THE CUSTOM

The Rogatchover Gaon, Rabbi Joseph Rosen (1858–1936), gave a famous halakhic basis for this practice. He explains that although there is a general principle of *shome'a ke'oneh*, that listening is considered as if you said it yourself, this does not apply in all cases. In a situation where the recitation must be done in a certain manner, only the recitation itself falls under *shome'a ke'oneh*, not the manner of the recitation. The recitation of Haman's ten sons must be done in one breath. Hearing the *shaliaḥ tzibbur* say these names does not fulfill the "one breath" detail, so the

2 Rema, *Shulḥan Arukh, Oraḥ Ḥayim* 690:17.

3 For example, Yaakov Spiegel in his book *Pitḥei Tefilla UMoed* (Elkana: Michlelet Orot Yisrael, 2010), 205 states that he did not find this custom mentioned before Avraham Danzig did so in *Ḥayei Adam*.

4 *Ḥayei Adam* (Vilna, 1819), 155:22.

5 So too in Yissachar Dov Weinberger, *Edut BeYehosef – Minhagei Vizhnitz, Ḥodshei HaḤoref* (Bnei Brak, 2002), 291–92. The custom is not mentioned at all in Moshe Harari, *Mikra'ei Kodesh: Hilkhot Purim* (Jerusalem: Mercaz Harav, 1994), chapter 7:21, 130.

congregation has to do this part themselves.[6] Rabbi Zevin included this explanation in his book *HaMoadim BeHalakha*, and it is the most popular explanation for the custom.[7]

The concept of a limitation of this type to the concept *shome'a ke'oneh* can be found in other cases as well. Rabbi Yaakov Emden (1697–1776) opposed calling up people who are blind to the Torah for *aliyot*, explaining that *shome'a ke'oneh* is not applicable because the Torah portion must be read from the scroll itself, and it does not suffice to hear it from another person reading the Torah. It therefore cannot be transferred by *shome'a ke'oneh*.[8] Another example is given by Rabbi Joseph B. Soloveitchik in his *Beit HaLevi*, who explains that "*shome'a ke'oneh* is only applicable when all that is needed is recital alone," and therefore it would not apply to *Birkat Kohanim*, which has an additional component of being said in a loud voice.[9] It has also been suggested that *shome'a ke'oneh* would not apply to telling the story of the exodus from Egypt on Seder night, since that must be done in question-and-answer format, rather than simply as a recital.[10]

However, the Ḥazon Ish, Rabbi Avraham Karelitz (1878–1953), opposed this understanding of *shome'a ke'oneh*. He states that "the principle of *shome'a ke'oneh* unifies the listener and the one reciting, one with speech and the other through listening, until the recitation also applies to the listener. Thus, even regarding commandments where recitation alone is not enough, and there are certain conditions regarding the recitation, the listener still fulfills the commandment by listening." The Ḥazon Ish explains that the listener is included in everything the one reciting does, including the actions related to the manner of recitation. He proves his

6 *Tzafnat Paane'aḥ*, vol. 4 (on Rambam's *Sefer Haflaa*) (Piotrkow, 1903), *hashmatot* to *hilkhot gerushin*, chapter 2, halakha 16, 57a. He also states that the reason it is customary to write the names of Haman's sons in very large letters in the Megilla is to indicate that the congregation has to recite it for themselves.

7 Shlomo Zevin, *HaMoadim BeHalakha* (Jerusalem: HaMachon HaTalmud HaYisraeli HaShalem, 1980), 241.

8 *She'elat Yaavetz* (Lemberg, 1884), 47b, question 75.

9 *Beit HaLevi al HaTorah* (Jerusalem, 1985), end of the section on Hanukka, 87.

10 Ishmael Cohen, *Shevaḥ Pesaḥ* (Warsaw, 1894), Maggid, *siman* 2, 4b. See also David Alexander Milinofsky, *Sefer Imrei David* (Bnei Brak, 1982), *siman* 3, 11.

approach with the reading of the Megilla itself, which must be done from a scroll, yet the congregation, through *shome'a ke'oneh,* fulfills their obligation by listening, even though they are not looking at the scroll. In this view, the congregants are not considered to be reciting the Megilla by heart, because even the aspect of reading from a scroll is transferred through *shome'a ke'oneh.*[11] Rabbi Moshe Sternbuch understands *shome'a ke'oneh* in a similar manner and writes that he is baffled by the approach of the Rogatchover Gaon. He gives the example of the mitzva of hearing the shofar blasts, which also have to be done in one breath and is transferred through *shome'ah ke'oneh,* and infers that the same would apply to the reading of the names of Haman's sons.[12]

Aside from this, the approach of the Rogatchover Gaon is difficult since, according to his understanding of *shome'a ke'oneh,* the congregation would have to say the names of Haman's sons in one breath, and yet there is no record of this being the custom.[13] While Rabbi Moshe Sternbuch writes that the congregation should follow the Rogatchover Gaon,[14] it does not appear that anyone is actually careful to say it in one breath.

Based on this explanation, the *Ḥayei Adam*'s opposition to this practice was founded on his understanding of *shome'a ke'oneh,* which presumably was at odds with that of the Rogatchover Gaon.[15] Although the Rogatchover's explanation is innovative, it does not appear to be the impetus for the practice, but rather a justification for something that was already being done. Furthermore, the *Ḥayei Adam* described the practice as a "stupid custom" which seems overly harsh and inappropriate if it was simply a disagreement over the concept of *shome'a ke'oneh.*

---

11 *Ḥazon Ish, Oraḥ Ḥayim* 29:3.

12 Moshe Sternbuch, *Teshuvot VeHanhagot,* vol. 2 (Jerusalem, 1994), *Oraḥ Ḥayim siman* 358, 301.

13 See Yosef Hacohen, "BeInyan Shome'a KeOneh BeSefirat HaOmer," *Or Torah* (Tevet 5763/2002), 180, note 2. Also found in Dekel Cohen, *Sefer Eliashiv HaCohen* (Bnei Brak, 2009), *siman* 46, 291.

14 Sternbuch, *Teshuvot VeHanhagot, Oraḥ Ḥayim siman* 358, 302.

15 Different versions of the exact difference of opinion can be found in Milinofsky, *Sefer Imrei David, siman* 3, 12; Yitzhak Mirsky, *Hegyonei Halakha BeInyan Shabbat UMoadim* (Jerusalem: Mossad HaRav Kook, 1988), 114; David Barda, *Revid HaZahav* (Tiberias, 1996), *Oraḥ Ḥayim, siman* 11, 34.

## OTHER EXPLANATIONS FOR THE CUSTOM

Rabbi Avraham Hayim Naeh states that it was the custom in Hebron for the children to make a lot of noise during the reading of the names of Haman and his sons. However, since the reader would say them quickly in one breath, there was not enough time for noisemaking. In order to give the children more of an opportunity to make noise, the congregation would say these names before the reader.[16]

We do find accounts from Persia and Egypt that children would make noise at the mention of not only Haman but also his sons,[17] and it is easy to see how a custom to make noise when Haman's name is read would extend to his sons' names as well. However, it should be noted that even in those communities there is no record that the congregation said the names out loud.[18] The *Ḥayei Adam* was not familiar with the custom of the congregation reading the names aloud presumably because in his community the children did not make noise at this point.

According to this explanation, the community reads the names simply to provide time for children to make noise. However, this is not in line with the current practice where children do not make any noise while the congregants say the names of Haman's sons aloud.

My grandfather, Rabbi Eliezer Cohen, who served as the rabbi of Congregation Agudas Aḥim in Brooklyn, told me many years ago that he felt that the custom arose because the *shaliaḥ tzibbur* would pause to take a deep breath before reading the names of Haman's sons. Some congregants thought that this pause was the *shaliaḥ tzibbur* waiting for them to say something out loud, the same way he pauses for the verses traditionally read that way. Once a few people started saying it out loud the reader had to wait for them to finish, and so the custom was born. It became more widespread because other congregants, when they saw that the *shaliaḥ tzibbur* stopped for them, assumed that this was supposed to

---

16 Avraham Hayim Naeh, *Ketzot HaShulḥan*, vol. 3 (Jerusalem, 1978), notes to Purim, *siman* 3.

17 Asher Waserteil, ed., *Yalkut Minhagim* (Jerusalem, 1996), 325, 412, 462. There (p. 412) it states that in Egypt, "the rabbis ruled not to make noise during [the reading of the name] Haman since it disrupts hearing the Megilla, rather to do this during the reading of the [names of the] sons of Haman."

18 Letter by Boaz Moredchai in *HaMaayan* 217 (2006), 56:3, 91.

be done. It was for this reason that the *Ḥayei Adam* labeled the practice a "stupid custom."

### THE CUSTOM TO RECITE VERSES ALOUD

There is an ancient custom, mentioned as early as the *Geonim*, that certain verses from the Megilla are said aloud by the congregation. The Rema writes that there are four such verses (*Oraḥ Ḥayim* 690:17), but there are a few different versions in rabbinic literature regarding exactly which verses to say aloud.

Rav Saadia Gaon states that there are two verses of redemption said aloud by the congregation: "The Jews had light and gladness, and joy and honor" (Est. 8:16) and "For Mordekhai the Jew was second unto King Aḥashverosh, and great among the Jews, and accepted by most of his brethren; seeking the good of his people and speaking peace to all his seed" (10:3).[19] *Seder Rav Amram Gaon* includes an additional verse in the name of Rav Saadia Gaon: "And Mordekhai went forth from the presence of the king in royal apparel of blue and white, and with a great crown of gold, and with a robe of fine linen and purple; and the city of Shushan shouted and was glad" (8:15).[20] These verses, with the addition of Esther 10:3, are the four that the Rema writes are customarily said aloud.

Other authorities list five verses;[21] a popular addition is "On that night the king's sleep was disturbed; and he ordered to bring the book of records of the chronicles, and they were read before the king" (Est. 6:1), which marks the turning point of the story and the beginning of the salvation.[22] Different communities added other verses. For example, it was reported that in Djerba it was customary to say six verses out loud,

---

19 Israel Davidson, Simha Assaf and Yissachar Yoel, eds., *Siddur Rav Saadia Gaon* (Jerusalem: Reuven Mass, 2000), 369.

20 Daniel Goldschmidt, ed., *Seder Rav Amram Gaon*, (Jerusalem: Mossad HaRav Kook, 2004), 101.

21 Regarding the different customs, see Yaakov Spiegel in his book *Pitḥei Tefilla UMoed* (Elkana: Michlelet Orot Yisrael, 2010), 195–99.

22 Spiegel, *Pitḥei Tefilla UMoed*, 201–4; Moshe Harari, *Mikra'ei Kodesh: Hilkhot Purim* (Jerusalem: Mercaz Harav, 1994), chapter 7:24, 131; Simha Rabinowitz, *Piskei Teshuvot*, vol. 6 (Jerusalem, 1997), 690:6, 552.

in addition to all the verses of chapter 10.[23] The *Arukh HaShulḥan* (*Oraḥ Ḥayim* 690:23) states that it was customary to recite aloud from the end of Esther 9:6, "five hundred men," through the names of Haman's sons, because "that is the main part of the redemption."

In the 1300s, Rabbi Avraham ben Natan HaYarḥi explained in *Sefer HaManhig* that the reason those four verses were read aloud by the congregation was "in order to increase joy,"[24] and the Abudraham wrote that it was "to increase joy for the children and for all... in order to awaken their hearts,"[25] so it is not unusual to find that some communities added more verses for congregational recital.

In fact, we find this exact practice recorded by Rabbi Yosef Yuspa Cashman Segal in his book *Noheg KeTzon Yosef*, which provides a record of the customs of the Frankfurt am Main community. This book was first published in 1718, thirty years before Rabbi Avraham Danzig was born. There we find that "the congregation reads the verses of redemption aloud, including, 'There was a certain Jew...' (Est. 2:5), 'And Mordekhai went forth...' (8:15), 'The Jews had light...' (8:16), [the verses listing] the ten sons of Haman, 'For Mordekhai the Jew...' (10:3), and the *shaliaḥ tzibbur* repeats them afterward, and does not say them along with the congregation because they might not hear him as they are reciting it themselves."[26] Here we have the same four verses that the Rema mentioned, with the addition of the verses listing Haman's sons. This is the earliest record of the custom for the congregation to say the names of Haman's sons out loud. This practice is included in other books of the customs of Frankfurt[27] as well as in books of Chabad customs[28] and the customs of the Djerba community.[29]

---

23 Spiegel, *Pitḥei Tefilla UMoed*, 203.

24 Y. Refael, ed., *Sefer HaManhig* (Jerusalem: Mossad HaRav Kook, 1978), 243.

25 *Sefer Abudraham* (Jerusalem: Machon Even Yisrael, 1995), 228.

26 Yosef Yuspa Cashman Segal, *Noheg KeTzon Yosef* (Tel Aviv, 1969), 200, Purim, *siman* 6.

27 Zvi Leitner, *Minhagei Frankfurt – Ḥelek HaMoadim* (Jerusalem, 1982), 111, Purim customs, *siman* 1.

28 Asher Waserteil, ed., *Yalkut Minhagim* (Jerusalem, 1996), 297.

29 Ibid., 526.

From this we can now understand that communities were accustomed to saying the names of Haman's sons out loud because they were viewed as part of the special verses of joy and redemption that are recited aloud by the congregation. Once some of the congregation said the names out loud and the *shaliaḥ tzibbur* had to wait anyway, it is natural that the custom would have spread.

### A DIFFERENT WAY TO UNDERSTAND THE *ḤAYEI ADAM*

If indeed some communities were accustomed to reading the names of Haman's sons out loud, why would this anger Rabbi Danzig so much that he would call it a "stupid custom"? There were many variations of which verses to say, and adding more verses does not seem particularly offensive. It may be that since the list of Haman's sons does not seem to be a section that can be termed a "verse of redemption," Rabbi Danzig saw no reason to add it. However, the Talmud in Megilla (16b) explicitly notes that the ten sons of Haman are listed in two columns, reminiscent of a special *shira*,[30] and we have already noted that the *Arukh HaShulḥan* (*Oraḥ Ḥayim* 690:23) called that section "the main part of the redemption."

With this in mind, it seems we need to understand what Rabbi Danzig was upset about in a different way.[31] Rabbi Alexander Ziskind of Grodno (d. 1794) wrote *Yesod VeShoresh HaAvoda*, an influential book of instruction on living a religious life. It was first published in 1782 and includes many practices related to the proper observance of mitzvot. He writes that individuals should say the names of Haman's sons themselves, even if they hear the rest of the Megilla from the reader. This is because the *shaliaḥ tzibbur* tends to say it so quickly, in one breath, that it is difficult to hear this part properly.[32] Here is a source that instructs people to say the names of Haman's sons along with the reader, and it is this practice that Rabbi Danzig termed a

---

30 See also Eliakim Devoraks, *BeShvilei HaMinhag – Shabbat UMoadim*, vol. 3 (Jerusalem, 1998), 127.

31 On this, see the letter by Moshe Chadad in *HaMaayan* 217 (2006), 56:3, 91–92.

32 Shlomo Shefer, ed., *Yesod VeShoresh HaAvoda* (Bnei Brak, 1987), 136, *shaar* 12, chapter 5.

"stupid custom," since if many people do this, the rest of the congregation will not be able to hear the reader.

From the way the practice is described in *Ḥayei Adam* (145:22), the *Kitzur Shulḥan Arukh* (141:14), the *Mishna Berura* (690:52), and by the Rogatchover Gaon, there is no clear indication whether the congregation says the names of Haman along with or directly before the *shaliaḥ tzibbur*. However, it is clear from Rabbi Yaakov Sofer in his *Kaf HaḤayim* (*Oraḥ Ḥayim* 690:91) that his understanding of the *Ḥayei Adam* was that he opposed saying the names *along* with the reader, as Rabbi Sofer makes a distinction between what the *Ḥayei Adam* was referring to and the practice of some to say the names before the reader. Rabbi Ovadia Yosef explicitly states that the Rogatchover Gaon was justifying the practice to say the names along with the reader, and this is what the *Ḥayei Adam* came out against.[33] Rabbi Moshe Sternbuch also explains the practice in exactly this way. Although he does not refer to *Yesod VeShoresh HaAvoda*, he explains that the simple reason for the practice is the concern that the reader might not correctly enunciate the names of Haman's sons in his rush to say them all in one breath.[34]

It should be noted that while the Rogatchover Gaon seems to be justifying a popular custom that already existed,[35] it is only Rabbi Alexander Ziskind in *Yesod VeShoresh HaAvoda* that actually instructed people to do this as a matter of meticulous Megilla reading. The *Ḥayei Adam* opposed that ruling. Based on this, there was never any opposition to adding the recital of the names of Haman's sons to the list of verses that congregants say aloud before the *shaliaḥ tzibbur* reads them, but only to saying the names at the same time as the *shaliaḥ tzibbur*. Additionally, the instruction of *Yesod VeShoresh HaAvoda* is directed to particularly pious and meticulous individuals, rather than to the congregation as a congregational practice which might disrupt the reading of the Megilla, and it is this that the *Ḥayei Adam* opposed.

---

33 Yitzhak Yosef, ed., *Yalkut Yosef – Moadim* (Jerusalem, 1988), 299, *siman* 34.

34 Moshe Sternbuch, *Teshuvot VeHanhagot*, vol. 2 (Jerusalem, 1994), *Oraḥ Ḥayim siman* 358, 302. This approach is brought in the name of *Aḥaronim* in Yehoshua Yoel Weinberg, "Hilkhot UMinhagei Keriat HaMegilla" in *Paamei Yaakov BeSdeh HaHalakha*, Kislev 5766 (2005), 241.

35 David Milinofsky, *Sefer Imrei David* (Bnei Brak, 1982), *siman* 3, 11.

## CONCLUSION

We now see that in the 1700s there were two customs regarding the congregational recital of the names of Haman's sons: the earlier practice reported in *Noheg KeTzon Yosef*, to say it aloud before the *shaliaḥ tzibbur* did so, and the instruction of *Yesod VeShoresh HaAvoda* to say it together with the *shaliaḥ tzibbur*. Since the earliest mention of the practice is as a festive recital in *Noheg KeTzon Yosef*, it is possible that while at first only some communities added this to the other festive verses, over time people may have thought that it was mandatory for a halakhic reason, in the event that the recital of the *shaliaḥ tzibbur* was unintelligible at this part. The fact that the Rema did not list this as one of the verses to be read aloud as an expression of joy may have contributed to this impression. Thus the custom developed that in places where the reader did not pause to give everyone a chance to say the names out loud, some people said the names along with the reader, in addition to those meticulous individuals following the instructions of *Yesod VeShoresh HaAvoda*. This is what the *Ḥayei Adam* so vehemently opposed. The current practice of reading the names aloud before the *shaliaḥ tzibbur* is simply a continuation of the custom that originated in Frankfurt am Main, as reported in *Noheg KeTzon Yosef*.

*Chapter 26*

# Reading Song of Songs, Ruth, Lamentations, and Ecclesiastes

The reading of *Megillat Esther* on Purim is dealt with extensively in the Mishna and Talmud in Tractate Megilla. Today it is customary to read Song of Songs on Passover, the Book of Ruth on Shavuot, Lamentations on Tisha BeAv, and Ecclesiastes on Sukkot. None of these readings are mentioned in the Talmud. In this chapter we will trace the origin of this custom, the ways it was performed, and the reasons given for it.

## THE TRADITIONAL CONNECTIONS BETWEEN THE HOLIDAYS AND THE MEGILLOT

### *Song of Songs*

A possible conceptual source for reading Song of Songs on Passover is found at the end of Rav Saadia Gaon's introduction to his commentary to Song of Songs. He states there: "And when Solomon reigned and sat on his throne in the last days of Passover he prophesized in Song of Songs (ניבא בשיר השירים)." The source for this idea is unknown, but it may explain the connection between Song of Songs and the last days of Passover, when it is customarily read.[1]

The earliest source that provides explanations for reading each of the Megillot on a particular holiday is the eleventh-century work *Maḥzor Vitry*. *Maḥzor Vitry* explains that Song of Songs is read on Passover because it was thought to hint to the redemption of the Israelites: "I have likened you, my darling, to a mare in Pharaoh's chariots" (Song of Songs 1:9).[2] In the 1300s, Rabbi Avraham ben Natan HaYarḥi reiterated the explanation found in *Maḥzor Vitry* in his work *Sefer HaManhig*,[3] which was in turn quoted by the Abudraham.[4] Additionally, many verses in Song of Songs are interpreted in Song of Songs Rabba as referring to the exodus,[5] and there are also kabbalistic connections between Passover and Song of Songs.[6]

Another idea is that many songs are associated with Passover: the Song of the Sea, Hallel sung at night and at the Seder, the song to be sung in the future in the *haftara* of the last day of Passover in the Diaspora. Song of Songs is an appropriate addition to this holiday of songs.[7]

### The Book of Ruth

The earliest explanation for why the Book of Ruth is read on Shavuot is found in the beginning of *Midrash Rut Zuta*. The midrash asks, "What is the connection between Ruth and Atzeret, so that it is read on Atzeret, the time of the giving of the Torah? To teach you that the Torah is given only through suffering and poverty. And so it is written, 'Your tribe dwells there; O God, in Your goodness You provide for the needy' (Ps. 68:11).

1 S. *Wertheimer, Geon HaGeonim*, vol. 1 (Jerusalem, 1925), 81, note 49.

2 Simon Hurwitz, ed., *Maḥzor Vitry* (Nuremberg: J. Bulka, 1923), 304.

3 Y. Refael, ed., *Sefer HaManhig* (Jerusalem: Mossad HaRav Kook, 1978), 416–17.

4 *Sefer Abudraham* (Jerusalem, 1995), 266.

5 See, for example, Song of Songs Rabba 1:2 and 1:7. See also Shmuel Gelbard, *Otzar Taamei HaMinhagim* (Petach Tikvah: Mifal Rashi, 1995), 296.

6 See J. D. Eisenstein, *Otzar Dinim UMinhagim* (New York, 1917), 414.

7 Amos Chacham, *Daat Mikra: Shir HaShirim* (Jerusalem: Mossad HaRav Kook, 1990), 15.

The Torah said before the Holy One, blessed be He, 'Master of the Universe, make my portion with the tribe of the needy, for if the wealthy deal with me they will become haughty, but when they are needy and deal with me, they know that they are hungry, as it is said, "Folly was placed on lofty heights, while rich men sat in low estate" (Eccl. 10:6).'"[8] It is not clear when this midrash was composed. Most opinions range from the tenth through twelfth century, though some give a much earlier date.[9] This explanation is also mentioned at the end of the eleventh-century work *Midrash Lekaḥ Tov* on Ruth,[10] with slightly different phrasing. Later, this explanation was quoted in *Yalkut Shimoni Rut* (end of *remez* 596), and from there in *Magen Avraham* (*Oraḥ Ḥayim* 490:8).

After bringing the explanation found in *Rut Zuta, Midrash Lekaḥ Tov* on Ruth offers another reason to read Ruth on Shavuot: "Since this Megilla is all *ḥesed,* and the Torah is all *ḥesed,* as it is said, "The law of kindness (*torat ḥesed*) is on her tongue' (Prov. 31:26), and the Torah was given on the holiday of Shavuot."[11]

*Maḥzor Vitry* explains that Ruth is read on Shavuot because it takes place during the harvest (Ruth 1:22),[12] and also because Ruth underwent a conversion and accepted the Torah, just as the Israelites did at Sinai.[13] In addition to these two new explanations, *Maḥzor Vitry* also quotes the explanation from *Rut Zuta,* adding that R. Yehuda b.

8 S. Buber, ed., *Midrash Zuta* (Vilna: Romm, 1925), 39, 1:1. See the discussion of this teaching in Hayim Yosef David Azulai, *Simḥat HaRegel* (Lemberg, 1863), *limmud* 3, 5.

9 Anat Reizel, *Introduction to the Midrashic Literature* (Alon Shvut: Tevunot, 2011), 178 [Hebrew].

10 S. Bamberger, ed., *Peirush Lekaḥ Tov – Rut* (Mainz: Lehman, 1887), 46.

11 Ibid., 47.

12 Note, however, that Ruth takes place "at the beginning of the barley harvest" (Ruth 1:22), which is actually at Passover, when the *omer* of barley is offered, while Shavuot is the time of the wheat harvest (Ex. 34:22). Ruth 2:23 mentions that Ruth "gleaned until the barley harvest and the wheat harvest were finished," so the narrative did continue into the time of Shavuot.

13 See Yevamot 46b. Abraham Hershowitz (*Minhagei Yeshurun* [Vilna, 1899], *siman* 135, 74) explains that based on this, Ruth is read specifically on the second day of Shavuot because that was the day when the Israelites made a covenant to accept the Torah and said, "We shall do and we shall listen."

Barzilai explains that when the Israelites left Egypt through suffering they were redeemed, and so too Ruth lived through famine and then accepted the Torah and converted.[14] As with the explanation *Maḥzor Vitry* gave for Song of Songs, these explanations were also quoted in *Sefer HaManhig*,[15] and then by the Abudraham.[16] He was in turn quoted by Rabbi Moshe Isserles in *Darkhei Moshe* (490:1), making the two explanations in the *Maḥzor Vitry* the most well-known classic explanations for reading Ruth on Shavuot.

In the 1500s, Rabbi Mordekhai Jaffe explained that Leviticus 23:15–21 speaks about Shavuot, and following immediately, Leviticus 23:22 states, "When you reap the harvest of your land you shall not reap all the way to the edges of your field, or gather the gleanings of your harvest; you shall leave them for the poor and the stranger." This is exactly what Boaz fulfilled, so it is fitting to read the Book of Ruth on Shavuot.[17]

Later works added more explanations to these. Rabbi Alexander Schorr (1673–1737), in his book *Beḥor Shor*, suggests that King David is the connection between the Book of Ruth and Shavuot. He explains that Ruth was written to provide the lineage of King David, who, according to Y. Ḥagiga (2:3), died on Shavuot. Rabbi Schorr reasons that since God completes the years of the righteous (so that they are born and die on the same date), David must have been born on Shavuot,[18] so it is appropriate to read Ruth on the day of the birth of King David, in

14 Simon Hurwitz, ed., *Maḥzor Vitry* (Nuremberg: J. Bulka, 1923), 344. Note that the association with leaving Egypt would make it appropriate for Ruth to be read on Passover as well.

15 Y. Refael, ed., *Sefer HaManhig* (Jerusalem: Mossad HaRav Kook, 1978), 416–17.

16 *Sefer Abudraham* (Jerusalem, 1995), 266.

17 Mordekhai Jaffe, *Levush HaḤur* (Bardichev, 1818), *siman* 494:2. It may also be that the reading of Ruth was meant to instruct the listeners regarding the charity given to the poor at harvest season. See Feivel Meltzer, *Daat Mikra: Rut* (Jerusalem: Mossad HaRav Kook, 1990), 20, note 56.

18 Although there is no explicit early source that David was born on Shavuot, Y. Berakhot 2:1, Y. Rosh HaShana 1:1, and Y. Moed Katan 3:7 all refer to David living "full days" based on I Chronicles 17:11: "When your days are done and you follow your fathers." Thanks to Avi Levine for finding these references.

his honor.[19] Rabbi Schorr seems to be the originator of this particular explanation, which proved to be very popular. This same explanation is found, without attribution, in the book *Binyan Ariel* by Rabbi Shaul Levinstam (1717–97), head of the Amsterdam *beit din*,[20] and in the writings of many other later figures.[21]

Rabbi Hayim Yosef David Azulai (the Ḥida, 1724–1806) makes another connection based on *Gematria*: At first Ruth observed only the seven Noahide laws, and when she accepted the Torah, she took on 606 more commandments. The name Ruth (רות) has the same numerical value of 606 (תר"ו), so on Shavuot, when all of Israel accepted an additional 606 commandments, it is fitting to read the Book of Ruth.[22]

The introduction to the Book of Ruth printed in the Sephardic *Maḥzor Moadei Hashem* mentions another reason. It states there that we read Ruth on Shavuot to teach us that "Ruth attained perfection only through her good choices and diligent effort to enter under the wings

19 Alexander Schorr, *Beḥor Shor* (Zitomir, 1868), 26, commentary on Bava Batra 13b. This is the source quoted by Hayim Yosef David Azulai in *Birkei Yosef, Oraḥ Ḥayim* 494:11. There he refers to Schorr by his major work on the laws of *sheḥita, Simla Ḥadasha*. Zevin mentions this explanation in his *HaMoadim BeHalakha* (Jerusalem, 1980), 393, referring to Schorr by another of his works, *Tevuot Shor*. Abraham Hershowitz (*Minhagei Yeshurun* [Vilna, 1899], *siman* 135, 75) explains that based on this, Ruth is read specifically on the second day of Shavuot because that was the day King David was buried.

20 Shaul Levinstam, *Binyan Ariel* (Cracow, 1905), 248. This is the source mentioned by Avraham Sperling in *Sefer Taamei HaMinhagim UMekorei haDinim* (Lemberg: David Roth, 1928), 74a and in Feivel Meltzer, *Daat Mikra: Rut* (Jerusalem: Mossad HaRav Kook, 1990), 21, note 57.

21 For example, Schorr is quoted in *Shaarei Teshuva, Oraḥ Ḥayim* 494:7, Avraham Khalfon, *Ḥayei Avraham* (Livorno, 1826), 41b, *siman* 282 (in later editions, *siman* 289). See also Nachman Zelnik, *Sefer Atzeret – Ḥag HaShavuot* (Jerusalem: Machon Harry Fischel, 1989), 211–12.

22 Hayim Yosef David Azulai, *Birkei Yosef, Oraḥ Ḥayim* 494:11. See there for another explanation based on the *Gematria* explanation. This explanation is quoted in Yitzhak Lipetz, *Sefer Mataamim* (Warsaw, 1890), 57, *siman* 59, and from there in J. D. Eisenstein, *Otzar Dinim UMinhagim* (New York, 1917), 383, and Shmuel Gelbard, *Otzar Taamei HaMinhagim* (Petach Tikvah: Mifal Rashi, 1995), 307.

of the Divine Presence; so too should each person whose heart prods him to attain happiness, and not rely on his background and lineage."[23]

Rabbi Yehudah Leib Alter, author of the *Sfat Emet*, explains that Ruth was chosen to be read on the day we commemorate the giving of the Torah because the entire story of Ruth is based on the rabbinic interpretation in Yevamot 76b of Deuteronomy 23:4, which states, "No Ammonite or Moabite shall be admitted into the congregation of the Lord." It is argued that this applies only to males and not females. Reading Ruth on this day shows that the Oral and Written Torah are inseparable and comprise one unit.[24]

Taking this idea further, Rabbi Yehuda Leib Maimon (Fishman) explains that the reading of Ruth on Shavuot was instituted to invalidate the position of the Karaites and uphold the veracity of the Oral Law. Shavuot was a contentious holiday because the rabbinic interpretation of Leviticus 23:15 conflicted with that of the Karaites. That verse states, "And you shall count for yourselves from the day after the Sabbath... seven full weeks." The rabbis interpreted "the day after the Sabbath" to mean the day after the first day of Passover, and the Karaites believed that it refers to the day after the Shabbat that falls during Passover. Thus, according to rabbinic tradition, Shavuot was always celebrated on the sixth of Sivan but on different days of the week, while according to the Karaites, Shavuot always fell on a Sunday but on different calendar dates. The founder of the Karaite movement was Anan, who was of Davidic descent. Reading Ruth on Shavuot was tantamount to saying to the Karaites that if you do not accept the rabbinic interpretations, your founder himself would not be considered a legitimate member of the Jewish people, as it would have been prohibited for Boaz to marry Ruth.[25] Therefore, the reading of Ruth on Shavuot is part of the polemic against the Karaites.

---

23 *Moadei Hashem* (Livorno, 1872), 190a. This book was first published in 1839. A hasidic take on this basic idea can be found in Yehuda Aryeh Leib Alter, *Sfat Emet – Bemidbar* (Petrikov, 1905), Shavuot 5644, 36.

24 Yehuda Aryeh Leib Alter, *Sfat Emet – Bemidbar* (Petrikov, 1905), Shavuot 5633, 23. See also Eliyahu Kitov, *Sefer HaTodaa*, vol. 2 (Jerusalem: Beit Hotzaat Sefarim, 1958), 301.

25 Yehuda Leib Maimon, *Ḥagim UMoadim* (Jerusalem: Weiss, 1943), 269–70. This idea is also found in Maimon's series of articles "*Midei Ḥodesh BeḤodsho*," in *Sinai*

While these multiple explanations indicate that possibly a confluence of factors led to reading the Book of Ruth on Shavuot,[26] a certain progression can be noted in the interpretations given over time. The earliest explanation, found in both *Rut Zuta* and *Midrash Lekaḥ Tov,* was based on an understanding that the Torah is associated with suffering. This explanation fell by the wayside over time and was replaced with more positive associations, such as the theme of *ḥesed*. We then find many explications in the time of the *Rishonim* based on textual elements and themes in the Book of Ruth itself, such as acceptance of the Torah and the harvest season. It was only much later that a connection was made with King David.

### *Lamentations*

The associations between Lamentations and Tisha BeAv are far more obvious than those between other Megillot that are read on a particular holiday. The Talmud in Taanit (30a) states that it is prohibited to read from the Tanakh on Tisha BeAv, as this creates joy. One of the exceptions noted is *Kinnot,* a term used to refer to Lamentations, which deals in its entirety with the destruction of the Temple and Jerusalem.[27] While the Talmud adds that one is allowed to read Lamentations on Tisha BeAv, it does not record a custom to specifically do so. However, in the Talmud Yerushalmi (Shabbat 16:1) we do read of rabbis studying Lamentations on the eve of Tisha BeAv that fell on Shabbat.

### *Ecclesiastes*

*Maḥzor Vitry* explains that Ecclesiastes is read on Shabbat Ḥol HaMoed of Sukkot or Shemini Atzeret because of the verse "Distribute portions to seven or even to eight" (Eccl. 11:2), which was understood as referring to the seven days of Sukkot and the eighth day of Shemini Atzeret.[28]

---

35 (1953), 158–59, later collected in his book *Midei Ḥodesh BeḤodsho* (Jerusalem: Mossad HaRav Kook, 1962).

26 Feivel Meltzer, *Daat Mikra: Rut* (Jerusalem: Mossad HaRav Kook, 1990), 20.

27 Yehiel Zvi Moskovitz, *Daat Mikra: Eikha* (Jerusalem: Mossad HaRav Kook, 1990), 3–5.

28 See Eiruvin 40b. See note 30 in Simon Hurwitz, ed., *Maḥzor Vitry* (Nuremberg: J. Bulka, 1923), 441. This explanation is also brought in Salomon Buber, ed., *Siddur*

It also mentions the verse in I Kings 8:2, "All the men of Israel gathered (*vayikahalu*) before King Solomon at the feast, in the month of *Etanim*, that is, the seventh month." This was taken as a hint for reading Ecclesiastes at this time of year.[29]

*Sefer HaManhig* expands on the relationship between Ecclesiastes and Shemini Atzeret noted in *Maḥzor Vitry* with another explanation of the connection between Ecclesiastes and the above-mentioned verse, "Distribute portions to seven or even to eight." Since the harvest is collected at this time of year, it was considered appropriate to provide a reminder about the commandments to give tithes and the priestly portion. This is also the time when vows are due (Rosh HaShana 4b).[30] Additionally, Avraham ben Nathan HaYarḥi explains that Sukkot was the time of year for gathering the people together, particularly to chastise them,[31] so it was appropriate to read Ecclesiastes then. Nathan HaYarḥi notes that he heard these reasons from others; they are not his own ideas.[32] These explanations are also quoted in the Abudraham.[33]

*Magen Avraham* (490:8) gives another explanation, that since Sukkot is a time of joy (Lev. 23:40; Deut. 16:14, 15), and in Ecclesiastes 2:2 it says, "Of merriment, 'What good is that?'" it is appropriate to read Ecclesiastes on Sukkot. While this would seem to be a reason not to read Ecclesiastes on Sukkot, as it seems to be pointing out that joy is pointless, it is usually explained that Ecclesiastes denigrates only foolish revelry, and Sukkot is a time of spiritual joy.[34]

A more general explanation for reading these three Megillot over these three holidays is based on the teaching of R. Yoḥanan in Song of Songs Rabba (1:10), which states that Song of Songs reflects the youthful practice of composing songs and poems, and Ecclesiastes reflects the thinking of an old man looking back on life. The three pilgrimage festivals follow the agricultural cycle, from its beginning on Passover in

---

*Rashi* (Berlin: Ḥevrat Mekitzei Nirdamim, 1911) 104, *siman* 222.

29 Hurwitz, *Maḥzor Vitry*, 440–41.

30 Ecclesiastes5:3–4 warns not to delay the fulfillment of vows.

31 See Deut. 31:10; see also I Kings 8:2.

32 Y. Refael, ed., *Sefer HaManhig* (Jerusalem: Mossad HaRav Kook, 1978), 416–17.

33 *Sefer Abudraham* (Jerusalem, 1995), 266.

34 See Yehuda Shaviv, "*Kohelet* on Sukkot," *HaMaayan* 41, no.1 (Tishrei 5761), 13–14.

the spring, to the harvest of Shavuot, to the end of the cycle on Sukkot, so that a Megilla appropriate for each phase in this cycle and each corresponding phase of life is read on each holiday.[35]

### THE EARLY VERSION OF THE CUSTOM

The earliest source for the reading of all of these Megillot, except for Ecclesiastes, is *Masekhet Soferim.*

Reading Song of Songs on Passover and Ruth on Shavuot is described in *Masekhet Soferim* 14:16:[36] "Song of Songs is read on the last nights of the additional day of the holiday in the Diaspora, half on one night, half on the second night. Ruth is read on the night after the first day of Atzeret – up to half – and is completed on the night after the last day of the holiday. Some say: In all we begin on the Saturday night before the holiday." *Soferim* concludes that this is all based on custom. Ecclesiastes is not mentioned as being read at any time during the year.[37]

This method of reading the Megillot is similar to the way an additional reading of *Megillat Esther* is described in *Masekhet Soferim,* where it is noted that the "congregation reads together" the Megilla in two halves on the two Saturday nights of Adar preceding Purim. The first five chapters are read on one Saturday night, and the last five chapters are read on the following Saturday night. This custom is presented after

---

35 See J. D. Eisenstein, *Otzar Dinim UMinhagim* (New York, 1917), 414; Mordechai Zer-Kavod, *Daat Mikra: Kohelet* (Jerusalem: Mossad HaRav Kook, 1990), 6.

36 In some editions 14:17 or 14:18.

37 Some versions of *Masekhet Soferim* include Ecclesiastes in the list of Megillot over which a blessing is recited (in *Soferim* 14:3). For example, the versions of *Masekhet Soferim* quoted in Simon Hurwitz, ed., *Maḥzor Vitry* (Nuremberg: J. Bulka, 1923), 344, *siman* 312, note 20; 706, *siman* 527; Alexander Suslin, ed., *Sefer HaAguda* (Cracow, 1575), 227b; Mordekhai, Megilla, *siman* 784. The Vilna Gaon also added Ecclesiastes to the list in *Soferim* 14:3; see *Biur HaGra, Oraḥ Ḥayim* 490:9. See also M. Higger, *Masekhet Soferim* (New York, 1937), 251; Shmuel Wasserstein, *Masekhet Soferim* (Jerusalem, 2001), 119–20. Ecclesiastes does not appear in the versions of *Masekhet Soferim* quoted in *Sefer Abudraham* (Jerusalem, 1995), 266; *Hagahot Meimoniot, Hilchot Taanit,* 5:2 and in the section "*Minhagei Tisha BeAv*" at the end of *Hilchot Taanit* chapter 5; Asher Siev, ed., *Shut Rema* (Jerusalem, 1970), number 35, 197, see there note 31. Even the versions of *Masekhet Soferim* that do include Ecclesiastes do not mention it being read at any particular time of year.

stating the rule that one must read *Megillat Esther* on both Purim eve and day, a ruling also found in Megilla 4a. The first mishna in Tractate Megilla discusses additional days when Esther can be read, and Megilla 1b brings the teaching of R. Natan that "the entire month is fit for reading the Megilla." This demonstrates that there is the possibility of a certain amount of leeway regarding when a Megilla is read relative to the holiday it is associated with, something also seen in the first mishna of Tractate Megilla, where the 11th, 12th, 13th, 14,th and 15th of Adar are all presented as viable days for the reading of *Megillat Esther*. The reading on the Saturday nights preceding Purim seems not to have been led by a *shaliaḥ tzibbur*, since it is described as the congregation reading together.[38] It would seem that this is also the way *Masekhet Soferim* understood that Song of Songs and Ruth were read.

We see that Megillot were read in parts on the evenings after Shabbat or a holiday.[39] That the additional holiday day in the Diaspora figures so prominently in this custom suggests that it may not have been practiced in Israel at all.[40] However, *Masekhet Soferim* has long been considered a work of Palestinian provenance,[41] and this chapter in particular is thought to have been greatly influenced by the Talmud Yerushalmi,[42] so this may be the Diaspora version of an Israeli custom to read the Megillot.

Regarding the reading of Lamentations, *Masekhet Soferim* (18:4) states: "Some read the Book of Lamentations in the evening, and some

38 Yitzhak Landa, *Masekhet Soferim – Mikra Soferim* (Suwalki, Poland, 1862), 29a, note 11.

39 Although *Soferim* explicitly discusses reading on Saturday night after Shabbat (מוצאי שבת), the other readings are described as taking place on "the night of the holiday" (לילי יום טוב), which for the second day of the holiday would seem to indicate once the holiday is over. However, sometimes the usage of the term ליל can indicate the late afternoon right before actual nightfall, as in the mishna in Nedarim 63b, according to the understanding of Rabbeinu Nissim there, *ad shaa*. However, others interpret this mishna differently; see Rashash.

40 Wasserstein, *Masekhet Soferim*, 132.

41 Debra Reed Blank, "It's Time to Take Another Look at 'Our Little Sister' *Soferim*: A Bibliographical Essay," *The Jewish Quarterly Review* 90, no. 1/2, 2, 4.

42 M. Higger, *Masekhet Soferim* (New York, 1937), 23, section 3:8.

delay reading it until the morning after the Torah reading."[43] This section is understood as reflecting the custom in Israel,[44] which is also seen in Y. Shabbat 16:1, where we find rabbis studying Lamentations on the eve of Tisha BeAv, planning to finish it on Tisha BeAv itself. This shows that there was some flexibility regarding when the reading took place, something noted in *Masekhet Soferim* regarding Song of Songs and Ruth as well. This flexibility is reflected in later practices regarding the Megillot, as we will see.

The nighttime reading of Lamentations became the dominant custom. It is already indicated in Lamentations Rabba (*petiḥta* 17), where it is mentioned that people go from eating and drinking at a meal just before the eve of Tisha BeAv to reading Lamentations.[45] Many early works, such as *Maḥzor Vitry*[46] and *Hagahot Meimoniot*,[47] mention the reading of Lamentations only at night. While the *Tur* (*Oraḥ Ḥayim* 559) brings both the custom to read Lamentations at night, as well as the approach of *Masekhet Soferim* that some read Lamentations in the morning, it is clear that he presents the night reading as the standard approach.[48] Based on the *Tur*, Rabbi Isaiah Horowitz in *Shenei Luḥot HaBrit* states that although Lamentations is read publicly only at night, it is appropriate for God-fearing individuals to read Lamentations again in the daytime.[49] This idea is presented in the *Mishna Berura* (559:2).

*Maḥzor Vitry* has the readings of Song of Songs, Ruth, and Ecclesiastes all taking place during the daytime of the holiday. The nighttime readings and Saturday night readings before the holiday found in *Masekhet Soferim* were no longer customary in the time of *Maḥzor Vitry*. For example, *Maḥzor Vitry* states that Song of Songs is

43 In some editions 18:5.

44 Higger, *Masekhet Soferim*, 27.

45 See the commentary of David Luria on this midrash.

46 Simon Hurwitz, ed., *Maḥzor Vitry* (Nuremberg: J. Bulka, 1923), 224.

47 Both in *Hilkhot Taanit*, 5:2 and in the section "*Minhagei Tisha BeAv*" at the end of *Hilkhot Taanit* chapter 5, *Hagahot Meimoniot* mentions *Masekhet Soferim* regarding the custom to read Lamentations on Tisha BeAv in general, and to do so with a blessing, but a daytime reading is not mentioned.

48 See *Beit Yosef* (*Oraḥ Ḥayim* 559), *aval*.

49 Isaiah Horowitz, *Shenei Luḥot HaBrit*, vol. 2 (Jerusalem: Machon Shaarei Ziv, 1993), *Masekhet Taanit, ner mitzva siman* 1, 89.

read before the Torah reading on the morning of Shabbat Ḥol HaMoed, and if there is no Shabbat Ḥol HaMoed, it is read on the last day of Passover.[50]

While the night readings are no longer common, Rabbi Yitzhak Landa notes that his community's custom in nineteenth-century Poland was that in addition to the daytime readings, Song of Songs was read on the first two nights of Passover, and Ruth was read on the first night of Shavuot.[51]

Similarly, while the divided readings are no longer common, they remained customary in some communities, mostly Sephardic. The nineteenth-century prayer book *Moadei Hashem*, subtitled "according to the custom of the holy Sephardic community," writes that Song of Songs is read before Minḥa, half on the seventh day of Passover and half on the eighth.[52] Ruth is also read at Minḥa, divided over the two days of Shavuot.[53] The second part of Ruth begins with Ruth 3:8, "In the middle of the night, the man gave a start and pulled back – there was a woman lying at his feet!" This represents a turning point in the story.[54] A Romanian prayer book gives two options for where the first part of Ruth ends, either with Ruth 2:4 or 3:12, which could also be considered turning points in the story.[55] A divided reading of Song of Songs over the seventh and eighth days of Passover is also found among the Jews of Libya[56] and Georgia.[57]

Some communities divided up the Megillot into even smaller sections. The Romanian community read Song of Songs and Ecclesiastes in four parts, one part after Minḥa on the first two and last two days

---

50 Hurwitz, *Maḥzor Vitry*, 304.

51 Yitzhak Landa, *Masekhet Soferim – Mikra Soferim* (Suwalki, Poland, 1862), 29b, notes 12 and 13.

52 *Moadei Hashem* (Livorno, 1872), 175a.

53 Ibid., 190a.

54 Ibid., 202b.

55 *Siddur Tefillot HaShana LeMinhag Kehillot Romania* (Venice, 1523), 182b, 189b.

56 Frija Zuartz, "Customs of the Jews of Libya," 382, 11:13 in Asher Waserteil, ed., *Yalkut Minhagim* (Jerusalem, 1996).

57 Asher Chadad, "Customs of the Jews of Georgia," in Waserteil, *Yalkut Minhagim*, 256, 9:18.

of the holiday.[58] A similar division for Song of Songs is recorded as a Bukharian custom.[59]

*Siddur Knesset HaGedola* describes a Yemenite custom of reading the Megillot before Minḥa and divided into parts. The first four chapters of Song of Songs were read on the seventh day of Passover, and the rest on the eighth. In Israel, since there is no eighth day, the reading took place over Shabbat Ḥol HaMoed and the seventh day, or if there was no Shabbat Ḥol HaMoed, then on the first and seventh days of Passover. Similarly, Ecclesiastes was read in two parts over Shemini Atzeret and Simḥat Torah,[60] and in Israel in three parts over the first day of Sukkot, Shabbat Ḥol HaMoed, and Shemini Atzeret. Ruth was also read over the two days of Shavuot, ending with Ruth 2:12 on the first day and completing the rest on the second day. Since there is no option to divide Ruth in Israel, it was all read at one time.[61] The original custom in Yemen was clearly to always have a divided reading of the Megillot, similar to that described in *Masekhet Soferim*.

While many Sephardic communities no longer followed the divided reading of the Megillot upon their relocation in Israel,[62] among some communities this custom was preserved as much as possible even in Israel. Similarly, while the nighttime readings were no longer customary, an aspect of the original custom was perpetuated by having the readings take place not in the morning, but in the afternoon, connected to Minḥa.[63]

### THE ORIGIN OF THE CUSTOM

The original custom to read these Megillot at night seems to be connected to the ruling in the Mishna (Shabbat 115a) that books from

58 *Siddur Tefillot HaShana LeMinhag Kehillot Romania*, 130a, 404a.

59 Giora Pozilov, "Customs of the Jews of Buchara," 216, 11:43 in Waserteil, *Yalkut Minhagim*.

60 Alternatively, half on Shabbat Ḥol HaMoed and half on Simḥat Torah. Waserteil, *Yalkut Minhagim*, Shimon Gridi, "Customs of the Jews of Yemen," 545, 4:7.

61 Yosef Tzubiri, *Siddur Knesset HaGedola*, vol. 2 (Tel Aviv, 1976), 327.

62 Asher Chadad, "Customs of the Jews of Georgia," in Waserteil, *Yalkut Minhagim*, 256, 9:18.

63 The custom in Amsterdam is reported to have shifted around World War II from daytime readings of the Megillot to Minḥa time. Yehuda Berelman, *Minhagei Amsterdam* (Jerusalem: Machon Yerushalayim, 2002), 44, chapter 3, 7:7.

Ketuvim (the Writings) were not read on Shabbat "because of neglect of the *beit midrash*." The term *beit midrash* here refers to the time when rabbis would give a public lecture (*pirka*) on Shabbat. Rashi explains that this lecture was delivered on Shabbat before the Musaf service, after which the congregation would come to the synagogue for Musaf.[64] This *shiur* functioned to provide halakhic instruction to working people who did not have time to study during the week. It is the forerunner of the sermon that today takes place at this point in the service.[65] Rashi, in the name of his teacher, Rabbi Yitzhak HaLevi, explains that "Ketuvim draw the heart" and their study would cause people not to attend the public lecture, so the study of Ketuvim was banned during that time.[66] The Talmud in Shabbat 116b records the custom in Nehardea: "Nehardea was Shmuel's town, and in Nehardea they *paskei sidra* with Ketuvim at Minḥa on Shabbat." The Talmud explains that this is in keeping with Shmuel's view that Ketuvim may be studied as long as it was "not the time of the *beit midrash*."[67] By the time of the Shabbat meal,[68] and certainly by the time of Minḥa, this lecture was over,[69] so the *paskei sidra* did not interfere with the lecture.

What does *paskei sidra* mean? Rabbeinu Tam explains that it refers to a practice to read a *haftara* from Ketuvim at Minḥa on Shabbat.[70] *Tosafot* state that "there are places where it is customary to do

64 Rashi, Berakhot 28b, *lo*.

65 See Leopold Zunz, *HaDerashot BeYisrael* (Hebrew translation of *Die Gottesdienstliche Vorträge der Juden Historisch Entwickelt*) (Jerusalem: Bialik Institute, 1974), 170–73.

66 Rashi, Shabbat 115a, *bein she'ein*, in the name of Rabbeinu Yitzhak HaLevi.

67 Yosef Ingbar, *Minḥat Yosef* (Lakewood, NJ, 2009), 41, uses the Shabbat morning ban on studying Ketuvim to explain why the *Birkat HaMazon* on weekdays uses the form *magdil*, quoting from Ps. 18:51, while on Shabbat and holidays the form *migdol* is used from the parallel verse, II Sam. 22:51. This is to hint to the ban on Ketuvim on Shabbat and holidays during the time of the *beit midrash* lecture.

68 Rashi, Shabbat 116b, *bazman shelo*. See Zunz, *HaDerashot BeYisrael*, 167, notes 92, 94.

69 Leading to the ruling that Ketuvim may be read from Minḥa and on, Y. Shabbat 16:1, *Masekhet Soferim* 15:3. Philo reports that these lessons lasted "till about the late afternoon"; see Folker Siegert, "The Sermon as an Invention of Hellenistic Judaism," in Alexander Deeg, Walter Homolka, and Heinz-Gunther Schottler, eds., *Preaching in Judaism and Christianity* (Berlin: Walter de Gruyter, 2008), 35; Zunz, *HaDerashot BeYisrael*, 164–66, 170–71.

70 *Tosafot*, Shabbat 24a, *she'ilmalei*; Megilla 21a, *ve'ein maftirin*.

this,"[71] indicating that the custom was still practiced in certain places even in the time of the *Tosafot*.[72] However, the term *pasek sidra* in other instances in the Talmud always refers to study rather than a liturgical reading, usually in connection with the study of Ketuvim in particular.[73] For example, in Bava Batra 164b we read that R. Shimon was *pasek sidra* in Psalms, with no connection to a *haftara*, or even Shabbat. Rabbeinu Gershom explains that R. Shimon was learning one of the five sections of the book of Psalms. In Shabbat 152a it says that R. Kahana was *pasek sidra* in Ecclesiastes, and in Avoda Zara 19a it states that after being *paskei sidra* and completing the book they were studying, Levi asked that Proverbs be brought in for study while R. Shimon asked for Psalms. Similarly, in Yoma 77a, Rav is described as *pasek sidra*, which Rashi explains as studying a section of Tanakh. In Shabbat 116b Rashi explains that it was customary to read a portion of Ketuvim in the *beit midrash*.[74] Rabbi Isaiah di Trani (Rid) therefore explains, counter to Rabbeinu Tam, that this *paskei sidra* was a study session devoted to Ketuvim rather than a *haftara* reading.[75]

From the references above it would seem that the Talmud in Shabbat 116b shows that, at least in Nehardea, there was some kind of communal study of Ketuvim that took place in such a way that the regular *beit midrash* was unaffected.[76] It may have been formalized as a

71 *Tosafot*, Megilla 21a, *ve'ein maftirin*.

72 The *Tosafot* printed in Megilla are understood to be those of Yehudah of Paris (Sir Leon), (1166–1224). See Ephraim Urbach, *The Tosaphists: Their History, Writings and Methods* (Jerusalem: Bialik Institute, 1954), 617. See also Ismar Elbogen, *Jewish Liturgy: A Comprehensive History* (Philadelphia: Jewish Publication Society, 1993), 150, note 8, where based on Yehuda b. Barzilai, *Sefer HaIttim* (Cracow: Ḥevrat Mekitzei Nirdamim, 1903), 289, he discusses whether the custom of *paskei sidra* in Ketuvim still existed in the time of the *Geonim* and early *Rishonim*.

73 See Samuel Mirsky, "Mekorot HaHalakha BeMidrashim," *Talpioth*, Nisan 5707 (1947), 122, note 20; Marc Hirshman, *The Stabilization of Rabbinic Culture, 100 CE–350 CE* (Oxford: Oxford University Press, 2009), 72.

74 Rashi, Shabbat 116b, *paskei*.

75 Shlomo Werthheimer, ed., *Sefer HaMakhria* (Jerusalem: Ktav Yad VeSefer, 1998), item 31, 162.

76 See Zvi Gombo, *Or Zvi – Shabbat*, vol. 2 (Bnei Brak, 2000), 141, where it is suggested that the initial reading of a selection from Ketuvim was followed by individual study.

*haftara*, but it was most likely a *derasha* and study session.[77] As Eliezer Levi concludes, "There can be no doubt that a regular reading of the Hagiographa is what is meant."[78] It has been suggested that this is the origin of the custom to recite certain psalms or study *Pirkei Avot* on Shabbat afternoons at Minḥa time,[79] such as the custom to read Psalm 92 aloud after the Shabbat Minḥa Torah reading.[80] The custom of saying Psalm 111 after the Shabbat Minḥa Torah reading was also explained as a remnant of the custom to have a *haftara* from the Ketuvim at that point in the service. It is for this reason that that particular chapter was chosen, as it contains ten verses, the minimum for a *haftara* reading.[81] Note that Psalm 112, the other psalm that is traditionally read after the Torah reading on Shabbat Minḥa, is also ten verses long, and so may also be a vestige of the Ketuvim *haftara*.[82]

This practice is reflected in the statement in *Masekhet Soferim* (14:4) that "one who reads the Ketuvim must say, 'Blessed are You... who commanded us to read holy writings' (*bekitvei hakodesh*)." The simple understanding of this ruling is that it is referring to the communal reading of a selection from Ketuvim on Shabbat afternoons.[83] While

77 Eliezer Levi, *Yesodot HaTefilla* (Tel Aviv: Avraham Zioni, 1958), 322.

78 Ismar Elbogen, *Jewish Liturgy: A Comprehensive History* (Philadelphia: Jewish Publication Society, 1993), 150.

79 Eliezer Dinner, *Zikhron Avraham Moshe* (Jerusalem, 1945), 64, on Megilla 21a; Shlomo Elkayam, "*Maḥzor* Fez as a Source for Ancient Prayer Customs," *Hemdaat* 6, 17–18 [Hebrew].

80 Yosef Tzubiri, *Siddur Knesset HaGedola*, vol. 1 (Tel Aviv, 1976), 523.

81 A ten-verse *haftara* is mentioned in Megilla 23b. The *haftara* for *Ki Tetzeh* is ten verses long. Yisrael Chaim Friedman, *Likkutei Mahariḥ*, vol. 2 (Sighet, 1900), 73b–74a. See also Reuven Margaliot, *Nitzotzei Or* (Jerusalem: Mossad HaRav Kook, 2002), 40, who gives this basic explanation and adds a kabbalistic explanation as well.

82 Shmuel Weingarten, "Reishitan shel HaHaftarot," *Sinai* 83 (1978), 126.

83 Yitzhak Landa, *Masekhet Soferim – Mikra Soferim* (Suwalki, Poland, 1862), 27a; Shmuel Wasserstein, *Masekhet Soferim* (Jerusalem, 2001), 121. Mordekhai (Megilla, *siman* 783) explains that this blessing was recited when reading one of the Megillot written as part of the Ketuvim rather than on its own scroll, but this is difficult as there is no example of two different blessings recited over the same thing. Furthermore, it appears that this interpretation is based on a textual variant of this part of *Masekhet Soferim*. See Yehuda Heschel Levenberg, "Regarding Blessings over Reading the Megilla and Reading the Writings," *Oraita*, vol. 11, Adar 5751 (1991), 73, 74 [Hebrew].

the Torah was read on Shabbat, Mondays, and Thursdays, and selections from the Prophets were read as the *haftara* on Shabbat and holidays, there was no mechanism to familiarize people with the Ketuvim. This was remedied by the institution of the study of Ketuvim on Shabbat afternoons,[84] a practice still found in some Sephardic communities,[85] as well as the North African custom to recite a different psalm each week at the conclusion of Shabbat Minḥa, usually chosen with a connection to the week's Torah reading.[86]

An example of a system for studying Ketuvim used by Ashkenazic communities in Germany was found in a manuscript from 1326. There we read that Psalms, Proverbs, Job, Daniel, and Ezra-Nehemiah were studied on Shabbat before Minḥa over the course of the weeks between Shavuot and Rosh HaShana. It is significant that it is prefaced by an introductory remark: "This is the order of our custom to read the entire Ketuvim and *Avot* a little before Minḥa, and the five Megillot over the festivals,"[87] which puts the Megillot in the general context of the cycle of reading Ketuvim.

The reading of Proverbs, Job, and Daniel in the late afternoon on Shabbat during the summer months is found in many Sephardic communities.[88] Moroccan communities based their study on the arrangement

84 Shlomo Rapoport, *Erekh Millin*, vol. 1 (Prague, 1852), 174, paragraph 10; Levenberg, "Regarding Blessings over Reading the Megilla and Reading the Writings," 75.

85 Ezra Zion Melamed, *Pirkei Minhag VeHalakha* (Jerusalem: Kiryat Sefer, 1970), 84.

86 Amram Aburabia, *Netivei Am* (Petach Tikvah, 2006), 192, *siman* 284:1; David Ovadia, *Nahagu HaAm* (Jerusalem: Machon Yismach Lev, 2000), 37, *siman* 29. There he lists the customary psalms for every week as recited by the community of Sefrou, Morrocco. Reciting specific psalms on particular Shabbatot is an ancient custom; see Jacob Mann, *The Bible as Read and Preached in the Old Synagogue* (Hoboken, NJ: Ktav, 1971), 15.

87 A. Kirsch, "Hagiographen Lection am Sabbatnachmittag Ein Schwaebischer (altzuercher) Minhag," MGWJ (Monatsschrift fuer Geschichte und Wissenschaft des Judentums) 12 (December, 1880), 543–48. This is discussed in Yissachar Jacobson, *Ḥazon HaMikra* (Tel Aviv: Sinai, 1989), 33.

88 See the two articles on this subject by Tovia Preschel in the newspaper *HaDoar*. An article from 1 Sivan 5726 deals with the custom to learn Proverbs on Shabbat afternoons, and an article from 24 Sivan 5737 discusses the custom to learn Job and Daniel on Shabbat afternoons. Reprinted in the second volume of his collected writings, *Maamarei Tuvia* (Jerusalem: Mossad HaRav Kook, 2017).

found in the book *Arbaa Gevi'im*, where Proverbs, Job, and Daniel are divided into sections, called *hafsakot*, and read before Shabbat Minḥa from Passover to the beginning of Elul,[89] using the cantillation of the Megillot.[90] There also is an almost identical Algerian custom to read these books after Shabbat Minḥa. What is particularly interesting about the Algerian custom is that Lamentations is also included in the cycle, between Job and Daniel, read in two parts on the two Shabbatot before Tisha BeAv,[91] recalling the divided reading of Megillot in *Masekhet Soferim*.

The midrash *Agadat Bereshit* (ca. tenth century) contains material for the Torah reading and *haftara* for every Shabbat as well as a selection from Ketuvim,[92] and the proem verses for the aggadic midrashim on the Torah were almost all taken from Ketuvim, all evidence that study of Ketuvim took place regularly.[93] It may be that these aggadic *derashot* were given on Shabbat afternoons, while the halakhic *derashot*, the *pirka*, took place earlier in the day, before Musaf. The fact that these midrashim originated in Israel suggests that in Nehardea they heard about and followed an Israeli custom of studying Ketuvim on Shabbat afternoons.[94]

89 *Arbaa Gevi'im* (Livorno, 1935); Proverbs begins there on page 157. See Shlomo Elkayam, "*Maḥzor* Fez as a Source for Ancient Prayer Customs," *Hemdaat* 6, 19, note 36 [Hebrew].

90 David Ovadia, *Nahagu HaAm* (Jerusalem: Machon Yismach Lev, 2000), 37, *siman* 29.

91 Yaakov Partosh, "The Order of Prayers According to the Custom of the Jews of Algeria," *Tagim* 1 (1968), 71–72 [Hebrew].

92 Ismar Elbogen, *Jewish Liturgy: A Comprehensive History* (Philadelphia: Jewish Publication Society, 1993), 151.

93 Shlomo Rapoport, *Erekh Millin*, vol. 1 (Prague, 1852), 171, paragraph 7. See Shmuel Weingarten, "Reishitan shel HaHaftarot," *Sinai* 83 (1978), 128, where he notes that the opening verses of sections 4–6 of Genesis Rabba are taken from Psalm 104, *Barkhi Nafshi*, customarily recited after the Shabbat Minḥa from Sukkot to Passover. See also Gunter Stemberger, "The *Derashah* in Rabbinic Times," in Alexander Deeg, Walter Homolka, and Heinz-Gunther Schottler, eds., *Preaching in Judaism and Christianity* (Berlin: Walter de Gruyter, 2008), 21.

94 Rapoport, *Erekh Millin*, vol. 1, 174, paragraph 10. There he notes that Nehardea had a particular connection to the community in Israel.

A remnant of the afternoon sermon relating to Ketuvim may be seen in the custom of the Jews of Georgia, whose rabbi would give a sermon relating to the theme of Song of Songs before Minḥa on the last days of Passover when it was read.[95]

The idea of studying Ketuvim in the late afternoon and evenings can shed light on the mishna in Yoma 1:6, where we learn that in order to help the high priest stay up on Yom Kippur night, the books of Job, Ezra, Chronicles, and Daniel would be read to him. It is not a coincidence that these are all from the Ketuvim, which was usually read late in the day.

The ancient practice of evening study of Ketuvim may even be reflected in the reading of *Megillat Esther*. The Ri explains that although a *Sheheḥeyanu* blessing is said for the Purim evening Megilla reading, another *Sheheḥeyanu* must be said for the daytime reading, because that reading is the "main expression of publicizing the miracle,"[96] implying that only the daytime reading was recognizable as something out of the ordinary. Rav Joseph B. Soloveitchik comments that the nighttime reading functions only to prepare people for the daytime reading, allowing them to understand it better after having reviewed it the night before.[97] Thus the evening reading can be viewed as part of the regular study of Ketuvim, while the daytime Purim reading was the truly unique reading, demonstrating that it was a special obligatory reading.

The schedule for reading Megillot described in *Masekhet Soferim* can now be seen as a mechanism for providing a framework for studying them. All study takes place "after hours," such as when the regular *beit midrash* study was over, Saturday night, festival nights, and, in the case of Lamentations, the day of Tisha BeAv, when regular Torah study was prohibited.[98] The custom of reading Megillot at night seems to be an outgrowth of the convention to read Ketuvim at times that did not conflict with the *beit midrash*. Note that Rashi gives "Midrash of Song of Songs and Midrash of Ecclesiastes" as examples of what was studied

95 Asher Chadad, "Customs of the Jews of Georgia," in Asher Waserteil, ed., *Yalkut Minhagim* (Jerusalem, 1996), 256, 9:18.

96 *Tosafot*, Megilla 4a, *ḥayav*.

97 Michel Zalman Sirkin, *Hararei Kedem*, vol. 1 (Jerusalem, 2000), *siman* 203, 335.

98 Taanit 30a.

on Shabbat afternoons,[99] confirming that the time for studying Ketuvim in general, and Megillot in particular, was the afternoon.[100]

The verse from Ecclesiastes quoted in *Maḥzor Vitry* to explain why it is read on Ḥol HaMoed Sukkot, "Distribute portions to seven or even to eight" (11:2), would seem to indicate that all seven days of Sukkot are equally valid for reading Ecclesiastes, yet the preferred custom noted there was to read it on Shabbat Ḥol HaMoed.[101] It may be that the Ashkenazic custom to read Song of Songs and Ecclesiastes on Shabbat Ḥol HaMoed of Passover and Sukkot when possible,[102] rather than on the last days of the festivals, is reflective of the same early custom to study Ketuvim at some point on Shabbat.

Customs varied as to how the Megillot were read, either by individuals on their own or by a *shaliaḥ tzibbur*. Regarding Lamentations, we find in the *Kol Bo* that there were various customs: in some places each individual read it on their own, and in other places the *shaliaḥ tzibbur* read it aloud while everyone else followed along silently. The *Kol Bo* notes that in his community the custom was for each person to read it on their own.[103] The Maharil quotes different customs for different Megillot, as he states regarding Lamentations: "And he recites '*al mikra Megilla*' before beginning Lamentations,"[104] but regarding Ruth and Song of Songs, the Maharil states: "Each person recites the blessing '*al*

99 Rashi, Shabbat 116b, *shonin*.

100 R. Meir gave a lesson involving Ecclesiastes and Job on Shabbat in Y. Ḥagiga 2:1, though it is not indicated whether this took place in the afternoon. See the discussion of this case in Gunter Stemberger, "The *Derashah* in Rabbinic Times," 14, in Alexander Deeg, Walter Homolka, and Heinz-Gunther Schottler, eds., *Preaching in Judaism and Christianity* (Berlin: Walter de Gruyter, 2008).

101 Hayim Palagi (*Yafeh Lalev* [Izmir, 1876], *Oraḥ Ḥayim* 663:2) explains that "portions to seven" is a reference to Shabbat.

102 Israel Elfenbein, ed., *Sefer Minhagim d-bei Rabbi Meir ben Barukh m-Rothenburg* (New York: Jewish Theological Seminary of America, 1938), 28; Simon Hurwitz, ed., *Maḥzor Vitry* (Nuremberg: J. Bulka, 1923), 304, 440, 446.

103 *Kol Bo* (Jerusalem: Even Yisroel, 1997), 249, *siman* 62.

104 Shlomo Spitzer, *Sefer Maharil* (Jerusalem: Machon Yerushalayim, 1989), 251.

*mikra Megilla*' before it,"[105] indicating that these Megillot were read by individuals on their own.[106]

Rabbi Moshe Isserles discusses this matter at length in a responsum regarding whether to recite blessings over reading these Megillot. He explains that only Lamentations was read by an individual for the congregation, and the others were not read in this manner,[107] which follows the description of the Maharil. He concludes that therefore only Lamentations is recited with a blessing, because the others are recited individually. Rabbi Isserles addresses the discrepancy with what it says in *Masekhet Soferim* and explains that there they are all recited with blessings, either because at the time of writing the custom was for one person to read aloud for the whole congregation, or because they were read in the context of the custom of reading Ketuvim as a *haftara* at Minḥa on Shabbat. Since the previous chapter in *Masekhet Soferim* deals with *ḥaftarot*, Rabbi Isserles suggests that this chapter dealing with the Megillot is a continuation of the general customs of *haftarot*.[108] This approach, highlighted by Rabbi Isserles, confirms that originally the reading of the Megillot was a variation on the practice of the afternoon reading of Ketuvim.

We have seen that reading the Megillot began as part of a general system of learning Ketuvim, and at first this was done in the late afternoon or evening. However, as this custom waned in popularity, in many Ashkenazic communities reading the Megillot was shifted to a time of day that seemed more appropriate, namely during the morning service, when the reading of both the Torah and *haftara* took place. Some communities, however, did retain the original custom of reading the Megillot when the Ketuvim were previously studied. For example, the custom of

105 Ibid., 147, 161.

106 Shlomo Zevin, *HaMoadim BeHalakha* (Jerusalem: Yad HaRav Herzog, 1980), 391. However, regarding Ecclesiastes this language is not used; rather, it says, "On it is recited the blessing *al mikra Megilla*," but it could be because there the main idea being stressed is that a blessing is said over Ecclesiastes at all, as there were varying opinions on this matter; see *Sefer Maharil*, 380, and notes 9 and 10 there.

107 Asher Siev, ed., *Shut Rema* (Jerusalem, 1970), number 35, 195.

108 Asher Siev, ed., *Shut Rema* (Jerusalem, 1970), number 35, 197.

Italian,[109] Yemenite, and other communities was to read Song of Songs after Minḥa on the seventh day of Passover;[110] the Algerian custom was to read Song of Songs after the Minḥa *Amida* on the last day of Passover[111] and the entire Book of Ruth after the Minḥa *Amida* on the second day of Shavuot;[112] and the custom of the Jews of Afghanistan was to read Ruth in the synagogue right before Minḥa.[113] The Tunisian custom was for each family to read Ruth together after the meal on Shavuot, and an additional reading took place in the synagogue for those who did not do so at home.[114] Note that Ruth was read specifically after the meal, which is when the *beit midrash* was no longer in session according to Rashi. The original evening readings may also be reflected in the custom to read Song of Songs at night after the Passover Seder and on Friday afternoons, either right before or right after Minḥa.[115]

The divided and afternoon readings of the Megillot were preserved mainly by Sephardic communities, who maintained the cycle of Ketuvim study more than Ashkenazim. Among the Ashkenazic communities, where the Ketuvim cycle was largely forgotten, reading the Megillot was transformed into a daytime reading of the whole Megilla, using the daytime reading of Esther as a model. However, even where the Megillot are read in the daytime, they are read before the regular Torah reading.[116] At first glance this is unusual, since the general rule is that that which is more common is done first. Indeed, *Megillat Esther* is read on Purim day after the Torah reading, but this is not the case for

109 *Maḥzor Kol HaShana Kefi Minhag Kehillat Kodesh Italiani*, vol. 1 (Livorno, 1856), 131a.

110 Amos Chacham, *Daat Mikra: Shir HaShirim* (Jerusalem: Mossad HaRav Kook, 1990), 15.

111 Eliyahu Gig, *Zeh HaShulḥan*, vol. 2 (Algiers, 1889), 129, *siman* 52.

112 Ibid., 136, *siman* 58:7.

113 Giora Pozilov, "Customs of the Jews of Afghanistan," in Asher Waserteil, ed., *Yalkut Minhagim* (Jerusalem, 1996), 46, 19:13.

114 Mordechai Satbon and Avraham Hatel, "Customs of the Jews of Tunisia," in Asher Waserteil, ed., *Yalkut Minhagim* (Jerusalem, 1996), 515, 14:3.

115 See Amos Chacham, *Daat Mikra: Shir HaShirim* (Jerusalem: Mossad HaRav Kook, 1990), 15.

116 Simon Hurwitz, ed., *Maḥzor Vitry* (Nuremberg: J. Bulka, 1923), 440, 446; S. Buber, ed., *Siddur Rashi* (Berlin: Ḥevrat Mekitzei Nirdamim, 1910), 104, 147.

the other Megillot. Rabbi Sternbuch explains that this distinction is because reading the other Megillot is only a custom; they are read earlier so that whoever comes late will at least hear the Torah reading, which is obligatory.[117] Based on what we have said, we can also explain that placing a reading from Ketuvim after the Torah reading would put it right where the *pirka* would take place, something that the Talmud specifically warned against. *Megillat Esther* is read then in order to demonstrate its special status, and that it in fact overrides Torah study (Megilla 3a).[118]

No explanation is provided in *Masekhet Soferim* as to why these particular books should be read on these particular occasions, although reading Lamentations on Tisha BeAv seems self-evident. The connections drawn between Ruth, Song of Songs, and Ecclesiastes and Shavuot, Passover, and Sukkot, respectively, are many and varied, often involving thematic connections and textual allusions. These kinds of connections are also found in explanations tying a specific *haftara* to a particular Torah reading,[119] which is to be expected, since as we saw, reading the Megillot was itself a variation of the general custom to read from the Ketuvim over the course of the year in a way that paralleled the *haftara* from the Prophets.

It may well be that *Masekhet Soferim* made no inherent connection between each Megilla and the holiday on which it was read, and that it was merely a coincidence that they reached that stage as part of the Ketuvim learning cycle. It is also possible that the Megillot were the Ketuvim portion associated with the Torah reading on these occasions, rather than with the holiday itself. This being the case, Song of Songs could have been the Ketuvim reading connected to the Torah reading of the last day of Passover, which includes the Song of the Sea. Similarly,

117 Rabbi Moshe Sternbuch, *Teshuvot VeHanhagot*, vol. 1 (Jerusalem, 1992), 226, *siman* 323.

118 There is a classic question noted by many *Aḥaronim* regarding the rule stated in Megilla 3a that Torah study is canceled in order to read Esther, since Esther itself is part of the Bible and should be considered Torah study. The simple explanation is that generally the study of Ketuvim specifically was set aside at the time of public lectures, and it is this public study that was canceled in order to read Esther.

119 See the explanations for the *haftarot* given in Yissachar Jacobson, *Ḥazon HaMikra* (Tel Aviv: Sinai, 1989).

Ruth parallels verses and themes found in the Torah readings right before and right after Shavuot.[120] There are a number of examples of these.[121] This is particularly significant in light of the custom reported in *Masekhet Soferim* that part of Ruth was read the Saturday night before Shavuot.

## ADDENDUM: THE SPECIAL CASE OF ECCLESIASTES

*Maḥzor Vitry* and *Siddur Rashi* are the earliest sources for the custom of reading Ecclesiastes on Sukkot. They both state that it is ideally read on Shabbat Ḥol HaMoed of Sukkot, and if that is not possible, for example in a year when there is no Shabbat Ḥol HaMoed, it is read on Shemini Atzeret.[122]

Why was Ecclesiastes not mentioned in *Masekhet Soferim*? The most obvious reason is that Ecclesiastes may have been viewed as less than suitable for communal study. Mishna Eduyot 5:3 records that Beit Hillel held that the scroll of Ecclesiastes can render a person's hands impure, like all other biblical books, but Beit Shammai did not agree. This indicates that it was not clear that Ecclesiastes had the same level of sanctity as the other parts of Tanakh. Similarly, the Talmud in Shabbat 30b tells us that "R. Yehuda b. R. Shmuel b. Shilat said in the name of Rav: The Sages wished to hide Ecclesiastes because its words are self-contradictory," but they did not, "because its beginning is religious teaching and its end is religious teaching." Explanations are given to resolve what appeared to be contradictions within Ecclesiastes. Although Ecclesiastes

120 One of the oldest elements in the fixing of the Torah portion according to Megilla 31b is completing *Beḥukkotai* before Shavuot, which then became completing *Parashat Bemidbar* before Shavuot as well; see *Tosafot* there, *Moshe*.

121 For instance, in *Parashat Bemidbar*: Num. 3:4 and Ruth 1:5 (death of brothers), Num. 4:18, and Ruth 4:10 (cutting off); in *Parashat Naso*: Num. 5:8 and Ruth 3:12 (a redeemer), Num. 6:24 and Ruth 2:4 ("May God bless you"), Num. 6:27 and Ruth 4:14 (a name in Israel); and in *Parashat Behaalotekha*: Numbers 10: 29–30, where Yitro returns home "to my land and to my family," a reverse parallel of Ruth. See an elaboration of all these in Chaim Chamiel, "Megillat Rut BeAtzeret," *Turei Yeshurun* 31 (May 1972), 8–9.

122 The sources for reading Ecclesiastes on Shabbat Ḥol HaMoed of Sukkot are: Hurwitz, *Maḥzor Vitry*, 440; S. Buber, ed., *Siddur Rashi* (Berlin: Ḥevrat Mekitzei Nirdamim, 1910), 104, *siman* 222.The sources for reading Ecclesiastes on Shemini Atzeret are: Hurwitz, *Maḥzor Vitry*, 446; Buber, *Siddur Rashi*, 147, *siman* 307.

was ultimately accepted as a holy book worthy of inclusion in Tanakh, perhaps its public study was downplayed because some verses seem to present contradictions and ideas not in accordance with standard religious thinking. This idea is given credence by Rabbi Shalom of Neustadt, teacher of the Maharil. He stated that while blessings are recited over the other Megillot, it is customary not to recite a blessing over Ecclesiastes, because "it does not contain matters of holiness."[123] Similarly, Rabbi Israel Bruna (Mahari Bruna) states that although the Rabbis ultimately decided not to hide Ecclesiastes, there was never a command to read it, since it was not written with the holy spirit of *ruaḥ hakodesh,* so no blessing is recited over reading it.[124]

The unique status of Ecclesiastes may also be seen in the fact that most Sephardic communities did not have a custom to read Ecclesiastes publicly at all.[125] As we have seen, the Sephardic practice more closely adhered to the original custom as recorded in *Masekhet Soferim,* with divided readings taking place later in the day, but Ecclesiastes was not included.

There may be hints to the controversial nature of Ecclesiastes even in places where it was read. *Sefer HaManhig* states that it was customary in France to read Ecclesiastes in the synagogue on Shemini Atzeret before reading the Torah portion, while in Provence it would be read individually in the sukka. He advises that it is better to read it publicly in the synagogue since many people are not proficient enough to read

---

123 Shlomo Spitzer, ed., *Hilkhot UMinhagei Rabbeinu Shalom MeNeustadt* (Jerusalem: Machon Yerushalayim, 1997), 7, no. 121.

124 *Shut Mahari Bruna* (Jerusalem, 1973), 54, *siman* 66. Mordekhai Jaffe (*Levush HaḤur* [Bardichev, 1818], *siman* 663:2) also brings this as a reason a blessing is not recited over Ecclesiastes, although he wonders about this answer since most opinions agree that it was written "with a spirit of prophecy." *Magen Avraham* (*Oraḥ Ḥayim* 662:1) states that all agree that no blessing is recited over the reading of Ecclesiastes. *Maḥatzit HaShekel* (490:9) states that the only explanation for that is because at first the rabbis thought Ecclesiastes should be hidden away. However, the Vilna Gaon (*Oraḥ Ḥayim* 490:9) says that since it was decided to accept Ecclesiastes as part of Tanakh, it has the same status as any other Megilla and a blessing should be recited over it.

125 Abraham Idelsohn, *Jewish Liturgy and Its Development* (New York: Henry Holt and Company, 1932), 200.

it on their own.[126] This may be a reference to the ideas found in Ecclesiastes as well as the difficult words themselves. Ecclesiastes should thus be read specifically in a synagogue setting where the rabbi can address and interpret any difficult verses.

Having seen that the Megillot were originally part of a cycle of studying Ketuvim, it may be that Ecclesiastes was originally not associated with Sukkot for a more technical reason. The lists of the Ketuvim learning cycles from the various Jewish communities apply to the summer months, when Shabbat and Yom Tov afternoons are long. Some cycles began on Passover, some on Shavuot, ending by Rosh HaShana. Song of Songs, Ruth, and Lamentations all coincide with the festivals of this time period; only Ecclesiastes is read in the autumn. It may be due to a combination of factors that Ecclesiastes was excluded from the early version of the custom described in *Masekhet Soferim*. With twelve chapters, it is the longest Megilla, the afternoon is relatively short during Sukkot, and its content was considered somewhat controversial. Only later, when the summer Ketuvim cycle was forgotten and the Megillot were more explicitly associated with particular holidays did Ecclesiastes come to fill a void as the Megilla associated with Sukkot. Thus it is no coincidence that Sephardic communities, which best preserved the summer Ketuvim cycle, tend not to have a custom to read Ecclesiastes on Sukkot.

---

126 Y. Refael, ed., *Sefer HaManhig* (Jerusalem: Mossad HaRav Kook, 1978), 416–17.

*Chapter 27*

# *LaOmer/BaOmer*: The Approach of Rav Saadia Gaon

### THE CLASSIC DISCUSSION

There have been many discussions about the formula used for counting the Omer, whether it is more correct to say *laOmer* (לעומר) or *baOmer* (בעומר). Generally, *baOmer* is considered the Ashkenazic term, and *laOmer* is the term used in Sephardic communities and those who follow the approach of Rabbi Isaac Luria, the Ari.[1] In truth, we find that most Ashkenazic *Rishonim* who included a form of the word "Omer" in the blessing wrote that *laOmer* is said.[2] This is the approach detailed in the *Mishna Berura* (489:8), which states, "In most authorities the form is *laOmer*," whether Ashkenazic or Sephardic.[3] The clear source among

1 Simha Rabinowitz, *Piskei Teshuvot*, vol. 5 (Jerusalem, 1995), 489:5, 272–73.

2 For example, *Oraḥ Ḥayim, Hilkhot Sefirat HaOmer siman* 2, 3; *Kol Bo, siman* 55; *Sefer HaPardes, Shaar HaMaaseh*; Rabbeinu Yeruham, *Toldot Adam VeḤava, netiv* 5, part 4.

3 *Shaarei Teshuva* (489:8) notes that "also in the way people speak *laOmer* is more common."

Ashkenazic *Rishonim* of the custom to say *baOmer* is Isaac Tirnau's *Sefer Minhagim*.[4] This appears to be the source for the parenthetical insertion[5] of the term *baOmer* in the formula of the blessing found in the *Shulḥan Arukh* (*Oraḥ Ḥayim* 589:1), despite the fact that most authorities preferred *laOmer*.

From a grammatical perspective, Biblical Hebrew used both the prefix *be-* and *le-* to denote the counting of days within a fixed time period, for example, "On the fifteenth day of the second month (לחדש השני)" (Ex. 16:1), and "On the fifteenth day of the eighth month (בחדש השמיני)" (I Kings 12:33). The term for month, *ḥodesh*, originally meant Rosh Ḥodesh, meaning "the renewal of the month," and when people said "x days *laḥodesh*" it meant "x days since Rosh Ḥodesh." However, the phrase "x days *baḥodesh*" referred to the day within the time period we call a month, the way we understand the word *ḥodesh* nowadays. Whatever the case, the meaning is the same.

It may well be that when counting the Omer, the term *laOmer* indicated "since the Omer offering was brought," while *baOmer* meant "within the time period we call the Omer." Since the term "Omer" can refer to either the *omer* of barley used in the sacrifice commonly referred to as the Omer, or the time period of the counting of the Omer, both terms can be viewed as linguistically appropriate.[6] The *Taz* (489:3), however, notes that *baOmer* is more appropriate, since "it means 'within,' which is not the case with *lamed*, which can be interpreted as referring to the offering," and when the Omer is counted on the first night the sacrifice had not yet been offered, as it was brought only the following morning.

## THE GEONIC APPROACH

These sources do not factor in the version of the blessing found in the oldest known prayer books, *Seder Rav Amram Gaon* and *Siddur Rav*

4 Shlomo Spitzer, ed., *Sefer HaMinhagim LeRabbeinu Isaac Tirnau* (Jerusalem: Machon Yerushalayim, 2000), 56.

5 Regarding the parenthetical additions in the *Shulḥan Arukh*, see Daniel Sperber, *Minhagei Yisrael*, vol. 1 (Jerusalem: Mossad HaRav Kook, 1989), 179, note 6.

6 This is based on the response I received from the Academy of the Hebrew Language (question #54107), sent by Tamar Katzir, and based on the explanation of her colleague Dr. Keren Dubnov.

*Saadia Gaon,* dating from the geonic period. The section on counting the Omer is missing in all manuscripts of *Seder Rav Amram Gaon* that we have today. All we have preserved from the *Rishonim* is Rav Amram Gaon's ruling in the case of a person who forgot to count one night, but we have no evidence of his formula for counting the Omer.[7] However, the formula for blessing and counting the Omer does appear in *Siddur Rav Saadia Gaon.* This was first printed from a manuscript in 1941,[8] and was not known to the earlier rabbinic authorities who discussed the formula for counting the Omer.

Rav Saadia Gaon gives four examples of the formula for counting. On the first day, the formula is "now is one day *baOmer*" (האידנא חד יומא בעומרא), on the second it is "two days *baOmer*" (תרי יומי בעומרא), on the seventh it is "seven days *baOmer* which is one week" (יומאי שבעה יומי בעומרא דהון חד שבועא). All these examples use the term *baOmer.* The last example given is counting the night of the fifth of Sivan, forty-nine days *daOmer,* which are seven full weeks (יומאי ארבעין ותשעה יומי דעומרא דהוון שבעה שבועי שלמי).[9]

This approach matches that found in the name of Rav Hai Gaon as reported by Rabbi Yitzhak ibn Giat (Ritz Giat, 1038–89), regarding a person who missed one night of counting and wants to make it up.[10] In the course of the halakhic discussion, the formula for counting is mentioned, "it is now two days *baOmer*" (האידנא תרי יומי בעמרא).[11] The same term (בעומרא) is also found in the discussion of this topic in *Shibbolei HaLeket,* quoting "the responsa of the *Geonim.*"[12]

7 Daniel Goldschmidt, ed., *Seder Rav Amram Gaon* (Jerusalem: Mossad HaRav Kook, 2004), part 2, right before *siman* 90, 126.

8 See the introduction of Simha Assaf in Israel Davidson, Simha Assaf and Yissachar Yoel, eds., *Siddur Rav Saadia Gaon* (Jerusalem: Reuven Mass, 2000).

9 *Siddur Rav Saadia Gaon* (Jerusalem: Reuven Mass, 2000), 154.

10 Salomon Buber, ed., *Shibbolei HaLeket HaShalem* (Jerusalem: Zichron Aharon, 2012), part 2, 367, note 45.

11 *Hilkhot Ritz Giat, Hilkhot Ḥadash VeSefirat HaOmer,* 342.

12 *Shibbolei HaLeket, Din Sefirat HaOmer UBirkhata, siman* 234, 109. Sometimes *Shibbolei HaLeket* is quoted as saying דעומרא instead of בעומרא; see, for example, Avraham Shapira, *Minḥat Avraham,* vol. 3 (Jerusalem, 2003), *siman* 21, 209, but in all manuscripts of *Shibbolei HaLeket* it is בעומרא.

The sources above indicate that the geonic approach was to count in the vernacular, Aramaic, and to use the term *baOmer*, in the sense of "within the time period we call the Omer." This is the current practice in the Yemenite community today.[13] Thus, while most *Rishonim* preferred the term *laOmer*, in the geonic literature *baOmer* is the common form. It is not clear why Saadia Gaon changed the formula for the last night, making it *daOmer*.[14] Some have suggested that maybe *baOmer* is no longer appropriate once the Omer period is concluded on that last night,[15] but another explanation is possible.

## A FLEXIBLE APPROACH

The book *Sefer HaOra*, from the school of Rashi, states that after blessing and counting, the term "Omer" should be mentioned. In the same sentence, two examples are given, **יום אחד בעומר** (*baOmer*) and **שבעה ימים לעומר** (*laOmer*).[16] No explanation is offered for changing the phrase, and there does not seem to be any reason to do so. It could be suggested that, following the logic of the *Taz*, it does not make sense to say *laOmer* on the first night, before the sacrifice was brought, so on that night one should say *baOmer*, and one can then say *laOmer* on subsequent nights. But since no explicit reason is given for making a change, it is reasonable to conclude that there is simply no substantial difference between the two terms and either can be used. The *Arukh HaShulḥan* (*Oraḥ Ḥayim* 489:9) takes this view: "Regarding the formula *baOmer* or *laOmer*, there is no determination (אין הכרע)" regarding which one should be recited.

This approach is logical, considering that when the Rashba was asked whether one must include "today is x days *laOmer*, or can you say today is x (without mentioning the Omer at all)," he explained that it is only necessary to count, to state the number, and there is no need

13 Moshe Gavra, *Meḥkarim BeSiddurei Teiman*, vol. 3 (Bnei Brak: HaMakhon LeḤeker Ḥakhmei Teiman, 2010), 261; Eliyahu Katz, *She'elot UTeshuvot Be'er Eliyahu – Yoreh De'ah* (Jerusalem, 2002), *siman* 97, 117.

14 In contemporary Yemenite siddurim, the form is always *baOmer*, even on the forty-ninth night. See Moshe Gavra, *Meḥkarim BeSiddurei Teiman*, vol. 3 (Bnei Brak: HaMakhon LeḤeker Ḥakhmei Teiman, 2010), 262.

15 Katz, *She'elot UTeshuvot Be'er Eliyahu – Yoreh De'ah*, *siman* 97, 118.

16 Salomon Buber, ed., *Sefer HaOra* (Lemberg, 1905), *siman* 91, 106.

to add the term *laOmer* as it was already stated in the blessing that this is a counting of the Omer. However, although "it is all the same, it is more appropriate to say today is x days *laOmer* to make it more explicit (כדי לבאר יותר)."[17] Based on this, since neither *baOmer* nor *laOmer* are necessary, and are only added "to make it more explicit," both phrases are acceptable.

Returning to *Siddur Rav Saadia Gaon*, we can see that it also employs two versions of the phrase, *baOmer* and *daOmer*, with no explanation, indicating that it also saw them as interchangeable. Of course, over time this flexible approach would give way to viewing one form as more accurate and therefore more acceptable than the other, but the earliest textual evidence for adding any Omer term in the counting attests to the fact that all forms were considered equally appropriate.

17 *She'elot UTeshuvot HaRashba* (Jerusalem: Machon Yerushalayim, 1997), part 1, *siman* 457, 241.

# Stripes, Hats, and Fashion

There are certain elements of clothing today that are recognized as distinctly Jewish, even to non-Jews. The fact that these elements were not inherently Jewish and really had no particular connection to Jewishness at all teaches us that certain symbols can be transformed over time from something universal to decidedly Jewish, all due to changes in fashion.[1]

### TALLIT STRIPES

Today, the Ashkenazic tallit almost always has either black or blue stripes. The idea of having these stripes is not mandated anywhere in Jewish sources, yet it is ubiquitous.

The standard color of the non-blue tzizit fringes is white, as found in the Mishna (Menaḥot 4:1): "The [absence of] blue [in tzitzit] does not invalidate the white; neither does the [absence of] white invalidate the

1 This chapter will focus on the clothing worn by Jewish men. For a study of changes in the understanding of modest fashion as it relates to Orthodox Jewish women, see Yehuda Henkin, *Understanding Tzniut: Modern Controversies in the Jewish Community* (Jerusalem, 2008).

blue." White was also understood to be the color of the garment itself, as we find in Tractate Shabbat 153a: "'At all times let your clothes be white' (Eccl. 9:8); this is tzitzit." Rashi explains that this means the garment that the tzitzit are attached to is white. The *Shulḥan Arukh* (*Oraḥ Ḥayim* 9:5) states that those who are particular in their observance of commandments make the fringes the same color as the tallit garment itself, which is customarily white, and this is the Sephardic practice, to have an all-white tallit. Even if there is a design of stripes on the tallit, the stripes are white as well. This was taken seriously enough that there is halakhic discussion regarding the propriety of wearing a tallit that is no longer purely white due to the passage of time or to perspiration from the wearer.[2]

There are symbolic and mystical reasons for an all-white tallit. The kabbalist Rabbi Bahya ben Asher (1255–1340) in his comments on Numbers 15:38, where he discusses tzitzit, explains the famous aggadic passage in Rosh HaShana 17b, where God instructs Moses how to pray in a manner that the Israelites will be forgiven for their sins. "It teaches that God wrapped Himself in a tallit, like a cantor, and showed Moses at Mount Sinai, telling him that whenever the Israelites sin, he should do this and God would forgive them.... When it speaks of wrapping it means in a white tallit, since white is the symbol of forgiveness and atonement; just as red is a symbol of sin so white is a symbol of forgiveness. This is what is written, 'If your sins are as red as wool, they will become white as snow' (Is. 1:18)." Although the talmudic text does not indicate the color of the tallit God was wrapped in, Rabbi Bahya writes that it was all white, symbolizing the attribute of mercy.

This idea of a white tallit representing mercy is also discussed by Rabbi Shlomo Luria (Maharshal, 1510–73) in his explanation of the same passage in Rosh HaShana 17b. Based on this, he writes that he is careful to have a completely white tallit, including the thread used to sew the various parts together, as well as the *atara* of the tallit, the band of material worn near the neck.[3] This approach was popularized by Rabbi Hayim Yosef

2 See Simha Rabinowitz, *Piskei Teshuvot*, vol. 1 (Jerusalem, 2006), 9:6, 111, and note 51 there.

3 Shlomo Luria, *Yam shel Shlomo – Yevamot* (Szczecin, 1862), *siman* 3, 1b. Maharsha brings this same idea from "an old book of kabbalistic wisdom" in his comments to

David Azulai (Ḥida, 1724–1806) in his work on the *Shulḥan Arukh*[4] and in the commentary *Shaarei Teshuva* (9:4), which accompanies all standard printed versions of the *Shulḥan Arukh* and *Mishna Berura*.

There are halakhic sources that discuss adding color to the standard white tallit. The Rema, in his commentary on *Shulḥan Arukh* (*Oraḥ Ḥayim* 9:5), notes that Ashkenazic Jews make the fringes white even if the garment is colored. Rabbi David HaLevi Segal (*Taz*, c. 1586–1667), in his commentary on *Shulḥan Arukh* (*Oraḥ Ḥayim* 9:6), writes that the corners of the tallit (*kanaf*) should be white to match the color of the tzizit strings.

Rabbi Eliyahu Spira (1660–1712), in his commentaries *Eliya Zuta* (9:4) and *Eliya Rabba* (9:5), notes that his grandfather, Rabbi Aaron Shimon Spira (1599–1679), chief rabbi of Prague and Bohemia, wore a tallit with blue on the edges. Rabbi Eliyahu Spira conjectures that this was done as a way to remember the blue thread of *tekhelet* that was no longer in use. This is quoted by Rabbi Joseph ben Meir Teomim (1727–92) in his *Peri Megadim* (*Eshel Avraham* 9:6), who notes that this is customary and that it is also customary to have blue on the edge of the tallit katan. This explanation by the *Peri Megadim* is quoted in the popular *Sefer Taamei HaMinhagim UMekorei HaDinim*.[5] This is the basis for the popular traditional explanation that the blue stripes on the tallit recall the *tekhelet* thread.[6]

The black stripes often found on the tallit have traditionally been explained as a substitute for the blue ones, since the Rambam (*Mishneh Torah, Hilkhot Tzizit* 2:8) mentions that black resembles the color of *tekhelet*. In some contemporary works the black stripes are explained as "a remembrance or memorial to the destruction of the Holy Temple and the exile."[7]

---

Rosh HaShana 17b. See also Simha Rabinowitz, *Piskei Teshuvot*, vol. 1 (Jerusalem, 2006), 9:6, 111, and note 49 there.

4 Hayim Yosef David Azulai, *Birkei Yosef – Oraḥ Ḥayim* (Jerusalem, 2019), *shiurei berakha*, notes 1 and 2 on 9:5.

5 Avraham Sperling, *Sefer Taamei HaMinhagim UMekorei HaDinim* (Jerusalem, 1999), 10, *siman* 15.

6 Hertzel Hillel Yitzhak, *Tzel HeHarim: Tzitzit* (Jerusalem, 2006), 90, note 39.

7 Wayne D. Dosick, *Living Judaism: The Complete Guide to Jewish Belief, Tradition, and Practice* (New York: HarperOne, 1995), 223.

However, in all these explanations, no rationale is offered for the specific design, which incorporates stripes on either side of the garment, rather than any other mark of blue or black, and why the stripes are specifically positioned a few inches from the edge.

In ancient Rome, there were different toga designs "to indicate precisely the status or the nature of the wearer." The normal toga/tunic of the average male citizen was called *pura* (indicating clean, clear) to describe its natural off-white color. The senatorial class had their togas decorated with broad, vertical, purple stripes of about three inches wide; this kind of stripe was known as the *latus clivus*. Members of the equestrian class were permitted to have narrow stripes (about one inch wide) on their togas, and this type of stripe was called the *angustus clavus*.[8] The stripes ran down either side of the garment, close to the edge, but not touching the edge itself.[9] A purple stripe on a garment was considered a symbol of special status.[10] Other groups of men wore tunics with *clavi* (stripes) of various widths.[11]

Material evidence from archaeological findings indicates that Jews in the Roman era "did not have any distinctive national costume"; however, "the customary dress of tunic and mantle (tallit) was altered to conform with Jewish law," *shaatnez* and tzitzit in particular.[12] While Jewish garments did not appear radically different from others at the time, these changes could make them identifiable as Jews.[13]

---

8 Shelly Stone, "The Toga: From National to Ceremonial Costume," 15, and Norma Goldman, "Reconstructing Roman Clothing," 221, in Judith Lynn Sebesta and Larissa Bonfante, eds., *The World of Roman Costume* (Madison, WI, 2001).

9 Goldman, "Reconstructing Roman Clothing," in Sebesta and Larissa Bonfante, *The World of Roman Costume*, 221.

10 Laetitia La Follette, "The Costume of the Roman Bride," in Sebesta and Bonfante, *The World of Roman Costume*, 62, note 19.

11 Lena Larsson Loven, "Roman Art: What Can It Tell Us About Dress and Textiles? A Discussion on the Use of Visual Evidence as Sources for Textile Research," in Mary Harlow and Marie-Louise Nosch, eds., *Greek and Roman Textiles and Dress: An Interdisciplinary Anthology* (Oxford, 2014), 274.

12 Lucille Roussin, "Costume in Roman Palestine: Archaeological Remains and the Evidence from the Mishnah," in Sebesta and Bonfante, *The World of Roman Costume*, 188. "Mantle" is the term used for a tallit, 183.

13 Faith Pennick Morgan, *Dress and Personal Appearance in Late Antiquity* (Leiden, 2018), 26. See also Steven Fine, "How Do You Know a Jew When You See One?

Because of this, it seems that "the fact that the tallit is striped is probably because of the tradition of *clavi* bands."[14] In the 1960s, Yigael Yadin discovered striped *tallitot* dating from the Bar Kokhba period,[15] These tallitot "are the most ancient garments which are known to have been worn by Jews," and were found to have "long horizontal stripes over the whole fabric… this is still the Jewish tallit today."[16]

These stripes are also seen on the tunics in the artwork of the Dura-Europos synagogue (mid–third century CE). "Moses' garment is decorated with dark horizontal stripes which make its decoration identical to that of the second century remains. One cannot insist too strongly on the importance of what may seem to be only a minor detail of representation: Jewish art and the archeology of Eretz Israel thus combine to produce a single image of the Jewish costume in the period of the Mishna."[17]

These ancient purple lines persisted as the blue or black lines on tallitot to this day,[18] and would famously become incorporated into the flag of the State of Israel.[19] There is a certain irony that Jews have preserved an element of fashion prevalent among Romans, the destroyers

---

Reflections on Jewish Costume in the Roman World," in Leonard Jay Greenspoon, ed., *Fashioning Jews: Clothing, Culture, and Commerce* (West Lafayette, IN, 2013), 20.

14 Susan Karla Greenberg, *Tallitot: History and Design* (Madison, 1975), 19.

15 Yigael Yadin, *The Finds from the Bar Kokhba Period in the Cave of Letters*, vol. 1 (Jerusalem, 1963), chapter 11.

16 Elisabeth Revel-Neher, *The Image of the Jew in Byzantine Art* (Oxford, 1992), 52–53. See the pattern for replicating a Roman tunic, which looks just like a tallit, Norma Goldman, "Reconstructing Roman Clothing," in Sebesta and Bonfante, *The World of Roman Costume*, 222.

17 Revel-Neher, *The Image of the Jew in Byzantine Art*, 52–53.

18 Although brightly colored *tallitot* were popularized by Zalman Schachter Shalomi since his time as a Camp Ramah counselor in the 1960s as part of his "do-it-yourself religious artifacts" projects, and would have an impact on more people over the following decades, particularly among members of the Renewal and Havurah movements, the original design, of a plain white garment with simple parallel stripes, dating from ancient Roman times, remains the most popular tallit design to this day. See Chava Weissler, "Performing Kabbalah in the Jewish Renewal Movement," in Boaz Huss, ed., *Kabbalah and Contemporary Spiritual Revival* (Beer Sheva, 2011), 28.

19 See Daniel Sperber, *Minhagei Yisrael*, vol. 5 (Jerusalem, 1998), 207–8, note 5. On the history of the tallit stripe design on the flag of the State of Israel, see Ari Chwat, *Leharim et HaDegel* (Jerusalem, 2014), 25–31.

of the Second Temple and the Jewish state of that time, and have now incorporated it into the flag of the contemporary rebirth of the State of Israel. Although it is popular to say that "blue and white, the colors associated with the State of Israel and its flag, originated as the 'Jewish colors' because of the tallit,"[20] it is more accurate to go further back in history and say that they are Jewish colors because the Jews maintained the fashion of the *clavi* long after the Romans vanished.

Although these stripes are ubiquitous on Ashkenazic tallitot, it was never suggested that they are a halakhic requirement. As Rabbi Yechiel Michel Epstein (*Arukh HaShulḥan, Oraḥ Ḥayim* 9:26) points out, the blue on the edge of a tallit is for purposes of beauty only (לנוי בעלמא).[21]

## HASIDIC CLOTHING

The Fourth Lateran Council of 1215 and the regulations that followed insisted that Jews be visually distinguishable from Christians; this distinctiveness took the form of specific badges or hats that Jews had to wear.[22] The thirteenth-century *Takkanot Shum* of the Jewish communities of the Rhineland and rabbinic ordinances that followed had more general rules: that Jews were not to cut their hair or beards like Christians, that they should not wear *shaatnez*, and that they should generally not dress like Christians.[23] The idea of Jewish attire in the sense of an entire Jewish look, such as the easily identifiable hasidic look recognized today, emerged later, and was established by the eighteenth century.[24]

A description of the clothing of Frankfurt Jews published in 1714 relates that "the Jews wear black coats, black hats, generally clothes of

---

20 Michael Strassfeld, *A Book of Life: Embracing Judaism as a Spiritual Practice* (Woodstock, VT, 2006), 198.

21 See also *Mishna Berura*, 9:16, which states that the blue stripes are halakhically insignificant.

22 Francoise Piponnier and Perrine Mane, *Dress in the Middle Ages* (New Haven, 1997), 136–37.

23 Cornelia Aust, "From Noble Dress to Jewish Attire: Jewish Appearances in the Polish-Lithuania Commonwealth and the Holy Roman Empire," in Cornelia Aust, Denise Klein, and Thomas Weller, eds., *Dress and Cultural Difference in Early Modern Europe* (Berlin, 2019), 91.

24 Cornelia Aust, "From Noble Dress to Jewish Attire" (Berlin, 2019), 90.

dark color and around the neck a collar made of linen; the older and more distinguished ones also a round white linen ruff... which, in addition to the beret, have their origin in the former Spanish costume," common in sixteenth- and seventeenth-century Spain. German Jews adopted this clothing and retained it "when it became otherwise unfashionable."[25] The Spanish black cloak and ruff had fallen out of fashion in the Christian world, and became the dress of the relatively conservative Jewish communities of Frankfurt am Main and Furth.[26] A similar development occurred in Poland with what came to be known as hasidic clothing.

What is today identified as hasidic dress began as the fashion of the Polish nobility. "In traditional (Jewish) men's dress, from at least the sixteenth century, styles were influenced by those of the Polish gentry (*szlachta*), which itself had borrowed many elements from Turkish and other Near Eastern dress. While the *szlachta* abandoned certain types of clothing for newer fashions, in Jewish society the styles endured for a much longer period."[27] One example is the Varangian cap and caftan, which, "in the sixteenth century... became the national costume" of Poland.[28] The Varangians, a term used in the Byzantine Empire for Vikings, ruled the medieval state of Kievan Rus between the ninth and eleventh centuries and settled among many territories of modern Belarus, Russia, and Ukraine, impacting that region in many ways, including dress. Rather than being a particularly Jewish item of clothing, "in Eastern Europe, on the contrary, the *shtreimel* in the seventeenth century was no more a specifically Jewish hat" than others. While fashions changed, and "under the rule of the French and Saxon kings, new modes began to prevail and as in many other aspects of Polish life western fashions were adopted... Polish Jewry developed a strict conservatism." This "led to the favoring of the headgear most common at the time, namely the

---

25 Ibid., 94.

26 Ibid., 111.

27 Goldberg-Mulkiewicz, Olga. 2010. "Dress," entry in YIVO Encyclopedia of Jews in Eastern Europe. https://yivoencyclopedia.org/article.aspx/Dress (accessed November 20, 2019).

28 Raphael Straus, "The 'Jewish Hat' as an Aspect of Social History," *Jewish Social Studies* 4:1 (January, 1942), 70.

*shtreimel*." The Jews "clung to the Varangian cap longer and more intensely than any other community."[29]

The difference in headgear among various hasidic groups was "largely influenced by climatic conditions."[30] Over time, various homiletic and symbolic interpretations have been given, such as the comment by the Baal Shem Tov's student Rabbi Pinhas Shapiro of Koretz (1726–91) that the word "Shabbat" stands for "*shtreimel* in place of tefillin" (שטריימל במקום תפילין).[31] The general character of Polish Jewish men's clothing from the mid-eighteenth century "was similar in general type of the cut, length and folding to the men's national costume. The Jewish caftans were made according to the cut of the Polish zupan and were of similar length, that is, usually ankle reaching. They distinguished themselves, however, by darker color, often black."[32] The darker colors, considered more modest, are in accordance with the ruling of the Rema (*Shulḥan Arukh, Yoreh De'ah* 178:1), that one may not mimic non-Jewish clothing chosen "for the sake of licentiousness. For example, they are accustomed to wearing red clothing, which is princely clothing, and other clothing that is similarly immodest."

While members of the Polish nobility "increasingly adapted to a more Western European style of clothing, incorporating and adapting new fashionable cuts and accessories," Jews retained traditional garments.[33] "Jews, encumbered by pogroms, economic deprivations and mandatory dress codes… remained attired in… garb that now increasingly appeared anachronistic and distinctively Jewish."[34] Inventories and wanted posters from the mid-eighteenth century in Poland indicate that by then Jews wore zupans and caftans, while Christians did not.[35] This would become the clothing identified as hasidic garb today.

29 Ibid., 71.

30 Tzvi Rabinowicz, *The Encyclopedia of Hasidism* (Northvale, NJ, 1996), 94.

31 Aharon Wertheim, *Halakhot VeHalikhot BeḤasidut* (Jerusalem, 1960), 197.

32 Irena Turnau, "The Dress of the Polish Jews in the 17th and 18th centuries," *Proceedings of the World Congress of Jewish Studies* 10 (1989), D:2, 104–5.

33 Cornelia Aust, "From Noble Dress to Jewish Attire" (Berlin, 2019), 100.

34 Eric Silverman, *A Cultural History of Jewish Dress* (New York, 2013), 122.

35 Aust, "From Noble Dress to Jewish Attire," 103.

Hasidic leaders forcefully encouraged the retention of the old fashions, particularly Rabbi Menahem Mendel of Rimanov (1745–1815), a major hasidic leader in Poland. He wrote several times that new fashions are a cause of new diseases and troubles.[36] In 1815 he issued a set of thirteen communal ordinances, three of which were aimed at specifically prohibiting men and women from wearing "new fashions" (מאדע חדשה). A tailor who made such clothing was to be fined the first time, and expelled from the tailor's guild if it happened again.[37] We also have many homilies and exhortations in the name of Rabbi Sholom Rokeach (1781–1855), the first Belzer Rebbe, regarding the importance of not changing fashions according to the styles of the Gentiles.[38]

In the nineteenth century, large segments of German Jewish society "participated in the development of a bourgeois society and adopted the respective sartorial style," effectively putting an end to a specific Jewish attire in those areas.[39] Meanwhile, the majority of the Polish Jewish population continued to wear their distinctive fashions, resisting integration into the general society. In that era, "sartorial differentiation was not compatible with a modernizing ethos of homogeneity," which sometimes resulted in government decrees against clothing seen as particularly Jewish.[40] Still, many traditional Jews preserved old Polish fashions, which would become known as hasidic dress since those original fashions were no longer in use in general society and less traditional Jews adapted to modern trends. Despite various folkloric explanations for hasidic clothing, the simple explanation of its origin is that it mimicked the style of the wealthy and honorable in Polish society.[41]

---

36 See Menachem Mendel of Rimanov, *Menaḥem Tzion* (Jerusalem, 2007), 261–62, 295–98.

37 Menachem Mendel of Rimanov, *Ateret Menaḥem* (Bilgoraj, 1910), 12, items 1, 5, and 11.

38 Avraham Sperling, *Sefer Taamei HaMinhagim UMekorei HaDinim* (Jerusalem, 1999), 553 in the notes.

39 Aust, "From Noble Dress to Jewish Attire," 112.

40 Glenn Dynner, "The Garment of Torah: Clothing Decrees and the Warsaw Career of the First Gerer Rebbe," in Glenn Dynner and Francois Guesnet, eds., *Warsaw: The Jewish Metropolis* (Leiden, 2015), 102.

41 Aryeh David Wasserman, *Otzar HaKippa*, vol. 2 (Jerusalem, 2014), 505. This is a two-volume work whose second volume deals comprehensively with the obligation

## MEN'S HATS

The Rambam (*Hilkhot Tefilla* 5:5) and the *Shulḥan Arukh* (*Oraḥ Ḥayim* 91:6) state that "it is the way of scholars and their students not to pray when they are not wrapped," something accomplished by covering the head with a tallit.[42] A similar ruling is found in *Shulḥan Arukh* (*Oraḥ Ḥayim* 8:2), where it states that "it is appropriate that one covers his head with a tallit."[43] Rabbi Yosef Karo writes that this is based on the Talmud in Shabbat 10a, which says, "R. Ashi said: I saw that R. Kahana, when there is suffering in the world, would remove his cloak and clasp his hands and pray. He said that he did so as a servant before his master. When there is peace in the world, he would dress, and cover himself, and wrap himself, and pray, and he said that he did so in fulfillment of the verse 'Prepare to greet your God, Israel' (Amos 4:12)."[44] Rashi explains that R. Kahana would remove his cloak in times of suffering so as not to appear important, and we can see that in peaceful times he wrapped himself in an important garment.

Distinct from this is the matter of wearing a hat in particular for prayer. Rabbi Abraham Danzig in *Ḥayei Adam* (22:8), published in the early 1800s, states regarding proper attire for prayer: "And he puts a hat on his head the way he walks in the street."[45] Similarly, the *Mishna Berura* (91:11) states that "in our times during *tefilla* one must put a hat on their head the way he walks in the street," as this is the manner of standing before "important people." Both the *Ḥayei Adam* and the *Mishna Berura* require a hat because that is "the way he walks in the street." Similar language is used in *Arukh HaShulḥan* (*Oraḥ Ḥayim* 91:6), which explains that a hat is needed for prayer "like how one walks in the street," and that "the general rule is that one must pray in clothing that is worn in the street."

This view of wearing a hat reflects the fact that "in the nineteenth and early twentieth centuries, hats were worn by members of all social

---

to wear a hat.

42 See also *Mishna Berura* 91:6.

43 See *Mishna Berura* 8:4 regarding the opinions about whether this means for *Shemoneh Esreh* only or the entire service.

44 *Kesef Mishna, Hilkhot Tefilla* 5:5.

45 וישים כובע בראשו כדרך שהולך ברחוב.

classes, including the lowest social strata," and that "hats in previous centuries were worn in what we would now call the public sphere."[46] Writing in 1948, George Orwell stated that "even thirty or forty years ago, indeed, bare-headed men were booed at in the street.... Then, for no very clear reason, hatlessness became respectable."[47]

US President John F. Kennedy (Hatless Jack) is often credited with the demise of the wearing of hats as a societal norm among men.[48] In fact, although Kennedy's choice to remove his top hat for his inaugural speech may have aided the process, hat sales had already been on the decline for decades.[49] In 1899, the *North Adams Transcript*, in an article entitled "What's the Use of a Hat?" reported that "nobody wears them anymore. Nobody, that is, except for a few old fogies who imagine that they are duty bound to wear hats."[50] *Hat Life*, the journal for hat sellers, ran an eight-page special report in November 1934, "Hatlessness: What Shall We Do About It?"[51] A study by the Grey Advertising Agency in 1947 found that 57 percent of men in the twenty-five-to-thirty-five age bracket preferred not to wear a hat. On the other hand, 78 percent of men over the age of forty-five liked to wear hats. Only 15 percent of men under twenty said they preferred wearing a hat to going bareheaded. This led the report to conclude that "the younger the man was, the less he cared for hats."[52] Various reasons were given by younger men for not wearing hats, the biggest factors being "don't feel comfortable," "hat is a nuisance," "habit," and "just don't like to wear one."[53]

By the late 1940s and early 1950s the hat industry was in free fall, with the situation worsening over time. "Men's dress hat sales in the

46 Diana Crane, *Fashion and Its Social Agendas: Class, Gender, and Identity in Clothing* (Chicago, 2000), 83.

47 George Orwell, "George Gissing," first published in *London Magazine* (June 1960), written in 1948.

48 Nicholas Storey, *History of Men's Fashion: What the Well-Dressed Man Is Wearing* (Barnaby, 2008), 130.

49 Maria Mackinney-Valentin, *Fashioning Identity: Status Ambivalence in Contemporary Fashion* (London, 2017), 7.

50 Neil Steinberg, *Hatless Jack* (New York, 2004), 248.

51 Ibid., 254.

52 Ibid., 211.

53 Ibid., 212.

United States in 1960 were half of what they had been a decade earlier."[54] There were three major popular theories explaining why men were not wearing hats: World War II veterans had to wear hats as soldiers and now they were rebelling against this, private automobiles, which were increasing in number, provided little space for a driver to wear a hat, and President Kennedy did not wear a hat (actually removing the hat he wore) during his inaugural address.[55] However, historians believe that in America men stopped wearing hats primarily because younger people no longer wished to conform to what they perceived as outdated societal conventions.[56] In 1925 the *New York Times* noted that the rejection of hat wearing became a fad among college students that "spread to the young business man and even to his father."[57] Hats were perceived as a symbol of conformity to be abandoned.[58] A telling comment is found in a 1944 *Chicago Daily News* column, where a young reporter writes that he and his friends "resented the bland uniformity of the dumb-looking hat," and "wouldn't be caught dead in a hat."[59] This reflected the trend among younger people to favor a relaxation of the rules of formal etiquette and to feel that they "operate at all times as spontaneous individuals."[60]

By the time President Kennedy famously discarded his hat, young men already considered the hat a superfluous item of clothing, similar to the current trend of wearing more casual work attire without neckties.[61] As George Orwell said, "This is an interesting example of the changes in outlook that can suddenly make an all-powerful taboo seem ridiculous."[62]

Following this, in a society that no longer considers a hat to be an essential item, it is thus no longer relevant for proper prayer attire either, as noted in the *Mishna Berura* (91:11): "It all depends on the custom of

---

54 Ibid., xix.

55 Ibid.

56 Ibid., 220.

57 Ibid., 233.

58 Ibid., 232.

59 Ibid., 218.

60 Alison Lurie, *The Language of Clothes* (New York, 1981), 179.

61 Steinberg, *Hatless Jack*, 256, n.7.

62 George Orwell, "George Gissing."

the places."[63] Rabbi Eliezer Waldenberg (1915–2006), when asked about wearing a hat for prayer, wrote that based on the wording of the *Ḥayei Adam* there could be a leniency for those that don't wear a hat in the street, but since the *Mishna Berura* emphasizes that one must dress in the manner that one does when meeting important people, if a person wears a hat on that occasion, he should do so for prayer as well.[64] The implication remains that if a person doesn't wear a hat even when meeting important people, he would not be required to do so for prayer either.[65]

The Rambam presents a similar opinion in *Hilkhot Tefilla* 5:5: "Before beginning the service, one's dress should first be adjusted and one's personal appearance made trim and neat, as it is said, 'O worship the Lord in the beauty of holiness' (Ps. 96:9). One should not stand in prayer wearing a money belt, nor bareheaded, nor barefoot, where the local custom is not to stand in the presence of the great without shoes." Rabbi Yosef Karo in *Kesef Mishna* comments that this would exclude people living in Arab lands, where it was acceptable to stand barefoot in front of important people, and that if nobody cared whether or not shoes were worn in front of someone important, the same would apply for prayer as well.[66]

### HATS FOREVER

Among certain groups, hat wearing is still considered significant. "Hats still have a place in African American communities, where being perfectly turned out for church and recreation still carries the meaning it once did for the population at large – as a sign of respectability and success."[67] This was a phenomenon most commonly associated with women's "church hats," and today it is still a distinguishing feature among some Orthodox

---

63 Simha Rabinowitz, *Piskei Teshuvot*, vol. 1 (Jerusalem, 2006), 91:3, 720.

64 Eliezer Waldenberg, *Tzitz Eliezer*, vol. 13 (Jerusalem, 1984), 13:1, 33 and 13:4, 34.

65 See Aryeh David Wasserman, *Otzar HaKippa*, vol. 2 (Jerusalem, 2014), 43–44.

66 See Wasserman, *Otzar HaKippa*, vol. 2, 45–46. This also led to a discussion of whether it is appropriate to wear a jacket draped over the shoulders during prayer, or to have one arm sticking out of the jacket, as this would not be done in the presence of an important figure. See there, 57–59.

67 Steinberg, *Hatless Jack*, 294.

Jews, particularly those associated with the Lithuanian tradition,[68] who retain this article of clothing even when the fashion trend has been mostly abandoned by the rest of society.

In contemporary rabbinic writings it is not unusual to find the opinion that nowadays Jews must still wear hats.[69] The Klausenberger Rebbe, Rabbi Yekutiel Yehudah Halberstam (1905–94), states in *Divrei Yatziv* that even if people no longer wear hats in the streets and public places, this should not influence a person, since "the custom of the foolish is nothing."[70] Similarly, Rabbi Moshe Sternbuch states that although some claim that since in Israel people appear before ministers without a hat and jacket then one may pray that way as well, this is not the case. He contends that this practice of appearing without a hat and jacket before important people was learned from non-Jews, who picked it up from Communists, who wished to demonstrate that everyone is equal, everyone is a "comrade." Therefore the fashion of the outside world to abandon hats in formal and public settings should not impact Jews.[71] While attributing hatlessness to communist influence is debatable, we have seen that it did originate with the trend of young men abandoning what they considered old-fashioned ideas and conformity, arguably things that Rabbi Sternbuch values.

The result of these rulings is that although hats began as an article of clothing that were expected to be worn by men in public situations, thus giving it the status of an item of clothing required for prayer, the reverse fashion trend is not considered an acceptable reason to no longer wear hats during prayer. The hat has now been transformed into a Jewish ritual item that cannot be forfeited.

However, as the *Mishna Berura* (91:11) states, wearing a hat is customary when standing before "important people." In a society where the important people themselves neither wear hats nor expect them to be worn by people meeting them, it may seem unnecessary to

68 Wasserman, *Otzar HaKippa*, vol. 2, 502.

69 For example, Moshe Tzuriel, *Otzrot HaMusar* (Jerusalem, 2002), 1175; Wasserman, *Otzar HaKippa*.

70 Yekutiel Yehudah Halberstam, *She'elot UTeshuvot Divrei Yatziv, Oraḥ Ḥayim*, vol. 1 (Kiryat Sanz, Netanya, 2004), 60:8, 125. מנהג שוטים אינו כלום.

71 Moshe Sternbuch, *Teshuvot VeHanhagot*, vol. 4 (Jerusalem, 2001), *siman* 26, 23.

still require a hat for prayer. When asked this directly by a questioner, who pointed out that in many places in Israel and the United States it is not customary to walk in the street with a hat, Rabbi Hayim Kanievsky responded that "even in our times also most people wear a hat and jacket when meeting with important people."[72] Of course, in a society where it is still customary to wear hats for formal occasions and public appearances, wearing a hat would be considered important for prayer as well.[73] Thus, the very fact that a certain community retains the fashion of wearing a hat in the public sphere, although abandoned by society at large, creates an obligation to maintain this practice. This is pointed out by Rabbi Shlomo Blumenkrantz, who states that although the general society no longer wears hats in the public arena, the "*benei Torah*" do. And even though they may not wear a hat when visiting an important person in the secular or Gentile world, they still wear a hat when visiting a Torah scholar. This leads to his conclusion that a hat is still necessary for prayer.[74] Maintaining this fashion creates a loop which reinforces the continuation of the fashion.

## CONCLUSION

*Pesikta DeRav Kahane* (*Parashat Beshalaḥ* 11:6) brings the famous teaching of R. Ḥuna in the name of Bar Kappara that in the merit of four things the Israelites were redeemed from Egypt: "They did not change their names, they did not change their language, they did not speak *lashon hara*, and no one among them was promiscuous." There are various versions of this teaching, but although often included in the list, the statement "they did not change their clothing" is not found in the early midrashic literature.[75] It is first attested to in the eleventh century work *Midrash Lekaḥ Tov* (Ex. 6:6).[76] This variant reading is understood to have arisen due to the fact that in the ancient world Jews fundamentally "wore

72 Hayim Kanievsky, *Daat Nota*, vol. 1 (Bnei Brak, 2009), 280, question 102.

73 Simha Rabinowitz, *Piskei Teshuvot*, vol. 1 (Jerusalem, 2006), 91:3, 721.

74 Shlomo Blumenkrantz, *Barukh Tzuri* (Brooklyn, NY, 1972), 12, *siman* 12:2.

75 Salomon Buber, ed., *Pesikta* (Lvov, 1868), 83b, note 66. See also Moshe Svar, *Mikhlol HaMaamarim VehaPitgamim* (Jerusalem, 1987), 348.

76 See the discussion in Menachem Kasher, *Torah Sheleima – Shemot*, vol. 8 (Jerusalem, 1992), 239, *miluim* 3.

clothing that was indistinguishable from that of non-Jews."[77] By contrast, medieval European Jews did dress distinctly, often not by choice.[78]

However, when choosing to adopt distinctive dress, Jews "had always adopted the dress from the surrounding nation, preserving some elements that distinguished them from the strangers and determined their national membership."[79] This is part of the "pre-modern ethos that condoned and sometimes required visible distinction among estates, social classes, and residents of different locales."[80] As fashions changed, so did the way Jewish people dressed, while still preserving certain distinguishing elements. So long as the non-Jewish clothing was not considered immodest, changing styles was not viewed as problematic.[81]

Even so, certain fashion trends which were not originally perceived as particularly Jewish were vigorously preserved by Jews even when discarded by local society. In such cases, the item of clothing morphed into something that was perceived as a mark of traditional Jewish values or custom, and in some cases as even ritually or spiritually significant. Over time, the outside world as well would then start to view these fashion relics as emblematic of Jewish culture, reinforcing and cementing their elevation, transformation, and even conversion, for example from Roman to distinctively Jewish.

Hats, once a staple of men's fashion in the Western world, went through such a metamorphosis. With the advent of various forces of

---

77 Shaye J. D. Cohen, *The Beginnings of Jewishness: Boundaries, Varieties, Uncertainties* (Berkeley, 1999), 31. See the discussion there on pages 30–34. There are specific exceptions, such as black shoes, which according to Taanit 22a seem to have not been normative for Jews to wear, although according to Rabbeinu Tam (Bava Kama 59b, *Tosafot*, s.v. *havei*), this may refer to the shoelaces rather than the shoes themselves.

78 Steven Fine, "How Do You Know a Jew When You See One? Reflections on Jewish Costume in the Roman World," in Leonard Jay Greenspoon, ed., *Fashioning Jews: Clothing, Culture, and Commerce* (West Lafayette, IN, 2013), 20, and 26, note 13.

79 Irena Turnau, "The Dress of the Polish Jews in the 17th and 18th centuries," *Proceedings of the World Congress of Jewish Studies* 10 (1989), D:2, 102.

80 Glenn Dynner, "The Garment of Torah: Clothing Decrees and the Warsaw Career of the First Gerer Rebbe," in Glenn Dynner and Francois Guesnet, eds., *Warsaw: The Jewish Metropolis* (Leiden, 2015), 101.

81 See the responsum by Moshe Feinstein on this topic (*Iggerot Moshe, Yoreh De'ah* 1:81), dated 1952.

social change in the early 1900s, formal hats became less popular in general society. This trend continues today with the acceptance of more casual dress for men, while in the Orthodox world, the older, more formal fashions have persisted.

In the case of the tallit stripes, although designing tallitot with stripes is an ancient practice, it was never mandated by halakha, and while nice explanations were given for their presence, having them on one's tallit was not particularly encouraged. It remains in the realm of a popular fashion choice, although certainly one that is widespread and considered traditional. By contrast, in certain circles hat wearing has evolved beyond a fashion choice into a halakhic obligation, thus giving it the special status of a fashion trend that can never end by virtue of its being viewed as mandated by halakha.

# *Conclusion*

When I began researching this book on the history and development of various customs, I did so without having a particular thesis in mind. I was not seeking to advance any particular agenda. My intent was simply to determine the origins of practices that we seem to take for granted. However, over the years, certain underlying mechanisms became apparent regarding the development of Jewish customs, and it emerged that there are a few examples of each in this book.

## THE DISSEMINATION OF INDIVIDUAL PRACTICES

We have seen that some customs began as something only certain people or groups did, such as adding special *HaRaḥaman* prayers in *Birkat HaMazon*. Saying *Al Tira* after *Aleinu* began as a custom of the Jews of Provence taken on by Ibn Shushan, and it has since become standard in most prayer books today. *Ḥai rotel* also started this way, as something two childless men began one year at Meron.

## THE ALLURE OF THE DEFINITE

An important factor in the spreading of customs is the desire for people to feel that they are doing the right thing. This expresses itself in their wanting to be guided in the "right way" to do something, even if in fact there are many ways to do it.

For example, we have seen that saying *baOmer* or *laOmer* is not actually a necessary part of counting the Omer, and either term is fine if one chooses to add them. Today, however, there are different practices regarding which word is "correct," because it is difficult for some to accept the premise that either way, or not at all, is just fine. The addition of *Al Tira* after *Aleinu* has this component as well – of the many post-Shaḥarit additions, which were all originally considered optional, this one became the prayer that you were "supposed to" recite.

The idea of pointing to the Torah with a particular finger (the pinky) spread based on this premise as well. While very few can explain why they do this, everyone feels that they are doing it in the very particular way that it should be done. Rather than being satisfied with the general instruction about the lifting of the arms found in *Shulḥan Arukh*, a more particular and specific instruction resonates with someone concerned with choosing the correct way of responding during *hagbaha*, even though it lacks textual support.

Similarly, concerning the recitation of *Taḥanun* on Mondays and Thursdays, we saw that originally there were many different options regarding which verses to add, leaving up to the individual or the prayer leader the choice of what to include. Today, prayer books list all of them together as one long segment, no longer suggesting that individual sections may be chosen. It seems that rather than making a choice, people want to make sure that what they are saying is "correct," so they say all possible options. Today, most people don't know that originally they were expected to choose what they wanted to say.

An extreme example of this type of conformity is the date chosen to commemorate the death of Rachel, where the date in the Book of Jubilees, a sectarian work, was preferred over that given in the Midrash, because having a definite date (the eleventh of Ḥeshvan) was more appealing than the general time period of springtime found in rabbinic literature.

## CROSS-CULTURAL CUSTOMS RETAINED BY JEWS

Observant Jews are by definition conservative in their practice, retaining the rituals and lifestyle of previous generations. This extends to practices that are not Jewish per se, or at least were not originally viewed as particularly Jewish, but were retained along with related halakhic practices. An example of this is the wedding canopy. While there were originally many different explanations for the form the *ḥuppa* should take, as the Rema notes in *Shulḥan Arukh, Even HaEzer* 55:1, it became associated with a cloth canopy that was extensively used. This cloth canopy was actually the baldachin, a canopy of state used in the Middle Ages to cover the thrones or altars of important personages such as royalty.[1] While once a common cross-cultural European practice, over time it was retained primarily by Jews and became associated with Jewish weddings, even though it began as a standard way of showing honor, much like the modern-day red carpet. While the world shifted to other ways of providing VIP treatment, Jewish people continued using this canopy at weddings, and so this form of *ḥuppa* became a classic symbol of a Jewish wedding.[2]

In this book we observed the same process regarding wearing costumes on Purim, particularly dressing up as the opposite gender, something considered festive among the non-Jews in certain European countries. This became a general way to express festivity even among Jews, despite an unequivocal Torah prohibition. Similarly, certain fashion trends that were once popular in the world at large eventually disappeared among the general population but the Jewish people retained these styles, and today they are considered identifiers of the Jewish people. This is the case with striped togas and dress hats.

Similar is the case of covering mirrors in the home of a mourner. We saw that this was once a widespread practice across numerous cultures based on a certain view of how spirits function in relation to mirrors. At the time, many Jews also accepted these premises, not as part of their faith, but as an understanding of how the world works, "the science of the time," one could say. Once large numbers of people in the outside world abandoned this practice, it came to be associated with Jewish mourning customs. In this manner, a general custom became viewed as a Jewish one, with a selection of Jewish associations offered

1 Daniel Sperber, *Minhagei Yisrael*, vol. 8 (Jerusalem: Mossad HaRav Kook, 2007), 51–65.

2 See also Eliyahu Bechor, *Sefer HaTishbi* (Basel, 1601), 34.

for it. These explanations are needed to understand a practice that was originally taken as a given because that was what everybody did.

Both covering mirrors and having a *ḥuppa* were given symbolic meaning in popular Jewish literature, the former to show that physicality and vanity must be put aside during mourning,[3] and the latter as a symbol of the home of the newly married couple.[4] However, this symbolism was added only once these customs were no longer well-known practices in the wider world and became something that was not obviously recognized and understood in its original context.

Another example of this phenomenon is the use of salt water as a dip for vegetables. Once a common salad dressing, salt water is now part of a particularly Jewish ritual that symbolizes the bitter tears of our enslaved ancestors. The same process has taken place with the use of a feather in the search for *ḥametz*. Once it was a standard cleaning tool, now it has acquired symbolic meaning.

Is dipping a vegetable in salt water a Jewish custom? Is covering mirrors? Is getting married under a *ḥuppa*? There are many things that Jewish people do that the outside society does as well, for example, wearing belts or drinking coffee. These cannot be considered Jewish customs. There are certain things that are associated with Jews specifically, such as eating bagels and cream cheese or deli sandwiches, at least in the United States. As Jewish people do not give these practices any symbolic meaning, for our purposes it seems that they cannot be considered Jewish customs. However, what of a case where a practice was once cross-cultural, shared by Jews and non-Jews alike, but over time was dropped by the majority of the wider world and retained primarily by Jews? And what if, with the passage of time, Jews no longer recalled the original context of these practices, and gave them a new, symbolic meaning, one that carries a Jewish message? It would seem that the practice would now be transformed into a Jewish custom. This can also be the case when other cultures do retain their original practice, which for

---

3 See, for example, Maurice Lamm, *The Jewish Way in Death and Mourning* (New York: Jonathan David Publishers, 1969), 103.

4 See, for example, Hayim Shafner, *The Everything Jewish Wedding Book* (Avon, MA: Adams, 2009), 84–85.

one reason or another, usually geographical, Jewish people are no longer aware of. For example, braided bread for special occasions is still a very popular Ukrainian practice, but because that is not known to most Jewish people, the practice is perceived as exclusively Jewish.

Sometimes, however, these customs do not persevere, despite the conservative nature of Jewish practice. An example we saw was the tradition of not slaughtering geese during the Egyptian days. Although the concept of Egyptian days was once widespread, today it is fairly obscure. Why did the Jewish version of this practice disappear as well? It would seem that it is due to a combination of inter-related factors. No "Jewish" reason was given for the practice, at least none that captured the imagination, and it affected only a small group, the geese slaughterers, so it was never very widespread in the first place. It is likely that because it was not relevant to the masses, no compelling Jewish reason was ever given for it. Thus, the practice faded into obscurity, despite its being recorded by the Rema in the *Shulḥan Arukh*. When a common practice fades from general usage and also fails to acquire a Jewish meaning, it is dropped from Jewish practice as well.

As culinary, sartorial, and societal trends change in the world, Jewish people who cling to what was previously common practice are in essence laying the foundation for what, in generations to come, may be transformed into Jewish customs.

For example, today among many Jews, even strictly observant ones, it is understood that a birthday is celebrated, and it is done so with a special cake decorated with candles and singing a particular song.[5] This is true even though there are no early sources in Jewish literature that instruct someone to celebrate their birthday annually, and certainly not in this specific manner.[6] Yet it is celebrated that way in many Jewish

5 Presenting cakes with candles and singing "Happy Birthday" can now be found in halakhic literature. See, for example, Avishalom Monitzer, *Yeladim KeHalakha* (Rosh HaAyin, 2003), 196, *siman* 7; Yisrael Naftali Krauss, *Naḥalat Yisrael* (Bnei Brak, 2008), 428.

6 See J. McClintock and J. Strong, *Cyclopedia of Biblical, Theological and Ecclesiastical Literature*, vol. 1 (New York, 1895), 817. "[The Jews] regarded birthday celebrations as parts of idolatrous worship... and this probably on the account of the idolatrous rites with which they were observed in honor of those who were regarded as the patron

households, although it is certainly not based on any Jewish practice.[7] It is simply the way the world around us celebrates birthdays, and so we do too. Imagine a world two hundred years from now, when perhaps new and different ways are accepted for birthday commemoration, and yet Jews persist in using a cake with candles to emulate the way their grandparents celebrated. What if a future rabbinic authority then devises a clever Jewish symbolism for these particular practices?

## ḤUKKAT AKUM

When one becomes aware of the fact that certain customs began as cross-cultural practices and then developed into specifically Jewish ones, a halakhic difficulty is raised – that of *ḥukkat akum*, the prohibition against following the laws and practices of non-Jews (Lev. 18:3). In codifying this rule, the *Shulḥan Arukh* (*Yoreh De'ah, siman* 178) focuses on not changing one's appearance to look like a non-Jew. The Rema adds, based on the ruling of Rabbi Joseph Colon (Maharik, c. 1420–80), that the prohibition applies to "a matter that they have as a custom or rule and there is no reason for it, where there is a concern of 'the ways of the Amorite' (superstition) and that they have an aspect of idolatry from their forefathers, but something that is customary for a purpose… or is done for honor or another reason, is allowed." Based on this, the baldachin would not be prohibited in its modern guise as a *ḥuppa*, as it functions as a symbol of honor. But what of covering mirrors, which is based on superstition?

While some of the customs that we have seen here may have begun as superstitions from our perspective, my understanding is that they were not considered that way to the communities who originally practiced them. A superstition is an irrational practice, but in earlier times, when the world appeared to be filled with many unknown and

gods of the day on which the party was born." For a discussion of the development of Jewish birthday celebrations, see Israel Ta-Shma, "Al Yom HaHuledet BeYisrael," *Zion* 67 (2002), 19–24; Michael Avioz, "Birthday," *Bar-Ilan University Weekly Dvar Torah Page*, #577 (2004).

7 For a popular history of birthday celebrations, see Charles Panati, *Extraordinary Origins of Everyday Things* (New York: Harper and Row, 1987), 31–33; Tad Tuleja, *Curious Customs* (New York: Harmony Books, 1987), 25–26.

incomprehensible forces, conventions that we regard as superstitions today made some kind of sense. Just as the Talmud refers to astrological ideas that were considered the science of the time but today are categorized as superstition, so too is the case with other practices that made sense to people of a certain period, based on their world view and Zeitgeist.

With this understanding of *ḥukkat akum*, we can say that the prohibition applies to adopting a non-Jewish practice in a time and place where it has been demonstrated to be superstitious. In the case of covering mirrors, for example, by the time it could be viewed by people as a groundless superstition it had received rabbinic interpretations, recasting the practice as symbolic of ideas consistent with Jewish views of death and mourning. Thus, while clearly originating as a cross-cultural practice now understood according to our modern scientific views to be superstition, the custom to cover mirrors has become infused with new meaning, and survives today as a "Jewish" custom.[8]

The Vilna Gaon (*Shulḥan Arukh, Yoreh De'ah* 178:8) has a more stringent approach to *ḥukkat akum*, disputing the approach found in the Maharik and the Rema that any non-Jewish practice done for a reason is permitted. Instead, he argues that anything that emulates non-Jews is prohibited. The only practices that are permitted are "anything that we would do irrespective of them." In discussing this view, Rabbi Moshe Feinstein explains that even according to the Vilna Gaon, if Jews do something "of their own accord" (מסברת עצמן), even if it is also a non-Jewish practice, it would not be prohibited.[9] I would suggest that according to this understanding of *ḥukkat akum*, a custom that was never performed in order to emulate a non-Jewish practice per se, but simply in order to live in accordance with the mechanisms and forces present in the world as was understood by general society at that time, would not be *ḥukkat akum*. Jews did not cover mirrors in order to copy the mourning rituals of their non-Jewish neighbors; they did it to protect

---

8 Once, after speaking about the custom of covering mirrors in my community of Neve Daniel, the *rav* of the community, Matania Ben Shachar, referred to it as a custom that "underwent conversion."

9 Moshe Feinstein, *Iggerot Moshe, Yoreh De'ah* (New York, 1973), 2:168, 281.

themselves and the deceased from negative spiritual elements, which they understood as a fact of their reality.

### WHAT NOW?

What makes a custom Jewish? Is anything that Jews practice a Jewish custom? Not if everyone else is doing it as well. But once only Jews continue to practice it and a Jewish interpretation is given to it, it would seem that it morphs into a Jewish custom, despite its pedigree or lack thereof. Does this mean we have to keep it? Must the custom be perpetuated?

My understanding is that the term "have to keep it" is not really applicable to customs. Unlike halakha, customs have their origin with the masses. Only later do the rabbinic authorities give reasons and justifications for them in accordance with Jewish concepts and approaches. While halakha functions in a top-down manner, from authorities to the people, customs fundamentally work in the opposite way. They begin as a grassroots practice which later becomes justified, and even codified, by the authorities. It is for this reason that customs have fluidity; they are primarily in the hands of the common Jew. If the practice resonates with people, if the rabbinic explanations make sense to the masses, if the custom fills a human need, it will survive. Otherwise, it will slowly, or even not so slowly, fade away. Do you have to keep it? That is a question only you can answer.

# *Bibliography*


Abraham, David, ed. *Kol Bo*. Jerusalem: 2007.

Abrahams, Israel. "Jewish Ethical Wills." *The Jewish Quarterly Review* 3, no. 3 (April 1891): 436–84.

———. *The Book of Delight and Other Papers*. Philadelphia, PA: Jewish Publication Society of America, 1912.

———. *Hebrew Ethical Wills*. Philadelphia, PA: Jewish Publication Society, 1976.

Abramsky, Yaakov. *Ḥazon Yeḥezkel*. Bnei Brak: 2009.

Aburabia, Amram. *Netivei Am*. Petach Tikvah: 2006.

Adler, Elchanan. *Tzvi Tifara*. Passaic: 2017.

Adler, Menachem, ed. *Tal Orot HaKadmon*. Jerusalem: HaKetav VeHaMikhtav, 1996.

Aescoly, A.Z. *Sefer HaFalashim*. Jerusalem: Reuven Mass, 1943.

Afjin, Avner. *Divrei Shalom*. Vol. 4. Rosh HaAyin: 2003.

Aharon, Uri. "Melodies for Shir HaMaalot in Frankfurt am Main." *Duchan* 16. 2005.

Ahrend, Aaron. "Bride Going Around the Bridegroom – Study of a Marriage Custom." *Sidra* 7 (1991): 5–11.

Albeck, Shalom, ed. *Sefer HaEshkol*. Jerusalem: Wagschall, 1984.

Alfas, B.Z. *Mekor Dima – Shas Teḥina Ḥadasha*. Vilna: 1928.

Alkabetz, Shlomo. *Manot HaLevi*. Jerusalem: 2002.

Allen, Barbara. "The 'Image on Glass': Technology, Tradition, and the Emergence of Folklore." *Western Folklore* 41, no. 2 (April 1982): 85–103.

Aliner, A. "*Al Minhagei Keriat HaTorah VeHaHaftara BaAretz UVaGola.*" *Shana BeShana*. Jerusalem: 1964.

Alter, Yehuda Aryeh Leib. *Sfat Emet – Bemidbar*. Petrikov, Belarus: 1905.

Amar, Moshe. *Sefer She'eilot UTeshuvot R. Astruc b. David ibn Sangi.* Ramat Gan: Bar-Ilan University Press, 1982.

Aminach, Noach and Yosef Nitzan. *Gedolei HaAchronim*. Jerusalem: Jewish Agency, 2000.

Andrews, Tamara. *Nectar and Ambrosia: An Encyclopedia of Food in World Mythology*. Santa Barbara, CA: ABC-CLIO, 2000.

Angel, Shlomo, ed. *Sefer Tashbetz*. Jerusalem: Machon Yerushalayim, 2010.

Anshin, Natan. *Sippurim Yerushalmi'im*. Vol. 4. Jerusalem: Daat-HaMeimei, 1997.

Aptowitzer, Avigdor, ed. *Sefer Ra'aviah*. Vol. 1. Berlin: 1912.

Arnow, David. *Creating Lively Passover Seders: A Sourcebook of Engaging Tales, Texts & Activities*. Woodstock, VT: Jewish Lights, 2004.

Asad, Yehuda. *She'eilot UTeshuvot Yehuda Yaaleh, Oraḥ Ḥayim*. Lemberg: 1873.

Ashkenazi, Natan. *Birkat HaMazon im Peirush R. Ashkenazi*. Lublin: 1575.

Ashton, Dianne. *Hanukkah in America: A History*. New York: New York University Press, 2013.

Assaf, Simha. *Mekorot LeToldot HaḤinukh BeYisrael.* Tel Aviv: Dvir, 1925.

———, ed. *Sifran shel Rishonim. Sefer Minhagot*. Jerusalem: Ḥevrat Mekitzei Nirdamim, 1934.

Aubrey, John. *Remains of Gentilism and Judaism, 1686–87*. London: Satchell, Peyton, 1881.

Auerbach, Aharon and Yitzhak Triger, eds. *Halikhot Shlomo: Nisan–Av*. Jerusalem: Yeshivat Halikhot Shlomo, 2007.

Aust, Cornelia. "From Noble Dress to Jewish Attire: Jewish Appearances in the Polish-Lithuania Commonwealth and the Holy Roman Empire." In *Dress and Cultural Difference in Early Modern Europe*, edited by Cornelia Aust, Denise Klein, and Thomas Weller, 90–112. Berlin: De Gruyter, 2019.

Aviner, Shlomo. *Piskei Shlomo*. Vol. 1. Beit El: Sifriat Chava, 2013.

Avitan, David, ed. *Birkei Yosef*. Jerusalem: Siach Yisrael, 2005.

Avraham, Yissakhar. *Haggada shel Pesaḥ – Mateh Yissakhar*. Petrikov, Belarus: 1913.

Ayish, Yehuda. *Beit Yehuda*. Livorno: 1746.

Azariya de Rossi. *Meor Einayim*. Vilna: 1865.

Azulai, Hayim Yosef David. *Birkei Yosef*. Livorno: 1776. Jerusalem: 2019.

———. *Petaḥ Einayim*. Livorno: 1790.

———. *LeDavid Emet*. Jerusalem: 1847.

———. *Simḥat HaRegel*. Lemberg: 1863.

———. *Avodat HaKodesh*. Warsaw: 1874.

———. *Maḥzik Berakha, Oraḥ Ḥayim*. Vol. 5. Jerusalem: Yahadut, 1989.

———. *Otzrot Ḥayim: Tikkun Seuda*. Jerusalem: Ahavat Shalom, 1999.

Bachrach, Yair Hayim. *Mekor Ḥayim*. Vol. 2. Jerusalem: Machon Yerushalayim, 1983.

Bacon, Josephine. "Kalach, Kolatch, Kulitch – Challah?" In *Oxford Symposium on Food and Cookery, 1990: Feasting and Fasting: Proceedings*, edited by Harlan Walker, 53–54. London: Prospect Books, 1990.

Baer, Seligman. *Seder Avodat Yisrael*. Roedelheim: 1901.

———. *Siddur Avodat Yisrael*. Roedelheim: 1868.

Bagamilsky, Shmuel Pesaḥ. "*BeInyan Amirat Savri Maranan*." In *Kovetz He'arot HaTemimim VeAnshei Shlomenu*. Vol. 3. Morristown, NJ: 1988.

Bamberger, S., ed. *Peirush Lekaḥ Tov – Ruth*. Mainz: Lehman, 1887.

Bandi, Tavala. *Haggada shel Pesaḥ*. Frankfurt am Main: Slavatsky, 1898.

Baneth, Eduard. *Der Sederabend: Ein Vortrag*. Berlin: Poppelauer, 1904.

Bar-Ilan, Meir. *From Volozhin to Jerusalem*. Vol. 2. Tel Aviv: Pilei, 1939.

———. *Divrei Gad HaḤozeh*. Rehovot: Meir Bar-Ilan, 2015.

Bar-Lev, Yechiel, ed. *Maggid Meisharim*. Petach Tikvah: 1990.

Barda, David. *Revid HaZahav*. Tiberias: 1996.

Barnett, Abraham Natan. *Haggada shel Pesaḥ im Likkutim Neḥemadim*. Jerusalem: 1959.

Barzam, Moshe. *Imrot Moshe*. Bnei Brak: 2004.

Baumgarten, Joseph M. "The Calendars of the Book of Jubilees and the Temple Scroll." *Vetus Testamentum* 37, no. 1 (1987): 71–78.

Becher, Mordechai. *Gateway to Judaism: The What, How and Why of Jewish Life.* Brooklyn, NY: Shaar Press, 2005.

Bechor, Eliyahu. *Sefer HaTishbi.* Basel: 1601.

Becker, Hayim S. *Yalkut LeMoadim: Haggada shel Pesaḥ.* Jerusalem: HaTeḥiya, 1968.

Behar, Moshe and Zvi Ben-Dor Benite, eds. *Modern Middle Eastern Jewish Thought: Writings on Identity, Politics, and Culture, 1893–1958.* Waltham, MA: Brandeis University Press, 2013.

Belkin, Samuel. "*Midrash Tadshe* or *Midrash DeRav Pinḥas ben Yair,* an Ancient Hellenistic Midrash." *Horeb* 11 (Nisan 1951).

Bell, C.C. "Fifth of November Customs." *Folklore* 14, no. 1 (1903): 185–88.

Bell, Dean Phillip. *Jewish Identity in Early Modern Germany: Memory, Power and Community.* New York: Routledge, 2016.

Ben-David, Yehuda Levi. *Sefer Kara Ravatz.* Jerusalem: Birkei Yosef, 1996.

Ben-Dov, Jonathan. "Tradition and Innovation in the Calendar of Jubilees." In *Enoch and the Mosaic Torah: The Evidence of Jubilees,* edited by Gabrielle Boccaccini and Giovanni Ibba, 276–293. Leiden: Brill, 2007.

———. "The History of Pentecontad Time Units (I)." In *A Teacher for All Generations: Essays in Honor of James C. VanderKam,* vol. 1, edited by Eric F. Mason, 93–111. Leiden: Brill, 2012.

Ben-Harush, Pinhas. *Mei Pinḥas.* Ashdod: 2011.

Ben-Shem, Meir David, ed. *Sefer HaNer LeRav Zechariah ben Rav Yehuda Agmati.* Jerusalem: Machon Torah Shleimah, 1958.

Ben-Shimon, Refael Aharon. *Nahar Mitzrayim.* Alexandria: 1908.

Ben-Shushan, Yitzhak. *BeFi Yesharim – Haggada shel Pesaḥ.* Rishon LeZion: Agudat Maḥzikei Torah Etz HaḤayim, 1986.

Ben-Simchon, Refael. *Yahadut Magreb.* Jerusalem: Machon Bnei Yissachar, 1998.

Benayahu, Meir. *Sefer Zikaron LeRav Yitzhak Nissim.* Vol. 6: *Maamadot UMoshavot.* Jerusalem: Yad HaRav Nissim, 1985.

Bender, A.P. "Beliefs, Rites and Customs of the Jews Connected with Death, Burial and Mourning." *The Jewish Quarterly Review* 6, no. 2 (1894): 317–47.

Berelman, Yehuda. *Minhagei Amsterdam.* Jerusalem: Machon Yerushalayim, 2002.

Berger, Avigdor. *Minhagei Betziat Leḥem Mishna*. Jerusalem: Dfus Alon, 2002.

Berger, Shneur Zalman. *Noda BeShe'arim*, 2010.

Bergman, Asher. *Haggada shel Pesaḥ – Arzei HaLevanon*. Vol. 2. Bnei Brak: Mishor, 1999.

Bergman, Meir Zvi. *Sefer Shaarei Ora*. Jerusalem: 2001.

Berkowitz, Matthew. *The Lovell Haggadah*. Jerusalem: The Schechter Institute of Jewish Studies, 2008.

Berlin, Adele. *The JPS Bible Commentary: Esther*. Philadelphia, PA: Jewish Publication Society, 2001.

———, ed. *The Oxford Dictionary of the Jewish Religion*, 2nd ed. Oxford: Oxford University Press, 2011.

Berlin, I.P. *Minei Targuma*. Breslau: 1831.

Berliner, Abraham. *Ketavim Nivḥarim*. Vol. 1. Jerusalem: Mossad HaRav Kook, 1969.

Berman, Howard. *The New Union Haggadah – Revised Edition*. New York, NY: CCAR Press, 2014.

Berman, Samuel. *Midrash Tanhuma-Yelammedenu: An English Translation of Genesis and Exodus*. Hoboken, NJ: Ktav, 1996.

Bik, Moshe Zvi Aryeh, ed. *Amudei Shamayim*. 1962.

Bing, Yehezkel. *Siddur HaRashash*. Bnei Brak: Divrei Shalom, 2009.

Birnbaum, Philip. *Haggadah*. New York: Hebrew Publishing Company, 1953.

Bistritzky, Levi. *Siddur Shaar Menaḥem*. Tzfat: Ḥasdei Lev, 2008.

Biton, Eliyahu. *Sefer Netivot HaMaarav*. Jerusalem: Machon Bnei Yissachar, 1998.

———. *Netivot HaMaarav HaShalem*. Jerusalem: 2007.

———. *Naḥalat Avot*. Biria, 2006.

Blank, Debra Reed. "It's Time to Take Another Look at 'Our Little Sister' Soferim: A Bibliographical Essay." *Jewish Quarterly Review* 90, nos. 1–2 (1999): 1–26.

Blinder, Yaakov. *The Haggadah of the Roshei Yeshivah – Book Two*. Brooklyn, NY: Mesorah Publications, 1999.

Bloch, Abraham. *The Biblical and Historical Background of Jewish Customs and Ceremonies*. New York: Ktav, 1980.

Bloch, Joseph. *La Haggadah de Paque*. Paris: 1950.

Blum, Yehuda Zvi. *She'eirit Yehuda.* Jerusalem: 1972.
Blumenkrantz, Shlomo. *Baruch Tzuri.* Brooklyn, NY: 1972.
Boeckler, A.M. "'Service for the Souls': The Origin of Modern Memorial Services, 1819 to 1938." In *May God Remember: Memory and Memorializing in Judaism – Yizkor,* edited by Lawrence A. Hoffman, 113–27. Woodstock, VT: Jewish Lights, 2013.
Bombach, Avraham, ed. *Mor UKetzia.* Jerusalem: Machon Yerushalayim, 1996.
Brach, Shaul. *Tov Devarcha.* Munkacs: 1940.
Brand, John. *Observations on the Popular Antiquities of Great Britain: Chiefly Illustrating the Origin of Our Vulgar and Provisional Customs, Ceremonies, and Superstitions.* London: George Bell and Sons, 1893.
Brandeis, B.J. *Leshon Ḥakhamim.* Prague: 1815.
Brandwein, Eliezer. *Degel Machaneh Yehuda.* Brooklyn, NY: Imre Shefer, 2011.
Braun, I. *Tanya Rabbati.* Jerusalem: 2011.
Braun, Shlomo Zalman. *Kitzur Shulchan Aruḥ: She'arim Metzuyanim BeHalakha.* Vol. 4. New York: Feldheim, 1951.
Brendris, Shmariah. *Iyun Tefilla.* Lvov: 1849.
Brillman, Yehuda. *Minhagei Amsterdam.* Jerusalem: Machon Yerushalayim, 2001.
Brisman, Shimeon. *A History and Guide to Judaic Dictionaries and Concordances. Part 1: Dictionaries.* Hoboken, NJ: Ktav, 2000.
Brody, Robert, ed. *Responsa of Rav Natronai Gaon.* Jerusalem: Ofeq Institute, 1994.
———. *The Geonim of Babylonia and the Shaping of Medieval Jewish Culture.* New Haven, CT: Yale University Press, 1998.
Brown, Amy. *Understanding Food: Principles and Preparation.* Stamford, CT: Cengage Learning, 2015.
Buber, Salomon, ed. *Pesikta.* Lvov: 1868.
———, ed. *Siddur Rashi.* Berlin: Ḥevrat Mekitzei Nirdamim, 1911.
———, ed. *Sefer HaOra.* Lemberg: 1905.
———, ed. *Midrash Zuta.* Vilna: Romm, 1925.
———, ed. *Shibbolei HaLeket HaShalem.* Jerusalem: Zichron Aharon, 2012.

Bublil, Moshe. *Simḥat Banim.* 2006.

Buleh, Menachem. *Daat Mikra: Yirmeyahu.* Jerusalem: Mossad HaRav Kook, 1983.

Bulka, Reuven. *The Haggadah for Pesah.* Jerusalem: Machon Pri Haaretz, 1985.

Burne, Charlotte Sophia. "Presidential Address." *Folklore* 22, no. 1 (1911): 14–40.

———. *The Handbook of Folklore.* London: Sidgwick and Jackson, Ltd., 1914.

Burridge, Kate. *Weeds in the Garden of Words: Further Observations on the Tangled History of the English Language.* Cambridge: Cambridge University Press, 2005.

Bush, Lawrence and Jeffrey Dekro. "From *Gelt* to *Tzedakah.*" *Tikkun* 15, no. 6 (2000): 49.

Cameron, Morag. "Highland Fisher-Folk and Their Superstitions." *Folklore* 14, no. 3 (1903): 300–306.

Carlà-Uhink, Filippo. "Between the Human and the Divine: Cross-Dressing and Transgender Dynamics in the Graeco-Roman World." In *TransAntiquity: Cross-Dressing and Transgender Dynamics in the Ancient World,* edited by Domitilla Campanile, Filippo Carlà-Uhink, and Margherita Facell, 3–37. London: Routledge, 2017.

Cassel, Paulus. *An Explanatory Commentary on Esther: With Four Appendices Consisting of the Second Targum Translated from the Aramaic with Notes: Mithra: The Winged Bulls of Persepolis: and Zoroaster.* Edinburgh: T & T Clark, 1888.

Chacham, Amos. *Daat Mikra: Sefer Tehillim.* Vol. 2. Jerusalem: Mossad HaRav Kook, 1990.

———. *Daat Mikra: Shir HaShirim.* Jerusalem: Mossad HaRav Kook, 1990.

Chajes, J.H. *Between Worlds: Dybbuks, Exorcists, and Early Modern Judaism.* Philadelphia, PA: University of Pennsylvania Press, 2003.

Chambers, Robert. *Book of Days: A Miscellany of Popular Antiquities in Connection with the Calendar.* Whitefish, MT: Kessinger, 2004. Reprint of the original 1869 edition.

Chamiel, Chaim. "*Megillat Rut BeAtzeret.*" *Turei Yeshurun* 31 (May 1972).

Chananiah, Asher. *She'eilot UTeshuvot Shaarei Yosher*. Vol. 3. Jerusalem: 2005.

Chanoch Zundel ben Yosef. *Mitzhalot Ḥatanim*. Johannesberg, Germany: 1854.

Chardonnens, Laszlo Sandor. "Anglo-Saxon Prognostics: A Study of the Genre with a Text Edition." PhD diss., Leiden University, 2006.

———. *Anglo-Saxon Prognostics, 900–1100: Study and Texts*. Leiden: Brill, 2007.

Charney, Yosef Yehuda. *Sefer Masaot*. St. Petersburg: 1884.

Chavatzelet, Avraham. "*Birkat HaNehenin LeRav Yehuda ibn Shushan*." *Moriah* 72 (1983).

Chavel, Hayim, ed. *Rabbeinu Baḥye, Biur al HaTorah*. Jerusalem: Mossad HaRav Kook, 1990.

Chazzan, Yitzhak. *Ko LeḤai – Haggada shel Pesaḥ*. Jerusalem: Alfa, 1986.

———. *She'eilot UTeshuvot Yeḥaveh Daat*. Vol. 3. Jerusalem: Otiot, 2008.

Chesner, Yehuda. *Siaḥ Tefilla*. Ofakim: 2003.

Chill, Abraham. *The Minhagim: The Customs and Ceremonies of Judaism, Their Origins and Rationale*. New York: Sepher-Hermon Press, 1979.

Clarke, John. *Looking at Laughter: Humor, Power and Transgression in Roman Visual Culture*. Berkley: University of California Press, 2007.

Coggeshall, William T. *The Journeys of Abraham Lincoln*. Columbus: Ohio State Journal, 1865.

Cohen, Aharon Mendel. *Kelilat Ḥatanim*. Cairo: 1910.

Cohen, Baruch. *Barukh HaShulḥan*. Vol. 4. Bnei Brak: 1986.

Cohen, Daniel. *What Will They Say About You When You're Gone?: Creating a Life of Legacy*. Deerfield Beach, FL: Health Communications, 2016.

Cohen, David. *Shpola*. Haifa: Sokolofsky, 1965.

———. "*He'arot BeInyanei Tefilla*." *HaDarom* 50 (1980).

———. *Gvul Yaavetz*. Vol. 1. Brooklyn, NY: 1987.

———. *Sefer Yemei Ḥanukka*. Jerusalem: 2005.

Cohen, Gerson David. "The Story of the Four Captives." *Proceedings of the American Academy for Jewish Research* 29 (1960–1961): 55–131.

Cohen, Ishmael. *Shevaḥ Pesaḥ*. Warsaw: 1894.

Cohen, Meir. *Sefer Pesaḥ KeHalakha*. Ashdod: 1997.

Cohen, Shaye J.D. *The Beginnings of Jewishness: Boundaries, Varieties, Uncertainties*. Berkley, CA: University of California Press, 1999.

Cohen, Steven, and Kenneth Brander, eds. *The Yeshiva University Haggada*. New York: Student Organization of Yeshiva University, 1985.

Cohen, Yitzhak Yosef. *Ḥakhmei Hungaria VeHaSafrut HaToranit Bah*. Jerusalem: Machon Yerushalayim, 1997.

Cohen, Yonatan Binyamin. *Haggada shel Pesaḥ – Nefesh Yonatan*. Sighet: 1925.

Cohen, Yosef. *Sefer VaYeshev Yosef*. Printed in *BeKaneh Eḥad*. Vol. 3. Ashdod: 2016.

Cohn, Gabriel and Harold Fisch, eds. *Prayer in Judaism: Continuity and Change*. Northvale, NJ: Jason Aronson, 1996.

Cohn-Sherbok, Dan. *Dictionary of Jewish Biography*. New York: Continuum, 2005.

Cole, Susan Guettel. "Finding Dionysus." In Daniel Ogden, ed. *A Companion to Greek Religion*, 327–41. Oxford: Blackwell, 2010.

Conforte, David. *Korei HaDorot*. Jerusalem: Ahavat Shalom, Yad Samuel Franco, 2008.

Cooper, John. *Eat and Be Satisfied: A Social History of Jewish Food*. Northvale, NJ: Jason Aronson, 1993.

Cooperstein, Barukh Mordechai. *Ezer MiKodesh*. Jerusalem: 1993.

Corbit, Robert McClain. *History of Jones County, Iowa*. Vol. 1. Chicago: S. J. Clarke, 1910.

Corinaldi, Michael. "The Relationship Between the *Beta Yisrael* Tradition and the *Book of Jubilees*." In *Jews of Ethiopia*, edited by Oliver Leaman. New York: Routledge, 2005.

Coronel, Nachman Nathan, ed. *Seder Rav Amram Gaon*. Warsaw: 1865.

Courtney, M.A. "Cornish Feasts and 'Feasten' Customs" *Folklore* 4, no. 2 (1886): 109–132.

Coyte, Mary Ellen, Peter Gilbert, and Vicky Nicholis, eds. *Spirituality, Values and Mental Health: Jewels for the Journey*. London: Jessica Kingsley, 2007.

Crane, Diana. *Fashion and Its Social Agendas: Class, Gender, and Identity in Clothing*. Chicago, IL: University of Chicago Press, 2000.

Craven, Toni. *Artistry and Faith in the Book of Judith*. Chico, CA: Scholars Press, 1983.

Cravens, Craig Steven. *Culture and Customs of the Czech Republic and Slovakia*. Westport, CT: Greenwood, 2006.

Crawford, Sidnie White. *The Temple Scroll and Related Texts*. Sheffield: Sheffield Academic Press, 2000.

Crump, William. *Encyclopedia of New Year's Holidays Worldwide*. Jefferson, NC: McFarland, 2008.

Da Fano, Menahem Azariya. *She'eilot UTeshuvot HaRema MiPano*. Jerusalem: 1963.

———. *Sefer Gilgulei Neshamot*. Lublin: 1907.

Dachbash, Hizkiya. *Tiklal* (Shami). Rosh HaAyin, 2005.

Dandroivitch, Yisrael. "Are We Really Not Fulfilling the Commandment to Burn Chametz?" *Moriah* 10–12. 2016.

Danzig, Avraham. *Ḥayei Adam*. Vilna: 1819.

David ben Aryeh Leib of Lida. *Divrei David*. Brooklyn, NY: Tiferet Bachurim d-Bobov, 2006.

David ibn Zimra. *Magen David*. Amsterdam: 1713.

Davidson, Israel, Simha Assaf, and Yissachar Yoel, eds. *Siddur Rav Saadia Gaon*. Jerusalem: Reuven Mass, 2000.

Dayan, Nissim. *Naeh Zivam*. Bnei Brak: 2002.

De Sola Pool, David and Tamar. *The Haggadah of Passover*. New York: Jewish Welfare Board, 1943.

De Vidas, Eliyahu. *Reshit Ḥokhma*. Mukachevo, Ukraine: 1943.

Debs, Wayland. *Popular Beliefs and Superstitions: A Compendium of American Folklore*. Vol. 1. G.K. Hall, 1981.

Deitch, E. *Sefer Duda'ei HaSadeh*. Seini: 1929.

Deitch, Hayim Yehuda Segal. *Seder Haggada shel Pesaḥ: Kol Yehuda*. Satmar: 1937.

Dekker, Rudolf and Lotte van de Pol. *The Tradition of Female Cross-Dressing in Early Modern Europe*. London: Macmillan Press, 1989.

Dembińska, Maria. *Food and Drink in Medieval Poland: Rediscovering a Cuisine of the Past*. Philadelphia, PA: University of Pennsylvania Press, 1999.

Demetrio, Francisco R. *Encyclopedia of Philippine Folk Beliefs and Customs*. Vol. 2. Cagayan de Oro City, Philippines: Xavier University, 1991.

Deutsch, Moshe. *Or Ganuz*. Vol. 2. London: 1996.

Devilsky, David, ed. *Sefer Ra'aviah*. Vol. 2. Bnei Brak: 2005.

Devlitzky, Seriah. *Zeh HaShulḥan*. Bnei Brak: 1958.

Devoraks, Eliyakim. *BeShvilei HaMinhag – Shabbat UMoadim*. Vol. 2. Jerusalem: Imrei David, 1997. Vol. 3. Jerusalem: 1998.

Diamant, Anita. *The Jewish Wedding Now*. New York: Simon and Schuster, 2001.

Dinner, Eliezer. *Zikhron Avraham Moshe*. Jerusalem: 1945.

Diskin, Mordechai. *Divrei Mordekhai*. Jerusalem: 1889.

Docken, Frank. *Herod as a Composite Character in Luke-Acts*. Tubingen, Germany: Mohr Siebeck, 2014.

Dodwell, Charles Reginald. *Anglo-Saxon Gestures and the Roman Stage*. Cambridge: Cambridge University Press, 2000.

Domb, Yonatan Shraga, ed. *Shu"t Rabbeinu Yaakov Weil*. Vol. 1. Jerusalem: Machon Yerushalayim, 2000.

Donnely, Catherine, ed. *The Oxford Companion to Cheese*. Oxford: Oxford University Press, 2016.

Dosick, Wayne. *Living Judaism: The Complete Guide to Jewish Belief, Tradition and Practice*. New York: HarperOne, 1995.

Dow, James. *German Folklore: A Handbook*. Westport, CT: Greenwood Press, 2006.

Drukman, Hayim. *Netiot Haaretz*. Kfar Darom: Makhon HaTorah VeHaAretz, 2004.

Dubarle, A.M. *Judith: Formes et Sens des Diverses Traditions – Tome II: Textes*. Rome: Institut Biblique Pontifical, 1966.

Dubnow, Nissan David. *Eḥad Mi Yode'a*. Tzfat: Chish, 2008.

Duke Estroff, Sharon. *Can I Have a Cell Phone for Hanukkah?: The Essential Scoop on Raising Modern Jewish Kids*. New York: Broadway Books, 2007.

Dunat (Donath), Moshe Eliezer. *Dibburei Emet*. Bardiow: Horovitz, 1931.

Duncan, Leland L. "Fairy Beliefs and Other Folklore: Notes from County Leitrim." *Folklore* 7, no. 2 (1896): 161–83.

Dunner, "*Mishnato shel Moreinu HaRav, ztz"l*." *Kol HaTorah* 65 (Nisan 5768/2008).

Dynner, Glenn. "The Garment of Torah: Clothing Decrees and the Warsaw Career of the First Gerer Rebbe." In *Warsaw: The Jewish*

*Metropolis: Essays in Honor of the 75th Birthday of Professor Antony Polonsky*, edited by Glenn Dyner and Francois Guesnet, 91–127. Leiden: Brill, 2015.

Efrati, Yaakov. *Vavim LeAmudim*. Vol. 3. Jerusalem: 2002.

Ehrenreich H.Z. *Shaarei Ḥayim* on *Shaarei Ephraim*. Irsava: 1932.

Ehrenreich, Hayim Yehuda, ed. *Sefer HaPardes*. Budapest: 1924.

Ehrenreich, Hayim Zvi. *Ketzei HaMateh* commentary on *Mateh Ephraim*. New York: Kol Aryeh, 1959.

Ehrenreich, Shlomo Zalman, ed. *Iggeret HaTiyul*. Jerusalem: HaTechiya, 1957.

Eichorn, Yissachar Dov. *Pi Kohen*. Jerusalem: 2010.

Einfeld, Natan. *Minḥat Natan – Aggada*. Bnei Brak: 2007.

Eisenstein, J.D. *Otzar Midrashim*. New York: Noble Offset Printers, 1915.

———. *Otzar Dinim UMinhagim*. New York: 1917.

———. *Haggada: Seder Ritual for Passover Eve*. New York: Hebrew Publishing Company, 1928.

Ela, A. "Working Evil by a Duck's Foot." *Folklore* 28, no. 3 (1917): 322.

Elbogen, Ismar. *Jewish Liturgy: A Comprehensive History*. Philadelphia, PA: The Jewish Publication Society, 1993.

Eleazar of Worms. *Sefer HaRokeaḥ HaGadol*. Jerusalem: 1966.

Elfenbein, Israel. *Sefer Minhagim DeBei Rabbi Meir ben Barukh MiRotenburg*. New York: Jewish Theological Seminary of America, 1938.

Elias, Joseph. *Haggadah shel Pesach*. Brooklyn, NY: Mesorah, 1977.

Eliram, Shlomo. *Harei At Mekudeshet*. Jerusalem: 1993.

Eliyahu, Mordechai. *Siddur Kol Eliyahu HaShalem*. Jerusalem: Darkhei Horaa LeRabbanim, 2002.

———. *Kitzur Shulḥan Arukh*. Jerusalem: 2009.

Eliyahu of Vilna. *Yahel Or*. Vilna: Romm, 1882.

Elkayam, Shlomo. "Maḥzor Fez as a Source for Ancient Prayer Customs." *Hemdaat* 6.

Emanuel, Simha, ed. *Rabbi Eleazar of Worms: Derasha LePesaḥ*. Jerusalem: Ḥevrat Mekitzei Nirdamim, 2006.

Emden, Yaakov. *She'eilat Yaavetz*. Lemberg: 1884.

———. *Siddur Beit Yaakov*. Lemberg: 1904.

———. *Amudei Shamayim*. Altona: 1745. Altona: 1748. 1962 facsimile edition.

Emert, Phyllis Raybin. *The Pretzel Book*. New Hope, PA: Woodsong Graphics, 1984.
Englishman, Michael. *163256: A Memoir of Resistance*. Waterloo, Ontario: Wilfrid Laurier University Press, 2007.
Epstein, Abraham. *Mikadmonot Hayehudim*. Vienna: 1887.
Epstein, M.M. *Levush Mordekhai – Bava Kama*. Jerusalem: 1957.
Epstein, Steve. "The Source of the Addition of *Tehillat Hashem* after *Shir HaMaalot*." In *Ḥiddushei Torah@NDS* 12. 2011.) [Hebrew].
Epstein, Yechiel Michel. *Kitzur Shenei Luḥot HaBrit*. Amsterdam: 1721. Jerusalem: 1944.
Erlich, Avi. *Ancient Zionism: The Biblical Origins of the National Idea*. New York: Free Press, 1995.
Escapa, Yosef. *Rosh Yosef*. Izmir: 1658.
Etshalom, Yitzhak. "*Al HaDima VeAl HaRina – Iyun BeMizmor* 126." *Megadim* 42 (2005).
Eybeschutz, Yonatan. *Ye'arot Devash*. Jerusalem: Machon Or HaSefer, 1988.
Falk, Daniel Keith. *Daily, Sabbath and Festival Prayers in the Dead Sea Scrolls*. Leiden: Brill, 1998.
Falk, David. *Sefer Inyano Shel Yom*. Jerusalem: 2004.
Farbstein, Esther. *Hidden in Thunder: Perspectives on Faith, Halacha and Leadership During the Holocaust*. Jerusalem: Mossad HaRav Kook, 2007.
Feinhandler, Yisroel. *Avnei Yashpeh*. Jerusalem: 1999.
Feinstein, David. *The Kol Dodi Haggadah*. Brooklyn, NY: Mesorah Publications, in conjunction with Mesivta Tifereth Jerusalem, 1990.
Feinstein, Moshe. *Iggerot Moshe, Yoreh De'ah*. Vol. 2. New York: 1973.
Feldman, Y. *Areshet Sefateinu*. Vol. 4. Brooklyn, NY: 1965.
———. S. *Sefer Yisrael BeMaamadam*. New Square, NY: 2005.
Feldman, Yirmiyahu. *Divrei Yirmeyahu – Kiddushin*. Jerusalem: Machon Yerushalayim, 1984.
Feliks, Yehuda. *Nature and Land in the Bible*. Jerusalem: Reuven Mass, 1992.
Ferguson, Everett. *Backgrounds of Early Christianity*. Grand Rapids, MI: William B. Eerdmans, 2003.

Fine, Lawrence. *Physician of the Soul, Healer of the Cosmos: Isaac Luria and His Kabbalistic Fellowship.* Stanford, CA: Stanford University Press, 2003.

Fine, Steven. "How Do You Know a Jew When You See One? Reflections on Jewish Costume in the Roman World." In *Fashioning Jews: Clothing, Culture, and Commerce,* edited by Leonard Jay Greenspoon, 19–28. West Lafayette, IN: 2013.

Finkelstein, M. *Tosefet Ḥayim* on *Ḥayei Adam.* Warsaw: 1888.

Firth, Raymond. *Symbols: Public and Private.* London: Allen and Unwin, 1973.

Fisher, Alexander J. *Music, Piety, and Propaganda: The Soundscape of Counter-Reformation Bavaria.* Oxford: Oxford University Press, 2014.

Fisher, Shlomo. "'Do Not Let Wickedness Dwell in Our Tents' (On Forgeries in Books and Books Containing Deceptive Ideas)." *Tzfunot* 3 (Nisan 5749).

Fishman, Talya. "Rhineland Pietist Approaches to Prayer and the Textualization of Rabbinic Culture in Medieval Northern Europe." *Jewish Studies Quarterly* 11, no. 4 (2004): 313–331.

Fogel, Moshe. "The Sabbatean Character of Hemdat Yamim: A Reexamination." *Jerusalem Studies in Jewish Thought* 16, no. 2 (2001).

Folger, Chaim Ben-Zion. *Shevach Pesach.* Monsey, NY: Eastern Book Press, 2013.

Forbes, Bruce David. *Christmas: A Candid History.* Los Angeles: University of California Press, 2007.

Forta, Arye. *Examining Religions: Judaism.* Oxford: Heinemann Educational, 1995.

Frazer, James. "Some Popular Superstitions of the Ancients." *Folklore* 1, no. 2 (1890): 145–71.

———. *The Golden Bough.* New York: MacMillan, 1900. Cambridge: Cambridge University Press, 1913.

Freehof, Solomon B. "The Origin of the Tahanun." *Hebrew Union College Annual* 2 (1925): 339–50.

———. *Recent Reform Responsa.* Cincinnati, OH: Hebrew Union College Press, 1960.

———. "Hazkarath Neshamoth." *Hebrew Union College Annual* 36 (1965): 179–89.

Friedland, E.L. "The Atonement Memorial Service in the American Mahzor." *Hebrew Union College Annual* 55 (1984): 243–82.

Friedland, Eric L. "Yizkor: A Microcosm of Liturgical Interconnectivity." In *May God Remember: Memory and Memorializing in Judaism – Yizkor*, edited by Lawrence A. Hoffman, 104–12. Woodstock, VT: Jewish Lights, 2013.

Friedlander, Hayim. *Siftei Ḥayim: Moadim.* Vol. 2. Bnei Brak: 1993.

Friedman, Avraham Tsevi, *Sefer Otzar Halakhot.* Vol. 2. Brooklyn, NY: Hamatik Printing, 2007.

Friedman, Yaakov, ed. *Leket Yosher – Oraḥ Ḥayim.* Berlin, 1903.

Friedman, Yisrael Chaim. *Likkutei Mahariḥ.* Vol. 1. Jerusalem, 2013. Vol. 2. Sighet, 1900. Jerusalem, 1965. Vol. 3. New York, 1965.

Friedman, Yoel, ed. *HaTorah VeHaAretz.* Jerusalem: Hemed, 2001.

Frenkel, Yonah. *Midrash VeAggada.* Tel Aviv: The Open University of Israel, 1996.

Freiman, Jacob, ed. *The Sefer HaMaḥkim of R. Nathan ben Yehuda.* Kharkov: 1909.

———. "*Sefer Amarcal al Hilkhot Yayin Nesekh.*" In *LeDavid Zvi.* Berlin: 1914.

Freundel, Barry. *Why We Pray What We Pray: The Remarkable History of Jewish Prayer.* Jerusalem: Urim, 2010.

Friend, Tuvia. *Moadim LeSimḥa.* Jerusalem: Otzar HaPoskim, 2000.

Frohlich, Ida. "Enoch and Jubilees." In *Enoch and Qumran Origins: New Light on a Forgotten Connection*, edited by Gabriele Boccaccini, 141–47. Grand Rapids, MI: Eerdmans, 2005.

Frojimovics, Kinga, ed. *Jewish Budapest: Monuments, Rites and History.* Budapest: Central European University Press, 1999.

Frumkin, Aryeh Loeb. *Seder Tefilla KeMinhag Ashkenaz im Seder Rav Amram HaShalem.* Vol. 1. Jerusalem: 1912.

Gaguine, Shemtob. *Keter Shem Tov.* Vol. 1. Jerusalem: 1960. Vol. 2. London: 1934. Vol. 6. London: Shraga, 1955.

Gald, Yechiel Michel. *Sefer Darkhei Ḥayim VeShalom.* Munkacs, 1940.

Ganzfried, Shlomo. *Kitzur Shulḥan Arukh.* Lemberg: 1884. Warsaw: 1901. Lublin: 1905. Vilna: 1915. Hebrew Publishing Company, 1927. Jerusalem: 1944. Basel: 1945. Jerusalem: Mossad HaRav Kook, 1973.

Garnsey, Peter. *Food and Society in Classical Antiquity*. Cambridge: Cambridge University Press, 1999.

Gaster, Theodor. *Myth, Legend, and Custom in the Old Testament*. New York: Harper and Row, 1969.

Gavra, Moshe. *Meḥkarim BeSiddurei Teiman*. Bnei Brak: HaMakhon LeḤeker Ḥakhmei Teiman, 2010.

———. *HaTiklal HaMadai HaMehudar*. Bnei Brak: HaMakhon LeḤeker Ḥakhmei Teiman, 2012.

Gelbard, Shmuel. *Otzar Taamei HaMinhagim*. Petach Tikva: Mifal Rashi, 1996.

Gereboff, Joel. "One Nation, with Liberty and Haggadahs for All." In *Key Texts in American Jewish Culture*, edited by Jack Kugelmass, 275–92. New Brunswick, NJ: Rutgers University Press, 2003.

Gershon, Reuven David and Moshe David Shvicha. "*Seder HaShulḥan LeRabbi Naftali*." In *Birkat Menaḥem*. Cleveland, OH: Machon Nahor Safra, 2007.

Gig, Eliyahu. *Zeh HaShulḥan*. Algeria: 1888–1889.

Gilbert, Arthur. *The Passover Seder: Pathways Through the Haggadah*. New York: Ktav, 1965.

Giman, Elazar. *Sifran shel Tzaddikim*. Lublin: 1928.

Ginzberg, Louis. *Genizah Studies in Memory of Doctor Solomon Schechter*. Vol. 2. New York: Jewish Theological Seminary, 1929.

Glass, Lillian. *Say It… Right: How to Talk in Any Social or Business Situation*. New York: Putnam's Sons, 1991.

Glatzer, Nahum, ed. *The Passover Haggadah*. New York: Schocken Books, 1953.

Glick, Shmuel. *Or LeAvel*. Efrat: 1991.

———. *Or Noga Aleihem*. Efrat: Keter, 1997.

Gold, Yechiel Michel. *Darkhei Ḥayim VeShalom*. Munkacz: 1940. Brooklyn, NY: 1987.

Goldberg, Avraham. "Rabbinic and Biblical Shabbat Prohibitions." *Sinai* 46 (Tishrei 1959).

Goldberg, Chaim. *Pnei Barukh*. Jerusalem: 1986.

Goldberger, Dov. *Osim Seder – Haggada shel Pesaḥ*. Tel Aviv: Yedioth Ahronoth, 2004.

Goldhaber, Yechiel. *Sefer Minhagei HaKehillot*. Vol. 2. Jerusalem: 2007.

Goldin, Hyman, trans. *Kitzur Shulchan Aruch, Code of Jewish Law*. New York: Hebrew Publishing Co., 1963.

Goldish, Matt. *Jewish Questions: Responsa on Sephardic Life in the Early Modern Period*. Princeton, NJ: Princeton University Press, 2008.

Goldman, Norma. "Reconstructing Roman Clothing." In *The World of Roman Costume*, edited by Judith Lynn Sebesta and Larissa Bonfante, 213–40. Madison, WI: University of Wisconsin Press, 2001.

Goldreich, Yair. "*Sidrei Tefilla BaKehilla.*" *Shnot Ḥayim* (2007).

Goldschmidt, Aryeh, ed. *Maḥzor Vitry*. Vol. 1. Jerusalem: Otzar HaPoskim, 2004.

Goldschmidt, Daniel. *Die Pessach-Haggada*. Berlin: Schocken, 1937.

———. *Haggada shel Pesaḥ*. Tel Aviv: Schocken, 1947.

———. *Maḥzor LeYamim HaNora'im – Yom Kippur*. Jerusalem: 1970.

———. *Maḥzor Sukkot, Shemini Atzeret VeSimḥat Torah*. Jerusalem: 1981.

———, ed. *Seder Rav Amram Gaon*. Jerusalem: Mossad HaRav Kook, 2004.

———. *Yeshuat Daniel*. Modiin Illit, 2013.

Goldschmidt, Shlomo, ed. *Seder Rav Amram Gaon*. Jerusalem: Mossad HaRav Kook, 2004.

Goldstein, J.A. *II Maccabees – A New Translation with Introduction and Commentary*. New York: Doubleday, 1983.

Golinkin, David. *Responsa in a Moment: Halakhic Responses to Contemporary Issues*. Vol. 4. Jerusalem: Schechter Institute of Jewish Studies, 2017.

Gombo, Zvi. *Or Zvi – Shabbat*. Vol. 2. Bnei Brak: 2000.

Gomme, Laurence. "Rules Concerning Perilous Days." *Folklore* 24, no. 1 (1913): 121–23.

Grattan, J.H.G. and C.W. Singer. *Anglo-Saxon Magic and Medicine, Illustrated Specially from the Semi-Pagan*. London: Oxford University Press, 1952.

Grayzel, Solomon. "Hasmonean Coins." In *Hanukkah: The Feast of Lights*, edited by Emily Solis-Cohen, 91–92. Philadelphia, PA: Jewish Publication Society of America, 1965.

Greco, Gina L. and Christine M. Rose, trans. *The Good Wife's Guide: A Medieval Household Book*. Ithaca, NY: Cornell University Press, 2009.

Green, Aaron. *The Revised Haggadah*. London: George Routledge and Sons, 1897. London: George Routledge and Sons, 1929.

Greenberg, Irving. *The Jewish Way: Living the Holidays*. New York: Simon and Schuster, 1988.

Greenberg, Susan Karla. *Tallitot: History and Design*. Thesis, University of Wisconsin-Madison, 1975.

Greenblatt, Ephraim. *Rivevos Ephraim*. Vol. 1. Memphis, TN: 1975. Vol. 2. Brooklyn, NY: Deutsch Printing and Publishing Co., 1978. Vol. 6. Brooklyn, NY: Mazel, 1993. Vol. 7. Brooklyn, NY: Mazel, 1995.

Greenboim, David Efraim. *Haggada VeAggadta*. Modiin Illit: 2004.

Greenwald, Yaakov. *VaYaged Yaakov*. Brooklyn, NY: 2008.

Greenwald, Yekutiel Yehuda (Leopold). *Kol Bo al Aveilut*. New York: Moria, 1947.

Gries, Ze'ev. *Safrut HaHanhagot*. Jerusalem: Bialik Institute, 1989.

Grig, Lucy. *Popular Culture in the Ancient World*. Cambridge: Cambridge University Press, 2017.

Grintz, Yehoshua. *Sefer Yehudit*. Jerusalem: Bialik Institute, 1957.

Gross, Mordechai. *Iggreta DeḤedvata*. Vol. 18. Bnei Brak: 2015.

Gross, Shalom. *Afiat Matza HaShalem*. Jerusalem: 1983.

Gross, Shlomo, ed. *Divrei Torah al Haggada shel Pesaḥ*. Ramat Beit Shemesh: Or Yechezkel, 2008.

Grossberg, Chanoch Zundel. *Zer HaTorah*. Jerusalem: 1979.

Grossfeld, Bernard. *The Two Targums of Esther*. Translated with Apparatus and Notes. Collegeville, MN: Liturgical Press, 1991.

Grossman, Avraham. *The Early Sages of France: Their Lives, Leadership and Works*. Jerusalem: Magnes Press, 2001.

———. *The Early Sages of Ashkenaz*. Jerusalem: Magnes Press, 2001.

Gruen, Erich. *Heritage and Hellenism: The Reinvention of Jewish Tradition*. Berkeley: University of California Press, 1998.

Guggenheimer, Heinrich. *The Scholar's Haggadah*. Northvale, NJ: Jason Aronson, 1998.

Haas, S. *Kerem Shlomo*. Pressburg: 1848.

Haberman, Avraham Meir. "*Minhagei HaKehilla BeVermiza Mitokh Sefer HaMinhagim shel Rav Yuspa Shamash*." *Sinai* 79, nos. 5–6 (1976).

Haberman, A., ed. *Even Boḥen*. Tel Aviv: Machbaroth Lesifrut Publishing House, 1956.

Haberman, A. *Ḥadashim Gam Yeshanim*. Jerusalem: Reuven Mass, 1971.
Hacker, Joseph and Yaron Harel, eds. *The Scepter Shall Not Depart from Judah: Leadership, Rabbinate and Community in Jewish History: Studies Presented to Professor Shimon Schwarzfuchs*. Jerusalem: Bialik Institute, 2011.
Hacohen, Aviad. *The Tears of the Oppressed: An Examination of the Agunah Problem – Background and Halakhic Sources*. Jersey City, NJ: Ktav, 2004.
Hacohen, Elazar. *Haggada Zikhron Niflaot*. Warsaw: 1880.
Hacohen, Eliyahu. *Shevet Mussar*. Jerusalem: 1989.
Hacohen, Menachem. *Sefer Ḥayei Adam – Kelulot*. Jerusalem: Keter, 1986.
Hacohen, Naftali Yaakov. *Otzar HaGedolim*. Bnei Brak: 1966.
Hacohen, Shushan. *Peraḥ Shushan*. Jerusalem: 1977.
Hacohen, Yosef. "*BeInyan Shome'a KeOneh BeSefirat HaOmer*." *Or Torah* (Tevet 5763/2002).
Hahn, Joseph Juspa. *Sefer Yosef Ometz*. Frankfurt am Main: 1723.
HaKohen, Aharon. *Orḥot Ḥayim*. Jerusalem: Sela, 1956.
Halachmi, David. *Ḥakhmei Yisrael*. Bnei Brak: Tiferet Hasefer, 1980.
HaLevi, Naftali Hertz. *Siddur HaGra*. Jerusalem: 1895.
Halberstam, Yekutiel Yehudah. *Divrei Yatziv*. Jerusalem: Shefa Ḥayim, 1997.
———. *She'eilot UTeshuvot Divrei Yatziv, Oraḥ Ḥayim*. Vol. 1. Kiryat Sanz, Netanya: 2004.
Hallamish, Moshe. *Kabbalah: In Liturgy, Halakha and Customs*. Ramat Gan: Bar-Ilan University Press, 2000.
———. *Hanhagot Kabbaliot BeShabbat*. Jerusalem: Orchot, 2006.
Hamburger, Binyamin Shlomo. "*Shnei Ḥuppot BeYom HaNisuin*." *Or Yisrael* 21 (Tishrei 5761/2001).
———. "Synagogue Customs for Ashkenazim in Israel and the Diaspora." *Yerushateinu* 2 (2008) [Hebrew].
Hammer, Jill. "Holle's Cry: Unearthing a Birth Goddess in a German Jewish Naming Ceremony." *Nashim: A Journal of Jewish Women's Studies and Gender Issues* 9 (2005): 62–87.
Hand, Wayland D., ed. *The Frank C. Baum Collection of North Carolina Folklore*. Durham, NC: Duke University Press, 1964.
Handelman, Maxine Segal. *Jewish Every Day: The Complete Handbook for Early Childhood Teachers*. Denver, CO: ARE Publishing, 2000.

Harari, Moshe. *Mikra'ei Kodesh: Hilkhot Purim*. Jerusalem: Mercaz HaRav, 1994.

———. *Mikra'ei Kodesh: Yom Kippur*. Jerusalem: 2003.

Hastings, James, ed. *Encyclopedia of Religion and Ethics*. Edinburgh: T & T Clark, 1913. New York: Charles Scribner's Sons, 1916.

Havlin, Shlomo Zalman, ed. *Sefer Kol Bo*. Jerusalem: Even Yisroel, 1997.

Hayim, Yosef. *Ben Ish Ḥai – Halakhot*. Jerusalem: Siach Yisrael, 1985.

———. *Otzrot Ḥayim – Yamim UZemanim – Moadim 1*. Jerusalem: Ahavat Shalom, 1996.

———. *Sefer Ben Ish Ḥai HaMeshulav*. Bnei Brak: Machon HaRav Matzliach, 2005.

Heina, Yehuda Arye Leib. *Likkutei Yehuda, Devarim* 1. Jerusalem: 1972.

Heinzelmann, Ursula. *Food Culture in Germany*. Westport, CT: Greenwood Press, 2008.

Henshke, David, *Festival Joy in Tannaitic Discourse*. Jerusalem: Magnes Press, 2007.

Herr S. and S. Shrira. *Toldot HaSifrut HaTalmudit*. Tel Aviv: Haskala LaAm, 1937.

Hershler, Shimon, ed. *Ḥanukkat HaBayit*. Bnei Brak: Machon Nachlat Zvi, 1991.

———. *Seh LaBayit*. London: 2010.

Hershler, Moshe, ed. *Siddur of R. Solomon ben Samson of Garmaise*. Jerusalem: Hemed, 1971.

———, ed. *Siddur Rabbeinu Shlomo*. Jerusalem: 1972.

———. *Maaseh Yehudit*. In *Genuzot I*. Jerusalem: Moznaim, 1984.

Hershler, Moshe and Yehudah Hershler, eds. *Peirushei Siddur HaTefilla LaRokeaḥ*. Jerusalem: Machon HaRav Hershler, 1992.

Hershovitz, Avraham. *Otzar Kol Minhagei Yeshurun. Sefer Minhagei Yeshurun*. Warsaw: 1899. Vilna: 1899. St. Louis, MO: 1918. Lemberg: 1929.

Hewitt, Sarah Rochel, ed. *Beginners Passover Haggadah*. New York: National Jewish Outreach Program, 2010.

Higger, Michael. *Halakhot VaAggadot*. New York: 1933.

———, ed. *Masekhet Soferim*. New York: Dbei Rabanan, 1937.

———. "*Sefer Amarcal al Hilkhot Pesaḥim*." In *Sefer HaYovel LeAlexander Marx*. New York: Jewish Theological Seminary, 1950.

Hilevitz, Alter. "Taanit Esther." *Sinai* 64 (1968).

———. *Ḥikkrei Zemanim*. Vol. 1. Jerusalem: Mossad HaRav Kook, 1976.

Hill, Thomas D. "Perchta the Belly Slitter and Án Hrísmagi: 'Laxdœla Saga' Cap. 48–49." *The Journal of English and Germanic Philology* 106, no. 4 (2007): 516–23.

Hirshman, Marc. *The Stabilization of Rabbinic Culture, 100 CE – 350 CE: Texts on Education and Their Late Antique Context*. Oxford: Oxford University Press, 2009.

Hobden, Fiona. *The Symposion in Ancient Greek Society and Thought*. Cambridge: Cambridge University Press, 2013.

Hoenig, Sidney. *Hanukkah: The Feast of Lights*. Philadelphia, PA: Jewish Publication Society of America, 1937.

———. *The Haggadah of Passover with Introductory Notes and Supplement*. New York: Shulsinger Brothers, 1950.

Hoffman, Lawrence. *The Canonization of the Synagogue Service*. Notre Dame, IN: University of Notre Dame Press, 1979.

———, ed. *My People's Prayer Book: Tachanun and Concluding Prayers*. Woodstock, VT: Jewish Lights, 2002.

———. "The Liturgy of Confession: What It Is and Why We Say It." In *We Have Sinned: Sin and Confession in Judaism*, edited by Lawrence A. Hoffman, 13–31. Woodstock, VT: Jewish Lights, 2012.

———, ed. *May God Remember: Memory and Memorializing in Judaism – Yizkor*. Woodstock, VT: Jewish Lights, 2013.

Hoffman, Lawrence, and David Arnow, eds. *My People's Passover Haggadah: Traditional Texts, Modern Commentaries*. Woodstock, VT: Jewish Lights, 2008.

Hofmeister, Shlomo. *Seder Zemirot Yeshurun*. Vienna: Yeshurun, 2016.

Holzberg, Moshe Zvi. "*Biur Makkot Mitzrayim*." *Kovetz Beit Aharon* 33 (Shvat-Adar 5751/1991).

Horovitz, Mordechai HaLevi (Markus). *Rabbanei Frankfurt*. Jerusalem: Mossad HaRav Kook, 1972.

Horowitz, Avraham Halevi, *Orkhot Rabbeinu*. Vol. 1. Bnei Brak: 1991.

Horowitz, Isaiah. *Shenei Luḥot HaBrit*. Jerusalem: Oz VeHadar, 1992. Jerusalem: Machon Shaarei Ziv, 1993.

Horowitz, Isaiah. *Siddur HaShelah, Shaar HaShamayim*. Amsterdam: 1717.

Horowitz, Isaiah. *Haggadat HaShelah HaShalem*. Jerusalem: Ahavat Shalom, 2001.

Horowitz, Levi Yitzchak. *Seder Haggada Shel Pesaḥ – Ezrat Avoteinu*. Jerusalem: New England Chassidic Center, 1997.

Horvitz, Avraham. *Orḥot Rabbeinu HaKehillot Yaakov*. Vol. 3. Bnei Brak: 1998.

Hrabák, Josef. *Výbor z české literatury od počátků po dobu Husovu* (Committee on Czech Literature: From the Beginning to the Time of Hus). Prague: Czechoslovak Academy of Sciences, 1957.

Hurwitz, Simon. *Maḥzor Vitry*. Nuremberg: J. Bulka, 1923.

Huss, Boaz. *The Zohar: Reception and Impact*. Liverpool, England: Liverpool University Press, 2016.

Hutchins, Kristin. "Candle Making." In *All Things Dickinson: An Encyclopedia of Emily Dickinsons's World*. Vol. 1, edited by Wendy Martin. Santa Barbara, CA: Greenwood, 2014.

Idelsohn, A.Z. *Jewish Liturgy and Its Development*. New York: Henry Holt, 1932.

Inbari, Motti. *Messianic Religious Zionism Confronts Israeli Territorial Compromises*. Cambridge: Cambridge University Press, 2012.

Ingbar, Yosef. *Minḥat Yosef*. Lakewood, NJ: 2009.

Insoll, Timothy. *Case Studies in Archaeology and World Religion: The Proceedings of the Cambridge Conference*. Oxford: Archaeopress, 1999.

Israelzon, Moshe. *Haggada shel Pesaḥ*. Jerusalem: Machon Keren Re'em, 2006.

Isaacs, Ronald. *Bubbe Meises: Jewish Myths, Jewish Realities*. Jersey City, NJ: Ktav, 2008.

Issac, Pinhas. *Peninei Pardes – Haggada shel Pesaḥ*. Rishon LeZion: 1995.

Isserles, Justine. "Some Hygiene and Dietary Calendars in Hebrew Manuscripts from Medieval Ashkenaz." In *Time, Astronomy, and Calendars in the Jewish Tradition*, edited by Sacha Stern and Charles Burnett, 273–326. Leiden: Brill, 2014.

Isserlin, Israel. *Leket Yosher*. Berlin: 1903.

Issitt, Micah and Carlyn Main. *Hidden Religion: The Greatest Mysteries and Symbols of the World's Religious Beliefs*. Santa Barbara, CA: ABC-CLIO, 2014.

Jacobson, Bernhard S. (Yissachar). *Pesach: Arbeitsplan und Stoffsammlung*. Hamburg: 1936.

Jacobson, Yissachar. *Netiv Binah*. Vol. 1. Tel Aviv: Sinai, 1991. Vol. 2. Tel Aviv: Sinai, 1987.

———. *Ḥazon HaMikra*. Tel Aviv: Sinai, 1989.

Jaffe, Mordekhai. *Levush HaḤur*. Berdychiv: 1818. Jerusalem: 2004.

Jamieson, John. *An Etymological Dictionary of the Scottish Language*. Edinburgh, Scotland: Abernathy and Walker, 1818.

Jellinek, Adolph. *Beit HaMidrash*. Jerusalem: Wahrman Books, 1967.

Johnston, Reginald Fleming. *Lion and Dragon in Northern China*. London: Murray, 1910.

Justman, H. *MeOtzareinu HaYashan – Bereshit*. Tel Aviv: Mofet, 1976.

Justman, Moshe Bunem. *Haggada shel Pesaḥ mit a Modern Yiddish Iberzetzing – Fun Unzer Alten Otzar*. Warsaw, Poland: Yehudiah, 1938.

Kacirk, Jeffrey. *Forgotten English*. New York: Quill, 1997.

Kaganoff, Benzion. *A Dictionary of Jewish Names and Their History*. Northvale, NJ: Jason Aronson, 1996.

Kahana, Kalman. *Ḥeker VeIyun*. Tel Aviv: Melen, 1960.

Kahane, N. *Orḥot Ḥayim – Oraḥ Ḥayim*. Sighet, 1898.

Kahane, Yaakov Zev. *She'eilot UTeshuvot She'erit Yaakov*. Vilna: 1895.

Kahane, Yitzhak Zev, ed. *Teshuvot, Pesakim UMinhagim shel Rav Meir ben Rav Barukh MiRotenburg*. Jerusalem: Mossad HaRav Kook, 1957.

Kahn, Shlomo. *From Twilight to Dawn: The Traditional Passover Haggadah*. New York: Scribe, 1960.

Kaidanover, Z.H. *Kav HaYashar*. Frankfurt am Main: 1706. Constantinople: 1732.

Kamil, Reuven. *Shaar Reuven*. Jerusalem: 2006.

Kanarfogel, Ephraim. *Peering Through the Lattices: Mystical, Magical and Pietistic Dimensions in the Tosafist Period*. Detroit, MI: Wayne University Press, 2000.

Kanievsky, Chaim. *Daat Nota*. Vol. 1. Bnei Brak: 2009.

Kaplan, Aryeh. *Made in Heaven: A Jewish Wedding Guide*. New York: Moznaim, 1983.

Kaplan, Mordechai. *New Haggadah*. New York: Behrman's, 1941.

Kaplan, Steven. *The Beta Israel (Falasha) in Ethiopia: From Earliest Times to the Twentieth Century*. New York: New York University Press, 1992.

Karl, Zvi. *Meḥkarim BeToldot HaTefilla*. Tel Aviv: Twersky, 1950.

Karmi, Mordechai. *Maamar Mordekhai*. Vol. 4. Jerusalem: Oz VeHadar, 1995.

Karp, Moshe Mordechai. *Hilkhot Ḥag BeḤag – Purim*. Jerusalem: 2002.

———. *Hilkhot Ḥag BeḤag – Rosh Ḥodesh VeKiddush Levana*. Jerusalem: 2015.

Kasher, Menachem. *The Passover Haggadah*. New York: American Biblical Encyclopedia Society, 1957.

———. *Torah Sheleima – Shemot*. Vol. 8. Jerusalem: 1992.

Katz, Avraham Yitzhak, ed. *Midrash Rabbi David HaNaggid – Bereshit*. Jerusalem: Mossad HaRav Kook, 1964.

Katz, Eliyahu. *She'eilot UTeshuvot Be'er Eliyahu – Yoreh De'ah*. Jerusalem: 2002.

Katz, Moshe. *VaYaged Moshe*. Jerusalem: 1973.

Katz, Shmuel, ed. *HaRabbanut HaReshit LeYisrael: Shivim Shana LeYisoda*. Vol. 2. Jerusalem: 2002.

Katz-Hyman, Martha B. and Kym S. Rice, eds. *World of a Slave: Encyclopedia of the Material Life of Slaves in the United States*. Santa Barbara, CA: Greenwood Press, 2011.

Katzenelbogen, Mordechai Leib, ed. *Torat Ḥayim, Megillat Esther*. Jerusalem: Mossad HaRav Kook, 2006.

Kelly, Sarah. "Specialty Baking in Germany, Austria and Switzerland." In *National and Regional Styles of Cookery: Proceedings: Oxford Symposium 1981*, edited by Alan Davidson, 148–63. London: Prospect Books, 1981.

Kenapo, Yosef. *Haggada shel Pesaḥ – Zevaḥ Pesaḥ*. Livorno: 1875.

Khalfon, Avraham. *Ḥayei Avraham*. Livorno: 1826.

Kiel, Yehuda. *Daat Mikra: Shmuel*. Vol. 1. Jerusalem: Mossad HaRav Kook, 1981.

Kinarti, Amichai, ed. Joseph Juspa Hahn. *Sefer Yosef Ometz*. Shaalvim: Machon Shlomo Aumann, 2016.

Kipnes, Paul and Michelle November. *Jewish Spiritual Parenting: Wisdom, Activities, Rituals and Prayers for Raising Children with Spiritual*

*Balance and Emotional Wholeness*. Woodstock, VT: Jewish Lights, 2015.

Kirsch, A. "Hagiographen Lection am Sabbatnachmittag Ein Schwaebischer. (altzuercher) Minhag." MGWJ (Monatsschrift fuer Geschichte und Wissenschaft des Judentums) 12 (December 1880).

Kiss, Attila, ed. *The Iconography of the Fantastic: Eastern and Western Traditions of European Iconography* 2. Szeged: University of Szeged, 2002.

Kitov, Eliyahu. *Sefer HaToda'a*. Jerusalem: Beit Hotza'at Sefarim, 1958.

———. *Haggada shel Pesaḥ: Yalkut Tov*. Jerusalem: Alef, 1961.

Klatzkin, Eliyahu. *Kuntres LeDugma*. Lublin: 1921.

Klatzkin, Jacob. "Eliyahu Klatzkin." In *Jewish Leaders, 1750–1940*, edited by Leo Jung, 317–41. New York: Bloch, 1954.

Klein, Eliyahu. *A Mystical Haggadah: Passover Meditations, Teachings, and Tales*. Berkeley, CA: North Atlantic Books, 2008.

Klein, Menashe. *Meshane Halakhot*. Vol. 7. Jerusalem: 2008.

Klein, Zev. *Haggada shel Pesaḥ – Ḥokhma im Naḥala*. Buenos Aires: Julio Kaufman, 1948.

Klopholtz, Israel and Natan Ortner, eds. *Haggada shel Pesaḥ – Midrash BeḤiddush*. Bnei Brak: 1965.

Klopholtz, Israel, ed. *Maharash (Imrei Kodesh)*. Tel Aviv: 1965.

Kluger, Avraham Zvi. *Rav Ḥesed*. Beit Shemesh: 2018.

Kochavi, Yaakov. *Darakh Kokhav MiYaakov*. Bnei Brak: 2006.

Kohler, George. *Reading Maimonides' Philosophy in 19th Century Germany: The Guide to Religious Reform*. New York: Springer, 2012.

Kolatch, Alfred J. *The Family Seder – A Traditional Passover Haggadah for the Modern Home*. New York: Jonathan David, 1967.

———. *The Jewish Book of Why*. New York: Jonathan David, 1981.

Konav, M.M. *Maḥzor LeShemini Atzeret VeLeSimḥat Torah*. Roedelheim: 1832.

———. *Minḥa Ḥadasha – Maḥzor LeYom Kippur*. Krotoschin, Poland: 1838.

Kook, Avraham Yitzhak. *Orot HaKodesh*. Vol. 3. Jerusalem: Mossad HaRav Kook, 1950.

———. *Ein Ayah – Shabbat*. Vol. 1. Jerusalem: Machon HaRav Zvi Yehuda Kook, 1993.

Kook, Refael. *Kehunat Refael.* Jerusalem: 2008.
Korech, Asher. *Kehillat Galina.* Jerusalem: Weiss, 1950.
Koren, Irit. "The Bride's Voice: Religious Women Challenge the Wedding Ritual." *Nashim* 10 (2005).
Kornfeld, Pinhas Simha. *Maarekhet HaShulḥan.* Bnei Brak: 1995.
Korsia, Shimon. *Sefer Orot HaḤag.* Jerusalem: 2006.
Krauss, Samuel. "Aus Der Jüdischen Volksküche" (From the Jewish National Cuisine). *Mitteilungen Zur Jüdischen Volkskunde* 18, nos. 1–2 (53) (1915).
Krauss, Yisrael Naftaly. *Naḥalat Yisrael.* Bnei Brak: 2008.
Krispin, Mordechai. *Divrei Mordekhai.* Salonika: 1836.
Kroizer, Shmuel. *Yalkut MeAm Loez, Devarim.* Jerusalem: Wagshal, 1969.
Kugel, James. *The Bible As It Was.* Cambridge, MA: Harvard University Press, 1997.
Kulp, Joshua and David Golinkin. *The Schechter Haggadah: Art, History and Commentary.* Jerusalem: Schechter Institute of Jewish Studies, 2009.
Kuperstock, Yitzhak. *Meorot Natan.* Jerusalem: 1998.
Kvamme, Torstein O. *The Christmas Carolers' Book in Song and Story.* Miami, FL: Hall and McCreary, 1935.
La Follette, Laetitia. "The Costume of the Roman Bride." In *The World of Roman Costume,* edited by Judith Lynn Sebesta and Larissa Bonfante, 54–64. Madison, WI: University of Wisconsin Press, 2001.
Labovitz, Gail. *Marriage and Metaphor: Constructions of Gender in Rabbinic Literature.* Lanham: Lexington Books, 2009.
Lamm, Maurice. *The Jewish Way in Death and Mourning.* New York: Jonathan David, 1969.
———. *The Jewish Way in Love and Marriage.* New York: Jonathan David, 1980.
Landa, Isaac. *Mikra Soferim.* Suwalki, Poland: 1862.
Landa, Menachem Mendel. *Siddur Tzluta DeAvraham.* Vol. 1. Tel Aviv: Grafika, 1958. Vol. 2. Tel Aviv: Grafika, 1961.
Landa, Yitzhak. *Masekhet Soferim – Mikra Soferim.* Suwalki, Poland: 1862.
Landau, Bezalel. *Haggada shel Pesaḥ – LeAvot ULeBanim.* Jerusalem: Mifal Torah MiTzion, 1972.
Landau, Yaakov. *Agur.* Piotrków: 1883.

Landau, Reuven. *HaOtzar MiSippurei Tzadikkim.* Warsaw: 1937.

Landoy, Bezalel. *Masa Meron.* Jerusalem: Usha, 1966.

Landshut, Eliezer. *Siddur Hegayon Lev.* Königsberg: Adolph Samter, 1845.

Lange, Isaak S., ed. *Derashot Maharaḥ Or Zarua.* Jerusalem: 1972.

Langer, Ruth. *To Worship God Properly: Tensions Between Liturgical Custom and Halakhah in Judaism.* Cincinnati, OH: Hebrew Union College Press, 1998.

———. "Biblical Texts in Jewish Prayers: Their History and Function." In *Jewish and Christian Liturgy and Worship: New Insights into Its History and Interaction,* edited by Albert Gerhards and Clemens Leonhard, 63–90. Leiden: Brill, 2007.

Langer, Ruth. "'We Do Not Even Know What to Do!': A Foray into the Early History of Tahanun." In *Seeking the Favor of God: Volume 3: The Impact on Penitential Prayer Beyond Second Temple Judaism,* edited by Mark J. Boda, Richard Falk, and Rodney Werline, 39–70. Atlanta, GA: Society of Biblical Literature, 2008.

Laufer, Nathan. *Leading the Passover Journey: The Seder's Meaning Revealed, The Haggadah's Story Retold.* Woodstock, VT: Jewish Lights, 2005.

Lauterbach, J. "The Ceremony of Breaking Glass at Weddings." *Hebrew Union College Annual* 2 (1925): 351–80.

Lavut, Avraham David. *Shaar HaKollel.* Vilna: 1912. Brooklyn, NY: Kehot, 2005.

Lehmann, Menashe. "*Maḥzor Ketav Yad Lehmann VeHaTashbetz Shebetokho.*" In *Kovetz al Yad.* Jerusalem: Ḥevrat Mekitzei Nirdamim, 1985.

Lehrman, S.M. *Jewish Customs and Folklore.* London: Shapiro, Valentine and Co., 1949.

Leibovitz, Yehuda, ed. *Ritva – Hilkhot Seder HaHaggada.* Jerusalem: Mossad HaRav Kook, 1983.

Leiman, Shnayer Z. "*Sefarim HaḤashudim BeShabtaut.*" In *Sefer HaZikaron Le-Rav Moshe Lipshitz.* New York: 1996.

———. "Rabbinic Openness to General Culture in the Early Modern Period in Western and Central Europe." In *Judaism's Encounter with Other Cultures,* edited by Jacob J. Schacter, 143–216. Northvale, NJ: Jason Aronson, 1997.

———. "The Adventure of The Maharal of Prague in London: R. Yudl Rosenberg and the Golem of Prague." *Tradition* 36, no. 1 (2002): 26–58.

Leiter, Moshe. *Mamlekhet Kohanim*. Modiin Illit: 2002.

Leiter, Moshe Chaim. "*She'iltot BeInyanei Ḥanukka*." *Yeshurun* 19 (2007).

Leitner, Zvi. *Minhagei Frankfurt – Ḥelek HaMoadim*. Jerusalem: 1982.

Leonhard, Clemens. *The Jewish Pesach and the Origins of the Christian Easter*. Berlin: Walter de Gruyter, 2006.

Lerner, M.B. "*Massekhet Soferim*." In *The Literature of the Sages. First Part: Mishna, Tosefta, Talmud, External Tractates,* edited by Shmuel Safrai, 397–400. Assen/Maastricht: Van Gorcum, 1987.

Leser, Yosef. *Haggada shel Pesaḥ – Maatayim Sheloshim VeShemoneh Peirushim*. Cracow, Poland: 1905.

Lev, Baruch. *There Is No Such Thing as Coincidence…and Other Stories of Divine Providence*. Jerusalem: Feldheim, 2003.

Levenberg, Yehuda Heschel. "Regarding Blessings over Reading the Megilla and Reading the Writings." *Oraita* 11 (Adar 5751/1991).

Levi, Chanan. *BeShvilei HaḤodashim*. Rechasim: Tiferet Ram, 2001.

Levi, Eliezer. *Yesodot HaTefilla*. Tel Aviv: Avraham Zioni, 1958.

Levi, John. *A Family Haggadah*. Melbourne, Australia: Melbourne Books, 2002.

Levin, Yehuda Leib. *Ḥiddushei HaRim*. Jerusalem: Nachliel, 1965.

Levine Gera, Deborah. "The Jewish Textual Traditions." In *The Sword of Judith: Jewish Studies Across the Disciplines,* edited by Kevin Brine, Elena Ciletti, and Hernike Lähnemann, 23–40. Cambridge: Open Book Publishers, 2010.

———. "Shorter Medieval Hebrew Tales of Judith." In *The Sword of Judith: Jewish Studies Across the Disciplines,* edited by Kevin Brine, Elena Ciletti, and Hernike Lähnemann, 81–96. Cambridge: Open Book Publishers, 2010.

Levinsohn, Isaac Baer. *Yalkut Ribal*. Warsaw: 1878.

Levinson, Avraham. "*LeRikkudei Am BeYisrael*." *Reshumot*. Vol. 3. Tel Aviv: Dvir, 1947.

Levinstam, Shaul. *Binyan Ariel*. Cracow: 1905.

Levovitch, Yitzhak Zvi. *Shulḥan HaEzer*. Vol. 2. Dej: 1932.

Lewinsky, Yom Tov. *Sefer HaMoadim: Rosh Ḥodesh, Ḥanukka, Ḥamisha Asar BiShvat*. Tel Aviv: Dvir, 1961.

———. *Eileh Moadei Yisrael*. Tel Aviv: Achiasaf, 1987.

Lewy, Hildegard and Julius Lewy. "The Origin of the Week and the Oldest West Asiatic Calendar." *Hebrew Union College Annual* 17 (1942–1943): 1–152.

Lewy, Yosef. *Minhag Yisrael Torah*. Brooklyn, NY: Fink Graphics, 1990. Jerusalem: Frank, 1994.

Lewysohn, A. *Mekorei Minhagim*. Berlin: 1847.

Lieber, Laura. "Confessing from A to Z: Penitential Forms in Early Synagogue Poetry." In *Seeking the Favor of God: Volume 3: The Impact on Penitential Prayer Beyond Second Temple Judaism*, edited by Mark J. Boda, Richard Falk, and Rodney Werline, 99–125. Atlanta, GA: Society of Biblical Literature, 2008.

Lieberman, Yitzhak. *Sefer Ḥag HaAssif – Halakhot UMinhagim*. Bnei Brak: 1991.

———. *Sefer Ḥag HaMatzot – Halakhot UMinhagim*. Bnei Brak: 2003.

Libermann, Saul. *Shki'in*. Jerusalem: Shalem Books. 1992.

Lifshitz, Eliezer Meir. *Ktavim*. Vol. 1. Jerusalem: Mossad HaRav Kook, 1947.

Lifshitz, Joseph Isaac. "*Av HaRahamim*: On the 'Father of Mercy' Prayer." In *Death in Jewish Life – Burial and Mourning Customs Among Jews of Europe and Nearby Communities*, edited by Stefan C. Reif, Andreas Lehnardt and Avriel Bar-Levav, 141–54. Berlin: De Gruyter, 2014.

Lindemann, Oliver, Ahmad Alipour, and Martin H. Fischer. "Finger Counting Habits in Middle Eastern and Western Individuals." *Journal of Cross-Cultural Psychology* 42, no. 4 (2011): 566–78.

Lipetz, Yitzhak. *Sefer Mataamim*. Warsaw: 1890, 1894, 1899, 1910.

Loewy, Joseph and Joseph Guens. *Service for the First Nights of Passover*. Vienna: Joseph Schlesinger, 1929.

Lorberbaum, Yaakov. *Siddur Derekh HaḤayim*. Vienna: 1859.

Lovén, Lena Larsson. "Roman Art: What Can It Tell Us About Dress and Textiles? A Discussion on the Use of Visual Evidence as Sources for Textile Research." In *Greek and Roman Textiles and Dress: An*

*Interdisciplinary Anthology*, edited by Mary Harlow and Marie-Louise Nosch, 260–79. Philadelphia, PA: Oxbow Books, 2015.

Löw, Binyamin Zev (Lev). *Sefer Divrei Yirmeyahu – Drashot*. Satmar: Meir Lev Hirsch, 1934.

Low, George. *History of Orkneys: Introduced by a Description of the Islands and Their Inhabitants*. Kirkwall, Scotland: Orkney Heritage Society, 2001.

Lowenberg, Miriam Elizabeth. *Food and People*. Hoboken, NJ: Wiley, 1979.

Lowinger, David Samuel. *Yehudit – Shoshana*. Budapest: 1940.

Lowy, Yosef. *Minhag Yisrael Torah*. Vol. 1. Brooklyn, NY: 1994.

Luncz, A.M. "History of the Jews in Palestine, Part I." *Jerusalem Year Book* 2 (1887).

Luria, Shlomo. *Yam shel Shlomo – Yevamot*. Szczecin, Poland: 1862.

Lurie, Alison. *The Language of Clothes*. New York: Random House, 1981.

Macdonald, James. *Religion and Myth of Africa*. London: D. Nutt, 1883.

Macey, Samuel L. *Patriarchs of Time: Dualism in Saturn-Cronus, Father Time, the Watchmaker Go and Father Christmas*. Athens, GA: University of Georgia Press, 2010.

Machfud, Sagiv, ed. *Tiklal – Etz Ḥayim*. Bnei Brak: Nusach Teiman, 2012.

Machfutz, Meir Eliyahu. *Inyanei Ḥuppa*. Kfar Chabad: 2015.

Machon Ofeq. "*Peirush Rabbeinu Yitzḥak Karkosha LeHilkhot HaRif LeMasekhet Rosh HaShana*." *Yeshurun* 6 (Av 5759/1999).

Mackinney-Valentin, Maria. *Fashioning Identity: Status Ambivalence in Contemporary Fashion*. London: Bloomsbury Academic, 2017.

Maged, Aron. *Beit Aharon*. Vol. 3. Brooklyn, NY: E. Grossman's, 1965. Vol. 13. New York: Balshon, 1978.

Maged, Aron. *Beit Aharon: Klalei HaShas*. Vol. 10. Brooklyn, NY: Deutsch, 1975.

Magnus, Shulamit. "Pauline Wengeroff and the Voice of Jewish Modernity." In *Gender and Judaism: The Transformation of Tradition*, edited by Tamar Rudavsky, 181–90. New York: NYU Press, 1995.

———. "Kol Ishah: Women and Pauline Wengeroff's Writing of an Age." *Nashim* 7 (2004).

Maier, Johann. *The Temple Scroll*. Sheffield: JSOT Press, 1985.

Maimon, Yehuda Leib. *Ḥagim UMoadim*. Jerusalem: Weiss, 1943.

Malka, Yoel. *Netivei Halakha*. Emmanuel, 1994.
Mandel, Nathan. *Passover Haggadah*. New York: 1954.
Mandelbaum, Bernard, ed. *Pesikta de Rav Kahane*. New York: Jewish Theological Seminary of America, 1987.
Manley, Johanna. *Grace After Grace: The Psalter and the Holy Fathers*. Crestwood, NY: Monastery Books, 2003.
Mann, Jacob. *The Bible as Read and Preached in the Old Synagogue*. Hoboken, NJ: Ktav, 1971.
Marber, Gershon. *Darkhei HaḤayim*. Bilgoraj: Neta Kronenberg, 1937.
Margaliot, Ephraim. *Shaarei Ephraim*. Dubno: 1820.
Margaliot, Reuven. *Haggada shel Pesaḥ – Be'er Miriam, Kehillat Moshe*. Tel Aviv: Margaliot, 1937.
———, ed. *Sefer Ḥasidim*. Jerusalem: Mossad HaRav Kook, 1990.
———. *Nitzotzei Or*. Jerusalem: Mossad HaRav Kook, 2002.
Margalit, Eran Moshe, *Haggadat Likutei Sfat Emet*. Or Etzion, 2009.
Marks, Gil. *The World of Jewish Cooking*. New York: Simon and Schuster, 1996.
———. *Encyclopedia of Jewish Food*. Hoboken, NJ: John Wiley and Sons, 2010.
McClintock, J. and J. Strong. *Cyclopedia of Biblical, Theological and Ecclesiastical Literature*. New York: 1895.
Medini, H. *Sdeh Ḥemed – Asifat Dinim*. Warsaw: 1896.
Melamed, Ezra Zion. *Pirkei Minhag VeHalakha*. Jerusalem: Kiryat Sefer, 1970.
Melchior-Bonnet, Sabine. *The Mirror: A History*. London: Routledge, 2001.
Meller, Shimon Yosef. *The Brisker Rav: The Life and Times of Maran HaGaon HaRav Yitzchok Ze'ev HaLevi Soloveichik zt"l*. Vol. 1. Jerusalem: Feldheim, 2007.
Meltzer, Feivel. *Daat Mikra: Ruth*. Jerusalem: Mossad HaRav Kook, 1990.
Meltzer, Shimshon, trans. *MeOtzareinu HaYashan*. Tel Aviv: Modiin, 1976.
Menahem ben Zerah. *Sefer Tzeida LaDerekh*. Livorno: 1859.
Menahem Mendel of Rimanov. *Ateret Menaḥem*. Bilgoraj: 1910.
———. *Menaḥem Tzion*. Jerusalem: 2007.
Menatzpach, Y. (Shamash). *Minhagim DeKehillat Kodesh Vermiza*. Jerusalem: 1988.

Mendelbaum, David. *Gibborei HaḤayil*. Bnei Brak: 2009.

Messas, Yosef. *Naḥalat Avot*. Vol. 3. Jerusalem: Otzrot Yosef, 1977.

Metzger, Yona and Nachum Langental. *BeMaagalei HaḤayim – BeḤayei HaAdam*. Tel Aviv: Yedioth Ahronoth, 1988.

Meyer, Michael. "Women in the Thought and Practice of the European Jewish Reform Movement." In *Gender and Jewish History*, edited by Marion Kaplan and Deborah Dash Moore, 139–57. Bloomington, IN: Indiana University Press, 2011.

Mezlomian, Yishai. *Segulot Rabboteinu*. Holon: 2014.

Michael, Geraldine and Frank N. Wills, Jr. "The Development of Gestures in Three Subcultural Groups." *Journal of Social Psychology* 79, no. 1 (1969): 35–41.

Milgram, Abraham. *Jewish Worship*. Philadelphia, PA: Jewish Publication Society of America, 1971.

Milinofsky, David Alexander. *Sefer Imrei David*. Bnei Brak: 1982.

Mirsky, Samuel. "*Mekorot HaHalakha BeMidrashim*." *Talpioth* (Nisan 5707/1947).

———. *She'iltot – Genesis* 2. Jerusalem: Sura, 1961.

Mirsky, Yitzhak. *Hegyonei Halakha BeInyan Shabbat UMoadim*. Jerusalem: Mossad HaRav Kook, 1988.

Mizrachi, Yosef Hayim. *Od Yosef Ḥai*. Jerusalem: 2005.

Mondshein, Yehoshua. *Otzar Minhagei Chabad, Nisan Iyar Sivan*. Jerusalem: Heichal Menachem, 1996.

Monitzer, Avishalom. *Yeladim KeHalakha*. Rosh HaAyin: 2003.

Moore, Carey A. *The Anchor Bible – Esther*. Garden City, NY: Doubleday, 1971.

———. *Daniel, Esther and Jeremiah: The Additions – The Anchor Bible*. New York: Doubleday, 1977.

———. *Judith – Anchor Bible Series*. Garden City, NY: Doubleday, 1985.

Morgan, Faith Pennick. *Dress and Personal Appearance in Late Antiquity: The Clothing of the Middle and Lower Classes*. Leiden: Brill, 2018.

Morgan, James L. *Culinary Creation: An Introduction to Foodservice and World Cuisine*. New York: Buttersworth-Heinemann, 2006.

Morgenstern, Matthias. *From Frankfurt to Jerusalem: Isaac Breuer and the History of the Secession Dispute in Modern Jewish Orthodoxy*. Leiden: Brill, 2002.

Moshe ben Avraham of Przemyśl. *Mateh Moshe*. Frankfurt: 1719.

Moshe ben Makhir. *Seder HaYom*. Venice: 1599.

Moskovitz, Yechiel Zvi. *Daat Mikra: Eikha*. Jerusalem: Mossad HaRav Kook, 1990.

Moua, Mai. *Culturally Intelligent Leadership: Leading Through Intercultural Interactions*. New York: Business Expert Press, 2010.

Moussaieff, Arieh, Neta Rimmerman, Tatiana Bregman, Alex Straiker, Christian C. Felder, Shai Shoham, Yoel Kashman, Susan M. Huang, Hyosang Lee, Esther Shohami, Ken Mackie, Michael J. Caterina, J. Michael Walker, Ester Fride, Raphael Mechoulam. "Incensole acetate, an incense component, elicits psychoactivity by activating TRPV3 channels in the brain." *FASEB Journal* 22, no. 8 (2008): 3024–34.

Movshovitz, Yosef Eliyahu Halevi, ed. *Haggada shel Pesaḥ im Peirush HaGra*. Jerusalem: Mossad HaRav Kook, 2009.

———. *Maaseh Rav*. Jerusalem: Mossad HaRav Kook, 2016.

Mualem, Yitzhak. *Aggadata DePisḥa*. Beitar Illit: Machon Ohalei Avraham Yaakov, 2003.

Munk, Derenbourg, Franck and Zotenberg. *Catalogues des Manuscrits Hébreux et Samaritains de la Bibliothèque Impériale/Manuscrits Orientaux*. Paris: 1866.

Munk, Eliyahu. *Olam HaTefillot*. Vol. 1. Jerusalem: Mossad HaRav Kook, 1992.

Murgoci, A. "Customs Connected with Death and Burial Among the Romanians." *Folklore* 30 (1919): 89–102.

Musabi, Pinhas. *Pinḥas Yepallel*. Jerusalem: 2006.

Mutzfi, Bentzion. *Shivat Tzion – Shabbat*. Vol. 1. Jerusalem: 2005.

Nachshoni, Yehuda. *Rabbeinu Moshe Sofer*. Jerusalem: Mashabim, 1981.

Naeh, Avraham Hayim, *Ketzot HaShulḥan*. Jerusalem: 1928, 1978.

Najman, Hindy. *Seconding Sinai: The Development of Mosaic Discourse in Second Temple Judaism*. Leiden: Brill, 2003.

Naor, Bezalel. *Post-Sabbatian Sabbatianism: Study of the Underground Messianic Movement*. Spring Valley, NY: Orot, 1999.

Nathanson, Meir. "The Law Regarding Preparing Salt Water for Seder Night, Particularly When It Falls on Shabbat." *Tzohar* 2 (1998).

Nebenzal, Avigdor. *Yerushlayim BeMoadeha – Pesaḥ*. Jerusalem: Machon Keren Re'em, 2006.

Nelson, Mildred B. "An Image: Borrowed and New." *Western Folklore* 29, no. 4 (1970): 247–50.

Neubauer, Abraham. "The Early Settlement of the Jews in Southern Italy." *Jewish Quarterly Review* 4 (1892): 606–25.

Neusner, Noam. "The Pinkie Paradox." *Jerusalem Post Magazine*, June 13, 2003.

Neuwirth, Yehoshua. *Shemirat Shabbat KeHilkhatah*. Vol. 2. Jerusalem: Moriah, 1988.

Newlands, Carole E. *Statius' Silvae and the Poetics of Empire*. Cambridge: Cambridge University Press, 2004.

Nieuwsma, Heddi and Dorian Rollin. *Swiss Bread: A Culinary Journey with 42 Sweet and Savory Recipes*. Basel: Helvetiq, 2020.

Nigal, Gedaliah. "*Peirusho shel R. Yosef Yaavatz LeRut*." *Sinai* 76 (1975).

Nissenbaum, Stephen. *The Battle for Christmas: A Cultural History of America's Most Cherished Holiday*. New York: Vintage Books, 1997.

Nissim, Yitzhak. "*HaHagahot al Shulḥan Arukh*." In *Rabbi Yosef Karo*, edited by Yitzhak Refael. Jerusalem: Mossad HaRav Kook, 1969.

Nulman, Macy. *The Encyclopedia of Jewish Prayer*. Northvale, NJ: Jason Aronson, 1996.

Oberlander, Gedalia. "Avoiding Eating Nuts and Sour Foods on the High Holidays." *Kovetz Or Yisrael* 1, no. 17 (Tishrei 5760/1999, year 5) [Hebrew].

———. *Minhag Avotenu BeYadenu – Shabbat Kodesh*. Monsey, NY: Merkaz Halacha, 2010.

Olevski, Natan Neta. *Neta Revai*. Jerusalem: Machon Yerushalayim, 1995.

Olson, S. Douglas, trans. *Athenaeus, The Learned Banqueters*. Cambridge, MA: Harvard University Press, Loeb Classical Library, 2009.

Orenstein, Avraham. *Encyclopedia LeTaarei Kavod BeYisrael*. Vol. 3. Tel Aviv: Netzach, 1963.

Orenstein, Yehuda. *Tal Yerushalayim*. Jerusalem: 1988.

Ormos, Istvan. "David Kaufmann and His Collection." In papers presented at the David Kaufmann Memorial Conference, November 29, 1999, edited by Éva Apor, 127–96. Budapest: Library of the Hungarian Academy of Sciences, 2002.

Orwell, George. "George Gissing." *London Magazine*, June 1960.

Otzen, Benedikt. *Tobit and Judith*. London: Sheffield Academic Press, 2002.

Ovadia MiBartenura. *Darkhei Tziyon*. Kolomya: 1886.
Ovadia, David. *Nahagu HaAm*. Jerusalem: Machon Yismach Lev, 2000.
Oved, Ephraim. *Haggada shel Pesaḥ*. Bnei Brak: 2004.
Pakshar, Menachem Mendel. *Invei HaGefen*. Jerusalem: 1985.
Palagi, Hayim. *Sefer Ḥayim*. Salonika: 1863.
———. *Ruaḥ Ḥayim*. Izmir: 1876.
———, *Lev Ḥayim*. Vol. 2. Izmir: 1876.
———. *Sefer Nefesh HaḤayim*. Jerusalem: Chen Chayyim, 2004.
Palagi, Rachamim. *Yafeh LaLev*. Izmir: 1876.
Panati, Charles. *Extraordinary Origins of Everyday Things*. New York: Harper and Row, 1987.
Partosh, Yaakov. "The Order of Prayers According to the Custom of the Jews of Algeria." *Tagim* 1 (1968).
Patai, Raphael and Emanuel S. Goldsmith. *Thinkers and Teachers of Modern Judaism*. New York: Paragon House, 1994.
Patton, Kimberley Christine. *Religion of the Gods: Ritual, Paradox, and Reflexivity*. Oxford: Oxford University Press, 2009.
Patton, Lewis, ed. *The International Critical Commentary – The Book of Esther*. Edinburgh: T & T Clark, 1976.
Pelov, Aharon. *Otzroteihem shel Tzaddikim*. Jerusalem: 2012.
Pennick, Nigel. *The Pagan Book of Days: A Guide to the Festivals, Traditions, and Sacred Days of the Year*. Rochester, VT: Destiny Books, 1992.
Peretz, Michael. *Siddur Ohalei Shem*. Jerusalem: 2007.
Perlman, Natan. "*Minhag Rabboteinu SheEin Omrim HaPiyut Dvai Haser*." *Kovetz Beit Aharon VeYisrael* 180 (Elul 5771/2011).
Perlov, Aaron. *Birkat HaMazon – Karnei Hod*. Jerusalem: 2014.
Perser, Israel Meir. *Haggada shel Pesaḥ Abrabanel – Zevaḥ Pesaḥ*. Jerusalem: Mossad HaRav Kook, 2007.
Petuchowski, Jakob J. *Prayerbook Reform in Europe: The Liturgy of European Liberal and Reform Judaism*. New York: World Union for Progressive Judaism, 1968.
Pigg, Daniel. "Imagining Urban Life and Its Discontents: Chaucer's 'Cook's Tale' and Masculine Identity." In *Urban Space in the Middle Ages and the Early Modern Age*, edited by Albrecht Classen, 395–408. Berlin: Walter de Gruyter, 2009.

Pilot, Andie. *Helvetic Kitchen: Swiss Cooking*. Basel: Bergli, 2017.

Pinhas, Eliyahu Dov, ed. *Mekor Ḥayim*. Jerusalem: Machon Yerushalayim, 1984.

Pinches, T.G. "Sabbath (Babylonian)." In *Encyclopedia of Religion and Ethics*, edited by James Hastings. New York: Charles Scribner's Sons, 1919.

Pinchuk, Aharon. *Mateh Aharon*. Jerusalem: 1980.

Piponnier, Françoise and Perrine Mane. *Dress in the Middle Ages*. New Haven, CT: Yale University Press, 1997.

Poliakoff, Manuel. *Minhagei Lita: Customs of Lithuanian Jewry and a Litvishe Rav's Perspective on Life and Halachah*. Baltimore, MD: M.M. Poliakoff, 2008.

Pollack, Aharon. *Beito Naaveh Kodesh*. Vol. 1. Bnei Brak: Machon Zichron Aharon, 1999.

Pollack, Menachem Segal. *Ḥelek Levi*. Szechenyi: Friedman Miskolc, 1934.

Postgate, Nicholas. "The Bread of Assur." *Iraq* 77 (2015): 159–72.

Poppers, Meir. *Or Tzaddikim*. Warsaw: 1889.

Prener, Tuvia. *Shalmei Moed*. Jerusalem: 2004.

Preschel, Tovia. *Maamarei Tuvia*. Jerusalem: Mossad HaRav Kook, 2017.

Preuss, Julius. *Biblical and Talmudic Medicine*. Translated by Fred Rosner. Northvale, NJ: Jason Aronson, 1993.

Printz, Elchanan. *Avnei Derekh*. Vol. 7. Jerusalem: 2013. Vol. 8. Jerusalem: 2014.

———. *She'eilot UTeshuvot Avnei Derekh*. Vol. 7. Jerusalem: 2014.

Prinz, Deborah R. *On the Chocolate Trail: A Delicious Adventure Connecting Jews, Religions, History, Travel, Rituals and Recipes to the Magic of Cacao*. Woodstock, VT: Jewish Lights, 2012.

Quait, David. *Sefer Sukkat David*. Jerusalem: 2005.

Raban, Zeev. *The Bezalel Haggada*. Tel Aviv: Sinai, 1965.

Rabbinovicz, R.N. *Dikdukei Soferim*. Vol. 10. Munich: 1879.

Rabinowicz, Tzvi. *The Encyclopedia of Hasidism*. Northvale, NJ: Jason Aaronson, 1996.

Rabinowitz, David. *Hagadah shel Pesach – Livnat Sapir*. Brooklyn, NY: 1949.

Rabinowitz, Gamliel. *Gam Ani Odekha – Responsa of Rabbi Yisrael Pesaḥ Feinhandler*. Bnei Brak: 2016.

Rabinowitz, Simha. *Piskei Teshuvot*. Vol. 1. Jerusalem: 2006. Vol. 2. Jerusalem: 2002. Vol. 3. Jerusalem: 2009, 2011. Vol. 5. Jerusalem: 1995. Vol. 6. Jerusalem: 1997.

Rabinowitz, Yehoshua Heschel. *Erkhei Yehoshua*. Jerusalem: 1995.

Radford, Edwin and Mona Radford. *Encyclopedia of Superstitions*. New York: Philosophical Library, 1949.

Rafael, Yitzhak, ed. *Sefer HaManhig LeRabbi Avraham BeRebbi Natan HaYarḥi*. Jerusalem: Mossad HaRav Kook, 1978.

Raffeld, M. "Components and Combinations in the *Yizkor* Prayers of the North Italian Ashkenaz Community." *HaMaayan* 53, no. 1 (2012) [Hebrew].

Raiskin, Shlomi. "Lighting Lamps on Yom Kippur Eve in the Synagogue." *Magal* 15 (2007).

Raizel, Anat. *Introduction to the Midrashic Literature*. Alon Shvut, Israel: Tevunot-Michlelet Herzog, 2011.

Rakocz, Yoetz Kim Kadish. *Siaḥ Sarfei Kodesh*. Vol. 3. Bnei Brak: 1989.

Rakovsky, Yaakov. *Arukhat Bat Ami*. Vol. 4. Jerusalem: 1993.

Rand, Michael Aryeh. *Kehilkhot Pesaḥ*. Ashdod: 2011.

Raphael, S. *Yizkor: From Mourning of Mega-Death to Soul-Guiding*. Philadelphia, PA: 2013.

Rapoport, Shlomo. *Erekh Millin*. Vol. 1. Prague: 1852.

Rappel, Goel. *Moreshet Am VeAretz*. Tel Aviv: Yedioth Ahronoth, 2002.

Raskin, Levi Yitzchak, ed. *Siddur Rabbeinu HaZaken im Tziyunim, Mekorot, VeHe'arot*. Brooklyn, NY: Kehot, 2004.

———, *Seder Birkat HaMazon*. London: 2013.

Ratzabi, Yitzhak. *Shulḥan Arukh HaMekutzar*. Bnei Brak: 1995, 2001.

Ravitzky, Aviezer. "Covenant of Faith or Covenant of Fate? Competing Orthodox Conceptions of Secular Jews." In *Creation and Re-Creation in Jewish Thought:*

*Festschrift in honor of Joseph Dan on the Occasion of his Seventieth Birthday*, edited by Rachel Elior and Peter Schafer, 271–307. Tübingen, Germany: Mohr Siebeck, 2005.

Reider, Freda. *The Hallah Book: Recipes, History, and Traditions*. New York: Ktav, 1987.

Reider, Joseph. "Secular Currents in Synagogal Chant in America: 1918." In *The Value of Sacred Music: An Anthology of Essential Writings,*

*1801–1918*, edited by Jonathan L. Friedman, 138–46. Jefferson, NC: McFarland, 2009.

Reif, S.C., A. Lehnardt, and A. Bar-Levav, eds. *Death in Jewish Life – Burial and Mourning Customs Among Jews of Europe and Nearby Communities*. Berlin: De Gruyter, 2014.

Reifman, Yaakov. "Notes on Targum Megillat Esther and Kohelet." *Zion: Ephemerides Hebraicae* (1840–1841).

Reimer, Daniel Mordechai. *Sefer Tefillat Ḥayim*. Beitar: Tzror HaḤayim, 2004.

Remler, Pat. *Egyptian Mythology A–Z*. New York: Chelsea House, 2000.

Revel-Neher, Elisabeth. *The Image of the Jew in Byzantine Art*. Oxford: Pergamon Press, 1992.

Rhys, John. "Manx Folk-lore and Superstitions." *Folklore* 3 (1892): 325–41.

Ricardo, Israel. *Tefillat Kol Peh*. Amsterdam: 1993.

Rickels, Laurence. *The Vampire Lectures*. Minneapolis, MN: University of Minnesota Press, 1999.

Riddle, John M. *Dioscorides on Pharmacy and Medicine*. Austin, TX: University of Texas Press, 1985.

Rifkind, Isaac. *Yidishe Gelt*. New York: Academy for Jewish Research, 1959.

Rimon, Yosef Zvi. *Haggada MiMekorah*. Jerusalem: Mossad HaRav Kook, 2002.

Ringel, Yissachar. *Adir BaMarom*. Brooklyn, NY: Makhon Tal Orot, 2003.

Riskin, Shlomo. *The Passover Haggadah*. New York: Ktav, 1983.

———. *Around the Family Table: A Comprehensive "Bencher" and Companion for Shabbat and Festival Meals and Other Family Occasions with Insight and Commentary*. Jerusalem: Urim, 2005.

Rokach, Yeshaya. *Yalkut Yashar*. Bilgoraj, Poland: 1937.

Rosen, Joseph. *Tzafnat Paaneaḥ*. Vol. 4. Piotrkow, Poland: 1903.

Rosenau, William and Alois Kaiser. *Home-Service for Passover Eve*. New York: Bloch, 1905.

Rosenfeld, Moshe, ed. *Birkat Ephraim*. London: 1979.

Rosenruas, Lior. *Birkat HaShulḥan*. Bnei Brak: 2011.

Rosenthal, Shabbtai. *Haggada shel Pesaḥ – Geonei VeḤakhmei Yerushalayim*. Jerusalem: Mifal Moreshet Yerushalayim, 1996.

Rosenwasser, Moshe. "Hidden *Midrashim* as Sources for the *Piyyut Odekha.*" *HaMaayan* 43, no. 2 (2002): 30.

Rosner, Fred. *Medicine in the Bible and Talmud: Selections from Classical Jewish Sources.* Hoboken, NJ: Ktav, 1977.

Roth, C. *The Frankfurt Memorbuch.* Jerusalem: 1965.

Rothschild, Yaakov. "Shabbat *Zemirot* of the Jews of Southern Germany and the Customs Connected to Them." *Duchan* 7 (1964).

Roussin, Lucille. "Costume in Roman Palestine: Archaeological Remains and the Evidence from the Mishnah." In *The World of Roman Costume,* edited by Judith Lynn Sebesta and Larissa Bonfante, 182–90. Madison, WI: University of Wisconsin Press, 2001.

Roy, Christian. *Traditional Festivals: A Multicultural Encyclopedia.* Santa Barbara, CA: ABC-CLIO, 2005.

Rubenstein, Refael. *Sefer Birkat Refael BeInyanei Ḥanukka.* Jerusalem: 1984.

Rubin, Menachem Mendel. *Masa Meron.* Jerusalem: 1889.

Russof, David. *VeAmartem Ko LeḤai.* Jerusalem: Otzar HaTorah, 2006.

Rutgers, Leonard Victor. *The Jews in Late Ancient Rome: Evidence of Cultural Interaction in the Roman Diaspora.* Leiden: Brill, 1995.

Sacks, Jonathan. *Rabbi Jonathan Sacks's Haggadah.* New York: Continuum, 2010.

Samet, Moshe. *HaḤadash Assur min HaTorah.* Jerusalem: Carmel, 2005.

Samet, Yisrael. "The Meaning of *Ḥuppa* Customs – Part 2." *Tzohar* 10 (2001) [Hebrew].

Samovar, Larry A., Richard E. Porter, and Edwin R. McDaniel. *Communication Between Cultures.* Boston, MA: Wadsworth, 2007.

Samuel, Maurice. *Haggadah for Passover.* New York: Hebrew Publishing Company, 1942.

Sanders, E.P. *Judaism: Practice and Belief 63 BCE–66 CE.* London: SCM Press, 1994.

Sansom, William. *A Book of Christmas.* New York: McGraw-Hill, 1968.

Sapir, Sinai. *Olat Ḥodesh.* Warsaw: 1847.

Sarason, Richard S. "The Persistence and Trajectories of Penitential Prayer in Rabbinic Judaism." In *Seeking the Favor of God: Volume 3: The Impact on Penitential Prayer Beyond Second Temple Judaism,* edited by Mark Boda, Richard Falk, and Rodney Werline, 1–38. Atlanta, GA: Society of Biblical Literature, 2008.

Satz, Yitzhak, ed. *New Responsa of Rabbi Yaacov Molin – Maharil*. Jerusalem: Machon Yerushalayim, 1977.

Satz, Yitzchak, David Yitzchaki, and David Salmon, eds. *Birkat HaMazon LeMoreinu HaRav Shabbtai Sofer*. Toronto, ON: Otzreinu, 2002.

Savitz, Menachem. *Yismaḥ Lev*. Lakewood, NJ: 2004.

Schachter, Hershel. *Kavod HaRav*. New York: Student Organization of Yeshiva University, 1992.

———. *MiPninei HaRav*. New York: 2001.

Scharfstein, Sol. *Understanding Jewish Holidays and Customs: Historical and Contemporary*. Hoboken, NJ: Ktav, 1999.

Schauss, Hayyim. *Guide to Jewish Holy Days: History and Observance*. New York: Schocken Books, 1938.

Scherman, Nosson, ed. *The Haggadah Treasury*. New York: Mesorah, 1978. In conjunction with Zeirei Agudath Israel of America.

———, ed. *The Complete ArtScroll Machzor – Yom Kippur*. Brooklyn, NY: Mesorah, 1986.

———, ed. *The ArtScroll Siddur*. Brooklyn, NY: Mesorah, 1990.

———, ed. *Zemiros and Bircas Hamazon*. Brooklyn, NY: Mesorah, 1998.

Scherman, Nosson and Yitzchok Zev Scherman. *ArtScroll Youth Haggadah*. Brooklyn, NY: Mesorah, 1995.

Scheuer, Joseph, ed. *Siddur Schma Kolenu*. Basel: Morascha Verlag, 2000.

Schick, Shlomo Zvi. *Siddur Rashban*. Vienna: 1894.

Schiff, David Tevele. *Lashon Zahav*. London: Mechon Rav Chesed Trust, 1997.

Schiffman, Lawrence. *The Courtyards of the House of the Lord: Studies on the Temple Scroll*. Leiden: Brill, 2008.

Schigel, Avraham. *Doleh UMashkeh*. Kiryat Sefer: 2007.

Schneerson, Dov Ber. *Torat Ḥayim – Bereshit*. Brooklyn, NY: Otzar Chasidim, 2002.

Schneerson, Menachem Mendel. *Shaarei Halakha UMinhag – Oraḥ Ḥayim*. Vol. 2. Jerusalem: Heichal Menachem, 1993.

Scholem, Gershom. *Major Trends in Jewish Mysticism*. Jerusalem: Schocken, 1954.

Schorr, Alexander. *Beḥor Shor*. Zitomir: 1868.

Schostak, Zev. *Why Is This Night Different?* New York: ArtScroll Studios, 1977.

Schwab, Hermann. *Jewish Rural Communities in Germany*. London: Cooper Book Company, 1957.

Schwartz, Joseph. *Ginzei Yosef*. Deva, Romania: Markowitz and Friedman, 1930.

*Sefer HaKaneh*. Cracow: Yosef Fischer, 1894.

*Sefer HaMinhagim*. Brooklyn, NY: Kehot Publication Society, 1993.

Seff, Yitzhak, ed. *She'eilot UTeshuvot Maharil HaḤadashot*. Jerusalem: Machon Yerushalayim, 1991.

Segal, Michael. *The Book of Jubilees: Rewritten Bible, Redaction, Ideology and Theology*. Leiden: Brill, 2007.

Segal, Yosef Yuspa Cashman. *Noheg KeTzon Yosef*. Tel Aviv: 1969.

Senn, Frank. *Protestant Spiritual Traditions*. Eugene, OR: Wipf and Stock, 2000.

Setbon, David. *Alei Hadas*. Kiryat Sefer: 2010.

Setel, Yaakov Yisrael, ed. *Sefer Gematriot*. Jerusalem: 2005.

Shafner, Hayim. *The Everything Jewish Wedding Book*. Avon, MA: Adams, 2009.

Shakespear, J. "The Religion of Manipur." *Folklore* 7, no. 4 (1896): 409–55.

Shalom, Sharon. *From Sinai to Ethiopia: The Halachic and Conceptual World of Ethiopian Jewry*. Tel Aviv: Miskal-Yedioth Ahronoth Books, 2012.

Shammash, Yospe. *Minhagim of the Worms Community*. Jerusalem: Machon Yerushalayim, 1988.

Shapira, Aryeh Leib, ed. *Haggada shel Pesaḥ – Olellot Ephraim*. Zhitomir: 1863.

Shapira, Avraham. *Minḥat Avraham*. Jerusalem: 2003.

Shapira, Dan. "Judaeo-Persian Translations of Old Persian Lexica: A Case of Linguistic Discontinuity." In *Persian Origins – Early Judaeo-Persian and the Emergence of New Persian: Collected Papers of the Symposium, Göttingen 1999*, edited by Ludwig Paul, 221–42. Wiesbaden, Germany: Harrassowitz Verlag, 2003.

Shaviv, Yehuda. "Kohelet on Sukkot." *HaMaayan* 41, no. 1 (Tishrei 5761).

Shavmer, Shmuel. *Siḥot Talmidei Ḥakhamim*. Tel Aviv: 1950.

Shechter, Yitzhak. *Yashiv Yitzḥak*. Netanya: 2004.

Shefer, Shlomo, ed. *Yesod VeShoresh HaAvoda*. Bnei Brak: 1987.

Shehada, Housni Alkhateeb. *Mamluks and Animals: Veterinary Medicine in Medieval Islam*. Leiden: Brill, 2013.

Sheinfeld, Yehuda. *Oseri LeGefen*. Vol. 8. Jerusalem: 2002. Vol. 12. Jerusalem: 2006.

Shelneger, Eliakim. *Kitzur Shulḥan Arukh im Divrei Mishna Berura*. Be'er Yaakov, 1990.

Shillel, Yosha Leib. *Minhagei Baal HaḤatam Sofer*. Pressburg: 1930.

Shlezinger, Eliyahu. *Eleh Hem Moadai*. Jerusalem: 2001.

Shlezinger, Moshe. *Zimrat HaLevi*. Zikhron Meir, 2010.

Shneerson, B., ed. *Sefer HaRoke'aḥ HaGadol*. Jerusalem: 1967.

Shragai, Eliyahu. "Takkanot UMinhagim BeYisrael." *Shana BeShana* (5748/1987).

Shrum, Rebecca. *Mirroring Others/Fashioning Selves: A History of the Looking Glass in America*. PhD diss., University of South Carolina, 2007.

Siegert, Folker. "The Sermon as an Invention of Hellenistic Judaism." In *Preaching in Judaism and Christianity*, edited by Alexander Deeg, Walter Homolka and Heinz-Gunther Schottler, 25–44. Berlin: Walter de Gruyter, 2008.

Siev, Asher, ed. *Shut Rema*. Jerusalem: 1970.

Silberman, Shoshana. *A Family Haggadah*. Minneapolis, MN: Kar-Ben, 1987.

Silverman, Eric. *A Cultural History of Jewish Dress*. London: Bloomsbury, 2013.

Silverman, Morris. *Passover Haggadah with Explanatory Notes and Original Readings*. Hartford, CT: Prayer Book Press, 1959.

Simner, Zecharia. *Sefer Zekhira VeInyanei Segulot*. Hamburg: 1709.

Simon, Chanan. *The Why Haggadah*. New York: Beit Shammai, 1989.

Simons, Chaim. "Eating Cheese and *Levivot* on Chanukah." *Sinai* 115 (1995).

Sirkin, Michel Zalman. *Hararei Kedem*. Vol. 1. Jerusalem: 2000.

Smila, Ilan. *Ilana DeḤaye*. Lod: 2012.

Smith, Andrew, ed. *The Oxford Companion to American Food and Drink*. New York: Oxford University Press, 2007.

Smith, John. "Perchta the Belly-Slitter and Her Kin: A View of Some Traditional Threatening Figures, Threats and Punishments." *Folklore* 115, no. 2 (2004): 167–86.

Snodgrass, Mary Ellen. *Encyclopedia of Kitchen History*. New York: Fitzroy Dearborn, 2004.

Sofer, Moses. *Ḥatam Sofer: Derashot*. New York: Avraham Yitzchak Friedman, 1961.

Sofer, Yaakov Shalom. *Torat Ḥayim*. Vol. 4. Paks, Hungary: 1911.

Solomon, Matityahu. "This Night Two Times." *Kol HaTorah* 13 (Nisan 1983).

Soloveitchik, Yosef Dov, *Beit HaLevi al HaTorah*. Jerusalem: 1985.

Sonnenfeld, Yosef Hayim. *Ḥokhmat Ḥayim*. Jerusalem: 2002.

Sperber, Daniel. *Minhagei Yisrael*. Vol. 1. Jerusalem: Mossad HaRav Kook, 1989. Vol. 2. Jerusalem: 1991. Vol. 3. Jerusalem: 1994. Vol. 4. Jerusalem: 1995. Vol. 5. Jerusalem: 1998. Vol. 6. Jerusalem: 1998. Vol. 7. Jerusalem: 2003. Vol. 8. Jerusalem: 2007.

———. *On Changes in Jewish Liturgy: Options and Limitations*. Jerusalem: Urim, 2010.

Sperber, Miriam. *MiSippurei HaSavta*. Jerusalem: 1986.

Sperling, Abraham. *Sefer Taamei HaMinhagim UMekorei HaDinim*. Lemberg: 1928. Jerusalem: Shai Lamora, 1999.

Spiegel, Yaakov. *Pitḥei Tefilla UMoed*. Elkana: Michlelet Orot Yisrael, 2010.

Spira, Hayim Elazar. *Nimukei Oraḥ Ḥayim*. Brooklyn, NY: Emes Publishing Institute, 2004.

Spira, Nathan Natan. *Seder Birkat HaMazon im Peirush Moreinu Rav Natan Spira MiHorodna*. Lublin: 1574.

Spitzer, Shlomo. "*Yediot al Rabbi Dossa HaYevani MiḤiburo al HaTorah.*" In *Sefer Zikaron LeRav Yitzḥak Nissim*. Vol. 4. Jerusalem: Yad HaRav Nissim, 1984.

———, ed. *Sefer Maharil*. Jerusalem: Machon Yerushalayim, 1989.

———, ed. *Hilkhot UMinhagei Rabbeinu Shalom MeNeustadt*. Jerusalem: Machon Yerushalayim, 1997.

———, ed. *Sefer HaMinhagim LeRabbeinu Isaac Tirnau*. Jerusalem: Machon Yerushalayim, 2000.

Staiman, Mordechai. *"His Name is Aaron" and other Amazing Chassidic Stories and Songs*. Brooklyn, NY: Otzar Sifrei Lubavitch, 2002.

Stanov, Yitzhak. *Siddur VaYe'ater Yitzḥak*. Berlin: 1785.

Stechishin, Savella. *Traditional Ukrainian Cookery*. London: Trident Press, 1991.

Stein, Ephraim. *Sefer Avodat Ephraim*. Vol. 1. Bnei Brak: Machon Zecher Shaul, 1996.

Steinberg, Neil. *Hatless Jack*. New York: Plume, 2004.

Steinberg, Paul. *Celebrating the Jewish Year: The Winter Holidays: Hanukkah, Tu B'shevat, Purim*. Philadelphia, PA: Jewish Publication Society, 2007.

Steinsaltz, Adin. *HaSiddur VeHaTefilla*. Tel Aviv: Yedioth Ahronoth, 1994.

Stell, Yaakov Yisrael. "*Tefillat Neshamot HaNiftarim BeVeit HaKnesset*." *Yerushateinu* 3 (Elul 5769/2009).

———. "*Ḥomot Yeriḥo: Minyanan, Tivan, VeInyanan*." *Kovetz Ḥitzei Gibborim* 10 (Nisan 5777/2017).

Stemberger, Günter. "The Derashah in Rabbinic Times." In *Preaching in Judaism and Christianity*, edited by Alexander Deeg, Walter Homolka and Heinz-Gunther Schottler, 7–21. Berlin: Walter de Gruyter, 2008.

Stern, Bezalel. *BeTzel HaḤokhma*. Bnei Brak: 1982.

———. *Ohalekha BeAmitekha*. Jerusalem: 2005.

Stern, Moshe. *Be'er Moshe*. Jerusalem: 1984.

Stern, Shmuel Eliezer. *Seder Erusin VeNisuin LeRabboteinu HaRishonim*. Bnei Brak: 1990.

———, ed. *Meorot HaRishonim*. Vol. 1. Jerusalem: Machon Yerushalayim, 2001.

Stern, Yehiel Mikhel. *Sefer Gedolei HaDorot*. Jerusalem: Minchat Yisrael, 1996.

Sternbuch, Moshe. *Teshuvot VeHanhagot*. Vol. 1. Jerusalem: 1992. Vol. 2. Jerusalem: 1994. Vol. 4. Jerusalem: 2001.

Sternhell, Isaac. *Kokhavei Yitzḥak*. Vol. 1. Brooklyn, NY: Balshon Printing, 1969.

Stessel, Zahava. *Wine and Thorns in Tokay Valley: Jewish Life in Hungary*. Cranbury, NJ: Associated University Presses, 1995.

Stone, Michael. "Astronomy in the Apocrypha." *Maḥanayim* 125 (Tishrei 1971).

Stone, Shelly. "The Toga: From National to Ceremonial Costume." In *The World of Roman Costume*, edited by Judith Lynn Sebesta and Larissa Bonfante, 13–45. Madison, WI: University of Wisconsin Press, 2001.

Storey, Nicholas. *History of Men's Fashion: What the Well-Dressed Man Is Wearing*. Barnsley, South Yorkshire, England: 2008.

Strachov, A.B. "Miscellanea Meterologica Slavica: 'Breaking' the Rainbow in Poles'e." *Die Welt der Slaven* 33 (1988): 336–53.

Strassfeld, Michael. *A Book of Life: Embracing Judaism as a Spiritual Practice*. Woodstock, VT: Jewish Lights, 2006.

Straus, Raphael. "The 'Jewish Hat' as an Aspect of Social History." *Jewish Social Studies* 4, no. 1 (1942): 59–72.

Streane, A.W. *Cambridge Bible for Schools and Colleges: Esther*. Cambridge: Cambridge University Press, 1907.

Suslin, Alexander, ed. *Sefer HaAguda*. Cracow: 1575.

Susskind, Alexander. *Yesod VeShoresh HaAvoda*. Jerusalem: 1940.

Svar, Moshe, *Mikhlol HaMaamarim VeHaPitgamim*. Jerusalem: 1987.

Sweeney, Marvin A. "Sefirah at Qumran: Aspects of the Counting Formulas for the First-Fruits Festivals in the Temple Scroll." *Bulletin of the American Schools of Oriental Research* 251 (1983): 61–66.

Ta-Shma, Israel. "Where Were *Sefer HaKaneh* and the *Pelia* composed?" In *The Jacob Katz Jubilee Volume*. Jerusalem: Magnes Press, 1980 [Hebrew].

———. *Early Franco-German Ritual and Custom*. Jerusalem: Magnes Press, 1999.

———. "*Al Yom HaHuledet BeYisrael*." *Zion* 67 (2002).

———. *The Early Ashkenazic Prayer: Literary and Historical Aspects*. Jerusalem: Magnes Press, 2003.

Tabory, Joseph. *The Passover Ritual Throughout the Generations*. Tel Aviv: HaKibbutz HaMeuḥad, 2002.

———. *The JPS Commentary on the Haggadah: Historical Introduction, Translation and Commentary*. Philadelphia, PA: Jewish Publication Society, 2008.

Tal, Shlomo. *Siddur Rinat Yisrael*. Jerusalem: 1972. Jerusalem: Moreshet, 1981.
Tamar, Yissachar. *Alei Tamar, Yerushalmi: Zera'im*. Vol. 1. Givatayim, Israel: Atir, 1979.
———. *Alei Tamar, Yerushalmi: Seder Moed*. Vol. 1. Alon Shvut: Chorev, 1992.
Taub, Shaul Yedidya Elazar. *Haggada shel Pesaḥ – Ishei Yisrael*. Warsaw: 1938. Brooklyn, NY: Vaad Agudat Chasidei Modzitz, 1947.
Taub, Yehuda. *Otzar HaHalakhot – Pesaḥ, part 1*. Jerusalem: 1983.
Tawil, Yitzhak. *Mekadesh Yisrael VeHaZemanim*. Jerusalem: 2005.
Tchernowitz, Hayim. *Toldot HaPoskim*. Vol. 3. New York: 1947.
Teeter, Emily. *Religion and Ritual in Ancient Egypt*. Cambridge: Cambridge University Press, 2011.
Teichtel, Yissachar Shlomo. *Mishneh Sakhir*. Vol. 2. Jerusalem: Machon Keren Re'em, 2013.
Teitelbaum, Hanoch. *She'eilot UTeshuvot Yad Ḥanokh*. Brooklyn, NY: 1999.
Teomim, Aharon. *Mateh Aharon*. Frankfurt am Main: 1710.
Teshenzer, Yehuda. *Shaarei Yemei HaPesaḥ*. Ofakim: 2008.
Thomas, N.W. "Animal Superstitions and Totemism." *Folklore* 11, no. 3 (1900): 227–67.
Thompson, Stith. *The Motif-Index of Folk Literature*. Copenhagen and Bloomington, IN: Indiana University Press, 1955–1958.
Tidhar, David. *Encyclopedia of the Founders and Builders of Israel*. Tel Aviv: 1997.
Tirani, D. *Ikkarei HaDat*. Florence: 1806.
Tobias, Hanokh. *Alim LeTrufa*, no. 381 (Av 5763/2003).
Tolles, Delight. *The Banquet-Libations of the Greeks*. Ann Arbor, MI: Edwards Brothers, 1943.
Toussaint-Samat, Maguelonne. *A History of Food*. Chichester, West Sussex, England: John Wiley and Sons, 2009.
Trachtenberg, Joshua. *Jewish Magic and Superstition: A Study in Folk Religion*. New York: Atheneum, 1984.
Traktin, Baruch and Zev Hershkovitz. *Encyclopedia LeYahadut Romania*. Vol. 1. Jerusalem: Mossad HaRav Kook, 2012.
Tukachinsky, Y.M. *Gesher HaḤayim*. Jerusalem: 1960.

Tuleja, Tad. *Curious Customs: The Stories Behind 296 Popular American Rituals*. New York: Harmony Press, 1987.

Tunic, Avner. *Mayim Ḥayim*. Bnei Brak: 2003.

Turnau, Irena. "The Dress of the Polish Jews in the 17th and 18th centuries." In *Proceedings of the World Congress of Jewish Studies, Division D, Volume II: Art, Folklore and Music*, 101–8. Jerusalem: World Congress of Jewish Studies, 1989.

Twersky, Avraham. *Magen Avraham*. Vol. 2. Lublin: 1887.

Tzoref, Aharon. *Mevasser Tov*, 2010.

Tzubiri, Yosef. *Siddur Knesset HaGedola*. Tel Aviv: 1976.

Tzuriel, Moshe. *Otzrot HaMussar*. Jerusalem: 2002.

———. *Otzrot HaRaya*. Vol. 3. Rishon LeZion: Yeshivat Hesder Rishon LeZion, 2002.

———. *Otzrot HaTorah*. Bnei Brak: 2005.

Urbach, Ephraim. *The Tosaphists: Their History, Writings and Methods*. Jerusalem: Bialik Institute, 1954.

———, ed. *Arugat HaBosem*. Vol. 1. Jerusalem: Ḥevrat Mekitzei Nirdamim, 1939. Vol. 3. Jerusalem: 1962. Vol. 4. Jerusalem: 1963.

———. "*Mishmarot* and *Maamadot*." *Tarbiz* 42, nos. 3–4 (1973).

Vallee, F.G. "Burial and Mourning Customs in a Hebridean Community." *The Journal of the Royal Anthropological Institute of Great Britain and Ireland* 85, nos. 1–2 (1955): 119–30.

VanderKam, James C. *The Book of Jubilees*. Sheffield, England: Sheffield Academic Press, 2001.

Venderofsky, Y. *Minhagei Beit Yaakov*. New York: 1911.

Verner, Shlomo. *MiShulḥanam shel Gedolei Yerushalayim*. Jerusalem: Machon Keren Re'em, 2008.

Vidislefsky, Chanoch and Aryeh Leib Pepper, eds. *Birkat HaMazon – Pninei Maharal*. Ashdod: Mechon Maharal Tzintz, 2010.

Viski, Karoly. *Hungarian Peasant Customs*. Budapest: Dr. George Vajna, 1932.

Vital, Hayim. *Pri Etz Ḥayim*. Dubrovno, Belarus: 1804.

———. *Shaar HaMitzvot*. Jerusalem: 1905.

———. *Shaar HaKavanot*. Jerusalem: 1961. Jerusalem: Yerid HaSefarim, 2005.

Vizhonsky, N. "Should One Leave for *Yizkor*?" *Teḥumin* 17 (1997) [Hebrew].

Wahrmann, Nachum. *Ḥagei Yisrael UMoadeihem*. Tel Aviv: Achiasaf, 1970.

Waldenberg, Eliezer. *Tzitz Eliezer*. Vol. 12. Jerusalem: 1976. Vol. 13. Jerusalem: 1984.

Wallach, Shalom Meir. *Meilo shel Shmuel*. Bnei Brak: 1998.

Walner, M.D. *Ḥemdat Zvi*. Tel Aviv: 1973.

Waltz, Yisrael. *Ḥok LeYisrael*. Jerusalem: 1974.

Waserteil, Asher, ed. *Yalkut Minhagim*. Jerusalem: Ministry of Education and Culture, 1977. Jerusalem: 1996.

Wasserman, Ari. *Hegyonei HaParashah*. New York: Feldheim, 2008.

Wasserman, Aryeh David. *Otzar HaKippa*. Vol. 2. Jerusalem: 2014.

Wasserstein, Shmuel, ed. *Masekhet Soferim*. Jerusalem: 2001.

Wayne, Tiffany, ed. *Feminist Writings from Ancient Times to the Modern World: A Global Sourcebook and History*. Santa Barbara, CA: ABC-CLIO, 2011.

Webster, Thomas. *An Encyclopedia of Domestic Economy*. New York: Harper and Brothers, 1845.

Wecowski, Marek. *The Rise of the Greek Aristocratic Banquet*. Oxford: Oxford University Press, 2014.

Wehl, Yaakov. *The Haggadah with Answers: The Classic Commentators Respond to Over 200 Questions*. Brooklyn, NY: Mesorah, 1997.

Weil, Yaakov. *Torat Shabbat*. Karlsruhe, Germany: 1839.

Weil, Yedidya. *Haggada shel Pesaḥ im Biur Marbeh LeSapper*. Karlsruhe: 1791.

Wein, Berel. *The Pesach Haggadah: Through the Prism of Experience and History*. New York: Shaar Press, 2004.

Weinberg, Yehoshua Yoel. "*Hilkhot UMinhagei Keriyat HaMegilla*." In *Paamei Yaakov BeSdeh HaHalakha* (Kislev 5766/2005).

Weinberger, Yissachar Dov. *Edut BeYehosef – Minhagei Vizhnitz, Ḥodshei HaḤoref*. Bnei Brak: 2002.

Weinberger, Yosef. *Edut BeYehosef*. Bnei Brak: 2006.

Weinfeld, Avraham. *Lev Avraham*. Vol. 1. Brooklyn, NY: Balshon, 1977.

Weingarten, Shmuel. "*Reishitan shel HaHaftarot*." *Sinai* 83 (1978).

Weingarten, Susan. "Food, Sex, and Redemption in *Megillat Yehudit* (the Scroll of Judith)." In *The Sword of Judith: Jewish Studies Across the*

*Disciplines*, edited by Kevin Brine, Elena Ciletti, and Henrike Lähnemann. 97–125. Cambridge: Open Book Publishers, 2010.

Weingarten, Yaakov. *HaSeder HaArukh*. Vol. 2. Jerusalem: Machon Otzar HaMoadim, 1992.

Weingarten, Yosef David. *Darkhei Horaa*. Vol. 7. Jerusalem: 2006.

Weinstock, Moshe. *Siddur HaGeonim VeHaMekubalim VeHaḤasidim*. Vol. 18. Jerusalem: 1981. Vol. 20. Jerusalem: 1980.

Weinstock, Yisrael. *Maagalei HaNigleh VeHaNistar*. Jerusalem: Mossad HaRav Kook, 1970.

Weiss, Abner. *Death and Bereavement: A Halakhic Guide*. New York: Union of Orthodox Jewish Congregations of America, 1991.

Weiss, I. *Kuntres Devek Tov*, appended to the end of Y. Teichtel's *Mishneh Sakhir*. Baridow: 1924.

Weiss, Meir. "*Barkhi Nafshi*: Ps. 104." In *Mikraot KeKavanatam*. Jerusalem: Mossad Bialik, 1988.

Weiss, Shaul Yehezkel, *Haggada shel Pesaḥ – Otzar Divrei HaMefarshim*. London: 2010.

Weiss, Yitzhak. *Minḥat Yitzḥak*. Vol. 2. Jerusalem: 1993.

Weissler, Chava. "Performing Kabbalah in the Jewish Renewal Movement." In *Kabbalah and Contemporary Spiritual Revival*, edited by Boaz Huss, 39–74. Beer Sheva: Ben-Gurion University of the Negev, 2011.

Weissman Joselit, Jenna. *The Wonders of America: Reinventing Jewish Culture, 1880–1950*. New York, Hill & Wang, 1994.

Wengeroff, Pauline and Shulamit Magnus, trans. *Memoirs of a Grandmother: Scenes from the Cultural History of the Jews of Russia in the Nineteenth Century*. Vol. 1. Stanford, CA: Stanford University Press, 2010.

Wertheim, Aharon. *Halakhot VeHalikhot BeḤasidut*. Jerusalem: Mossad HaRav Kook, 1960. Jerusalem: Mossad HaRav Kook, 2003.

Wertheimer, Shlomo. *Geon HaGeonim*. Vol. 1. Jerusalem: 1925.

———, ed. *Abudraham HaShalem*. Jerusalem: 1963.

———, ed. *Sefer HaMakhria*. Jerusalem: Ktav Yad VeSefer, 1998.

Westropp, Thomas J. "A Folklore Survey of County Clare." *Folklore* 21, no. 2 (1911): 180–99.

Wexler, Paul. *Two-Tiered Relexification in Yiddish*. Berlin: Walter de Gruyter, 2002.

Whiteley, Suzanne Mehler. *Appel Is Forever: A Child's Memoir*. Detroit, MI: Wayne State University Press, 1999.

Wiener, Nancy. *Beyond Breaking the Glass: A Spiritual Guide to Your Jewish Wedding*. New York: CCAR, 2001.

Wilhelm, Nachman. *Haggada shel Pesaḥ – Ata Beḥartanu*. Bnei Brak: 2010.

Williams, Victoria R. *Celebrating Life Customs Around the World: From Baby Showers to Funerals. Vol. 1: Birth and Childhood*. Santa Barbara, CA: ABC-CLIO, 2017.

Wills, Lawrence M., ed. *Ancient Jewish Novels: An Anthology*. Oxford: Oxford University Press, 2002.

Wintermute, O.S. "Jubilees (Second Century B.C.): A New Translation and Introduction." In *The Old Testament Pseudepigrapha. Vol. 2: Expansions of the Old Testament and Legends, Wisdom, and Philosophical Literature, Prayers, Psalms, and Odes, Fragments of Lost Judeo-Hellenistic Works*, edited by James H. Charlesworth, 35–142. New York: Doubleday, 1985.

Wise, Michael Owen. *A Critical Study of the Temple Scroll from Qumran Cave 11*. Chicago, IL: The Oriental Institute of the University of Chicago, 1990.

Witcover, Paul. *Zora Neale Hurston: Author*. New York: Chelsea House, 1991.

Wolfson, Moshe. *Emunat Itekha*. Vol. 2. Jerusalem: 2004.

Wolfson, Ron. *Hanukkah: The Family Guide to Spiritual Celebration*. Woodstock, VT: Jewish Lights, 2001.

Wolski, Nathan, trans. *The Zohar: Pritzker Edition*. Vol. 10. Stanford, CA: Stanford University Press, 2016.

Wright, A.R. "Some Chinese Folklore." *Folklore* 14, no. 3 (1903): 292–98.

Wunder, Meir. *Encyclopedia LeḤakhmei Galitzia*. Vol. 2. Jerusalem: Machon LeHantzaḥat Yahadut Galitzia, 1982. Vol. 6. Jerusalem: 2005.

Yaakov Yosef of Polonne. *Toldot Yaakov Yosef*. Vol. 1. Jerusalem: Machon Daat UTevuna, 2009.

Yaari, Avraham, ed. *Iggerot Eretz Yisrael*. Ramat Gan: Massada, 1971.

———. *Toldot Ḥag Simḥat Torah*. Jerusalem: Mossad HaRav Kook, 1998.

Yadin, Yigael. *The Finds from the Bar Kokhba Period in the Cave of Letters, Volume 1.* Jerusalem: Israel Exploration Society, 1963.

———. *The Temple Scroll.* Jerusalem: Israel Exploration Society, 1977.

Yahuda, Abraham. *Ever VaArev.* New York: Shulsinger Bros., 1946.

Yarom, Natan Zvi. *Birkat HaMazon BeMeḥitzat HaḤafetz Ḥayim.* Modiin Illit: Mechon Mishnat HaḤafetz Ḥayim, 2014.

Yates, J.K. *Global Engineering & Construction.* Hoboken, NJ: John Wiley and Sons, 2007.

Yedidya, Assaf. "Orthodox Reactions to Wissenschaft Des Judentums." *Modern Judaism* 31, no. 1 (2010): 69–94.

Yehuda b. Barzilai. *Sefer HaIttim.* Cracow: Ḥevrat Mekitzei Nirdamim, 1903.

Yerushalmi, Shmuel, ed. *Tzror HaḤayim.* Jerusalem: 1966.

Yevrov, Nachum. *Kitzur Hilkhot Avelut UBikkur Ḥolim.* Jerusalem: 2001.

Yevrov, Zvi. *Derekh Siḥa.* Bnei Brak: Or HaḤayim, 2004.

———. *Birkat HaMazon im Biur MiMaran HaGraḥ Kanievsky.* Bnei Brak: 2009.

Yisrael, Meir. *Birkat HaMazon HaMevoar.* Bnei Brak: Keter Chaim, 2011.

Yisraeli, Yaakov. *Beit Karlin-Stolin.* Tel Aviv: Keren Yaakov VeRachel, 1982.

Yitzhak, Hertzel Hillel. *Tzel HeHarim: Tzitzit.* Jerusalem: 2006.

Yoffie, Alan. *Sharing the Journey: The Haggadah for the Contemporary Family.* New York: CCAR Press, 2012.

Yonge, C. D., trans. *The Deipnosophists, or Banquet of the Learned.* London: R. Clay, 1854.

———, trans. *The Works of Philo.* Peabody, MA: Hendrikson, 1993.

Yosef bar Moshe. *Leket Yosher.* Berlin: 1873.

Yosef Hayim of Baghdad. *Sefer Ben Ish Ḥai.* Baghdad: 1902. Jerusalem: 1932.

Yosef, Yitzhak, ed. *Yalkut Yosef – Moadim.* Jerusalem: 1988.

Young, Jason R. *Rituals of Resistance: African Atlantic Religion in Kongo and the Lowcountry South in the Era of Slavery.* Baton Rouge: Louisiana State University Press, 2007.

Yuval, Israel. J. "Vengeance and Damnation, Blood and Defamation: From Jewish Martyrdom to Blood Libel Accusations." *Zion* 58, no. 1 (1993): 33–90.

Zamlong, Azriel Chaim. *Eser Niflaot*. Piotrkow, Poland: 1932.
Zecharia, Naftali ben David. *Birkat HaMazon*. Venice: 1603.
Zeitlin, Solomon, ed. *The Book of Judith*. Leiden: Brill, 1972.
Zeleznik, Aharon, ed. *She'eilot UTeshuvot Rashba*. Vol. 3. Jerusalem: Machon Yerushalayim, 1996.
Zeller, Yitzhak. *Yalkut Yitzḥak*. Vol. 4. Warsaw: 1900.
Zelnik, Nachman. *Sefer Atzeret – Ḥag HaShavuot*. Jerusalem: Machon Harry Fischel, 1989.
Zer-Kavod, Mordechai. *Daat Mikra: Kohelet*. Jerusalem: Mossad HaRav Kook, 1990.
———. *Daat Mikra: Ezra Neḥemya*. Jerusalem: Mossad HaRav Kook, 1994.
Zevin, Shlomo. *HaMoadim BeHalakha*. Jerusalem: Machon HaTalmud HaYisraeli HaShalem, 1980.
Ziegler, Aharon. *Halakhic Positions of Rabbi Joseph B. Soloveitchik*. Northvale, NJ: Jason Aronson, 1998, 2001.
Zigelman, Eliezer Zvi. *Naḥalei Emuna*. Lublin: 1935.
Zilber, Binyamin. *Az Nidabru*. Vol. 11. Bnei Brak: 1980.
Zilber, Ephraim. *Sdeh Yerushlayim*. Tchernowitz, 1883.
Zilber, Yechiel Avraham. *Birur Halakha Talitaa*. Bnei Brak: 1995.
Zilberstein, Yitzhak and Moshe Rothchild. *Torat HaYoledet*. Bnei Brak: Machon Halakha VeRefua, 2011.
Zimmer, Yitzhak (Eric). "*Kefiat HaMitta BeAvelut VeGilgulei Hilkhata VeHanhagata*." *Sinai* 115 (1995).
———. "The Custom of *Matnat Yad*." *Yerushateinu* 3 (2009) [Hebrew].
———. "The Customs of *Matnat Yad* and *Yizkor*." In *The Scepter Shall Not Depart from Judah: Leadership, Rabbinate and Community in Jewish History: Studies Presented to Professor Shimon Schwarzfuchs*, edited by Joseph Hacker and Yaron Harel, 71–88. Jerusalem: The Bialik Institute, 2011 (Hebrew).
Zimmerman, Martha. *Celebrating Biblical Feasts: In Your Home or Church*. Minneapolis, MN: Bethany House, 2004.
Zinberg, Israel. *A History of Jewish Literature: The Haskalah Movement in Russia*. Cincinnati, OH: Hebrew Union College Press, 1978.
Zinger, Yehuda. *Ziv HaMinhagim*. Jerusalem: Dror, 1970. Jerusalem: Kollel Ziv HaMinhagim, 2000.

Zinner, Gavriel. *Nitei Gavriel: Hilkhot Pesaḥ*. Vol. 1. Jerusalem: Shemesh, 2002. Vol. 2. Jerusalem: 1997.

———. *Nitei Gavriel: Hilkhot Nesuin*. Vol. 2. Jerusalem: Shemesh, 1998.

———. *Nitei Gavriel: Yom Tov*. Vol. 2. Jerusalem: Shemesh, 1998.

———. *Nitei Gavriel: Ḥanukka*. Jerusalem: Shemesh, 1999.

———. *"BeDin Birkat Erusin VeNisuin LeKama Ḥatanim BeVat Eḥad." Kovetz Beit Aharon VeYisrael* 81, no. 3 (Shvat–Adar 5759/1999).

———. *Nitei Gavriel: Hilkhot Purim*. Jerusalem: Congregation Nitei Gavriel, 2000.

———. *Nitei Gavriel: Hilkhot Avelut*. Jerusalem: Shemesh, 2000, 2001.

———. *Nitei Gavriel: Children's Haircuts, Bringing Them to Cheder and Chumash Parties*. Jerusalem: 2001.

Zion, Mordechai. *Kum Hithalekh BaAretz*. Maale Adumim: 2015.

Zion, Noam and David Dishon. *The Family Participation Haggadah: A Different Night*. Jerusalem: Shalom Hartman Institute, 1997.

Zis, Avraham. *Minhagei Komarna*. Tel Aviv: 1964.

Zivon, Hayim Shimon Dov. *Shivi'im Temarim: Tzavaat Rabbi Yehuda HaḤasid*. Warsaw: 1900.

Zivotofsky, Avi. "What's the Truth About... Hallel on Pesach?" *Jewish Action* 60, no. 3 (Spring 5760/2000). Available at: jewishaction.com/issues/spring-2000/.

Zlicha, Yosef Ezra. "Regarding the Signs Eaten on Rosh HaShana Night." *Or Torah* 13, no. 296 (Elul 5752/1992).

Zrok, Refael. *Zekhor LeRefael*. Bat Yam: 2009.

Zuckerman, Hayim. *Birkat Ḥayim al Moadim*. Vol. 2. Tel Aviv: 1971.

Zuckermann, Ghil'ad. "'Ety*myth*ological Othering' and the Power of 'Lexical Engineering' in Judaism, Islam and Christianity: A Socio-Philo(sopho)logical Perspective." In *Explorations in the Sociology of Language and Religion*, edited by Tope Omoniyi and Joshua A. Fishman, 237–58. Amsterdam: John Benjamins, 2006.

Zunz, Leopold. *Die Ritus Synagogalen Gottesdientes*. Berlin: J. Springer, 1859.

———. *Literaturgeschichte der Synagogalen Poesie*. Frankfurt am Main: Gerschel, 1865.

———. *Nachtrag zur Literaturgeschichte der synagogalen Poesie*. Berlin: 1867.

———. *HaDerashot BeYisrael.* Hebrew translation of *Die Gottesdienstliche Vorträge der Juden Historisch Entwickelt.* Jerusalem: Bialik Institute, 1974.

# Source Index

## SHULḤAN ARUKH

### *Oraḥ Ḥayim*

### *Yoreh De'ah*



### *Even HaEzer*

# Subject and Name Index

*The fonts used in this book are from the Arno family*

*Maggid Books*
*The best of contemporary Jewish thought from*
*Koren Publishers Jerusalem Ltd.*